JAVA DEVELOPER'S GUIDE

murach's beginning Java 2 JDK 5

Doug Lowe
Joel Murach
Andrea Steelman

MIKE MURACH & ASSOCIATES, INC.
3484 W. Gettysburg Ave., Suite 101 • Fresno, CA 93722-7801
www.murach.com • murachbooks@murach.com

Authors: Doug Lowe
Joel Murach
Andrea Steelman

Editor: Anne Boehm

Cover Design: Zylka Design

Production: Judy Taylor

2 books for Java programmers

Murach's Beginning Java 2, JDK 5
Murach's Java Servlets and JSP

5 books for .NET programmers

Murach's C#
Murach's Beginning Visual Basic .NET
Murach's VB.NET Database Programming with ADO.NET
Murach's ASP.NET Web Programming with VB.NET
Murach's SQL for SQL Server

5 books for IBM mainframe programmers

Murach's OS/390 and z/OS JCL
Murach's Mainframe COBOL
Murach's CICS for the COBOL Programmer
Murach's CICS Desk Reference
DB2 for the COBOL Programmer, Part 1

For their advice and support, we offer a special thanks to...

Kathy Cupp, Oklahoma City Community College
David J. Meinhardt, Southwest Missouri State University
Thomas Paul, Hofstra University

Printed in the United States of America

10 9 8 7 6 5 4 3 2 1
ISBN: 1-890774-29-4

Contents

Expanded contents

Section 1 Essential Java skills

Chapter 12 How to work with dates and strings

Chapter 13 How to handle exceptions

Chapter 14 How to work with threads

Introduction

Since its release in 1996, the Java language has established itself as one of the leading languages for object-oriented programming. Today, despite competition from Microsoft's .NET Platform, Java continues to be one of the leading languages for application development, especially for web applications. And that's going to continue for many years to come, for several reasons.

First, developers can obtain Java and a wide variety of tools for working with Java for free. In contrast, Microsoft's .NET programming tools are expensive. Second, Java code can run on any modern operating system. In contrast, code generated by the .NET Platform can only run on the Windows operating system. Third, Java's development is guided largely by the Java community, and the source code for the Java API is freely available. In contrast, the .NET Platform is tightly controlled by Microsoft.

Who this book is for

This book is for anyone who wants to learn the core features of the Java language. It works if you have no programming experience at all. It works if you have programming experience with another language. It works if you already know an older version of Java and you want to get up-to-speed with the latest version. And it works if you've already read three or four other Java books and still don't know how to develop a real-world application.

If you're completely new to programming, the prerequisites are minimal. You just need to be familiar with the operation of the platform that you're using. If, for example, you're developing programs using Windows on a PC, you should know how to use Windows to perform tasks like opening, saving, printing, closing, copying, and deleting files.

What version of Java this book supports

This book is designed to work with Java 2 Platform, Standard Edition 5.0 (J2SE 5.0). This version of the Java 2 Platform includes the Java Development Kit (JDK). For marketing reasons, Sun sometimes refers to this version of the JDK as JDK 5.0. However, from a developer's point of view, this version of the JDK is commonly referred to as version 1.5.0 or just 1.5.

As you work with JDK 5.0, please keep in mind that all Java versions are upwards-compatible. That means that everything in this book will also work with any future versions of the JDK.

How to get the software you need

You can download all of the software that you need to use with this book for free from the Internet. To make that easier for you, chapter 1 shows you how to download and install the JDK from the web site for Sun Microsystems. It also shows you how to download and install TextPad, a text editor that's designed for working with Java. As you will quickly see when you read this book, that's all the software you need for developing professional Java applications on your own.

What operating systems this book supports

As you will see when you download Java, the Sun web site provides JDKs that work with the Windows, Linux, and Solaris operating systems. In addition, as this book goes to press, the Macintosh OS X operating system comes with JDK 1.4. Before long, you should be able to upgrade this JDK to JDK 5.0 so you'll be able to develop 5.0 applications like the ones in this book on a Mac.

However, since most Java development today is done under Windows, this book uses Windows to illustrate any platform-dependent procedures. As a result, if you're working on another platform, you may need to download information from the Sun web site about how to do some of those procedures on your system. Fortunately, these platform-dependent procedures are few and far between.

Why you'll learn faster and better with this book

Like all our books, this one has features that you won't find in competing books. That's why we believe that you'll learn faster and better with our book than with any other. Here are just three of those features.

- To help you develop applications at a professional level, this book presents complete, non-trivial applications. For example, chapter 17 presents a complete Product Maintenance application that uses presentation classes, business classes, and database classes. You won't find real-world applications like this in other Java books, even though studying these types of applications is the best way to master Java development.
- All of the information in this book is presented in our unique paired-pages format, with the essential syntax, guidelines, and examples on the right page and the perspective and extra explanation on the left page. This helps you learn more while reading less, and it helps you quickly find the information that you need when you use this book for reference.
- The exercises at the end of each chapter give you a chance to try out what you've just learned and to gain valuable, hands-on experience with Java. They guide you through the development of some of the book's applications, and they challenge you to apply what you've learned in new ways. Because we provide the starting code for these exercises from our web site, you get the maximum amount of practice in a minimum of time.

What you'll learn in this book

Unlike competing books, this one focuses on the practical, everyday features that you'll need for developing professional Java applications. Here's a quick tour of what this book covers.

- In section 1, you'll quickly master the basics of the Java language. In chapter 1, you'll learn how to install and configure the JDK and its documentation. In chapter 2, you'll learn how to write complete console applications that use the Scanner class to get input from a user. And by the end of chapter 5, you'll know how to code bulletproof applications that use custom methods to validate user input and how to use the BigDecimal class to make accurate calculations for decimal data.
- In section 2, you'll learn how to use Java for object-oriented programming. In chapter 6, you'll learn how to create and use your own classes, which is the basis for developing applications that are easier to test, debug, and maintain. Then, in chapters 7 through 9, you'll learn how to develop more sophisticated classes that use inheritance, interfaces, packages, type-safe enumerations, and the factory pattern. In addition, you'll learn how to use the three-tiered architecture that's used by most professionals.
- In section 3, you'll learn more of the core Java features that you'll use all the time. In chapters 10 through 14, for instance, you'll learn how to work with arrays, collections, dates, strings, and exceptions. And in chapter 15, you'll learn how to use threads so your applications can perform two or more tasks at the same time. Along the way, you'll learn new 5.0 features like enhanced for loops, typed collections, generics, autoboxing, assertions, and the StringBuilder class.
- In section 4, you'll learn how to develop graphical user interfaces (GUIs) with Java. First, you'll learn how to use Swing components to develop real-world GUI applications that handle events, validate data, and populate objects. Then, you'll learn how to develop applets, a special type of Java application that can be downloaded from the Internet and run within a web browser.
- Because storing data is critical to most applications, section 5 shows you how to store the data for objects in a file or database. In chapter 19, you'll learn how to work with text files and binary files, including random-access files. In chapter 20, you'll learn how to work with XML documents and files. And in chapter 21, you'll learn how to use JDBC to work with databases.

How our downloadable files make learning easier

To make learning easier, you can download the source code for the applications presented in this book. Then, you can view the complete code for these applications as you read each chapter, and you can compile and run these applications to see how they work.

In addition, you can download the source code that you need to do the exercises in this book. That way, you don't have to start every exercise from scratch. This takes the busywork out of doing these exercises. For more information about these downloads, please see appendix A.

Support materials for trainers and instructors

If you're a trainer or instructor who would like to use this book for a course, we offer your students a Student Workbook that can be downloaded from our web site (www.murach.com). This Workbook includes study aids like objectives, new term lists, and self-study questions, plus projects that ask the students to develop applications from scratch (unlike the exercises in the book).

We also offer an Instructor's CD that includes everything else you need for running an effective course. That includes a complete set of PowerPoint slides, multiple-choice tests, and solutions to the exercises and projects. Taken together, this book and the Instructor's CD make a powerful teaching package.

To download a sample of this Instructor's CD and to find out how to get the complete CD, please visit our web site at www.murach.com and click on the Instructors link. Or, if you prefer, call Kelly at 1-800-221-5528 or send her an email at kelly@murach.com.

About *Murach's Java Servlets and JSP*

Since web programming is one of the primary uses of Java, we also offer a book on web programming called *Murach's Java Servlets and JSP*. It shows you how to use Java servlets and JavaServer Pages as you develop professional web applications. If you read that book, you'll discover that Java web programming requires most of the skills that are presented in this book. In fact, you need to know everything that's in this book except the GUI skills in section 4. That's why *Murach's Java Servlets and JSP* is the ideal companion to this book.

Please let us know how this book works for you

When we started this book, our goals were (1) to teach you Java as quickly and easily as possible and (2) to teach you the practical Java concepts and skills that you need for developing real-world business applications. Now, we sincerely hope that we've succeeded. So if you have any comments about this book, we'd appreciate hearing from you at murachbooks@murach.com.

Thanks for buying this book. Thanks for reading it. And good luck with your Java programming.

Doug Lowe, Author | Joel Murach, Author | Andrea Steelman, Author

Section 1

Essential Java skills

This section gets you started quickly with Java programming. First, chapter 1 shows you how to compile and run Java applications, and chapter 2 introduces you to the basic skills that you need for developing Java applications. When you complete these chapters, you'll be able to write, test, and debug simple applications of your own.

After that, chapter 3 presents the details for working with numeric data. Chapter 4 presents the details for coding control statements. And chapter 5 shows you how to validate the data that's entered by the user. These are the essential skills that you'll use in almost every Java application that you develop. When you finish these chapters, you'll be able to write solid programs of your own. And you'll have the background that you need for learning how to develop object-oriented programs.

1

How to get started with Java

Before you can begin learning the Java language, you need to install Java and learn how to use some tools for working with Java. So that's what you'll learn in this chapter. Since most Java developers use Windows, the examples in this chapter show how to use Java with Windows. However, the principles illustrated by these examples apply to all operating systems including Linux, Mac (OS X), and Solaris.

Introduction to Java

In 1996, Sun Microsystems released a new programming language called Java. This language had great promise as a language that could be used on all platforms. Today, Java has fulfilled much of that promise and has established itself as one of the most widely used object-oriented programming languages.

Toolkits and platforms

Figure 1-1 describes all major releases of Java to date starting with version 1 and ending with version 5. Throughout Java's history, Sun has used the terms *Java Development Kit* (*JDK*) and *Software Development Kit* (*SDK*) to describe the Java toolkit. In version 5 of Java, Sun favors the term *JDK*. In this book, we'll use the term *JDK* since it's the most current term. In practice, though, SDK and JDK are often used interchangeably.

Versions 1.2 through 5 of the JDK are sometimes referred to as *Java 2* because they both run under the *Java 2 Platform*. This book will show you how to use the *Java 2 Platform, Standard Edition* (*J2SE*). Once you master the Standard Edition, you will have all the skills you need for learning how to use the *Java 2 Platform, Enterprise Edition* (*J2EE*).

Java compared to C++

When Sun's developers created Java, they tried to keep the syntax for Java similar to the syntax for C++ so it would be easy for C++ programmers to learn Java. In addition, they designed Java so its applications can be run on any computer platform. In contrast, C++ needs to have a specific compiler for each platform. Java was also designed to automatically handle many operations involving the creation and destruction of memory. This led to improved productivity for Java programmers, and it's a key reason why it's easier to develop programs and write bug-free code with Java than with C++.

To provide these features, the developers of Java had to sacrifice some speed (or performance) when compared to C++. For many types of applications, however, Java's relative slowness is not an issue.

Java compared to C#

Microsoft's new Visual C# language is similar to Java in many ways. Like Java, C# uses a syntax that's similar to C++ and that automatically handles memory operations. Also like Java, C# applications can run on any system that has the appropriate interpreter. Currently, however, only Windows provides the interpreter needed to run C# applications. In addition, C# applications are optimized for Windows. Because of that, C# is a good choice for developing applications for a Windows-only environment. However, many of the server computers that store critical enterprise data use Solaris or Linux. As a result, Java remains popular for developing programs that run on these servers.

Java timeline

Year	Month	Event
1996	January	Sun releases Java Development Kit 1.0 (JDK 1.0).
1997	February	Sun releases Java Development Kit 1.1 (JDK 1.1).
1998	December	Sun releases the Java 2 Platform with version 1.2 of the Software Development Kit (SDK 1.2).
1999	August	Sun releases Java 2 Platform, Standard Edition (J2SE).
	December	Sun releases Java 2 Platform, Enterprise Edition (J2EE).
2000	May	Sun releases J2SE with version 1.3 of the SDK.
2002	February	Sun releases J2SE with version 1.4 of the SDK.
2004	September	Sun releases J2SE with version 5.0 (instead of 1.5) of the JDK.

Operating systems supported by Sun

Windows (NT, 95, 98, 2000, XP)
Solaris
Linux
Macintosh (OS X)

Java compared to C++

Feature	Description
Syntax	Java syntax is similar to C++ syntax.
Platforms	Compiled Java code can be run on any platform that has a Java interpreter. C++ code must be compiled once for each type of system that it is going to be run on.
Speed	C++ runs faster than Java, but Java is getting faster with each new version.
Memory	Java handles most memory operations automatically, while C++ programmers must write code that manages memory.

Java compared to C#

Feature	Description
Syntax	Java syntax is similar to C# syntax.
Platforms	Like compiled Java code, compiled C# code (MSIL) can be run on any system that has the appropriate interpreter. Currently, only Windows has an interpreter for MSIL.
Speed	C# runs faster than Java.
Memory	Both C# and Java handle most memory operations automatically.

Description

- Versions 1.0, 1.1, and 5.0 of the Java toolkit are called the *Java Development Kit*, or *JDK*.
- Versions 1.2, 1.3, and 1.4 of the Java toolkit are called the *Software Development Kit*, or *SDK*.
- The *Java 2 Platform, Standard Edition (J2SE)* supports versions 1.2 to 5.0 of the JDK.
- The *Java 2 Platform, Enterprise Edition (J2EE)* can be used to create enterprise-level, server-side applications.

Figure 1-1 Introduction to Java

Applications, applets, and servlets

Figure 1-2 describes the three types of programs that you can create with Java. First, you can use Java to create *applications*. This figure shows an application that uses a *graphical user interface* (*GUI*) to get user input and perform a calculation. In this book, you'll be introduced to a variety of applications with the emphasis on GUI applications that get data from files and databases.

One of the unique characteristics of Java is that you can use it to create a special type of web-based application known as an *applet*. For instance, this figure shows an applet that works the same way as the application above it. The main difference between an application and an applet is that an applet can be downloaded from a web server and can run inside a Java-enabled browser. As a result, you can distribute applets via the Internet or an intranet.

Although applets can be useful for creating a complex user interface within a browser, they have their limitations. First, you need to make sure a plug-in is installed on each client machine to be able to use the newer Java GUI components (such as Swing components). Second, since an applet runs within a browser on the client, it's not ideal for working with resources that run on the server, such as enterprise databases.

To provide access to enterprise databases, many developers use the Enterprise Edition of the Java 2 Platform (J2EE) to create applications that are based on servlets. A *servlet* is a special type of Java application that runs on the server and can be called by a client, which is usually a web browser. This is also illustrated in this figure. Here, you can see that the servlet works much the same way as the applet. The main difference is that the code for the application runs on the server.

When a web browser calls a servlet, the servlet performs its task and returns the result to the browser, typically in the form of an HTML page. For example, suppose a browser requests a servlet that displays all unprocessed invoices that are stored in a database. Then, when the servlet is executed, it reads data from the database, formats that data within an HTML page, and returns the HTML page to the browser.

When you create a servlet-based application like the one shown here, all the processing takes place on the server and only HTML is returned to the browser. That means that anyone with an Internet or intranet connection, a web browser, and adequate security clearance can access and run a servlet-based application. Because of that, you don't need to install any special software on the client.

To make it easy to store the results of a servlet within an HTML page, the J2EE specification provides for *JavaServer Pages* (JSPs). Most developers use JSPs together with servlets when developing server-side Java applications. Although servlets and JSPs aren't presented in this book, we cover this topic in a companion book, *Murach's Java Servlets and JSP*. For more information about this book, please visit our web site at www.murach.com.

An application

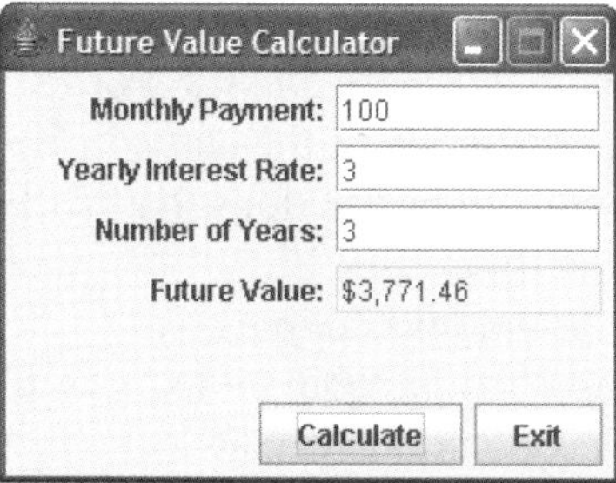

An applet

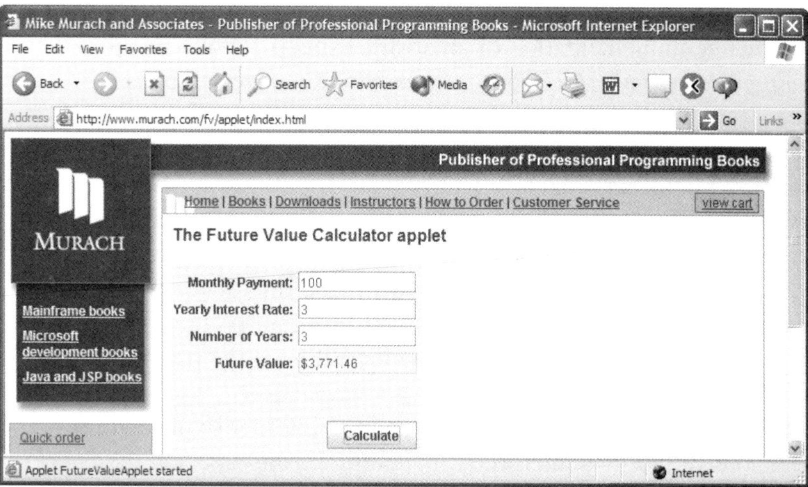

A servlet

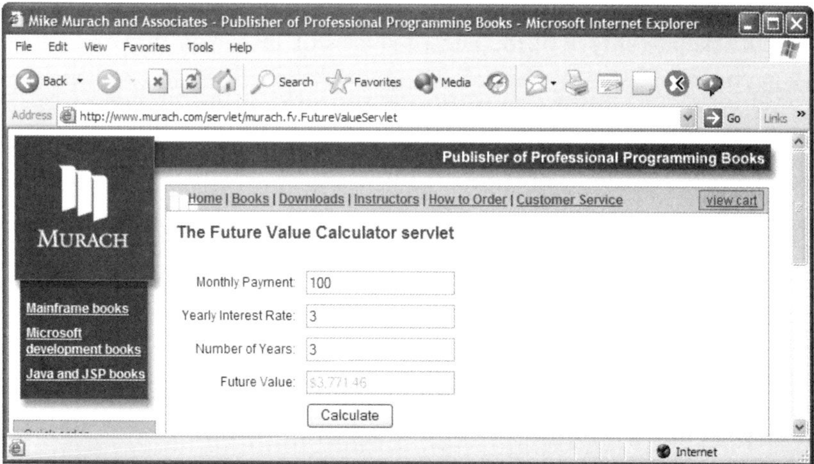

Description

- You can run the applet and servlet versions of the Future Value Calculator application shown above by going to www.murach.com/fv.

Figure 1-2 Applications, applets, and servlets

How Java compiles and interprets code

When you develop a Java application, you develop one or more *classes*. For each class, you write the Java statements that direct the operation of the class. Then, you use a Java tool to translate the Java statements into instructions that can be run by the computer. This process is illustrated in figure 1-3.

To start, you can use any text editor to enter and edit the Java *source code* for a class. These are the Java statements that tell the application what to do. Then, you use the *Java compiler* to compile the source code into a format known as Java *bytecodes*. At this point, the bytecodes can be run on any platform that has a *Java interpreter* to *interpret* (or translate) the Java bytecodes into code that can be understood by the underlying operating system. The Java interpreter is a concrete implementation of an abstract specification known as the *Java virtual machine (JVM)*. As a result, these two terms are often used interchangeably.

Since Java interpreters are available for all major operating systems, you can run Java on most platforms. This is what gives Java applications their *platform independence*. In contrast, C++ requires a specific compiler for each type of platform that its programs are going to run on.

In addition, some web browsers like Netscape and the Internet Explorer are Java enabled. In other words, these browsers contain Java interpreters. This allows applets, which are bytecodes that are downloaded from the Internet or an intranet, to run within a web browser.

The problem with this is that both Netscape and the Internet Explorer only support older versions of the Java interpreter. In addition, Netscape and the Internet Explorer support slightly different subsets of the Java language. To solve this problem, Sun has developed a tool known as the *Java Plug-in*, which lets the user upgrade the interpreter to a later version. This makes it possible to develop applets that take advantage of the latest features of Java. You'll learn more about this in chapter 18.

How Java compiles and interprets code

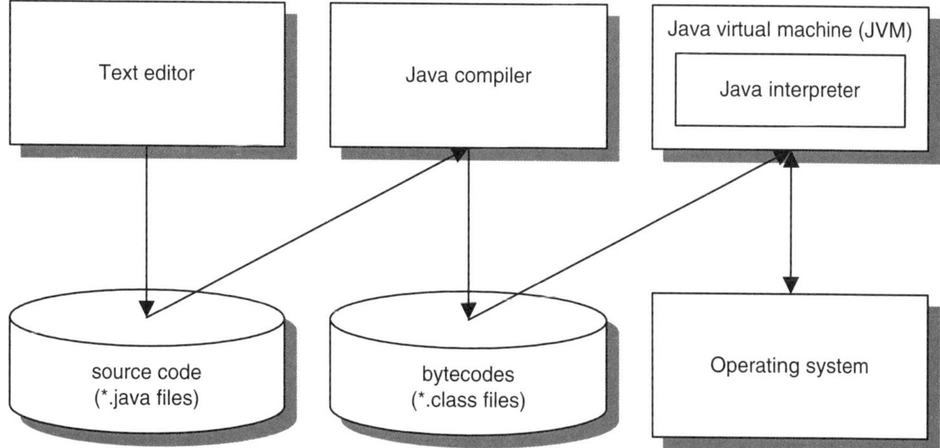

Description

- When you develop a Java application, you develop one or more *classes.*
- You can use any text editor to create, edit, and save the *source code* for a Java class. Source code files have the *java* extension.
- The *Java compiler* translates Java source code into a *platform-independent* format known as Java *bytecodes.* Files that contain Java bytecodes have the class extension.
- The *Java interpreter* executes Java bytecodes. Since Java interpreters exist for all major operating systems, Java bytecodes can be run on most platforms. A Java interpreter is an implementation of a *Java virtual machine (JVM).*
- Some web browsers like Netscape and the Internet Explorer contain Java interpreters. This lets applets run within these browsers. However, both Netscape and the Internet Explorer only provide older versions of the Java interpreter.
- Sun provides a tool known as the *Java Plug-in* that allows you to specify the version of the Java virtual machine that you want to use.

Figure 1-3 How Java compiles and interprets code

How to prepare your system for using Java

Before you can develop Java applications, the JDK must be installed on your system. In addition, your system may need to be configured to work with the JDK. Once you install the JDK, you'll be ready to create your first Java application.

How to install the JDK

Figure 1-4 shows how to install the JDK. To start, you download the exe file for the setup program for the most recent version of the JDK from the Java web site. Then, you navigate to the directory that holds the exe file, run the setup file, and respond to the resulting dialog boxes.

Since Sun periodically updates the Java web site, we've kept the procedure shown in this figure somewhat general. As a result, you may have to do some searching to find the current version of the JDK. In general, you can start by looking for products for the Java 2 Platform, Standard Edition. Then, you can find the most current version of the JDK for your operating system.

By the way, all of the examples in this book have been tested against version 5.0 of the JDK. Since Java has a good track record of being upwards compatible, however, these examples should work equally well with later versions of the JDK.

The Java web site

`java.sun.com`

How to download the JDK from the Java web site

1. Go to the Java web site.
2. Locate the list of Java products, and display the page for the Java 2 Platform, Standard Edition.
3. Display the J2SE Downloads page and select the link for the most current JDK version that's available for your operating system.
4. Click the Download link for the JDK (not the JRE), and follow the instructions.
5. Save the exe file for the setup program to your hard disk.

How to install the JDK

- Run the exe file and respond to the resulting dialog boxes. When you're prompted for the JDK directory, use the default directory. For most Windows systems, the default directory is C:\Program Files\Java\jdk1.5.0 for version 5 of the JDK.

Notes

- For more information about installing the JDK, you can refer to the Java web site.
- If you are installing the Windows version of the JDK, you can perform either an offline or an online installation. An online installation is faster because only a small setup file is downloaded. However, you must remain online during the entire installation so the required files can be installed.
- You can click the "How long will it take" link to determine how long it will take to download the setup program based on its size and the speed of your modem. For a 56K modem, for example, it will take about 2 hours and 13 minutes to download the Windows version of JDK 5.0 (about 44MB).

Figure 1-4 How to install the JDK

A summary of the directories and files of the JDK

Figure 1-5 shows the directories and files that are created when you install the JDK. Here, the JDK is stored in the C:\Program Files\Java\jdk1.5.0 directory. This directory has multiple subdirectories, but the bin, jre, lib, and docs directories are the most important.

The *bin* directory holds all the tools necessary for developing and testing a program, including the Java compiler. Later in this chapter, you'll learn how to use these tools to compile and run Java applications. The *lib* directory contains libraries and support files required by the development tools.

The *jre* directory contains the Java interpreter, or *Java Runtime Environment* (*JRE*), that's needed to run Java applications once they've been compiled. Although the JDK uses this internal version of the JRE, you can also download a standalone version of the JRE from the Java web site. Once you're done developing a Java application, for example, you can distribute the standalone JRE to other computers so they can run your application.

The *docs* directory can be used to store the Java documentation. Later in this chapter, you'll learn how to download and install this documentation.

In the JDK directory, you can find an HTML *readme* file that contains much of the information that's presented in this figure as well as more technical and detailed information about the JDK. You can view the HTML file with a web browser.

The JDK directory also contains the src.zip file. This is a compressed file that holds the source code for the JDK. If you want to view the source code, you can extract the source files from this zip file. If you're curious to see the Java code of the JDK, you may want to do that once you understand Java better.

When you work with Windows, you'll find that it sometimes uses the terms *folder* and *subfolder* to refer to directories and subdirectories. For consistency, though, we use the term *directory* throughout this book. In practice, these terms are often used interchangeably.

The default directory for the JDK on a Windows machine

```
C:\Program Files\Java\jdk1.5.0\bin
```

Four important subdirectories of the JDK

Directory	Description
bin	The Java development tools and commands
jre	The root directory of the Java Runtime Environment (JRE)
lib	Additional libraries of code that are required by the development tools
docs (optional)	The on-line documentation that you can download (see figure 1-15)

Two important files stored in the JDK directory

File	Description
readme.html	An HTML page that provides information on Java 2, including system requirements, features, and documentation links.
src.zip	A zip file containing the source code for the J2SE API. If you use a zip tool such as WinZip to extract these directories and files, you can view the source code for the JDK.

Description

- The *Java Runtime Environment* (*JRE*) is the Java interpreter that allows you to run compiled programs in Java. The jre directory is an internal copy of the runtime environment that works with the JDK. You can also download a standalone version of the JRE for computers that don't have the JDK installed on them.

Figure 1-5 A summary of the directories and files of the JDK

How to set the command path

Figure 1-6 shows you how to configure Windows to make it easier to work with the JDK. If you're not using Windows, you can refer to the Java web site to see what you need to do to configure Java for your system.

To configure Windows to work with the JDK, you need to add the bin directory to the *command path*. That way, Windows will know where to look to find the Java commands that you use.

If you're using a recent version of Windows like Windows 2000, NT, or XP, you can use the first procedure in this figure to set the command path. When you find the Path variable in the Environment Variables, you can usually add the path for the Java bin directory to the end of the list of paths. To do that, you type a semicolon and the complete path (shaded at the top of this figure). However, if you've installed previous versions of Java on your system, you need to make sure that the path for Java 5.0 is in front of the path for earlier versions.

If you're using an older version of Windows like Windows 95, 98, or ME, you can use the second procedure in this figure to edit the Path or Set Path command in the *autoexec.bat* file. This is the file that is automatically executed every time you start your computer. After you edit the file, you can restart your computer to run the autoexec.bat file and establish the new path. Then, you can enter *path* at the command prompt to make sure that the bin subdirectory of the JDK directory is now in the command path.

Whenever you edit the command path, be careful! Since the command path may affect the operation of other programs on your PC, you don't want to delete or modify any of the other paths. You only want to add one directory to the command path. If that doesn't work, be sure that you're able to restore the command path to its original condition.

If you don't configure Windows in this way, you can still compile and run Java programs, but it's more difficult. For instance, instead of typing a command like this to compile a Java class

```
javac
```

you may need to type this command:

```
\Program Files\Java\jdk1.5.0\bin\javac
```

As you can see, then, setting the command path makes this much simpler. That's why it's so important to get this set right.

A typical Path command

```
path=C:\Windows;C:\Program Files\Java\jdk1.5.0\bin
```

How to set the path for Windows 2000/NT/XP

1. Depending on how your system is set up, (1) go to the Start menu, and select the Control Panel, or (2) go to the Start menu, select Settings, and select the Control Panel.
2. Edit the environment variables for your system.
   - For 2000, select the System icon, the Advanced tab, and the Environment Variables button.
   - For NT, select the System icon and the Environment tab.
   - For XP, select the Performance and Maintenance icon, the System icon, the Advanced tab, and the Environment Variables button.
3. If you haven't installed earlier versions of Java, type a semicolon and the path for the bin subdirectory of JDK 1.5 to the far right of the list of paths. Otherwise, add the 1.5 path followed by a semicolon before the paths for earlier JDK versions.

How to set the path for Windows 95/98/ME

1. Start the Windows Explorer and navigate to the autoexec.bat file, which should be stored in the root drive (c:\autoexec.bat).
2. Right-click on the autoexec.bat file and select the Edit command. This should open the file in a text editor.
3. If the file doesn't contain a Path or Set Path command, enter "path=" at the beginning of the file followed by the bin subdirectory of JDK 1.5. If the file does contain a Path or Set Path command and you haven't installed earlier versions of Java, type a semicolon at the end of the command followed by the path of the bin subdirectory of JDK 1.5. However, if you have installed earlier Java versions, add the 1.5 path followed by a semicolon before the paths of any earlier versions.
4. Save the file and exit the text editor.
5. To have the new path take effect, run the autoexec.bat file by restarting your computer.

How to check the current path

- Start a Command Prompt or DOS Prompt as described in figure 1-12. Then, enter the Path command by typing the word path. This will display the current path statement.

Description

- The *command path* on a Windows system tells Windows where to look for the commands that it is told to execute. When you use Java tools, you need to add the path for the jdk1.5.0\bin directory that's shown above.

Notes

- For more information about setting the path for Windows or for information about configuring non-Windows operating systems, you can refer to the Java web site.

Figure 1-6 How to set the command path

How to set the class path

The *class path* is used to tell the operating system where to look for the Java files that you create. When you compile a class, for example, the operating system needs to know where to find the source code (.java files) for that class. Similarly, when you run a program, the operating system needs to know where to find the bytecodes (.class files) for that class.

By default, the class path for a Windows system includes the current directory, which is usually all you need. Then, before you compile or run a program from a command prompt, you simply change to the directory that contains the .java or .class files. You'll learn more about how to display and work from the command prompt later in this chapter.

The operating system also uses the class path when you compile or run a program using some Java tools such as TextPad. In that case, the tool automatically changes the current directory to the directory where the source code and class files for the program you're compiling or running are stored.

So as long as the class path for your system includes the current directory, the tool will work correctly. If the class path doesn't include the current directory, however, you'll need to add it before the tool will work correctly. Figure 1-7 describes how you do that.

To set the class path, you use the same techniques that you use for setting the command path (see figure 1-6), but you add a path to the Classpath list instead of the Path list. Specifically, you add a dot (.) for the current directory followed by a semicolon at the start of the list of paths. This is illustrated in the class path at the top of this figure.

To determine what the current class path is, you can enter *set* at the prompt. This runs the Set command, which displays a variety of settings, including the class path. This will also show you whether you've successfully added the current directory.

A typical Classpath command

```
classpath=.;c:\java\classes;
```

When and how to modify the class path

- If your system doesn't have a Classpath command, the default class path will allow you to run all of the programs described in this book. As a result, you won't need to modify the class path.
- If your system has a Classpath command that doesn't include the current directory, you need to add the current directory to the class path.
- To modify the class path, follow the procedure shown in figure 1-6 for modifying the command path, but modify the Classpath command instead. To include the current directory in the class path, just code a period for the directory followed by a semicolon at the start of the list of paths as shown above.

How to check the current class path

- Start a Command Prompt or DOS Prompt as described in figure 1-12, and enter the Set command by typing the word *set*. This will display a variety of settings including the current class path.

Description

- The *class path* tells the JDK where to find the .java and .class files you create. The class path is used when you compile or run a program. By default, the class path is the current directory.

Note

- For more information about configuring the class path or for information about configuring non-Windows operating systems, you can refer to the Java web site.

Figure 1-7 How to set the class path

How to use TextPad to work with Java

Once the JDK is installed and configured for your operating system, you're ready to create your first application. Since most Java development is still done under Windows, this topic shows how to install and use a free trial version of TextPad, one of the most popular *text editors* that's designed for Java development.

Unfortunately, TextPad only runs under Windows. As a result, if you're using a non-Windows computer, you'll need to search the web to find a text editor for Java development that runs on the operating system that you're using. Fortunately, you can find a variety of these types of text editors on the web, and many of them are available for free (freeware) or for a small fee (shareware).

How to install TextPad

Figure 1-8 shows how to download and install a free trial version of TextPad. Once you save the exe for the setup file to your hard disk, you simply run this file and respond to the resulting dialog boxes. Since this version of TextPad is a trial version, you should pay for TextPad if you decide to use it beyond the initial trial period. Fortunately, this program is relatively inexpensive (about $30), especially when you consider how much time and effort it can save you.

The TextPad web site

`www.textpad.com`

How to download TextPad

1. Go to the TextPad web site.
2. Find the Free Trial version of TextPad and save the exe file for the setup program to your hard disk. This should take just a few minutes.

How to install TextPad

- Run the exe file and respond to the resulting dialog boxes.

Notes

- The trial version of TextPad is free, but if you like TextPad and continue to use it, you can pay the small fee of approximately $30 to purchase it.
- The examples in this chapter were created with version 4.7 of TextPad.
- Although TextPad is a popular text editor for doing Java development under Windows, it doesn't run on Linux, Macintosh, or Solaris. As a result, if you're using a non-Windows operating system, you'll need to find a text editor for Java development that runs on your operating system. For example, VI and Emacs are two popular text editors for Linux.

Figure 1-8 How to install TextPad

How to use TextPad to save and edit source code

Figure 1-9 shows how to use TextPad to save and edit source code. In short, you can use the standard Windows shortcut keystrokes and menus to enter, edit, and save your code. You can use the File menu to open and close files. You can use the Edit menu to cut, copy, and paste text. And you can use the Search menu to find and replace text. In addition, TextPad color codes the code in the source files so it's easier to recognize the Java syntax.

When you save Java source code, you must give the file the same name as the class name. Since Java is a *case-sensitive* language, you must also use the same capitalization in the file and class names. If you don't, you'll get an error message when you try to compile the code. In this figure, for example, you can see that "TestApp" is used for both the class name and the file name.

You must also save a Java source file with the four-letter *java* extension. When you use TextPad to save your source code, you can use the Save As Type drop-down list in the Save As dialog box to apply this extension. However, if you're using a text editor that isn't designed for working with Java, you may need to add the *java* extension to the end of the file name and enclose the file name in quotation marks like this: "TextApp.java". Otherwise, the text editor may truncate the extension to jav or change the capitalization in the file name. This will lead to errors when you try to compile the source code.

You must also save Java source code in a standard text-only format such as the *ASCII format* or the *ANSI format*. By default, TextPad saves code in the ANSI format and that's usually what you want. If, however, you need to save a file in another format such as Unicode, TextPad can do that too.

The TextPad text editor with source code in it

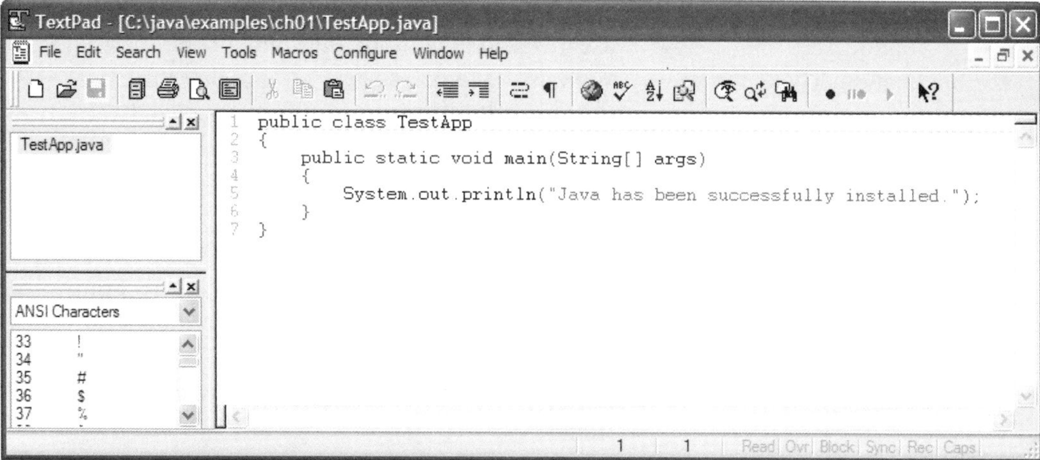

TextPad's Save As dialog box

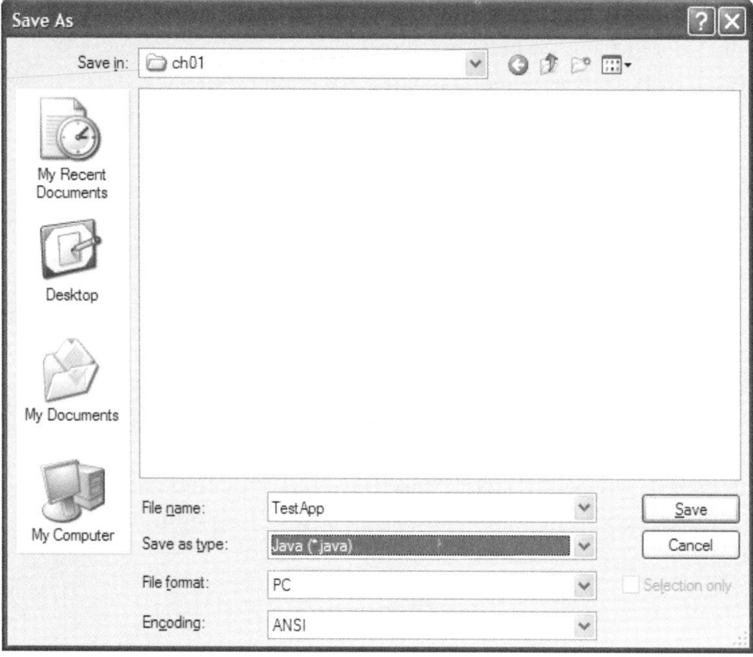

How to enter, edit, and save source code

- To enter and edit source code, you can use the same techniques that you use for working with any other Windows text editor.
- To save the source code, select the Save command from the File menu (Ctrl+S). Then, enter the file name so it's exactly the same as the class name, and select the Java option from the Save As Type list so TextPad adds the four-letter java extension to the file name.

Figure 1-9 How to use TextPad to save and edit source code

How to use TextPad to compile source code

Figure 1-10 shows how to use TextPad to compile the source code for a Java application. The quickest way to do that is to press Ctrl+1 to execute the Compile Java command of the Tools menu. If the source code compiles cleanly, TextPad will generate a Command Results window and return you to the original source code window.

However, if the source code doesn't compile cleanly, TextPad will leave you at a Command Results window like the one shown in this figure. In this case, you can read the error message, switch to the source code window, correct the error, and compile the source code again. Since each error message identifies the line number of the error, you can make it easier to find the error by selecting the Line Number option from the View menu. That way, TextPad will display line numbers as shown in this figure.

When you have several Java files open at once, you can use the Document Selector pane to switch between files. In this figure, only two documents are open (TestApp and Command Results), but you can open as many files as you like. You can also use the Window menu and standard Windows keystrokes (Ctrl+F6 and Ctrl+Shift+F6) to switch between windows.

To edit as efficiently as possible, you can use the View menu to set the editing options for a single file. And you can use the Configure→Preferences command to set the options for all files. In particular, you may want to turn the Line Number option on, and you may want to set the tab settings so you can easily align the code in an application.

How to use TextPad to run an application

Once you've compiled the source code for an application, you can run that application by pressing Ctrl+2. In this figure, the application prints text to the *console*. As a result, TextPad starts a console window like the one shown in this figure. Then, you can usually press any key to end the application and close the window. Sometimes, however, you may need to click on the Close button in the upper right corner of the window to close it.

The Tools menu

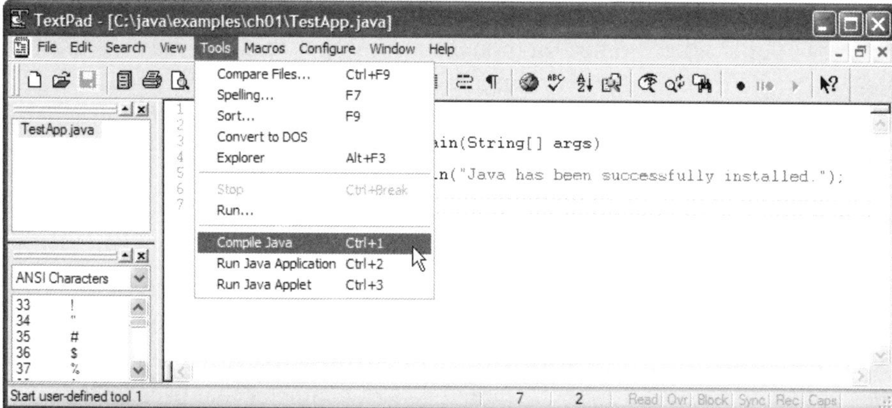

A compile-time error

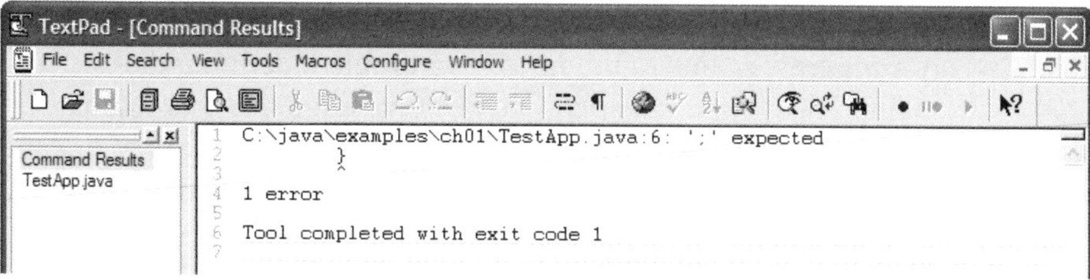

Text printed to the console

```
C:\WINDOWS\System32\cmd.exe
Java has been successfully installed.
Press any key to continue . . .
```

How to compile and run an application

- To compile the current source code, press Ctrl+1 or select Tools→Compile Java.
- To run the current application, press Ctrl+2 or select Tools→Run Java Application.
- If you encounter compile-time errors, TextPad will print them to a window named Command Results. To switch between this window and the source code window, press Ctrl+F6 or use the Document Selector pane that's on the left side of the TextPad window.
- When you print to the *console*, a DOS window like the one above is displayed. To close the window, press any key or click the Close button in the upper right corner.

How to display line numbers and set options for one source file

- To display the line numbers for the source code, select View→Line Numbers.
- To set formatting options like tab settings, select View→Document Properties.

How to display line numbers and set the options for all source files

- Select Configure→Preferences. Then, in the Preferences dialog box, click on the type of default that you would like to set, and check or uncheck the appropriate options. For instance, to display line numbers for all files, click on View and click on Line Numbers.

Figure 1-10 How to use TextPad to compile and run an application

Common error messages and solutions

Figure 1-11 summarizes some common error messages that you may encounter when you try to compile or run a Java application. The first two errors illustrate *compile-time errors*. These are errors that occur when the Java compiler attempts to compile the program. In contrast, the third error illustrates a *runtime error*. That is an error that occurs when the Java interpreter attempts to run the program but can't do it.

The first error message in this figure involves a syntax error. When the compiler encounters a syntax error, it prints two lines for each error. The first line prints the name of the *.java file, followed by a colon, the line number for the error, another colon, and a brief description of the error. The second line prints the code that caused the error, including a caret character that tries to identify the location where the syntax error occurred. In this example, the caret points to the right brace, but the problem is that the previous line didn't end with a semicolon.

The second error message in this figure involves a problem defining the *public class* for the file. The compiler displays an error message like this when the file name for the *.java file doesn't match the name of the public class defined in the source code. For example, the TextApp.java file must contain this code

```
public class TestApp{
```

If the name of the file doesn't match the name of the public class (including capitalization), the compiler will give you an error like the one shown in this figure. You'll learn more about the syntax for defining a public class in the next chapter.

The third error message in this figure occurs if you try to run an application that doesn't have a main method. You'll learn how to code a main method in the next chapter. For now, just realize that every application must contain a main method. To correct the error shown in this figure, then, you must add a main method to the class or run another class that has a main method.

Most of the time, the information displayed by an error message will give you an idea of how to fix the problem. Sometimes, though, the compiler gets confused and doesn't give you accurate error messages. In that case, you'll need to double-check all of your code. You'll learn more about debugging error messages like these as you progress through this book.

A common compile-time error message and solution

Error:

```
C:\java\examples\ch01\TestApp.java:6: ';' expected
          }
          ^
```

Description: The first line in this error message displays the file name of the *.java file, a number indicating the line where the error occurred, and a brief description of the error. The second line displays the line of code that may have caused the error with a caret symbol (^) below the location where there may be improper syntax.

Solution: Edit the source code to correct the problem and compile again.

Another common compile-time error message and solution

Error:

```
C:\java\examples\ch01\TestApp.java:1: class testapp is
public, should be declared in a file named testapp.java

public class testapp
       ^
```

Description: The *.java file name doesn't match the name of the public class. You must save the file with the same name as the name that's coded after the words "public class". In addition, you must add the java extension to the file name.

Solution: Edit the class name so it matches the file name (including capitalization), or change the file name so it matches the class name. Then, compile again.

A common runtime error message and solution

Error:

```
Exception in thread "main" java.lang.NoSuchMethodError:
main
```

Description: The class doesn't contain a main method.

Solution: Run a different class that does have a main method, or enter a main method for the current class.

Description

- When you compile an application that has some statements that aren't coded correctly, the compiler cancels the compilation and displays messages that describe the *compile-time errors*. Then, you can fix the causes of these errors and compile again.
- When the application compiles without errors (a "clean compile") and you run the application, a *runtime error* occurs when the Java Virtual Machine can't execute a compiled statement. Then, the application is cancelled and an error message is displayed.

Figure 1-11 Common error messages and solutions

How to use the command prompt to work with Java

If you're using TextPad, you can use its commands to compile and run most of your Java applications. Even so, there may be times when you will need to compile and run Java applications from the *command prompt*. And if you're using another text editor that doesn't provide compile and run commands, you can use the command prompt to compile and run all of your Java applications.

How to compile source code

Figure 1-12 shows how to use a command prompt to compile and run applications. In particular, this figure shows how to use the Windows command prompt, sometimes called the *DOS prompt*.

To start, you enter the change directory (cd) command to change the current directory to the directory that holds the application. In this figure, for example, you can see that the directory has been changed to c:\java\examples\ch01 because that's the directory that contains the TestApp.java file. Then, to compile the application, you use the *javac command* to start the Java compiler. When you enter the javac command, you follow it by a space and the complete name of the *.java file that you want to compile. Since Java is case-sensitive, you need to use the same capitalization that you used when you saved the *.java file.

If the application doesn't compile successfully, you can use your text editor to correct and resave the *.java file, and you can compile the program again. Since this means that you'll be switching back and forth between the text editor and the command prompt, you'll want to leave both windows open.

When you compile an application successfully, the Java compiler will create a *.class file that has the same file name as the *.java file. For example, a successful compilation of the TestApp.java file will create the TestApp.class file. This *.class file is the file that contains the Java bytecodes that can be run by the Java interpreter.

How to run an application

To run a program from the command prompt, you use the *java command* to start the Java interpreter. Although you need to use the proper capitalization when you use the java command, you don't need to include an extension for the file. When you enter the java command correctly, the Java interpreter will run the *.class file for the application.

Running a Java program often displays a graphical user interface like the one shown in figure 1-2. However, you can also print information to the console and get input from the console. For example, the TestApp file in this figure prints a single line of text to the console.

The commands for compiling and running an application

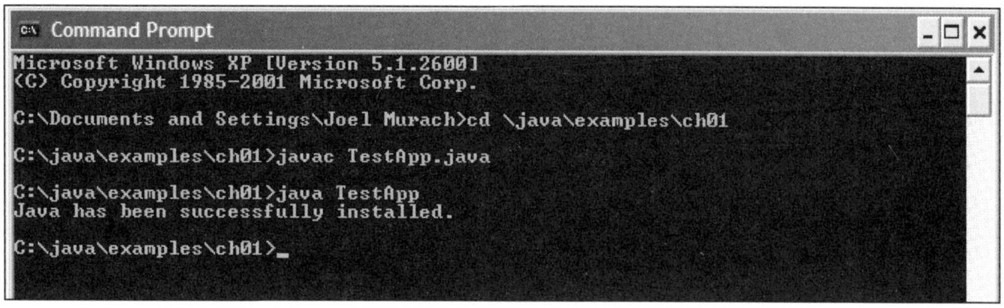

```
Command Prompt
Microsoft Windows XP [Version 5.1.2600]
(C) Copyright 1985-2001 Microsoft Corp.

C:\Documents and Settings\Joel Murach>cd \java\examples\ch01

C:\java\examples\ch01>javac TestApp.java

C:\java\examples\ch01>java TestApp
Java has been successfully installed.

C:\java\examples\ch01>_
```

Syntax to compile an application

```
javac ProgramName.java
```

Syntax to run an application

```
java ProgramName
```

Description

- The *command prompt* is the prompt that indicates that the operating system is waiting for the next command. This prompt usually shows the current directory, and it always ends with >.
- In Windows, the command prompt is sometimes referred to as the *DOS prompt* or the *DOS window*. You can enter DOS commands at the DOS prompt.

Operation

- To open a command prompt in Windows, click on the Start button, find MS-DOS Prompt or Command Prompt, and select it. If its location isn't obvious, try looking in Accessories.
- To change the current directory to the directory that contains the file with your source code, use the change directory command (cd) as shown above.
- To compile the source code, enter the Java compile command (javac), followed by the file name (including the java extension). Since this is a case-sensitive command, make sure to use the same capitalization that you used when naming the file.
- If the code compiles successfully, the compiler generates another file with the same name, but with class as the extension. This file contains the bytecodes.
- If the code doesn't compile successfully, the java compiler generates error messages for the compile-time errors. Then, you must switch back to your text editor, fix the errors, save your changes, and compile the program again.
- To run the compiled version of your source code, enter the Java command (java), followed by the program name (without any extension). Since this is a case-sensitive command, make sure to use the same capitalization that you used when naming the file.

Note

- The code shown in the command prompt above will only work if the bin subdirectory of the JDK 5.0 directory has been added to the command path as shown in figure 1-6.

Figure 1-12 How to use the command prompt to compile and run an application

How to compile source code with a switch

Most of the time, you can use TextPad's compile command or the plain javac command shown in the last figure to compile Java source code. Sometimes, however, you need to supply a *switch* to use certain features of the javac command as summarized in figure 1-13.

Note in the syntax summary in this figure that the brackets around the switch name indicate that it's optional. In addition, the ellipsis (...) indicates that you can code as many switches as you need. You'll see this notation used throughout this book.

When new versions of Java become available, the designers of Java mark some older features as *deprecated*. When a feature is deprecated, it means that its use is not recommended and it may not be supported in future versions of Java. As a result, you should try to avoid using deprecated features whenever possible.

The first example in this figure shows how to use the deprecation switch to get more information about code that uses deprecated features of the JDK. As you can see, if you don't use this switch, you'll get a brief message that indicates that your code uses deprecated features. On the other hand, if you use this switch, you'll get detailed information about the code that uses deprecated features including the line number for that code. That makes it easier to modify your code so it doesn't use these features.

The second example shows how to use the source switch to compile code so it can run on another computer that's using an older Java interpreter. In particular, this example shows how to compile code so it can run on a computer with version 1.4 of the JRE. When you use this switch, though, you won't be able to use the new features of Java 5. As a result, you shouldn't use this switch if want to use the new Java 5 features that are presented in this book.

This figure also shows how to use a switch with TextPad. To do that, you begin by selecting the Configure→Preferences command, which displays the Preferences dialog box. Then, you expand the Tools group and select Compile Java, which displays the options for compiling Java. At that point, you can add a switch by typing it at the end of the parameters in the Parameters text box. In this figure, for example, the deprecation switch has been added to the end of the Parameters text box. As a result, the deprecation feature will be on for future TextPad sessions until you remove it from this dialog box.

Keep in mind, though, that you don't need to use either of the two switches shown in this figure as you use this book. Since the book is designed to teach you Java 5, you shouldn't need the source switch to specify the use of an earlier version. Since this book doesn't teach the deprecated features, you shouldn't need more information about them. However, you may occasionally need to use one or both of these switches.

Syntax to compile source code with a switch

```
javac ProgramName.java -switch1Name [-switch2Name]...
```

Two javac switches

Name	Description
deprecation	You can use this switch to get additional information about any deprecated features that your source code uses.
source	You can use this switch followed by the version number (1.3 or 1.4) to compile code that works with older versions of the Java interpreter.

How to compile code that uses deprecated features

Without the deprecation switch (you get notes)

```
C:\java\ch01>javac LoanCalculatorFrame.java
Note: LoanCalculatorFrame.java uses or overrides a deprecated API.
Note: Recompile with -Xlint:deprecation for details.
```

With the deprecation switch (you get details)

```
C:\java\ch01>javac LoanCalculatorFrame.java -deprecation
LoanCalculatorFrame.java:34: warning: [deprecation] show() in
java.awt.Window has been deprecated
                frame.show();
                     ^
1 warning
```

How to compile code with the source and deprecation switches

```
C:\java1.5\ch01>javac TestApp.java -source 1.4 -deprecation
```

The Preferences dialog box for TextPad with the deprecation switch on

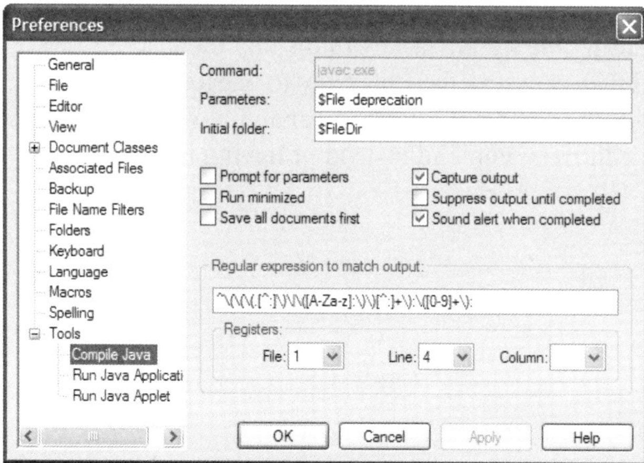

Description

- If you want to use the Java 1.5 features and you don't want to get the extra information for *deprecated features*, you don't need to set any switches.
- To use a switch with TextPad, select Configure→Preferences, expand the Tools group, select the Compile Java group, and add the switch to the end of the Parameters text box.

Figure 1-13 How to compile source code with a switch

Essential DOS skills for working with Java

Figure 1-14 summarizes some of the most useful commands and keystrokes for working with DOS. In addition, it shows how to install and use a DOS program called DOSKey, which makes entering and editing DOS commands easier. If you're going to use DOS to work with Java, you should review these DOS commands and keystrokes, and you will probably want to turn on the DOSKey program if it isn't already on. If you aren't going to use DOS, of course, you can skip this figure.

At the top of this figure, you can see a DOS window that shows two DOS commands and a directory listing. Here, the first command changes the current directory to c:\java\exercises\ch01. The next command displays a directory listing. If you study this listing, you can see that this directory contains two files with one line of information for each file. At the right side of each line, you can see the complete file names for these two files (TestApp.class and TestApp.java), and you can see the capitalization for these files as well.

If you master the DOS commands summarized in this figure, you should be able to use DOS to work with Java. To switch to another drive, type the letter of the drive followed by a colon. To change the current directory to another directory, use the cd command. To display a directory listing for the current directory, use the dir command. Although DOS provides many more commands that let you create directories, move files, copy files, and rename files, you can also use the Windows Explorer to perform those types of tasks.

Although you don't need to use the DOSKey program, it can save you a lot of typing and frustration. If, for example, you compile a program and you encounter a syntax error, you will need to use a text editor to fix the error in the source code. Then, you will need to compile the program again. If you're using DOSKey, you can do that by pressing the up-arrow key to display the last command that was executed and then pressing the Enter key to execute the command. And if you make a mistake when entering a command, you can use the left- and right-arrow keys to edit the command instead of having to enter the entire command again.

A directory listing

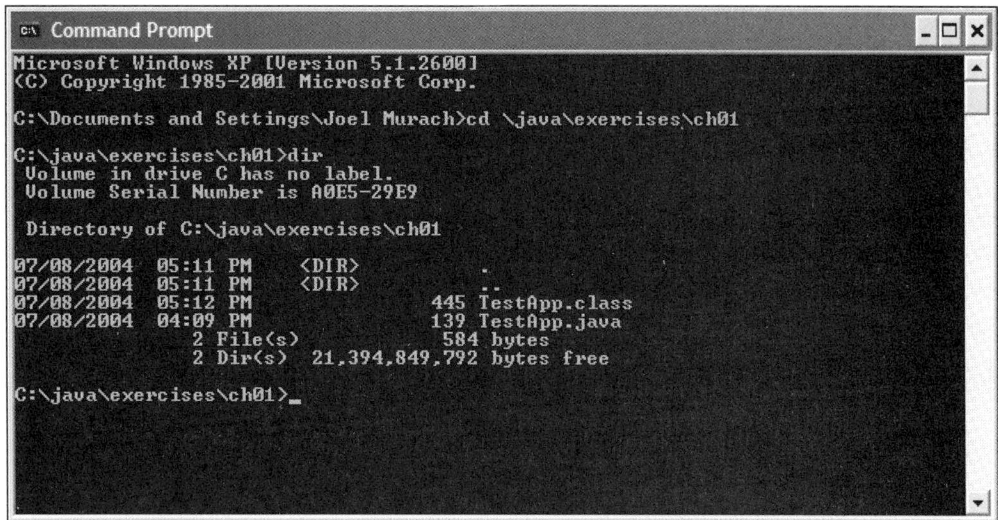

Command Prompt
Microsoft Windows XP [Version 5.1.2600]
(C) Copyright 1985-2001 Microsoft Corp.
C:\Documents and Settings\Joel Murach>cd \java\exercises\ch01
C:\java\exercises\ch01>dir
Volume in drive C has no label.
Volume Serial Number is A0E5-29E9
Directory of C:\java\exercises\ch01
07/08/2004 05:11 PM <DIR> .
07/08/2004 05:11 PM <DIR> ..
07/08/2004 05:12 PM 445 TestApp.class
07/08/2004 04:09 PM 139 TestApp.java
2 File(s) 584 bytes
2 Dir(s) 21,394,849,792 bytes free
C:\java\exercises\ch01>_

A review of DOS commands and keystrokes

Command	Description
dir	Displays a directory listing.
dir /p	Displays a directory listing that pauses if the listing is too long to fit on one screen.
cd \	Changes the current directory to the root directory for the current drive.
cd ..	Changes the current directory to the parent directory.
cd *directory name*	Changes the current directory to the subdirectory with the specified name.
letter:	Changes the current drive to the drive specified by the letter. For example, entering d: changes the current drive to the d drive.

How to start the DOSKey program

- To start the DOSKey program, enter "doskey /insert" at the command prompt.
- To automatically start the DOSKey program for all future sessions, add the "doskey/insert" statement after the "path" statement in the autoexec.bat file. For help on editing the autoexec.bat file, see the second procedure in figure 1-6.

How to use the DOSKey program

Key	Description
Up or down arrow	Cycles through previous DOS commands in the current session.
Left or right arrow	Moves cursor to allow normal editing of the text on the command prompt.

Figure 1-14 Essential DOS skills for working with Java

How to use the documentation for the J2SE API

When you write Java code, you'll often need to look up information about the *Application Program Interface* (*API*) for the J2SE. The API provides the Java classes that you can use as you build your Java applications. Since Sun provides HTML-based documentation for the J2SE API, you can browse this documentation with any web browser to get the detailed information you need about any Java class.

How to install the API documentation

Although you can use your browser to view the documentation for the J2SE API from the Java web site, you will want to install this documentation on your hard drive instead. That way, you can browse the documentation more quickly, and you can browse it even if you aren't connected to the Internet.

To download and install this documentation, you can use the procedure shown in figure 1-15. Since the documentation comes in a compressed format called a *zip file*, you need to use an unzip tool to extract the HTML pages from the zip file. When you use this tool, it creates a docs directory that contains many files and subdirectories. Although you can store the docs directory anywhere you like, it's common to store it as a subdirectory of the JDK directory.

If your operating system doesn't include a tool for working with zip files, you can download one from the web. For example, WinZip is a popular program for working with zip files. You can download a free evaluation copy from www.winzip.com.

How to download the API documentation

1. Go to the Java web site (java.sun.com).
2. Go to the download page for the version of the JDK that you're using (see figure 1-4) and find the hyperlink for the API documentation download.
3. Follow the instructions for the download and save the zip file to your hard drive.

How to install the API documentation

- Extract all files in the zip file to your hard drive. This will create a directory named docs that contains several files and subdirectories.
- Although it's common to store the API documentation in the JDK directory (usually C:\Program Files\Java\jdk1.5.0 for version 5), you can store it anywhere you like.

Description

- The *Application Programming Interface*, or *API*, provides all the classes that are included as part of the JDK. To learn about these classes, you can use the API documentation.
- You can view the API documentation from the Java web site, or you can download and install it on your system.

Notes

- You can click the "How long will it take" link to determine how long it will take to download the zip file based on its size and the speed of your modem. For a 56K modem, for example, it will take about 2 hours and 16 minutes to download 46MB.
- If you're using an older operating system that doesn't automatically work with zip files, you may need to use a tool such as WinZip to extract the files from the zip file. To download a free evaluation copy of WinZip, go to www.winzip.com.

Figure 1-15 How to install the API documentation

How to navigate the API documentation

Figure 1-16 shows how to navigate the documentation for the J2SE API. To start, you point your web browser to the index page that's stored in the docs\api directory. To do that for the first time, use the Windows Explorer to navigate to the docs\api directory and double-click on the index.html file, or enter the location of this page into the address area of your web browser:

```
C:\Program Files\Java\jdk1.5.0\docs\api\index.html
```

Since you'll need to access this page often as you learn about Java, you should use your web browser's favorites or bookmark feature to mark this page. Then, the next time you need to use this page, you can go right to it.

To browse the Java documentation, you need to know that all the classes in the Java API are organized into *packages*. As a result, the index page for the documentation provides a way to navigate through packages and classes. To start, you can select a package from the upper left frame. When you do, the lower left frame displays all the classes in that package. Then, you can select a class to display information about that class in the right frame.

As you progress through this book, you'll learn about many different packages and classes, and you'll learn much more about how packages and classes work. Along the way, you can always use the documentation for the Java API to help clarify the discussion or further your knowledge.

The index for the documentation

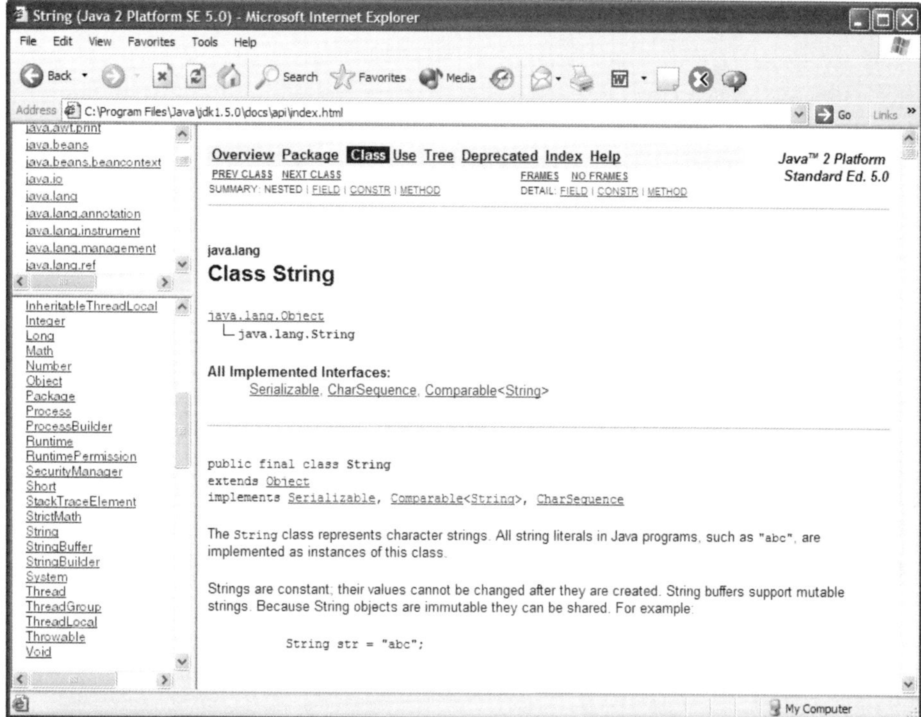

Description

- If you've installed the API documentation on your hard drive, you can display an index like the one shown above by using your web browser to go to the index.html file in the docs\api directory. If you haven't installed the documentation, you can browse through it on the Java web site.
- Related classes in the Java API are organized into *packages*, which are listed in the upper left frame of the documentation page. When you select a package, all the classes for that package are listed in the lower left frame.
- You can select a class from the lower left frame to display the documentation for that class in the right frame. You can also select the name of the package at the top of the lower left frame to display information about the package and the classes it contains.
- Once you display the documentation for a class, you can scroll through it or click on a hyperlink to get more information.
- The documentation for a class usually provides a wide range of information, including a summary of all of its methods. You'll learn more about methods and how they're used throughout this book.
- To make it easier to access the API documentation, you should bookmark the index page. To do that with the Internet Explorer, select the Add To Favorites command from the Favorites menu and accept the default name for the page or assign your own name to it. Then, you can redisplay this page later by selecting it from the Favorites menu.

Figure 1-16 How to navigate the API documentation

Introduction to Java IDEs

Many *Integrated Development Environments* (*IDEs*) are available for working with Java. A typical IDE provides not only a text editor, but also tools for compiling, running, and debugging code as well as tools for designing user interfaces. To illustrate the range of Java IDEs available, I'll present an overview of two IDEs. Keep in mind, however, that a search of the web will show that dozens of other IDEs are also available for working with Java.

Overview of Eclipse

Eclipse is a popular IDE that's available for free from www.eclipse.org. The first screen in figure 1-17 shows the window you use to edit code using Eclipse. As you work with the code editor, Eclipse can help you complete your code and notify you of potential compile-time errors. In addition, Eclipse will automatically compile your programs for you when you run them. And when you run a program that prints text to the console, Eclipse displays that text in the Console window.

The second screen in this figure shows the windows that are displayed when you use Eclipse to debug a program. Here, you can use the code editor to set breakpoints, and you can use the buttons in the toolbar to step through your code. As you do, you can use the top-right window to view the values of all of the active variables. If you've used any modern debugging tool, you should understand how this works.

Eclipse also provides many other advanced features that aren't available from a simple tool like TextPad. For example, you can use Eclipse with JUnit, which helps you test each part of an application, and also with Ant, which helps you document, package, and deploy your applications.

When we recommend using a professional IDE

Although a professional IDE like Eclipse can make it easier to develop Java applications, we don't recommend that you use one when you're learning Java for two reasons. First, this type of IDE will often generate code for you, which won't help you learn how to write the code for yourself. Second, an IDE like this is a complex tool with operational details that are themselves difficult to learn.

Once you've got a solid grasp on the use of Java, though, a professional IDE can make working with Java easier. In particular, it can make it easier to develop graphical user interfaces and to debug your code. As a result, we recommend that you start using one of these tools after you've mastered the core Java skills.

Of course, we realize that this choice is a personal one. Some talented programmers prefer the simplicity and speed of a text editor to the complexity and sluggishness of a professional IDE. Conversely, some students prefer learning with an IDE despite the additional learning curve that it presents. With or without an IDE, though, this book will help you master the core Java skills.

The Eclipse code editor

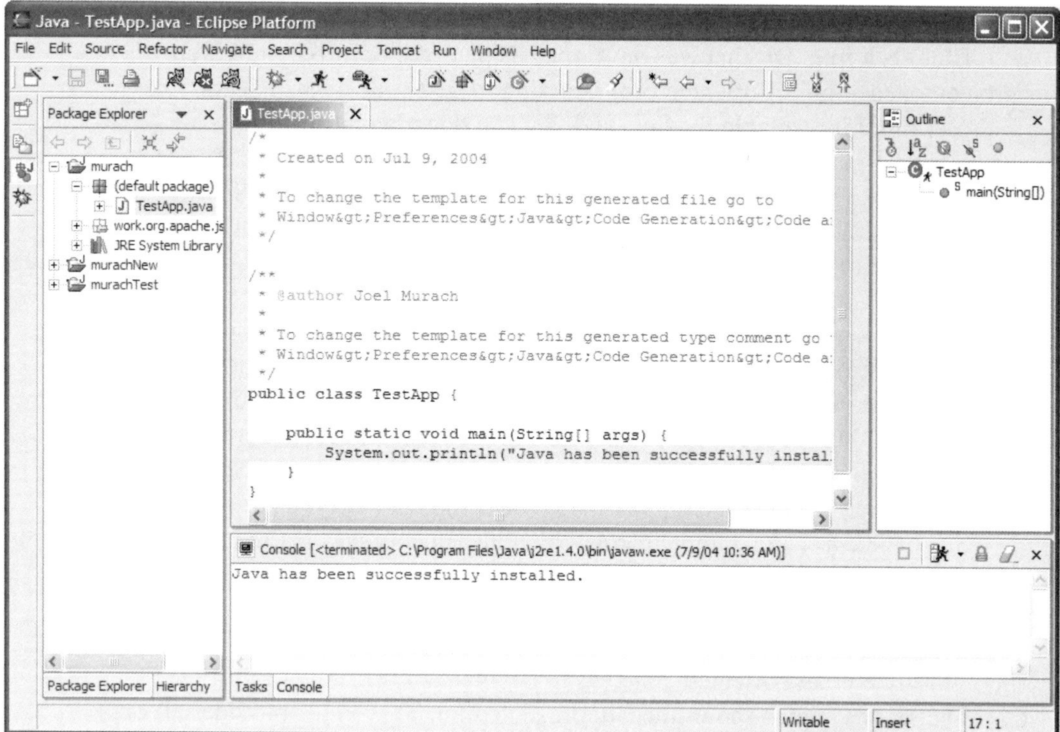

The Eclipse debugger

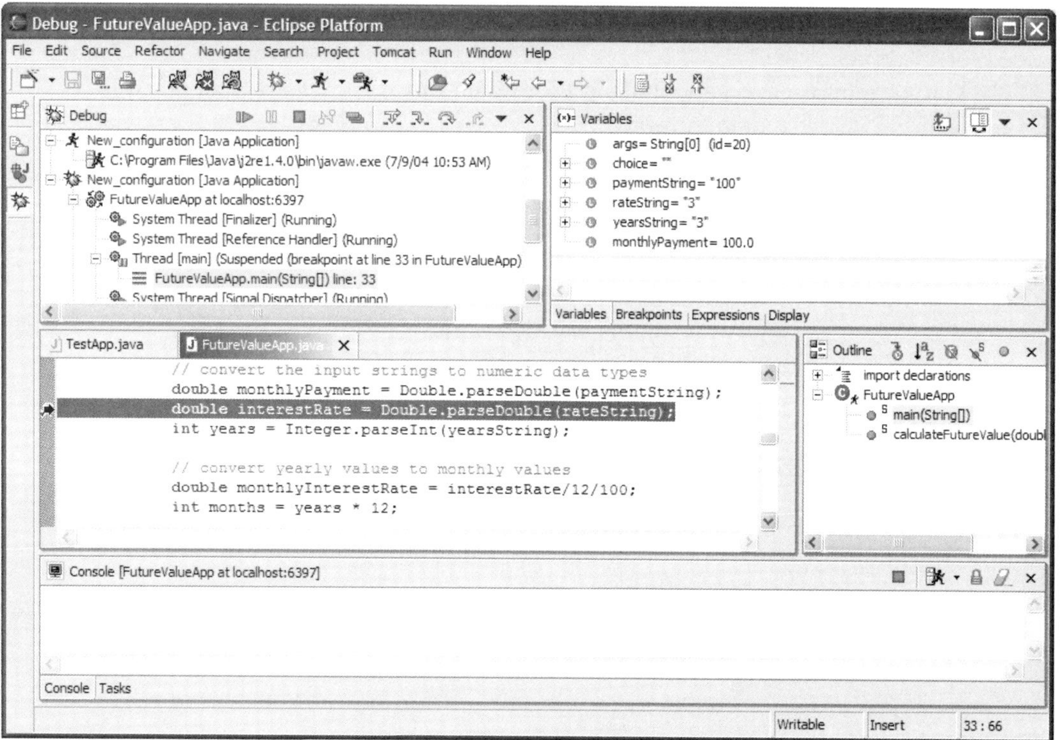

Figure 1-17 Two views of a professional IDE named Eclipse

Overview of BlueJ

BlueJ is a free IDE that was developed as part of a university research project to teach object-oriented programming to first year Java students. Like Eclipse, BlueJ is available for free, and you can download it from www.bluej.org. Although BlueJ doesn't provide as many features as a professional IDE like Eclipse, it provides some of the advantages of an IDE without some of the drawbacks. For example, BlueJ includes a debugger that's easy for students to learn. As a result, if you're new to object-oriented programming, you might want to try using BlueJ.

The first screen in figure 1-18 shows how BlueJ maintains a diagram of all classes in a project. This diagram can help students visualize how the classes in a project work together. In this diagram, the arrows with closed heads show that the Book and Software classes inherit the Product class. In contrast, the other arrows show that the ProductDB class uses the Product, Book, and Software classes and that the ProductApp class uses the Product and ProductDB classes.

Since the BlueJ diagram is interactive, it also encourages learning. For instance, you can right-click on any class to compile the code for a class, to edit or view the code for the class, to experiment with the class, and to explore the class. While this provides little benefit to an experienced programmer, it can help illustrate object-oriented concepts to beginners.

The second screen shows the BlueJ code editor. This editor provides all of the features that you would expect from a text editor that's designed for working with Java. In fact, it provides many of the same features as TextPad, including a Compile command that allows you to compile code directly from the code editor.

For more information about using BlueJ with this book, please visit our web site at:

```
www.murach.com/bluej
```

Here, you'll find a PDF file that shows how to download and install BlueJ. This file also shows how to use BlueJ to work with the applications presented in this book.

A BlueJ project

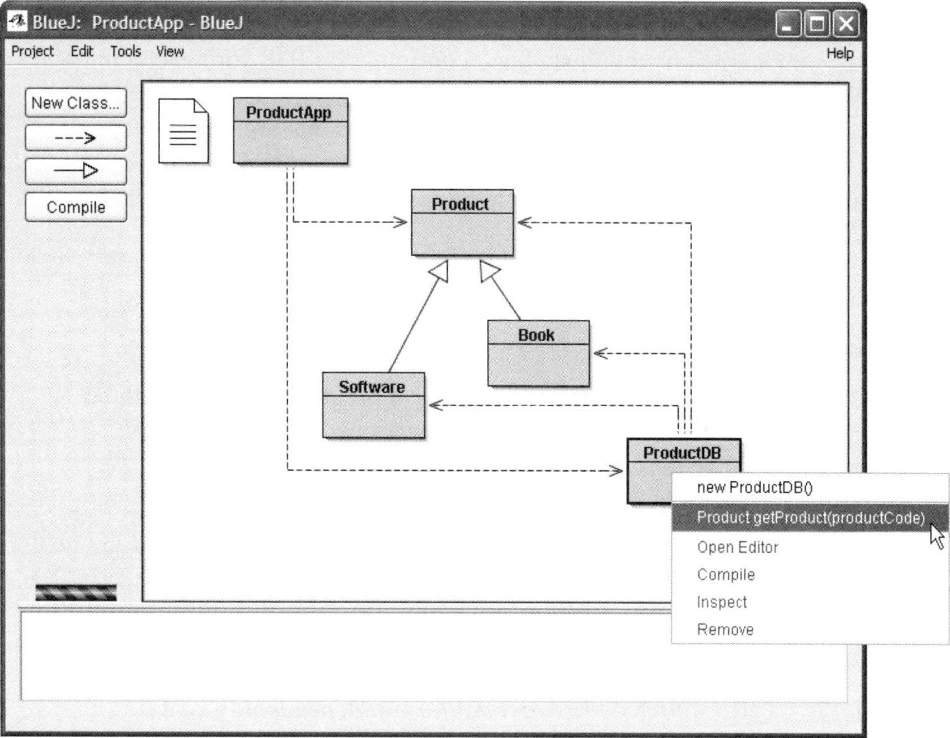

The BlueJ code editor

ProductApp

Class Edit Tools Options

Compile | Undo | Cut | Copy | Paste | Find... | Find Next | Close | Implementation

```
import java.util.Scanner;

public class ProductApp
{
    public static void main(String args[])
    {
        // welcome the user to the program
        System.out.println("Weclome to the Product Selector");
        System.out.println();

        // perform 1 or more selections
        String choice = "y";
        while (choice.equalsIgnoreCase("y"))
        {
            // get the input scanner
            Scanner sc = new Scanner(System.in);
            System.out.print("Enter product code: ");
            String productCode = sc.nextLine();  // read entire line

            // use the ProductDB class to get the Product object
            Product p = ProductDB.getProduct(productCode);

```

File saved

saved

Figure 1-18 Two views of a student IDE named BlueJ

Perspective

In this chapter, you learned how to install and configure the JDK for developing Java programs. You learned how to use TextPad to enter, edit, compile, and run a program. You learned how to use the command prompt to compile and run programs. And you learned how to install and view the API documentation for the JDK. With that as background, you're ready to learn how to write your own Java applications.

Summary

- You use the *Java Development Kit* (*JDK*) to develop Java programs. This used to be called the *Software Development Kit* (*SDK*) for Java. Versions 1.2 through 5.0 of the JDK run under the *Java 2 Platform, Standard Edition* (*J2SE*) so they are sometimes referred to as *Java 2*.
- You can use the J2SE platform to create *applications* and a special type of Internet-based application known as an *applet*. In addition, you can use the *Java 2 Platform, Enterprise Edition* (*J2EE*) to create server-side applications using *servlets* and *JavaServer Pages* (*JSPs*).
- The *Java compiler* translates *source code* into a *platform-independent* format known as Java *bytecodes*. Then, the *Java interpreter*, or *Java Runtime Environment* (*JRE*), translates the bytecodes into instructions that can be run by a specific operating system. A Java interpreter is an implementation of a *Java virtual machine* (*JVM*).
- When you use the JDK with Windows, you should add the bin directory (usually C:\Program Files\Java\jdk1.5.0\bin) to the *command path* and you should add the current directory to the *classpath*.
- A *text editor* that's designed for working with Java provides features that make it easier to enter, edit, and save Java code.
- Some text editors such as TextPad include commands for compiling and running Java applications. You can also use the *command prompt* to enter the commands for compiling and running an application.
- When you compile a program, you may get *compile-time errors*. When you run a program, you may get *runtime errors*.
- To compile code from the command prompt, you use the *javac command* to start the Java compiler. To run an application from the command prompt, you use the *java command* to start the Java interpreter.
- You can get detailed information about any class in the J2SE by using a web browser to browse the HTML-based documentation for its *Application Programming Interface* (*API*).
- Once you've mastered the basics of Java, an *Integrated Development Environment* (*IDE*) can make working with Java easier.

Before you do the exercises for this chapter

Before you do any of the exercises in this book, you need to download the folders and files for this book from our web site (www.murach.com) and install them on your system. For complete instructions, please refer to appendix A. Then, you should follow the procedures shown in this chapter to install and configure the JDK (figure 1-4 through 1-7), TextPad (figure 1-8) or an equivalent text editor, and the documentation for the Java API (figure 1-15).

Exercise 1-1 Use TextPad to develop an application

This exercise will guide you through the process of using TextPad to enter, save, compile, and run a simple application.

Enter and save the source code

1. Start TextPad by clicking on the Start button and selecting Programs or All Programs→TextPad.
2. Enter this code (type carefully and use the same capitalization):

```
public class TestApp
{
    public static void main(String[] args)
    {
        System.out.println(
            "This Java application has run successfully");
    }
}
```

3. Use the Save command in the File menu to display the Save As dialog box. Next, navigate to the c:\java1.5\ch01 directory and enter TestApp in the File name box. If necessary, select the Java option from the Save as Type combo box. Then, click on the Save button to save the file.

Compile the source code and run the application

4. Press Ctrl+1 to compile the source code. If you get an error message, read the error message, edit the text file, save your changes, and compile the application again. Repeat this process until you get a clean compile (the code is displayed with no error messages).
5. Press Ctrl+2 to run the application. This application should display a console window that says “This Java application has run successfully” followed by a line that reads “Press any key to continue…”.
6. Press any key. This should close the console window. If it doesn’t, click on the Close button in the upper right corner of the window to close it.

Introduce and correct a compile-time error

7. In the TextPad window, delete the semicolon at the end of the System.out.println statement. Then, press Ctrl+1 to compile the source code. TextPad should display an error message that indicates that the semicolon is missing in the Command Results window.

8. In the Document Selector pane, click on the TestApp.java file to switch back to the source code, and press Ctrl+F6 twice to toggle back and forth between the Command Result window and the source code. Then, select View→Line Numbers to display the line numbers for the source code lines.
9. Correct the error and compile the file again (this automatically saves your changes). This time the file should compile cleanly, so you can run it again and make sure that it works correctly.
10. Select Configure→Preferences, click on View, and check Line Numbers. That will add line numbers to the source statements in all your applications. If you want to look through the other options and set any of them, do that now. When you're done, close the file and exit TextPad.

Exercise 1-2 Use any Java development tool to develop an application

If you aren't going to use TextPad to develop your Java programs, you can try whatever tools you are going to use with this generic exercise.

Use any text editor to enter and save the source code

1. Start the text editor and enter this code (type carefully and use the same capitalization):

```
public class TestApp
{
    public static void main(String[] args)
    {
        System.out.println(
            "This Java application has run successfully");
    }
}
```

2. Save this code in the c:\java1.5\ch01 directory in a file named "TestApp.java".

Compile the source code and run the application

3. Compile the source code. If you're using a text editor that has a compile command, use this command. Otherwise, use your command prompt to compile the source code. To do that, start your command prompt and use the cd command to change to the c:\java1.5\ch01 directory. Then, enter the javac command like this (make sure to use the same capitalization):

```
javac TestApp.java
```

4. Run the application. If you're using a text editor that has a run or execute command, use this command. Otherwise, use your command prompt to run the application. To do that, enter the java command like this (make sure to use the same capitalization):

```
java TestApp
```

5. When you enter this command, the application should print "This Java application has run successfully" to the console window.

Exercise 1-3 Use the command prompt to run any compiled application

This exercise shows how to use the command prompt to run any Java application.

1. Open the command prompt window. Then, change the current directory to c:\java1.5\ch01.
2. Use the java command to run the LoanCalculatorApp application. This application calculates the monthly payment for a loan amount at the interest rate and number of years that you specify. This shows how the JRE can run any application whether or not it has been compiled on that machine. When you're done, close the application to return to the command prompt.

Exercise 1-4 Navigate the API documentation

This exercise will give you some practice using the API documentation to look up information about a class.

1. Start a web browser and navigate to the index page that contains the API documentation for the JDK (usually C:\Program Files\Java\jdk1.5.0\docs\api\index.htm). This page should look like the one shown in figure 1-16.
2. Bookmark this page so you can easily access it later. To do that with the Internet Explorer, select the Add To Favorites item from the Favorites menu. Then, close your web browser.
3. Start your web browser again and use the bookmark to return to the API documentation for the JDK. To do that with the Internet Explorer, select the Java 2 Platform SE item from the Favorites menu.
4. Select the java.lang package in the upper left frame and notice that the links in the lower left frame change. Select the System class from this frame to display information about it in the right frame.
5. Scroll down to the Field Summary area in the right frame and click on the out link for the standard output stream. When you do, an HTML page that gives some information about how to use the standard output stream will be displayed. In the next chapter, you'll learn more about using the out field of the System class to print data to the console.
6. Continue experimenting with the documentation until you're comfortable with how it works. Then, close the browser.

2

Introduction to Java programming

Once you've got Java on your system, the quickest and best way to *learn* Java programming is to *do* Java programming. That's why this chapter shows you how to write complete Java programs that get input from a user, make calculations, and display output. When you finish this chapter, you should be able to write comparable programs of your own.

Basic coding skills

This chapter starts by introducing you to some basic coding skills. You'll use these skills for every Java program you develop. Once you understand these skills, you'll be ready to learn how to write simple programs.

How to code statements

The *statements* in a Java program direct the operation of the program. When you code a statement, you can start it anywhere in a coding line, you can continue it from one line to another, and you can code one or more spaces anywhere a single space is valid. In the first example in figure 2-1, the statements aren't shaded.

To end most statements, you use a semicolon. But when a statement requires a set of braces { }, it ends with the right brace. Then, the statements within the braces are referred to as a *block* of code.

To make a program easier to read, you should use indentation and spacing to align statements and blocks of code. This is illustrated by the program in this figure and by all of the programs and examples in this book.

How to code comments

Comments are used in Java programs to document what the program does and what specific blocks and lines of code do. Since the Java compiler ignores comments, you can include them anywhere in a program without affecting your code. In the first example in figure 2-1, the comments are shaded.

A *single-line comment* is typically used to describe one or more lines of code. This type of comment starts with two slashes (//) that tell the compiler to ignore all characters until the end of the current line. In the first example in this figure, you can see four single-line comments that are used to describe groups of statements. The fifth comment is coded after a statement to describe what that statement does. This type of comment is sometimes referred to as an *end-of-line comment*.

The second example in this figure shows how to code a *block comment*. This type of comment is typically used to document information that applies to a block of code. This information can include the author's name, program completion date, the purpose of the code, the files used by the code, and so on.

Although many programmers sprinkle their code with comments, that shouldn't be necessary if you write code that's easy to read and understand. Instead, you should use comments only to clarify code that's difficult to understand. In this figure, for example, an experienced Java programmer wouldn't need any of the single-line comments.

One problem with comments is that they may not accurately represent what the code does. This often happens when a programmer changes the code, but doesn't change the comments that go along with it. Then, it's even harder to understand the code because the comments are misleading. So if you change the code that you've written comments for, be sure to change the comments too.

An application consists of statements and comments

```
import java.util.Scanner;

public class InvoiceApp
{
    public static void main(String[] args)
    {
        // display a welcome message
        System.out.println("Welcome to the Invoice Total Calculator");
        System.out.println();  // print a blank line

        // get the input from the user
        Scanner sc = Scanner.create(System.in);
        System.out.print("Enter subtotal:   ");
        double subtotal = sc.nextDouble();

        // calculate the discount amount and total
        double discountPercent = .2;
        double discountAmount = subtotal * discountPercent;
        double invoiceTotal = subtotal - discountAmount;

        // format and display the result
        String message = "Discount percent: " + discountPercent + "\n"
                       + "Discount amount:  " + discountAmount + "\n"
                       + "Invoice total:    " + invoiceTotal + "\n";
        System.out.println(message);
    }
}
```

A block comment that could be coded at the start of a program

```
/*
 * Date:     9/1/04
 * Author:   A. Steelman
 * Purpose:  This program uses the console to get a subtotal from the user.
 *           Then, it calculates the discount amount and total
 *           and displays these values on the console.
 */
```

Description

- Java *statements* direct the operations of a program, while *comments* are used to help document what the program does.
- You can start a statement at any point in a line and continue the statement from one line to the next. To make a program easier to read, you should use indentation and extra spaces to align statements and parts of statements.
- Most statements end with a semicolon. But when a statement requires a set of braces { }, the statement ends with the right brace. Then, the code within the braces can be referred to as a *block* of code.
- To code a *single-line comment*, type // followed by the comment. You can code a single-line comment on a line by itself or after a statement. A comment that's coded after a statement is sometimes called an *end-of-line comment*.
- To code a *block comment*, type /* at the start of the block and */ at the end. You can also code asterisks to identify the lines in the block, but that isn't necessary.

Figure 2-1 How to code comments and statements

How to create identifiers

As you code a Java program, you need to create and use *identifiers*. These are the names in the program that you define. In each program, for example, you need to create an identifier for the name of the program and for the variables that are used by the program.

Figure 2-2 shows you how to create identifiers. In brief, you must start each identifier with a letter, underscore, or dollar sign. After that first character, you can use any combination of letters, underscores, dollar signs, or digits.

Since Java is case-sensitive, you need to be careful when you create and use identifiers. If, for example, you define an identifier as CustomerAddress, you can't refer to it later as Customeraddress. That's a common compile-time error.

When you create an identifier, you should try to make the name both meaningful and easy to remember. To make a name meaningful, you should use as many characters as you need, so it's easy for other programmers to read and understand your code. For instance, netPrice is more meaningful than nPrice, and nPrice is more meaningful than np.

To make a name easy to remember, you should avoid abbreviations. If, for example, you use nwCst as an identifier, you may have difficulty remembering whether it was nCust, nwCust, or nwCst later on. If you code the name as newCustomer, though, you won't have any trouble remembering what it was. Yes, you type more characters when you create identifiers that are meaningful and easy to remember, but that will be more than justified by the time you'll save when you test, debug, and maintain the program.

For some common identifiers, though, programmers typically use just one or two lowercase letters. For instance, they often use the letters *i*, *j*, and *k* to identify counter variables. You'll see examples of this later in this chapter.

Notice that you can't create an identifier that is the same as one of the Java *keywords*. These 50 keywords are reserved by the Java language and are the basis for that language. To help you identify keywords in your code, Java-enabled text editors and Java IDEs display these keywords in a different color than the rest of the Java code. For example, TextPad displays keywords in blue. As you progress through this book, you'll learn how to use almost all of these keywords.

Valid identifiers

```
InvoiceApp          $orderTotal        i
Invoice             _orderTotal        x
InvoiceApp2         input_string       TITLE
subtotal            _get_total         MONTHS_PER_YEAR
discountPercent     $_64_Valid
```

The rules for naming an identifier

- Start each identifier with a letter, underscore, or dollar sign. Use letters, dollar signs, underscores, or digits for subsequent characters.
- Use up to 255 characters.
- Don't use Java keywords.

Keywords

```
boolean     if          interface   class       true
char        else        package     volatile    false
byte        final       switch      while       throws
float       private     case        return      native
void        protected   break       throw       implements
short       public      default     try         import
double      static      for         catch       synchronized
int         new         continue    finally     const
long        this        do          transient   goto
abstract    super       extends     instanceof  null
```

Description

- An *identifier* is any name that you create in a Java program. These can be the names of classes, methods, variables, and so on.
- A *keyword* is a word that's reserved by the Java language. As a result, you can't use keywords as identifiers.
- When you refer to an identifier, be sure to use the correct uppercase and lowercase letters because Java is a case-sensitive language.

Figure 2-2 How to create identifiers

How to declare a class

When you write Java code, you store your code in a *class*. As a result, to write a Java program, you must write at least one class. As you learned in chapter 1, the code for each class is stored in a *.java file, and the compiled code is stored in a *.class file. To write a class, you must begin with a *class declaration* like the ones shown in figure 2-3.

In the syntax for declaring a class, the boldfaced words are Java keywords, and the words that aren't boldfaced represent code that the programmer supplies. The bar (|) in this syntax means that you have a choice between the two items that the bar separates. In this case, the bar means that you can start the declaration with the public keyword or the private keyword.

The public and private keywords are *access modifiers* that control the *scope* of a class. Usually, a class is declared public, which means that other classes can access it. In fact, you must declare one (and only one) public class for every *.java file. Later in this book, you'll learn when and how to use private classes.

After the public keyword and the class keyword, you code the name of the class using the basic rules for creating an identifier. When you do, it's a common coding convention to start a class name with a capital letter and to use letters and digits only. It's also common to start every word within the name with a capital letter. We also recommend that you use a noun or a noun that's preceded by one or more adjectives for your class names. In this figure, all four class names adhere to these rules and guidelines.

After the class name, the syntax summary shows a left brace, the statements that make up the class, and a right brace. It's a good coding practice, though, to type your ending brace right after you type the starting brace, and then type your code between the two braces. That prevents missing braces, which is a common compile-time error.

The two InvoiceApp classes in this figure show how a class works. Here, the class declaration and its braces are shaded and the code for the class is between the braces. In this simple example, the class contains a single block of code that displays a message. You'll learn more about how this code works in the next figure.

Notice that the only difference between the two classes in this figure is where the opening braces for the class and the block of code within the class are placed. Some programmers prefer to code the brace on a separate line because they think that the additional vertical spacing makes the code easier to read. Others prefer to code the brace immediately following the class or method name because it saves vertical space and because they believe that it is equally easy to read. Although either technique is acceptable, we've chosen to use the first technique for this book whenever possible.

As you learned in the last chapter, when you save your class on disk, you save it with a name that consists of the public class name and the *java* extension. As a result, you save the class in this figure with the name InvoiceApp.java.

The syntax for declaring a class

```
public|private class ClassName
{
    statements
}
```

Typical class declarations

```
public class InvoiceApp{}
public class ProductOrderApp{}
public class Product{}
public class ProductOrder{}
```

A public class named InvoiceApp

```
public class InvoiceApp                              // declare the class
{                                                    // begin the class
    public static void main(String[] args)
    {
        System.out.println("Welcome to the Invoice Total Calculator");
    }
}                                                    // end the class
```

The same class with different brace placement

```
public class InvoiceApp{                              // declare and begin the class
   public static void main(String[] args){
      System.out.println("Welcome to the Invoice Total Calculator");
   }
}                                                     // end the class
```

The rules for naming a class

- Start the name with a capital letter.
- Use letters and digits only.
- Follow the other rules for naming an identifier.

Naming recommendations for classes

- Start every word within a class name with an initial cap.
- Each class name should be a noun or a noun that's preceded by one or more adjectives.

Description

- When you develop a Java application, you code one or more *classes* for it. For each class, you must code a *class declaration*. Then, you write the code for the class within the opening and closing braces of the declaration.
- The public and private keywords are *access modifiers* that control what parts of the program can use the class. If a class is public, the class can be used by all parts of the program.
- Most classes are declared public, and each file must contain one and only one public class. The file name for a class is the same as the class name with *java* as the extension.

Figure 2-3 How to declare a class

How to declare a main method

Every Java program contains one or more *methods*, which are pieces of code that perform tasks (they're similar to *functions* in some programming languages). The *main method* is a special kind of method that's automatically executed when the class that holds it is run. All Java programs contain a main method that starts the program.

To code a main method, you begin by coding a *main method declaration* as shown in figure 2-4. For now, you can code every main method declaration using the code exactly as it's shown, even if you don't understand the code. Although this figure gives a partial explanation for each keyword in the method, you can skip that if you like because you'll learn more about each of these keywords as you progress through this book. We included this summary for those who are already familiar with object-oriented programming.

As you can see in this figure, the main method of the InvoiceApp class is coded within the class declaration. To make this structure clear, the main method is indented and the starting and ending braces are aligned so it's easy to see where the method begins and ends. Then, between the braces, you can see the one statement that this main method performs.

The syntax for declaring a main method

```
public static void main(String[] args)
{
    statements
}
```

The main method of the InvoiceApp class

```
public class InvoiceApp
{
    public static void main(String[] args)
    {                                         // begin main method
        System.out.println("Welcome to the Invoice Total Calculator");
    }                                         // end main method
}
```

Description

- A *method* is a block of code that performs a task.
- Every Java application contains one *main method* that you can declare exactly as shown above. This is called the *main method declaration.*
- The statements between the braces in a main method declaration are run when the program is executed.

Partial explanation of the terms in the main method declaration

- The *public* keyword in the declaration means that other classes can access the main method. The *static* keyword means that the method can be called directly from the other classes without first creating an object. And the *void* keyword means that the method won't return any values.
- The *main* identifier is the name of the method. When you code a method, always include parentheses after the name of the method.
- The code in the parentheses lists the *arguments* that the method uses, and every main method receives an argument named *args*, which is defined as an array of strings.

Figure 2-4 How to declare a main method

How to work with numeric variables

In this topic, you'll learn how to work with numeric variables. This will introduce you to the use of variables, assignment statements, arithmetic expressions, and two of the eight primitive data types that are supported by Java. Then, you can learn all the details about working with the primitive data types in the next chapter.

How to declare and initialize variables

A *variable* is used to store a value that can change as the program executes. Before you can use a variable, you must *declare* its data type and name, and you must *assign* a value to it to *initialize* it. The easiest way to do that is shown in figure 2-5. Just code the data type, the variable name, the equals sign, and the value that you want to assign to the variable.

This figure also summarizes two of the eight Java *data types*. You can use the *int* data type to store *integers*, which are numbers that don't contain decimal places (whole numbers), and you can use the *double* data type to store numbers that contain decimal places. In the next chapter, you'll learn how to use the six other primitive data types, but these are the two that you'll probably use the most.

As you can see in the summary, the double data type can be used to store very large and very small numbers with up to 16 significant digits. In case you aren't familiar with E notation, .123456E+7 means .123456 times 10^7, which is 1234560. And 1234E-5 means 1234 times 10^{-5}, which is .01234. Here, the first example has six significant digits, and the second one has four significant digits. For business applications, you usually don't need to use this notation, and 16 significant digits are usually enough. In the next chapter, though, you'll learn how you can go beyond that 16 digit limitation whenever that's necessary.

To illustrate the declaration of variables, the first example in this figure declares an int variable named scoreCounter with an initial value of 1. And the second example declares a double variable named unitPrice with an initial value of 14.95. When you assign values to double types, it's a good coding practice to include a decimal point, even if the initial value is a whole number. If, for example, you want to assign the number 29 to the variable, you should code the number as 29.0.

If you follow the naming recommendations in this figure as you name the variables, it will make your programs easier to read and understand. In particular, you should capitalize the first letter in each word of the variable name, except the first word, as in scoreCounter or unitPrice. This is commonly referred to as *camel notation*.

When you initialize a variable, you can assign a *literal* value like 1 or 14.95 to a variable as illustrated by the examples in this figure. However, you can also initialize a variable to the value of another variable or to the value of an expression like the arithmetic expressions shown in the next figure.

Two of the eight primitive data types

Type	Bytes	Description
int	4	Integers from -2,147,483,648 to 2,147,483,647.
double	8	Numbers with decimal places that range from –1.7E308 to 1.7E308 with up to 16 significant digits.

How to declare and initialize a variable in one statement

Syntax

```
type variableName = value;
```

Examples

```
int scoreCounter = 1;              // initialize an integer variable
double unitPrice = 14.95;          // initialize a double variable
```

How to code assignment statements

```
int quantity = 0;                  // initialize an integer variable
int maxQuantity = 100;             // initialize another integer variable

// two assignment statements
quantity = 10;                     // quantity is now 10
quantity = maxQuantity;            // quantity is now 100
```

Description

- A *variable* stores a value that can change as a program executes.
- Java provides for eight *primitive data types* that you can use for storing values in memory. The two that you'll use the most are the int and double data types. In the next chapter, you'll learn how to use the other primitive data types.
- The *int* data type is used for storing *integers* (whole numbers). The *double* data type is used for storing numbers that can have one or more decimal places.
- To *initialize* a variable, you *declare* a data type and *assign* an initial value to the variable. As default values, it's common to initialize integer variables to 0 and double variables to 0.0.
- An *assignment statement* assigns a value to a variable. This value can be a literal value, another variable, or an expression like the arithmetic expressions that you'll learn how to code in the next figure. If a variable has already been declared, the assignment statement doesn't include the data type of the variable.

Naming recommendations for variables

- Start variable names with a lowercase letter and capitalize the first letter in all words after the first word.
- Each variable name should be a noun or a noun preceded by one or more adjectives.
- Try to use meaningful names that are easy to remember.

Figure 2-5 How to declare and initialize variables

How to code assignment statements

After you declare a variable, you can assign a new value to it. To do that, you code an *assignment statement*. In a simple assignment statement, you code the variable name, an equals sign, and a new value. The new value can be a literal value or the name of another variable as shown in figure 2-5. Or, the new value can be the result of an expression like the arithmetic expressions shown in figure 2-6.

How to code arithmetic expressions

To code simple *arithmetic expressions*, you can use the four *arithmetic operators* that are summarized in figure 2-6. As the first group of statements shows, these operators work the way you would expect them to with one exception. If you divide one integer into another integer, any decimal places are truncated. In contrast, if you divide a double into a double, the decimal places are included in the result.

If you code more than one operator in an expression, all of the multiplication and division operations are done first, from left to right. Then, the addition and subtraction operations are done, from left to right. If this isn't the way you want the expression to be evaluated, you can use parentheses to specify the sequence of operations in much the same way that you use parentheses in algebraic expressions. In the next chapter, you'll learn more about how this works.

When you code assignment statements, it's common to code the same variable on both sides of the equals sign. For example, you can add 1 to the value of a variable named counter with a statement like this:

```
counter = counter + 1;
```

In this case, if counter has a value of 5 when the statement starts, it will have a value of 6 when the statement finishes. This concept is illustrated by the second and third groups of statements.

What happens when you mix integer and double variables in the same arithmetic expression? The integers are *cast* (converted) to doubles so the decimal places can be included in the result. To retain the decimal places, though, the result variable must be a double. This is illustrated by the fourth group of statements.

The basic operators that you can use in arithmetic expressions

Operator	Name	Description
+	Addition	Adds two operands.
-	Subtraction	Subtracts the right operand from the left operand.
*	Multiplication	Multiplies the right operand and the left operand.
/	Division	Divides the right operand into the left operand. If both operands are integers, then the result is an integer.

Statements that use simple arithmetic expressions

```
// integer arithmetic
int x = 14;
int y = 8;
int result1 = x + y;          // result1 = 22
int result2 = x - y;          // result2 = 6
int result3 = x * y;          // result3 = 112
int result4 = x / y;          // result4 = 1

// double arithmetic
double a = 8.5;
double b = 3.4;
double result5 = a + b;       // result5  = 11.9
double result6 = a - b;       // result6  = 5.1
double result7= a * b;        // result7 = 28.9
double result8 = a / b;       // result8  = 2.5
```

Statements that increment a counter variable

```
int invoiceCount = 0;
invoiceCount = invoiceCount + 1;                  // invoiceCount = 1
invoiceCount = invoiceCount + 1;                  // invoiceCount = 2
```

Statements that add amounts to a total

```
double invoiceAmount1 = 150.25;
double invoiceAmount2 = 100.75;
double invoiceTotal = 0.0;
invoiceTotal = invoiceTotal + invoiceAmount1;     // invoiceTotal = 150.25
invoiceTotal = invoiceTotal + invoiceAmount2;     // invoiceTotal = 251.00
```

Statements that mix int and double variables

```
int result9 = invoiceTotal / invoiceCount         // result11 = 125
double result10 = invoiceTotal / invoiceCount     // result12 = 125.50
```

Description

- An *arithmetic expression* consists of one or more *operands* and *arithmetic operators*.
- When an expression mixes the use of int and double variables, Java automatically *casts* the int types to double types. To retain the decimal places, the variable that receives the result must be a double.
- In the next chapter, you'll learn how to code expressions that contain two or more operators.

Figure 2-6 How to code arithmetic expressions

How to work with string variables

In the topics that follow, you'll learn some basic skills for working with strings. For now, these skills should be all you need for many of the programs you develop. Keep in mind, though, that many programs require extensive string operations. That's why chapter 12 covers strings in more detail.

How to create a String object

A *string* can consist of any letters, numbers, and special characters. To declare a string variable, you use the syntax shown in figure 2-7. Although this is much like the syntax for declaring a numeric variable, a String *object* is created from the String class when a string variable is declared. Then, the string data is stored in that object. When you declare a string variable, you must capitalize the String keyword because it is the name of a class, not a primitive data type.

In the next topic and in chapter 6, you'll learn much more about classes and objects. For now, though, all you need to know is that string variables work much like numeric variables, except that they store string data instead of numeric data.

When you declare a String object, you can assign a *string literal* to it by enclosing the characters within double quotes. You can also assign an *empty string* to it by coding a set of quotation marks with nothing between them. Finally, you can use the null keyword to assign a *null value* to a String object. That indicates that the value of the string is unknown.

How to join and append strings

If you want to *join*, or *concatenate*, two or more strings into one, you can use the + operator. For example, you can join a first name, a space, and a last name as shown in the second example in this figure. Then, you can assign that string to a variable. Notice that when concatenating strings, you can use string variables or string literals.

You can also join a string with a primitive data type. This is illustrated in the third example in this figure. Here, a variable that's defined with the double data type is appended to a string. When you use this technique, Java automatically converts the double value to a string.

You can use the + and += operators to *append* a string to the end of a string that's stored in a string variable. If you use the + operator, you need to include the variable on both sides of the = operator. Otherwise, the assignment statement will replace the old value with the new value instead of appending the old value to the new value. Since the += operator provides a shorter and safer way to append strings, this operator is commonly used.

The syntax for declaring and initializing a string variable

```
String variableName = value;
```

Example 1: How to declare and initialize a string

```
String message1 = "Invalid data entry.";
String message2 = "";
String message3 = null;
```

Example 2: How to join strings

```
String firstName = "Bob";                      // firstName is Bob
String lastName = "Smith";                     // lastName is Smith
String name = firstName + " " + lastName;      // name is Bob Smith
```

Example 3: How to join a string and a number

```
double price = 14.95;
String priceString = "Price: " + price;
```

Example 4: How to append one string to another with the + operator

```
firstName = "Bob";                      // firstName is Bob
lastName = "Smith";                     // lastName is Smith
name = firstName + " ";                 // name is Bob followed by a space
name = name + lastName;                 // name is Bob Smith
```

Example 5: How to append one string to another with the += operator

```
firstName = "Bob";                      // firstName is Bob
lastName = "Smith";                     // lastName is Smith
name = firstName + " ";                 // name is Bob followed by a space
name += lastName;                       // name is Bob Smith
```

Description

- A *string* can consist of any characters in the character set including letters, numbers, and special characters like *, &, and #.
- In Java, a string is actually a String object that's created from the String class that's part of the Java API.
- To specify the value of a string, you can enclose text in double quotation marks. This is known as a *string literal*.
- To assign a *null value* to a string, you can use the null keyword. This means that the value of the string is unknown.
- To assign an *empty string* to a String object, you can code a set of quotation marks with nothing between them. This means that the string doesn't contain any characters.
- To *join* (or *concatenate*) a string with another string or a data type, use a plus sign. Whenever possible, Java will automatically convert the data type so it can be used as part of the string.
- When you *append* one string to another, you add one string to the end of another. To do that, you can use assignment statements.
- The += operator is a shortcut for appending a string expression to a string variable.

Figure 2-7 How to create and use strings

How to include special characters in strings

Figure 2-8 shows how to include certain types of special characters within a string. In particular, this figure shows how to include backslashes, quotation marks, and control characters such as new lines, tabs, and returns in a string. To do that, you can use the *escape sequences* shown in this figure.

As you can see, each escape sequence starts with a backslash. The backslash tells the compiler that the character that follows should be treated as a special character and not interpreted as a literal value. If you code a backslash followed by the letter *n*, for example, the compiler will include a new line character in the string. You can see how this works in the first example in this figure. If you omitted the backslash, of course, the compiler would just include the letter *n* in the string value. The escape sequences for the tab and return characters work similarly, as you can see in the second example.

To code a string literal, you enclose it in double quotes. If you want to include a double quote within a string literal, then, you must use an escape sequence. This is illustrated in the third example. Here, the \" escape sequence is used to include two double quotes within the string literal.

Finally, you need to use an escape sequence if you want to include a backslash in a string literal. To do that, you code two backslashes as shown in the fourth example. If you code a single backslash, the compiler will treat the next character as a special character. That will cause a compiler error if the character isn't a valid special character. And if the character is a valid special character, the results won't be what you want.

Common escape sequences

Sequence	Character
`\n`	New line
`\t`	Tab
`\r`	Return
`\"`	Quotation mark
`\\`	Backslash

Example 1: New line

String

```
"Code: JSPS\nPrice: $49.50"
```

Result

```
Code: JSPS
Price: $49.50
```

Example 2: Tabs and returns

String

```
"Joe\tSmith\rKate\tLewis"
```

Result

```
Joe     Smith
Kate    Lewis
```

Example 3: Quotation marks

String

```
"Type \"x\" to exit"
```

Result

```
Type "x" to exit
```

Example 4: Backslash

String

```
"C:\\java\\files"
```

Result

```
C:\java\files
```

Description

- Within a string, you can use *escape sequences* to include certain types of special characters.

Figure 2-8 How to include special characters in strings

How to use Java classes, objects, and methods

So far, you've learned how to create String objects from the String class in the Java API. As you develop Java applications, though, you need to use dozens of different Java classes and objects. To do that, you need to know how to import Java classes, how to create objects from Java classes, and how to call Java methods.

How to import Java classes

In the API for the J2SE, groups of related classes are organized into *packages*. In figure 2-9, you can see a list of some of the commonly used packages. Since the java.lang package contains the classes that are used in almost every Java program (such as the String class), this package is automatically made available to all programs.

To use a class from a package other than java.lang, though, you'll typically include an import statement for that class at the beginning of the program. If you don't, you'll still be able to use the class, but you'll have to qualify it with the name of the package that contains it each time you refer to it. Since that can lead to a lot of unnecessary typing, we recommend that you always code an import statement for the classes you use.

When you code an import statement, you can import a single class by specifying the class name, or you can import all of the classes in the package by typing an asterisk (*) in place of the class name. The first two statements in this figure, for example, import a single class, while the next two import all of the classes in a package. Although it requires less code to import all of the classes in a package at once, importing one class at a time clearly identifies the classes you're using.

As this figure shows, Java provides two different technologies for building a graphical user interface (GUI) that contains text boxes, command buttons, combo boxes, and so on. The older technology, known as the *Abstract Window Toolkit* (*AWT*), was used with versions 1.0 and 1.1 of Java. Its classes are stored in the java.awt package. Since version 1.2 of Java, though, a new technology known as *Swing* has been available. The Swing classes are stored in the javax.swing package. In general, many of the newer package names begin with javax instead of java. Here, the x indicates that these packages can be considered extensions to the original Java API.

In addition to the packages provided by the Java API, you can get packages from third party sources, either as shareware or by purchasing them. For more information, check the Java web site. You can also create packages that contain classes that you've written. You'll learn how to do that in chapter 9.

Common packages

Package name	Description
java.lang	Provides classes fundamental to Java, including classes that work with primitive data types, strings, and math functions.
java.text	Provides classes to handle text, dates, and numbers.
java.util	Provides various utility classes including those for working with collections.
java.io	Provides classes to read data from files and to write data to files.
java.sql	Provides classes to read data from databases and to write data to databases.
java.applet	An older package that provides classes to create an applet.
java.awt	An older package called the *Abstract Window Toolkit* (AWT) that provides classes to create graphical user interfaces.
java.awt.event	A package that provides classes necessary to handle events.
javax.swing	A newer package called *Swing* that provides classes to create graphical user interfaces and applets.

The syntax of the import statement

```
import packagename.ClassName;
   or
import packagename.*;
```

Examples

```
import java.text.NumberFormat;
import java.util.Scanner;
import java.util.*;
import javax.swing.*;
```

How to use the Scanner class to create an object

With an import statement

```
Scanner sc = new Scanner(System.in);
```

Without an import statement the package name is required as a qualifier

```
java.util.Scanner sc = new java.util.Scanner(System.in);
```

Description

- The API for the J2SE provides a large library of classes that are organized into *packages*.
- All classes stored in the java.lang package are automatically available to all Java programs.
- To use classes that aren't in the java.lang package, you can code an import statement as shown above. To import one class from a package, specify the package name followed by the class name. To import all classes in a package, specify the package name followed by an asterisk (*).

Figure 2-9 How to import Java classes

How to create objects and call methods

To use a Java class, you usually start by creating an *object* from a Java *class*. As the syntax in figure 2-10 shows, you do that by coding the Java class name, the name that you want to use for the object, an equals sign, the new keyword, and the Java class name again followed by a set of parentheses. Within the parentheses, you code any *arguments* that are required by the *constructor* of the object that's defined in the class.

In the examples, the first statement shows how to create a Scanner object named sc. The constructor for this object requires just one argument (System.in), which represents console input. In contrast, the second statement creates a Date object named now that represents the current date, but its constructor doesn't require any arguments. As you go through this book, you'll learn how to create objects with constructors that require two or more arguments, and you'll see that a single class can provide more than one constructor for creating objects.

When you create an object, you can think of the class as the template for the object. That's why the object can be called an *instance* of the class, and the process of creating the object can be called *instantiation*. Whenever necessary, you can create more than one object or instance from the class. For instance, you often use several String objects in a single program.

Once you've created an object from a class, you can use the *methods* of the class. To *call* one of these methods, you code the object name, a dot (period), and the method name followed by a set of parentheses. Within the parentheses, you code the arguments that are required by the method.

In the examples, the first statement calls the nextDouble method of the Scanner object named sc to get data from the console. The second statement calls the toString method of the Date object named now to convert the date and time that's stored in the object to a string. Neither one of these methods requires an argument, but you'll soon see some that do.

Besides methods that you can call from an object, some classes provide *static methods* that can be called directly from the class. To do that, you substitute the class name for the object name as illustrated by the third set of examples. Here, the first statement calls the toString method of the Double class, and the second statement calls the parseDouble method of the Double class. Both of these methods require one argument.

Incidentally, you can also use the syntax shown in this figure to create a String object. However, the preferred way to create a String object is to use the syntax shown in figure 2-7. Once a String object is created, though, you use the syntax in this figure to use one of its methods. You'll see examples of this later in this chapter.

In the pages and chapters that follow, you'll learn how to use dozens of classes and methods. For now, though, you just need to focus on the syntax for creating an object from a class, for calling a method from an object, and for calling a static method from a class. Once you understand that, you're ready to learn how to research the Java classes and methods that you might want to use.

How to create an object from a class

Syntax

```
ClassName objectName = new ClassName(arguments);
```

Examples

```
Scanner sc = new Scanner(System.in);    // creates a Scanner object named sc
Date now = new Date();                  // creates a Date object named now
```

How to call a method from an object

Syntax

```
objectName.methodName(arguments)
```

Examples

```
double subtotal = sc.nextDouble();    // get a double entry from the console
String currentDate = now.toString(); // convert the date to a string
```

How to call a static method from a class

Syntax

```
ClassName.methodName(arguments)
```

Examples

```
String sPrice = Double.toString(price);         // convert a double to a string
double total = Double.parseDouble(userEntry); // convert a string to a double
```

Description

- When you create an *object* from a Java class, you are creating an *instance* of the *class*. Then, you can use the *methods* of the class by *calling* them from the object.
- Some Java classes contain *static methods*. These methods can be called directly from the class without creating an object.
- When you create an object from a class, the *constructor* may require one or more *arguments*. These arguments must have the required data types, and they must be coded in the correct sequence separated by commas.
- When you call a method from an object or a class, the method may require one or more arguments. Here again, these arguments must have the required data types and they must be coded in the correct sequence separated by commas.
- Although you can use the syntax shown in this figure to create a String object, the syntax in figure 2-7 is the preferred way to do that. Once a String object is created, though, you call its methods from the object as shown above.
- In this book, you'll learn how to use dozens of the Java classes and methods that you'll use the most in your applications. You will also learn how to create your own classes and methods.

Figure 2-10 How to create objects and call methods

How to use the API documentation to research Java classes

If you refer back to the list of keywords in figure 2-2, you can see that the Java language consists of just 50 keywords that you can master with relative ease. What's difficult about using Java, though, is mastering the hundreds of classes and methods that your applications will require. To do that, you frequently need to study the API documentation that comes with Java, and that is one of the most time-consuming aspects of Java programming.

Figure 2-11 summarizes some of the basic techniques for navigating through the API documentation. Here, you can see the start of the documentation for the Scanner class, which goes on for many pages. To get there, you click on the package name in the upper left frame and then on the class name in the lower left frame.

If you scroll through the documentation for this class, you'll get an idea of the scale of the documentation that you're dealing with. After a few pages of descriptive information, you come to a summary of the eight constructors for the class. After that, you come to a summary of the dozens of methods that the class offers. That in turn is followed by more detail about the constructors, and then by more detail about the methods.

At this point in your development, this is far more information than you can handle. That's why one of the goals of this book is to introduce you to the dozens of classes and methods that you'll use in most of the applications that you develop. Once you've learned those, the API documentation will make more sense to you, and you'll be able to use that documentation to research classes and methods that aren't presented in this book. To get you started with the use of objects and methods, the next topic will show you how to use the Scanner class.

It's never too early to start using the documentation, though. So by all means use the documentation to get more information about the methods that are presented in this book and to research the other methods that are offered by the classes that are presented in this book. After you learn how to use the Scanner class, for example, take some time to do some research on that class. You'll get a chance to do that in exercise 2-4.

The documentation for the Scanner class

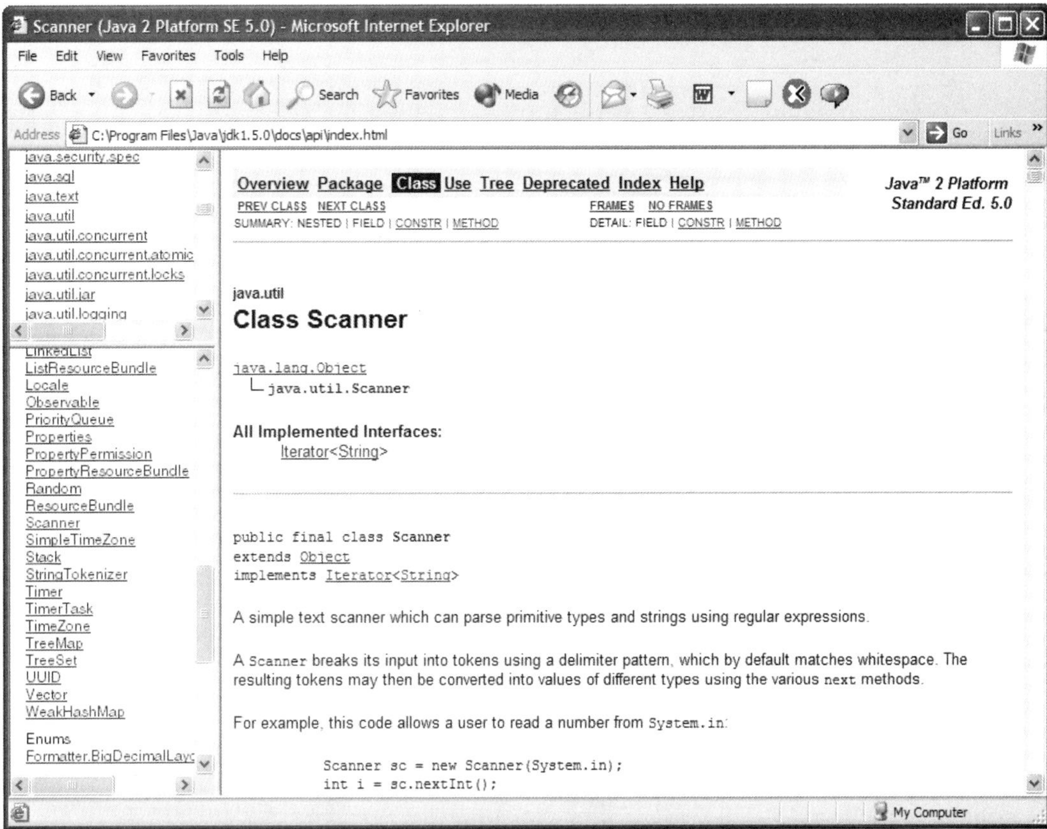

Description

- The Java J2SE API contains thousands of classes and methods that can help you do most of the tasks that your applications require. However, researching the Java API documentation to find the classes and methods that you need is one of the most time-consuming aspects of Java programming.
- If you've installed the API documentation on your hard drive, you can display an index by using your web browser to go to the index.html file in the docs\api directory. If you haven't installed the documentation, you can browse through it on the Java web site.
- You can select the name of the package in the top left frame to display information about the package and the classes it contains. Then, you can select a class in the lower left frame to display the documentation for that class in the right frame.
- Once you display the documentation for a class, you can scroll through it or click on a hyperlink to get more information.
- To make it easier to access the API documentation, you should bookmark the index page. Then, you can easily redisplay this page whenever you need it.

Figure 2-11 How to use the API documentation to research Java classes

How to use the console for input and output

Most of the applications that you write will require some type of user interaction. In particular, most applications will get input from the user and display output to the user. With version 1.5 of Java, the easiest way to get input is to use the new Scanner class to retrieve data from the console. And the easiest way to display output is to print it to the console.

How to use the System.out object to print output to the console

To print output to the *console*, you can use the println and print methods of the System.out object as shown in figure 2-12. Here, System.out actually refers to an instance of the PrintStream class, where out is a public variable that's defined by the System class. From a practical point of view, though, you can just think of System.out as an object that represents console output. And you don't need to code any other statements in your program to create that object.

Both the println and print methods require a string argument that specifies the data to be printed. The only difference between the two is that the println method starts a new line after it displays the data, and the print method doesn't.

If you study the examples in this figure, you shouldn't have any trouble using these methods. For instance, the first statement in the first example uses the println method to print the words "Welcome to the Invoice Total Calculator" to the console. The second statement prints the string "Total: " followed by the value of the total variable (which is automatically converted to a string by this join). The third statement prints the value of the variable named message to the console. And the fourth statement prints a blank line since no argument is coded.

Because the print method doesn't automatically start a new line, you can use it to print several data arguments on the same line. For instance, the three statements in the second example use the print method to print "Total: ", followed by the total variable, followed by a new line character. Of course, you can achieve the same result with a single line of code like this:

```
System.out.print("Total: " + total + "\n");
```

or like this:

```
System.out.println("Total: " + total);
```

This figure also shows an application that uses the println method to print seven lines to the console. In the main method of this application, the first four statements set the values for four variables. Then, the next seven statements print a welcome message, a blank line, the values for the four variables, and another blank line.

When you work with console applications, you should know that the appearance of the console may differ slightly depending on the operating system. The example in this figure shows a console for Windows. Even if the console looks a little different, however, it should work the same.

Two methods of the System.out object

Method	Description
`println(data)`	Prints the data argument followed by a new line character to the console.
`print(data)`	Prints the data to the console without starting a new line.

Example 1: The println method

```
System.out.println("Welcome to the Invoice Total Calculator");
System.out.println("Total: " + total);
System.out.println(message);
System.out.println();           // print a blank line
```

Example 2: The print method

```
System.out.print("Total: ");
System.out.print(total);
System.out.print("\n");
```

Example 3: An application that prints data to the console

```
public class InvoiceApp
{
    public static void main(String[] args)
    {
        // set and calculate the numeric values
        double subtotal = 100;          // set subtotal to 100
        double discountPercent = .2;    // set discountPercent to 20%
        double discountAmount = subtotal * discountPercent;
        double invoiceTotal = subtotal - discountAmount;

        // print the data to the console
        System.out.println("Welcome to the Invoice Total Calculator");
        System.out.println();
        System.out.println("Subtotal:         " + subtotal);
        System.out.println("Discount percent: " + discountPercent);
        System.out.println("Discount amount:  " + discountAmount);
        System.out.println("Total:            " + invoiceTotal);
        System.out.println();
    }
}
```

The console output

```
C:\WINNT\System32\cmd.exe
Welcome to the Invoice Total Calculator

Subtotal:         100.0
Discount percent: 0.2
Discount amount:  20.0
Total:            80.0

Press any key to continue . . .
```

Description

- Although the appearance of a console may differ from one system to another, you can always use the print and println methods to print data to the console.

Figure 2-12 How to use the System.out object to print output to the console

How to use the Scanner class to read input from the console

Figure 2-13 shows how you can use the Scanner class to read input from the console. To start, you create a Scanner object by using a statement like the one in this figure. Here, sc is the name of the scanner object that is created and System.in represents console input, which is the keyboard. You can code this statement this way whenever you want to get console input.

Once you've created a Scanner object, you can use the next methods to read data from the console, but the method you use depends on the type of data you need to read. To read string data, for example, you use the next method. To read integer data, you use the nextInt method. And to read double data, you use the nextDouble method.

To use one of these methods, you code the object name (sc), a period (dot), the method name, and a set of parentheses. Then, the method gets the next user entry. For instance, the first statement in the examples gets a string and assigns it to a string variable named name. The second statement gets an integer and assigns it to an int variable named count. And the third statement gets a double and assigns it to a double variable named subtotal.

Each entry that a user makes is called a *token*, and a user can enter more than one token before pressing the Enter key. To do that, the user separates the entries by one or more space, tab, or return characters. This is called *whitespace*. Then, each next method gets the next token that has been entered. If, for example, you press the Enter key (a return character), type 100, press the Tab key, type 20, and press the Enter key again, the first token is 100 and the second one is 20.

This means that an entry error will occur if the user accidentally types a space or tab in the middle of an entry. In chapter 5, though, you'll learn how to prevent this type of error.

Similarly, if the user doesn't enter the type of data that the next method is looking for, an error occurs and the program ends. In Java, an error like this is also known as an *exception*. If, for example, the user enters a double value when the nextInt method is executed, an exception occurs. You'll also learn how to prevent this type of error in chapter 5.

Although this figure only shows methods for working with String, int, and double types, the Scanner class includes methods for working with most of the other data types that you'll learn about in the next chapter. It also includes methods that let you check what type of data the user entered. As you'll see in chapter 5, you can use these methods to avoid exceptions by checking the data type before you issue the next method.

The Scanner class

```
java.util.Scanner
```

How to create a Scanner object

```
Scanner sc = new Scanner(System.in);
```

Common methods of a Scanner object

Method	Description
`next()`	Returns the next token stored in the scanner as a String object.
`nextInt()`	Returns the next token stored in the scanner as an int value.
`nextDouble()`	Returns the next token stored in the scanner as a double value.

How to use the methods of a Scanner object

```
String name = sc.next();
int count = sc.nextInt();
double subtotal = sc.nextDouble();
```

Description

- To create a Scanner object, you use the new keyword. To create a Scanner object that gets input from the *console*, specify System.in in the parentheses.
- To use one of the methods of a Scanner object, code the object name, a dot (period), the method name, and a set of parentheses.
- When one of the next methods of the Scanner class is run, the application waits for the user to enter data with the keyboard. To complete the entry, the user presses the Enter key.
- Each entry that a user makes is called a *token*. A user can enter two or more tokens by separating them with *whitespace*, which consists of one or more spaces, a tab character, or a return character.
- The entries end when the user presses the Enter key. Then, the first next method that is executed gets the first token, the second next method gets the second token, and so on.
- If the user doesn't enter the type of data that the next method expects, an error occurs and the program ends. In Java, this type of errors is called an *exception*. You'll learn more about this in chapter 5.
- Since the Scanner class is in the java.util package, you'll want to include an import statement whenever you use this class.

Note

- The Scanner class was introduced in version 5.0 of the JDK.

Figure 2-13 How to use the Scanner class to read input from the console

Examples that get input from the console

Figure 2-14 presents two examples that get input from the console. The first example starts by creating a Scanner object. Then, it uses the print method of the System.out object to prompt the user for three values, and it uses the next methods of the Scanner object to read those values from the console. Because the first value should be a string, the next method is used to read this value. Because the second value should be a double, the nextDouble method is used to read it. And because the third value should be an integer, the nextInt method is used to read it.

After all three values are read, a calculation is performed using the int and double values. Then, the data is formatted and the println method is used to display the data on the console. You can see the results of this code in this figure.

Unlike the first example, which reads one value per line, the second example reads three values in a single line. Here, the first statement uses the print method to prompt the user to enter three integer values. Then, the next three statements use the nextInt method to read those three values. This works because a Scanner object uses whitespace (spaces, tabs, or returns) to separate the data that's entered at the console into tokens.

Example 1: Code that gets three values from the user

```
// create a Scanner object
Scanner sc = new Scanner(System.in);

// read a string
System.out.print("Enter product code: ");
String productCode = sc.next();

// read a double value
System.out.print("Enter price: ");
double price = sc.nextDouble();

// read an int value
System.out.print("Enter quantity: ");
int quantity = sc.nextInt();

// perform a calculation and display the result
double total = price * quantity;
System.out.println();
System.out.println(quantity + " " + productCode
    + " @ " + price + " = " + total);
System.out.println();
```

The console after the program finishes

```
C:\WINNT\System32\cmd.exe
Enter product code: cshp
Enter price: 49.50
Enter quantity: 2

2 cshp @ 49.5 = 99.0

Press any key to continue . . .
```

Example 2: Code that reads three values from one line

```
// read three int values
System.out.print("Enter three integer values: ");
int i1 = sc.nextInt();
int i2 = sc.nextInt();
int i3 = sc.nextInt();

// calculate the average and display the result
int total = i1 + i2 + i3;
int avg = total / 3;
System.out.println("Average: " + avg);
System.out.println();
```

The console after the program finishes

```
C:\WINNT\System32\cmd.exe
Enter three integer values: 99 88 92
Average: 93

Press any key to continue . . .
```

Figure 2-14 Examples that get input from the console typewriter

How to code simple control statements

As you write programs, you need to determine when certain operations should be done and how long repetitive operations should continue. To do that, you code *control statements* like the if/else and while statements. This topic will get you started with the use of these statements, but first you need to learn how to write expressions that compare numeric and string variables.

How to compare numeric variables

Figure 2-15 shows how to code *Boolean expressions* that use the six *relational operators* to compare two primitive data types. This type of expression evaluates to either true or false based on the result of the comparison, and the operands in the expression can be either variables or literals.

For instance, the first expression in the first set of examples is true if the value of the variable named discountPercent is equal to the literal value 2.3. The second expression is true if the value of subtotal is not equal to zero. And the sixth example is true if the value of the variable named quantity is less than or equal to the value of the variable named reorderPoint.

Although you shouldn't have any trouble coding simple expressions like these, you must remember to code two equals signs instead of one for the equality comparison. That's because a single equals sign is used for assignment statements. As a result, if you try to code a Boolean expression with a single equals sign, your code won't compile.

When you compare numeric values, you usually compare values of the same data type. However, if you compare different types of numeric values, Java will automatically cast the less precise numeric type to the more precise type. For example, if you compare an int type to a double type, the int type will be cast to the double type before the comparison is made.

How to compare string variables

Because a string is an object, not a primitive data type, you can't use the relational operators to compare strings. Instead, you must use the equals or equalsIgnoreCase methods of the String class that are summarized in figure 2-15. As you can see, both of these methods require an argument that provides the String object or literal that you want to compare with the current String object.

In the examples, the first expression is true if the value in the string named userEntry equals the literal value "Y". In contrast, the second expression uses the equalsIgnoreCase method so it's true whether the value in userEntry is "Y" or "y". Then, the third expression shows how you can use the not operator (!) to reverse the value of a Boolean expression that compares two strings. Here, the expression will evaluate to true if the lastName variable is *not* equal to "Jones". The fourth expression is true if the string variable named code equals the string variable named productCode.

Relational operators

Operator	Name	Description
`==`	Equality	Returns a true value if both operands are equal.
`!=`	Inequality	Returns a true value if the left and right operands are not equal.
`>`	Greater Than	Returns a true value if the left operand is greater than the right operand.
`<`	Less Than	Returns a true value if the left operand is less than the right operand.
`>=`	Greater Than Or Equal	Returns a true value if the left operand is greater than or equal to the right operand.
`<=`	Less Than Or Equal	Returns a true value if the left operand is less than or equal to the right operand.

Examples of conditional expressions

```
discountPercent == 2.3    // equal to a numeric literal
subtotal != 0             // not equal to a numeric literal
years > 0                 // greater than a numeric literal
i < months                // less than a variable
subtotal >= 500           // greater than or equal to a numeric literal
quantity <= reorderPoint  // less than or equal to a variable
```

Two methods of the String class

Method	Description
`equals(String)`	Compares the value of the String object with a String argument and returns a true value if they are equal. This method makes a case-sensitive comparison.
`equalsIgnoreCase(String)`	Works like the equals method but is not case-sensitive.

Examples

```
userEntry.equals("Y")                  // equal to a string literal
userEntry.equalsIgnoreCase("Y")        // equal to a string literal
(!lastName.equals("Jones"))            // not equal to a string literal
code.equalsIgnoreCase(productCode)     // equal to another string variable
```

Description

- You can use the *relational operators* to compare two numeric operands and return a *Boolean value* that is either true or false.
- To compare two numeric operands for equality, make sure to use two equals signs. If you only use one equals sign, you'll code an assignment statement, and your code won't compile.
- If you compare an int with a double, Java will cast the int to a double.
- To test two strings for equality, you must call one of the methods of the String object. If you use the equality operator, you will get unpredictable results (more about this in chapter 4).

Figure 2-15 How to compare numeric and string variables

How to code if/else statements

Figure 2-16 shows how to use the *if/else statement* (or just *if statement*) to control the logic of your applications. This statement is the Java implementation of a control structure known as the *selection structure* because it lets you select different actions based on the results of a Boolean expression.

As you can see in the syntax summary, you can code this statement with just an if clause, you can code it with one or more else if clauses, and you can code it with a final else clause. In any syntax summary, the ellipsis (...) means that the preceding element (in this case the else if clause) can be repeated as many times as it is needed. And the brackets [ ] mean that the element is optional.

When an if statement is executed, Java begins by evaluating the Boolean expression in the if clause. If it's true, the statements within this clause are executed and the rest of the if/else statement is skipped. If it's false, Java evaluates the first else if clause (if there is one). Then, if its Boolean expression is true, the statements within this else if clause are executed, and the rest of the if/else statement is skipped. Otherwise, Java evaluates the next else if clause.

This continues with any remaining else if clauses. Finally, if none of the clauses contains a Boolean expression that evaluates to true, Java executes the statements in the else clause (if there is one). However, if none of the Boolean expressions are true and there is no else clause, Java doesn't execute any statements.

If a clause only contains one statement, you don't need to enclose that statement in braces. This is illustrated by the first statement in the first example in this figure. However, if you want to code two or more statements within a clause, you need to code the statements in braces. The braces identify the block of statements that is executed for the clause.

If you declare a variable within a block, that variable is available only to the other statements in the block. This can be referred to as *block scope*. As a result, if you need to access a variable outside of the block, you should declare it before the if statement. You'll see this illustrated by the program at the end of this chapter.

When coding if statements, it's a common practice to code one if statement within another if statement. This is known as *nesting* if statements. When you nest if statements, it's a good practice to indent the nested statements and their clauses. Since this allows the programmer to easily identify where the nested statement begins and ends, this makes the code easier to read. In this figure, for example, Java only executes the nested statement if the customer type is "R". Otherwise, it executes the statements in the outer else clause.

The syntax of the if/else statement

```
if (booleanExpression) {statements}
[else if (booleanExpression) {statements}] ...
[else {statements}]
```

Example 1: If statements without else if or else clauses

With a single statement

```
if (subtotal >= 100)
    discountPercent = .2;
```

With a block of statements

```
if (subtotal >= 100)
{
    discountPercent = .2;
    status = "Bulk rate";
}
```

Example 2: An if statement with an else clause

```
if (subtotal >= 100)
    discountPercent = .2;
else
    discountPercent = .1;
```

Example 3: An if statement with else if and else clauses

```
if (customerType.equals("T"))
    discountPercent = .4;
else if (customerType.equals("C"))
    discountPercent = .2;
else if (subtotal >= 100)
    discountPercent = .2;
else
    discountPercent = .1;
```

Example 4: Nested if statements

```
if (customerType.equals("R"))
{                                          // begin nested if
    if (subtotal >= 100)
        discountPercent = .2;
    else
        discountPercent = .1;
}                                          // end nested if
else
    discountPercent = .4;
```

Description

- An *if/else statement*, or just *if statement*, always contains an if clause. In addition, it can contain one or more else if clauses, and a final else clause.
- If a clause requires just one statement, you don't have to enclose the statement in braces. You can just end the clause with a semicolon.
- If a clause requires more than one statement, you enclose the block of statements in braces.
- Any variables that are declared within a block have *block scope* so they can only be used within that block.

Figure 2-16 How to code if/else statements

How to code while statements

Figure 2-17 shows how to code a *while statement*. This is one way that Java implements a control structure know as the *iteration structure* because it lets you repeat a block of statements. As you will see in chapter 4, though, Java also offers other implementations of this structure.

When a while statement is executed, the program repeats the statements in the block of code within the braces *while* the expression in the statement is true. In other words, the statement ends when the expression becomes false. If the expression is false when the statement starts, the statements in the block of code are never executed.

Because a while statement loops through the statements in the block as many times as needed, the code within a while statement is often referred to as a *while loop*. Here again, any variables that are defined within the block have block scope, which means that they can't be accessed outside the block.

The first example in this figure shows how to code a loop that executes a block of statements while a variable named choice is equal to either "y" or "Y". In this case, the statements within the block get input data from the user, process it, and display output. This is a common way to control the execution of a program, and you'll see this illustrated in detail in the next figure.

The second example shows how to code a loop that adds the numbers 1 through 4 to a variable named sum. Here, a *counter variable* (or just *counter*) named i is initialized to 1 and the sum variable is initialized to zero before the loop starts. Then, each time through the loop, the value of i is added to sum and one is added to i. When the value of i becomes 5, though, the expression in the while statement is no longer true and the loop ends. The use of a counter like this is a common coding practice, and single letters like *i, j,* and *k* are commonly used as the names of counters.

When you code loops, you must be careful to avoid *infinite loops*. If, for example, you forget to code a statement that increments the counter variable in the second example, the loop will never end because the counter will never get to 5. Then, you have to press Ctrl+C or close the console to cancel the application so you can debug your code.

The syntax of the while loop

```
while (booleanExpression)
{
    statements
}
```

Example 1: A loop that continues while choice is "y" or "Y"

```
String choice = "y";
while (choice.equalsIgnoreCase("y"))
{
    // get the invoice subtotal from the user
    Scanner sc = new Scanner(System.in);
    System.out.print("Enter subtotal:   ");
    double subtotal = sc.nextDouble();

    // the code that processes the user's entry goes here

    // see if the user wants to continue
    System.out.print("Continue? (y/n): ");
    choice = sc.next();
    System.out.println();
}
```

Example 2: A loop that adds the numbers 1 through 4 to sum

```
int i = 1;
int sum = 0;
while (i < 5)
{
    sum = sum + i;
    i = i + 1;
}
```

Description

- A *while statement* executes the block of statements within its braces as long as the Boolean expression is true. When the expression becomes false, the while statement skips its block of statements so the program continues with the next statement in sequence.
- The statements within a while statement can be referred to as a *while loop*.
- Any variables that are declared in the block of a while statement have block scope.
- If the Boolean expression in a while statement never becomes false, the statement never ends. Then, the program goes into an *infinite loop*. You can cancel an infinite loop by closing the console window or pressing Ctrl+C.

Figure 2-17 How to code while loops

Two illustrative applications

You have now learned enough about Java to write simple applications of your own. To show you how you can do that, this chapter ends by presenting two illustrative applications.

The Invoice application

Figure 2-18 shows the console and code for an Invoice application. Although this application is simple, it gets input from the user, performs calculations that use this input, and displays the results of the calculations. It continues until the user enters anything other than "Y" or "y" in response to the Continue? prompt.

The Invoice application starts by displaying a welcome message at the console. Then, it creates a Scanner object named sc that will be used in the while loop of the program. Although this object could be created within the while loop, that would mean that the object would be recreated each time through the loop, and that would be inefficient.

Before the while statement is executed, a String object named choice is initialized to "y". Then, the loop starts by getting a double value from the user and storing it in a variable named subtotal. After that, the loop uses an if/else statement to calculate the discount amount based on the value of subtotal. If, for example, subtotal is greater than or equal to 200, the discount amount is .2 times the subtotal (a 20% discount). If that condition isn't true but subtotal is greater than or equal to 100, the discount is .1 times subtotal (a 10% discount). Otherwise, the discount amount is zero. When the if/else statement is finished, an assignment statement calculates the invoice total by subtracting discountAmount from subtotal.

At that point, the program displays the discount percent, discount amount, and invoice total on the console. Then, it displays a message that asks the user if he or she wants to continue. If the user enters "y" or "Y", the loop is repeated. Otherwise, the program ends.

Although this application illustrates most of what you've learned in this chapter, you should realize that it has a couple of shortcomings. First, the numeric values that are displayed should be formatted with two decimal places since these are currency values. In the next chapter, you'll learn how to do that type of formatting.

Second, an exception will occur and the program will end prematurely if the user doesn't enter one valid double value for the subtotal each time through the loop. This is a serious problem that isn't acceptable in a professional program, and you'll learn how to prevent problems like this in chapter 5.

In the meantime, if you're new to programming, you can learn a lot by writing simple programs like the Invoice program. That will give you a chance to become comfortable with the coding for input, calculations, output, if/else statements, and while statements. And that will prepare you for the chapters that follow.

The console input and output for a test run

```
C:\WINNT\system32\cmd.exe
Welcome to the Invoice Total Calculator

Enter subtotal:   150
Discount percent: 0.1
Discount amount:  15.0
Invoice total:    135.0

Continue? (y/n): _
```

The code for the application

```
import java.util.Scanner;

public class InvoiceApp
{
    public static void main(String[] args)
    {
        // welcome the user to the program
        System.out.println("Welcome to the Invoice Total Calculator");
        System.out.println();  // print a blank line

        // create a Scanner object named sc
        Scanner sc = new Scanner(System.in);

        // perform invoice calculations until choice isn't equal to "y" or "Y"
        String choice = "y";
        while (choice.equalsIgnoreCase("y"))
        {
            // get the invoice subtotal from the user
            System.out.print("Enter subtotal:   ");
            double subtotal = sc.nextDouble();

            // calculate the discount amount and total
            double discountPercent = 0.0;
            if (subtotal >= 200)
                discountPercent = .2;
            else if (subtotal >= 100)
                discountPercent = .1;
            else
                discountPercent = 0.0;
            double discountAmount = subtotal * discountPercent;
            double total = subtotal - discountAmount;

            // display the discount amount and total
            String message = "Discount percent: " + discountPercent + "\n"
                           + "Discount amount:  " + discountAmount + "\n"
                           + "Invoice total:    " + total + "\n";
            System.out.println(message);

            // see if the user wants to continue
            System.out.print("Continue? (y/n): ");
            choice = sc.next();
            System.out.println();
        }
    }
}
```

Figure 2-18 The Invoice application

The Test Score application

Figure 2-19 presents another Java application that will give you more ideas for how you can apply what you've learned so far. If you look at the console input and output for this application, you can see that it lets the user enter one or more test scores. To end the application, the user enters a value of 999. Then, the application displays the number of test scores that were entered, the total of the scores, and the average of the scores.

If you look at the code for this application, you can see that it starts by displaying the instructions for using the application. Then, it declares and initializes three variables, and it creates a Scanner object that will be used to get console input.

The while loop in this program continues until the user enters a test score that's greater than 100. To start, this loop gets the next test score. Then, if that test score is less than or equal to 100, the program adds one to scoreCount, which keeps track of the number of scores, and adds the test score to scoreTotal, which accumulates the total of the scores. The if statement that does this is needed, because you don't want to increase scoreCount and scoreTotal if the user enters 999 to end the program. When the loop ends, the program calculates the average score and displays the score count, total, and average.

To include decimal places in the score average, this program declares scoreTotal and averageScore as a double data types. Declaring scoreTotal as a double type causes the score average to be calculated with decimal places. Declaring the averageScore variable as a double type allows it to store those decimal places.

To allow statements outside of the while loop to access the scoreTotal and scoreCount variables, this program declares these variables before the while loop. If these variables were declared inside the while loop, they would only be available within that block of code and couldn't be accessed by the statements that are executed after the while loop. In addition, the logic of the program wouldn't work because these variables would be reinitialized each time through the loop.

Here again, this program has some obvious shortcomings that will be addressed in later chapters. First, the data isn't formatted properly, but you'll learn how to fix that in the next chapter. Second, an exception will occur and the program will end prematurely if the user enters invalid data, but you'll learn how to fix that in chapter 5.

The console input and output for a test run

```
C:\WINNT\system32\cmd.exe
Please enter test scores that range from 0 to 100.
To end the program enter 999.

Enter score: 90
Enter score: 80
Enter score: 75
Enter score: 999

Score count:   3
Score total:   245.0
Average score: 81.66666666666667

Press any key to continue . . .
```

The code for the application

```
import java.util.Scanner;

public class TestScoreApp
{
    public static void main(String[] args)
    {
        // display operational messages
        System.out.println(
            "Please enter test scores that range from 0 to 100.");
        System.out.println("To end the program enter 999.");
        System.out.println();  // print a blank line

        // initialize variables and create a Scanner object
        double scoreTotal = 0.0;
        int scoreCount = 0;
        int testScore = 0;
        Scanner sc = new Scanner(System.in);

        // get a series of test scores from the user
        while (testScore <= 100)
        {
            // get the input from the user
            System.out.print("Enter score: ");
            testScore = sc.nextInt();

            // accumulate score count and score total
            if (testScore <= 100)
            {
                scoreCount = scoreCount + 1;
                scoreTotal = scoreTotal + testScore;
            }
        }

        // display the score count, score total, and average score
        double averageScore = scoreTotal / scoreCount;
        String message = "\n"
                       + "Score count:   " + scoreCount + "\n"
                       + "Score total:   " + scoreTotal + "\n"
                       + "Average score: " + averageScore + "\n";
        System.out.println(message);
    }
}
```

Figure 2-19 The Test Score application

How to test and debug an application

In chapter 1, you were introduced to the compile-time errors that can occur when you compile an application (see figure 1-11). Once you've fixed those errors, you're ready to test and debug the application as described in this topic. Then, in the next two chapters, you'll learn several more debugging techniques. And when you do the exercises, you'll get lots of practice testing and debugging.

How to test an application

When you *test* an application, you run it to make sure the application works correctly. As you test, you should try every possible combination of valid and invalid data to be certain that the application works correctly under every set of conditions. Remember that the goal of testing is to find errors, or *bugs*, not to show that an application program works correctly.

As you test, you will encounter two types of bugs. The first type of bug causes a *runtime error*. (In Java, this type of error is also known as a *runtime exception*.) A runtime error causes the application to end prematurely, which programmers often refer to as "crashing" or "blowing up." In this case, an error message like the one in figure 2-20 is displayed, and this message shows the line number of the statement that was being executed when the crash occurred.

The second type of bug produces inaccurate results when the application runs. These bugs occur due to *logical errors* in the source code. For instance, the second example in this figure shows the output for the Test Score application. In this case, the final totals were displayed and the application ended before the user entered any input data. This type of bug can be more difficult to find and correct than a runtime error.

How to debug an application

When you *debug* a program, you find the cause of the bugs, fix them, recompile, and test again. As you progress through this book and your programs become more complex, you'll see that debugging can be one of the most time-consuming aspects of programming.

To find the cause of runtime errors, you can start by finding the source statement that was running when the program crashed. You can usually do that by studying the error message that's displayed. In the first console in this figure, for example, you can see that the statement at line 20 was running when the program crashed. That's the statement that used the nextDouble method of the Scanner object, and that indicates that the problem is invalid input data. For now, you can ignore this bug. In chapter 5, you'll learn how to fix it.

To find the cause of incorrect output, you can start by figuring out why the application produced the output that it did. For instance, you can start by asking why the second application in this figure didn't prompt the user to enter any test scores. Once you figure that out, you're well on your way to fixing the bug.

A runtime error that occurred while testing the Invoice application

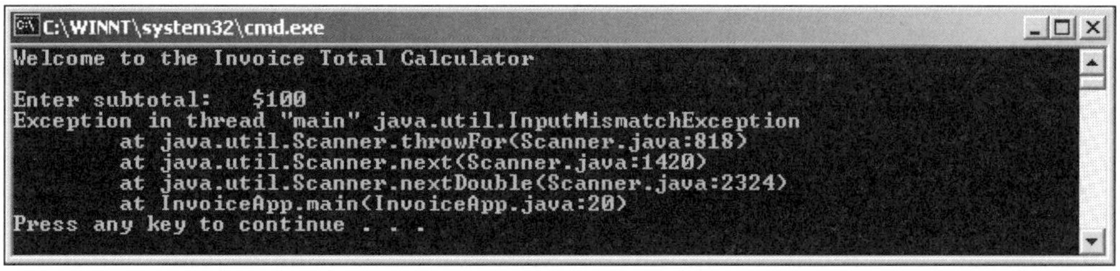

```
C:\WINNT\system32\cmd.exe
Welcome to the Invoice Total Calculator

Enter subtotal:   $100
Exception in thread "main" java.util.InputMismatchException
        at java.util.Scanner.throwFor(Scanner.java:818)
        at java.util.Scanner.next(Scanner.java:1420)
        at java.util.Scanner.nextDouble(Scanner.java:2324)
        at InvoiceApp.main(InvoiceApp.java:20)
Press any key to continue . . .
```

Incorrect output produced by the Test Score application

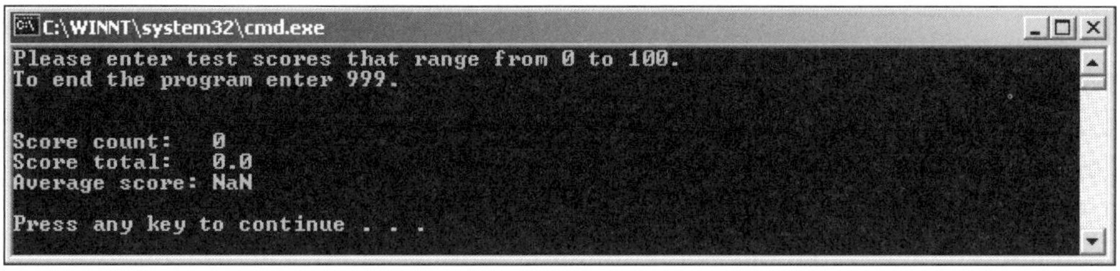

```
C:\WINNT\system32\cmd.exe
Please enter test scores that range from 0 to 100.
To end the program enter 999.


Score count:   0
Score total:   0.0
Average score: NaN

Press any key to continue . . .
```

Debugging tips

- For a runtime error, go to the line in the source code that was running when the program crashed. That should give you a strong indication of what caused the error.
- For incorrect output, first figure out how the source code produced that output. Then, fix the code and test the application again.

Description

- To *test* an application, you run it to make sure that it works properly no matter what combinations of valid and invalid data you enter. The goal of testing is to find the errors (or *bugs*) in the application.
- To *debug* an application, you find the causes of the bugs and fix them.
- One type of bug leads to a *runtime error* (also known as a *runtime exception*) that causes the program to end prematurely. This type of bug must be fixed before testing can continue.
- Even if an application runs to completion, the results may be incorrect due to *logical errors*. These bugs must also be fixed.

Figure 2-20 How to test and debug an application

Perspective

The goal of this chapter has been to get you started with Java programming and to get you started fast. Now, if you understand how the Invoice and Test Score applications in figures 2-18 and 2-19 work, you've come a long way. You should also be able to write comparable programs of your own.

Keep in mind, though, that this chapter is just an introduction to Java programming. So in the next chapter, you'll learn the details about working with data. In chapter 4, you'll learn the details about using control statements. And in chapter 5, you'll learn how to prevent and handle runtime exceptions.

Summary

- The *statements* in a Java program direct the operation of the program. The *comments* document what the program does.
- You must code at least one public *class* for every Java program that you write. The *main method* of this class is executed when you run the class.
- *Variables* are used to store data that changes as a program runs, and you use *assignment statements* to assign values to variables. Two of the most common *data types* for numeric variables are the int and double types.
- A *string* is an object that's created from the String class, and it can contain any characters in the character set. You can use the plus sign to *join* a string with another string or a data type, and you can use assignment statements to *append* one string to another. To include special characters in strings, you can use *escape sequences*.
- Before you use many of the classes in the Java API, you should code an import statement for the class or for the *package* that contains it.
- When you use a *constructor* to create an *object* from a Java class, you are creating an *instance* of the class. There may be more than one constructor for a class, and a constructor may require one or more *arguments*.
- You *call* a *method* from an object and you call a *static method* from a class. A method may require one or more arguments.
- One of the most time-consuming aspects of Java programming is researching the classes and methods that your programs require.
- You can use the methods of a Scanner object to read data from the *console*, and you can use the print and println methods of the System.out object to print data to the console.
- You can code *if statements* to control the logic of a program based on the true or false values of *Boolean expressions*. You can code *while statements* to repeat a series of statements until a Boolean expression becomes false.
- *Testing* is the process of finding the errors or bugs in an application. *Debugging* is the process of fixing the bugs.

Before you do the exercises for this chapter

If you didn't do it already, you should install and configure Java 1.5, the Java API documentation, and TextPad or an equivalent text editor as described in chapter 1. You also need to download and install the folders and files for this book from our web site (www.murach.com) before you start the exercises for this chapter. For complete instructions, please refer to appendix A.

Exercise 2-1 Test the Invoice application

In this exercise, you'll compile and test the Invoice application that's presented in figure 2-18. That will give you a better idea of how this program works.

1. Start your text editor and open the file named InvoiceApp.java that you should find in the c:\java1.5\ch02 directory. Then, compile the application, which should compile with no errors.
2. Test this application with valid subtotal entries like 50, 150, 250, and 1000 so it's easy to see whether or not the calculations are correct.
3. Test the application with a subtotal value like 233.33. This will show that the application doesn't round the results to two decimal places. But in the next chapter, you'll learn how to do that.
4. Test the application with an invalid subtotal value like $1000. This time, the application should crash. Study the error message that's displayed and determine which line of source code was running when the error occurred.
5. Restart the application, enter a valid subtotal, and enter 20 when the program asks you whether you want to continue. What happens and why?
6. Restart the application and enter two values separated by whitespace (like 1000 20) before pressing the Enter key. What happens and why?

Exercise 2-2 Modify the Test Score application

In this exercise, you'll modify the Test Score application that's presented in figure 2-19. That will give you a chance to write some code of your own.

1. Open the file named TestScoreApp.java in the c:\java1.5\ch02 directory, and save the program as ModifiedTestScoreApp.java in the same directory. Then, change the class name to ModifiedTestScoreApp and compile the class.
2. Test this application with valid data to see how it works. Then, test the application with invalid data to see what will cause exceptions. Note that if you enter a test score like 125, the program ends, even though the instructions say that the program ends when you enter 999.
3. Modify the while statement so the program only ends when you enter 999. Then, test the program to see how this works.
4. Modify the if statement so it displays an error message like "Invalid entry, not counted" if the user enters a score that's greater than 100 but isn't 999. Then, test this change.

Exercise 2-3 Modify the Invoice application

In this exercise, you'll modify the Invoice application. When you're through with the modifications, a test run should look something like this:

```
C:\WINNT\system32\cmd.exe
Weclome to the Invoice Total Calculator

Enter subtotal:   100
Discount percent: 0.1
Discount amount:  10.0
Invoice total:    90.0

Continue? (y/n): 0

Enter subtotal:   500
Discount percent: 0.25
Discount amount:  125.0
Invoice total:    375.0

Continue? (y/n): n

Number of invoices: 2
Average invoice:    232.5
Average discount:   67.5

Press any key to continue . . .
```

1. Open the file named InvoiceApp.java that's in the c:\java1.5\ch02 directory, and save the program as ModifiedInvoiceApp.java in the same directory. Then, change the class name to ModifiedInvoiceApp.
2. Modify the code so the application ends only when the user enters "n" or "N". As it is now, the application ends when the user enters anything other than "y" or "Y". To do this, you need to use a not operator (!) with the equalsIgnoreCase method. This is illustrated by the third example in figure 2-15. Then, compile this class and test this change by entering 0 at the Continue? prompt.
3. Modify the code so it provides a discount of 25 percent when the subtotal is greater than or equal to $500. Then, test this change.
4. Using the Test Score application as a model, modify the Invoice program so it displays the number of invoices, the average invoice amount, and the average discount amount when the user ends the program. Then, test this change.

Exercise 2-4 Use the Java API documentation

This exercise steps you through the Java API documentation for the Scanner, String, and Double classes. That will give you a better idea of how extensive the Java API is.

1. Go to the index page of the Java API documentation as described in chapter 1. If you did the exercises for that chapter, you should have it bookmarked.
2. Click the java.util package in the upper left window and the Scanner class in the lower left window to display the documentation for the Scanner class. Then, scroll through this documentation to get an idea of its scope.
3. Review the constructors for the Scanner class. The constructor that's presented in this chapter has just an InputStream object as its argument. When you code that argument, remember that System.in represents the InputStream object for the console.
4. Review the methods of the Scanner class with special attention to the next, nextInt, and nextDouble methods. Note that there are three next methods and two nextInt methods. The ones used in this chapter have no arguments. Then, review the has methods in the Scanner class. You'll learn how to use some of these in chapter 5.
5. Go to the documentation for the String class, which is in the java.lang package, and note that it offers a number of constructors. In this chapter, though, you learned the shortcut for creating String objects because that's the best way to do that. Now, review the methods for this class with special attention to the equals and equalsIgnoreCase methods.
6. Go to the documentation for the Double class, which is also in the java.lang package. Then, review the static parseDouble and toString methods that you'll learn how to use in the next chapter.

If you find the documentation difficult to follow, rest assured that you'll become comfortable with it before you finish this book. Once you learn how to create your own classes, constructors, and methods, it will make more sense.

3

How to work with data

In chapter 2, you learned how to use two of the eight primitive data types as you declared and initialized variables and coded assignment statements that used simple arithmetic expressions. Now, you'll learn all of the details that you need for working with variables and data types at a professional level.

Basic skills for working with data

In this topic, you'll learn about the six primitive data types that weren't presented in chapter 2. Then, you'll learn the fundamentals for working with all of the data types.

The eight primitive data types

Figure 3-1 shows the eight *primitive data types* provided by Java. You can use these eight data types to store six types of numbers, characters, and true or false values.

In chapter 2, you learned how to use the int data type for storing *integers* (whole numbers). But as this figure shows, you can also use three other data types for integers. Most of the time, you can use the int type for working with integers, but you may need to use the *long* type if a value is too big for the int type. Although the use of the *short* and *byte* types is less common, you can use them when you're working with smaller integers and you need to save system resources.

In chapter 2, you also learned how to use the double data type for storing numbers with decimal places. But as this figure shows, you can also use the *float* data type for those numbers. The values in both of these data types are stored as *floating-point numbers* that can hold very large and very small values, but with a limited number of *significant digits*. For instance, the double type with its 16 significant digits provides for numbers like 12,345,678,901,234.56 or 12,345,678.90123456 or 12.34567890123456. Since the double type has more significant digits than the float type, you'll use the double type for most floating-point numbers.

To express the value of a floating-point number, you can use *scientific notation*. This lets you express very large and very small numbers in a sort of shorthand. To use this notation, you type the letter *e* or *E* followed by a power of 10. For instance, 3.65e+9 is equal to 3.65 times 10^9 (or 3,650,000,000), and 3.65e-9 is equal to 3.65 times 10^{-9} (or .00000000365).

You can use the *char* type to store one character. Since Java uses the two-byte *Unicode character set*, it can store practically any character from any language around the world. As a result, you can use Java to create programs that read and print Greek or Chinese characters. In practice, though, you'll usually work with the characters that are stored in the older one-byte *ASCII character set*. These characters are the first 256 characters of the Unicode character set.

Last, you can use the *boolean* type to store a true value or a false value. This data type is typically used to represent a condition that can be true or false.

The eight primitive data types

Type	Bytes	Use
byte	1	Very short integers from -128 to 127.
short	2	Short integers from -32,768 to 32,767.
int	4	Integers from -2,147,483,648 to 2,147,483,647.
long	8	Long integers from -9,223,372,036,854,775,808 to 9,223,372,036,854,775,807.
float	4	Single-precision, floating-point numbers from -3.4E38 to 3.4E38 with up to 7 significant digits.
double	8	Double-precision, floating-point numbers from –1.7E308 to 1.7E308 with up to 16 significant digits.
char	2	A single Unicode character that's stored in two bytes.
boolean	1	A *true* or *false* value.

Description

- A *bit* is a binary digit that can have a value of one or zero. A *byte* is a group of eight bits. As a result, the number of bits for each data type is the number of bytes multiplied by 8.
- *Integers* are whole numbers, and the first four data types above provide for integers of various sizes.
- *Floating-point numbers* provide for very large and very small numbers that require decimal positions, but with a limited number of *significant digits*. A *single-precision number* provides for numbers with up to 7 significant digits. A *double-precision number* provides for numbers with up to 16 significant digits.
- The *double* data type is commonly used for business programs because it provides the precision (number of significant digits) that those programs require.
- The *Unicode character set* provides for over 65,000 characters with two bytes used for each character.
- The older *ASCII character set* that's used by most operating systems provides for 256 characters with one byte used for each character. In the Unicode character set, the first 256 characters correspond to the 256 ASCII characters.
- A *boolean* data type holds a *true* or *false* value.

Technical notes

- To express the value of a floating-point number, you can use *scientific notation* like 2.382E+5, which means 2.382 times 10^5 (a value of 238,200), or 3.25E-8, which means 3.25 times 10^{-8} (a value of .0000000325). Java will sometimes use this notation to display the value of a float or double data type.
- Because of the way floating-point numbers are stored internally, they can't represent the exact value of the decimal places in some numbers. This can cause a rounding problem in some business applications. Later in this chapter, you'll learn how to use the BigDecimal class to solve these rounding problems.

Figure 3-1 The eight primitive data types

How to initialize variables

In chapter 2, you learned how to *declare* and *initialize* a *variable*. This information is repeated in figure 3-2, but with some new information. In particular, it shows how to use separate statements to declare and initialize the variable. It also shows how to declare and initialize some of the data types that weren't presented in chapter 2.

Although you usually declare and initialize a variable in one statement, it occasionally makes sense to do it in two. For instance, you may want to declare a variable at the start of a coding routine without giving it a starting value because its value won't be set until later on.

The one-statement examples in this figure show how to declare and initialize various types of variables. Here, the third and fourth examples show how to assign values to the float and long types. To do that, you need to add a letter after the value. For a float type, you add an *f* or *F* after the value. For a long type, you add an *L*. You can also use a lowercase *l*, but it's not a good coding practice since the lowercase L can easily be mistaken for the number 1. If you omit the letter in one of these assignments, you'll get a compile-time error.

The fifth statement shows how you can use scientific notation as you assign a value to a variable. Then, the sixth and seventh examples show that you can assign a character to the char type by enclosing a character in single quotes or by supplying the integer that corresponds to the character in the Unicode character set. And the eighth example shows how to initialize a variable named valid as a boolean type with a false value.

The last example shows that you can declare and initialize two or more variables in a single statement. Although you may occasionally want to do this, it's usually better to declare and initialize one variable per statement. That way, it's easier to read your code and to modify it later on.

How to initialize constants

A *constant* is used in a Java program to store a value that can't be changed as the program executes, and many of the skills for initializing variables also apply to initializing constants. However, you begin the initialization statement for a constant with the *final* keyword. As a result, constants are sometimes called *final variables*. In addition, it's a common coding convention to use all uppercase letters for the name of a constant and to separate the words in the name with an underscore.

How to initialize a variable in two statements

Syntax

```
type variableName;
variableName = value;
```

Example

```
int counter;                   // declaration statement
counter = 1;                   // assignment statement
```

How to initialize a variable in one statement

Syntax

```
type variableName = value;
```

Examples

```
int counter = 1;               // initialize an int variable
double price = 14.95;          // initialize a double variable
float interestRate = 8.125F;   // F indicates a floating-point value
long numberOfBytes = 20000L;   // L indicates a long integer
double distance = 3.65e+9;     // scientific notation
char letter = 'A';             // stored as a two-digit Unicode character
char letter = 65;              // integer value for a Unicode character
boolean valid = false;         // where false is a keyword
int x = 0, y = 0;              // initialize 2 variables with 1 statement
```

How to initialize a constant

Syntax

```
final type CONSTANT_NAME = value;
```

Examples

```
final int DAYS_IN_NOVEMBER = 30;
final double SALES_TAX = .075;
```

Description

- A *variable* stores a value that can change as a program executes, while a *constant* stores a value that can't be changed.
- To *initialize* a variable or constant, you *declare* its data type and *assign* an initial value. As default values, it's common to initialize integer variables to 0, floating-point variables to 0.0, and boolean variables to false.
- To initialize more than one variable for a single data type in a single statement, use commas to separate the assignments.
- To identify float values, you must type an *f* or *F* after the number. To identify long values, you must type an *l* or *L* after the number.

Naming conventions

- Start variable names with a lowercase letter and capitalize the first letter in all words after the first word.
- Capitalize all of the letters in constants and separate words with underscores.
- Try to use meaningful names that are easy to remember as you code.

Figure 3-2 How to initialize variables and constants

How to code assignment statements and arithmetic expressions

In chapter 2, you learned how to code *assignment statements* that used simple *arithmetic expressions* to assign the value of the expression to a variable. These expressions used the first four *arithmetic operators* in figure 3-3. Now, this figure summarizes all of the other Java arithmetic operators. These operators indicate what operations are to be performed on the *operands* in the expression, which can be either *literals* or variables.

In this figure, the first five operators work on two operands. As a result, they're referred to as *binary operators*. For example, when you use the subtraction operator (-), you subtract one operand from another.

In contrast, the last four operators work on one operand. As a result, they're referred to as *unary operators*. For example, you can code the negative sign operator (-) in front of an operand to reverse the value of the operand. Although you can also code the positive sign operator (+) in front of an operand, it doesn't change the value of the operand so it's rarely used as a unary operator.

While the addition (+), subtraction (-), and multiplication (*) operators are easy to understand, the division (/) and modulus (%) operators are more difficult. If you're working with integer data types, the division operator returns an integer value that represents the number of times the left operand will fit into the right operand. Then, the modulus operator returns an integer value that represents the remainder (which is the amount that's left over after dividing the right operand by the left operand). However, if you're working with non-integer data types, the division operator returns a value that uses decimal places to indicate the result of the division, and that's usually what you want.

When you code an increment (++) or decrement (--) operator, you can *prefix* the operand by coding the operator before the variable. Then, the increment or decrement operation is performed before the rest of the statement is executed. Conversely, you can *postfix* the operand by coding the operator after the variable. Then, the increment or decrement operation isn't performed until after the statement is executed.

Often, an entire statement does nothing more than increment a variable like this:

```
counter++;
```

Then, both the prefix and postfix forms will yield the same result. However, if you use the increment and decrement operators as part of a larger statement, you'll need to use the prefix and postfix forms of these operators to control when the operation is performed. More about that in a moment.

Since each char type is a Unicode character that has a numeric code that maps to an integer, you can perform some integer operations on char types. For instance, this figure shows an example of how you can use the increment operator to change the numeric value for a char variable from 67 to 68, which changes the character from *C* to *D*.

Arithmetic operators

Operator	Name	Description
+	Addition	Adds two operands.
-	Subtraction	Subtracts the right operand from the left operand.
*	Multiplication	Multiplies the right operand and the left operand.
/	Division	Divides the right operand into the left operand. If both operands are integers, then the result is an integer.
%	Modulus	Returns the value that is left over after dividing the right operand into the left operand.
++	Increment	Adds 1 to the operand (x = x + 1).
--	Decrement	Subtracts 1 from the operand (x = x - 1).
+	Positive sign	Promotes byte, short, and char types to the int type.
-	Negative sign	Changes a positive value to negative, and vice versa.

Examples of simple assignment statements

```
int x = 14;
int y = 8;
int result1 = x + y;          // result1 = 22
int result2 = x - y;          // result2 = 6
int result3 = x * y;          // result3 = 112
int result4 = x / y;          // result4 = 1
int result5 = x % y;          // result5 = 6
int result6 = -y + x;         // result6 = 6
int result7 = --y;            // result7 = 7
int result8 = ++x;            // result8 = 15, x = 15

double a = 8.5;
double b = 3.4;
double result9 = a + b;       // result9 = 11.9
double result10 = a - b;      // result10 = 5.1
double result11 = a * b;      // result11 = 28.90
double result12 = a / b;      // result12 = 2.5
double result13 = a % b;      // result13 = 1.7
double result14 = -a + b;     // result14 = -5.1
double result15 = --a;        // result15 = 7.5
double result16 = ++b;        // result16 = 4.4

// character arithmetic
char letter1 = 'C';           // letter1 = 'C'  Unicode integer is 67
char letter2 = ++letter1;     // letter2 = 'D'  Unicode integer is 68
```

Description

- An *arithmetic expression* consists of *operands* and *arithmetic operators*. The first five operators above are called *binary operators* because they operate on two operands. The next four are called *unary operators* because they operate on just one operand.
- An *assignment statement* consists of a variable, an equals sign, and an expression. When the assignment statement is executed, the value of the expression is determined and the result is stored in the variable.

Figure 3-3 How to code arithmetic expressions and assignment statements

How to use the shortcut assignment operators

When coding assignment statements, it's common to code the same variable on both sides of the equals sign. This is illustrated by the first group of statements in figure 3-4. That way, you can use the current value of the variable in an expression and update the variable by assigning the result of the expression to it. You saw this illustrated in chapter 2.

Since it's common to write statements like this, the Java language provides the five shorthand *assignment operators* shown in this figure. Although these operators don't provide any new functionality, you can use them to write shorter code.

If, for example, you need to increment or decrement a variable by a value of 1, you can use a shortcut operator. For example:

```
month = month + 1;
```

can be coded with a shortcut operator as

```
month += 1;
```

which is equivalent to

```
month++;
```

Similarly, if you want to add the value of a variable named nextNumber to a summary field named sum, you can do it like this:

```
sum += nextNumber;
```

which is equivalent to

```
sum = sum + nextNumber;
```

The techniques that you use are mostly a matter of preference because the code is easy to read and maintain either way you code it.

Assignment operators

Operator	Name	Description
=	Assignment	Assigns a new value to the variable.
+=	Addition	Adds the operand to the starting value of the variable and assigns the result to the variable.
-=	Subtraction	Subtracts the operand from the starting value of the variable and assigns the result to the variable.
*=	Multiplication	Multiplies the operand by the starting value of the variable and assigns the result to the variable.
/=	Division	Divides the operand by the starting value of the variable and assigns the result to the variable. If the operand and the value of the variable are both integers, the result is an integer.
%=	Modulus	Derives the value that is left over after dividing the right operand by the value in the variable, and then assigns this value to the variable.

Statements that use the same variable on both sides of the equals sign

```
count = count + 1;          // count is increased by 1
count = count - 1;          // count is decreased by 1
total = total + 100.0;      // total is increased by 100.0
total = total - 100.0;      // total is decreased by 100
price = price * .8;         // price is multiplied by 8
sum = sum + nextNumber;     // sum is increased by value of nextNumber
```

Statements that use the shortcut operators to get the same results

```
count += 1;                 // count is increased by 1
count -= 1;                 // count is decreased by 1
total += 100.0;             // total is increased by 100.0
total -= 100.0;             // total is decreased by 100.0
price *= .8;                // price is multipled by 8
sum += nextNumber;          // sum is increased by the value of nextNumber
```

Description

- Besides the equals sign, Java provides for the five other *assignment operators* shown above. These operators provide a shorthand way to code common assignment operations.

Figure 3-4 How to use the shortcut assignment operators

How to work with the order of precedence

Figure 3-5 gives more information about coding arithmetic expressions. In particular, it gives the *order of precedence* of the arithmetic operations. This means that all of the prefixed increment and decrement operations in an expression are done first, followed by all of the positive and negative operations, and so on. If there are two or more operations at the same order of precedence, the operations are done from left to right.

Because this sequence of operations doesn't always work the way you want it to, you may need to override the sequence by using parentheses. Then, the expressions in the innermost sets of parentheses are done first, followed by the next sets of parentheses, and so on. Within the parentheses, though, the operations are done left to right by the order of precedence. In general, you should use parentheses to dictate the sequence of operations whenever there's any doubt about it.

The need for parentheses is illustrated by the first example in this figure. Because parentheses aren't used in the first expression that calculates the price, the multiplication operation is done before the subtraction operation, which gives an incorrect result. In contrast, because the subtraction operation is enclosed in parentheses in the second expression, this operation is performed before the multiplication operation, which gives a correct result.

The second example in this figure shows how parentheses can be used in a more complicated expression. Here, three sets of parentheses are used to calculate the current value of an investment account after a monthly investment amount is added to it, monthly interest is calculated, and the interest is added to it. If you have trouble following this, you can plug the initial values into the expression and evaluate it one set of parentheses at a time:

```
(5000 + 100) * (1 + (.12 / 12))
(5000 + 100) * (1 + .01)
(5100 * 1.01)
5151
```

If you have trouble creating an expression like this for a difficult calculation, you can often code it in a more direct way. To illustrate, this figure shows another way to calculate the current value. Here, the first statement adds the monthly investment amount to the current value. The second statement calculates the interest. And the third statement adds the interest to the current value. This not only takes away the need for parentheses, but also makes it easier to follow what's going on.

The third example in this figure shows the differences between the use of prefixed and postfixed increment and decrement operators. With prefixed operators, the variable is incremented or decremented before the result is assigned. With postfixed operators, the result is assigned before the operations are done. Because this can get confusing, it's best to limit these operators to simple expressions.

The order of precedence for arithmetic operations

1. Increment and decrement
2. Positive and negative
3. Multiplication, division, and remainder
4. Addition and subtraction

Example 1: A calculation that uses the default order of precedence

```
double discountPercent = .2;             // 20% discount
double price = 100;                      // $100 price
price = price * 1 - discountPercent;     // price = $99.8
```

The same calculation with parentheses that specify the order of precedence

```
price = price * (1 - discountPercent);   // price = $80
```

Example 2: An investment calculation based on a monthly investment and yearly interest rate

```
double currentValue = 5000;          // current value of investment account
double monthlyInvestment = 100;      // amount added each month
double interestRate = .12;           // yearly interest rate
currentValue = (currentValue + monthlyInvestment) * (1 + (interestRate/12));
// currentValue = 5100 * 1.01 = 5151
```

Another way to calculate the current value of the investment account

```
currentValue += monthlyInvestment;                       // add investment
// calculate interest
double monthlyInterest = currentValue * interestRate / 12;
currentValue += monthlyInterest;                         // add interest
```

Example 3: Prefixed and postfixed increment and decrement operators

```
int a = 5;
int b = 5;
int y = ++a;      // a = 6, y = 6
int z = b++;      // b = 6, z = 5
```

Description

- Unless parentheses are used, the operations in an expression take place from left to right in the *order of precedence*.
- To specify the sequence of operations, you can use parentheses. Then, the operations in the innermost sets of parentheses are done first, followed by the operations in the next sets, and so on.
- When you use an increment or decrement operator as a *prefix* to a variable, the variable is incremented or decremented and then the result is assigned. But when you use an increment or decrement operator as a *postfix* to a variable, the result is assigned and then the variable is incremented or decremented.

Figure 3-5 How to work with the order of precedence

How to work with casting

As you develop Java programs, you'll frequently need to convert data from one data type to another. To do that, you use a technique called *casting*, which is summarized in figure 3-6.

As you can see, Java provides for two types of casting. *Implicit casts* are performed automatically and can be used to convert data with a less precise type to a more precise type. This is called a *widening conversion* because the new type is always wide enough to hold the original value. For instance, the first statement in this figure causes an integer value to be converted to a double value.

Java will also perform an implicit cast on the values in an arithmetic expression if some of the values have more precise data types than other values. This is illustrated by the next three statements in this figure. Here, the variables d, i, and j are used in an arithmetic expression. Notice that d is declared with the double data type, while i and j are declared with the int data type. Because of that, both i and j will be converted to double values when this expression is evaluated.

A *narrowing conversion* is one that casts data from a more precise data type to a less precise data type. With this type of conversion, the less precise data type may not be wide enough to hold the original value. In that case, you must use an *explicit cast*.

To perform an explicit cast, you code the data type in parentheses before the variable that you want to convert. When you do this, you should realize that you may lose some information. This is illustrated by the first example in this figure that performs an explicit cast. Here, a double value of 93.75 is cast to an int value of 93. An explicit cast is required in this example, however, because Java won't automatically cast a double value to an integer value since an integer value is less precise.

When you use explicit casting in an arithmetic expression, the casting is done before the arithmetic operations. This is illustrated by the last two examples of explicit casts. In the last example, two integer types are cast to double types before the division is done so the result will have decimal places if they are needed. Without explicit casting, the expression would return an integer value that would then be cast to a double.

When you code an explicit cast, an exception may occur at runtime if the JRE isn't able to perform the cast. As a result, you should use an explicit cast only when you're sure that the JRE will be able to perform the cast.

Although you typically cast between numeric data types, you can also cast between the int and char types. That's because every char value corresponds to an int value that identifies it in the Unicode character set. Since there's no possible loss of data, you can implicitly cast between these data types. However, if you prefer, you can also code these casts explicitly.

How implicit casting works

Casting from less precise to more precise data types

byte→short→int→long→float→double

Examples

```
double grade = 93;                  // convert int to double

double d = 95.0;
int i = 86, j = 91;
double average = (d+i+j)/3;        // convert i and j to double values
                                   // average = 90.666666...
```

How you can code an explicit cast

Syntax

```
(type) expression
```

Examples

```
int grade = (int) 93.25;            // convert double to int (grade = 93)

double d = 95.0;
int i = 86, j = 91;
double average = ((int)d+i+j)/3;    // convert d to int value (average = 90)

double result = (double) i / (double) j;     // result has decimal places
```

How to cast between char and int types

```
char letterChar = 65;              // convert int to char (letterChar = 'A')
char letterChar2 = (char) 65;      // this works too
int letterInt = 'A';               // convert char to int (letterInt = 65)
int letterInt2 = (int) 'A';        // this works too
```

Description

- If you assign a less precise data type to a more precise data type, Java automatically converts the less precise data type to the more precise data type. This can be referred to as an *implicit cast* or a *widening conversion.*
- When you code an arithmetic expression, Java implicitly casts the less precise data types to the most precise data type.
- To code an assignment statement that assigns a more precise data type to a less precise data type, you must use parentheses to specify the less precise data type. This can be referred to as an *explicit cast* or a *narrowing conversion.*
- You can also use an explicit cast in an arithmetic expression. Then, the casting is done before the arithmetic operations.
- Since each char value has a corresponding int value, you can implicitly or explicitly cast between these types.

Figure 3-6 How to work with casting

How to use Java classes for working with data types

As you learned in chapter 2, Java provides hundreds of classes that provide methods that you can use in your programs. Now, you'll learn about four of the classes that you'll use often when working with data types.

How to use the NumberFormat class

When you use numeric values in a program, you often need to format them. For example, you may want to apply a standard currency format to a double value. To do that, you need to add a dollar sign and commas and to display just two decimal places. Similarly, you may want to display a double value in a standard percentage format. To do that, you need to add a percent sign and move the decimal point two digits to the right.

To do this type of formatting, Java provides the NumberFormat class, which is summarized in figure 3-7. Since this class is part of the java.text package, you'll usually want to include an import statement for this class before you begin working with it.

Once you import this class, you can call one of its static methods to return a NumberFormat object. As you learned in chapter 2, you can call static methods directly from a class. In other words, you code the name of the class, followed by the dot operator, followed by the method. For instance, the first example calls the static getCurrencyInstance method directly from the NumberFormat class.

Once you use a static method to return a NumberFormat object, you can call non-static methods from that object. To do that, you code the name of the object, followed by the dot operator, followed by the method. For instance, the first example calls the non-static format method from the NumberFormat object named currency. This returns a string that consists of a dollar sign plus the value of the price variable with two decimal places. In this format, negative numbers are enclosed in parentheses.

The second example shows how to format numbers with the percent format. The main difference between the first and second examples is that you use the getPercentInstance method to create a NumberFormat object that has the default percent format. Then, you can use the format method of this object to format a number as a percent. In this format, negative numbers have a leading minus sign.

The third example shows how to format numbers with the number format, and how to set the number of decimal places for a NumberFormat object. Here, the format is changed from the default of three decimal places to just one decimal place. In this format, negative numbers also have a leading minus sign.

The fourth example shows how you can use one statement to create a NumberFormat object and use its format method. Although this example accomplishes the same task as the second example, it doesn't create a variable for the NumberFormat object that you can use later in the program. As a result, you should only use code like this when you need to format just one number.

The NumberFormat class

```
java.text.NumberFormat
```

Three static methods of the NumberFormat class

Method	Returns a NumberFormat object that ...
`getCurrencyInstance()`	Has the default currency format ($99,999.99).
`getPercentInstance()`	Has the default percent format (99%).
`getNumberInstance()`	Has the default number format (99,999.999).

Three methods of a NumberFormat object

Method	Description
`format(anyNumberType)`	Returns a String object that has the format specified by the NumberFormat object.
`setMinimumFractionDigits(int)`	Sets the minimum number of decimal places.
`setMaximumFractionDigits(int)`	Sets the maximum number of decimal places.

Example 1: The currency format

```
double price = 11.575;
NumberFormat currency = NumberFormat.getCurrencyInstance();
String priceString = currency.format(price);        // returns $11.58
```

Example 2: The percent format

```
double majority = .505;
NumberFormat percent = NumberFormat.getPercentInstance();
String majorityString = percent.format(majority);   // returns 50%
```

Example 3: The number format with one decimal place

```
double miles = 15341.253;
NumberFormat number = NumberFormat.getNumberInstance();
number.setMaximumFractionDigits(1);
String milesString = number.format(miles);          // returns 15,341.3
```

Example 4: Two NumberFormat methods that are coded in one statement

```
String majorityString = NumberFormat.getPercentInstance().format(majority);
```

Description

- You can use one of the three static methods to create a NumberFormat object. Then, you can use the methods of that object to format one or more numbers.
- When you use the format method, the result is automatically rounded by using a rounding technique called half-even. This means that the number is rounded up if the preceding digit is odd, but the extra decimal places are truncated if the preceding digit is even.
- Since the NumberFormat class is in the java.text package, you'll want to include an import statement when you use this class.

Figure 3-7 How to use the NumberFormat class

When you use the format method of a NumberFormat object, the numbers are automatically rounded by a technique called *half-even*, which rounds up if the preceding digit is odd, but rounds down if the preceding digit is even. If, for example, the currency format is used for a value of 123.455, the formatted result is $123.46, which is what you would expect. But if the value is 123.445, the result is $123.44. Although this is okay for many applications, it can cause problems in others. You'll learn more about this later in this chapter.

How to use the Math class

The Math class provides a few dozen methods for working with numeric data types. Some of the most useful ones for business applications are presented in figure 3-8.

The first group of examples shows how to use the round method. Here, the first statement rounds a double type to a long type, and the second statement rounds a float type to an int type. Note, however, that this method only rounds to an integer value so it's not that useful.

The second group of examples shows how to use the pow method to raise the first argument to the power of the second argument. This method returns a double value and accepts two double arguments. However, since Java automatically converts any arguments of a less precise numeric type to a double, the pow method accepts all of the numeric types. In this example, the first statement is equal to 2^2, the second statement is equal to 2^3, and the third and fourth statements are equal to 5^2.

In general, the methods of the Math class work the way you would expect. Sometimes, though, you may need to cast numeric types to get the methods to work the way you want them to. For example, the pow method returns a double type. So if you want to return an int type, you need to cast the double type to an int type as shown in the fourth pow example.

The third group of examples shows how to use the sqrt method to get the square root of a number, and the fourth group shows how to use the max and min methods to return the greater or lesser of two values. If you study these examples, you shouldn't have any trouble understanding how they work.

The fifth group of examples shows how to use the random method to generate random numbers. Since this method returns a random double value greater than or equal to 0.0 and less than 1.0, you can return any range of values by multiplying the random number by another number. In this example, the first statement returns a random double value greater than or equal to 0.0 and less than 100.0. Then, the second statement casts this double value to a long data type. A routine like this can be useful when you want to generate random values for testing a program.

If you have the right mathematical background, you shouldn't have any trouble using these or any of the other Math methods. If you've taken a course in trigonometry, for example, you should be able to understand the trigonometric methods that the Math class provides.

The Math class

```
java.lang.Math
```

Common static methods of the Math class

Method	Description
`round(float or double)`	Returns the closest long value to a double value or the closest int value to a float value. The result has no decimal places.
`pow(number, power)`	Returns a double value of a double argument (number) that is raised to the power of another double argument (power).
`sqrt(number)`	Returns a double value that's the square root of the double argument.
`max(a, b)`	Returns the greater of two float, double, int, or long arguments.
`min(a, b)`	Returns the lesser of two float, double, int, or long arguments.
`random()`	Returns a random double value greater than or equal to 0.0 and less than 1.0.

Example 1: The round method

```
long result = Math.round(1.667);        // result is 2
int result = Math.round(1.49F);         // result is 1
```

Example 2: The pow method

```
double result = Math.pow(2, 2);         // result is 4.0 (2*2)
double result = Math.pow(2, 3);         // result is 8.0 (2*2*2)
double result = Math.pow(5, 2);         // result is 25.0 (5 squared)
int result = (int) Math.pow(5, 2);      // result is 25 (5 squared)
```

Example 3: The sqrt method

```
double result = Math.sqrt(20.25);       // result is 4.5
```

Example 4: The max and min methods

```
int x = 67;
int y = 23;
int max = Math.max(x, y);               // max is 67
int min = Math.min(x, y);               // min is 23
```

Example 5: The random method

```
double x = Math.random() * 100;     // result is a value >= 0.0 and < 100.0
long result = (long) x;             // converts the result from double to long
```

Description

- You can use the static methods of the Math class to perform common arithmetic operations. This figure summarizes the methods that are the most useful for business applications.
- When a method requires one or more arguments, you code them between the parentheses, separating multiple arguments with commas.
- In some cases, you need to cast the result to the data type that you want.

Figure 3-8 How to use the Math class

How to use the Integer and Double classes

Figure 3-9 shows how to use a few of the constructors and static methods that are provided by the Integer and Double classes. Since these classes can be used to create objects that wrap around the primitive types, they are sometimes referred to as *wrapper classes*. Wrapper classes also exist for the other six primitive data types.

The first group of statements in this figure shows how to create Integer and Double objects that can store int and double data types. This is useful when you want to provide an int or double data type as an argument to a method, but the method requires that the argument be an object, not a data type. You'll see how this works in a later chapter. Once you create an Integer or Double object, you can use any of the methods of these classes to work with the data it contains.

Note, however, that these classes also provide static methods that you can use without creating objects. For instance, the second group of statements in this figure shows how to use the static toString method to convert a primitive type to a string. Here, the first statement converts the int variable named counter to a string and returns the value to a string variable named counterString. The second statement converts the double variable named price to a string and returns that value to the string variable named priceString.

Similarly, the third group of statements shows how to use the static parse methods to convert strings to primitive types. Here, the first statement uses the parseInt method of the Integer class to convert a string to an int data type. The second statement uses the parseDouble method of the Double class to convert a string to a double data type. Once these statements have been executed, you can use the quantity and price variables in arithmetic expressions.

But what happens if the string contains a non-numeric value like "ten" that can't be parsed to an int or double type? In that case, the parseInt or parseDouble method will cause a runtime error known as an exception. Using Java terminology, you can say that the method will *throw an exception*. In chapter 5, you'll learn how to *catch* the exceptions that are thrown by these methods.

Constructors for the Integer and Double classes

Constructor	Description
Integer(int)	Constructs an Integer object from an int data type.
Double(double)	Constructs a Double object from a double data type.

Two static methods of the Integer class

Method	Description
parseInt(stringName)	Attempts to convert the String object that's supplied as an argument to an int type. If successful, it returns the int value. If unsuccessful, it throws an exception.
toString(intName)	Converts the int value that's supplied as an argument to a String object and returns that String object.

Two static methods of the Double class

Method	Description
parseDouble(stringName)	Attempts to convert the String object that's supplied as an argument to a double type. If successful, it returns the double value. If unsuccessful, it throws an exception.
toString(doubleName)	Converts the double value that's supplied as an argument to a String object and returns that String object

How to create Integer and Double objects

```
Integer quantityDoubleObject = new Integer(quantity);
Double priceDoubleObject = new Double(price);
```

How to use static methods to convert primitive types to String objects

```
String counterString = Integer.toString(counter);
String priceString = Double.toString(price);
```

How to use static methods to convert String objects to primitive types

```
int quantity = Integer.parseInt(quantityString);
double price = Double.parseDouble(priceString);
```

Description

- The Integer and Double classes are known as *wrapper classes* since they can be used to construct Integer and Double objects that contain (wrap around) int and double values. This can be useful when you need to pass an int or double value to a method that only accepts objects, not primitive data types.
- These classes also provide static methods that you can use for converting values from these data types to strings and vice versa. And every primitive type has a wrapper class that works like the Integer and Double classes.
- If the parseInt and parseDouble methods can't successfully parse the string, they will cause an error to occur. In Java terminology, this is known as *throwing an exception*. You'll learn how to handle or *catch* exceptions in chapter 5.

Figure 3-9 How to use the Integer and Double classes

The formatted Invoice application

To illustrate some of the skills you've just learned, figure 3-10 shows the console and code for an enhanced version of the Invoice application that was presented in chapter 2. This time, the application does a few more calculations and formats the results before displaying them. You can see the results for one user entry in the console that's in this figure.

The code for the application

In chapter 2, you saw how the console looks when displayed by Windows. In this figure, the console is displayed in a platform-neutral format that's easy to read. This is the format that will be used to display console output for the rest of this book.

The shaded code in this figure identifies the primary changes to the Invoice application of the last chapter. First, two new values are calculated. Sales tax is calculated by multiplying the total before tax by .05. And the invoice total is calculated by adding the sales tax to the total before tax.

Second, currency and percent objects are created by using the methods of the NumberFormat class. Then, the format methods of these objects are used to format the five values that have been calculated by this application. This shows how one currency object can be used to format two or more values. The result of each use of the format method is a string that is added to the message that eventually gets displayed.

Although this application is now taking on a more professional look, you should remember that it still has some shortcomings. First, it doesn't handle the exception that's thrown if the user doesn't enter a valid number at the console. You'll learn how to fix that problem in chapter 5. Second, because of the way rounding works with the NumberFormat methods, the results may not always come out the way you want them to. You'll learn more about that next.

The console for the formatted Invoice application

```
Enter subtotal:    150.50
Discount percent: 10%
Discount amount:   $15.05
Total before tax: $135.45
Sales tax:         $6.77
Invoice total:     $142.22

Continue? (y/n):
```

The code for the formatted Invoice application

```
import java.util.Scanner;
import java.text.NumberFormat;

public class InvoiceApp
{
    public static void main(String[] args)
    {
        // create a Scanner object and start while loop
        Scanner sc = new Scanner(System.in);
        String choice = "y";
        while (choice.equalsIgnoreCase("y"))
        {
            // get the input from the user
            System.out.print("Enter subtotal:   ");
            double subtotal = sc.nextDouble();

            // calculate the results
            double discountPercent = 0.0;
            if (subtotal >= 100)
                discountPercent = .1;
            else
                discountPercent = 0.0;
            double discountAmount = subtotal * discountPercent;
            double totalBeforeTax = subtotal - discountAmount;
            double salesTax = totalBeforeTax * .05;
            double total = totalBeforeTax + salesTax;

            // format and display the results
            NumberFormat currency = NumberFormat.getCurrencyInstance();
            NumberFormat percent = NumberFormat.getPercentInstance();
            String message =
                "Discount percent: " + percent.format(discountPercent) + "\n"
              + "Discount amount:  " + currency.format(discountAmount) + "\n"
              + "Total before tax: " + currency.format(totalBeforeTax) + "\n"
              + "Sales tax:        " + currency.format(salesTax) + "\n"
              + "Invoice total:    " + currency.format(total) + "\n";
            System.out.println(message);

            // see if the user wants to continue
            System.out.print("Continue? (y/n): ");
            choice = sc.next();
            System.out.println();
        }
    }
}
```

Figure 3-10 The formatted Invoice application

How to analyze the data problems in the Invoice application

The console at the top of figure 3-11 shows more output from the Invoice application in figure 3-10. But wait! The results for a subtotal entry of 100.05 don't add up. If the discount amount is $10.00, the total before tax should be $90.05, but it's $90.04. Similarly, the sales tax for a subtotal entry of .70 is shown as $0.03, so the invoice total should be $0.73, but it's shown as is $0.74. What's going on?

To analyze data problems like this, you can add *debugging statements* to a program like the ones in this figure. These statements display the unformatted values of the result fields so you can see what they are before they're formatted. This is illustrated by the console at the bottom of this figure, which shows the results for the same entries as the ones in the console at the top of this figure.

If you look at the unformatted results for the first entry (100.05), you can easily see what's going on. Because of the way NumberFormat rounding works, the discount amount value of 10.005 and the total before tax value of 90.045 aren't rounded up. However, the invoice total value of 94.54725 is rounded up. With this extra information, you know that everything is working the way it's supposed to, even though you're not displaying the results you want.

Now, if you look at the unformatted results for the second entry (.70), you can see another type of data problem. In this case, the sales tax is shown as .034999999999999996 when it should be .035. This happens because floating-point numbers, which are binary, aren't able to exactly represent some decimal fractions. As a result, the formatted value is $0.03 when it should be rounded up to $0.04. However, the unformatted invoice total is correctly represented as 0.735, which is rounded to a formatted $0.74. And here again, it looks like Java can't add.

Although trivial errors like these are acceptable in many applications, they are unacceptable in some business applications. And for those applications, you need to provide solutions that deliver the results that you want. (Imagine getting an invoice that didn't add up!)

One solution is to write your own code that does the rounding so you don't need to use the NumberFormat class to do the rounding for you. As you go through this book, you'll learn how to use classes and methods that will help you do that. However, that still doesn't deal with the fact that some decimal fractions can't be accurately represented by floating-point numbers. To solve that problem as well as the other data problems, the best solution is to use the BigDecimal class that you'll learn about next.

Output data that illustrates a problem with the Invoice application

```
Enter subtotal:   100.05
Discount percent: 10%
Discount amount:  $10.00
Total before tax: $90.04
Sales tax:        $4.50
Invoice total:    $94.55

Continue? (y/n): y

Enter subtotal:   .70
Discount percent: 0%
Discount amount:  $0.00
Total before tax: $0.70
Sales tax:        $0.03
Invoice total:    $0.74

Continue? (y/n):
```

Statements that you can add to the program to help analyze this problem

```
// debugging statements that display the unformatted fields
// these are added before displaying the formatted results
String debugMessage = "\nUNFORMATTED RESULTS\n"
                    + "Discount percent: " + discountPercent + "\n"
                    + "Discount amount:  " + discountAmount + "\n"
                    + "Total before tax: " + totalBeforeTax + "\n"
                    + "Sales tax:        " + salesTax + "\n"
                    + "Invoice total:    " + total + "\n"
                    + "\nFORMATTED RESULTS";
System.out.println(debugMessage);
```

The unformatted and formatted output data

```
Enter subtotal:   100.05

UNFORMATTED RESULTS
Discount percent: 0.1
Discount amount:  10.005
Total before tax: 90.045
Sales tax:        4.50225
Invoice total:    94.54725

FORMATTED RESULTS
Discount percent: 10%
Discount amount:  $10.00
Total before tax: $90.04
Sales tax:        $4.50
Invoice total:    $94.55

Continue? (y/n): y

Enter subtotal:   .70

UNFORMATTED RESULTS
Discount percent: 0.0
Discount amount:  0.0
Total before tax: 0.7
Sales tax:        0.034999999999999996
Invoice total:    0.735

FORMATTED RESULTS
Discount percent: 0%
Discount amount:  $0.00
Total before tax: $0.70
Sales tax:        $0.03
Invoice total:    $0.74

Continue? (y/n):
```

Figure 3-11 How to analyze the data problems in the Invoice application

How to use the BigDecimal class for working with decimal data

The BigDecimal class is designed to solve two types of problems that are associated with floating-point numbers. First, the BigDecimal class can be used to exactly represent decimal numbers. Second, it can be used to work with numbers that have more than 16 significant digits.

The constructors and methods of the BigDecimal class

Figure 3-12 summarizes a few of the constructors that you can use with the BigDecimal class. These constructors accept an int, double, long, or string argument and create a BigDecimal object from it. Because floating-point numbers are limited to 16 significant digits and because these numbers don't always represent decimal numbers exactly, it's often best to construct BigDecimal objects from strings rather than doubles.

Once you create a BigDecimal object, you can use its methods to work with the data. In this figure, for example, you can see some of the BigDecimal methods that are most useful in business applications. Here, the add, subtract, multiply, and divide methods let you perform those operations. The compareTo method lets you compare the values in two BigDecimal objects. And the toString method converts the value of a BigDecimal object to a string.

This figure also includes the setScale method, which lets you set the number of decimal places (*scale*) for the value in a BigDecimal object as well as the rounding mode. For example, you can use the setScale method to return a number that's rounded to two decimal places like this:

```
salesTax = salesTax.setScale(2, RoundingMode.HALF_UP);
```

In this example, RoundingMode.HALF_UP is a value in the RoundingMode enumeration that's summarized in this figure. The scale and rounding mode arguments work the same for the divide method.

Enumerations are similar to classes, and you'll learn more about them in chapter 9. For now, you can code the rounding mode as HALF_UP because it provides the type of rounding that is normal for business applications. However, you need to import the RoundingMode enumeration at the start of the application unless you want to qualify the rounding mode like this:

```
java.math.RoundingMode.HALF_UP
```

If you look at the API documentation for the BigDecimal class, you'll see that it provides several other methods that you may want to use. This class also provides many other features that you may want to become more familiar with.

The BigDecimal class

`java.math.BigDecimal`

Constructors of the BigDecimal class

Constructor	Description
`BigDecimal(int)`	Creates a new BigDecimal object with the specified int value.
`BigDecimal(double)`	Creates a new BigDecimal object with the specified double value.
`BigDecimal(long)`	Creates a new BigDecimal object with the specified long value.
`BigDecimal(String)`	Creates a new BigDecimal object with the specified String object. Because of the limitations of floating-point numbers, it's often best to create BigDecimal objects from strings.

Methods of the BigDecimal class

Methods	Description
`add(value)`	Returns the value of this BigDecimal object after the specified BigDecimal value has been added to it.
`compareTo(value)`	Compares the value of the BigDecimal object with the value of the specified BigDecimal object and returns -1 if less, 0 if equal, and 1 if greater.
`divide(value, scale, rounding-mode)`	Returns the value of this BigDecimal object divided by the value of the specified BigDecimal object, sets the specified scale, and uses the specified rounding mode.
`multiply(value)`	Returns the value of this BigDecimal object multiplied by the specified BigDecimal value.
`setScale(scale, rounding-mode)`	Sets the scale and rounding mode for the BigDecimal object.
`subtract(value)`	Returns the value of this BigDecimal object after the specified BigDecimal value has been subtracted from it.
`toString()`	Converts the BigDecimal value to a string.

The RoundingMode enumeration

`java.math.RoundingMode`

Two of the values in the RoundingMode enumeration

Values	Description
`HALF_UP`	Round towards the "nearest neighbor" unless both neighbors are equidistant, in which case round up.
`HALF_EVEN`	Round towards the "nearest neighbor" unless both neighbors are equidistant, in which case round toward the even neighbor.

Description

- The BigDecimal class provides a way to perform accurate decimal calculations in Java. It also provides a way to store numbers with more than 16 significant digits.
- You can pass a BigDecimal object to the format method of a NumberFormat object, but NumberFormat objects limit the results to 16 significant digits.

Figure 3-12 The constructors and methods for the BigDecimal class

How to use BigDecimal arithmetic in the Invoice application

Figure 3-13 shows how you can use BigDecimal arithmetic in the Invoice application. To start, look at the console output when BigDecimal is used. As you can see, this solves both the rounding problem and the floating-point problem so it now works the way you want it to.

To use BigDecimal arithmetic in the Invoice application, you start by coding an import statement that imports all of the classes and enumerations of the java.math package. This includes both the BigDecimal class and the RoundingMode enumeration. Then, you use the constructors and methods of the BigDecimal class to create the BigDecimal objects, do the calculations, and round the results when necessary.

In this figure, the code starts by constructing BigDecimal objects from the subtotal and discountPercent variables, which are double types. To avoid conversion problems, though, the toString method of the Double class is used to convert the subtotal and discountPercent values to strings that are used in the BigDecimal constructors.

Since the user may enter subtotal values that contain more than two decimal places, the setScale method is used to round the subtotal entry after it has been converted to a BigDecimal object. However, since the discountPercent variable only contains two decimal places, it isn't rounded. From this point on, all of the numbers are stored as BigDecimal objects and all of the calculations are done with BigDecimal methods.

In the statements that follow, only discount amount and sales tax need to be rounded. That's because they're calculated using multiplication, which can result in extra decimal places. In contrast, the other numbers (total before tax and total) don't need to be rounded because they're calculated using subtraction and addition. Once the calculations and rounding are done, you can safely use the NumberFormat objects and methods to format the BigDecimal objects for display.

When working with BigDecimal objects, you may sometimes need to create one BigDecimal object from another BigDecimal object. However, you can't supply a BigDecimal object to the constructor of the BigDecimal class. Instead, you need to call the toString method from the BigDecimal object to convert the BigDecimal object to a String object. Then, you can pass that String object as the argument of the constructor as illustrated by the last statement in this figure.

Is this a lot of work just to do simple business arithmetic? Relative to some other languages, you would have to say that it is. In fact, it's fair to say that this is a weakness of Java. In contrast, languages like Microsoft's C# and Visual Basic .NET provide a decimal data type that can have up to 28 significant digits along with a Round method in the Math class that's easy to use with decimal data. However, once you get the hang of working with the BigDecimal class, you should be able to solve floating-point and rounding problems with ease.

The Invoice application output when BigDecimal arithmetic is used

```
Enter subtotal:    100.05
Subtotal:          $100.05
Discount percent: 10%
Discount amount:   $10.01
Total before tax: $90.04
Sales tax:         $4.50
Invoice total:     $94.54

Continue? (y/n): y

Enter subtotal:    .70
Subtotal:          $0.70
Discount percent: 0%
Discount amount:   $0.00
Total before tax: $0.70
Sales tax:         $0.04
Invoice total:     $0.74

Continue? (y/n):
```

The import statement that's required for BigDecimal arithmetic

```
import java.math.*;  // imports all classes and enumerations in java.math
```

The code for using BigDecimal arithmetic in the Invoice application

```
// convert subtotal and discount percent to BigDecimal
BigDecimal decimalSubtotal = new BigDecimal(Double.toString(subtotal));
decimalSubtotal = decimalSubtotal.setScale(2, RoundingMode.HALF_UP);
BigDecimal decimalDiscountPercent =
    new BigDecimal(Double.toString(discountPercent));

// calculate discount amount
BigDecimal discountAmount =
    decimalSubtotal.multiply(decimalDiscountPercent);
discountAmount = discountAmount.setScale(2, RoundingMode.HALF_UP);

// calculate total before tax, sales tax, and total
BigDecimal totalBeforeTax = decimalSubtotal.subtract(discountAmount);
BigDecimal salesTaxPercent = new BigDecimal(".05");
BigDecimal salesTax = salesTaxPercent.multiply(totalBeforeTax);
salesTax = salesTax.setScale(2, RoundingMode.HALF_UP);
BigDecimal total = totalBeforeTax.add(salesTax);
```

How to create a BigDecimal object from another BigDecimal object

```
BigDecimal total2 = new BigDecimal(total.toString());
```

Description

- With this code, all of the result values are stored in BigDecimal objects, and all of the results have two decimal places that have been rounded correctly when needed.
- Once the results have been calculated, you can use the NumberFormat methods to format the values in the BigDecimal objects without any fear of rounding problems. However, the methods of the NumberFormat object limits the results to 16 significant digits.

Figure 3-13 How to use BigDecimal arithmetic in the Invoice application

Perspective

If this chapter has succeeded, you should now be able to work with whatever primitive data types you need in your applications. You should be able to use the NumberFormat, Math, Double, and Integer classes whenever you need them. And you should be able to use the BigDecimal class to solve the problems that are associated with floating-point numbers.

Summary

- Java provides eight *primitive data types* to store *integer*, *floating-point*, *character*, and *boolean* values.
- *Variables* store data that changes as a program runs. *Constants* store data that doesn't change as a program runs. You use *assignment statements* to assign values to variables.
- You can use *arithmetic operators* to form *arithmetic expressions*, and you can use some *assignment operators* as a shorthand for some types of arithmetic expressions.
- Java can *implicitly cast* a less precise data type to a more precise data type. Java also lets you *explicitly cast* a more precise data type to a less precise data type.
- You can use the NumberFormat class to apply standard currency, percent, and number formats to any of the primitive numeric types.
- You can use the static methods of the Math class to perform mathematical operations such as rounding numbers and calculating square roots.
- You can use the constructors of the Double and Integer *wrapper classes* to create objects that wrap double and int values. You can also use the static methods of these classes to convert strings to numbers and vice versa.
- You can use the constructors of the BigDecimal class to create objects that store decimal values that aren't limited to 16 significant digits. Then, you can use the methods of these objects to do the calculations that your programs require.

Exercise 3-1 Test the Invoice application

In this exercise, you'll compile and test the formatted Invoice application that's presented in figure 3-10.

1. Open the file named FormattedInvoiceApp.java that you should find in the c:\java1.5\ch03 directory. Then, compile and run the application. As you test the application, enter the three subtotal values that are shown in figures 3-10 and 3-11 to see how the program works and to see what the problems are.
2. To better understand what is happening, add debugging statements like those in figure 3-11 so the program displays two sets of data for each entry: first the unformatted output, then the formatted output. When you add debugging statements, you should try to do it in a way that makes them easy to remove when you're through debugging.
3. Test the application again with a range of entries so you clearly see what the data problems are when you study the unformatted and formatted results.

Exercise 3-2 Modify the Test Score application

In this exercise, you'll use some of the skills that you learned in this chapter as you modify the Test Score application that you worked with in the last chapter, but you won't use BigDecimal arithmetic.

1. Open the file named ModfiedTestScoreApp.java that you should find in the c:\java1.5\ch02 directory if you did exercise 2-2. If you didn't do that exercise, open TestScoreApp instead.
2. Save the file as EnhancedTestScoreApp.java in the ch03 directory, and change the class name in the file to EnhancedTestScoreApp. Then, compile and run the program to refresh your memory about how it works.
3. Use the += operator to increase the scoreCount and scoreTotal fields. Then, test this to make sure that it works.
4. As the user enters test scores, use the methods of the Math class to keep track of the minimum and maximum scores. When the user enters 999 to end the program, display these scores at the end of the other output data. Now, test these changes to make sure that they work. (This step can be challenging if you're new to programming, but you'll learn a lot by doing it.)
5. Change the variable that you use to total the scores from a double to an int data type. Then, use casting to cast the score count and score total to doubles as you calculate the average score and save that average as a double. Now, test that change.
6. Use thc NumberFormat class to round the average score to one decimal place before displaying it at the end of the program. Then, test this change. Note that the rounding method that's used doesn't matter in a program like this.

Exercise 3-3 Create a new application

In this exercise, you'll develop an application that will give you a chance to use your new skills. This application asks the user to enter a file size in megabytes (MB) and then calculates how long it takes to download that file with a 56K analog modem (you won't need to use BigDecimal arithmetic). The output from this application should look something like this:

```
Welcome to the Download Time Estimator

This program calculates how long it will take to
download a file with a 56K analog modem.

Enter file size (MB): 50

A "56K" modem will take 2 hours 44 minutes 6 seconds

Continue? (y/n):
```

1. Instead of starting this application from scratch, open the file named FormattedInvoiceApp.java in the ch03 directory. Then, save it with the name DownloadTimeApp.java, and change its class name to DownloadTimeApp.
2. Delete the code that you won't need for this application, and modify the code that remains so it provides for the basic operation of the program without the calculations. These first two steps are an efficient way to start any new application because you don't have to re-enter the routine code.
3. Add the code that that calculates the hours, minutes, and seconds needed to download this file with a 56K analog modem. To do the calculations, assume that a 56K modem can transfer data at the rate of 5.2 kilobytes (KB) per second. Then, add the code for displaying the results. (You also need to know that 1 MB is equal to 1,024 KB).
4. Compile and run the application. Enter a value of 50 for the file size to be sure that the calculated value is the same as shown above. Then, enter other values to see how they work.

Exercise 3-4 Use BigDecimal arithmetic

To get some practice with BigDecimal arithmetic, this exercise has you modify the Test Score application so it uses BigDecimal arithmetic.

1. Open EnhancedTestScoreApp in the ch03 directory or your last version of the Test Score application in the ch02 directory. Then, save the file as BDTestScoreApp in ch03, and change the class name to BDTestScoreApp.
2. Modify the program so it uses BigDecimal arithmetic to calculate the average test score with the result rounded to one decimal place. Be sure to use the appropriate toString methods of either the Double or Integer classes so the BigDecimal objects are constructed from string values. Then, test this change with a range of values.

4

How to code control statements

In chapter 2, you learned how to code simple if and while statements to control the execution of your applications. Now, you'll learn more about coding these statements. You'll learn how to code the other control statements that Java offers. And you'll learn how to code your own static methods, which will help you divide your applications into manageable parts.

How to code Boolean expressions

In chapter 2, you learned how to code the *Boolean expressions* that control the operation of your control statements. These are expressions that evaluate to either true or false. To start, this topic repeats some of the information that you learned before, but in a larger context.

How to compare primitive data types

Figure 4-1 shows how to use the six *relational operators* to code a Boolean expression that compares *operands* that are primitive data types. In a Boolean expression, an operand can be a literal, a variable, an arithmetic expression, or a keyword such as true or false.

The first three expressions in this figure use the equality operator (==) to test if the two operands are equal. To use this operator, you must code two equals signs instead of one. That's because a single equals sign is used for assignment statements. As a result, if you try to code a Boolean expression with a single equals sign, your code won't compile.

The next expression uses the inequality operator (!=) to test if a variable is not equal to a numeric literal. The two expressions after that use the greater than operator (>) to test if a variable is greater than a numeric literal and the less than operator (<) to test if one variable is less than another. And the two expressions after that use the greater than or equal operator (>=) and less than or equal operator (<=) to compare operands.

The last two expressions in this figure illustrate that you don't need to the == or != operator when you use a boolean variable in an expression. That's because, by definition, a boolean variable evaluates to a boolean value. As a result,

```
isValid == true
```

is the same as

```
isValid
```

and

```
!isValid
```

is the same as

```
isValid == false
```

Although the first and last expressions may be easier for a beginning programmer to understand, the second and third expressions are commonly used by professional programmers.

When comparing numeric values, you usually compare values of the same data type. However, if you compare different types of numeric values, Java will automatically cast the less precise numeric type to the more precise type. For example, if you compare an int type to a double type, the int type will be cast to the double type before the comparison is made.

Relational operators

Operator	Name	Description
==	Equality	Returns a true value if both operands are equal.
!=	Inequality	Returns a true value if the left and right operands are not equal.
>	Greater Than	Returns a true value if the left operand is greater than the right operand.
<	Less Than	Returns a true value if the left operand is less than the right operand.
>=	Greater Than Or Equal	Returns a true value if the left operand is greater than or equal to the right operand.
<=	Less Than Or Equal	Returns a true value if the left operand is less than or equal to the right operand.

Examples of Boolean expressions

```
discountPercent == 2.3     // equal to a numeric literal
letter == 'y'              // equal to a char literal
isValid == false           // equal to the false value

subtotal != 0              // not equal to a numeric literal

years > 0                  // greater than a numeric literal
i < months                 // less than a variable

subtotal >= 500            // greater than or equal to a numeric literal
quantity <= reorderPoint   // less than or equal to a variable

isValid                    // isValid is equal to true
!isValid                   // isValid is equal to false
```

Description

- You can use the relational operators to create a Boolean expression that compares two operands and returns a boolean value that is either true or false.
- If you compare two numeric operands that are not of the same type, Java will convert the less precise operand to the type of the more precise operand before doing the comparison.
- By definition, a boolean variable evaluates to a boolean value of true or false.

Figure 4-1 How to compare primitive data types

How to compare strings

As you learned in chapter 2, a string is an object, not a primitive data type, so you can't use the relational operators to compare strings. Instead, you must use the equals or equalsIgnoreCase method of the String class as shown by the expressions at the start of figure 4-2.

Both of these methods require an argument that provides the String object or literal that you want to compare with the current object. The difference between the two is that the equals method is case-sensitive while the equalsIgnoreCase method is not.

If you call the equals or equalsIgnoreCase method from a string that contains a null, however, Java will throw an exception. To avoid that, you can use the equality operator (==) or the inequality operator (!=) to check whether a string contains a null before you use the equals or equalsIgnoreCase method. This is illustrated by the last two expressions at the start of this figure.

The next block of code shows what happens when you test two strings for equality with the == operator. Here, the code asks you to enter values for two different strings. No matter what values you enter, though, the equals comparison that follows will be false. If, for example, you enter "abc" for both strings, the equals test will be false.

That's because all object variables are *reference types*, which means that they don't actually contain the data like primitive types do. Instead, reference types refer to (or point to) the data, which is held in another area of internal storage. For these types, the equality and inequality operators test to see whether the variables refer to the same object. If they do, they're considered equal. But if they refer to two different objects, they're considered unequal, even if the objects contain the same values.

What happens if you issue this statement?

```
string1 = string2;
```

The variable named string1 now refers to the same data that string2 refers to. As a result, the Boolean expression

```
(string1 == string2)
```

will be true because both variables will refer to the same object.

This just makes the point that you shouldn't use the equality and inequality operators to test whether two strings have the same values because these operators don't work that way. Since all objects are reference types, this holds true for other types of objects too. As a result, you'll learn other ways to test objects for equality as you progress through this book.

Two methods of the String class

Method	Description
`equals(String)`	Compares the current String object with the String object specified as the argument and returns a true value if they are equal. This method makes a case-sensitive comparison.
`equalsIgnoreCase(String)`	Works like the equals method but is not case-sensitive.

Expressions that compare two string values

```
firstName.equals("Frank")            // equal to a string literal
firstName.equalsIgnoreCase("Frank")  // equal to a string literal
firstName.equals("")                 // equal to an empty string

!lastName.equals("Jones")            // not equal to a string literal
!code.equalsIgnoreCase(productCode)  // not equal to another string variable

firstName == null                    // equal to a null value
firstName != null                    // not equal to a null value
```

Code that tests whether two strings refer to the same object

```
Scanner sc = new Scanner(System.in);
System.out.print("Enter string1: ");
String string1 = sc.next();
System.out.print("Enter string2: ");
String string2 = sc.next();

if (string1 == string2)        // this will be false no matter what you enter
    System.out.println("string1 = string2");
else
    System.out.println("string1 not = string2");
```

Description

- To test two strings to see whether they contain the same string values, you must call one of the methods of the String object.
- To test whether a string is null, you can use the equality operator (==) or the inequality operator (!=) with the null keyword.
- A string object is a *reference type*, not a primitive data type. That means that a string variable doesn't contain the data like a primitive type does. Instead, a string variable refers to (or points to) the data, which is in another location of computer memory.
- If you use the equality or inequality operator to compare two string variables, Java tests to see whether the two strings refer to the same String object. If they do, the expression is true. If they don't, it's false.

Technical note

- Because Java stores string literals in pools to reduce duplication, the equality and inequality tests for strings may not work as shown above when two String objects are assigned the same literal value.

Figure 4-2 How to compare strings

How to use the logical operators

Figure 4-3 shows how to use the *logical operators* to code a Boolean expression that consists of two or more Boolean expressions. For example, the first expression uses the && operator. As a result, it evaluates to true if both the first expression *and* the second expression evaluate to true. Conversely, the second expression uses the || operator. As a result, it evaluates to a true value if either the first expression *or* the second expression evaluate to true.

When you use the && and || operators, the second expression is only evaluated if necessary. Because of that, these operators are sometimes referred to as the *short-circuit operators*. To illustrate, suppose the value of subtotal in the first example is less than 250. Then, the first expression evaluates to false. That means that the entire expression will return a false value. As a result, the second expression is not evaluated. Since this is more efficient than always evaluating both expressions, you'll want to use these operators most of the time.

However, there may be times when you want to evaluate both expressions regardless of the value that's returned by the first expression. For example, there may be times when the second expression performs an operation such as incrementing a variable or calling a method. In that case, you can use the & and | operators to make sure that the second expression is evaluated.

You can also use multiple logical operators in the same expression as illustrated by the fifth example. Here, the && and || operators connect three expressions. As a result, the entire expression is true if the first *and* second expressions are true *or* the third expression is true.

When you code this type of expression, the expression is evaluated from left to right based on this order of precedence: arithmetic operations first, followed by relational operations, followed by logical operations. For logical operations, And operations are performed before Or operations. If you need to change this sequence or if there's any doubt about the order of precedence, you can use parentheses to clarify or control this evaluation sequence.

If necessary, you can use the ! operator to reverse the value of an expression. However, this can create code that's difficult to read. As a result, you should avoid using the ! operators whenever possible. For example, instead of coding

```
!(subtotal < 100)
```

you can code

```
subtotal >= 100
```

Both expressions perform the same task, but the second expression is easier to read.

Logical operators

Operator	Name	Description
`&&`	And	Returns a true value if both expressions are true. This operator only evaluates the second expression if necessary.
`||`	Or	Returns a true value if either expression is true. This operator only evaluates the second expression if necessary.
`&`	And	Returns a true value if both expressions are true. This operator always evaluates both expressions.
`|`	Or	Returns a true value if either expression is true. This operator always evaluates both expressions.
`!`	Not	Reverses the value of the expression.

Examples

```
subtotal >= 250 && subtotal < 500
timeInService <=4 || timeInService >= 12

isValid == true & counter++ < years
isValid == true | counter++ < years

(subtotal >= 250 && subtotal < 500) || isValid == true

!(counter++ >= years)
```

Description

- You can use the *logical operators* to create a Boolean expression that combines two or more Boolean expressions.
- Since the && and || operators only evaluate the second expression if necessary, they're sometimes referred to as *short-circuit operators* and are slightly more efficient than the & and | operators.
- By default, Not operations are performed first, followed by And operations, and then Or operations. These operations are performed after arithmetic operations and relational operations.
- You can use parentheses to change the sequence in which the operations will be performed or to clarify the sequence of operations.

Figure 4-3 How to use the logical operators

How to code if/else and switch statements

In chapter 2, you were introduced to the if/else statement, but this topic will expand on that. This topic will also present the switch statement.

How to code if/else statements

Figure 4-4 reviews the use of the *if/else statement* (or just *if statement*). This is Java's implementation of the *selection structure*.

When an if statement is executed, Java begins by evaluating the Boolean expression in the if clause. If it's true, the statements within this clause are executed and the rest of the if/else statement is skipped. If it's false, Java evaluates the first else if clause (if there is one). Then, if its Boolean expression is true, the statements within this else if clause are executed, and the rest of the if/else statement is skipped. Otherwise, Java evaluates the next else if clause.

This continues with any remaining else if clauses. Finally, if none of the clauses contains a Boolean expression that evaluates to true, Java executes the statements in the else clause (if there is one). If none of the Boolean expressions are true and there is no else clause, Java doesn't execute any statements.

As the syntax shows, you code the statements for an if or else clause in braces. The braces are optional if a clause contains only one statement, as illustrated by the first example in this figure. They're required if the clause contains two or more statements, as illustrated by the second example.

Whenever you code a set of braces in Java, you are explicitly defining a *block* of code that may contain one or more statements. Then, any variables that are declared within those braces have *block scope*. In other words, they can't be accessed outside of that block. As a result, if you want to access the variable outside of the block, you must declare it before the block. This is illustrated by the second example.

However, in if/else statements, each clause automatically has block scope even if you don't code the braces. As a result, if you want to access the variable outside of the if/else statement, you must declare it before the if/else statement, as shown in the first example. In addition, if you try to declare a variable in an if/else clause without using braces, you'll get a compile-time error. That makes sense because the variable can't be used outside of the clause, and there aren't any additional statements within the clause to use it.

When coding if statements, it's a common practice to code one if statement within another if statement. This is known as *nesting* if statements, and it's illustrated by the third example in this figure. When you nest if statements, it's a good practice to indent the nested statements and their clauses since this allows the programmer to easily identify where each nested statement begins and ends.

Another good coding practice is to code the conditions with a logical structure and in a logical sequence. If necessary, you can also add comments to your code so it's easier to follow. As always, the easier your code is to read and understand, the easier it is to test, debug, and maintain.

The syntax of the if/else statement

```
if (booleanExpression) {statements}
[else if (booleanExpression) {statements}] ...
[else {statements}]
```

Example 1: An if statement with else if and else clauses

```
double discountPercent = 0.0;
if (subtotal >= 100 && subtotal <= 199)
    discountPercent = .1;
else if (subtotal >= 200 && subtotal <= 299)
    discountPercent = .2;
else if (subtotal >= 300)
    discountPercent = .3;
else
    discountPercent = .1;
```

Example 2: An if statement that contains two blocks of code

```
double discountPercent = 0.0;
if (customerType.equals("R"))
{                                           // start block
    discountPercent = .1;
    shippingMethod = "UPS";
}                                           // end block
else if (customerType.equals("C")
{                                           // start block
    discountPercent = .2;
    shippingMethod = "Bulk";
}                                           // end block
else
    shippingMethod = "USPS";
```

Example 3: Nested if statements

```
if (customerType.equals("R"))
{                                           // begin nested if
    if (subtotal >= 100)
        discountPercent = .2;
    else
        discountPercent =.1;
}                                           // end nested if
else
    discountPercent = .4;
```

Description

- If a clause in an if/else statement contains just one statement, you don't have to enclose the statement in braces. You can just end the clause with a semicolon. However, this statement can't declare a variable or it won't compile.
- If a clause requires more than one statement, you must enclose the *block* of statements in braces. Then, any variable that is declared within the block has *block scope* so it can only be used within that block.

Figure 4-4 How to code if/else statements

How to code switch statements

Figure 4-5 shows how to work with the *switch statement*. This is the Java implementation of a control structure known as the *case structure*, which lets you code different actions for different cases. The switch statement can sometimes be used in place of an if statement with else if clauses. However, since the switch statement can only be used with expressions that evaluate to an integer, this statement has limited use.

To code a switch statement, you start by coding the switch keyword followed by a switch expression that evaluates to one of the integer types. After the switch expression, you can code one or more *case labels* that represent the possible values of the switch expression. Then, when the switch expression matches the value specified by the case label, the statements after the label are executed.

You can code the case labels in any sequence, but you should be sure to follow each label with a colon. Then, if the label contains one or more statements, you can code a *break statement* after them to jump to the end of the switch statement. Otherwise, the execution of the program *falls through* to the next case label and executes the statements in that label. The *default label* is an optional label that identifies the statements to execute if none of the case labels are executed.

The first example in this figure shows how to code a switch statement that sets the description for a product based on the value of an int variable named productID. Here, the first case label assigns a value of "Hammer" to the productDescription variable if productID is equal to 1. Then, the break statement exits the switch statement. Similarly, the second case label sets the product description to "Box of Nails" if productID is equal to 2 and then exits the switch statement. If productID is equal to something other than 1 or 2, the default case label is executed. Like the other two case labels, this one sets the value of the productDescription variable and then exits the switch statement.

The second example shows how to code a switch statement that sets a day variable to "weekday" or "weekend" depending on the value of the integer in the variable named dayOfWeek. Here, the first break statement is coded after the case labels for 2, 3, 4, 5, and 6. As a result, day is set to "weekday" for any of those values. Similarly, whenever dayOfWeek equals 1 or 7, day is set to "weekend".

Although the last case label in both of these examples includes a break statement, that isn't necessary. If you omit it, program execution falls through to the statement that follows the switch statement. Even so, it's a good programming practice to code a break statement after the last case label.

When you code switch statements, you can nest one statement within another. You can also nest if/else statements within switch statements and switch statements within if/else statements. Here again, you should try to code the statements with a logical structure that is relatively easy to understand. If necessary, you can also add comments that clarify the logic of your code.

The syntax of the switch statement

```
switch (integerExpression)
{
    case label1:
        statements
        break;
    case label2:
        statements
        break;
    any other case statements
    default: (optional)
        statements
        break;
}
```

Example 1: A switch statement with a default label

```
switch (productID)
{
    case 1:
        productDescription = "Hammer";
        break;
    case 2:
        productDescription = "Box of Nails";
        break;
    default:
        productDescription = "Product not found";
        break;
}
```

Example 2: A switch statement that falls through case labels

```
switch (dayOfWeek)
{
    case 2:
    case 3:
    case 4:
    case 5:
    case 6:
        day = "weekday";
        break;
    case 1:
    case 7:
        day = "weekend";
        break;
}
```

Description

- The switch statement can only be used with an expression that evaluates to one of these integer types: char, byte, short, or int. The case labels represent the integer values of that expression, and these labels can be coded in any sequence.
- The switch statement transfers control to the appropriate *case label*. If control isn't transferred to one of the case labels, the optional *default label* is executed.
- If a case label doesn't contain a break statement, code execution will *fall through* to the next label. Otherwise, the break statement ends the switch statement.

Figure 4-5 How to code switch statements

An enhanced version of the Invoice application

To give you a better idea of how if/else statements can be used, figure 4-6 presents another enhanced version of the Invoice application. This time, the console prompts the user for two entries: customer type and subtotal.

In this application, if the user enters "R" or "C" for the customer type, the discount percent changes depending on the value of the subtotal. If, for example, the customer type is "R" and the subtotal is greater than or equal to 250, the discount percent is .2. Or, if the customer type is "C" and the subtotal is less than 250, the discount percent is .2.

Here, you can see that the conditions are coded in a logical order. For instance, the expressions in the nested if statement for customer type "R" go from a subtotal that's less than 100, to a subtotal that's greater than or equal to 100, to a subtotal that's greater than or equal to 250. That covers all of the possible subtotals from the smallest to the largest. Although you could code these conditions in other sequences, this sequence makes it easy to tell that all possibilities have been covered.

The console

```
Enter customer type (r/c): r
Enter subtotal:    100
Discount percent: 10%
Discount amount:   $10.00
Total:             $90.00

Continue? (y/n):
```

The code

```
import java.text.NumberFormat;
import java.util.Scanner;

public class InvoiceApp
{
    public static void main(String[] args)
    {
        Scanner sc = new Scanner(System.in);
        String choice = "y";

        while (!choice.equalsIgnoreCase("n"))
        {
            // get the input from the user
            System.out.print("Enter customer type (r/c): ");
            String customerType = sc.next();
            System.out.print("Enter subtotal:   ");
            double subtotal = sc.nextDouble();

            // get the discount percent
            double discountPercent = 0.0;
            if (customerType.equalsIgnoreCase("R"))
            {
                if (subtotal < 100)
                    discountPercent = 0;
                else if (subtotal >= 100 && subtotal < 250)
                    discountPercent = .1;
                else if (subtotal >= 250)
                    discountPercent = .2;
            }
            else if (customerType.equalsIgnoreCase("C"))
            {
                if (subtotal < 250)
                    discountPercent = .2;
                else
                    discountPercent = .3;
            }
            else
                discountPercent = .1;

            // the code to calculate, format, and display results goes here

            // the code to see if the user wants to contine goes here
        }
    }
}
```

Figure 4-6 The enhanced Invoice application

How to code loops

In chapter 2, you learned how to code while statements and while loops. Now, you'll review the coding for those loops and learn how to code two other Java statements that implement the *iteration structure*.

How to code while and do-while loops

Figure 4-7 shows how to use the *while statement* to code a *while loop*. Then, it shows how to code a *do-while loop*. The difference between these types of loops is that the Boolean expression is evaluated at the beginning of a while loop and at the end of a do-while loop. As a result, the statements in a while loop are executed zero or more times while the statements in a do-while loop are always executed at least once.

When coding while loops, it's common to use a *counter variable* to execute the statements in a loop a certain number of times. The first loop in this figure, for example, uses an int counter variable named i that's initialized to 1. Then, the last statement in the loop increments the counter variable with each iteration of the loop. As a result, the first statement in this loop will be executed as long as the counter variable is less than or equal to 36. As I've mentioned earlier, it is a common coding practice to name counter variables with single letters like *i, j,* and *k.*

Most of the time, you can use either of these two types of loops to accomplish the same task. For instance, the first example in this figure uses a while loop to calculate the future value of a series of monthly payments at a specified interest rate, and the second example uses a do-while loop to perform the same calculation.

When coding loops, it's important to remember that the code within a loop has block scope. As a result, any variables that are declared within the loop can't be used outside of the loop. That's why the variables that are needed outside of the loop have been declared outside of the loop. That way, you can use these variables after the loop has finished executing.

When you code loops, you usually want to avoid *infinite loops*. If, for example, you forget to code a statement that increments the counter variable, the loop will never end. Then, you have to press Ctrl+C or close the console to cancel the application so you can debug your code.

The syntax of the while loop

```
while (booleanExpression)
{
   statements
}
```

A while loop that calculates a future value

```
int i = 1;
int months = 36;
while (i <= months)
{
    futureValue = (futureValue + monthlyPayment) *
        (1 + monthlyInterestRate);
    i++;
}
```

The syntax of the do-while loop

```
do
{
   statements
}
while (booleanExpression);
```

A do-while loop that calculates a future value

```
int i = 1;
int months = 36;
do
{
    futureValue = (futureValue + monthlyPayment) *
        (1 + monthlyInterestRate);
    i++;
}
while (i <= months);
```

Description

- In a *while loop*, the condition is tested before the loop is executed. In a *do-while loop*, the condition is tested after the loop is executed.
- A while or do-while loop executes the block of statements within the loop as long as its Boolean expression is true.
- If a loop requires more than one statement, you must enclose the statements in braces. This identifies the block of statements that are executed by the loop, and any variables or constants that are declared in that block have block scope.
- If a loop requires just one statement, you don't have to enclose the statement in braces. However, that statement can't declare a variable or it won't compile.
- If the condition at the start of a while statement never becomes false, the statement never ends. Then, the program goes into an *infinite loop*. You can cancel an infinite loop by closing the console window or pressing Ctrl+C.

Figure 4-7 How to code while and do-while loops

How to code for loops

Figure 4-8 shows how to use the for statement to code *for loops*. This type of loop is useful when you need to increment or decrement a counter that determines how many times the loop is going to be executed.

To code a for loop, you start by coding the for keyword followed by three expressions enclosed in parentheses and separated by semicolons. The first expression is an initialization expression that gives the starting value for the counter variable. This expression can also declare the counter variable, if necessary. The second expression is a Boolean expression that determines when the loop will end. And the third expression is an increment expression that determines how the counter is incremented or decremented each time the loop is executed.

The first example in this figure shows how to use these expressions. First, the initialization expression declares the counter variable that's used to determine the number of loops and assigns an initial value to it. In this example, the counter variable is an int type named i, and it's initialized to 0. Next, a Boolean expression specifies that the loop will be repeated as long as the counter is less than 5. Then, the increment expression increments the counter by 1 at the end of each repetition of the loop.

Since the two loops in this example store the counter variable followed by a space in a string, this code stores the numbers 0 to 4 in a string variable like this:

```
0 1 2 3 4
```

Notice that you can code this loop using a single statement or using multiple statements. If you use more than one statement, though, you must enclose those statements in braces.

The second example calculates the sum of 8, 6, 4, and 2. Here, the sum variable is declared before the loop so it will be available outside of the loop. Within the parentheses of the for loop, the initialization expression initializes the counter variable to 8, the Boolean expression indicates that the loop will end when the counter variable is no longer greater than zero, and the increment expression uses an assignment operator to subtract 2 from the counter variable with each repetition of the loop. Within the loop, the value of the counter variable is added to the value that's already stored in the sum variable. As a result, the final value for the sum variable is 20.

The third example shows how to code a loop that calculates the future value for a series of monthly payments. Here, the loop executes one time for each month. If you compare this example with the examples in the previous figure, you can see how a for loop improves upon a while or do-while loop when a counter variable is required.

The syntax of the for loop

```
for(initializationExpression; booleanExpression; incrementExpression)
{
    statements
}
```

Example 1: A for loop that stores the numbers 0 through 4 in a string

With a single statement

```
String numbers = "";
for (int i = 0; i < 5; i++)
    numbers += i + " ";
```

With a block of statements

```
String numbers = "";
for (int i = 0; i < 5; i++)
{
    numbers += i;
    numbers += " ";
}
```

Example 2: A for loop that adds the numbers 8, 6, 4, and 2

```
int sum = 0;
for (int j = 8; j > 0; j -= 2)
{
    sum += j;
}
```

Example 3: A for loop that calculates a future value

```
for (int i = 1; i <= months; i++)
{
    futureValue = (futureValue + monthlyPayment) *
        (1 + monthlyInterestRate);
}
```

Description

- A *for loop* is useful when you need to increment or decrement a counter that determines how many times the loop is executed.
- Within the parentheses of a for loop, you code an initialization expression that gives the starting value for the counter, a Boolean expression that determines when the loop ends, and an increment expression that increments or decrements the counter.
- The loop ends when the Boolean expression is false.
- If necessary, you can declare the counter variable before the for loop. Then, this variable will be in scope after the loop finishes executing.

Figure 4-8 How to code for loops

The Future Value application

Now that you've learned the statements for coding loops, figure 4-9 presents an application that uses a for loop within a while loop. As the console for this application shows, the user starts by entering the values for the monthly payment that will be made, the yearly interest rate, and the number of years the payment will be made. Then, for each group of entries, the application calculates and displays the future value.

If you look at the code for this application, you can see that it uses a while loop to determine when the program will end. Within this loop, the program first gets the three entries from the user. Next, it converts these entries to the same time unit, which is months. To do that, the number of years is multiplied by 12, and the yearly interest rate is divided by 12. Besides that, the yearly interest rate is divided by 100 so it will work correctly in the future value calculation.

Once those variables are prepared, the program enters a for loop that calculates the future value. When the loop finishes, the program displays the result and asks whether the user wants to continue.

Because this application doesn't validate the user's entries, it will crash if the user enters invalid data. But you'll learn how to fix that in the next chapter. Otherwise, this application works the way you would want it to. In this case, rounding isn't an issue because the result is rounded just one time after the future value loop has finished.

Because it can be hard to tell whether an application with a loop is producing the right results, it often makes sense to add debugging statements within the loop while you're testing it. For instance, you could add this statement to the Future Value application as the last statement in the loop:

```
System.out.println("Debug: " + i + "     " + futureValue);
```

Then, one line will be displayed on the console each time through the loop so you can check to make sure that the calculations for the first few months are accurate. You will also be able to tell at a glance whether the loop was executed the right number of times.

The console

```
Enter monthly investment:   100
Enter yearly interest rate: 3
Enter number of years:      3
Future value:               $3,771.46

Continue? (y/n): y
```

The code

```
import java.util.Scanner;
import java.text.NumberFormat;

public class FutureValueApp
{
    public static void main(String[] args)
    {
        Scanner sc = new Scanner(System.in);
        String choice = "y";
        while (!choice.equalsIgnoreCase("n"))
        {
            // get the input from the user
            System.out.print("Enter monthly investment:   ");
            double monthlyInvestment = sc.nextDouble();
            System.out.print("Enter yearly interest rate: ");
            double interestRate = sc.nextDouble();
            System.out.print("Enter number of years:      ");
            int years = sc.nextInt();

            // convert yearly to monthly values and initialize future value
            double monthlyInterestRate = interestRate/12/100;
            int months = years * 12;
            double futureValue = 0.0;

            // use a for loop to calculate the future value
            for (int i = 1; i <= months; i++)
            {
                futureValue =
                    (futureValue + monthlyInvestment) *
                    (1 + monthlyInterestRate);
            }

            // format and display the result
            NumberFormat currency = NumberFormat.getCurrencyInstance();
            System.out.println("Future value:               "
                                 + currency.format(futureValue));
            System.out.println();

            // see if the user wants to continue
            System.out.print("Continue? (y/n): ");
            choice = sc.next();
            System.out.println();
        }
    }
}
```

Figure 4-9 The code for the Future Value application

How to code nested for loops

Like if and switch statements, you can also nest for loops, and that's illustrated by the code in figure 4-10. As with all nested statements, you should use indentation to clearly show the relationships between the statements.

The example in this figure shows how to use three nested for loops to display a table of future value calculations on the console. Here, the amount of the monthly investment is set to $100, the interest rates vary from 5.0% to 6.5%, and the number of years varies from 2 years to 4 years. Before the nested for loops are executed, another for loop adds the headings to the table string.

After that, the three nested loops add one row for each year to the table string. To do that, the outer loop iterates through the years (4, 3, and 2). Then, the code adds the year to the start of the row string. After that, the next loop iterates though the four interest rates (5%, 5.5%, 6%, and 6.5%) using the innermost loop to calculate the future value for each interest rate and to append these calculations to the row string. When this loop is finished, the top-level loop appends the row to the table string and clears the row string so it can be used again in the next iteration of the loop.

When all of the loops have been completed, the println method prints the table string to the console. This shows the lowest future value amount in the bottom left corner and the highest future value amount in the top right corner. To align these interest rates, this code uses spaces. Although it would be possible to use tab characters to align each column, tabs don't always align columns correctly.

The console

```
Monthly Payment: 100.0

       5.0%         5.5%         6.0%         6.5%
4    $5,323.58    $5,379.83    $5,436.83    $5,494.59
3    $3,891.48    $3,922.23    $3,953.28    $3,984.64
2    $2,529.09    $2,542.46    $2,555.91    $2,569.45
```

Nested for loops that print a table of future values

```
// get the currency and percent formatters
NumberFormat currency = NumberFormat.getCurrencyInstance();
NumberFormat percent = NumberFormat.getPercentInstance();
percent.setMinimumFractionDigits(1);

// set the monthly payment to 100 and display it to the user
double monthlyPayment = 100.0;
System.out.println("Monthly Payment: " + monthlyPayment);
System.out.println();

// declare a variable to store the table
String table  = "       ";

// fill the first row of the table
for (double rate = 5.0; rate < 7.0; rate += .5)
{
    table += percent.format(rate/100) + "         ";
}
table += "\n";

// loop through each row
for (int years = 4; years > 1; years--)
{
    // append the years variable to the start of the row
    String row = years + "    ";
    // loop through each column
    for (double rate = 5.0; rate < 7.0; rate += .5)
    {
        // calculate the future value for each rate
        int months = years * 12;
        double monthlyInterestRate = rate/12/100;
        double futureValue = 0.0;
        for (int i = 1; i <= months; i++)
        {
            futureValue =
                (futureValue + monthlyPayment) *
                (1 + monthlyInterestRate);
        }
        // add the calculation to the row
        row += currency.format(futureValue) + "    ";
    }
    table += row + "\n";
    row = "";
}

// display the table to the user
System.out.println(table);
```

Figure 4-10 How to code nested for loops that calculate future values

How to code break and continue statements

When you code loops, you usually want them to run to completion. Occasionally, though, an application may require that you jump out of a loop. To do that, you can use the break or continue statement.

How to code break statements

Figure 4-11 shows how to use the break statement and the labeled break statement to exit loops. If you need to exit the current loop, you can code a break statement. If you need to exit another loop in a set of nested loops, you can use the labeled break statement.

The first example shows how you can use the break statement to exit from an inner loop. Here, a while loop that generates random numbers is nested within a for loop. Notice that the Boolean expression for the while loop has been set to true. Because of that, this loop would execute indefinitely without a statement that explicitly jumps out of the loop. In this case, a break statement is used to exit from the loop when the random number that's generated is greater than 7. Then, control is returned to the for loop, which is executed until its Boolean expression is satisfied.

The second example shows how you can use the labeled break statement to exit an outer loop from an inner loop. To use a labeled break statement, you code a *label* for the loop that you want to exit. Then, to break out of the outer loop, you just type the break statement followed by the name of the label. This will transfer control to the statement that follows the outer loop.

The syntax of the break statement

```
break;
```

Example 1: A break statement that exits the inner loop

```
for (int i = 1; i < 4; i++)
{
    System.out.println("Outer " + i);
    while (true)
    {
        int number = (int) (Math.random() * 10);
        System.out.println("   Inner " + number);
        if (number > 7)
            break;
    }
}
```

The syntax of the labeled break statement

```
break labelName;
```

The structure of the labeled break statement

```
labelName:
loop declaration
{
    statements
    another loop declaration
    {
        statements
        if (conditionalExpression)
        {
            statements
            break labelName;
        }
    }
}
```

Example 2: A labeled break statement that exits the outer loop

```
outerLoop:
for (int i = 1; i < 4; i++)
{
    System.out.println("Outer " + i);
    while (true)
    {
        int number = (int) (Math.random() * 10);
        System.out.println("   Inner " + number);
        if (number > 7)
            break outerLoop;
    }
}
```

Description

- To jump to the end of the current loop, you can use the break statement.
- To jump to the end of an outer loop from an inner loop, you can label the outer loop and use the labeled break statement. To code a *label*, type the name of the label and a colon before a while, do-while, or for loop.

Figure 4-11 How to code break statements

How to code continue statements

Figure 4-12 shows how to use the continue statement and labeled continue statement to jump to the beginning of a loop. These statements work similarly to the break statements, but they jump to the beginning of a loop instead of the end of a loop. Like the break statements, you can use the unlabeled version of the statement to work with the current loop and you can use the labeled version of the statement to work with nested loops.

The first example shows how to use the continue statement to print 9 random numbers. In this example, the loop generates random numbers from 0 through 10 and prints them to the console. If the random number is less than or equal to 7, though, the continue statement jumps to the beginning of the loop. As a result, the println method that comes after the continue statement is only executed when the random number is greater than 7.

The second example shows how to use thc labeled continue statement to print the prime numbers from 1 through 19. In this example, the outer loop loops through the numbers 1 through 19, while the inner loop loops through all numbers from 2 through the outer number minus 1. Then, the remainder variable is set equal to the remainder of the outer loop counter divided by the inner loop counter. If the remainder equals 0, the continue statement causes control of the program to jump to the top of the outer loop. As a result, the outer loop continues with the next number. But if the remainder doesn't equal 0 at any point in the inner loop, which means the number is a prime number, the program finishes the inner loop and the println method prints the number to the console.

The syntax of the continue statement

```
continue;
```

Example 1: A continue statement that jumps to the beginning of a loop

```
for (int j = 1; j < 10; j++)
{
    int number = (int) (Math.random() * 10);
    System.out.println(number);
    if (number <= 7)
        continue;
    System.out.println("This number is greater than 7");
}
```

The syntax of the labeled continue statement

```
continue labelName;
```

The structure of the labeled continue statement

```
labelName:  <-------------------------------+
loop declaration                            |
{                                           |
    statements                              |
    another loop declaration                |
    {                                       |
        statements                          |
        if (conditionalExpression)          |
        {                                   |
            statements                      |
            continue labelName; ------------+
        }
    }
}
```

Example 2: A labeled continue statement that jumps to the beginning of the outer loop

```
outerLoop:
for(int i = 1; i < 20; i++)
{
    for(int j = 2; j < i-1; j++)
    {
        int remainder = i%j;
        if (remainder == 0)
            continue outerLoop;
    }
    System.out.println(i);
}
```

Description

- To skip the rest of the statements in the current loop and jump to the top of the current loop, you can use the continue statement.
- To skip the rest of the statements in the current loop and jump to the top of a labeled loop, you can add a label to the loop and use the labeled continue statement.
- To code a label, type the name of the label and a colon before a while, do-while, or for loop.

Figure 4-12 How to code continue statements

How to code and call static methods

So far, you've learned how to code applications that consist of a single method, the static main method that's executed automatically when you run a class. Now, you'll learn how to code and call other static methods. That's one way to divide the code for an application into manageable parts.

How to code static methods

Figure 4-13 shows how to code a *static method*. To start, you code an *access modifier* that indicates whether the method can be called from other classes (public) or just the class that it's coded in (private). Next, you code the static keyword to identify the method as a static method.

After the static keyword, you code a return type that identifies the type of data that the method will return. That return type can be either a primitive data type or a class like the String class. If the method doesn't return any data, you code the void keyword.

After the return type, you code a method name that indicates what the method does. A common coding convention is to use camel notation and to start each method name with a verb followed by a noun or by an adjective and a noun, as in calculateFutureValue.

After the method name, you code a set of parentheses. Within the parentheses, you declare the *parameters* that are required by the method. If a method doesn't require any parameters, you can code an empty set of parentheses. And if a method requires more than one parameter, you separate them with commas as shown by the second example. Later on, when you call the method, you pass arguments that correspond to these parameters.

At this point, you code a set of braces that contains the statements that the method will execute. If the method is going to return a value, these statements must include a *return statement* that identifies the variable or object to be returned. This is illustrated by the calculateFutureValue method in this figure.

When you code the return type, method name, and parameter list of a method, you form the *signature* of the method. As you might expect, each method must have a unique signature. However, you can code two or more methods with the same name but with different parameters. This is known as *overloading* a method, and you'll learn more about that in chapter 6.

How to call static methods

Figure 4-13 also shows how to *call* a static method that's coded within the same class. This is just like calling a static method from a Java class, but you don't need to code the class name. Then, if the method requires *arguments*, you code the arguments within parentheses, separating each argument with a comma. Otherwise, you code an empty set of parentheses.

The basic syntax for coding a static method

```
{public|private} static returnType methodName([parameterList])
{
   statements
}
```

A static method with no parameters and no return type

```
private static void printWelcomeMessage()
{
    System.out.println("Hello New User"); // This could be a lengthy message
}
```

A static method with three parameters that returns a double value

```
public static double calculateFutureValue(double monthlyInvestment,
double monthlyInterestRate, int months)
{
    double futureValue = 0.0;
    for (int i = 1; i <= months; i++)
    {
        futureValue = (futureValue + monthlyInvestment)
            * (1 + monthlyInterestRate);
    }
    return futureValue;
}
```

The syntax for calling a static method that's in the same class

```
methodName([argumentList])
```

A call statement with no arguments

```
printWelcomeMessage();
```

A call statement that passes three arguments

```
double futureValue = calculateFutureValue(investment, rate, months);
```

Description

- To allow other classes to access a method, use the public *access modifier*. To prevent other classes from accessing a method, use the private modifier.
- To code a method that returns data, code a return type in the method declaration and code a *return statement* in the body of the method. The return statement ends the execution of the method and returns the specified value to the calling method.
- Within the parentheses of a method, you can code an optional *parameter list* that contains one or more *parameters* that consist of a data type and name. These are the values that must be passed to the method when it is called.
- The name of a method along with its parameter list form the *signature* of the method, which must be unique.
- When you call a method, the *arguments* in the *argument list* must be in the same order as the parameters in the parameter list defined by the method, and they must have compatible data types. However, the names of the arguments and the parameters don't need to be the same.

Figure 4-13 How to code and call static methods

In practice, the terms *parameter* and *argument* are often used interchangeably. In this book, however, we'll use the term *parameter* to refer to the variables of a method declaration, and we'll use the term *argument* to refer to the variables that are passed to a method.

The Future Value application with a static method

To illustrate the use of static methods, figure 4-14 presents another version of the Future Value application. This time it uses a static method to calculate the future value. This method requires three arguments, and it includes the for loop that processes those arguments. When the loop finishes, the return statement returns the future value to the main method.

To use this statement, the body of the program prepares the three arguments in month units. Then, it calls the method and passes the three arguments to it. This simplifies the body of the program, and this illustrates how static methods can be used to divide a program into manageable components.

In this case, the call statement passes arguments that have the same variable names as the parameters of the method. Although this isn't necessary, it makes the code easier to follow. What is necessary, though, is that the arguments be passed in the same sequence as the parameters and with the same data types.

In the next chapter, you'll see other ways that static methods can be used. Then, in chapter 6, you'll see how static methods can be coded with the public keyword so they can be accessed by other classes. For now, though, you can code all of your static methods with the private access modifier.

The code

```
import java.util.Scanner;
import java.text.NumberFormat;

public class FutureValueApp
{
    public static void main(String[] args)
    {
        Scanner sc = new Scanner(System.in);
        String choice = "y";
        while (!choice.equalsIgnoreCase("n"))
        {
            // get the input from the user
            System.out.print("Enter monthly investment:   ");
            double monthlyInvestment = sc.nextDouble();
            System.out.print("Enter yearly interest rate: ");
            double interestRate = sc.nextDouble();
            System.out.print("Enter number of years:      ");
            int years = sc.nextInt();

            // convert yearly values to monthly values
            double monthlyInterestRate = interestRate/12/100;
            int months = years * 12;

            // call the future value method
            double futureValue = calculateFutureValue(
                monthlyInvestment, monthlyInterestRate, months);

            // format and display the result
            NumberFormat currency = NumberFormat.getCurrencyInstance();
            System.out.println("Future value:               "
                                  + currency.format(futureValue));
            System.out.println();

            // see if the user wants to continue
            System.out.print("Continue? (y/n): ");
            choice = sc.next();
            System.out.println();
        }
    }

    //  a static method that requires three arguments and returns a double
    private static double calculateFutureValue(double monthlyInvestment,
    double monthlyInterestRate, int months)
    {
        double futureValue = 0.0;
        for (int i = 1; i <= months; i++)
        {
            futureValue =
                (futureValue + monthlyInvestment) *
                (1 + monthlyInterestRate);
        }
        return futureValue;
    }
}
```

Figure 4-14 The Future Value application with a static method

Perspective

If this chapter has succeeded, you should now be able to use if, switch, while, do-while, and for statements. These are the Java statements that implement the selection, case, and iteration structures, and they provide the logic of an application. You should also be able to code and call your own static methods, which will help you divide your programs into manageable parts.

Summary

- You can use the *relational operators* to create *Boolean expressions* that compare primitive data types and return true or false values, and you can use the *logical operators* to connect two or more Boolean expressions.
- To determine whether two strings are equal, you can call the equals and equalsIgnoreCase methods from a String object.
- You can use *if/else statements* and *switch statements* to control the logic of an application, and you can *nest* these statements whenever necessary.
- You can use *while*, *do-while*, and *for loops* to repeatedly execute one or more statements until a Boolean expression evaluates to false, and you can nest these statements whenever necessary.
- You can use *break statements* to jump to the end of the current loop or a labeled loop, and you can use *continue statements* to jump to the start of the current loop or a labeled loop.
- To code a *static method*, you code an access modifier, the static keyword, its return type, its name, and a *parameter* list. Then, to return a value, you code a *return statement* within the method.
- To call a static method that's in the same class as the main method, you code the method name followed by an *argument* list.

Exercise 4-1 Test the Future Value application

In this exercise, you'll test the Future Value application that's presented in figure 4-9 in this chapter.

1. Open the FutureValueApp class stored in the ch04 directory. Then, compile and test it with valid data to see how it works.
2. To make sure that the results are correct, add a debugging statement within the for loop that calculates the future value. This statement should display the month and future value each time through the loop. Then, test the program with simple entries like 100 for monthly investment, 12 for yearly interest (because that's 1 percent each month), and 1 for year. When the debugging data is displayed, check the results manually to make sure they're correct.

Exercise 4-2 Enhance the Invoice application

In this exercise, you'll modify the nested if/else statements that are used to determine the discount percent for the Invoice application in figure 4-6. Then, you'll code and call a static method that determines the discount percent.

Open the application and change the if/else statement

1. Open the application named CodedInvoiceApp that's in the ch04 directory, save it as EnhancedInvoiceApp, and change the class name. Then, compile and run the application to see how it works.
2. Change the if/else statement so customers of type "R" with a subtotal that is greater than or equal to $250 but less than $500 get a 25% discount and those with a subtotal of $500 or more get a 30% discount. Next, change the if/else statement so customers of type "C" always get a 20% discount. Then, test the application to make sure this works.
3. Add another customer type to the if/else statement so customers of type "T" get a 40% discount for subtotals of less than $500, and a 50% discount for subtotals of $500 or more. Then, test the application.
4. Check your code to make sure that no discount is provided for a customer type code that isn't "R", "C", or "T". Then, fix this if necessary.

Code and call a static method that determines the discount percent

5. Code a static method named getDiscountPercent that has two parameters: customer type and subtotal. To do that efficiently, you can move the appropriate code from the main method of the application into the static method and make the required modifications.
6. Add code that calls the static method from the body of the application. Then, test to make sure that it works.

Exercise 4-3 Enhance the Test Score application

In this exercise, you'll enhance the Test Score application so it uses a while or a do-while loop plus a for loop. After the enhancements, the console for a user's session should look something like this:

```
Enter the number of test scores to be entered: 5

Enter score 1: 75
Enter score 2: 80
Enter score 3: 75
Enter score 4: 880
Invalid entry, not counted
Enter score 4: 80
Enter score 5: 95

Score count:   5
Score total:   405
Average score: 81
Minimum score: 75
Maximum score: 95

Enter more test scores? (y/n): y

Enter the number of test scores to be entered: 3

Enter score 1: 85
Enter score 2: 95
Enter score 3: 100

Score count:   3
Score total:   280
Average score: 93.3
Minimum score: 85
Maximum score: 100

Enter more test scores? (y/n):
```

1. Open the EnhancedTestScoreApp in ch03 that you developed for exercise 3-2. If you didn't do that exercise, you can work from an earlier version like the ModifiedTestScoreApp or the TestScoreApp that's in ch02. Then, save the application in the ch04 directory as EnhancedTestScoreApp, change the class name if necessary, and compile and test the application.
2. Change the while statement to a do-while statement, and test this change. Does this work any better than the while loop?
3. Enhance the program so it uses a while or do-while loop that controls whether the user enters more than one set of test scores. The statements in this loop should first ask the user how many test scores are going to be entered. Then, this number should be used in a for loop that gets that many test score entries from the user. When the loop ends, the program should display the summary data for the test scores, determine whether the user wants to enter another set of scores, and repeat the while loop if necessary. After you make these enhancements, test them to make sure they work.
4. If you didn't already do it, make sure that the code in the for loop doesn't count an invalid entry. In that case, an error message should be displayed and the counter decremented by one. Now, test to make sure this works.

5

How to validate input data

In the last three chapters, you learned how to code applications that get input from a user and perform calculations based on that input. However, if the user enters data that the application can't handle, an exception will occur and the application will crash.

Now, you'll learn how to validate the input data before processing it so problems like that won't occur. This is an essential skill when you're developing professional applications.

How to handle exceptions

To prevent your applications from crashing, you can write code that handles exceptions when they occur. This is known as *exception handling*, and it plays an important role in most applications.

How exceptions work

When an application can't do the operation it's trying to perform, Java *throws* an *exception*. An exception is an object that's created from one of the classes in the Exception hierarchy such as the ones shown in figure 5-1. Exception objects represent errors that have occurred, and they contain information about those errors. One of the most common causes of exceptions is invalid input data.

The Exception class that's at the top of the exception hierarchy defines the most general type of exception. The RuntimeException class is a *subclass* of the Exception class that defines a more specific type of exception. Similarly, the NoSuchElementException and IllegalArgumentException classes are subclasses of the RuntimeException class that define even more specific types of exceptions. Since the RuntimeException class represents exceptions that occur at runtime, none of the exceptions shown in this figure are checked by the compiler. In chapter 13, you'll learn about another type of exception that is checked by the compiler.

A well-coded application will *catch* any exceptions that are thrown and handle them. Exception handling can be as simple as notifying users that they must enter valid data. Or, for more serious exceptions, it may involve notifying users that the application is being shut down, saving as much data as possible, cleaning up resources, and exiting the application as smoothly as possible.

When you're testing an application, it's common to encounter exceptions that haven't been handled. For a console application, this will typically cause information about the exception to be displayed at the console. This information usually includes the name of the exception class, a brief message that describes the cause of the exception, and a *stack trace*. In this figure, for example, you can see the information that's displayed when the user enters an invalid double value for the Invoice application.

As you can see in this example, a stack trace is a list of the methods that were called before the exception occurred. These methods are listed in the reverse order from the order in which they were called. Each method includes a line number, which can help you find the statement that caused the exception in your source code. The stack trace in this figure, for example, indicates that line 15 of the main method of the InvoiceApp class threw an exception when it called the nextDouble method of the Scanner class.

One common situation where you'll need to handle exceptions is when you convert string data to numeric data. If, for example, the nextDouble method of the Scanner class can't convert the data the user enters to a double type, an InputMismatchException is thrown. Similarly, a NumberFormatException is

Some of the classes in the Exception hierarchy

```
Exception
    RuntimeException
        NoSuchElementException
            InputMismatchException
        IllegalArgumentException
            NumberFormatException
        ArithmeticException
        NullPointerException
```

The console after an InputMismatchException has been thrown

```
Enter subtotal:   $100
Exception in thread "main" java.util.InputMismatchException
        at java.util.Scanner.throwFor(Scanner.java:810)
        at java.util.Scanner.next(Scanner.java:1404)
        at java.util.Scanner.nextDouble(Scanner.java:2291)
        at InvoiceApp.main(InvoiceApp.java:15)
Press any key to continue . . .
```

Three methods that might throw an exception

Class	Method	Throws
Scanner	nextDouble()	InputMismatchException
Integer	parseInt(String)	NumberFormatException
Double	parseDouble(String)	NumberFormatException

Description

- An *exception* is an object that contains information about an error that has occurred. When an error occurs in a method, the method *throws* an exception.
- If an exception is thrown when you're testing a console application, some information about the exception, including its name and stack trace, is displayed at the console.
- A *stack trace* is a list of the methods that were called before the exception occurred. The list appears in reverse order, from the last method called to the first method called.
- All exceptions are *subclasses* of the Exception class. The Exception class represents the most general type of exception. Each successive layer of subclasses represents more specific exceptions.
- The class for an exception is usually stored in the same package as the class whose methods throw that type of exception. For instance, the InputMismatchException class is stored in the java.util package along with the Scanner class.

Figure 5-1 How exceptions work

thrown when a value of one data type can't be converted to another data type. This exception can be thrown by the parseDouble method of the Double class or the parseInt method of the Integer class.

The class for an exception is usually stored in the same package as the class that has the methods that throw that type of exception. For instance, the InputMismatchException is thrown by the Scanner class so the class for this exception is stored in the java.util package along with the Scanner class. As a result, if your application is going to use this exception object, it must import java.util.InputMismatchException or all of the classes in that package.

How to catch exceptions

To catch and handle exceptions, you use the *try statement* shown in figure 5-2. First, you code a try clause that contains a block of one or more statements that may cause an exception. Then, you code a catch clause immediately after the try clause. This clause contains the block of statements that will be executed if an exception is thrown by a statement in the try block. Since this block contains the code that handles the exception, it is known as an *exception handler*.

The example in this figure shows how you might use a try statement in the Invoice application. Here, the nextDouble method of the Scanner class is coded within a try clause, and a catch clause is coded for the InputMismatchException. Then, if the user enters a non-numeric value for the subtotal, the nextDouble method will throw an InputMismatchException and the code in the catch block will be executed. In order to catch that exception, though, the application must import the class for that exception, which is in the java.util package.

In this case, the catch block starts by calling the next method of the Scanner object to discard the incorrectly entered value. That way, the scanner won't try to retrieve this value the next time the nextDouble method is called. This is necessary because the nextDouble method isn't completed if an exception occurs. After this value is discarded, the second statement displays an error message. And finally, the continue statement jumps to the beginning of the loop, which causes the application to prompt the user to enter another subtotal. Of course, this assumes that the try/catch statement is coded within a while loop as shown in the next figure.

The catch block in this example will only be executed if the InputMismatchException is thrown. Since this exception is the only exception that's likely to be thrown in the try block, this is the clearest way to catch this exception. If you wanted the catch clause to catch other exceptions as well, however, you could name an exception higher up in the Exception hierarchy. For example, if you wanted to catch any runtime exception, you could code this catch clause:

```
catch(RuntimeException e)
```

And if you wanted to catch any exception, you could code this catch clause:

```
catch(Exception e)
```

You'll learn more about how this works in chapter 13.

The syntax for the try statement

```
try { statements }
catch(ExceptionClass exceptionName) { statements }
```

Two ways to import the InputMismatchException class

```
import java.util.InputMismatchException;
import.java.util.*;
```

A try statement that catches an InputMismatchException

```
double subtotal = 0.0;
try
{
    System.out.print("Enter subtotal:   ");
    subtotal = sc.nextDouble();
}
catch(InputMismatchException e)
{
    sc.next();      // discard the incorrectly entered double
    System.out.println("Error! Invalid number. Try again.\n");
    continue;       // jump to the top of the loop
}
```

Console output

```
Enter subtotal:   $100
Error! Invalid number. Try again.

Enter subtotal:
```

Description

- In a *try statement* (or *try/catch statement*), you code any statements that may throw an exception in a *try block*. Then, you can code a *catch block* that will handle any exceptions that may occur in the try block.
- When an exception occurs, any remaining statements in the try block are skipped and the statements in the catch block are executed.
- Any variables or objects that are used in both the try and catch blocks must be created before the try and catch blocks so both the try and catch blocks can access them.
- If you use a catch block to catch a specific type of exception, you must also import the package that contains that exception class.

Figure 5-2 How to catch exceptions

The Future Value application with exception handling

Figure 5-3 presents an improved version of the Future Value application that was presented in the last chapter. This version uses a try statement that's coded within the while loop to catch any exceptions that might be thrown when data is retrieved from the user.

To start, this application begins with an import statement that imports all of the classes in the java.util package. This includes the Scanner class and the InputMismatchException class. As a result, this application can use a Scanner object to get user input from the console, and it can catch the InputMismatchException object that may be thrown by the methods of the Scanner class.

To catch exceptions, all of the statements that get numeric input are coded within a try block. Then, if the user enters data with an invalid numeric format, the three statements in the catch block will be executed. The first statement uses the next method to discard the invalid entry. Then, the second statement displays a message that indicates that the entry is not a valid number. And finally, the continue statement causes execution to continue at the top of the while loop. That way, the user is prompted repeatedly until valid data is entered for all three values.

Although this technique works, it has two shortcomings. First, the user must start entering values from the beginning each time an exception is thrown even if some of the values were valid. Second, the application displays a generic error message that isn't as descriptive or helpful as it could be. Later in this chapter, you'll learn how to fix both of these shortcomings.

The code for the Future Value application with exception handling

```
import java.util.*;
import java.text.NumberFormat;

public class FutureValueExceptionApp
{
    public static void main(String[] args)
    {
        System.out.println("Welcome to the Future Value Calculator\n");
        Scanner sc = new Scanner(System.in);

        String choice = "y";
        while (choice.equalsIgnoreCase("y"))
        {
            double monthlyInvestment = 0.0;
            double interestRate = 0.0;
            int years = 0;
            try
            {
                System.out.print("Enter monthly investment:   ");
                monthlyInvestment = sc.nextDouble();
                System.out.print("Enter yearly interest rate: ");
                interestRate = sc.nextDouble();
                System.out.print("Enter number of years:      ");
                years = sc.nextInt();
            }
            catch(InputMismatchException e)
            {
                sc.next();      // discard the incorrectly entered number
                System.out.println("Error! Invalid number. Try again.\n");
                continue;       // jump to the top of the loop
            }

            double monthlyInterestRate = interestRate/12/100;
            int months = years * 12;
            double futureValue = calculateFutureValue(
                monthlyInvestment, monthlyInterestRate, months);

            NumberFormat currency = NumberFormat.getCurrencyInstance();
            System.out.println("Future value:               "
                             + currency.format(futureValue) + "\n");

            System.out.print("Continue? (y/n): ");
            choice = sc.next();
            System.out.println();
        }
    }

    private static double calculateFutureValue(double monthlyInvestment,
    double monthlyInterestRate, int months)
    {
        double futureValue = 0;
        for (int i = 1; i <= months; i++)
            futureValue = (futureValue + monthlyInvestment) *
                          (1 + monthlyInterestRate);
        return futureValue;
    }
}
```

Figure 5-3 The Future Value application with exception handling

How to validate data

Although you can use the try statement to catch and handle an exception caused by invalid data, it's usually best to prevent exceptions from being thrown whenever that's possible. To do that, you can use a technique called *data validation*. Then, when an entry is invalid, the application displays an error message and gives the user another chance to enter valid data. This is repeated until all the entries are valid.

How to prevent exceptions from being thrown

Figure 5-4 presents four methods of the Scanner class that you can use to prevent exceptions from being thrown. For instance, the first example in this figure illustrates how you can use the hasNextDouble method to check if the user has entered a string that can be converted to a double type. To do that, the hasNextDouble method is coded as the condition on an if statement. If this condition is true, the nextDouble method is called to retrieve the value.

If the condition on the if statement isn't true, it means that the user entered an invalid double value. In that case, the nextLine method is used to discard the entire line that the user entered. Then, an error message is displayed and the continue statement jumps to the beginning of the loop. This assumes, of course, that the if statement is coded within a loop like the while loop shown in figure 5-3.

When writing code like this, you can use the next method to discard the first string that the user enters. However, if the user enters two or more strings on a line, the next method will only discard the first string. Then, when the nextDouble method that follows is executed, it will attempt to read the next string in the line, without prompting the user for a new value. Since that's not what you want, you'll typically use the nextLine method instead of the next method to discard the remaining values in a line.

In the last chapter, you learned that if you call the equals or equalsIgnoreCase method from a string that contains a null, Java will throw an exception. Specifically, Java will throw a NullPointerException. To prevent this exception from being thrown, you can use code like that shown in the second example. To start, this code checks the value of a variable named customerType. If it isn't null, the code that follows calls the equals method. If it is, no processing is performed. Later in this book, you'll see why this type of code is often necessary.

Since code that checks user input without using exception handling runs faster than code that uses exception handling, you should avoid using exception handling to check user input whenever possible. In general, it's considered a good practice to use exception handling only when the situation is truly exceptional. For example, it's not exceptional that a user would accidentally enter a non-numeric value for a subtotal. As a result, you should use the methods of the Scanner class to prevent these types of exceptions whenever possible.

Methods of the Scanner class you can use to validate data

Method	Description
`hasNext()`	Returns true if the scanner contains another token.
`hasNextInt()`	Returns true if the scanner contains another token that can be converted to an int value.
`hasNextDouble()`	Returns true if the scanner contains another token that can be converted to a double value.
`nextLine()`	Returns any remaining input on the current line as a String object and advances the scanner to the next line.

Example 1: Code that prevents an InputMismatchException

```
double subtotal = 0.0;
System.out.print("Enter subtotal:   ");
if (sc.hasNextDouble())
    subtotal = sc.nextDouble();
else
{
    sc.nextLine();     // discard the entire line
    System.out.println("Error! Invalid number. Try again.\n");
    continue;          // jump to the top of the loop
}
```

Console output

```
Enter subtotal:   $100
Error! Invalid number. Try again.

Enter subtotal:
```

Example 2: Code that prevents a NullPointerException

```
if (customerType != null)
{
    if (customerType.equals("R"))
        discountPercent = .4;
}
```

Description

- The has methods of the Scanner class let you check whether additional data is available at the console and whether that data can be converted to a specific data type. You can use these methods to prevent an exception from being thrown when one of the next methods is called.
- You can use the nextLine method to retrieve and discard any additional data that the user enters on a line that isn't required by the application.
- When your code prevents an exception from being thrown, it runs faster than code that catches and then handles the exception.

Figure 5-4 How to prevent exceptions from being thrown

How to validate a single entry

When a user enters data in a console application, you may want to perform several types of data validation. In particular, it's common to perform the two types of data validation for numeric entries that are illustrated in figure 5-5.

First, if the application requires that the user enter a number at the prompt, you can use one of the has methods of the Scanner class to check that the string value the user entered can be converted to the appropriate numeric data type. Second, if the application requires that the user enter a number within a specified range, you can use if/else statements to check that the number falls within that range. This is known as *range checking*.

To repeat this checking until all the entries on the form are valid, you can use a while loop like the one shown in this figure. This loop is executed repeatedly as long as the value of a boolean variable named isValid is false. Then, within the while loop, the first if/else statement checks whether the user entered a double value. If so, the nextDouble method is used to retrieve that value, and the isValid variable is set to true. If not, an error message is displayed.

If the value the user entered is valid, the second if/else statement checks the value to see if it is greater than 0 and less than 10000. If so, the data is valid and the while loop ends. Otherwise, an appropriate error message is displayed, and the isValid variable is set to false so the while loop will repeat.

In this code, the nextLine method is called after the first if/else statement to discard any unnecessary or invalid entries. For example, if the user enters

```
100 dollars
```

the nextDouble method converts 100 to a double value, and the nextLine method reads past the "dollars" string. Then, because the String object that's returned by the nextLine method isn't assigned to a variable, it's discarded. Similarly, if the user enters an invalid double value, it's discarded by the nextLine method.

Since all characters in a string are valid, you don't need to check string variables for that type of validity. In some cases, though, you need to check whether the characters that a string contains are acceptable to the application. If, for example, the user is asked to enter a one-character code that should only be R, C, or T, the application should check to make sure the user has entered one of those characters. That's easily done with an if statement.

Although this figure only shows how to check data that the user has entered at a command prompt, the same principles apply to other types of applications. In section 4, for example, you'll see how these principles can be used to validate entries for an application that uses a graphical user interface.

Code that gets a valid double value within a specified range

```
Scanner sc = new Scanner(System.in);
double subtotal = 0.0;
boolean isValid = false;
while (isValid == false)
{
    // get a valid double value
    System.out.print("Enter subtotal:   ");
    if (sc.hasNextDouble())
    {
        subtotal = sc.nextDouble();
        isValid = true;
    }
    else
    {
        System.out.println("Error! Invalid number. Try again.");
    }
    sc.nextLine();  // discard any other data entered on the line

    // check the range of the double value
    if (isValid == true && subtotal <= 0)
    {
        System.out.println("Error! Number must be greater than 0.");
        isValid = false;
    }
    else if (isValid == true && subtotal >= 10000)
    {
        System.out.println("Error! Number must be less than 10000.");
        isValid = false;
    }
}
```

Description

- When a user enters data, that data usually needs to be checked to make sure that it is valid. This is known as *data validation*.
- When an entry is invalid, the program needs to display an error message and give the user another chance to enter valid data. This needs to be repeated until the entry is valid. One way to code this type of validation routine is to use a while loop.
- Two common types of validity checking for a numeric entry are (1) to make sure that the entry has a valid numeric format, and (2) to make sure that the entry is within a valid range (known as *range checking*).

Figure 5-5 How to validate an entry

How to use generic methods to validate an entry

Almost all professional applications need to validate two or more entries. Instead of writing code that validates a specific entry then, it often makes sense to create generic methods like the ones shown in figure 5-6. These methods perform the same types of validation shown in the previous figure, but they work for any double entry instead of for a specific entry.

In this figure, the getDouble method checks to be sure that the user enters a double value. This method accepts two parameters: a Scanner object and a String object that contains the text for the prompt. Then, this method displays the prompt to the user and, if the user enters a valid double value, it uses the scanner to read that value. Finally, the return statement returns the value to the calling method.

The getDoubleWithinRange method accepts four parameters. The first two parameters are the same as those used by the getDouble method. The second two parameters contain double values that represent the minimum and maximum values that are accepted by the application. Within the while loop for this method, the first statement passes the Scanner object and the prompt string to the getDouble method to return a double value. Then, the if/else statement that follows checks if the double value returned by the getDouble method falls within the specified range. If so, the while loop ends and the double value is returned to the calling method. Otherwise, the getDouble method is called again until the user enters a value within the valid range.

Note that the public keyword is used as the access modifier for both of these methods. That way, the methods can be accessed and used by other classes. You'll learn more about that in the next chapter. If you're only going to use the methods within one class, though, the access modifier can be coded as private.

Once you understand how the getDouble and getDoubleWithinRange methods work, you can code methods for other numeric types. For example, you can code a getInt method that uses the hasNextInt method to be sure that the user enters a valid int value at the prompt. Similarly, you can code a getIntWithinRange method to check that an int value is within a specified range.

The code at the bottom of this figure shows how to call these methods to make sure a valid double value has been entered at the Subtotal prompt. The first statement creates the Scanner object that's needed by the getDouble method. Then, the second statement calls the getDouble method to get a valid double value for the subtotal. The third statement uses the getDoubleWithinRange method to get a valid double value for a subtotal that is greater than 0 and less than 10000. This shows that you can call the getDouble method directly if you don't need to check the range. If you need to check the range, however, you can call the getDoubleWithinRange method, which calls the getDouble method for you.

A method that gets a valid numeric format

```
public static double getDouble(Scanner sc, String prompt)
{
    double d = 0.0;
    boolean isValid = false;
    while (isValid == false)
    {
        System.out.print(prompt);
        if (sc.hasNextDouble())
        {
            d = sc.nextDouble();
            isValid = true;
        }
        else
        {
            System.out.println("Error! Invalid number. Try again.");
        }
        sc.nextLine();      // discard any other data entered on the line
    }
    return d;
}
```

A method that checks for a valid numeric range

```
public static double getDoubleWithinRange(Scanner sc, String prompt,
double min, double max)
{
    double d = 0.0;
    boolean isValid = false;
    while (isValid == false)
    {
        d = getDouble(sc, prompt);  // call the getDouble method
        if (d <= min)
        {
            System.out.println(
                "Error! Number must be greater than " + min + ".");
        }
        else if (d >= max)
        {
            System.out.println(
                "Error! Number must be less than " + max + ".");
        }
        else
            isValid = true;
    }
    return d;
}
```

Code that uses these methods to return two valid double values

```
Scanner sc = new Scanner(System.in);
double subtotal1 = getDouble(sc, "Enter subtotal: ");
double subtotal2 = getDoubleWithinRange(sc, "Enter subtotal: ", 0, 10000);
```

Description

- Because most applications need to check more than one type of entry for validity, it often makes sense to create and use generic methods for data validation.

Figure 5-6 How to use generic methods to validate an entry

The Future Value application with data validation

Figure 5-3 presented a version of the Future Value application that used a try statement to catch the most common exceptions that might be thrown. Now, you'll see an improved version of this application that uses generic methods to validate the user entries. This code prevents the most common exceptions from being thrown, and it provides more descriptive messages to the user.

The console

Figure 5-7 shows the console display when the user enters invalid data for the improved version of the Future Value application. Here, the error messages have been highlighted so you can see them more easily. For example, the first error message is displayed if the user doesn't enter a valid double value for the monthly investment. The second error message is displayed if the user enters a value that's out of range for the interest rate. And the third error message is displayed if the user doesn't enter a valid integer value for the years.

The Data Entry section in this figure uses descriptive error messages to identify the problem to the user, and it doesn't require that the user re-enter values that have already been successfully entered. In addition, it only uses the first value the user enters on a line, which is usually what you want. All other values are discarded.

After the user completes the Data Entry section, the Future Value application calculates the future value and displays it along with the user's entries in the Formatted Results section. This makes it easy to see what valid values the user entered, which is useful if the user has entered one or more invalid entries in the Data Entry section.

The console for the Future Value application

```
Welcome to the Future Value Calculator

DATA ENTRY
Enter monthly investment: $100
Error! Invalid decimal value. Try again.
Enter monthly investment: 100 dollars
Enter yearly interest rate: 120
Error! Number must be less than 30.0.
Enter yearly interest rate: 12.0
Enter number of years: one
Error! Invalid integer value. Try again.
Enter number of years: 1

FORMATTED RESULTS
Monthly investment:      $100.00
Yearly interest rate:    12.0%
Number of years:         1
Future value:            $1,280.93

Continue? (y/n):
```

Description

- The Data Entry section gets input from the user and displays an appropriate error message if the user enters an invalid numeric format or an invalid range.
- The Formatted Results section displays the data that was entered by the user along with the future value in a format that's easy to read.

Figure 5-7 The console for the Future Value application with data validation

The code

Figure 5-8 shows the code for this version of the Future Value application. On page 1, you can see the code for the main method. Because this code is similar to code you've already seen, you shouldn't have any trouble understanding how it works. The biggest difference is that it uses methods named getDoubleWithinRange and getIntWithinRange to validate the data entered by the user. In this case, the monthly investment must be a double that's greater than 0 and less than 1000, the yearly interest rate must be a double that's greater than 0 and less than 30, and the number of years must be an int that's greater than 0 and less than 100. As a result, even if the user enters the maximum values for each variable, the application will be able to calculate an accurate future value.

The getDouble and getDoubleWithinRange methods shown on page 2 of this listing are the ones presented in figure 5-6. As a result, if you have any trouble understanding how these methods work, you may want to review that figure. The getInt and getIntWithinRange methods on page 3 work like the getDouble and getDoubleWithinRange methods except that they validate an int value instead of a double value. In this application, all of the methods are coded with the public access modifier so they can be accessed from other classes.

As you review this code, notice how each method performs a specific task. For example, the getDouble and getInt methods prompt the user for an entry, validate the entry, and return the valid entry. Similarly, the calculateFutureValue method performs a calculation and returns the result. This is a good design because it leads to code that's reusable and easy to maintain. For example, you can use the getDouble and getInt methods with any console application that gets double or int values from the user. Although you can copy these methods from one application to another, you can also store them in classes that you can access from any application. You'll learn how to do that in the next chapter.

The code for the Future Value application with data validation Page 1

```
import java.util.*;
import java.text.*;

public class FutureValueApp
{
    public static void main(String[] args)
    {
        System.out.println("Welcome to the Future Value Calculator\n");

        Scanner sc = new Scanner(System.in);
        String choice = "y";
        while (choice.equalsIgnoreCase("y"))
        {
            System.out.println("DATA ENTRY");
            double monthlyInvestment = getDoubleWithinRange(sc,
                "Enter monthly investment: ", 0, 1000);
            double interestRate = getDoubleWithinRange(sc,
                "Enter yearly interest rate: ", 0, 30);
            int years = getIntWithinRange(sc,
                "Enter number of years: ", 0, 100);

            double monthlyInterestRate = interestRate/12/100;
            int months = years * 12;
            double futureValue = calculateFutureValue(
                monthlyInvestment, monthlyInterestRate, months);

            NumberFormat currency = NumberFormat.getCurrencyInstance();
            NumberFormat percent = NumberFormat.getPercentInstance();
            percent.setMinimumFractionDigits(1);

            String results =
                  "Monthly investment:\t"
                      + currency.format(monthlyInvestment) + "\n"
                + "Yearly interest rate:\t"
                      + percent.format(interestRate/100) + "\n"
                + "Number of years:\t"
                      +  years + "\n"
                + "Future value:\t\t"
                      + currency.format(futureValue) + "\n";

            System.out.println();
            System.out.println("FORMATTED RESULTS");
            System.out.println(results);

            System.out.print("Continue? (y/n): ");
            choice = sc.next();
            sc.nextLine();      // discard any other data entered on the line
            System.out.println();
        }
    }
```

Figure 5-8 The code for the Future Value application with data validation (part 1 of 3)

The code for the Future Value application with data validation Page 2

```
public static double getDouble(Scanner sc, String prompt)
{
    double d = 0.0;
    boolean isValid = false;
    while (isValid == false)
    {
        System.out.print(prompt);
        if (sc.hasNextDouble())
        {
            d = sc.nextDouble();
            isValid = true;
        }
        else
        {
            System.out.println
                ("Error! Invalid decimal value. Try again.");
        }
        sc.nextLine();  // discard any other data entered on the line
    }
    return d;
}

public static double getDoubleWithinRange(Scanner sc, String prompt,
double min, double max)
{
    double d = 0.0;
    boolean isValid = false;
    while (isValid == false)
    {
        d = getDouble(sc, prompt);
        if (d <= min)
        {
            System.out.println(
                "Error! Number must be greater than " + min + ".");
        }
        else if (d >= max)
        {
            System.out.println(
                "Error! Number must be less than " + max + ".");
        }
        else
            isValid = true;
    }
    return d;
}
```

Figure 5-8 The code for the Future Value application with data validation (part 2 of 3)

The code for the Future Value application with data validation Page 3

```
    public static int getInt(Scanner sc, String prompt)
    {
        int i = 0;
        boolean isValid = false;
        while (isValid == false)
        {
            System.out.print(prompt);
            if (sc.hasNextInt())
            {
                i = sc.nextInt();
                isValid = true;
            }
            else
            {
                System.out.println
                    ("Error! Invalid integer value. Try again.");
            }
            sc.nextLine();  // discard any other data entered on the line
        }
        return i;
    }

    public static int getIntWithinRange(Scanner sc, String prompt,
    int min, int max)
    {
        int i = 0;
        boolean isValid = false;
        while (isValid == false)
        {
            i = getInt(sc, prompt);
            if (i <= min)
                System.out.println(
                    "Error! Number must be greater than " + min + ".");
            else if (i >= max)
                System.out.println(
                    "Error! Number must be less than " + max + ".");
            else
                isValid = true;
        }
        return i;
    }

    public static double calculateFutureValue(double monthlyInvestment,
    double monthlyInterestRate, int months)
    {
        double futureValue = 0;
        for (int i = 1; i <= months; i++)
        {
            futureValue =
                (futureValue + monthlyInvestment) *
                (1 + monthlyInterestRate);
        }
        return futureValue;
    }
}
```

Figure 5-8 The code for the Future Value application with data validation (part 3 of 3)

Perspective

Now that you've completed this chapter, you should be able to write console applications that validate the input data that's entered by the users. As a result, the applications should never crash. That, of course, is the way professional applications should work.

At this point, you've learned a complete subset of Java and you know how to use some of the methods in a few of the classes in the Java API. But there's a lot more to Java programming than that. In particular, you need to learn how to create your own classes that have their own methods. That's the essence of object-oriented programming, and that's what you'll learn in the next section of this book.

Summary

- An *exception* is an object that's created from the Exception class or one of its *subclasses*. This object contains information about an error that has occurred.
- The *stack trace* is a list of methods that were called before an exception occurred.
- You can code a *try statement* to create an *exception handler* that will *catch* and handle any exceptions that are *thrown*. This is known as *exception handling*.
- *Data validation* refers to the process of checking input data to make sure that it's valid.
- *Range checking* refers to the process of checking an entry to make sure that it falls within a certain range of values.

Exercise 5-1 Add validation to the Invoice application

In this exercise, you'll add data validation to the Invoice application that you've worked on in previous chapters. To do that, you'll use exception handling. You'll also write and use some specific data validation methods.

1. Open the EnhancedInvoiceApp in the ch04 directory that you developed for exercise 4-2. If you didn't do that exercise, open CodedInvoiceApp in the ch04 directory. Either way, save the application as ValidatedInvoiceApp in the ch05 directory, change the class name, and compile and run the application.
2. As you test the application, enter an invalid customer type code to see what happens. Then, enter an invalid subtotal entry like $1000 to see what happens when the application crashes.

Validate the customer type code

3. Modify the application so it will only accept these customer type codes: r/c/t or just r/c, depending on which version of the program you're modifying. It should also discard any extra entries on the customer type line. If the user enters an invalid code, the application should display an error message and ask the user to enter a valid code. Now, test this enhancement.
4. Code a static method named getValidCustomerType that does the validation of step 3. This method should require one parameter that receives a Scanner object, and it should return a valid customer type code. The method should get an entry from the user, check it for validity, display an error message if it's invalid, and discard any other user entries whether or not the entry is valid. This method should continue getting user entries until one is valid.
5. After you've written this method, modify the application so it uses this method. Then, test this enhancement.

Validate the subtotal

6. Add a try statement so it catches any InputMismatchException that the nextDouble method of the Scanner class might throw. The catch block should display an error message and issue a continue statement to jump to the beginning of the while loop. It should also discard the invalid entry and any other entries on the line. To do this, you need to import the exception classes in the java.util package, and the best way to do that is to import all of the classes in this package. Now, test this enhancement.
7. Code a static method named getValidSubtotal that uses the hasDouble method of the Scanner class to validate the subtotal entry so the InputMismatchException won't occur. This method should require one parameter that receives a Scanner object, and it should return a valid subtotal. This method should get an entry from the user, check that it's a valid double value, check that it's greater than zero and less than 10000, display appropriate error messages if it isn't valid, and discard any other user entries whether or not the entry is valid. This should continue until the method gets a valid subtotal entry.
8. After you've written this method, modify the code within the try statement so it uses this method. Then, test this enhancement so you can see that an InputMismatchException is no longer caught by the catch block. (When the code in a try block calls a method, any exception that isn't handled by the method is passed back to the code in the try block.)

Discard any extra entries for the Continue prompt

9. Modify the code so the application will work right even if the user enters two or more entries when asked if he wants to continue. To do that, you need to discard any extra entries. Then, test this enhancement.

At this point, the application should be bulletproof. It should only accept valid entries for customer type and subtotal, and it should work even if the user makes two or more entries for a single prompt.

Exercise 5-2 Add validation to the Test Score application

In this exercise, you'll add data validation to the Test Score application that you enhanced for chapter 4. To do that, you'll use generic methods that you copy from the Future Value application. This will show you that generic validation methods can be used in a wide range of applications.

1. Open the EnhancedTestScoreApp in the ch04 directory that you developed for exercise 4-3. Then, save the application as ValidatedTestScoreApp in the ch05 directory, change the class name, and compile and run the application to refresh your memory about how it works.
2. Open the FutureValueValidationApp in the ch05 directory. Then, copy the generic getInt and getIntWithinRange methods from that application and paste them into ValidatedTestScoreApp.
3. Use the getInt and getIntWithinRange methods to validate (1) that the number of test scores that the user enters ranges from 5 through 35, and (2) that each test score ranges from 1 through 100. Then, test this enhancement.
4. Add code that discards any extra entries at the Continue prompt. Then, do your final testing to make sure that the application is bulletproof.

Section 2

Object-oriented programming with Java

In the first section of this book, you learned how to use classes that are provided as part of the Java API. For instance, you learned how to use the Math class to perform common arithmetic operations, and you learned how to use the NumberFormat class to format numeric values. That's one part of object-oriented programming.

Besides the classes provided by the API, though, you can create your own classes. That's the other part of object-oriented programming, and that's what the four chapters in this section teach you to do. Specifically, chapter 6 shows you how to create your own classes. Chapter 7 shows you how to use inheritance, one of the most important features of object-oriented programming. Chapter 8 shows you how to use interfaces. And chapter 9 presents other object-oriented skills.

Because each of the chapters in this section builds on the previous chapters, you should read these chapters in sequence. In addition, you should read all of the chapters in this section before going on to sections 3, 4, or 5. That's because many of the chapters in these sections rely on your knowledge of inheritance and interfaces.

6

How to define and use classes

This chapter shows you how to create and use your own classes in Java applications. Here, you'll learn how to create classes that include regular fields and methods as well as classes that contain static fields and methods. In addition, you'll see two complete applications that use several user-defined classes.

When you complete this chapter, you'll start to see how creating your own classes can help simplify the development of an application. As a bonus, you'll have a better understanding of how the Java API works.

An introduction to classes

The topics that follow introduce you to the concepts that you need to know before you create your own classes. That includes how you'll use classes in a typical business application, how the fields and methods of a class can be encapsulated within the class, and how a class relates to its objects.

How classes can be used to structure an application

Figure 6-1 shows how you can use classes to simplify the design of a business application using a *multi-layered architecture*, also called a *multi-tiered architecture*. In a multi-layered application, the classes that perform different functions of the application are separated into two or more layers, or tiers.

A *three-tiered* application architecture like the one shown in this figure consists of a presentation layer, a middle layer, and a database layer. In practice, the middle layer is sometimes eliminated and its functions split between the database and presentation layers. On the other hand, the design of some applications further develops the middle layer into additional layers.

The classes in the *presentation layer* handle the details of the application's user interface. So far, all of the applications you've seen have been console applications. In these applications, most of the presentation layer is handled by the main method, which may call methods of other classes. In section 4, though, you'll learn how to write Java applications that display a graphical user interface (GUI) that consists of multiple windows called frames. In these applications, a separate class is usually created for each frame displayed by the application.

The classes of the *database layer* are responsible for all of the database access that's required by the application. These classes typically include methods that connect to the database and retrieve, add, update, and delete information from the database. Then, the other layers can call these methods to access the database, leaving the details of database access to the database classes. Although we refer to this layer as the database layer, it can also contain classes that work with data that's stored in files.

The *middle layer* provides an interface between the database layer and the presentation layer. This layer often includes classes that correspond to business entities (for example, products and customers). It may also include classes that implement business rules, such as discount or credit policies. The classes in this tier are often referred to as *business classes*, and the objects that are created from these classes are often called *business objects*.

One advantage of developing applications with a tiered architecture is that it allows the work to be spread among members of a development team. For example, one group of developers might work on the database layer, another group on the middle layer, and still another group on the presentation layer.

Another advantage is that it allows classes to be shared among applications. In particular, the classes that make up the database and middle layers can be stored in packages that can be used by more than one project. You'll learn how to work with packages in chapter 9.

The architecture of a three-tiered application

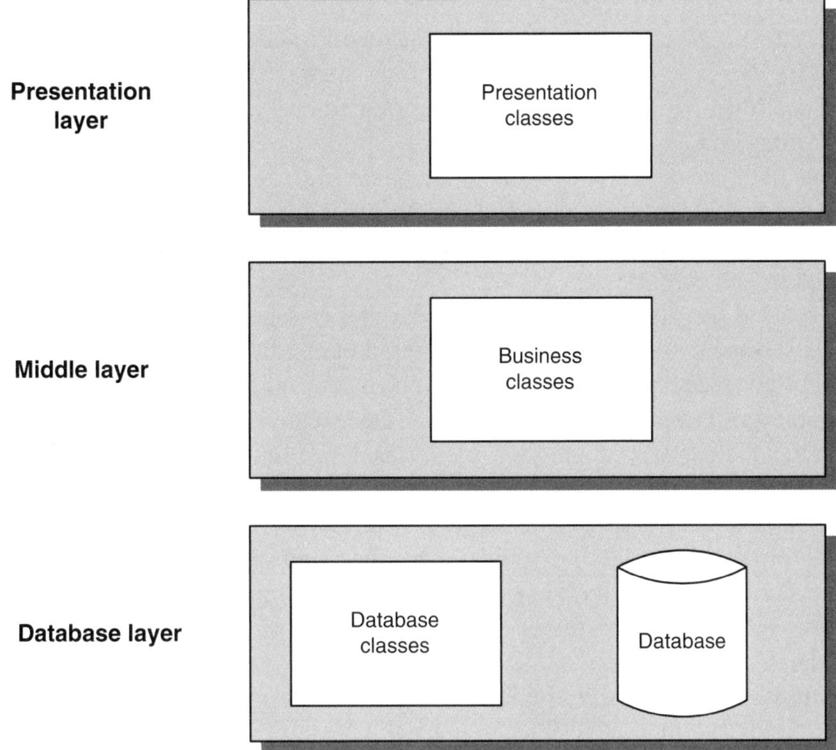

Description

- To simplify development and maintenance, many applications use a *three-tiered architecture* to separate the application's user interface, business rules, and database processing. Classes are used to implement the functions performed at each layer of the architecture.
- The classes in the *presentation layer* control the application's user interface. For a console application, the presentation layer consists only of a class with a main method and any other classes related to console input and output. For a GUI application, the user interface consists of at least one class for each window (called a *frame* in Java) that makes up the GUI.
- The classes in the *database layer* handle all of the application's data processing.
- The classes in the *middle layer*, which is sometimes called the *business rules layer*, act as an interface between the classes in the presentation and database layers. Sometimes, these classes correspond to business entities, such as customers or products, and sometimes these classes implement business rules, such as discount or credit policies. Often, the classes in this layer are referred to as *business classes*, and the objects created from them are called *business objects*.
- The classes that make up each layer are often stored in packages that can be shared among applications. For more information, see chapter 9.

Figure 6-1 How classes can be used to structure an application

How encapsulation works

Figure 6-2 shows a *class diagram* for a class named Product. This diagram uses *Unified Modeling Language* (*UML*), a modeling language that has become the industry standard for working with all object-oriented programming languages including Java.

In this class diagram, the class contains three *fields* and seven *methods*. Here, the minus sign (-) identifies fields and methods that are available only within the current class, while the plus sign (+) identifies fields and methods that are available to other classes.

In this case, all of the methods are available to other classes, but none of the fields are. However, the methods make the data stored by the fields available to other classes. For instance, the getCode method returns the value stored in the code field, and the setCode method assigns a new value to the code field.

This illustrates the concept of *encapsulation*, which is a fundamental concept of object-oriented programming. This means that the programmer can *hide*, or encapsulate, some fields and methods of a class, while *exposing* others. Since the fields (or data) of a class are typically encapsulated within a class, encapsulation is sometimes referred to as *data hiding*. In addition, though, the code that performs the methods of the class is also hidden from the classes that use the methods.

When you use a class, encapsulation lets you think of it as a black box that provides useful fields and methods. When you use the parseInt method of the Integer class, for example, you don't know how the method converts a string to an integer, and you don't need to know. Similarly, if you use the getPrice method of the Product class in this figure, you don't know how the method works, and you don't need to know.

This also means that you can change the code for a method within a class without affecting the classes that use the method. For instance, you can change the code for the getPrice method without changing the classes that use that method. This makes it easier to upgrade or enhance an application because you only need to change the classes that need upgrading.

A class diagram for the Product class

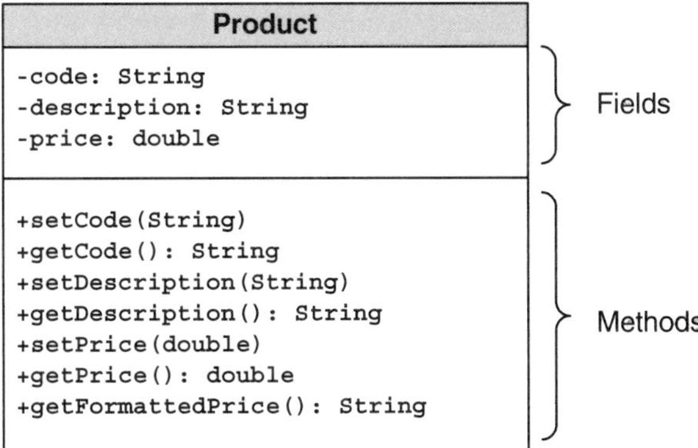

Description

- The *fields* of a class store the data of a class.
- The *methods* of a class define the tasks that a class can perform. Often, these methods provide a way to work with the fields of a class.
- *Encapsulation* is one of the fundamental concepts of object-oriented programming. This means that the class controls which of its fields and methods can be accessed by other classes. As a result, the fields in the class can be hidden from other classes, and the methods in a class can be modified or improved without changing the way that other classes use them.

UML diagramming notes

- *UML (Unified Modeling Language)* is the industry standard used to describe the classes and objects of an object-oriented application.
- The minus sign (-) in a UML *class diagram* marks the fields and methods that can't be accessed by other classes, while the plus sign (+) marks the fields and methods that can be accessed by other classes.
- For each field, the name is given, followed by a colon, followed by the data type.
- For each method, the name is given, followed by a set of parentheses. If a method requires parameters, the data type of each parameter is listed in the parentheses. Otherwise, the parentheses are left empty, and the data type of the value that's going to be returned is given after the colon.

Figure 6-2 How encapsulation works

The relationship between a class and its objects

Figure 6-3 uses UML diagrams to show the relationship between a class and its objects. In this figure, one class diagram and two *object diagrams* show how objects are created from a class. Here, the diagrams show only the fields, not the methods, of the class and its objects. In this case, two objects named product1 and product2 are created from the Product class.

Although an object diagram is similar to a class diagram, there are two differences. First, the name of the object diagram is underlined. Second, each field in an object diagram contains a value.

Once an *instance* of a class is created, it has an *identity* and a *state*. An object's identity is its address in internal memory, which is always unique. An object's state refers to the values that are stored by the object. For example, the states of the two Product objects in this figure are determined by the three values that they hold. As a program executes, the state of an object may change, but the identity of the object won't.

The relationship between a class and its objects

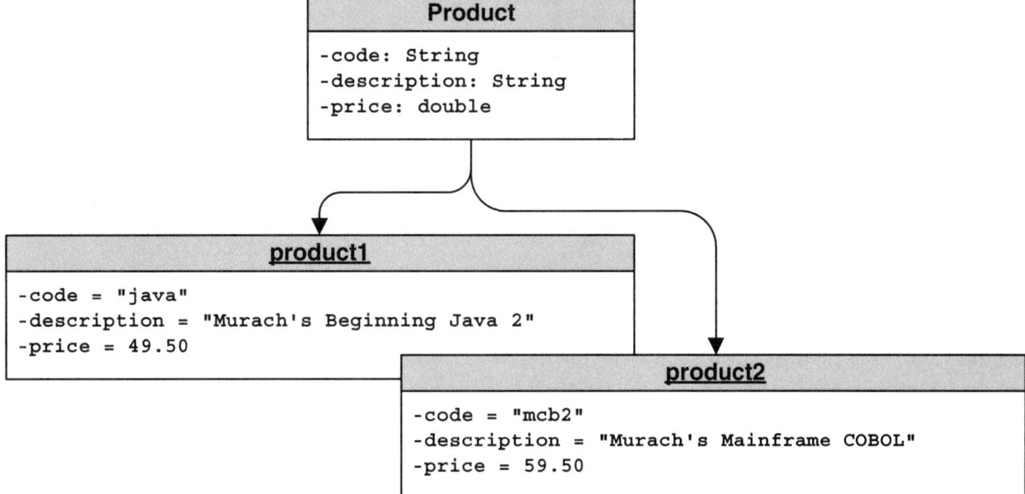

Description

- A *class* can be thought of as a template from which *objects* are made.
- An *object diagram* provides the name of the object and the values of the fields.
- Once an *instance* of a class is created, it has an *identity* (a unique address) and a *state* (the values that it holds). Although an object's state may change throughout a program, its identity never does.

Figure 6-3 The relationship between a class and its objects

How to code a class that defines an object

Now that you've learned some of the basic concepts for using classes, you're ready to learn the basic skills for creating your own classes. In the topics that follow, you'll learn how to create a business class named Product that you can use to work with products.

The code for the Product class

Figure 6-4 presents the code for the Product class. This code implements the fields and methods of the class diagram in figure 6-2. To start, the class declaration begins with an *access modifier*. In this case, the public keyword is used to declare the Product class so that other classes can access it.

The code within the class block defines the members of the Product class. In the next six pages, you'll learn the details of writing code like the code shown here. For now, I'll just present a preview of this code so you have a general idea of how it works.

The first three statements in this class are declarations for the fields of the class. The *fields* are the variables or constants that are available to the class and its objects. In this example, all three fields define *instance variables*, which store the data for the code, description, and price variables that apply to each Product object.

After the field declarations, this class declares the *constructor* of the Product class. This constructor creates an instance of the Product class and initializes its instance variables to their default values. As you'll see later in this chapter, you can also code constructors that accept parameters. Then, the constructor can use the parameter values to initialize the instance variables.

Next are the declarations for the methods of the Product class. In this class, the methods provide access to the values stored in the three fields. For each field, a *get method* returns the value stored in the field while a *set method* assigns a new value to the field. Of these methods, the getFormattedPrice method is the only method that does any work beyond getting or setting the value provided by the instance variable. This method applies the standard currency format to the price variable and returns the resulting string.

Although the Product class includes both a get and a set method for each field, you don't always have to code both of these methods for a field. In particular, it's common to code just a get method for a field so that its value can be retrieved but not changed. This can be referred to as a *read-only field*. Although you can also code just a set method for a field, that's uncommon.

The private and public keywords determine which members of a class are available to other classes. Since all of the instance variables of the Product class use the private keyword, they are only available within that class. The constructor and the methods, however, use the public keyword. As a result, they are available to all classes. Keep in mind, though, that you can include both public and private instance variables and methods in any class.

The Product class

```
import java.text.NumberFormat;

public class Product
{
    // the instance variables
    private String code;
    private String description;
    private double price;

    // the constructor
    public Product()
    {
        code = "";
        description = "";
        price = 0;
    }

    // the set and get accessors for the code variable
    public void setCode(String code)
    {
        this.code = code;
    }
    public String getCode()
    {
        return code;
    }

    // the set and get accessors for the description variable
    public void setDescription(String description)
    {
        this.description = description;
    }
    public String getDescription()
    {
        return description;
    }

    // the set and get accessors for the price variable
    public void setPrice(double price)
    {
        this.price = price;
    }
    public double getPrice()
    {
        return price;
    }

    // a custom get accessor for the price variable
    public String getFormattedPrice()
    {
        NumberFormat currency = NumberFormat.getCurrencyInstance();
        return currency.format(price);
    }
}
```

Figure 6-4 The code for the Product class

By the way, this class follows the three coding rules that are required for a *JavaBean*. First, it includes a constructor that requires no arguments. Second, all of the instance variables are private. Third, it includes get and set methods for all instance variables that you want to be able to access. As you progress with Java, you'll find that there are many advantages to creating classes that are also JavaBeans. For example, if you develop JavaServer Pages (JSPs) for a web application, you can use special JSP tags to create a JavaBean and to access its get and set methods.

Now that you've seen the code for the Product class, you might want to consider how it uses encapsulation. First, the three fields are hidden from other classes because they're declared with the private keyword. In addition, all of the code contained within the constructor and methods is hidden. Because of that, you can change any of this code without having to change the other classes that use this class.

How to code instance variables

Figure 6-5 shows how to code the instance variables that define the types of data that are used by the objects that are created from a class. When you declare an instance variable, you should use an access modifier to control its accessibility. If you use the private keyword, the instance variable can be used only within the class that defines it. In contrast, if you use the public keyword, the instance variable can be accessed by other classes. You can also use other access modifiers that give you finer control over the accessibility of your instance variables. You'll learn about those modifiers in the chapters that follow.

This figure shows four examples of declaring an instance variable. The first example declares a variable of the double type. The second one declares a variable of the int type. The third one declares a variable that's an object of the String class. And the last one declares an object from the Product class...the class that you're learning how to code right now.

Although instance variables work like regular variables, they must be declared within the class body, but not inside methods or constructors. That way, they'll be available throughout the entire class. In this book, all of the instance variables for a class are declared at the beginning of the class. However, when you read through code from other sources, you may find that the instance variables are declared at the end of the class or at other locations within the class.

The syntax for declaring instance variables

```
public|private primitiveType|ClassName variableName;
```

Examples

```
private double price;
private int quantity;
private String code;
private Product product;
```

Where you can declare instance variables

```
public class Product
{
    //common to code instance variables here
    private String code;
    private String description;
    private double price;

    //the constructors and methods of the class
    public Product(){}
    public void setCode(String code){}
    public String getCode(){ return code; }
    public void setDescription(String description){}
    public String getDescription(){ return description; }
    public void setPrice(double price){}
    public double getPrice(){ return price; }
    public String getFormattedPrice(){ return formattedPrice; }

    //also possible to code instance variables here
    private int test;
}
```

Description

- An instance variable may be a primitive data type, an object created from a Java class such as the String class, or an object created from a user-defined class such as the Product class.
- To prevent other classes from accessing instance variables, use the private keyword to declare them as private.

Figure 6-5 How to code instance variables

How to code constructors

Figure 6-6 shows how to code a constructor for a class. When you code one, it's a good coding practice to assign a value to all of the instance variables of the class as shown in the four examples. You can also include any additional statements that you want to execute within the constructor. For instance, the fourth example ends by calling two different get methods from the current class.

When you code a constructor, you must use the public access modifier and the same name, including capitalization, as the class name. Then, if you don't want to accept arguments, you must code an empty set of parentheses as shown in the first example. On the other hand, if you want to accept arguments, you code the parameters for the constructor as shown in the next three examples. When you code the parameters for a constructor, you must code a data type and a name for each parameter. For the data type, you can code a primitive data type or the class name for any class that defines an object.

The second example shows a constructor with three parameters. Here, the first parameter is a String object named code; the second parameter is a String object named description; and the third parameter is a double type named price. Then, the three statements within the constructor use these parameters to initialize the three instance variables of the class.

In this example, the names of the parameters are the same as the names of the instance variables. As a result, the constructor must distinguish between the two. To do that, it uses the this keyword to refer to the instance variables of the current object. You'll learn about other ways you can use this keyword later in this chapter.

The third example works the same as the second example, but it doesn't need to use the this keyword because the parameter names aren't the same as the names of the instance variables. In this case, though, the parameter names aren't very descriptive. As a result, the code in the second example is easier for other programmers to read than the code in the third example.

The fourth example shows a constructor with one parameter. Here, the first statement assigns the first parameter to the first instance variable of the class. Then, the second statement calls a method of a class named ProductDB to get a Product object for the specified code. Finally, the last two statements call methods of the Product object, and the values returned by these methods are assigned to the second and third instance variables.

When you code a constructor, the class name plus the number of parameters and the data type for each parameter form the *signature* of the constructor. You can code more than one constructor per class as long as each constructor has a unique signature. For example, the first two constructors shown in this figure have different signatures so they could both be coded within the Product class. This is known as *overloading* a constructor.

If you don't code a constructor, Java will create a *default constructor* that doesn't accept any parameters and initializes all instance variables to null, zero, or false. If you code a constructor that accepts parameters, though, Java won't

The syntax for coding constructors

```
public ClassName([parameterList])
{
    // the statements of the constructor
}
```

Example 1: A constructor that assigns default values

```
public Product()
{
   code = "";
   description = "";
   price = 0.0;
}
```

Example 2: A custom constructor with three parameters

```
public Product(String code, String description, double price)
{
    this.code = code;
    this.description = description;
    this.price = price;
}
```

Example 3: Another way to code the constructor shown above

```
public Product(String c, String d, double p)
{
    code = c;
    description = d;
    price = p;
}
```

Example 4: A constructor with one parameter

```
public Product(String code)
{
    this.code = code;
    Product p = ProductDB.getProduct(code);
    description = p.getDescription();
    price = p.getPrice();
}
```

Description

- The constructor must use the same name and capitalization as the name of the class.
- If you don't code a constructor, Java will create a *default constructor* that initializes all numeric types to zero, all boolean types to false, and all objects to null.
- To code a constructor that has parameters, code a data type and name for each parameter within the parentheses that follow the class name.
- The name of the class combined with the parameter list forms the *signature* of the constructor. Although you can code more than one constructor per class, each constructor must have a unique signature.
- In the second and fourth examples above, the this keyword is used to refer to an instance variable of the current object.

Figure 6-6 How to code constructors

create this default constructor. So if you need a constructor like that, you'll need to code it explicitly. To avoid this confusion, it's a good practice to code all of your own constructors. That way, it's easy to see which constructors are available to a class, and it's easy to check the values that each constructor uses to initialize the instance variables.

How to code methods

Figure 6-7 shows how to code the methods of a class. To start, you code an access modifier. Most of the time, you can use the public keyword to declare the method so it can be used by other classes. However, you can also use the private keyword to hide the method from other classes.

After the access modifier, you code the return type for the method, which refers to the data type that the method returns. After the return type, you code the name of the method followed by a set of parentheses. Within the parentheses, you code the parameter list for the method. Last, you code the opening and closing braces that contain the statements of the method.

Since a method name should describe the action that the method performs, it's a common coding practice to start each method name with a verb. For example, methods that set the value of an instance variable usually begin with *set*. Conversely, methods that return the value of an instance variable usually begin with *get*. In addition, methods that perform other types of tasks begin with verbs such as print, save, read, and write.

The first example shows how to code a method that doesn't accept any parameters or return any values. To do that, it uses the void keyword for the return type and it ends with a set of empty parentheses. When this method is called, it prints the instance variables of the Product object to the console, separating each instance variable with a pipe character (|).

The next three examples show how to code methods that return data. To do that, these methods specify a return type, and they include a return statement to return the appropriate variable. When coding a method like this, you must make sure that the return type that you specify matches the data type of the variable that you return. Otherwise, your code won't compile.

In the fourth example, the getFormattedPrice method uses a NumberFormat object to apply standard currency formatting to the double variable named price. This also converts the double variable to a String object. Then, the return statement returns the String object to the calling method.

The fifth and sixth examples show two possible ways to code a set method. In the fifth example, the method accepts a parameter that has the same name as the instance variable. As a result, the assignment statement within this method uses the this keyword to identify the instance variable. In the sixth example, the parameter has a different name than the instance variable. As a result, the assignment statement doesn't need to use the this keyword. Since the parameter name for both examples are descriptive, both of these examples work equally well.

The syntax for coding a method

```
public|private returnType methodName([parameterList])
{
   // the statements of the method
}
```

Example 1: A method that doesn't accept parameters or return data

```
public void printToConsole()
{
    System.out.println(code + "|" + description + "|" + price);
}
```

Example 2: A get method that returns a string

```
public String getCode()
{
   return code;
}
```

Example 3: A get method that returns a double value

```
public double getPrice()
{
   return price;
}
```

Example 4: A custom get method

```
public String getFormattedPrice()
{
    NumberFormat currency = NumberFormat.getCurrencyInstance();
    return currency.format(price);
}
```

Example 5: A set method

```
public void setCode(String code)
{
    this.code = code;
}
```

Example 6: Another way to code a set method

```
public void setCode(String productCode)
{
    code = productCode;
}
```

Description

- To allow other classes to access a method, use the public keyword. To prevent other classes from accessing a method, use the private keyword.
- To code a method that doesn't return data, use the void keyword for the return type. To code a method that returns data, code a return type in the method declaration and code a return statement in the body of the method.
- When you name a method, you should start each name with a verb. It's a common coding practice to use the verb *set* for methods that set the values of instance variables and to use the verb *get* for methods that return the values of instance variables.

Figure 6-7 How to code methods

How to overload methods

Figure 6-8 shows how to overload a method, which is similar to overloading a constructor. When you overload a method, you code two or more methods with the same name, but with unique combinations of parameters. In other words, you code methods with unique signatures.

For a method signature to be unique, the method must have a different number of parameters than the other methods with the same name, or at least one of the parameters must have a different data type. Note that the names of the parameters aren't part of the signature. So using different parameter names isn't enough to make the signatures unique. Also, the return type isn't part of the signature. As a result, you can't create two methods with the same name and parameters but different return types.

The purpose of overloading is to provide more than one way to invoke a given method. For example, this figure shows three versions of the printToConsole method. The first one accepts a String parameter named sep that's used to separate the code, price, and description of a Product object. Then, it prints the resulting string to the console.

The second method doesn't accept a parameter that specifies the separator string. Instead, it separates the code, price, and description with the pipe character. To do that, it calls the first printToConsole method and passes the pipe character to it. Although I could have just called the println method to print the line, calling an overloaded method can often prevent code duplication.

The third method accepts a String parameter for the separator along with a boolean parameter that indicates whether to print a blank line after printing the data to the console. This method begins by passing the sep parameter to the first printToConsole method. Then, it uses an if statement to determine whether to print a blank line.

When you refer to an overloaded method, the number of arguments you specify and their types determine which version of the method is executed. The three statements in this figure that call the printToConsole method illustrate how this works. Because the first statement doesn't specify an argument, it causes the second version of the printToConsole method to be executed. In contrast, the second statement specifies a String argument of four blank spaces and a boolean argument of true. As a result, it will cause the third version of the printToConsole method to be executed. Finally, the third statement specifies a single String argument, which causes the first version of the printToConsole method to be executed.

Example 1: A method that accepts one argument

```
public void printToConsole(String sep)
{
    System.out.println(code + sep + description +  sep + price);
}
```

Example 2: An overloaded method that provides a default value

```
public void printToConsole()
{
    printToConsole("|");    // this calls the method in the first example
}
```

Example 3: An overloaded method with two arguments

```
public void printToConsole(String sep, boolean printLineAfter)
{
    printToConsole(sep);    // this calls the method in the first example
    if (printLineAfter)
        System.out.println();
}
```

Code that calls these methods

```
Product p = ProductDB.getProduct("java");

p.printToConsole();
p.printToConsole("    ", true);
p.printToConsole("    ");
```

The console

```
java|Murach's Beginning Java 2|49.5
java    Murach's Beginning Java 2    49.5

java    Murach's Beginning Java 2    49.5
```

Description

- When you create two or more methods with the same name but with different parameter lists, the methods are overloaded. It's common to use overloaded methods to provide two or more versions of a method that work with different data types or that supply default values for omitted parameters.

How to use the this keyword

In figures 6-6 and 6-7, you saw how to use the this keyword to refer to an instance variable from a constructor or method. You can also use this keyword to call methods of the current object, to pass the current object to another method, and to call another constructor of the current class from the current constructor. Figure 6-9 shows you how to use this keyword.

The first line of the syntax summary shows how to refer to an instance variable of the current object. The second and third lines show how to call a constructor or method of the same class. And the fourth and fifth lines show how to pass the current object to a method of the object and to a static method of a class.

Since Java implicitly supplies the this keyword for all instance variables and methods, you don't usually need to code this keyword when referring to instance variables or methods. However, the first example is an exception to this rule. Here, the code, description, and price parameters in the constructor have the same names as the code, description, and price instance variables. As a result, you need to use the this keyword to explicitly identify the instance variables. Of course, another approach would be to change the parameter names so they aren't the same as the instance variable names.

The second example shows how to call the getPrice method of the current object. In this case, the this keyword isn't necessary because it would be added implicitly. However, it does make it clear that the getPrice method is a method of the current object.

The third example shows how to call another constructor in the same class. Specifically, this constructor uses the this keyword to call the constructor in the first example, and it passes three default values to it. This is an easy way to overload a constructor so it provides default values for missing parameters.

The fourth example shows how to use the this keyword to pass the current object to a method. In this example, a method named print sends the current object to the println method of the System.out object. As a result, the println method will print a representation of the current object to the console.

The fifth example works like the fourth example, but it shows that you can use the this keyword to pass the current object to a static method. In this case, a method named save saves the current object by calling the static saveProduct method of the ProductDB class.

The syntax for using the this keyword

```
this.variableName // refers to an instance variable of the current object
this(argumentList); // calls another constructor of the same class
this.methodName(argumentList) // calls a method of the current object
objectName.methodName(this) // passes the current object to a method
ClassName.methodName(this) // passes the current object to a static method
```

Example 1: How to refer to instance variables

```
public Product(String code, String description, double price)
{
    this.code = code;
    this.description = description;
    this.price = price;
}
```

Example 2: How to refer to methods

```
public String getFormattedPrice()
{
    NumberFormat currency = NumberFormat.getCurrencyInstance();
    return currency.format(this.getPrice);
}
```

Example 3: How to call a constructor

```
public Product()
{
    this("", "", 0.0);
}
```

Example 4: How to send the current object to a method

```
public void print()
{
    System.out.println(this);
}
```

Example 5: How to send the current object to a static method

```
public void save()
{
    ProductDB.saveProduct(this);
}
```

Description

- Since Java implicitly uses the this keyword for instance variables and methods, you don't need to explicitly code it unless a parameter has the same name as an instance variable.
- If you use the this keyword to call another constructor, the statement must be the first statement in the constructor.

Figure 6-9 How to use the this keyword

How to create and use an object

In earlier chapters, you learned how to create an object from a Java class and call the methods of that object. Now that you know how a class works, you should have a much better idea of what's happening when you do that. So in the next three topics, you'll review the skills for creating objects and using methods. Then, you'll see a class that creates a Product object, and you'll see a class that uses that object.

How to create an object

Figure 6-10 shows how to create an object with one and with two statements. Most of the time, you'll use one statement to create an object. However, as you'll scc later in this book, certain types of coding situations require you to create an object with two statements.

When you use two statements to create an object, the first statement declares the class and the name of the variable that the object will be assigned to. However, an instance of the object isn't actually created until the second statement is executed. This statement uses the new keyword to call the constructor for the object, which initializes the instance variables. Then, a reference to this object is assigned to the variable. At this point, you can use the variable to refer to the object.

When you send arguments to the constructor of a class, you must make sure that the constructor will be able to accept the arguments. To do that, you must send the right number of arguments, in the right sequence, and with data types that match the data types specified in the parameter list of the constructor. When a class contains more than one constructor, the constructor that matches the arguments that are sent is the constructor that will be executed.

The two-statement example in this figure creates a new Product object without passing any arguments to the constructor of the Product class. The same task is accomplished by the first one-statement example. Then, the second and third examples show how to send a single argument to the constructor of the Product class. Both of these statements send a String object, but the second example sends a literal while the third example sends a variable that refers to a String object. The fourth example sends three arguments to the constructor.

How to create an object in two statements

Syntax

```
ClassName variableName;
variableName = new ClassName(argumentList);
```

Example with no arguments

```
Product product;
product = new Product();
```

How to create an object in one statement

Syntax

```
ClassName variableName = new ClassName(argumentList);
```

Example 1: No arguments

```
Product product = new Product();
```

Example 2: One literal argument

```
Product product = new Product("java");
```

Example 3: One variable argument

```
Product product = new Product(productCode);
```

Example 4: Three arguments

```
Product product = new Product(code, description, price);
```

Description

- To create an object, you use the new keyword to create a new instance of a class. Each time the new keyword creates an object, Java calls the constructor for the object, which initializes the instance variables for the object.
- After you create an object, you assign it to a variable. When you do, a reference to the object is stored in the variable. Then, you can use the variable to refer to the object.
- To send arguments to the constructor, code the arguments between the parentheses that follow the class name. To send more than one argument, separate the arguments with commas.
- When you send arguments to the constructor, the arguments must be in the sequence and have the data types called for by the constructor.

Figure 6-10 How to create an object

How to call the methods of an object

Figure 6-11 shows how to call the methods of an object. By now, you should be familiar with the basic syntax for calling a method, so this figure should just be review. To start, you type the object name followed by the dot operator and the method name. Then, if the method requires arguments, you code the argument list between the parentheses, separating multiple arguments with commas. Otherwise, you code an empty set of parentheses.

The first two examples show two ways to call methods that don't return any data. The first example doesn't send an argument, while the second example sends an argument named productCode. In this case, the argument is a variable that represents a String object, but the argument could also be a literal value such as "java". Either way, you need to send the right number of arguments, and you need to match the data types of the arguments with the data types specified in the parameter list of the method.

The third and fourth examples show how to call a method that returns a value and assigns that value to a variable. In the third example, the getPrice method doesn't have any arguments, but it does return a value. Then, that value is assigned to a double variable named price. In the fourth example, the getFormattedPrice method sends a boolean variable as an argument that indicates whether a dollar sign should be included in the formatted value. This is a variation of the getFormattedPrice method you saw back in figure 6-4. Like that method, this method returns a string that is then stored in a string variable.

The fifth example shows how to call a method within an expression. Here, the expression includes a call to the getCode method, which returns a String object. Then, that String object is joined with three string literals, and the result is assigned to another String object.

How to call a method

Syntax

```
objectName.methodName(argumentList)
```

Example 1: Sends and returns no arguments

```
product.printToConsole();
```

Example 2: Sends one argument and returns no arguments

```
product.setCode(productCode);
```

Example 3: Sends no arguments and returns a double value

```
double price = product.getPrice();
```

Example 4: Sends an argument and returns a String object

```
String formattedPrice = product.getFormattedPrice(includeDollarSign);
```

Example 5: A method call within an expression

```
String message = "Code: " + product.getCode() + "\n\n"
               + "Press Enter to continue or enter 'x' to exit:";
```

Description

- To call a method that doesn't accept arguments, type an empty set of parentheses after the method name.
- To call a method that accepts arguments, enter the arguments between the parentheses that follow the method name. Here, the data type of each argument must match the data type that's specified by the method's parameters.
- To code more than one argument, separate the arguments with commas.
- If a method returns a value, you can code an assignment statement to assign the return value to a variable. Here, the data type of the variable must match the data type of the return value.

Figure 6-11 How to call the methods of an object

How primitive types and reference types are passed to a method

Figure 6-12 shows that *primitive types* are passed to a method one way, while *reference types* (objects) are passed in another way. Specifically, primitive types are *passed by value*, which means that a copy of the value is passed, not the value itself. In contrast, objects are *passed by reference*, which means that a pointer to the object is passed. Because of that, the method knows where the object's variables are so it can change them directly.

The first example shows how this works when a primitive data type is passed to a method that increases the value of the variable by 10%. In this case, the increasePrice method uses a return statement to return the increased value. Then, the code that calls this method reassigns the return value to the original variable. In other words, the method works with a copy of the value of the variable, but it can't modify the value in the variable itself.

The second example shows how this works when a reference type is passed to a method. Here, the return type for the increasePrice method is void, so no value is returned by the method. Instead, the getPrice and setPrice methods of the Product class are used to get and set the quantity variable itself. In other words, the method refers to the object and its data so that data is actually changed by the method.

In practice, you usually don't need to know how the values are passed. Most of the time, you won't directly modify a value stored in a parameter. Occasionally, though, you do need to be aware of the differences in the way that primitive types and objects are passed. When you do, you can refer back to this figure to refresh your memory about it.

Example 1: Primitive types are passed by value

A method that changes the value of a double type

```
static double increasePrice(double price) // returns a double
{
    return price *= 1.1;
}
```

Code that calls the method

```
double price = 49.5;
price = increasePrice(price);              // reassignment statement
System.out.println("price: " + price);
```

Result

```
price: 54.45
```

Example 2: Objects are passed by reference

A method that changes a value stored in a Product object

```
static void increasePrice(Product product)  // no return value
{
    double price = product.getPrice();
    product.setPrice(price *= 1.1);
}
```

Code that calls the method

```
Product product = ProductDB.getProduct("java");
System.out.println("product.getPrice(): " + product.getPrice());
increasePrice(product);                    // no reassignment necessary
System.out.println("product.getPrice(): " + product.getPrice());
```

Result

```
product.getPrice(): 49.5
product.getPrice(): 54.45
```

Description

- When a *primitive type* is passed to a method, it is *passed by value*. That means the method can't change the value of the variable itself. Instead, the method must return a new value that gets stored in the variable.
- When a *reference type* (an object) is passed to a method, it is *passed by reference*. That means that the method can change the data in the object itself, so a new value doesn't need to be returned by the method.

Figure 6-12 How primitive types and reference types are passed to a method

A ProductDB class that creates a Product object

Figure 6-13 presents a database class named ProductDB that provides the data processing required by an application that displays the data for a product. This class consists of a single static method named getProduct that returns a Product object based on the product code that's passed to it.

The code within the getProduct method starts by creating a Product object. If you look back to figure 6-4, you'll see that this causes the code and description fields to be set to empty strings and the price to be set to zero.

After the Product object is created, its setCode method is called to assign the product code that was passed to the getProduct method to the code field of this object. Next, the getProduct method uses an if/else statement to determine what values are assigned to the description and price fields of the Product object depending on the value of the product code. Notice that the setDescription and setPrice methods of the Product object are used to set these values. Also notice that if the product code doesn't match any of the specified products, this method sets the description to "Unknown" and it leaves the price at its default value of zero. Finally, this method returns the Product object.

Because this class doesn't retrieve the data for a product from a file or database, it isn't realistic. However, it does simulate the processing that would be done by a class like this. In fact, you could use code like this to test the basic functions of an application before you add the code that works with a file or database. In section 5 of this book, you'll learn how implement a class like this so it gets the required data from a file or a database.

The ProductDB class

```
public class ProductDB
{
    public static Product getProduct(String productCode)
    {
        // create the Product object
        Product p = new Product();

        // fill the Product object with data
        p.setCode(productCode);
        if (productCode.equalsIgnoreCase("java"))
        {
            p.setDescription("Murach's Beginning Java 2");
            p.setPrice(49.50);
        }
        else if (productCode.equalsIgnoreCase("jsps"))
        {
            p.setDescription("Murach's Java Servlets and JSP");
            p.setPrice(49.50);
        }
        else if (productCode.equalsIgnoreCase("mcb2"))
        {
            p.setDescription("Murach's Mainframe COBOL");
            p.setPrice(59.50);
        }
        else
        {
            p.setDescription("Unknown");
        }
        return p;
    }
}
```

Notes

- The ProductDB class provides the database layer that creates a Product object and gets the data for it from a file or database. In this case, though, the ProductDB class just simulates the processing that would be done by a database class.
- In a more realistic application, the database class would use the product code to retrieve the data for a product from a file or database and then fill the Product object with that data. It would also include methods for adding new products and for modifying and deleting existing products. You'll learn how to code classes like this in section 5.

Figure 6-13 A ProductDB class that returns a Product object

A ProductApp class that uses a Product object

Figure 6-14 presents a ProductApp class that uses the ProductDB class and the Product object it creates. As you can tell from the console at the top of this figure, this application prompts the user for a product code. Then, it retrieves and displays the description and price of that product.

The ProductApp class shown here contains the main method for the application, which means that this method is executed when the application starts. To make it easy to tell which class of an application contains the main method, it's common to add a suffix to the class name. In this book, we use "App" as the suffix as you've seen in all the applications we've presented to this point.

The main method in this class is similar to the other ones that you've seen. It uses a loop to retrieve and display the product data for each product code the user enters. The code that uses the Product class in this loop is highlighted. The first statement calls the getProduct method of the ProductDB class to create a Product object named product. Notice here that except for the capitalization, the object and class have the same name. That's possible because Java is a case-sensitive language.

Once the Product object is created and initialized, this program displays the product's description and price. To get that information, it calls the getDescription and getFormattedPrice methods of the Product object.

When you compile an application that uses fields or methods of a user-defined class, you need to be sure that your class path includes the current directory. If it doesn't, the compiler won't be able to find the class and it will display an error to that effect. To solve this problem, make sure that your class path is set as shown in figure 1-7 in chapter 1.

The console

```
Welcome to the Product Selector

Enter product code: java

SELECTED PRODUCT
Description: Murach's Beginning Java 2
Price:       $49.50

Continue? (y/n):
```

The ProductApp class

```
import java.util.Scanner;

public class ProductApp
{
    public static void main(String args[])
    {
        // display a welcome message
        System.out.println("Welcome to the Product Selector");
        System.out.println();

        // display 1 or more products
        Scanner sc = new Scanner(System.in);
        String choice = "y";
        while (choice.equalsIgnoreCase("y"))
        {
            // get the input from the user
            System.out.print("Enter product code: ");
            String productCode = sc.next();  // read the product code
            sc.nextLine();  // discard any other data entered on the line

            // get the Product object
            Product product = ProductDB.getProduct(productCode);

            // display the output
            System.out.println();
            System.out.println("SELECTED PRODUCT");
            System.out.println("Description: " + product.getDescription());
            System.out.println("Price:       " + product.getFormattedPrice());
            System.out.println();

            // see if the user wants to continue
            System.out.print("Continue? (y/n): ");
            choice = sc.nextLine();
            System.out.println();
        }
    }
}
```

Note

- This class contains the main method that provides the entry point for the Product application. In this book, we've used the suffix "App" to identify this type of class.

Figure 6-14 A ProductApp class that uses a Product object

How to code and use static fields and methods

In chapters 2 and 3, you learned how to call static methods from some of the classes in the Java API. In chapter 4, you learned how to code static methods in the same class as the main method. Now, you'll learn how to code static fields and methods in a separate class and how to call them from other classes.

How to code static fields and methods

Figure 6-15 shows how to code *static fields* and *static methods*. While instance variables and regular methods belong to an object that's created from a class, static fields and static methods belong to the class itself. As a result, they're sometimes called *class fields* and *class methods*.

The top of this figure shows how to code static fields. In short, you use a syntax that's similar to the syntax for a regular variable or constant. However, you use the static keyword so the variable or constant belongs to the class, not the object. Then, you supply an initial value for the variable or constant. Typically, the static variables of a class are declared with private access, but the static constants of a class are declared with public access. That way, other classes can access and use these constants.

The first example shows how to code a class that contains one static field and a static method. The static field is a constant that stores the number of months per year. The static method is similar to the calculateFutureValue method that you learned how to code in chapter 4. However, this method uses the static field named MONTHS_IN_YEAR, and it is coded in a separate class named FinancialCalculations. Note that since this class doesn't contain any non-static fields or methods, you don't need to code a constructor for this class.

The second example shows how you can add a static variable and a static method to the Product class. In this example, a static variable named objectCount counts the number of Product objects that are created from the Product class. This variable is declared as private so no other class can access it directly. Then, the constructor increments the static variable each time a new object is created from this class. Finally, the static getObjectCount method returns the static objectCount variable.

When you code a class that mixes regular fields and methods with static fields and methods, it's a good practice to keep your fields and methods organized. To do that, you can group your fields and methods by type (instance or static; variable or constant) and by access modifier (private or public). To illustrate, the second example lists all instance variables in a group, followed by the single static variable. For small classes, grouping fields and methods like this isn't critical. However, as your classes get longer, grouping can make your code easier to read and maintain.

How to declare static fields

```
private static int numberOfObjects = 0;
private static double majorityPercent = .51;
public static final int DAYS_IN_JANUARY = 31;
public static final float EARTH_MASS_IN_KG = 5.972e24F;
```

Example 1: A class that contains a static constant and a static method

```
public class FinancialCalculations
{
    public static final int MONTHS_IN_YEAR = 12;

    public static double calculateFutureValue(double monthlyPayment,
        double yearlyInterestRate, int years)
    {
        int months = years * MONTHS_IN_YEAR;
        double monthlyInterestRate = yearlyInterestRate/MONTHS_IN_YEAR/100;
        double futureValue = 0;
        for (int i = 1; i <= months; i++)
            futureValue = (futureValue + monthlyPayment) *
                (1 + monthlyInterestRate);
        return futureValue;
    }
}
```

Example 2: The Product class with a static variable and a static method

```
public class Product
{
    private String code;
    private String description;
    private double price;

    private static int objectCount = 0; // declare a static variable

    public Product()
    {
        code = "";
        description = "";
        price = 0;
        objectCount++;                    // update the static variable
    }

    public static int getObjectCount()  // get the static variable
    {
        return objectCount;
    }
    ...
```

Description

- You can use the static keyword to code *static fields* and *static methods*. Since static fields and static methods belong to the class, not to an object created from the class, they are sometimes called *class fields* and *class methods*.
- When you code a static method, you can only use static fields and fields that are defined in the method. You can't use instance variables in a static method because they belong to an instance of the class, not to the class as a whole.

Figure 6-15 How to code static fields and methods

How to call static fields and methods

Figure 6-16 shows how to call static fields and methods. As you would expect, you use the same syntax for calling static fields and methods from your own classes as you would for calling static fields and methods from the Java API.

To call a static field, you just code the class name, followed by the dot operator, followed by the field name. To illustrate, the first statement calls the PI field from the Math class. This field returns a double value for *pi*, which is the ratio of the circumference of a circle to its diameter. Then, the second statement calls the MONTHS_IN_YEAR field from the FinancialCalculations class in the previous figure.

The third statement shows how to call an objectCount field from the Product class. If you declare this static field as public in the Product class, you can use code like this to directly get or set this int value, which represents the number of objects that have been created from the Product class. However, if you declare this static field as private as shown in the previous figure, you can only use static methods to get or set its value. And if you only declare a get method, the field is a read-only field.

To call a static method, you code the class name, followed by the dot operator, followed by the name of the static method and a pair of parentheses. Within the parentheses, you code the arguments required by the method (if any). To illustrate, the first statement in the static method examples calls the static getCurrencyInstance method of the NumberFormat class. This method doesn't take any arguments, and it returns a NumberFormat object. The second statement calls the static parseInt method of the Integer class. This method takes a string argument, converts it to an int value, and returns that value. And the third statement uses the static pow method of the Math class to return the squared value of a variable named r.

The fourth statement calls the static calculateFutureValue method from the FinancialCalculations class described in the previous figure. This method accepts three arguments and returns the future value that's calculated based on the three arguments. Then, the eighth statement calls the static getObjectCount method of the Product class. This method returns the value stored in the static objectCount field.

The last statement in this figure shows how you can use both a static field and a static method in an expression. Here, the value that's returned by the static pow method of the Math class is multiplied by the static PI field of the Math class. Then, the result is assigned to a double variable named area.

Although the examples in this figure call static fields and methods from the classes that contain them, you can also call a static field or method from an object created from the class that contains it. For example, you can call the getObjectCount method from a Product object named product like this:

```
int productCount = product.getObjectCount();
```

To make it clear that a field or method is static, however, we recommend that you always call it from the class.

The syntax for calling a static field or method

```
className.FINAL_FIELD_NAME
className.fieldName
className.methodName(argumentList)
```

How to call static fields

From the Java API

```
Math.PI
```

From a user-defined class

```
FinancialCalculations.MONTHS_IN_YEAR
Product.objectCount    // if objectCount is declared as public
```

How to call static methods

From the Java API

```
NumberFormat currency = NumberFormat.getCurrencyInstance();
int quantity = Integer.parseInt(inputQuantity);
double rSquared = Math.pow(r, 2);
```

From user-defined classes

```
double futureValue = FinancialCalculations.calculateFutureValue(
    monthlyPayment, yearlyInterestRate, years);
int productCount = Product.getObjectCount();
```

A statement that calls a static field and a static method

```
double area = Math.PI * Math.pow(r, 2);  // pi times r squared
```

Description

- To call a static field, type the name of the class, followed by the dot operator, followed by the name of the static field.
- To call a static method, type the name of the class, followed by the dot operator, followed by the name of the static method, followed by a set of parentheses. If the method requires arguments, code the arguments within the parentheses, separating multiple arguments with commas.

Figure 6-16 How to call static fields and methods

How to code a static initialization block

When it takes more than one statement to initialize a static field, you can use a *static initialization block* to initialize the field as shown in figure 6-17. To start, you just code the static keyword followed by braces. Then, you code the statements of the block within the braces. The statements in this block are executed when the class is loaded, which happens when you call one of the class constructors or static methods.

In the example in this figure, the ProductDB class contains a static initialization block that executes several statements that initialize the static Connection object. This object is used by the some of the static methods in the class to connect to a database. Since a static initialization block runs as soon as any method of the class is called, this makes the Connection object available to the rest of the methods in the class.

For now, don't worry if you don't understand the code in the static block. The point is that it takes several statements to initialize the static Connection object. You'll learn more about these statements and how to connect to a database in chapter 21.

When to use static fields and methods

Now that you know how to code static fields and methods, you may wonder when to use them and when to use regular fields and methods. In general, when you need to create objects from a class, you should use regular fields and methods. That way, you can create several objects from a class, and each object has its own data in its own instance variables. Then, you can use the methods of each object to process that data.

In contrast, if you just need to perform a single task like a calculation, you can use a static method. Then, you send the method the arguments it needs, and it returns the result that you need without ever creating an object. As you progress through this book, you'll see many examples that will give you a better idea of when static fields and methods are appropriate.

The syntax for coding a static initialization block

```
public class className
{
    // any field declarations

    static
    {
        // any initialization statements for static fields
    }

    // the rest of the class
```

A class that uses a static initialization block

```
public class ProductDB
{
    private static Connection connection;         // static variable

    // the static initialization block
    static
    {
        try
        {
            Class.forName("sun.jdbc.odbc.JdbcOdbcDriver");
            String url = "jdbc:odbc:MurachProducts";
            String user = "Admin";
            String password = "";
            connection = DriverManager.getConnection(url, user, password);
        }
        catch (Exception e)
        {
            System.err.println("Error connecting to database.");
        }
    }

    // static methods that use the Connection object
    public static Product get(String code){}
    public static boolean add(Product product){}
    public static boolean update(Product product){}
    public static boolean delete(String code){}
}
```

Description

- To initialize the static variables of a class, you typically code the values in the declarations. If, however, a variable can't be initialized in a single statement, you can code a *static initialization block* that's executed when another class first calls any method of the static class.
- When a class is loaded, Java initializes all static variables and constants of the class. Then, it executes all static initialization blocks in the order in which they appear. (A class is loaded when one of its constructors or static methods is called.)

Figure 6-17 How to code a static initialization block

The Line Item application

The topics that follow present a Line Item application that calculates the total price for an invoice line item entered by the user. As you'll see, this application is more complex than the Product application you saw earlier in this chapter. As a result, it should give you a better feel for what you can do when you divide your applications into classes. It also illustrates how easy it is to use business and database classes in two or more applications.

The console

Figure 6-18 shows the console for the Line Item application. This application starts by prompting the user to enter a product code. Then, it prompts the user to enter a quantity for that product. Finally, it displays the data for the line item that's retrieved and calculated by the application.

The classes used by the Line Item application

Figure 6-18 also shows the classes used by the Line Item application. Here, the Product and ProductDB classes that you saw earlier are used again without any changes. Since you're already familiar with those classes, I'll focus on the other classes in this diagram.

The LineItem class defines three instance variables named product, quantity, and total. The product variable holds the Product object that's created by the ProductDB class based on the product code the user enters. The quantity variable holds the quantity the user enters. And the total variable holds the value that results by multiplying the quantity by the price of the product.

The LineItem class also defines seven methods. The first five are the get and set methods that provide access to the instance variables. In contrast, the private calculateTotal method is used by the getTotal method to calculate the line item total based on the quantity and price. The last method, getFormattedTotal, is similar to the getFormattedPrice method of the Product class. It applies the currency format to the line item total and returns it as a string.

The Validator class contains methods that are similar to the generic validation methods you saw in chapter 5. It includes methods for validating string, integer, and double input. You'll see the details of how these methods work in a minute.

Before I go on, you should notice the arrows between the ProductDB and Product classes and the LineItem and Product classes. This is a UML standard that's used to indicate that one class uses another. In this case, both the ProductDB and LineItem classes use the Product class. As you'll see in a minute, all of the classes shown here are also used by the class that contains the main method for the Line Item application.

The console

```
Welcome to the Line Item Calculator

Enter product code: java
Enter quantity:     2

LINE ITEM
Code:        java
Description: Murach's Beginning Java 2
Price:       $49.50
Quantity:    2
Total:       $99.00

Continue? (y/n):
```

The class diagrams

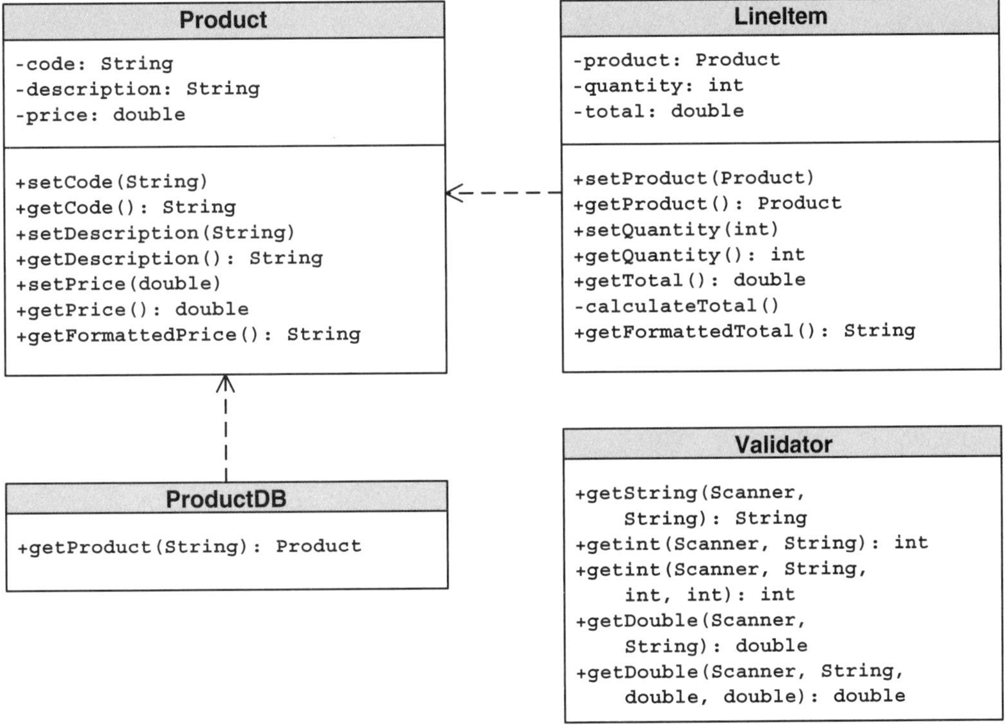

Description

- The Line Item application accepts a product code and quantity from the user, creates a line item using that information, and displays the result to the user.
- The Validator class is used to validate the data the user enters.
- The three instance variables of the LineItem class are used to store a Product object, the quantity, and the line item total. The get and set methods are used to get and set the values of these variables. The calculateTotal method is used to calculate the line item total, and the getFormattedTotal method is used to format the total as a currency value.

Figure 6-18 The classes used by the Line Item application

The LineItemApp class

Figure 6-19 shows the code for the LineItemApp class. This class contains the main method that gets the input from the user and displays the output to the user. To get the input, this method uses the static getString and getInt methods of the Validator class to get a valid product code and quantity.

After the main method gets valid user entries, it calls the getProduct method of the ProductDB class to get a Product object that corresponds to the product code that was entered by the user. Then, it creates a new LineItem object from the LineItem class by passing the Product object and the quantity entered by the user to the constructor of the LineItem class. Finally, this application uses the get methods of the Product and LineItem objects to get the output that's displayed.

Since you've already seen the Product and ProductDB classes, you shouldn't have much trouble understanding how the code in the LineItemApp class works. To understand it completely, however, you need to understand the code for the Validator and LineItem classes that's presented in the next two figures. As a result, you may want to refer back to this figure after you've had a chance to study these classes.

The Validator class

Figure 6-20 shows the code for the Validator class. This class contains five static methods: one getString method, two overloaded getInt methods, and two overloaded getDouble methods.

The getString method accepts a Scanner object and a string that prompts the user for input and returns a valid String value. This method uses the next method of the Scanner object to read the data that the user enters. Notice that, unlike the generic methods you saw in the last chapter for validating numeric data, this method doesn't include code to prevent an InputMismatchException. That's because the next method stores the data that's retrieved from the console as a string, so an InputMismatchException isn't possible. After the next method, the nextLine method is used to retrieve and discard any extra data the user may have entered at the console.

After the getString method are two methods named getInt. These methods work the same as the getInt and getIntWithinRange methods you saw in the last chapter. In this case, though, they have the same name so they are overloaded. Notice, however, that the second getInt method still calls the first getInt method to get a valid integer from the user. That way, this code doesn't have to be repeated in the second method.

Although they're not used by the Line Item application, the Validator class also includes two methods named getDouble. As you can see on page 2 of the code listing for this class, these methods provide the same functions as the getDouble and getDoubleWithinRange methods you saw in the last chapter, but this time they are overloaded methods. By including these methods, the Validator class can be used by any application that requires the user to enter a double type.

The LineItemApp class

```
import java.util.Scanner;

public class LineItemApp
{
    public static void main(String args[])
    {
        // display a welcome message
        System.out.println("Welcome to the Line Item Calculator");
        System.out.println();

        // create 1 or more line items
        Scanner sc = new Scanner(System.in);
        String choice = "y";
        while (choice.equalsIgnoreCase("y"))
        {
            // get the input from the user
            String productCode = Validator.getString(sc,
                "Enter product code: ");
            int quantity = Validator.getInt(sc,
                "Enter quantity:     ", 0, 1000);

            // get the Product object
            Product product = ProductDB.getProduct(productCode);

            // create the LineItem object
            LineItem lineItem = new LineItem(product, quantity);

            // display the output
            System.out.println();
            System.out.println("LINE ITEM");
            System.out.println("Code:        " + product.getCode());
            System.out.println("Description: " + product.getDescription());
            System.out.println("Price:       " + product.getFormattedPrice());
            System.out.println("Quantity:    " + lineItem.getQuantity());
            System.out.println("Total:       " +
                lineItem.getFormattedTotal() + "\n");

            // see if the user wants to continue
            choice = Validator.getString(sc, "Continue? (y/n): ");
            System.out.println();
        }
    }
}
```

Description

- After the user enters a valid product code and quantity, the getProduct method of the ProductDB class is called to get a Product object for the product with that code. Then, a new line item object is created with that product and quantity.
- The getCode, getDescription, and getFormattedPrice methods of the Product object are used to get the code, description, and price fields so they can be displayed at the console. The getQuantity and getFormattedTotal methods of the LineItem class are used to get the quantity and total.

Figure 6-19 The code of the LineItemApp class

The Validator class

Page 1

```
import java.util.Scanner;

public class Validator
{
    public static String getString(Scanner sc, String prompt)
    {
        System.out.print(prompt);
        String s = sc.next();  // read the user entry
        sc.nextLine();  // discard any other data entered on the line
        return s;
    }

    public static int getInt(Scanner sc, String prompt)
    {
        int i = 0;
        boolean isValid = false;
        while (isValid == false)
        {
            System.out.print(prompt);
            if (sc.hasNextInt())
            {
                i = sc.nextInt();
                isValid = true;
            }
            else
            {
                System.out.println(
                    "Error! Invalid integer value. Try again.");
            }
            sc.nextLine();  // discard any other data entered on the line
        }
        return i;
    }

    public static int getInt(Scanner sc, String prompt,
    int min, int max)
    {
        int i = 0;
        boolean isValid = false;
        while (isValid == false)
        {
            i = getInt(sc, prompt);
            if (i <= min)
                System.out.println(
                    "Error! Number must be greater than " + min + ".");
            else if (i >= max)
                System.out.println(
                    "Error! Number must be less than " + max + ".");
            else
                isValid = true;
        }
        return i;
    }
}
```

Figure 6-20 The code of the Validator class (part 1 of 2)

The Validator class

Page 2

```
    public static double getDouble(Scanner sc, String prompt)
    {
        double d = 0;
        boolean isValid = false;
        while (isValid == false)
        {
            System.out.print(prompt);
            if (sc.hasNextDouble())
            {
                d = sc.nextDouble();
                isValid = true;
            }
            else
            {
                System.out.println(
                    "Error! Invalid decimal value. Try again.");
            }
            sc.nextLine();  // discard any other data entered on the line
        }
        return d;
    }

    public static double getDouble(Scanner sc, String prompt,
    double min, double max)
    {
        double d = 0;
        boolean isValid = false;
        while (isValid == false)
        {
            d = getDouble(sc, prompt);
            if (d <= min)
                System.out.println(
                    "Error! Number must be greater than " + min + ".");
            else if (d >= max)
                System.out.println(
                    "Error! Number must be less than " + max + ".");
            else
                isValid = true;
        }
        return d;
    }
}
```

Description

- This class is part of the presentation layer for a console application. It can be called from the application's main method.

Figure 6-20 The code of the Validator class (part 2 of 2)

The LineItem class

Figure 6-21 shows the LineItem class that defines a line item for an invoice. Like the Product class, the LineItem class defines a business object in the application's middle tier. If you review the code for this object, you shouldn't have any trouble understanding how it works.

As you can see, this class contains two constructors. The first one initializes the instance variables to default values. Notice here that the product variable is initialized to a new Product object with default values. Although you could also assign a null value to the product variable, we don't recommend that. If you do assign a null, you'll get a NullPointerException if you try to use the variable before you assign an object to it.

The second constructor is the one the LineItemApp class uses to create a LineItem object. It accepts two parameters: a Product object and an int type that contains the quantity. The two statements of this constructor assign these two parameters to their corresponding instance variables.

After the constructors, the next five methods provide get and set methods for the three instance variables. These methods simply set or return the value of the corresponding instance variable. Note that the getTotal method calls the calculateTotal method to calculate the line item total. This method calls the getPrice method of the Product object to get the price of the product, multiplies the price by the quantity, and assigns the result to the total instance variable. The last method, getFormattedTotal, returns the line item total formatted as currency. To do that, it calls the getTotal method to calculate and return the total.

The LineItem class

```
import java.text.NumberFormat;

public class LineItem
{
    private Product product;
    private int quantity;
    private double total;

    public LineItem()
    {
        this.product = new Product();
        this.quantity = 0;
        this.total = 0;
    }

    public LineItem(Product product, int quantity)
    {
        this.product = product;
        this.quantity = quantity;
    }

    public void setProduct(Product product)
    {
        this.product = product;
    }

    public Product getProduct()
    {
        return product;
    }

    public void setQuantity(int quantity)
    {
        this.quantity = quantity;
    }

    public int getQuantity()
    {
        return quantity;
    }

    public double getTotal()
    {
        this.calculateTotal();
        return total;
    }

    private void calculateTotal()
    {
        total = quantity * product.getPrice();
    }

    public String getFormattedTotal()
    {
        NumberFormat currency = NumberFormat.getCurrencyInstance();
        return currency.format(this.getTotal);
    }
}
```

Figure 6-21 The code of the LineItem class

Perspective

Now that you've completed this chapter, you may be wondering why you should go to the extra effort of dividing an application into classes. The answer is twofold. First, dividing the code into classes makes it easier to use the classes in two or more applications. For example, any application that needs to work with product data can use the Product class. Second, using classes helps you separate the business logic and database processing of an application from the presentation elements. That can simplify the development of the application and make the application easier to maintain and enhance later on.

In this chapter, though, you've just learned the basic skills for creating and using classes. As you will soon see, there's a lot more to creating classes than what's presented here. And that's what the next three chapters are going to show you.

Summary

- In a *three-tiered architecture*, an application is separated into three layers. The *presentation layer* consists of the user interface. The *database layer* consists of the database and the database classes that work with it. And the *middle layer* provides an interface between the presentation layer and the database layer. Its classes are often referred to as *business classes*.
- The *Unified Modeling Language* (*UML*) is the standard modeling language for working with object-oriented applications. You can use UML *class diagrams* to identify the *fields* and *methods* of a class.
- *Encapsulation* lets you control which fields and methods within a class are *exposed* to other classes. When fields are encapsulated within a class, it's called *data hiding*.
- Multiple *objects* can be created from a single *class*. Each object can be referred to as an *instance* of the class.
- The data that makes up an object can be referred to as its *state*. Each object is a separate entity with its own state.
- A *field* is a variable or constant that's defined at the class level. An *instance variable* is a field that's allocated when an object is instantiated. Each object has a separate copy of each instance variable.
- Every class that contains instance variables has a *constructor* that initializes those variables.
- When you code the methods of a class, you often code public *get* and *set methods* that provide access to the fields of the class.
- If you want to code a method or constructor that accepts arguments, you code a list of *parameters* between the parentheses for the constructor or method. For each parameter, you must include a data type and a name.

- When coding a class, you can use the this keyword to refer to the current object.
- When Java passes a *primitive type* to a method, it passes a copy of the value. This is known as *passing by value*. When Java passes an object (a *reference type*) to a method, it passes a reference to the object. This is known as *passing by reference*.
- A *JavaBean* is a special type of Java class that follows a set of coding conventions.
- The name of a method or constructor combined with the list of parameter types is known as the *signature* of the method or constructor. You can *overload* a method or constructor by coding different parameter lists for constructors or methods that have the same name.
- When you use a class that contains only *static fields*, *static methods*, and *static initialization blocks*, you don't create an object from the class. Instead, you call these fields and methods directly from thc class.

Exercise 6-1 Enhance the Line Item application

This exercise guides you through the process of testing and enhancing the Line Item application that is presented in this chapter.

1. Open the LineItemApp, Validator, Product, LineItem, and ProductDB classes that are in the c:\java1.5\ch06\LineItem directory and review this code.
2. Compile all five classes. If the compiler throws an error that indicates that it can't "resolve" a class, you need to set your class path correctly as described in chapter 1. Once you've compiled these classes, run the LineItemApp class with valid codes like "java", "jsps", and "mcb2" to make sure that this application works correctly. Then, test it with an invalid code to see how that works.
3. Add another product to the ProductDB class. Its code should be "txtp", its description should be "TextPad", and its price should be $20.00. Then, compile just this class, and test the LineItemApp class again with the new product code. This shows that you can make a change to a class without affecting the other classes that use it.
4. Add a static field to the LineItem class that will count the number of objects that are created from the class as shown in figure 6-15. Next, add the code that increments this field each time an object is created from this class, and add a method named getObjectCount that gets the value of this field. Then, compile that class.
5. Modify the LineItemApp class so it uses the getObjectCount method and displays the object count on the console after it displays each line item. Then, compile and run that class to make sure that the changes in steps 4 and 5 work correctly.

Exercise 6-2 Use classes that have static methods in the Future Value application

This exercise guides you through the process of modifying the Future Value application so it uses classes that provide static methods.

1. Open the FutureValueValidationApp class that's in the ch05 directory and save it as FutureValueApp in the ch06\FutureValue directory. Then, change its class name to FutureValueApp.
2. Start a new class named Validator and save it in the same directory. Move the getDouble, getDoubleWithinRange, getInt, and getIntWithinRange methods into the Validator class. Next, change the name of the getDoubleWithinRange method to getDouble, and change the name of the getIntWithinRange method to getInt. This overloads the getDouble and getInt methods. Then, compile this class.
3. Modify the FutureValueApp class so it uses the methods in the Validator class. Then, compile and run that class to make sure that it works correctly.
4. Start a new class named FinancialCalculations, and save it in the same directory as the other classes. Move the calculateFutureValue method from the FutureValueApp class to the FinancialCalculations class, and make sure that the method is public. Then, compile this class.
5. Modify the FutureValueApp class so it uses the static calculateFutureValue method that's stored in the FinancialCalculations class. Then, compile and run this class to make sure that the application still works properly.

Exercise 6-3 Use objects in the Invoice application

In this exercise, you'll create an Invoice class and construct objects from it as you convert the Invoice application to an object-oriented application.

1. Open the InvoiceApp and Validator classes in the ch06\Invoice directory. This is yet another version of the Invoice application. Then, compile and run the classes to see how this application works.
2. Start a new class named Invoice and save it in the same directory. Then, write the code for this class so it provides all of the data and all of the processing for an Invoice object. Its constructor should require the subtotal and customer type as its only parameters, and it should initialize instance variables for discount percent, discount amount, and invoice total. Its methods should include the required get and set methods, plus a method named getInvoice that returns a string that contains all of the data for an invoice in a printable format. When you're done, compile the Invoice class.
3. Modify the code in the InvoiceApp class so it creates an Invoice object and uses its getInvoice method to get the formatted data for invoice. That should simplify this class considerably. Then, compile and test this class to make sure that this application works the way it did in step 1.

7

How to work with inheritance

Inheritance is one of the key concepts of object-oriented programming. It lets you create a class that's based on another class. As you'll see in this chapter, inheritance is used throughout the classes of the Java API. In addition, you can use it in the classes that you create.

An introduction to inheritance

Inheritance allows you to create a class that's based on another class. When used correctly, inheritance can simplify the overall design of an application. The following topics present an introduction to the basic concepts of inheritance.

How inheritance works

Figure 7-1 illustrates how inheritance works. When inheritance is used, a *subclass* inherits the fields, constructors, and methods of a *superclass*. Then, the objects that are created from the subclass can use these inherited members. The subclass can also provide its own members that *extend* the superclass, and it can *override* methods of the superclass by providing replacement definitions for them.

The two classes shown in this figure illustrate how this works. Here, the superclass is javax.swing.JFrame. That's the Java API class that you can use to create a GUI window, which is called a *frame*. As this figure shows, this class has several public fields and methods, such as the HIDE_ON_CLOSE field and the setTitle method. This class has many more methods than the ones shown here, though. This figure only shows a few representative ones.

The subclass in this figure is the ProductFrame class, and the diagram lists two groups of methods for this class. The first group shows the code that uses fields and methods that are inherited from the superclass. This sets some basic attributes of the frame, such as the title, location, and size. The second group includes two new methods that have been added to the subclass.

Incidentally, in this book, we'll primarily use superclass to refer to a class that another class inherits, and we'll use subclass to refer to a class that inherits another class. However, a superclass can also be called a *base* or *parent class*, and a subclass can also be called a *derived* or *child class*.

How inheritance works

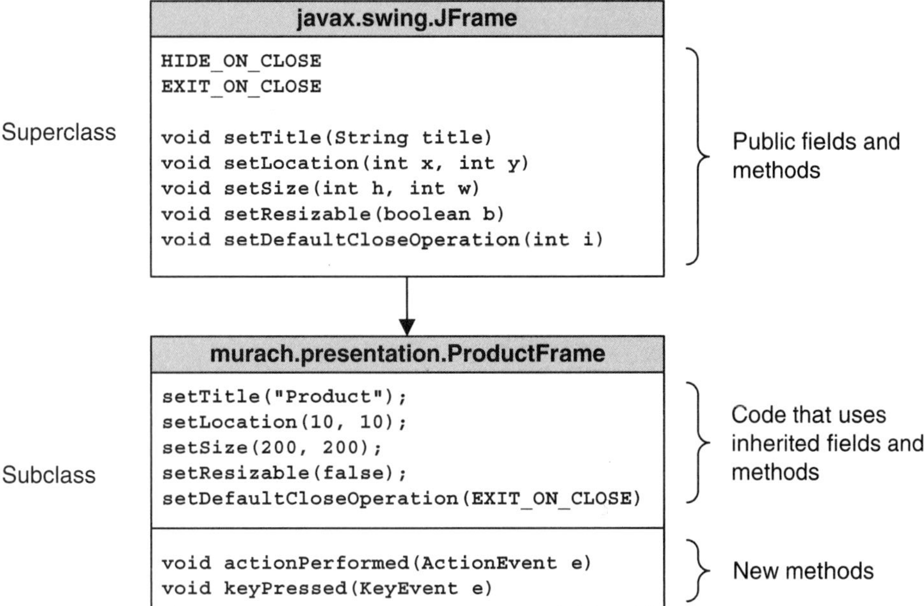
javax.swing.JFrame
HIDE_ON_CLOSE
EXIT_ON_CLOSE
void setTitle(String title)
void setLocation(int x, int y)
void setSize(int h, int w)
void setResizable(boolean b)
void setDefaultCloseOperation(int i)
Superclass
Public fields and methods
murach.presentation.ProductFrame
setTitle("Product");
setLocation(10, 10);
setSize(200, 200);
setResizable(false);
setDefaultCloseOperation(EXIT_ON_CLOSE)
void actionPerformed(ActionEvent e)
void keyPressed(KeyEvent e)
Subclass
Code that uses inherited fields and methods
New methods

Description

- *Inheritance* lets you create a new class based on an existing class. Then, the new class *inherits* the fields, constructors, and methods of the existing class.
- A class that inherits from an existing class is called a *derived class*, *child class,* or *subclass.* A class that another class inherits is called a *base class*, *parent class*, or *superclass*.
- A subclass can *extend* the superclass by adding new fields, constructors, and methods to the superclass. It can also *override* a method from the superclass with its own version of the method.
- To create a new window (called a *frame* in Java), you can code a class that inherits the JFrame class that's in the javax.swing package. Then, your frame will inherit all the fields and methods that are available to this class. Once you inherit the JFrame class, you can write code that uses the inherited fields and methods, you can add controls to the frame, and you can extend the frame by coding new fields and methods.

Figure 7-1 How inheritance works

How the Java API uses inheritance

Figure 7-2 shows a portion of the *inheritance hierarchy* that you can use to create a graphical user interface that uses windows, buttons, labels, text boxes, combo boxes, and so on. This illustrates how extensively inheritance is used throughout the Java API.

To start, all classes inherit the Object class in the java.lang package. Then, the Java API uses the classes in the *Abstract Windows Toolkit* (*AWT*) to define the classes for various GUI components. These classes are stored in the java.awt package. However, they are an older technology that was primarily used with versions 1.0 and 1.1 of Java.

Since version 1.2 of Java, a GUI technology known as *Swing* has been available. These classes are stored in the javax.swing package. These classes inherit classes in the java.awt package so they can use some of the code from these classes while improving and extending this code.

For example, the Component class in the java.awt package provides features that are common to all frames and controls. This class provides methods such as setLocation and setSize that set the location and size of the component. Because these methods are provided by the Component class, they are available to all awt and swing components including frames and the components that you place on frames such as buttons, labels, text boxes, and so on.

When you work with a class that inherits other classes, it's important to know that it can use fields and methods from any of the classes in its inheritance hierarchy. For example, the JFrame class can use fields and methods from the Frame, Window, Container, Component, and Object classes.

The shaded classes in this figure are the GUI components that you'll learn about in section 4 of this book. All of these classes are derived indirectly from the Component class. However, the JComponent class is the direct parent of the swing controls for buttons, text boxes, labels, and so on. Similarly, the Frame class is the direct parent of the swing frame.

For now, don't worry if you don't completely understand this figure. You'll learn all about using the JFrame class and the controls in the javax.swing package in section 4. The main point is that inheritance is a feature that's used extensively within the Java API.

The inheritance hierarchy for Swing forms and controls

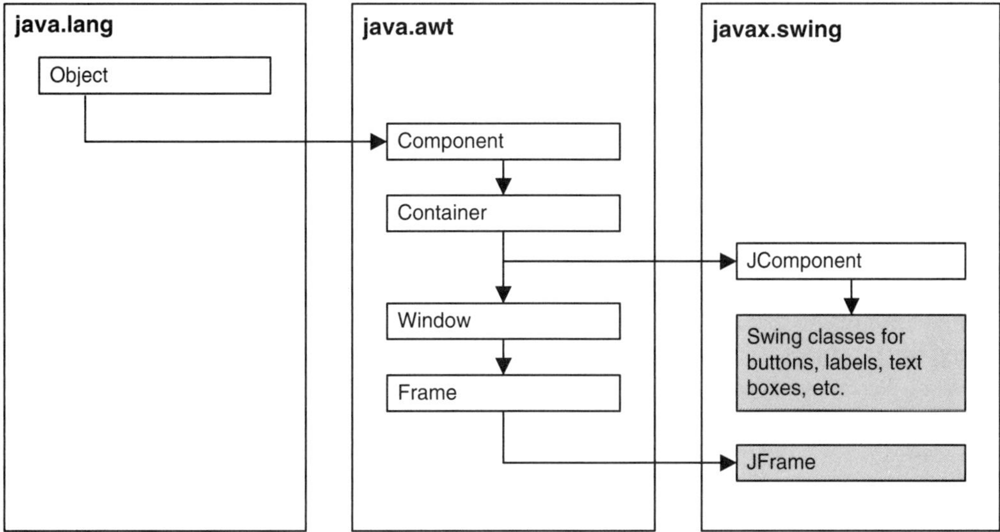

Description

- The Java API uses inheritance extensively in its own classes, so you often need to know what the *inheritance hierarchy* is as you use these classes. For example, you need to know that all classes ultimately inherit the Object class in the java.lang package.
- All *Swing* classes, which are stored in the javax.swing package, inherit the Component and Container classes in the java.awt package. This package contains the *Abstract Windows Toolkit* (*AWT*) classes.
- A class can use the fields and methods of any of its superclasses. For example, the JFrame class can use the fields and methods provided by the Frame, Window, Container, Component, and Object classes.

Figure 7-2 How the Java API uses inheritance

How the Object class works

Figure 7-3 summarizes the methods of the java.lang.Object class. Since every class automatically inherits these methods, they are available from every object. However, since subclasses often override these methods, these methods may work slightly differently from class to class. You'll learn more about working with these methods later in this chapter and in the next chapter.

Perhaps the most-used method of the Object class is the toString method. That's because the Java compiler implicitly calls this method when it needs a string representation of an object. For example, when you supply an object as the argument of the println method, this method implicitly calls the toString method of the object.

When you code a class, you typically override the toString method of the Object class to provide more detailed information about the object. Otherwise, the toString method will return the name of the class and the *hash code* of the object, which is a hexadecimal number that indicates the object's location in memory.

Unlike C++ and other languages that require you to manage memory, Java uses a mechanism known as the *garbage collector* to automatically manage memory. When the garbage collector determines that the system is running low on memory and that the system is idle, it frees the memory for any objects that don't have any more references to them. Before it does that, though, it calls the finalize method for each of those objects.

Although you can code a more specific finalize method for an object, that's generally not a good idea. Since you can't tell when the garbage collector will call this method, you can't be assured that your finalize method will be executed before the program terminates. Therefore, you shouldn't rely on the finalize method to handle any timely tasks.

On the other hand, if you were to write code for an object that uses non-Java calls to allocate memory, you should code a method for that object that releases those resources. Otherwise, Java won't free this memory, and you will create a "memory leak." If, for example, you code a method named "dispose" that releases all non-Java resources for an object, you can call that method whenever you need to free those resources.

The Object class

```
java.lang.Object
```

Methods of the Object class

Method	Description
`toString()`	Returns a String object containing the class name, followed by the @ symbol, followed by the hash code for this object. If that's not what you want, you can override this method as shown in figure 7-6.
`equals(Object)`	Returns true (boolean) if this object points to the same space in memory as the specified object. Otherwise, it returns false, even if both objects contain the same data. If that's not what you want, you can override the equals method as shown in figure 7-15.
`getClass()`	Returns a Class object that represents the type of this object. For more information, see figure 7-13.
`clone()`	Returns a copy of this object as an Object object. Before you can use this method, you must implement the Cloneable interface as shown in the next chapter.
`hashCode()`	Returns the hash code (int) for this object.
`finalize()`	Called by the garbage collector when the garbage collector determines that there are no more references to the object.

Description

- The Object class in the java.lang package is the superclass for all classes. In other words, every class inherits the Object class or some other class that ultimately inherits the Object class. As a result, the methods defined by the Object class are available to all classes.
- When creating classes, it's a common practice to override the toString and equals methods so they work appropriately for each class. For example, the toString method might return a value that uniquely identifies an object. And the equals method might compare two objects to see if their instance variables are equal.
- The *hash code* for an object is a hexadecimal number that identifies the object's location in memory.
- In general, you don't need to override the finalize method for an object, even though its default implementation doesn't do anything. That's because the *garbage collector* automatically reclaims the memory of an object whenever it needs to. Before it does that, though, it calls the finalize method of the object.

Figure 7-3 How the Object class works

How to use inheritance in your applications

In figure 7-1, you saw one way that you can use inheritance in your business applications. That is, you can create classes that inherit classes defined by the Java API. But it's also common to create classes that inherit classes that you define. This is illustrated in figure 7-4.

The inheritance hierarchy in this figure shows how you might use inheritance to create two classes that represent similar types of objects. In this case, the objects are different types of products—books and software—and the Product class is a superclass that defines the methods that are common to these objects. Then, the subclasses that define the Book and Software objects inherit all of the public methods of the Product class. In addition, each class adds a couple of methods that are unique to the class. In particular, the Book class adds the getAuthor and setAuthor methods, and the Software class adds the getVersion and setVersion methods.

An important aspect of inheritance is that you can use a subclass as an argument or return value for any method that is designed to work with the superclass. For example, if a method accepts a Product object, you can also pass a Book or a Software object to it. You'll see how this works in a moment.

Business classes for a Product Maintenance application

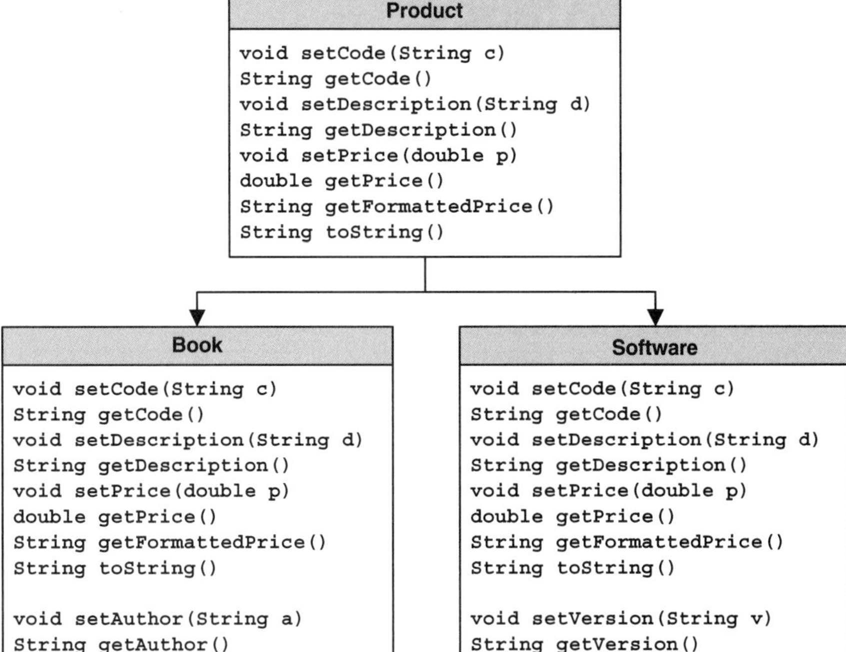

Description

- You can use inheritance in your applications to create generic superclasses that implement common elements of related subclasses. For example, if you need separate classes to represent distinct types of products, you can create a Product superclass. Then, you can use the Product class to create a separate subclass for each type of product.
- It's also common to create classes that inherit from classes that are defined by the Java API. For example, you might create a ProductFrame class that inherits the JFrame class as shown in figure 7-1.
- When you inherit a class, you can use the subclass whenever an instance of the superclass is called for. For example, if the Book class inherits the Product class as shown above, a Book object can be used whenever a Product object is called for.

Figure 7-4 How to use inheritance in your applications

Basic skills for working with inheritance

Now that you've been introduced to the basic concepts of inheritance, you're ready to see how inheritance is actually implemented in Java. In the topics that follow, you'll learn how to create both superclasses and subclasses. In addition, you'll learn how to take advantage of one of the major features of inheritance, called polymorphism.

How to create a superclass

Figure 7-5 shows how to create a class that can be used as a superclass for one or more subclasses. To do that, you define the fields, constructors, and methods of the class just as you would for any other class.

The Product class shown in this figure includes a toString method that overrides the toString method of the java.lang.Object class. This method returns a string that includes the code, description, and price for the product. As a result, any subclasses of this class can use this toString method. Or, they can override the toString method to provide their own code for that method.

The table in this figure lists several *access modifiers* you can use to indicate whether members of a superclass are accessible to other classes. By now, you should be familiar with the private and public access modifiers. To review, you use the private keyword for any fields or methods that you want only to be available within the current class. In contrast, you use the public keyword for any fields or methods that you want to be available to all other classes.

Beyond that, you may occasionally want to use the protected keyword to code *protected members*. A protected member is a member that can be accessed within the defining class, any class in the same package, and any class that inherits the defining class, but not by any other class. This lets subclasses access certain parts of the superclass without exposing those parts to other classes. For example, the Product class in this figure includes a static field named count that has protected access. As a result, any subclass of the Product class can access this field, regardless of whether the subclass is in the same package as the Product class. You'll see an example of how to use a field like this in the next figure.

You can also code a field or method without a modifier. Then, the classes in the same package will be able to access the field or method, but classes in other packages won't be able to do that.

Access modifiers

Keyword	Description
`private`	Available within the current class.
`public`	Available to classes in all packages.
`protected`	Available to classes in the same package and to subclasses.
no keyword coded	Available to classes in the same package.

The code for the Product superclass

```
import java.text.NumberFormat;

public class Product
{
    private String code;
    private String description;
    private double price;
    protected static int count = 0;   // a protected static variable

    public Product()
    {
        code = "";
        description = "";
        price = 0;
    }

    // get and set accessors for the code, description, and price
    // instance variables

    public String toString()  // override the toString method
    {
        String message =
            "Code:        " + code + "\n" +
            "Description: " + description + "\n" +
            "Price:       " + this.getFormattedPrice() + "\n";
        return message;
    }

    public static int getCount()   // create public access for the
    {                              // count variable
        return count;
    }
}
```

Description

- *Access modifiers* specify the accessibility of the members declared by a class. Public members are accessible to other classes, while private members are accessible only to the class in which they're declared.
- *Protected members* are accessible within the class in which they're declared. They can also be used by any class that inherits the class in which they're declared.
- A subclass can access the public and protected members of its superclass, but not the private members.

How to create a subclass

Figure 7-6 shows how to create a subclass. To indicate that a class is a subclass, you follow the class name on the class declaration with the extends keyword and the name of the superclass that the subclass inherits. For example, the code for the Book class shown in this figure specifies that the Book class extends the Product class. In other words, the Book class is a subclass of the Product class.

After you declare the subclass, you can extend the functionality of the superclass by adding fields, constructors, and methods. In this figure, for example, you can see that the Book class adds a new instance variable and a new constructor. It also adds new setAuthor and getAuthor methods, and it overrides the toString method defined by the Product class.

The constructor for the Book subclass starts by using the super keyword to call the default constructor of the Product class. This initializes the code, description, and price fields. Next, the author field is assigned a default value of an empty string. Finally, the count field, which was declared in the superclass with protected access, is incremented.

To override the toString method, you just code a toString method with the same signature as the toString method in the superclass. In this case, the method accepts no parameters and returns a string. The code within this method uses the super keyword to call the toString method of the superclass. This method returns a string representation of the Product object. Then, this code appends the author's name to this string. Finally, it returns the string.

The syntax for creating subclasses

To declare a subclass

```
public class SubclassName extends SuperClassName{}
```

To call a superclass constructor

```
super(argumentList)
```

To call a superclass method

```
super.methodName(argumentList)
```

The code for a Book subclass

```
public class Book extends Product
{
    private String author;

    public Book()
    {
        super();  // call constructor of Product superclass
        author = "";
        count++;  // update the count variable in the Product superclass
    }

    public void setAuthor(String author)
    {
        this.author = author;
    }

    public String getAuthor()
    {
        return author;
    }

    public String toString()  // override the toString method
    {
        String message =
            super.toString() +    // call method of Product superclass
            "Author:      " + author + "\n";
        return message;
    }
}
```

Description

- You can directly access fields that have public or protected access in the superclass.
- You can extend the superclass by adding new fields, constructors, and methods to the subclass.
- You can override methods in the superclass by coding methods in the subclass that have the same signatures as methods in the superclass.
- You use the super keyword to call a constructor or method of the superclass. If necessary, you can call constructors or methods that pass arguments to the superclass.

Figure 7-6 How to create a subclass

How polymorphism works

Polymorphism is one of the most important features of object-oriented programming and inheritance. As figure 7-7 shows, polymorphism lets you treat objects of different types as if they were the same type by referring to a superclass that's common to both objects. For example, consider the Book and Software classes that were presented in figure 7-4. Because these classes inherit the Product class, objects created from these classes can be treated as if they were Product objects.

One benefit of polymorphism is that you can write generic code that's designed to work with a superclass. Then, you can use that code with instances of any class that's derived from the superclass. For example, suppose you have a ProductDB class with an addRecord method that accepts a Product object as a parameter. Because the Book and Software classes are both derived from the Product class, the addRecord method will work with Book and Software objects.

The examples in this figure illustrate how polymorphism works. To start, the first three examples show the toString methods for the Product, Book, and Software classes. The Book version of the toString method adds the author's name to the end of the string that's returned by the toString method of the Product class. Similarly, the Software version adds the version number to the end of the string that's returned by the toString method of the Product class.

Then, the last example shows how polymorphism works with these classes. This code begins by creating an instance of the Book class, assigning it to a variable named b, and assigning values to its instance variables. After that, it creates an instance of the Software class, assigns it to a variable named s, and assigns values to its instance variables.

Next, a variable named p of type Product is declared, and the Book object is assigned to it. Then, the toString method of the Product class is called. When the JRE sees that the p variable refers to a Book object and that this object contains an overridden version of the toString method, it calls the overridden version of this method.

This example finishes by doing the same thing with the Software object. First, this Software object is assigned to the Product variable. Then, the toString method defined by the Product class is called, which causes the toString method of the Software class to be executed.

The key to polymorphism is that the decision on what method to call is based on the inheritance hierarchy at runtime. This can be referred to as *late binding*. At compile time, the compiler simply recognizes that a method with the specified signature exists.

Three versions of the toString method

The toString method in the Product superclass

```
public String toString()
{
    return "Code:        " + code + "\n" +
           "Description: " + description + "\n" +
           "Price:       " + this.getFormattedPrice() + "\n";
}
```

The toString method in the Book class

```
public String toString()
{
    return super.toString() +
        "Author:      " + author + "\n";
}
```

The toString method in the Software class

```
public String toString()
{
    return super.toString() +
        "Version:     " + version + "\n";
}
```

Code that uses the overridden methods

```
Book b = new Book();
b.setCode("java");
b.setDescription("Murach's Beginning Java 2");
b.setPrice(49.50);
b.setAuthor("Steelman");

Software s = new Software();
s.setCode("txtp");
s.setDescription("TextPad");
s.setPrice(27.00);
s.setVersion("4.7.3");

Product p;
p = b;
System.out.println(p.toString());  // calls toString from the Book class
p = s;
System.out.println(p.toString());  // calls toString from the Software class
```

Description

- *Polymorphism* is a feature of inheritance that lets you treat objects of different subclasses that are derived from the same superclass as if they had the type of the superclass. If, for example, Book is a subclass of Product, you can treat a Book object as if it were a Product object.
- If you access a method of a superclass object and the method is overridden in the subclasses of that class, polymorphism determines which method is executed based on the object's type. For example, if you call the toString method of a Product object, the toString method of the Book class is executed if the object is a Book object.

Figure 7-7 How polymorphism works

The Product application

Now that you've learned how to code superclasses and subclasses, the following topics present a version of the Product application that uses inheritance. This version of the application uses the Book and Software classes that were described in figure 7-4. In addition, it uses a ProductDB class that can return two distinct types of products: books and software.

The console

Figure 7-8 shows the console for this version of the Product application. As you can see, this application works much like the one you saw in chapter 6. However, there are three main differences. First, this application displays a fourth piece of information about each product, which varies depending on whether the product is a book or software. In particular, it displays an author for a book and a version number for software. Second, this application displays a count of the total number of objects it has created. Third, if the user enters an invalid product code, the application displays an appropriate error message.

The console for the Product application

```
Welcome to the Product Selector

Enter product code: java

Code:        java
Description: Murach's Beginning Java 2
Price:       $49.50
Author:      Andrea Steelman

Product count: 1

Continue? (y/n): y

Enter product code: txtp

Code:        txtp
Description: TextPad
Price:       $27.00
Version:     4.7.3

Product count: 2

Continue? (y/n): y

Enter product code: xxxx

No product matches this product code.

Product count: 2

Continue? (y/n):
```

Description

- This version of the Product application handles two types of products: books and software.
- If you enter the product code for a book, the information about the product includes an author.
- If you enter the product code for software, the information about the product includes a version number.

The ProductApp class

Figure 7-9 shows the code for this version of the ProductApp class. This code is similar to the code for the ProductApp class that was presented in chapter 6. However, in this version of the application, the product that's returned by the getProduct method of the ProductDB class is handled a little differently. That's possible because this method has been modified so it returns a null if the user enters an invalid product code. Otherwise, it returns a Book or Software object that corresponds to the product code. Note, however, that regardless of whether a Book or a Software object is returned, the object is stored in a Product variable.

The next statement tests the Product variable. If it contains a null, an error message is displayed. Otherwise, the println method is used to print the object that this variable refers to. If the object is a book, this causes the toString method of the Book class to be called to get its string representation. If it's software, it causes the toString method of the Software class to be called. In other words, this statement uses polymorphism to determine which method to call. If you look back to figure 7-8, you can see the differences in the information that's displayed by these two methods.

In this application, the product code that's entered by the user determines whether a Book object or a Software object is created. As a result, at compile time, the application doesn't know which version of the toString method it will call. At runtime, however, the JRE can determine what type of object has been returned, and it can call the appropriate method.

The code for the ProductApp class

```
import java.util.Scanner;

public class ProductApp
{
    public static void main(String args[])
    {
        // display a welcome message
        System.out.println("Weclome to the Product Selector");
        System.out.println();

        // perform 1 or more selections
        Scanner sc = new Scanner(System.in);
        String choice = "y";
        while (choice.equalsIgnoreCase("y"))
        {
            System.out.print("Enter product code: ");
            String productCode = sc.next();  // read the product code
            sc.nextLine();  // discard any other data entered on the line

            // get the Product object
            Product p = ProductDB.getProduct(productCode);

            // display the output
            System.out.println();
            if (p != null)
                System.out.println(p);
            else
                System.out.println("No product matches this product code.\n");

            System.out.println("Product count: " + Product.getCount() + "\n");

            // see if the user wants to continue
            System.out.print("Continue? (y/n): ");
            choice = sc.nextLine();
            System.out.println();
        }
    }
}
```

Figure 7-9 The code for the ProductApp class

The Product, Book, and Software classes

Figures 7-10 and 7-11 show the code for the Product superclass and its two subclasses, Book and Software. The Product class is shown in figure 7-10. Since you saw most of the code for this class in figure 7-5, you shouldn't have any trouble understanding how it works.

Similarly, the Book class shown in figure 7-11 is almost identical to the Book class presented in figure 7-6. The only difference is that the two statements in the toString method have been combined into a single statement.

The Software class shown in figure 7-11 works just like the Book class. After it extends the Product class, it declares a private instance variable named version. Next, it provides a parameterless constructor that creates a new Software object with default values and increments the count variable that was defined in the Product class. Finally, it provides setVersion, getVersion, and toString methods.

The toString method of the Software class overrides the toString method of the Product class. However, it uses the super keyword to call the toString method of the Product class, which returns a string that includes the code, price, and description. Then, it appends information about the software version to the end of this string.

The ProductDB class

Figure 7-12 shows the code for the getProduct method of the ProductDB class, which returns the Book and Software objects used by the Product application. Here, the return type for the getProduct method is a Product object. Since the Book and Software classes are subclasses of the Product class, however, this method can return both Book and Software objects.

Within the getProduct method, the first statement declares a Product variable named p and assigns a null value to it. Then, if the user doesn't enter a product code that matches a product, this null value will be returned.

If the product code that's passed to this method matches one of the valid book codes, a new Book object is created. Then, the instance variables for that object are set depending on the book code. Finally, that Book object is assigned to the Product variable.

If, on the other hand, the product code that's passed to this method matches the code for a software product, a new Software object is created and its instance variables are set. (Although only one valid software product is included in this example, additional products could have been included. In that case, a nested if statement like the one for the Book objects would have been used.) Then, that Software object is assigned to the Product variable.

The last statement in this method returns the Product variable to the calling method. In this case, the calling method is the main method of the ProductApp class. Because the Product variable can contain either a Book object, a Software object, or a null, it can then be processed as shown in figure 7-9.

The code for the Product class

```
import java.text.NumberFormat;

public class Product
{
    private String code;
    private String description;
    private double price;
    protected static int count = 0;

    public Product()
    {
        code = "";
        description = "";
        price = 0;
    }

    public void setCode(String code)
    {
        this.code = code;
    }
    public String getCode(){
        return code;
    }
    public void setDescription(String description)
    {
        this.description = description;
    }
    public String getDescription()
    {
        return description;
    }
    public void setPrice(double price)
    {
        this.price = price;
    }
    public double getPrice()
    {
        return price;
    }
    public String getFormattedPrice()
    {
        NumberFormat currency = NumberFormat.getCurrencyInstance();
        return currency.format(price);
    }
    public String toString()
    {
        return "Code:        " + code + "\n" +
               "Description: " + description + "\n" +
               "Price:       " + this.getFormattedPrice() + "\n";
    }
    public static int getCount()
    {
        return count;
    }
}
```

Figure 7-10 The code for the Product class

The code for the Book class

```
public class Book extends Product
{
    private String author;

    public Book()
    {
        super();
        author = "";
        count++;
    }

    public void setAuthor(String author)
    {
        this.author = author;
    }
    public String getAuthor()
    {
        return author;
    }
    public String toString()
    {
        return super.toString() +
            "Author:      " + author + "\n";
    }
}
```

The code for the Software class

```
public class Software extends Product
{
    private String version;

    public Software()
    {
        super();
        version = "";
        count++;
    }

    public void setVersion(String version)
    {
        this.version = version;
    }
    public String getVersion()
    {
        return version;
    }
    public String toString()
    {
        return super.toString() +
            "Version:     " + version + "\n";
    }
}
```

Figure 7-11 The code for the Book and Software classes

The code for the ProductDB class

```
public class ProductDB
{
    public static Product getProduct(String productCode)
    {
        // In a more realistic application, this code would
        // get the data for the product from a file or database
        // For now, this code just uses if/else statements
        // to return the correct product data

        Product p = null;

        if (productCode.equalsIgnoreCase("java") ||
           productCode.equalsIgnoreCase("jsps") ||
           productCode.equalsIgnoreCase("mcb2"))
        {
            Book b = new Book();
            if (productCode.equalsIgnoreCase("java"))
            {
                b.setCode(productCode);
                b.setDescription("Murach's Beginning Java 2");
                b.setPrice(49.50);
                b.setAuthor("Andrea Steelman");
            }
            else if (productCode.equalsIgnoreCase("jsps"))
            {
                b.setCode(productCode);
                b.setDescription("Murach's Java Servlets and JSP");
                b.setPrice(49.50);
                b.setAuthor("Andrea Steelman");
            }
            else if (productCode.equalsIgnoreCase("mcb2"))
            {
                b.setCode(productCode);
                b.setDescription("Murach's Mainframe COBOL");
                b.setPrice(59.50);
                b.setAuthor("Mike Murach");
            }
            p = b; // set Product variable equal to the Book object
        }
        else if (productCode.equalsIgnoreCase("txtp"))
        {
            Software s = new Software();
            s.setCode("txtp");
            s.setDescription("TextPad");
            s.setPrice(27.00);
            s.setVersion("4.7.3");
            p = s; // set Product variable equal to the Software object
        }
        return p;
    }
}
```

Figure 7-12 The code for the ProductDB class

More skills for working with inheritance

Now that you've learned the basics of inheritance and you've seen an application that uses it, you're ready to learn some additional techniques that are often required when you work with inheritance. That includes getting information about an object's type, casting objects, and comparing objects.

How to get information about an object's type

When Java runs an application, it uses a class named Class to keep track of all of the objects that it loads. For each object that it loads, Java creates a Class object that contains information about the object. This is sometimes referred to as *runtime type identification* (*RTTI*). Although the getName method is the most commonly used method of a Class object, this class and other related classes contain hundreds of methods that let you get a wide range of information about an object at runtime.

Figure 7-13 shows how you can use a Class object to get information about an object's type. To start, you call the getClass method of an object to return a Class object for that object. This works because the getClass method is a member of the Object class, so it's inherited by every object. Once you have the Class object, you can use its methods to get information about the object's type. The method you're most likely to use is getName, which returns a string that contains the name of its class.

The first example in this figure shows how this works. Here, the first statement creates a Book object and assigns it to a Product variable named p. Then, the second statement calls the getClass method to return a Class object that contains information about the object that's referred to by this variable. Finally, the third statement calls the getName method of the Class object to get the name of the class, and it displays it at the console. As you can see, the getClass method determines that the object that's stored in this variable is really a Book object even though the variable named p has a type of Product.

The second example in this figure shows how you can code an if statement to test an object's type. This example calls the getClass method from the variable named p to return a Class object. Then, it calls the getName method from the Class object that's returned to get a string object. Finally, it uses the equals method to see if the name of the class is equal to "Book".

The code in this example doesn't assign the Class and String objects returned by the getClass and getName methods to variables. Instead, it calls one method directly from another method. In other words, the code in this example is a more concise way of writing this code:

```
Class c = p.getClass();
String s = c.getName();
if (s.equals("Book"))
```

If you don't need to use the variables, though, there's no reason to create them.

The Class class

```
java.lang.Class
```

Common method

Method	Description
`getName()`	Returns a String object for the name of this Class object.

Example 1: Code that displays an object's type

```
Product p = new Book();  // create a Book object and assign it to a Product
                         // variable
Class c = p.getClass();  // get the Class object for the product
System.out.println("Class name: " + c.getName());  // print the object type
```

The console

```
Class name: Book
```

Example 2: Code that tests an object's type

```
Product p = new Book();  // create a Book object
if (p.getClass().getName().equals("Book"))
    System.out.println("This is a Book object");
```

The console

```
This is a Book object
```

Example 3: An easier way to test an object's type

```
Product p = new Book();  // create a Book object
if (p instanceof Book)
    System.out.println("This is a Book object");
```

The console

```
This is a Book object
```

Description

- Every object has a getClass method that returns a Class object that corresponds to the object's type.
- You can use the methods of the Class class to obtain information about any object, such as its name.
- The method shown above is only one of the more than 90 properties and methods of the Class class.
- You can use the instanceof operator to check if an object is an instance of a particular class.

Figure 7-13 How to get information about an object's type

Instead of using a class object to test an object's type, you can use the instanceof keyword. This is illustrated in the third example in figure 7-13. If you compare this code with the code in the second example, I think you'll agree that this is a much easier way to check if an object is an instance of a particular class.

How to cast objects

Another potentially confusing aspect of using inheritance is knowing when to cast inherited objects explicitly. The basic rule is that Java can implicitly cast a subclass to its superclass, but you must use explicit casting if you want to treat a superclass object as one of its subclasses. Figure 7-14 illustrates how this works.

To start, the first group of statements creates a Book object, assigns this object to a Book variable named b, and assigns values to the object's instance variables. Then, the second group of statements shows how you can cast a subclass to its superclass without explicitly coding a cast. The first statement in this group casts the Book object to a new Product variable named p. Since this cast goes up the inheritance hierarchy (from more data to less), you don't need to explicitly code the cast.

Once you perform a cast like this, you can't call methods that are specific to the subclass. For example, once you cast a Book object to a Product object, you can't call the setAuthor method of the Book object. However, you can call methods of the Product class such as the setDescription method.

The third group of statements shows how to explicitly cast a superclass to a subclass. Since this cast goes down the inheritance hierarchy (from less data to more), you need to code the class name within parentheses in the assignment statement before you code the name of the object you're casting. Here, the first statement casts a Product object to a Book object. This works because the Product object is actually the Book object that was created in the first group of statements. This makes all methods of the Book object available again and doesn't cause any of the data in the original Book object to be lost.

The fourth group of statements shows a cast that will cause a ClassCastException to be thrown. Here, the first statement creates a Product object. Then, the second statement attempts to cast this object to the Book type. Since the Product variable named p2 refers to an instance of the Product class, not an instance of the Book class, an exception will be thrown when this statement is executed.

Casting examples that use the Product and Book classes

```
Book b = new Book();
b.setCode("java");
b.setDescription("Murach's Beginning Java 2");
b.setAuthor("Andrea Steelman");
b.setPrice(49.50);

Product p = b;              // cast Book object to a Product object
p.setDescription("Test");  // OK - method in Product class
//p.setAuthor("Test");     // not OK - method not in Product class

b = (Book) p;               // cast the Product object back to a Book object
b.setAuthor("Test");        // OK - method in Book class

Product p2 = new Product();
Book b2 = (Book) p2;        // will throw a ClassCastException because
                            // p2 is a Product object not a Book object
```

Description

- Java can implicitly cast a subclass to a superclass. As a result, you can use a subclass whenever a reference to its superclass is called for. For example, you can specify a Book object whenever a Product object is expected because Book is a subclass of Product.
- You must explicitly cast a superclass object when a reference to one of its subclasses is required. For example, you must explicitly cast a Product object to Book if a Book object is expected. This only works if the Product object is a valid Book object. Otherwise, a ClassCastException will be thrown.
- Casting affects the methods that are available from an object. For example, if you store a Book object in a Product variable, you can't call the setAuthor method because it's defined by the Book class, not the Product class.

How to compare objects

Figure 7-15 shows how the equals method of the Object class works. In short, this method checks whether two variables refer to the same object, not whether two variables hold the same data. Since that's not usually the behavior you want when comparing objects for equality, many classes in the API, such as the String class, override this method. When you code your own classes, you'll often want to override this method too.

The first two examples in this figure show how the equals method of the Object class works when the Book class doesn't override the equals method. In the first example, the first two statements create two variables that refer to the same object. Since both variables point to the same space in memory, the expression that uses the equals method to compare these variables evaluates to true. In the second example, though, the first two statements create two objects that contain the same data. However, since these objects occupy different spaces in memory, the expression that uses the equals method to compare the variables that point to these objects evaluates to false. But that's usually not what you want.

The third example shows how to code an equals method in the Product class that overrides the equals method of the Object class. To start, this method uses the same signature as the equals method of the Object class, which returns a boolean value and accepts a parameter of the Object type. Then, an if statement uses the instanceof operator to make sure that the passed object is an instance of the Product class. If so, it casts the Object parameter to a Product object. Then, an if statement compares the three instance variables stored in the Product object with the instance variables stored in the current object. If all instance variables are equal, this statement returns true. Otherwise, it returns false. As a result, the first two examples in this figure will return a true value if the Product class contains this method.

The fourth example shows how to code an equals method in the LineItem class you saw in the last chapter that overrides the equals method of the Object class. The code for this method works the same as the code for the equals method of the Product class. However, because a LineItem object contains a Product object, the equals method of the LineItem class uses the equals method of the Product class. As a result, you must code an equals method for the Product class before this method will work.

How the equals method of the Object class works

Example 1: Both variables refer to the same object

```
Product product1 = new Product();
Product product2 = product1;
if (product1.equals(product2))                // expression returns true
```

Example 2: Both variables refer to different objects that store the same data

```
Product product1 = new Product();
Product product2 = new Product();
if (product1.equals(product2))                // expression returns false
```

How to override the equals method of the Object class

Example 3: The equals method of the Product class

```
public boolean equals(Object object)
{
    if (object instanceof Product)
    {
        Product product2 = (Product) object;
        if
        (
            code.equals(product2.getCode()) &&
            description.equals(product2.getDescription()) &&
            price == product2.getPrice()
        )
            return true;
    }
    return false;
}
```

Example 4: The equals method of the LineItem class

```
public boolean equals(Object object)
{
    if (object instanceof LineItem)
    {
        LineItem li = (LineItem) object;
        if
        (
            product.equals(li.getProduct()) &&
            quantity == li.getQuantity()
        )
            return true;
    }
    return false;
}
```

Description

- To test if two objects point to the same space in memory, you can use the equals method of the Object class.
- To test if two objects store the same data, you can override the equals method in the subclass so it tests whether all instance variables in the two objects are equal.

Figure 7-15 How to compare objects

How to work with the abstract and final keywords

The last two topics of this chapter show how you can require or restrict the use of inheritance in the classes you create by using the abstract and final keywords.

How to work with the abstract keyword

An *abstract class* is a class that can't be instantiated. In other words, you can't create an object directly from an abstract class. Instead, you can code a class that inherits an abstract class, and you can create an object from that class.

Figure 7-16 shows how to work with abstract classes. To declare an abstract class, you include the abstract keyword in the class declaration as shown in the Product class at the top of this figure. Within an abstract class, you can use the abstract keyword to code *abstract methods*. For example, the Product class shown here includes an abstract method named getDisplayText that returns a string. The declaration for this method includes the abstract keyword, it ends with a semicolon, and no method body is coded.

When you include abstract methods in an abstract class, you must override them in any class that inherits the abstract class. This is illustrated in the second example in this figure. Here, you can see that a class named Book that inherits the Product class overrides the abstract getDisplayText method that's defined by that class.

At this point, you may be wondering why you would use abstract classes. To help you understand, consider the Product application that's presented in this chapter. This application uses two types of product objects: Book objects and Software objects. However, there's nothing to stop you from creating instances of the Product class as well. As a result, the Product class hierarchy actually allows for three types of objects: Book objects, Software objects, and Product objects.

If that's not what you want, you can declare the Product class as an abstract class. Then, you can't create instances of the Product class. Instead, the Product class can only be used as the superclass for other classes. In addition, if you want to make sure that both the Book and Software classes implement the getDisplayText method, you can declare this method as abstract in the Product class.

Note that this doesn't mean that you can't declare variables of an abstract type. It only means that you can't use the new keyword with an abstract type to create an instance of the type. For example, if you declare the Product class as an abstract class, you can still declare a Product variable that holds Book or Software objects. But you can't use the new keyword with the Product class to create a Product object.

An abstract Product class

```
public abstract class Product
{
    private String code;
    private String description;
    private double price;

    // regular constructors and methods for instance variables

    public String toString()
    {
        return "Code:        " + code + "\n" +
               "Description: " + description + "\n" +
               "Price:       " + this.getFormattedPrice() + "\n";
    }

    abstract String getDisplayText();   // an abstract method
}
```

A class that inherits the abstract Product class

```
public class Book extends Product
{
    private String author;

    // regular constructor and methods for the Book class

    public String getDisplayText()   // implement the abstract method
    {
        return super.toString() +
            "Author:      " + author + "\n";
    }
}
```

Description

- An *abstract class* is a class that can be inherited by other classes but that you can't use to create an object. To declare an abstract class, code the abstract keyword in the class declaration.
- An abstract class can contain fields, constructors, and methods just like other superclasses. In addition, an abstract class can contain abstract methods.
- To create an *abstract method*, you code the abstract keyword in the method declaration and you omit the method body. Abstract methods cannot have private access. However, they may have protected or default access (no access modifier).
- When a subclass inherits an abstract class, all abstract methods in the abstract class must be overridden in the subclass.
- An abstract class doesn't have to contain abstract methods. However, any class that contains an abstract method must be declared as abstract.

Figure 7-16 How to work with the abstract keyword

How to work with the final keyword

Figure 7-17 shows how to use the final keyword to declare *final classes, final methods*, and *final parameters*. You can use this keyword whenever you want to make sure that no one will override or change your classes, methods, or parameters. When you declare a final class, other programmers won't be able to create a subclass from your class. When you declare a final method, other programmers won't be able to override that method. And when you declare a final parameter, other programmers won't be able to assign a new value to that parameter.

Why would you want to use final classes, methods, or parameters? First, for design reasons, you may not want other programmers to be able to change the behavior of a method or a class. Second, Java can execute final classes, methods, and parameters slightly faster than regular methods.

When should you use final classes and methods? For the sake of efficiency, you can use a final class or method whenever you're sure that no one else will want to inherit your class or override your methods. Often, though, it's hard to know when that's true. In addition, the performance gain is slight. As a result, you should avoid using final classes and methods unless you're certain that no one else will benefit by extending your class or by overriding a method in your class.

The first example shows how to declare a final class. This example declares the Book class that inherits the Product class as final. When you declare a final class like this, all methods in the class automatically become final methods.

The second example shows how to declare a final method. Since this method is in the Software class, which hasn't been declared as final, the class can still be inherited by other classes. However, any class that inherits the Software class won't be able to override the getVersion method.

The third example shows how you can declare final parameters when you're coding a method. Since you would rarely want to assign a new value to the variable that's supplied by the parameter, you can almost always declare parameters as final. However, the performance gain is slight, and the extra keyword clutters the code. As a result, you may or may not want to use final parameters, depending on the type of project that you're working on.

In most cases, you'll declare an entire class as final rather than declaring specific methods as final. Because of that, you typically won't need to worry about whether individual methods of a class are final. If you ever encounter final methods, however, you should now understand how they work.

Example 1: A final class

```
public final class Book extends Product
{
    // all methods in the class are automatically final
}
```

Example 2: A final method

```
public final String getVersion()
{
    return version;
}
```

Example 3: A final parameter

```
public void setVersion(final String version)
{
    // version = "new value"; // not allowed
    this.version = version;
}
```

Description

- To prevent a class from being inherited, you can create a *final class* by coding the final keyword in the class declaration.
- To prevent subclasses from overriding a method of a superclass, you can create a *final method* by coding the final keyword in the method declaration. In addition, all methods in a final class are automatically final methods.
- To prevent a method from assigning a new value to a parameter, you can code the final keyword in the parameter declaration to create a *final parameter*. Then, if a statement in the method tries to assign a new value to the parameter, the compiler will report an error.
- Coding the final keyword for classes and methods can result in a minor performance improvement for your application because the compiler doesn't have to allow for inheritance and polymorphism. As a result, it can generate more efficient code.

Figure 7-17 How to work with the final keyword

Perspective

Conceptually, this is one of the most difficult chapters in this book. Although the basic idea of inheritance isn't that difficult to understand, the complications of polymorphism, overriding, casting, and abstract and final classes are enough to make inheritance a difficult topic. So if you find yourself a bit confused right now, don't be disheartened. It will become clearer as you actually use the techniques you've learned here and see them used in the Java API.

The good news is that you don't have to understand every nuance of how inheritance works to use it. In fact, since all classes automatically inherit the Object class, you've already been using inheritance without even knowing it. Now that you've completed this chapter, though, you should have a better understanding of how the Java API works. In addition, you should have a better idea of how you can use inheritance to improve the design of your own classes.

Summary

- *Inheritance* lets you create a new class based on an existing class. The existing class is called the *superclass*, *base class*, or *parent class*, and the new class is called the *subclass*, *derived class*, or *child class*.
- A subclass inherits all of the fields and methods of its superclass. The subclass can *extend* the superclass by adding its own fields and methods, and it can *override* a method with a new version of the method.
- All classes inherit the java.lang.Object class, which provides methods such as toString, equals, and getClass.
- You can use *access modifiers* to limit the accessibility of the fields and methods declared by a class. *Protected members* can be accessed only by classes in the same package or by subclasses.
- In a subclass, you can use the super keyword to access the fields, constructors, and methods of the superclass.
- *Polymorphism* is a feature of inheritance that lets you treat subclasses as though they were their superclass.
- You can call the getClass method from any object to get a Class object that contains information about that object.
- You can use the instanceof operator to check if an object is an instance of a particular class.
- Java can implicitly cast a subclass type to its superclass type, but you must use explicit casting to cast a superclass type to a subclass type.
- *Abstract classes* provide code that can be used by subclasses. In addition, they can specify *abstract methods* that must be implemented by subclasses.

- You can use the final keyword to declare *final classes*, *final methods*, and *final parameters*. No class can inherit a final class, no method can override a final method, and no statement can assign a new value to a final parameter.

Exercise 7-1 Look at a class that inherits the JFrame class

This exercise lets you view and run a class that inherits the javax.swing.JFrame class.

1. Open the ProductFrame class that's stored in the c:\java1.5\ch07\FrameTest directory. When you review this code, notice how it inherits the JFrame class and calls methods inherited from this class. In addition, note that this class contains a main method that creates an instance of the ProductFrame and displays that instance.
2. Compile and run this class. This should display a frame. When you click on its close button, the frame should close. In section 4, you'll learn more about working with frames like this one. In particular, you'll learn how to add components such as buttons, labels, and text boxes.
3. Make a list of all the methods of the JFrame class that are called in this application. Then, using the documentation for the JFrame class from the Java API documentation, indicate whether the method is declared by the JFrame class or inherited from one of its superclasses. If the method is inherited, indicate which class it is inherited from.
4. Use your research from step 3 to determine which class inherited by the JFrame class actually declares the setVisible method. Then, modify the code in the main method so that the frame variable is declared as that type rather than as a JFrame type. Compile and run the application to verify that it still works properly.

Exercise 7-2 Create a Product application that uses inheritance

In this exercise, you'll create a Product application like the one presented in this chapter that uses inheritance. However, you will add an additional kind of product: compact discs. To make this application easier to develop, we'll give you most of the starting classes.

Create a new subclass named CompactDisc

1. Open the classes in the c:\java1.5\ch07\Product directory and review the code.
2. Add a class named CompactDisc that inherits the Product class. This new class should work like the Book and Software classes, but it should include public get and set methods for a private instance variable named artist. In addition, it should include a toString method that overrides the toString method in the Product class. This method should append the artist name to the end of the string.
3. Compile the CompactDisc class to make sure that it doesn't contain any syntax errors.

Modify the ProductDB class so it returns a CompactDisc object

4. Modify the ProductDB class so it creates at least one CompactDisc object. For example, this object might contain the following information:

```
Code:        sgtp
Description: Sgt. Pepper's Lonely Hearts Club Band
Price:       $15.00
Artist:      The Beatles
```

5. Compile this class and run the application to make sure it works.

Add a protected variable

6. Open the Product class and change the access modifier for the count variable from public to protected.
7. Compile this class, and then run the application one more time to make sure that the count is maintained properly.

Exercise 7-3 Modify the Product class to use the abstract keyword

In this exercise, you'll change the Product class in the Product application to an abstract class to see how that works. Then, you'll add an abstract method and implement it in the Book, Software, and CompactDisc subclasses.

Change the Product class to an abstract class

1. Still working with the Product application of exercise 7-2, add the abstract keyword to the Product class declaration and compile the class.
2. Open the ProductApp class, and add this statement before the statement that calls the getProduct method:

   ```
   Product pTest = new Product();
   ```

3. Compile the ProductApp class. You should get a message that says that the Product class is declared as abstract and cannot be instantiated.
4. Delete the statement you just added and compile the class again. Then, run the application to make sure it works.

Add an abstract method to the Product class

5. Add an abstract method named getDisplayText to the Product class. This method should accept no parameters, and it should return a String object. Compile this class.
6. Rename the toString methods in the Book, Software, and CompactDisc classes to getDisplayText, and compile these classes.
7. Modify the ProductApp class so it calls the getDisplayText method of a product object instead of the toString method. Then, compile this class, and run the application to be sure it works correctly.

Exercise 7-4 Modify the Book class to use the final keyword

In this exercise, you'll change the Book class in the Product application to a final class to see that a final class can't be inherited. Then, you'll create a final method to see that it can't be overridden.

Change the Book class to a final class

1. Still working with the Product application, add the final keyword to the Book class declaration and compile this class.
2. Create a class named UsedBook that inherits the Book class. You don't need to include any code in the body of this class. Then, compile this class. When you do, you should get a message that says the Book class can't be inherited because that class is final.

Add a final method

3. Remove the final keyword from the Book class declaration. Then, add the final keyword to the getDisplayText method of the Book class and compile this class.
4. Add a getDisplayText method to the UsedBook class to override the getDisplayText method of the Book class. You don't need to include any code in the body of this method. Then, compile this class. When you do, you should get a message that says the getDisplayText method can't be overridden because that method is final.

Exercise 7-5 Code an equals method for the Product and LineItem classes

In this exercise, you'll add an equals method to the Product and LineItem classes that you can use to compare the instance variables of two objects.

1. Open the EqualsTestApp class in the c:\java1.5\ch07\EqualsTest directory. This application creates and compares two Product objects and two LineItem objects using the equals method. Review this code to see how it works.
2. Compile the EqualsTestApp class, and run the application. Since the equals method isn't overridden in the Product or LineItem class, the output from this application should indicate that the comparisons are based on object references and not the data the objects contain.
3. Open the Product class, and add an equals method like the one shown in figure 7-15. Then, compile the Product class, and run the EqualsTestApp class again. This time, the output should indicate that the products are being compared based on their data and not their references.
4. Repeat step 2 for the LineItem class. This time, the comparisons for both the products and line items should be based on their data.

8

How to work with interfaces

The Java API defines hundreds of interfaces. Although most of them are intended for use by other classes in the API, you may need to use a few of these interfaces in your own applications. You'll learn how to use one of these interfaces, Cloneable, in this chapter. In addition, you'll learn how to create and use your own interfaces. As you'll see, interfaces are similar to abstract classes, but they have several advantages that make them easier to create and more flexible to use.

An introduction to interfaces

In some object-oriented programming languages, such as C++, a class can inherit more than one class. This is known as *multiple inheritance*. Although Java doesn't support multiple inheritance, it does support a special type of coding element known as an *interface*. An interface provides many of the advantages of multiple inheritance without some of the problems that are associated with it.

A simple interface

Figure 8-1 illustrates how you create and use an interface. Here, the first example shows the code for a simple interface named Printable. This code is similar to the code that defines a class and would be stored in a file named Printable.java. However, the code for an interface uses the interface keyword instead of the class keyword and contains only abstract methods.

The second example shows a Product class that *implements* the Printable interface. To implement the Printable interface, the declaration for the Product class uses the implements keyword followed by the name of the interface. Then, the body of the Product class implements the print method that's specified by the Printable interface.

The third example shows that a Product object that implements the Printable interface can be stored in a variable of the Printable type. In other words, an object created from a Product class that implements the Printable interface is both a Product object and a Printable object. As a result, you can use this object anywhere a Printable object is expected. You'll learn more about how this works later in this chapter.

Example 1: A Printable interface that defines a print method

```
public interface Printable
{
    public abstract void print();
}
```

Example 2: A Product class that implements the Printable interface

```
import java.text.NumberFormat;

public class Product implements Printable
{
    private String code;
    private String description;
    private double price;

    public Product(String code, String description, double price)
    {
        this.code = code;
        this.description = description;
        this.price = price;
    }

    // get and set methods for the fields

    public void print()  // implement the Printable interface
    {
        System.out.println("Code:\t\t" + code);
        System.out.println("Description:\t" + description);
        System.out.println("Price:\t\t" + this.getFormattedPrice());
    }
}
```

Example 3: Code that uses the print method of the Product class

```
Printable product =
    new Product("java", "Murach's Beginning Java 2", 49.50);
product.print();
```

Resulting output

```
Code:           java
Description:    Murach's Beginning Java 2
Price:          $49.50
```

Description

- An *interface* defines a set of public methods that can be implemented by a class. The interface itself doesn't provide any code to implement the methods. Instead, it merely provides the method signatures.
- A class that *implements* an interface must provide an implementation for each method defined by the interface.
- An interface can also define public constants. Then, those constants are available to any class that implements the interface.

Figure 8-1 A simple interface

Interfaces compared to abstract classes

At this point, you might be wondering how an interface compares to an abstract class. Figure 8-2 illustrates the similarities and differences. It also lists some of the advantages of each.

To start, both abstract classes and interfaces can contain abstract methods and static constants, and neither can be instantiated. However, an abstract class can also contain other types of fields, and it can define static and regular methods. In this respect, abstract classes are more powerful than interfaces.

A more important difference between abstract classes and interfaces is that a class can only inherit one other class—abstract or not—but it can implement more than one interface. This gives interfaces an important advantage over abstract classes. In short, interfaces are how Java provides some of the features of multiple inheritance.

To illustrate, suppose you want to create several types of products, such as books, software, and compact disks, and you want each type of product to have a print method that prints information about the product that's appropriate for the product type. You could implement this hierarchy using inheritance, with an abstract Product class at the top of the hierarchy and Book, Software, and CompactDisc classes that extend the Product class. Then, the Product class would provide features common to all products, such as a product code, description, and price. In addition, the Product class would declare an abstract print method, and the Book, Software, and CompactDisc classes would provide their own implementations of this method.

The drawback of this approach is that there are undoubtedly other objects in the applications that use these classes that can be printed as well. For example, objects such as invoices and customers have information that can be printed. Obviously, these objects wouldn't inherit the abstract Product class, so they'd have to define their own print methods.

In contrast, if you created a Printable interface like the one in this figure, it could be implemented by any class that represents an object that can be printed. One advantage of this is that it ensures consistency within the application by guaranteeing that any printable object will be printed using a method named print. Without the interface, some printable objects might use a method called print, while others might use methods with names like display or show.

More importantly, an interface defines a Java type, so any object that implements an interface is marked as that interface type. As a result, an object that's instantiated from a Book class that extends the Product class and implements the Printable interface is not only an object of type Book and of type Product, but also an object of type Printable. That means you can use the object, or any other object that implements the Printable interface, wherever a Printable type is called for. You'll see examples of this later in this chapter.

An abstract class compared to an interface

Abstract class
Variables Constants Static variables Static constants
Methods Static methods Abstract methods Abstract static methods

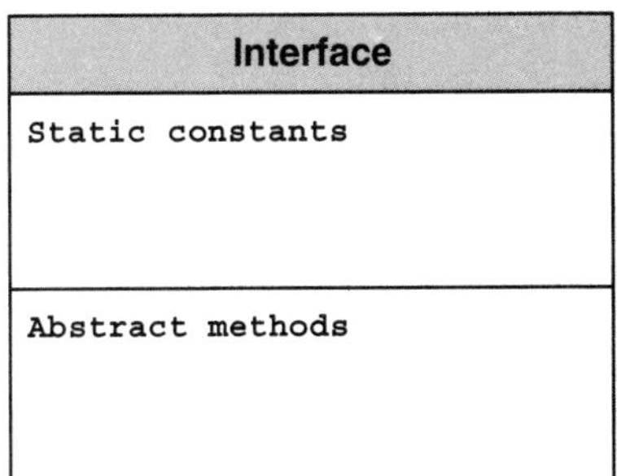

Example 1: A Printable interface

```
public interface Printable
{
    public abstract void print();
}
```

Example 2: A Printable abstract class

```
public abstract class Printable
{
    public abstract void print();
}
```

Advantages of an abstract class

- An abstract class can use instance variables and constants as well as static variables and constants. Interfaces can only use static constants.
- An abstract class can include regular methods that contain code as well as abstract methods that don't contain code. An interface can only define abstract methods.
- An abstract class can define static methods. An interface can't.

Advantages of an interface

- A class can only directly inherit one other class, but it can directly implement multiple interfaces.
- Any object created from a class that implements an interface can be used wherever the interface is accepted.

Figure 8-2 Interfaces compared to abstract classes

Some interfaces of the Java API

Almost every package in the Java API includes one or more interfaces. If you look in the API documentation, you'll see that the names of the interfaces are italicized. This makes it easy to differentiate between classes and interfaces.

To give you an idea of what some of the interfaces in the API do, figure 8-3 lists a few of the interfaces that you may need to use in your applications. The first table lists two general-purpose Java interfaces: Cloneable and Comparable. Of these interfaces, the one you're most likely to implement is Cloneable.

The Cloneable interface lets you identify objects that can safely use the clone method of the Object class. Since this interface contains no constants or methods, it is known as a *tagging interface*. Later in this chapter, you'll see an example of how to implement this interface for the Product and LineItem classes.

The Comparable interface provides a standard way for an object to compare itself with another object. However, most business classes don't have any real basis for determining whether one instance of the class is greater than or less than another. For example, how would you determine whether one product object is greater than or less than another product object? By comparing the product codes? The price? The amount of inventory on hand? One situation where you may need to use the comparable interface, however, is if you want to sort the elements in an array. You'll see an example of how to do that in chapter 10.

The second table lists several interfaces that you'll use as you develop graphical user interfaces. As you'll learn in section 4, a graphical user interface is a window that contains graphical components such as buttons, labels, and text boxes. A user can use a graphical user interface to interact with an application. To do that, the application must "listen" for events that occur on the window and its components. And that's where the interfaces shown in this figure come in to play.

Some interfaces in the java.lang package

Interface	Methods	Description
`Cloneable`	`None`	An interface that identifies the object as safe for cloning. When using this interface, it's recommended to override the protected clone method of the Object class.
`Comparable`	`int compareTo(Object o)`	Compares objects.

Some interfaces in the java.util and java.awt.event packages

Interface	Methods	Description
`EventListener`	`None`	An interface that identifies the object as an event listener.

`WindowListener`	`void windowActivated(WindowEvent e)`
	`void windowClosed(WindowEvent e)`
	`void windowClosing(WindowEvent e)`
	`void windowDeactivated(WindowEvent e)`
	`void windowDeiconified(WindowEvent e)`
	`void windowIconified(WindowEvent e)`
	`void windowOpened(WindowEvent e)`
		A type of event listener that listens for events that occur during a window's life.

`ActionListener`	`void actionPerformed(ActionEvent e)`	A type of event listener that listens for events that occur on GUI components such as text boxes, buttons, and combo boxes.

Description

- The Java API defines many interfaces that you can implement in your classes. In this chapter, you'll see an example of a class that implements the Cloneable interface.
- Since the Cloneable interface doesn't contain any methods and is primarily used to identify an interface as being safe for cloning, it's known as a *tagging interface*. Similarly, the EventListener interface is a tagging interface that identifies an interface as a type of EventListener.
- The WindowListener and ActionListener interfaces inherit the EventListener interface.
- This table only lists the most important members of each interface. For a complete description of these interfaces and a list of their members, see the documentation for the Java API.

Figure 8-3 Some interfaces of the Java API

How to work with interfaces

Now that you have an idea of what interfaces do, you're ready to learn the details of coding and implementing them.

How to code an interface

Figure 8-4 shows how to code an interface. To start, you code the public keyword, followed by the interface keyword, followed by the name of the interface. When you name an interface, it's common to end the name with a suffix of "able" or "er". For example, as you saw in figure 8-3, the Java API uses names like Cloneable, Comparable, EventListener, ActionListener, and so on.

The first example in this figure shows the code for the Printable interface. This interface contains a single abstract method named print that doesn't accept any arguments or return any data. As with all abstract methods, you don't code braces at the end of the method. Instead, you code a semicolon immediately after the parentheses.

The second example shows the code for an interface named ProductWriter. This interface contains three abstract methods: addProduct, updateProduct, and deleteProduct. All three of these methods accept a Product object as an argument and return a boolean value that indicates whether the operation was successful.

The third example shows how to code an interface that defines constants. In this case, an interface named DepartmentConstants defines three constants that map departments to integer values. You'll see how you can use constants like these in the next figure.

When you code an abstract method in an interface, you don't have to use the public and abstract keywords. That's because Java automatically supplies these keywords for all methods. Similarly, Java automatically supplies the public, static, and final keywords for constants. However, you can code these keywords if you think that they help clarify the code.

The fourth example shows the code for the Cloneable interface, which is a tagging interface. To code a tagging interface, you code an interface that doesn't contain any constants or methods. When a class implements a tagging interface, it often indicates that the class conforms to specifications made by that interface. For example, implementing the Cloneable interface in a class indicates that the class can be cloned. You'll learn more about how that works later in this chapter.

The syntax for declaring an interface

```
public interface InterfaceName
{
    type CONSTANT_NAME = value;              // declares a field
    returnType methodName([parameterList]);  // declares a method
}
```

Example 1: An interface that defines one method

```
public interface Printable
{
    void print();
}
```

Example 2: An interface that defines three methods

```
public interface ProductWriter
{
    boolean addProduct(Product p);
    boolean updateProduct(Product p);
    boolean deleteProduct(Product p);
}
```

Example 3: An interface that defines constants

```
public interface DepartmentConstants
{
    int ADMIN = 1;
    int EDITORIAL = 2;
    int MARKETING = 3;
}
```

Example 4: A tagging interface with no members

```
public interface Cloneable
{
}
```

Description

- Declaring an interface is similar to declaring a class except that you use the interface keyword instead of the class keyword.
- In an interface, all methods are automatically declared public and abstract, and all constants are automatically declared public, static, and final. Although you can code the public, abstract, and final keywords, they're optional.
- Interface methods can't be static.

Figure 8-4 How to code an interface

How to implement an interface

Figure 8-5 shows how to code a class that implements an interface. To do that, you code the implements keyword after the name of the class followed by the names of one or more interfaces separated by commas. In this figure, for example, you can see a class named Employee that implements both the Printable and DepartmentConstants interfaces.

A class that implements an interface must implement all of the methods defined by that interface. For example, because the Employee class implements the Printable interface, it must implement the print method declared by that interface. If this method isn't implemented, the class won't compile.

When a class implements an interface, it can use any of the constants defined by that interface. For example, since the Employee class implements the DepartmentConstants interface, this class can use the ADMIN, EDITORIAL, and MARKETING constants that are defined by that interface. In this example, the if statement in the print method uses these constants to determine what department name is included in the output.

To use a constant from an interface that's implemented by a class, you can code the name of the constant without any qualification as shown in this figure. If you want to, however, you can also code the name of the interface that defines the constant, followed by the dot operator, followed by the name of the constant. While this makes it clear where the value of the constant is stored, it also results in more code. Because of that, the interface name is typically omitted when referring to constants.

The syntax for implementing an interface

```
public class ClassName implements Interface1[, Interface2]...{}
```

A class that implements two interfaces

```
import java.text.NumberFormat;

public class Employee implements Printable, DepartmentConstants
{
    private int department;
    private String firstName;
    private String lastName;
    private double salary;

    public Employee(int department, String lastName, String firstName,
        double salary)
    {
        this.department = department;
        this.lastName = lastName;
        this.firstName = firstName;
        this.salary = salary;
    }

    public void print()
    {
        NumberFormat currency = NumberFormat.getCurrencyInstance();
        System.out.println("Name:\t" + firstName + " " + lastName);
        System.out.println("Salary:\t" + currency.format(salary));

        String dept = "";
        if (department == ADMIN)
            dept = "Administration";
        else if (department == EDITORIAL)
            dept = "Editorial";
        else if (department == MARKETING)
            dept = "Marketing";

        System.out.println("Dept:\t" + dept);
    }
}
```

Description

- To declare a class that implements an interface, you use the implements keyword. Then, you provide an implementation for each method defined by the interface.
- If you forget to implement a method that's defined by an interface that you're implementing, the compiler will issue an error message.
- A class that implements an interface can use any constant defined by that interface.

Figure 8-5 How to implement an interface

How to inherit a class and implement an interface

Figure 8-6 shows how to code a class that inherits another class and implements an interface. In particular, this figure shows how the Book class that you learned about in the previous chapter can inherit the Product class and implement the Printable interface. To do that, the declaration for the Book class uses the extends keyword to indicate that it inherits the Product class. Then, it uses the implements keyword to indicate that it implements the Printable interface. Finally, the Book class implements the print method specified by the Printable interface. As a result, an object created from the Book class can be used anywhere a Book, Product, or Printable object is required.

In figure 8-1, you saw a Product class that implements the Printable interface. If the Book class inherits this version of the Product class, it automatically implements the Printable interface, and it can use the print method implemented by the Product class. If you want to, however, you can include the implements keyword on the declaration for the Book class to clearly show that this class implements the Printable interface. In that case, though, you don't need to implement the print method since it's already implemented in the Product class. However, you can override this method.

The syntax for inheriting a class and implementing an interface

```
public class SubclassName extends SuperclassName implements Interface1
    [, Interface2]...{}
```

A Book class that inherits Product and implements Printable

```
public class Book extends Product implements Printable
{
    private String author;

    public Book(String code, String description, double price,
        String author)
    {
        super(code, description, price);
        this.author = author;
    }

    public void setAuthor(String author)
    {
        this.author = author;
    }

    public String getAuthor()
    {
        return author;
    }

    public void print()    // implement the Printable interface
    {
        System.out.println("Code:\t" + super.getCode());
        System.out.println("Title:\t" + super.getDescription());
        System.out.println("Author:\t" + this.author);
        System.out.println("Price:\t" + super.getFormattedPrice());
    }
}
```

Description

- A class can inherit another class and also implement one or more interfaces.
- If a class inherits another class that implements an interface, the subclass automatically implements the interface. However, you can code the implements keyword in the subclass for clarity.
- If a class inherits another class that implements an interface, the subclass has access to any methods of the interface that are implemented by the superclass and can override those methods.

Figure 8-6 How to inherit a class and implement an interface

How to use an interface as a parameter

Figure 8-7 shows how to code a method that uses an interface as the type for one of its parameters. When you do that, the statement that calls the method can pass any object that implements the interface to the method. Then, the method can call any of the methods that are defined by the interface and implemented by the object. You can use this type of code to create a flexible design that provides for processing objects created from different classes.

The first example in this figure shows a method named printMultiple that accepts two parameters. The first parameter is an object that implements the Printable interface, and the second parameter is an integer value that specifies the number of times to print the first parameter. Since the first parameter specifies Printable as the type, the printMultiple method doesn't know what type of object it will get, but it does know that the object will contain a print method. As a result, the code in the body of the method can call the print method.

In the second example, the printMultiple method is used to print two copies of a Product object to the console. This works because the Product class implements the Printable interface. Here, the first statement creates the Product object and assigns it to a variable of the Product type. Then, the second statement uses the printMultiple method to print two copies of the Product object.

The third example shows that you can also declare a variable using an interface as the type. Then, you can assign any object that implements the interface to the variable, and you can pass the variable to any method that accepts the interface as a parameter. As you can see, this code yields the same result as the second example, but it clearly shows that the Product object implements the Printable interface.

Example 1: A printMultiple method that prints multiple copies of a Printable object

```
private static void printMultiple(Printable p, int count)
{
    for (int i = 0; i < count; i++)
        p.print();
}
```

Example 2: Code that passes a Product object to the printMultiple method

```
Product product = new Product("java", "Murach's Beginning Java 2", 49.50);
printMultiple(product, 2);
```

Resulting output

```
Code:           java
Description:    Murach's Beginning Java 2
Price:          $49.50
Code:           java
Description:    Murach's Beginning Java 2
Price:          $49.50
```

Example 3: Code that passes a Printable object to the printMultiple method

```
Printable product =
    new Product("java", "Murach's Beginning Java 2", 49.50);
printMultiple(product, 2);
```

Resulting output

```
Code:           java
Description:    Murach's Beginning Java 2
Price:          $49.50
Code:           java
Description:    Murach's Beginning Java 2
Price:          $49.50
```

Description

- You can declare a parameter that's used by a method as an interface type. Then, you can pass any object that implements the interface to the parameter.
- You can also declare a variable as an interface type. Then, you can assign an instance of any object that implements the interface to the variable, and you can pass the variable as an argument to a method that accepts the interface type.

Figure 8-7 How to use an interface as a parameter

How to use inheritance with interfaces

Figure 8-8 shows how one interface can inherit other interfaces. To start, this figure presents three interfaces that don't use inheritance: ProductReader, ProductWriter, and ProductConstants. Then, it presents a ProductDAO interface that inherits the first three interfaces. This interface is named ProductDAO because it defines an object that provides data access for products. In other words, DAO stands for "Data Access Object." This is a common pattern and naming convention, so you may see it used in other applications you work on.

When an interface inherits other interfaces, any class that implements that interface must implement all of the methods declared by that interface and the inherited interfaces. For example, if a class implements the ProductDAO class, it must implement all of the methods defined by the ProductReader and ProductWriter classes. If it doesn't, the class must be declared as abstract so that no objects can be created from it.

When a class implements an interface that inherits other interfaces, it can use any of the constants stored in the interface or any of its inherited interfaces. For example, any class that implements the ProductDAO interface can use any of the constants in the ProductConstants interface.

When a class implements an interface that inherits other interfaces, you can use an object created from that class anywhere any of interfaces in the inheritance hierarchy are expected. If a class implements the ProductDAO interface, for example, an object created from that class can be passed to a method that accepts a ProductReader as a parameter. That's because any class that implements the ProductDAO interface must also implement the ProductReader interface.

The syntax for declaring an interface that inherits other interfaces

```
public interface InterfaceName
    extends InterfaceName1[, InterfaceName2]...
{
    // the constants and methods of the interface
}
```

Example 1: A ProductReader interface

```
public interface ProductReader
{
    Product getProduct(String code);
    String getProductsString();
}
```

Example 2: A ProductWriter interface

```
public interface ProductWriter
{
    boolean addProduct(Product p);
    boolean updateProduct(Product p);
    boolean deleteProduct(Product p);
}
```

Example 3: A ProductConstants interface

```
public interface ProductConstants
{
    int CODE_SIZE = 4;
    int DESCRIPTION_SIZE = 40;
}
```

Example 4: A ProductDAO interface that inherits these three interfaces

```
public interface ProductDAO
    extends ProductReader, ProductWriter, ProductConstants
{
}
```

Description

- An interface can inherit one or more other interfaces by specifying the inherited interfaces in an extends clause.
- An interface can't inherit a class.
- A class that implements an interface must implement all the methods declared by the interface as well as all the methods declared by any inherited interfaces unless the class is defined as abstract.
- A class that implements an interface can use any of the constants declared in the interface as well as any constants declared by any inherited interfaces.

Figure 8-8 How to use inheritance with interfaces

A Product Maintenance application that uses interfaces

To illustrate how interfaces work, the topics that follow present a Product Maintenance application that uses the interfaces presented in the previous figure to provide the data access for the application. As you'll see, when you use interfaces like this, you can separate the presentation layer of the application from the database layer. That's because the presentation layer only needs to know what interfaces the data access object implements. It doesn't need to know how the data is stored or processed.

The class diagram

Figure 8-9 shows the class diagram for the Product Maintenance application. Notice that the main class for the application, ProductMaintApp, uses the ProductDAO interface. As you saw in the last figure, the ProductDAO interface inherits the ProductConstants, ProductWriter, and ProductReader interfaces.

Because ProductDAO is an interface, it can't directly provide the data access functions for the application. That's where the ProductTextFile class comes in. It implements the ProductDAO interface by saving and retrieving product data from a text file. Notice, however, that there's no arrow going from the ProductMaintApp class to the ProductTextFile class. That's because the ProductMaintApp class isn't aware of the specific class that provides the data access. It knows only that the class it uses for data access implements the ProductDAO interface.

The key to this application is the DAOFactory class. As you'll see in a minute, this class has a single method named getProductDAO that returns an object that implements the ProductDAO interface. Then, after the ProductMaintApp class calls the getProductDAO method to get the ProductDAO object, it uses the methods of that object to handle the data access for the application. In short, the DAOFactory class insulates the ProductMaintApp class from the database layer of the application. This design pattern, called the *factory pattern*, is commonly used to provide flexibility in the application's database layer.

In this application, the getProductDAO method of the DAOFactory class returns an instance of the ProductTextFile class, which implements the ProductDAO interface with a text file. Because it uses the factory pattern, though, this implementation can easily be changed to a binary file, XML file, or a database such as MySQL, Oracle, or Microsoft SQL Server. To do that, you just provide another class that implements the ProductDAO interface, and you change the one statement in the DAOFactory class so it returns an object for that class.

The class diagram for the Product Maintenance application

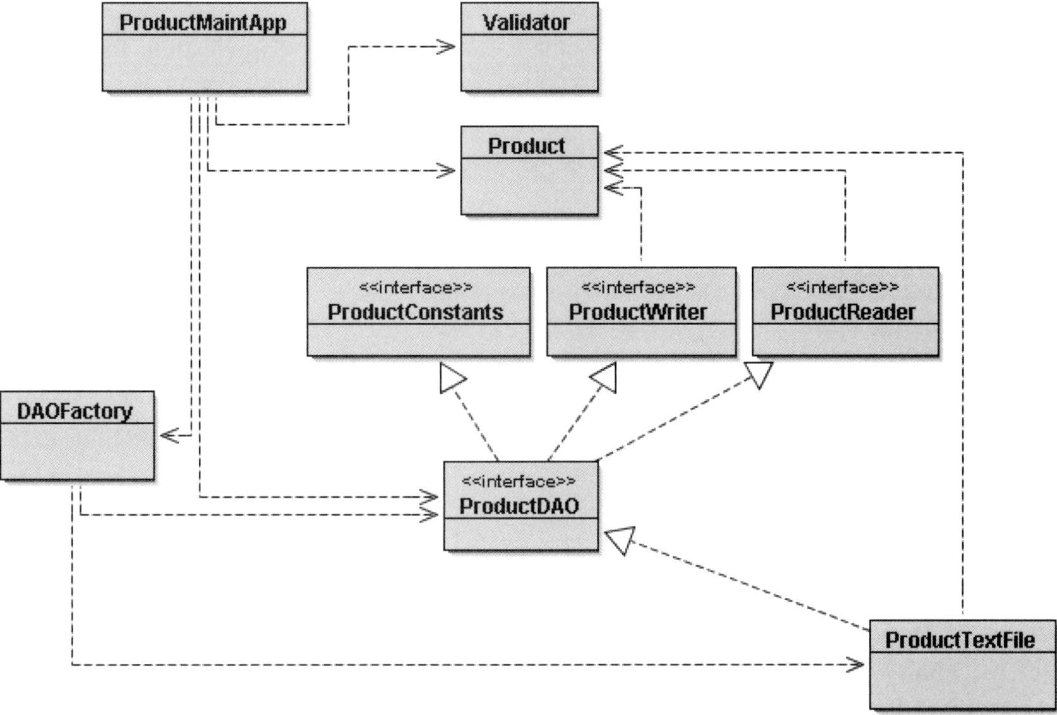

Classes and interfaces used by the Product Maintenance application

Class	Description	Figure
Product	Represents a Product object.	7-10 plus equals method in figure 7-15
Validator	Provides methods that accept and validate user input.	6-20 plus a method that gets a whole line
ProductConstants ProductReader ProductWriter ProductDAO	The interfaces used by the Product Maintenance application.	8-8
ProductTextFile	Implements the ProductDAO interface (which inherits the ProductReader, ProductWriter, and ProductConstants interfaces).	8-11 (outline only)
DAOFactory	Maps the ProductDAO interface to the ProductTextFile object. This is the only linkage between the ProductTextFile object and the rest of the application.	8-11
ProductMaintApp	Contains the main method for the Product Maintenance application.	8-12

Figure 8-9 The class diagram for the Product Maintenance application

The console

Figure 8-10 shows the console for the Product Maintenance application. To start, this application displays a welcome message and a list of five commands that are recognized by the application (list, add, del, help, and exit). When the user enters one of these commands, this application performs the appropriate action.

If the user enters the list command, the application displays a list of all the products that are currently stored in the file. A user might use this command after the add or del command to verify that a product has been added or deleted from the file.

If the user enters the add command, the application prompts the user to enter a code, description, and price for the product. Once the user makes these entries, the application adds the product to the file and displays an appropriate message to the user.

If the user enters the del command, the application prompts the user for the product's code. Once the user enters a code for a product that exists in the file, the application deletes the product and displays an appropriate message. However, if the user enters an invalid code, the application displays a message that indicates that the product couldn't be found.

If the user enters the help command, the application displays the menu of commands again. This command may come in handy if the menu has scrolled off the screen.

Although it's not shown here, alternate commands are provided for the delete and help commands. For example, the user can enter either "del" or "delete" to delete a product. Similarly, the user can enter either "help" or "menu" to display the menu of commands.

To exit from this application, the user enters the exit command. Then, the application displays a goodbye message and ends.

The console for the Product Maintenance application

```
Welcome to the Product Maintenance application

COMMAND MENU
list    - List all products
add     - Add a product
del     - Delete a product
help    - Show this menu
exit    - Exit this application

Enter a command: list

PRODUCT LIST
java    Murach's Beginning Java                        $49.50
jsps    Murach's Java Servlets and JSP                 $49.50
cshp    Murach's C#                                    $49.50
mcb2    Murach's Mainframe COBOL                       $59.50

Enter a command: del

Enter product code to delete: cshp

Murach's C# has been deleted.

Enter a command: add

Enter product code: txtp
Enter product description: TextPad 7.4
Enter price: 20

TextPad 7.4 has been added.

Enter a command: list

PRODUCT LIST
java    Murach's Beginning Java                        $49.50
jsps    Murach's Java Servlets and JSP                 $49.50
mcb2    Murach's Mainframe COBOL                       $59.50
txtp    TextPad 7.4                                    $20.00

Enter a command: exit

Bye.
```

Description

- When this application first starts, it displays a menu of the commands the user can enter. When the user enters one of these commands, the appropriate processing is performed. Otherwise, an error message is displayed.

The DAOFactory class

Figure 8-11 shows the DAOFactory class. This class contains one static method named getProductDAO that returns a ProductDAO object. In this case, the ProductDAO object is an instance of the ProductTextFile class. That's possible because the ProductTextFile class implements the ProductDAO interface. In fact, the two lines of code within this method could be condensed into this single line of code:

```
return new ProductTextFile();
```

The ProductTextFile class

Figure 8-11 also presents an outline of the ProductTextFile class. Because this class implements the ProductDAO interface, it must implement the methods defined by the ProductReader and ProductWriter interfaces that this interface inherits. You can see the declarations for the five methods defined by these interfaces in this figure.

Since an interface can only specify non-static methods, all of the methods in the ProductTextFile class are also non-static. As a result, the ProductTextFile class includes a constructor. When you create an object from this class, this constructor initializes the fields defined by the class. Then, you can call any of the methods from the ProductTextFile object.

If you look back at figure 8-8, you can see that the ProductConstants interface defines two constants: CODE_SIZE and DESCRIPTION_SIZE. Because the ProductDAO interface also inherits this interface, the ProductTextFile class can use these constants. These constants can be used in the getProductsString method to set the maximum number of characters that are displayed for the code and description fields. That way, the columns in the product list that's returned by this method can be aligned.

Because the code for implementing the methods shown in this figure uses some techniques that haven't been presented yet, it isn't shown here. In particular, the methods in this class use some of the techniques for working with collections that are covered in chapter 11, and they use some of the techniques for working with text files that are covered in chapter 19. If you're curious to see how this works, you can look ahead to chapter 19 to see a similar ProductTextFile class. You will also get a chance to review the code for this class when you do exercise 8-3. For now, though, you can focus on using the methods of this ProductTextFile class rather than on the implementation details.

Remember too that it's easy to change the way you implement the ProductDAO interface when you use the factory pattern. To do that, you create a new class that implements the interface with a binary file, XML file, or database. Then, you change the getProductDAO method in the DAOFactory class so it creates an object from the new class. Since those are the only classes that need to be changed, the factory pattern is commonly used when the implementation details are likely to change.

The code for the DAOFactory class

```
public class DAOFactory
{
    public static ProductDAO getProductDAO()
    {
        ProductDAO pDAO = new ProductTextFile();
        return pDAO;
    }
}
```

The code for the ProductTextFile class

```
public class ProductTextFile implements ProductDAO
{
    public ProductTextFile()
    {
        // code that initializes fields
    }

    //**************************************************
    // Implement the ProductReader interface
    //**************************************************
    public Product getProduct(String code)
    {
        // code that returns a Product
    }

    public String getProductsString()
    {
        // code that returns a String that lists all products

        // this code can use the CODE_SIZE and DESCRIPTION_SIZE
        // constants from the ProductConstants interface
        // to align the product data
    }

    //**************************************************
    // Implement the ProductWriter interface
    //***************************************************
    public boolean addProduct(Product p)
    {
        // code that adds a Product
    }

    public boolean deleteProduct(Product p)
    {
        // code that deletes a Product
    }

    public boolean updateProduct(Product p)
    {
        // code that updates a Product
    }
}
```

Figure 8-11 The DAOFactory and ProductTextFile classes

The ProductMaintApp class

Figure 8-12 shows the code for the ProductMaintApp class. To start, this class declares two static class variables. The first one is for a ProductDAO variable named productDAO that's set to a null. The second one is for a Scanner variable named sc that's also set to a null. Because these variables are defined at the class level, they are available to all the methods in the ProductMaintApp class.

After the main method displays a welcome message, the second group of statements assigns objects to the productDAO and sc variables. To get a ProductDAO object, the getProductDAO method of the DAOFactory class is called. This method actually returns a ProductTextFile object, but since the code that creates this object is in the DAOFactory class, the ProductMaintApp class has no direct knowledge of this. Instead, all of the methods of the ProductMaintApp class use the ProductDAO object.

Once the class variables have been set, the main method calls the displayMenu method that's shown on page 2 of this listing. This method displays a list of commands that are recognized by the Product Maintenance application. As a result, this list is displayed when the program starts to remind the user what commands are available.

After the main method displays the command menu, it enters a while loop. Within this loop, the application prompts the user for a command until the user enters the exit command. When the user enters this command, the application displays a goodbye message and exits. If the user enters an invalid command, the program displays an error message. Otherwise, the program calls a method to perform the requested function.

The code for the ProductMaintApp class **Page 1**

```
import java.util.Scanner;

public class ProductMaintApp
{
    // declare two class variables
    private static ProductDAO productDAO = null;
    private static Scanner sc = null;

    public static void main(String args[])
    {
        System.out.println(
            "Welcome to the Product Maintenance application\n");

        // set the class variables
        productDAO = DAOFactory.getProductDAO();
        sc = new Scanner(System.in);

        // display the command menu
        displayMenu();

        // perform 1 or more actions
        String action = "";
        while (!action.equalsIgnoreCase("exit"))
        {
            // get the input from the user
            action = Validator.getString(sc, "Enter a command: ");
            System.out.println();

            if (action.equalsIgnoreCase("list"))
                displayAllProducts();
            else if (action.equalsIgnoreCase("add"))
                addProduct();
            else if (action.equalsIgnoreCase("del") ||
                     action.equalsIgnoreCase("delete"))
                deleteProduct();
            else if (action.equalsIgnoreCase("help") ||
                     action.equalsIgnoreCase("menu"))
                displayMenu();
            else if (action.equalsIgnoreCase("exit"))
                System.out.println("Bye.\n");
            else
                System.out.println("Error! Not a valid command.\n");
        }
    }
```

Figure 8-12 The ProductMaintApp class (part 1 of 2)

If the user enters the list command, the displayAllProducts method is executed. This method displays a list of the products that are stored in the file. To do that, it calls the getProductsString method of the productDAO object to get a string that contains a list of the products. Then, it prints this string to the console.

If the user enters the add command, the addProduct method is executed. This method prompts the user to enter a product code, description, and price. To make sure that the user enters valid data, this application uses methods of the Validator class that was presented in chapter 6. For this application, though, a new method has been added to this class. This method, named getLine, uses the nextLine method of the Scanner class to get an entire line of data. It's used to validate the description the user enters. That's necessary because the description may consist of more than one word.

After the data has been gathered from the user, the addProduct method creates a Product object and sets its values. Then, it calls the addProduct method of the productDAO object to add the product to the file. Finally, this method displays a message to confirm that the product was successfully added.

If the user enters the del or delete command, the deleteProduct method is executed. This method prompts the user to enter a product code for the product. Then, it calls the getProduct method of the productDAO object to get a Product object that contains the data for the specified product. If no product is found with the specified product code, the Product variable, p, is set to null. In that case, a message is displayed to indicate that no product with that product code was found. Otherwise, the Product object is passed to the deleteProduct method of the productDAO variable to delete the product from the file. Finally, a message is displayed that indicates that this product has been deleted from the database.

This page of code shows that the linkage between the database layer and the presentation layer is minimal. In other words, none of the methods of the ProductTextFile class are called directly from the ProductMaintApp class. Instead, the ProductMaintApp class calls methods of the ProductDAO interface, which is implemented by the ProductTextFile class. As a result, it's easy to substitute another data storage mechanism. To do that, you can code another class that implements the ProductDAO interface. Then, you can modify the single line of code in the DAOFactory class that maps the ProductDAO interface to the appropriate implementing class. For example, you could code a class named ProductMySQL that stores product data in a MySQL database. Or, you could code a class named ProductXMLFile that stores the product data in an XML file.

This approach has some advantages and disadvantages. On the upside, this approach makes it easy to switch between data storage mechanisms. On the downside, this approach requires more code in the form of interfaces, and it increases the conceptual complexity of an application. As a result, if you're certain that you won't need to provide for other data storage mechanisms, you may want to keep things simple and call methods of the classes in the database layer directly. However, if you need to provide for varying data storage mechanisms, you may want to use interfaces as shown here.

The code for the ProductMaintApp class **Page 2**

```
    public static void displayMenu()
    {
        System.out.println("COMMAND MENU");
        System.out.println("list    - List all products");
        System.out.println("add     - Add a product");
        System.out.println("del     - Delete a product");
        System.out.println("help    - Show this menu");
        System.out.println("exit    - Exit this application\n");
    }

    public static void displayAllProducts()
    {
        System.out.println("PRODUCT LIST");
        System.out.println(productDAO.getProductsString());
    }

    public static void addProduct()
    {
        String code = Validator.getString(sc, "Enter product code: ");
        String description = Validator.getLine(
            sc, "Enter product description: ");
        double price = Validator.getDouble(sc, "Enter price: ");

        Product product = new Product();
        product.setCode(code);
        product.setDescription(description);
        product.setPrice(price);
        productDAO.addProduct(product);

        System.out.println();
        System.out.println(description + " has been added.\n");
    }

    public static void deleteProduct()
    {
        String code = Validator.getString(sc,
            "Enter product code to delete: ");

        Product p = productDAO.getProduct(code);

        System.out.println();
        if (p != null)
        {
            productDAO.deleteProduct(p);
            System.out.println(p.getDescription()
                + " has been deleted.\n");
        }
        else
        {
            System.out.println("No product matches that product code.\n");
        }
    }
}
```

Figure 8-12 The ProductMaintApp class (part 2 of 2)

How to implement the Cloneable interface

Occasionally, you may need to *clone* an object. When you clone an object, you create a new instance of the object that contains all the same data as the first object. To do that, you can call the clone method of the Object class. But first, you must implement the Cloneable interface that's in the java.lang package to tell the compiler that it's safe to use this method.

A Product class that implements the Cloneable interface

Figure 8-13 shows how to code a Product class that can be cloned. First, the Product class implements the Cloneable interface. This allows the Product class to call the clone method of the Object class. However, the clone method of the Object class has protected access. As a result, this method will only be available to subclasses and classes in the same package. To give public access to this method, the Product class overrides the clone method of the Object class and gives it public access. Then, the clone method of the Product class uses the super keyword to call the clone method of the Object class. This clones the product, which is then returned to the calling method.

Because the clone method of the Object class throws a CloneNotSupportedException, you must either throw or catch this exception when you override this method. In this example, you can see that the clone method in the Product class throws this exception. You'll learn more about throwing exceptions in chapter 13.

The code that uses the clone method of the Product class shows how the clone method works. Here, the first group of statements create a Product object and fill it with data. Then, the next statement uses the clone method to make a copy of the Product object. Since the clone method returns an Object type, this method casts the Object type to a Product type. At this point, the p1 and p2 variables both refer to their own copies of a Product object. As a result, you can change the price in one Product object without also changing the price in the other Product object.

By the way, it's a common mistake to try to clone an object using code like this:

```
Product p2 = p1;
```

However, this simply assigns the reference to an object that's stored in one variable to another variable. In other words, after executing this statement, both variables will refer to the same Product object. As a result, if you change the price in one variable, the price will also be changed in the other variable.

A Product class that implements the Cloneable interface

```
public class Product implements Cloneable
{
    private String code;
    private String description;
    private double price;

    // the code for the constructor and methods

    public Object clone() throws CloneNotSupportedException
    {
        return super.clone();
    }
}
```

Code that uses the clone method of the Product class

```
// create a new product
Product p1 = new Product();
p1.setCode("java");
p1.setDescription("Murach's Beginning Java 2");
p1.setPrice(49.50);

// clone the product
Product p2 = (Product) p1.clone();

// change a value in the cloned product
p2.setPrice(44.50);

// print the results
System.out.println(p1);
System.out.println(p2);
```

The result

```
Code:        java
Description: Murach's Beginning Java 2
Price:       $49.50

Code:        java
Description: Murach's Beginning Java 2
Price:       $44.50
```

Description

- You can use the clone method of the Object class to *clone* a user-defined class only if the user-defined class implements the Cloneable interface.
- Since the clone method in the Object class has protected access, it is only available to subclasses and other classes in the same package. To make this method available to all classes, you can override the clone method of the Object class with a clone method that has public access.
- The clone method returns an Object type. As a result, you may need to cast the result of this method to another type of class.
- The clone method of the Object class throws a CloneNotSupportedException. A class that overrides this method must throw or catch this exception or it won't compile.

Figure 8-13 A Product class that implements the Cloneable interface

A LineItem class that implements the Cloneable interface

The Product class that you saw in the previous figure contains only a primitive type (double) and two *immutable* objects (String). A String object is immutable because its value can't be changed. Instead, when you assign a new value to a string variable, the original String object is deleted and it's replaced with a new String object that contains the new value. To clone an object like this, you can simply call the clone method of the Object class.

In contrast, if a class contains *mutable* objects (objects that can be changed), the clone method of the Object class may not work properly. In that case, you'll need to override this method when you implement the Cloneable interface to be sure it works. Figure 8-14 shows how this works.

At the top of this figure, you can see a LineItem class that implements the Cloneable interface. Since this class contains an instance variable of a mutable object (a Product object), you must clone both the LineItem object and the Product object. So the first statement in the clone method clones the LineItem object by calling the clone method of the Object class. Because this method returns an Object type, that object is cast to a LineItem so it can be stored in a LineItem variable. At this point, you have two LineItem objects, but they both point to the same Product object.

To clone the Product object, the second statement calls the clone method of that object. Then, the object that's returned by that method is cast to a Product object and stored in a Product variable. The third statement assigns this object to the Product instance variable. At this point, each LineItem object points to its own copy of the Product object. As a result, this clone method will work properly for a LineItem object.

The code that uses the clone method of the LineItem class shows how this works. This code starts by creating a Product object and filling it with data. Then, it creates a LineItem object, supplying the data for the line item to the constructor. Next, the clone method of the LineItem object is called to clone the line item. To illustrate that both the line item and the product it contains have been cloned, the next two statements change the quantity of the second line item and the price of the product stored in that line item. Then, the last two statements print both LineItem objects to the console so you can see that the changes were applied only to the second line item and product.

A LineItem class that implements the Cloneable interface

```
public class LineItem implements Cloneable
{
    private Product product;
    private int quantity;
    private double total;

    // the code for the constructors and methods

    public Object clone() throws CloneNotSupportedException
    {
        LineItem li = (LineItem) super.clone();
        Product p = (Product) product.clone();
        li.setProduct(p);
        return li;
    }
}
```

Code that uses the clone method of the LineItem class

```
Product p1 = new Product();
p1.setCode("java");
p1.setDescription("Murach's Beginning Java 2");
p1.setPrice(49.50);

LineItem li1 = new LineItem(p1, 3);

// clone the line item
LineItem li2 = (LineItem) li1.clone();

// change values in the cloned LineItem and its Product object
li2.setQuantity(2);
li2.getProduct().setPrice(44.50);

// print the results
System.out.println(li1);
System.out.println(li2);
```

The result

```
Code: java
Description: Murach's Beginning Java 2
Price: $49.50
Quantity: 3
Total: $148.50

Code: java
Description: Murach's Beginning Java 2
Price: $44.50
Quantity: 2
Total: $89.00
```

Description

- To clone an object that contains an instance variable for a *mutable object*, you need to override the clone method and manually clone that object.

Perspective

In this chapter, you've learned how to use interfaces and how they can be used to improve the design of an application. That means that you should now be able to implement all types of classes that are commonly used in business applications. In the next chapter, though, you'll learn some additional object-oriented skills that will round out your knowledge of object-oriented programming.

Summary

- An *interface* is a special type of coding element that can contain static constants and abstract methods. Although a class can only inherit one other class, it can *implement* more than one interface.
- To implement an interface, a class must implement all the abstract methods defined by the interface. An interface can also inherit other interfaces, in which case the implementing class must also implement all the methods of the inherited interfaces.
- An interface defines a Java type. Because of that, you can use an object that's created from a class that implements an interface anywhere that interface is expected.
- When you *clone* an object, you make an identical copy of the object.
- Before you can use the clone method of the Object class, you need to implement the Cloneable interface. Then, you can override the clone method so it is public and so it works correctly with *mutable* objects.

Exercise 8-1 Create and work with interfaces

In this exercise, you'll create and implement the DepartmentConstants interface presented in this chapter. You'll also create and implement an interface named Displayable that's similar to the Printable interface.

Create the interfaces

1. Open the classes in the c:\java1.5\ch08\DisplayableTest directory.
2. Add an interface named DepartmentConstants that contains the three constants shown in figure 8-4. Compile the interface.
3. Add an interface named Displayable. This interface should contain a single method named getDisplayText that returns a String. Compile this interface.

Implement the interfaces

4. Edit the Product class so it implements the Displayable interface. The getDisplayText method in this class should format a string that can be used to display the product information. When you're done, compile this class.

5. Edit the Employee class so it implements the DepartmentConstants and Displayable interfaces. The getDisplayText method in this class should work like the one in the Product class, and it should use the constants in the DepartmentConstants interface to include the department name in the return value. When you're done, compile this class.

Use the classes that implement the interfaces

6. Display the DisplayableTestApp class.
7. Add code to this class that creates an Employee object, assigns it to a Displayable variable, and displays the information in the Employee object at the console. To get the information for an employee, you'll need to use the getDisplayText method of the Displayable interface.
8. Compile and run the application to make sure that it displays the employee information.
9. Repeat steps 7 and 8 for a Product object.

Exercise 8-2 Use an interface as a parameter

In this exercise, you'll use the Displayable interface you created and implemented in exercise 8-1 as a method parameter.

1. Open the classes in the c:\java 1.5\ch08\DisplayableTest directory and display the DisplayableTestApp class.
2. Add a method named displayMultiple that accepts a Displayable object and an integer and returns a string. The string returned by this method should contain the number of occurrences specified by the int parameter of the object specified by the Displayable parameter.
3. Modify the code in the main method so that it uses the displayMultiple method to display one occurrence of the employee information and two occurrences of the product information.
4. Compile and run the application to make sure it works correctly.

Exercise 8-3 Add an update function to the Product Maintenance application

In this exercise, you'll review the Product Maintenance application presented in this chapter. Then, you'll add an update function to this application.

Review and run the application

1. Open the files in the c:\java1.5\ch08\ProductMaintenance directory.
2. Review the code in each file to see how it works.
3. Run the application and try each of its functions. When you're comfortable with how it works, exit from the application.

Modify the application so it includes an update function

4. Add code to the ProductMaintApp class that lets the user update an existing product. To do that, you'll need to add an update command to the list of commands, and you'll need to add an updateProduct method that's executed if the user enters this command.
5. The updateProduct method should start by getting a valid product code from the user. Then, it should let the user update either the product's description or price. After the description or price of the Product object is updated, the updateProduct method should call the updateProduct method of the ProductDAO object to update the product.
6. Compile and run the ProductMaintApp class to make sure it works correctly.

Exercise 8-4 Implement the Cloneable interface

In this exercise, you'll implement the Cloneable interface for the Product and LineItem classes.

1. Open the classes in the c:\java1.5\ch08\CloneableTest directory. Display the ProductCloneApp class and review its code. Then, try to compile this class. The compilation will fail because the Cloneable interface hasn't been implemented in the Product class.
2. Implement the Cloneable interface for the Product class. Then, compile the Product and ProductCloneApp classes. If you implemented the Cloneable interface correctly, the ProductCloneApp class should compile.
3. Run the ProductCloneApp class to make sure it works correctly.
4. Repeat steps 1 through 3 for the LineItemCloneApp and LineItem classes.

9

Other object-oriented programming skills

In this chapter, you'll learn some other skills that are related to object-oriented programming. In particular, you'll learn how to create and use your own packages, how to document the classes in a package, when and how to combine two or more classes in one .java file, and how to create and use your own enumerations. When you finish this chapter, you should have all of the essential skills that you need for working with classes and enumerations in the real world.

How to work with packages

To make it easy for you to find and access classes, the Java API organizes its classes into packages. This allows you to import just the classes and packages that an application needs. Now, you'll learn how to organize your own classes into packages. You might want to do that to help keep track of the classes in an application that consists of a large number of classes. You might also want to do that to make it easy to reuse the classes in other applications or to distribute them to other developers.

How to store classes in a package

Before you store your classes in packages, you must create a directory structure for the packages. Then, you must store each class in the appropriate directory. This is illustrated in figure 9-1. Here, lineItem is the root directory for the Line Item application. This directory contains the .java file for the application along with the subdirectories for each package. Then, each subdirectory contains the classes for a package.

Although the packages in this example are stored in an application directory, that doesn't have to be the case. In particular, if you're creating packages that will be reused by other applications or developers, you may want to store them in a central location. For example, you might store them in the main java directory or in another directory you create specifically for packages.

When you create the directory structure for a package, keep in mind that each directory must correspond to the name you want to use for the package. For example, because the Product class is stored in the murach\business directory, the name of the package that contains it will be murach.business. Also keep in mind that packages can consist of more than two levels of subdirectories. However, two or three levels should be sufficient for most of the packages you develop.

When you name a package, you can use any name you wish. However, Sun recommends that you use your Internet domain name in reverse as a prefix. For example, since our Internet domain name is murach.com, all packages created by our company would begin with com.murach. Since each Internet domain name is unique, this ensures that your package names will be unique.

Even if you don't follow this convention, you should avoid using a generic name that might be used by someone else. For example, a package name of business is too generic, but murach.business is specific enough that it's unlikely to conflict with any other packages. In this book, we prefix all packages with the name murach.

Once you put a class in the correct directory, you code a package statement to identify the package that will contain it. This statement consists of the package keyword followed by the name of the package. In this figure, for example, you can see the package statements for the LineItem, Product, Validator, and ProductDB classes. Although you can code comments before this statement, the package statement must be the first statement in the file.

The directory structure for an application that uses packages

```
lineItem
    LineItemApp.java
    murach
        business
            Product.java
            LineItem.java
        database
            ProductDB.java
        presentation
            Validator.java
```

The LineItem class

```
package murach.business;

import java.text.NumberFormat;
import murach.business.Product;

public class LineItem{...}
```

The Product class

```
package murach.business;

import java.text.NumberFormat;

public class Product{...}
```

The ProductDB class

```
package murach.database;

import murach.business.Product;

public class ProductDB{...}
```

The Validator class

```
package murach.presentation;

import java.util.Scanner;

public class Validator{...}
```

Description

- The classes in a package should be saved in a subdirectory with a path that matches the name of the package. The package name should be unique so you don't have conflicts with other packages.
- To include a class in a package, code a package statement as the first statement in the file that defines the class. Then, include an import statement in any file that uses the package.
- You can use packages to organize the classes that make up an application. In that case, you should store the subdirectories that make up the package beneath the directory for the application as shown above.
- You can also use packages to make it easy to reuse a set of classes. In that case, you should store the subdirectories that make up the package in a central location, such as in the java directory.

Figure 9-1 How to store classes in a package

In addition to the package statements, import statements have also been added to the LineItem and ProductDB classes. That's necessary because once you store a class in a package, it can no longer be accessed directly by other classes. Instead, it must be imported into the class that uses it just like the classes of the Java API. In this case, both the LineItem and ProductDB classes use the Product class, so these classes must include import statements for this class.

How to compile the classes in a package

Some Java tools aren't able to compile classes that have been organized into packages. For example, once you store the LineItem and Product classes in the murach.business package, you can't use TextPad to compile the LineItem class because it depends on the Product class. Similarly, you can't use TextPad to compile the ProductDB class because it too depends on the Product class.

To compile classes like these, you can use the command prompt as shown in figure 9-2. To start, make sure that the class is saved in the correct directory, that the package statement it contains corresponds to that directory, and that it contains any necessary import statements. Then, open a command window and navigate to the directory that contains the package (the parent directory). If you're creating a package that consists of the classes used by a single application, that directory is probably the root directory for the application. In this figure, for example, the directory is java\lineItem.

After you change the directory, you issue the javac command followed by the path for the package and the name of the .java file you want to compile. When you specify the path, you can use either front or back slashes to separate the directories and the name of the .java file if you're using DOS. If you're using Linux, however, you must use front slashes. We use front slashes in our examples so that they will run under either DOS or Linux.

When you use the javac command to compile your source code, all related classes in the specified directory are compiled. For example, if you compile LineItem.java, Product.java will also be compiled because the Product class is used by the LineItem class. Although this works fine when you're compiling packages, you shouldn't depend on this feature as you're developing the classes. Instead, you should compile each class independently as you create it to make sure that it doesn't contain syntax errors.

How to compile the classes in a user-defined package

1. Make sure that the classes have all of the appropriate package and import statements as shown in the previous figure.
2. Start the command prompt and navigate to the directory that contains the package (the parent directory).
3. Use the javac command to compile the classes as shown below. To do this, you must include the subdirectories that correspond to the package name.

Syntax

```
c:\parentDir>javac packagePath/ClassName.java
```

Example

```
C:\java\lineItem>javac murach/business/LineItem.java
```

Description

- If you compile a class that uses another class in the same directory, both classes are compiled.
- Before you compile a class that imports another class in the package, you must compile the class it imports.
- Some Java tools, such as TextPad, can't compile a class that's in a package that depends on one or more classes in the same or in other user-defined packages. In that case, you need to use the javac command to compile the class.
- If you're using DOS, you can use either front slashes or back slashes to separate the names of the directories in the package and the name of the class file. If you're using Linux, however, you must use front slashes.

Figure 9-2 How to compile the classes in a package

How to make the classes of a package available to other classes

When you compile a class that contains a package statement, the class becomes part of a package and classes outside the package can't access it. To make a class within a package available to other classes, then, you can use one of the two techniques presented in figure 9-3. The technique you choose depends on whether you want to provide access to the classes in a single application or to the classes in any application.

If you want make a package available to a single application, you can just copy the directories and files of the package into the application's root directory. For example, suppose you're starting a new application named Invoice in the c:\java\invoice directory, and you want to use the classes in the murach.business package. To do that, you can just copy the murach\business directory into the c:\java\invoice directory.

If you want to make a package available to any application, you start by creating a *Java Archive (JAR) file* that contains the files for the package. To do that, you can use a command window to issue a jar command as shown in the first example in this figure. If this command is successful, the command window will display a list of the directories and files that have been added to the JAR file. Then, you must move the JAR file to the SDK's \jre\lib\ext subdirectory. This is the directory that the compiler looks in for extensions to the API libraries.

If you're going to be distributing a package commercially, you might not want to include the source code (.java files) for the package. In that case, you can remove the .java files from the package before you create the JAR file. Or, if you only want to distribute a single package, you can use a jar command like the one in the second example. This command specifies that only .class files should be included in the JAR file.

Regardless of how you choose to make packages available, you still need to code the necessary import statements for the classes that use these packages. For example, to use a class in the murach.business package, you must code an import statement like the first one shown in this figure. Or, if you prefer, you can code individual import statements for each class that you want to use.

How to make a package available to the classes in a single application

- Copy the directories and files of the package to the root directory of the application. For example, copy the murach directory and all of its subdirectories and files into the root directory for the application.

How to make a package available to the classes in any application

- Create a JAR file for the subdirectories and files of the package as shown below and then move that JAR file to the SDK's \jre\lib\ext directory.

Syntax for creating a JAR file for a package

```
c:\parentDir>jar cvf JARFilename.jar packagePath/*[.class]
```

Example 1: A statement that creates a JAR file for the murach packages

```
C:\java\lineItem>jar cvf murach.jar murach/*
```

Result

```
added manifest
adding: murach/business/(in = 0) (out= 0)(stored 0%)
adding: murach/business/LineItem.class(in = 1226) (out= 643)(deflated 47%)
adding: murach/business/LineItem.java(in = 1078) (out= 346)(deflated 67%)
adding: murach/business/Product.class(in = 1084) (out= 549)(deflated 49%)
adding: murach/business/Product.java(in = 940) (out= 308)(deflated 67%)
adding: murach/database/(in = 0) (out= 0)(stored 0%)
adding: murach/database/ProductDB.class(in = 829) (out= 541)(deflated 34%)
adding: murach/database/ProductDB.java(in = 1175) (out= 413)(deflated 64%)
adding: murach/presentation/(in = 0) (out= 0)(stored 0%)
adding: murach/presentation/Validator.class(in = 2057) (out= 1072)(deflated 47%)
adding: murach/presentation/Validator.java(in = 2357) (out= 571)(deflated 75%)
```

The statements for importing the classes in the packages

```
import murach.business.*;
import murach.database.*;
import murach.presentation.*;
```

Example 2: A statement that excludes the source files from a JAR file

```
C:\java\lineItem>jar cvf murach.business.jar murach/business/*.class
```

Description

- When you compile a class that contains a package statement, the class becomes part of the package and classes outside the package can't access it.
- Once you make a package available to an application, you can code import statements within the classes of the application to import the necessary classes of the package.
- If you don't want to include the source files for a package in a JAR file, you can include the .class extension in the file specification on the jar command. Then, only the class files will be included.

Figure 9-3 How to make the classes of a package available to other classes

How to use javadoc to document a package

If you develop classes that you intend to distribute to other programmers, you'll typically organize those classes into one or more packages as shown in the previous topics. In addition, you'll want to provide some documentation for your classes so other programmers can easily learn about the fields, constructors, and methods that are available to other classes. Fortunately, the SDK includes a utility named javadoc that makes it easy to generate HTML-based documentation for your classes. This documentation looks and works like the documentation for the Java API. In fact, the documentation for the Java API was generated using the javadoc utility.

How to add javadoc comments to a class

Figure 9-4 shows how to add simple *javadoc comments* to a class. A javadoc comment begins with /** and ends with */. Within a javadoc comment, any additional asterisks are ignored. Because of that, asterisks are commonly used as shown here to set the comments off from the rest of the code. For these comments to work, though, they must be coded directly above the class, field, constructor, or method that they describe.

The Product class with javadoc comments

```
package murach.business;

import java.text.NumberFormat;

/*************************************************************
 * The Product class represents a product and is used by
 * the LineItem and ProductDB classes.
 *************************************************************/
public class Product
{
    private String code;
    private String description;
    private double price;

    /*************************************************************
     * Creates a new Product with default values.
     *************************************************************/
    public Product()
    {
        code = "";
        description = "";
        price = 0;
    }

    /*************************************************************
     * Sets the product code to the specified String.
     *************************************************************/
    public void setCode(String code)
    {
        this.code = code;
    }

    /*************************************************************
     * Returns a String that represents the product code.
     *************************************************************/
    public String getCode(){
        return code;
    }
    .
    .
    .
```

Description

- A *javadoc comment* begins with /** and ends with */, and asterisks within the comment are ignored. You can use javadoc comments to describe a class and the public and protected fields, constructors, and methods it contains.
- A comment should be placed immediately above the class or member it describes. For a class, that means that the comment must be placed after any import statements.

How to use HTML and javadoc tags in javadoc comments

To help format the information that's displayed in the documentation for a class, you can include HTML and javadoc tags in your javadoc comments as shown in figure 9-5. Here, you can see that the *HTML tag* you're most likely to use is the Code tag. This tag can be used to display text in a monospaced font. In the Product class in this figure, for example, this tag is used to format the name of each class that's referred to in the class comment, and it's used to format the name of any object that's referred to in the other comments. Although it's not shown here, this tag is also commonly used to format references to primitive types.

The four *javadoc tags* shown here should be self-explanatory. You typically use the @author and @version tags in the class comment to document the author and current version of the class. Note that by default, this information isn't displayed in the documentation that's generated. Although you can specify that you want to include this information when you generate the documentation, that's usually not necessary.

You use the @param tag to describe a parameter that's accepted by a constructor or public method. In this figure, for example, you can see that a @param tag is used to document the code parameter used by the setCode method. Similarly, if a method returns a value, you can use the @return tag to describe that value. In this figure, the @return tag is used to document the String that's returned by the getCode method.

In addition to the tags shown here, you should realize that additional HTML and javadoc tags are available. For example, you can use the HTML I tag to italicize text, and you can use the B tag to boldface text. To create a hyperlink, you can use the javadoc @see tag. For more information on this tag and other javadoc tags, see the online documentation for the javadoc utility.

Common HTML tag used to format javadoc comments

HTML tag	Description
`<code></code>`	Displays the text between these tags with a monospaced font.

Common javadoc tags

Javadoc tag	Description
@author	Identifies the author of the class. Not displayed by default.
@version	Describes the current version of the class. Not displayed by default.
@param	Describes a parameter of a constructor or method.
@return	Describes the value that's returned by a method.

The Product class with comments that use HTML and javadoc tags

```
package murach.business;
import java.text.NumberFormat;
/*************************************************************
 * The <code>Product</code> class represents a product and is used
 * by the <code>LineItem</code> and <code>ProductDB</code> classes.
 * @author Joel Murach
 * @version 1.0.0
 *************************************************************/
public class Product{
    private String code;
    private String description;
    private double price;
    /*************************************************************
     * Creates a <code>Product</code> with default values.
     *************************************************************/
    public Product(){
        code = "";
        description = "";
        price = 0;
    }
    /*************************************************************
     * Sets the product code to the specified <code>String</code>.
     * @param code A <code>String</code> for the product code.
     *************************************************************/
    public void setCode(String code){
        this.code = code;
    }
    /*************************************************************
     * Returns a <code>String</code> that represents the product code.
     * @return A <code>String</code> for the product code.
     *************************************************************/
    public String getCode(){
        return code;
    }
    ...
```

Description

- Within a javadoc comment, you can code *HTML tags* to format the text that's displayed.
- You can also include *javadoc tags* to include special entries in the documentation.

Figure 9-5 How to use HTML and javadoc tags in javadoc comments

How to generate the documentation for a package

Figure 9-6 shows how to use the javadoc utility to generate the documentation for a package. To do that, you issue a javadoc command like the ones shown here. When you do, javadoc will create the docs directory you specify if it doesn't already exist. Then, it will generate the HTML pages for the documentation and store them in this directory.

The first example in this figure shows how you generate documentation for the classes in a single package. To do that, you just code the name of the package. The statement shown here, for example, generates documentation for the classes in the murach.business package.

Although you can generate documentation for a single package, it's more likely that you'll generate documentation for all related packages at once. To do that, you just list all of the packages as shown in the second example. The advantage of doing that is that you can access the documentation for any of the packages from a single page. In contrast, if you generate the documentation for each class separately, you have to access it separately.

Of course, you can also generate documentation for a single class. To do that, you just include the class path and name on the javadoc command. Since you're most likely to document classes that are stored in packages, however, you may never need to generate documentation for a single class.

How to view the documentation for a package

You can use a web browser to view the documentation for user-defined classes the same way that you view the documentation for the Java API. The main difference is that the index.html file for user-defined classes is stored in the directory you specify on the javadoc command. In this figure, for example, it's stored in the c:\java\lineItem\docs directory.

In the documentation in this figure, you can see that the three murach packages are listed in the upper left frame. Then, when I selected the murach.business package, the two classes in that package were listed in the lower left frame. Finally, when I selected the Product class, the documentation for that class was displayed in the right frame.

The documentation for the Product class indicates that the Product class is in the murach.business package. It also includes a brief description of the Product class, which was generated from the javadoc comment for the class. Next, it provides a summary of the constructors and methods of the class that are available to other classes, along with the descriptions I provided. If this class contained public or protected fields, the documentation would also include a summary of those fields. Finally, the documentation includes details of all the fields, constructors, and methods in the summaries. This is where you'll see any information provided with @param and @return tags. Note that the documentation doesn't expose the code that is encapsulated within the class. As a result, the documentation makes it easy for other programmers to use your classes without knowing the details of how they're implemented.

The syntax for generating documentation for one or more packages

```
C:\parentDir>javadoc -d docsDirectory packageName1 [packageName2]...
```

Example 1: A statement that generates documentation for a single package

```
C:\java\lineItem>javadoc -d c:\java\lineItem\docs\business murach.business
```

Example 2: A statement that generates documentation for three packages

```
C:\java\lineItem>javadoc -d c:\java\lineItem\docs murach.business
murach.database murach.presentation
```

The documentation that's generated by the second statement above

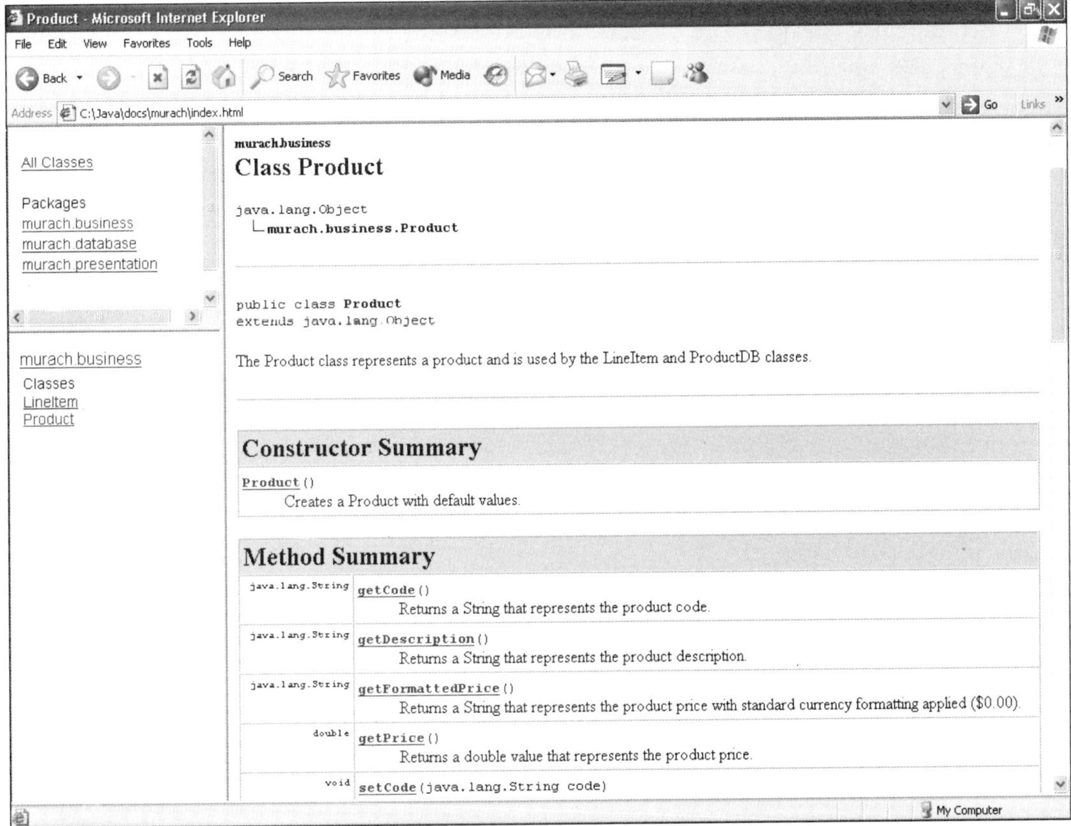

Description

- The javadoc tool lets you generate HTML-based documentation like the documentation for the Java API. You can use this tool to generate documentation for one or more packages. You can also use to it generate documentation for a single class.
- You can view the documentation that's generated by the javadoc command by starting a web browser and pointing to the index.html file that's created in the directory you specify.

Figure 9-6 How to generate and view the documentation for a package

How to code classes that are closely related

So far, all of the applications in this book have declared one class per file. Most of the time, that's how you want to code you classes. However, there are some coding situations in which two classes are so closely related that it makes sense to store them in the same file.

How to code more than one class per file

Figure 9-7 shows how to code more than one class per file. Here, the LineItem class is declared as the public class so it must be stored in a file named LineItem.java. However, the Product class is also stored in this file. To store this class in the LineItem.java file, it can't be declared with public access.

The advantage of coding classes in the same file is that you have fewer files to manage. Then, when you compile the code stored in the file, the compiler will generate the class files for all of the classes it contains. When you compile the LineItem file shown in this figure, for example, the compiler will generate the class files for both the LineItem and Product classes.

The disadvantage of coding classes in the same file is that it makes it more difficult to find the source code for the classes that aren't public. To modify the Product class, for example, you need to know that it's stored in the LineItem file. Because you can easily lose track of your classes when you use this technique, it usually makes sense to store the code for each class in a separate file. However, if two classes are so closely related that they don't make sense without each other, you may want to code them in the same file.

Two classes declared within the same file

```
import java.text.NumberFormat;

public class LineItem
{
    private Product product;
    private int quantity;
    private double total;
    .
    .
    .
}

class Product
{
    // body of Product class
}
```

The class files that are generated when the code above is compiled

```
LineItem.class
Product.class
```

Description

- When you code two or more classes in the same file, you can only have one public class in the file, and that class should be declared first.

Figure 9-7 How to code more than one class per file

An introduction to nested classes

You can code *nested classes* whenever you need to code a class that only makes sense within the context of another class. Most of the time, you won't need to use nested classes. Later in this book, however, you'll see how nested classes can be used when you develop graphical user interfaces.

Figure 9-8 shows the syntax and principles for coding nested classes. After you code the *outer class*, you can code *inner classes* and *static inner classes*. Since these types of classes are members of the outer class, they're sometimes called *member classes*.

The outer class in the first example in this figure works the same as the rest of the classes that you've been working with throughout this book. It must be declared public, and it must be stored in a file that has the same name as the class. Then, it can contain instance variables, static variables, constructors, methods, and static methods.

The first nested class shows the types of data that you can use in an inner class. Since an inner class has direct access to all private variables and methods of the outer class, you may want to use an inner class for some closely related classes. However, an inner class can't contain any static variables or methods.

The second nested class shows the types of data that you can use in a static inner class. Unlike regular inner classes, static inner classes are independent of the outer class. In fact, you can create an instance of the static inner class without referring to the outer class. As a result, static inner classes can't access any of the instance variables or methods of the outer class. However, they can access the static variables and methods of the outer class.

The second example in this figure shows how you can nest a class within a method. In this case, the class is known as a *local class* because it can only be called from within the method. In chapter 14, you will see a typical example of a local class.

If you compile the code for these examples, the compiler will generate the classes shown in this figure. Here, a dollar sign ($) separates the outer class and the inner class. This clearly shows that the inner classes are nested within the outer class.

Example 1: Two classes nested within another class

```
public class OuterClassName
{
    // can contain instance variables and methods
    // can contain static variables and methods

    class InnerClassName
    {
        // can contain instance variables and methods
        // can't contain static variables or methods
        // can access all variables and methods of OuterClass
    }

    static class StaticInnerClassName
    {
        // can contain instance variables and methods
        // can contain static variables and methods
        // can access static data from OuterClass
        // can't access instance variables or methods from OuterClass
    }
}
```

The class files generated for this class

```
OuterClassName.class
OuterClassName$InnerClassName.class
OuterClassName$StaticInnerClassName.class
```

Example 2: A class nested within a method

```
public class ClassName
{
    // code for the outer class

    public void methodName()
    {
        class InnerClassName
        {
            // code for the inner class
        }

        // code for the method
    }
}
```

The class files generated for this class

```
ClassName.class
ClassName$InnerClassName.class
```

Description

- Java has provided support for *nested classes* since version 1.1.
- When you nest classes, the *outer class* must be declared public and must have the same name as the file name of the class.
- Within an outer class, you can nest *inner classes* and *static inner classes*. Since the inner classes are members of the outer class, they are sometimes called *member classes*.
- A class can also be nested inside a method or any other type of block. These types of classes are sometimes called *local classes*.

Figure 9-8 An introduction to nested classes

How to work with enumerations

An *enumeration* is a set of related constants that define a type. Enumerations were introduced with Java 5.0. In chapter 3, you learned how to use the RoundingMode enumeration of the Java API to set the rounding mode for a BigDecimal object. Now, you'll learn how to create and use your own enumerations.

How to declare an enumeration

Figure 9-9 shows how to declare an enumeration. To do that, you code the public keyword, followed by the enum keyword, followed by the name of the enumeration. Then, within the enumeration, you code the names of one or more constants, separating each name with a comma.

Internally, each constant within the enumeration is assigned an integer value beginning with zero. For instance, in the ShippingType enumeration shown in the first example in this figure, the UPS_NEXT_DAY constant will have a value of zero, the UPS_SECOND_DAY constant will have a value of one, and so on. In most cases, though, you won't use these integer values.

When coding your own enumerations, it's common to store them in a separate file. That way, the enumeration will be available to all classes within the current package. However, you can also store your enumerations in the same file as a related class, and you can nest enumerations within a class. This works just like it does for classes.

How to use an enumeration

The next three examples in figure 9-9 show how you can use an enumeration. The second example shows that you can declare a variable as an enumeration type. Then, you can assign a constant in that enumeration to the variable. In this case, the UPS_SECOND_DAY constant is assigned to a ShippingType variable named secondDay.

The third example shows a getShippingAmount method that accepts a ShippingType enumeration as a parameter. Then, the code within the method compares the constant that's passed to the method with two of the constants in the enumeration to determine the shipping amount. The resulting double value is then passed back to the calling statement.

The fourth example shows a statement that calls the getShippingAmount method. This statement passes the UPS_SECOND_DAY constant of the ShippingType enumeration to the getShippingAmount method. Because of that, the method returns a double value of 5.99.

The statement that's commented out in the fourth example illustrates that you can't use an integer, or any other type, in place of an enumeration even though the constants in the enumeration are assigned integer values. In other words, enumerations are *type-safe*. This is in contrast to constants that are stored in classes or interfaces. This is one of several reasons that enumerations are generally preferred to constants.

The syntax for declaring an enumeration

```
public enum EnumerationName
{
    CONSTANT_NAME1[,
    CONSTANT_NAME2]...
}
```

Example 1: An enumeration that defines three shipping types

```
public enum ShippingType
{
    UPS_NEXT_DAY,
    UPS_SECOND_DAY,
    UPS_GROUND
}
```

Example 2: A statement that uses the enumeration and one of its constants

```
ShippingType secondDay = ShippingType.UPS_SECOND_DAY;
```

Example 3: A method that uses the enumeration as a parameter type

```
public static double getShippingAmount(ShippingType st)
{
    double shippingAmount = 2.99;
    if (st == ShippingType.UPS_NEXT_DAY)
        shippingAmount = 10.99;
    else if (st == ShippingType.UPS_SECOND_DAY)
        shippingAmount = 5.99;
    return shippingAmount;
}
```

Example 4: A statement that calls the method

```
double shippingAmount = getShippingAmount(ShippingType.UPS_SECOND_DAY);
// double shippingAmount2 = getShippingAmount(1); // Wrong type, not allowed
```

Description

- An *enumeration* contains a set of related constants. The constants are defined with the int type and are assigned values from 0 to the number of constants in the enumeration minus 1.
- An enumeration defines a type. Because of that, you can't specify another type where an enumeration type is expected. That means that enumerations are *type-safe*.

Figure 9-9 How to declare and work with enumerations

How to enhance an enumeration

Most of the time, the skills presented in figure 9-9 are the only ones you'll need for working with enumerations. You should know, however, that you can override methods that an enumeration inherits from the java.lang.Object and java.lang.Enum classes. You can also add your own methods. When you do that, you may want to use methods of the enumeration constants. Two of those methods are shown at the top of figure 9-10.

This figure also shows an enhanced version of the ShippingType enumeration. This enumeration includes a toString method that overrides the toString method of the Enum class. Without this method, the toString method of the Enum class would return the name of the constant.

Notice in this example that a semicolon is coded following the constants of the enumeration. That lets the compiler know that there are no more constants. Then, the toString method uses a series of if/else statements to return an appropriate string for each constant in the enumeration. To do that, it begins by using the ordinal method to return an int value for the constant. Then, it compares that value to integer values and returns a string that's appropriate for the current constant.

How to work with static imports

In addition to enumerations, Java 5.0 introduced a new feature known as *static imports*. This feature lets you simplify references to the constants in an enumeration. Figure 9-10 shows how.

To use the static import feature, you begin by coding a static import statement. This statement is similar to a regular import statement, but you code the static keyword after the import keyword, and you typically use the wildcard character (*) to import all of the constants of an enumeration. In this figure, for example, the static import statement specifies that all of the constants in the ShippingType enumeration in the murach.business package should be imported. (This assumes that the ShippingType enumeration has been stored in the murach.business package as described earlier in this chapter.)

Once you code a static import statement, you no longer need to code the name of the enumeration that contains the constants. For example, after you import the ShippingType enumeration, you no longer need to code the ShippingType qualifier when you refer to a constant in this enumeration. In this figure, for example, you can see a statement that refers to the UPS_GROUND constant of this enumeration.

In addition to using static imports to import enumerations, you can use them to import the static fields and methods of a class. For example, you could use a static import to import all the static fields and methods of the java.lang.Math class. Then, you could refer to those fields and methods without qualification.

Although you can save some typing by using static imports, they often result in code that's more difficult to read. That's because it may not be obvious where the constants, fields, and methods an application refers to are stored. As a result, you should use static imports only when they don't cause confusion.

Two methods of an enumeration constant

Method	Description
`name()`	Returns a String for the enumeration constant's name.
`ordinal()`	Returns an int value that corresponds to the enumeration constant's position.

How to add a method to an enumeration

An enumeration that overrides the toString method

```
public enum ShippingType
{
    UPS_NEXT_DAY,
    UPS_SECOND_DAY,
    UPS_GROUND;

    public String toString()
    {
        String s = "";
        if (this.ordinal() == 0)
            s = "UPS Next Day (1 business day)";
        else if (this.ordinal() == 1)
            s = "UPS Second Day (2 business days)";
        else if (this.ordinal() == 2)
            s = "UPS Ground (5 to 7 business days)";
        return s;
    }
}
```

Code that uses the toString method

```
ShippingType ground = ShippingType.UPS_GROUND;
System.out.println("toString: " + ground.toString() + "\n");
```

Resulting output

```
toString: UPS Second Day (2 business days)
```

How to work with static imports

How to code a static import statement

```
import static murach.business.ShippingType.*;
```

The code above when a static import is used

```
ShippingType ground = UPS_GROUND;
System.out.println("toString: " + ground.toString() + "\n");
```

Description

- All enumerations inherit the java.lang.Object and java.lang.Enum classes and can use or override the methods of those classes or add new methods.
- By default, the toString method of an enumeration constant returns the same string as the name method.
- You can use a *static import* to import all of the constants of an enumeration or all of the static fields and methods of a class. Then, you don't need to qualify the constant, field, or method with the name of the enumeration or class.

Figure 9-10 How to enhance an enumeration and work with static imports

Perspective

Now that you've finished this chapter, you should be able to package and document your classes so other programmers can use them. You should also be able to apply the appropriate technique for coding classes that are closely related, and you should be able to create and work with enumerations. With these skills, you'll be able to implement the classes, interfaces, and enumerations that are commonly used in business applications.

Summary

- You can organize the classes in your application by using a package statement to add them to a *package*. Then, you can use import statements to make the classes in that package available to other classes.
- You can use *javadoc comments* to document a class and its fields, constructors, and methods. Then, you can use the javadoc command to generate HTML-based documentation for your class.
- When two or more classes are closely related, it sometimes makes sense to store them all in one file or to *nest* them.
- You can use an *enumeration* to define a set of related constants as a type. Then, you can use the constants in the enumeration anywhere the enumeration is allowed.
- You can use *static imports* to import the constants of an enumeration or the static fields and methods of a class. Then, you can refer to the constants, fields, and methods without qualification.

Exercise 9-1 Package the classes in an application

This exercise guides you through the process of organizing the Product, LineItem, ProductDB, and Validator classes into packages. Then, it shows you how to modify the LineItemApp class so it uses those packages.

1. Copy the java files for the LineItemApp, LineItem, Product, ProductDB, and Validator classes from the c:\java1.5\ch06\LineItem directory to the c:\java1.5\ch09\LineItem directory.
2. Create subdirectories named murach\business, murach\database, and murach\presentation. Then, move the LineItem, Product, ProductDB, and Validator files into their appropriate subdirectories as shown in figure 9-1.
3. Add package and import statements to the Product, LineItem, ProductDB, and Validator classes as shown in figure 9-1.
4. Use the command prompt to compile these classes as shown in figure 9-2. Be sure to compile the Product class before you compile the ProductDB class. When you compile the LineItem class, it should compile both the Product and LineItem classes.

5. Open the LineItemApp class that's stored in the c:\java1.5\ch09\LineItem directory, and add import statements to import the three packages you just created. Then, compile and run this class to make sure the application is working correctly. When you're sure it is, close the class.
6. Open the LineItemApp class that's stored in the c:\java1.5\ch09\LineItemTester directory, and try to compile this class. You should get several compile-time errors. That's because the LineItemApp class can't find the three packages even though it includes the proper import statements.
7. Use a command window to create a JAR file named murach.jar that contains all three packages as shown in figure 9-3. Then, move the murach.jar file to the \jre\lib\ext subdirectory of your SDK directory.
8. Try to compile the LineItemApp class that's stored in the LineItemTester directory again. This time, it should compile. Then, run this class to make sure it works correctly.

Exercise 9-2 Document the murach packages

This exercise guides you through the process of adding javadoc comments to the Product and LineItem classes and using the javadoc tool to generate the API documentation for all the murach packages.

1. Open the Product and LineItem classes that are stored in the c:\java1.5\ch09\LineItem\murach\business directory.
2. Add javadoc comments like the ones shown in figure 9-4 for the LineItem class and its constructors and methods. Then, compile the class.
3. Add javadoc comments like the ones shown in figure 9-5 for the Product class and its constructor and methods. Then, compile the class.
4. Open a command window and use the javadoc command to generate the documentation for the murach.business, murach.database, and murach.presentation classes as shown in figure 9-6. When you're done, this documentation should be stored in the c:\java1.5\ch09\LineItem\docs directory.
5. Start your web browser, navigate to the c:\java1.5\ch09\LineItem\docs directory, and open the index.html page.
6. Click on the Validator class in the lower left frame to see the documentation that's generated for a class by default.
7. Click on the murach.business package to display just the LineItem and Product classes in the lower left frame. Then, click on the LineItem class to display its documentation. Notice that the details for the methods don't include a description of the parameters or return values.
8. Click on the Product class to display its documentation. Scroll to the method details to see how the descriptions of the parameters and return values are displayed.
9. When you're done experimenting, close your web browser.

Exercise 9-3 Code more than one file per class

In this exercise, you'll combine the code for two classes into a single file.

1. Open the code for the Customer and Address classes that are stored in the c:\java1.5\ch09\Classes directory. Cut the code from the Address class and paste it at the end of the Customer class. Delete the public modifier from the declaration of the Customer class, and save the file.
2. Delete the Address.java file. At this point, the c:\java1.5\ch09\Classes directory should only contain the Customer.java file and no .class files.
3. Compile the Customer class. Then, view the files in the c:\java1.5\ch09\Classes directory. Now, there should be .class files for both the Customer and Address classes. This shows that the Customer.java file now stores two classes.

Exercise 9-4 Create and use an enumeration

In this exercise, you'll create an enumeration and then use it in a test application.

1. Create an enumeration named CustomerType, and save it in the c:\java1.5\ch09\Enumeration directory. This enumeration should contain constants that represent three types of customers: retail, trade, and college.
2. Open the CustomerTypeApp class in the c:\java 1.5\ch09\Enumeration directory. Then, add a method to this class that returns a discount percent (.10 for retail, .30 for trade, and .20 for college) depending on the CustomerType variable that's passed to it.
3. Add code to the main method that declares a CustomerType variable, assigns a customer type to it, gets the discount percent for that customer type, and displays the discount percent. Compile and run the application to be sure that it works correctly.
4. Add a statement to the main method that displays the string returned by the toString method of the customer type. Then, compile and run the application again to see the result of this method.
5. Add a toString method to the CustomerType enumeration. This method should return a string that contains "Retail customer," "Trade customer," or "College customer" depending on the customer type. Compile this class, then run the CustomerTypeApp class again to view the results of the toString method.

Section 3

More Java essentials

This section consists of five chapters that show you how to use more of the core Java features. Chapter 10 presents the concepts and techniques you need to know to work with arrays. Chapter 11 shows you how to work with collections as well as a new feature of Java 5 called generics. Chapter 12 presents the most important skills for working with dates and strings. Chapter 13 provides additional information about handling exceptions. And chapter 14 shows you how to work with threads.

Except for chapter 11, each chapter in this section is treated as an independent unit. Because of that, you can read these chapters in any sequence you like. If, for example, you want to learn more about handling exceptions, you can read chapter 13 next. Or, if you want to learn about using dates and strings, you can read chapter 12 next. However, chapter 11 assumes that you know how to work with arrays, so you'll want to read chapter 10 before reading this chapter.

Once you've read chapters 10 and 11, which present skills that are critical to most Java applications, you can skip ahead to the remaining sections. If, for example, you want to learn how to develop a graphical user interface, you can skip to section 4. Or, if you want to learn how to store the data for your business objects in a file or database, you can skip to section 5. As you read those sections, you can skip back to the chapters in this section whenever necessary. For instance, since exception handling becomes more complicated when you store data in a database, you'll want to read chapter 13 before you read chapter 21.

10

How to work with arrays

In this chapter, you'll learn how to work with arrays, which are important in a variety of Java applications. For example, you can use a sales array to hold the sales amounts for each of the 12 months of the year. Then, you can use that array to perform calculations on those amounts. In this chapter, you'll learn the basic concepts and techniques for working with arrays.

Basic skills for working with arrays

In the topics that follow, you'll learn how to use an array to work with groups of primitive types or objects. First, you'll learn how to create an array. Next, you'll learn how to assign values to an array. Then, you'll see some examples that show how to work with arrays.

How to create an array

An *array* is an object that contains one or more items called *elements*, each of which is a primitive type such as an int or a double or an object such as a String or a custom type. All of the elements in an array must be of the same type. Thus, an int array can contain only integers, and a double array can contain only doubles. Note, however, that an array can contain elements that are derived from the array's base type. As a result, if you declare an array of type Object, the array can contain any type of object because all Java classes are ultimately derived from the Object class.

The *length* (or *size*) of an array indicates the number of elements that it contains. In Java, arrays have a fixed length. So once you create an array, you can't change its length. If your application requires that you change the length of an array, you should consider using one of the collection classes described in chapter 11 instead of an array.

Figure 10-1 shows several ways to create an array. To start, you must declare a variable that will be used to refer to the array. Then, you instantiate an array object and assign it to the variable. You can use separate statements to declare the array variable and instantiate the array, or you can declare the variable and instantiate the array in a single statement.

Notice that when you declare the array variable, you use an empty set of brackets to indicate that the variable is an array. You can code these brackets after the variable name or after the array type. Most programmers prefer to code the empty brackets after the array type to indicate that the array is an array of a particular type, but either technique is acceptable.

When you instantiate an array, you use another set of brackets to indicate the number of elements in the array. If you know the size of the array at compile time, you can code the number of elements as a literal or as a constant of type int. If you won't know the size of the array until run time, you can use a variable of type int to specify its size.

The first three examples show how to declare an array of double types. The first example simply declares an array variable without instantiating an array. The second example instantiates an array that holds four doubles and assigns it to the array variable declared in the first example. The third example combines these two statements into a single statement that both declares and instantiates the array.

The other group of examples in this figure show other ways to create arrays. The first two examples in this group create arrays of String and Product objects. And the last two examples use a constant and a variable to provide the length for an array of String objects.

The syntax for declaring and instantiating an array

Two ways to declare an array

```
type[] arrayName;
type arrayName[];
```

How to instantiate an array

```
arrayName = new type[length];
```

How to declare and instantiate an array in one statement

```
type[] arrayName = new type[length];
```

Examples of array declarations

Code that declares an array of doubles

```
double[] prices;
```

Code that instantiates an array of doubles

```
prices = new double[4];
```

Code that declares and instantiates an array of doubles in one statement

```
double[] prices = new double[4];
```

Other examples

An array of String objects

```
String[] titles = new String[3];
```

An array of Product objects

```
Product[] products = new Product[5];
```

Code that uses a constant to specify the array length

```
final int TITLE_COUNT = 100;           // array size set at compile time
String[] titles = new String[TITLE_COUNT];
```

Code that uses a variable to specify the array length

```
int titleCount = 100;                  // array size not set until run time
String[] titles = new String[titleCount];
```

Description

- An *array* can store more than one primitive type or object. An *element* is one of the items in an array.
- To create an array, you must declare a variable of the correct type and instantiate an array object that the variable refers to. You can declare and instantiate the array in separate statements, or you can combine the declaration and instantiation into a single statement.
- To declare an array variable, you code a set of empty brackets after the type or the variable name. Most programmers prefer coding the brackets after the array type.
- To instantiate an array, you use the new keyword and specify the *length*, or *size*, of the array in brackets following the array type. You can specify the length by coding a literal value or by using a constant or variable of type int.
- When you instantiate an array of primitive types, numeric types are set to zeros and boolean types to false. When you create an array of objects, they are set to nulls.

Figure 10-1 How to create an array

How to assign values to the elements of an array

Figure 10-2 shows how to assign values to the elements of an array. As the syntax at the top of this figure shows, you refer to an element in an array by coding the array name followed by an *index* in brackets. The index must be an int value starting at 0 and ending at one less than the size of the array. In other words, an index of 0 refers to the first element in the array, 1 refers to the second element, 2 refers to the third element, and so on.

The first three examples in this figure show how to assign values to the elements in an array by coding one statement per element. The first example creates an array of 4 double values, then assigns a literal value to each element. In this example, the first element holds the value 14.95, the second holds 12.95, the third holds 11.95, and the fourth holds 9.95. The second example creates an array that holds String objects and initializes the strings. And the third example creates an array that holds Product objects and initializes those objects.

If you specify an index that's outside of the range of the array, Java will throw an ArrayIndexOutOfBoundsException. For instance, the commented out line at the end of the first example in this figure refers to the element with index number 4. Because this array has only four elements, however, this statement would cause an ArrayIndexOutOfBoundsException. Although you can catch this exception, it's better to write your code so that it avoids using indexes that are out of bounds. You'll see examples of code like that in the next figure.

The syntax and examples at the bottom of this figure show how to create an array and assign values to the elements of the array in one statement. Here, you declare the array variable as usual. Then, you use the special assignment syntax to assign the initial values. With this syntax, you simply list the values you want assigned to the array within braces following the equals sign. Then, the number of values you list within the braces determines the size of the array that's created. The last three examples show how to use this special syntax to create the same arrays that were created by the first three examples in this figure.

The syntax for referring to an element of an array

```
arrayName[index]
```

Examples that assign values by accessing each element

Code that assigns values to an array of double types

```
double[] prices = new double[4];
prices[0] = 14.95;
prices[1] = 12.95;
prices[2] = 11.95;
prices[3] = 9.95;
//prices[4] = 8.95;  // this would throw ArrayIndexOutOfBoundsException
```

Code that assigns values to an array of String types

```
String[] names = new String[3];
names[0] = "Ted Lewis";
names[1] = "Sue Jones";
names[2] = "Ray Thomas";
```

Code that assigns objects to an array of Product objects

```
Product[] products = new Product[2];
products[0] = new Product("java");
products[1] = new Product("jsps");
```

The syntax for creating an array and assigning values in one statement

```
type[] arrayName = {value1, value2, value3, ...};
```

Examples that create an array and assign values in one statement

```
double[] prices = {14.95, 12.95, 11.95, 9.95};
String[] names = {"Ted Lewis", "Sue Jones", "Ray Thomas"};
Product[] products = {new Product("java"), new Product("jsps")};
```

Description

- To refer to the elements in an array, you use an *index* that ranges from zero (the first element in the array) to one less than the number of elements in the array.
- If you specify an index that's less than zero or greater than the upper bound of the array, an ArrayIndexOutOfBoundsException will be thrown when the statement is executed.
- You can instantiate an array and provide initial values in a single statement by listing the values in braces. The number of values you provide determines the size of the array.

Figure 10-2 How to assign values to the elements of an array

How to use for loops with arrays

For loops are commonly used to process the elements in an array one at a time by incrementing an index variable. Figure 10-3 shows how to process an array using a for loop.

The syntax at the top of this figure shows how to use the length field to return the length of an array. Since length is a field rather than a method, you don't need to include parentheses after it. The length field returns an int value that represents the length of the array. You'll typically use this value in the termination expression of a for loop to stop the loop after the last element has been processed.

The first example in this figure shows how to create an array of 10 int values and fill it with the numbers 0 through 9. Here, an int variable named i is used in the for loop both to index the array and to assign a value to each element in the array. Since the same variable is used to index the array and assign the element values, the value that's stored within each element is equal to the index for the element.

The second example shows how you can use a for loop to print the contents of an array to the console. Here, an array of doubles named prices is created with initial values. Then, a for loop is used to access each element of the array. The single statement within the loop prints each element of the array to the console as shown.

The third example shows how you can use a for loop to calculate the average of the prices array. This example assumes you've already created the prices array as shown in the previous example. Then, it uses a for loop to add the value of each array element to a variable named sum. When the for loop finishes, sum contains the total of all the prices in the array. Then, the average is calculated by dividing this total by the number of elements in the array.

The fourth example shows another way to calculate the average value for the prices array. In this example, the normal iterator expression of the for loop (i++) is replaced with an expression that adds the current element to the sum variable and increments the index variable. As a result, no statement is required within the loop. Because we think this type of clever coding obscures the purpose of the loop, we don't recommend you use it. However, you may see this type of coding in other applications, so you should be familiar with how it works.

The syntax for getting the length of an array

```
arrayName.length
```

Example 1: Code that puts the numbers 0 through 9 in an array

```
int[] values = new int[10];
for (int i = 0; i < values.length; i++)
{
   values[i] = i;
}
```

Example 2: Code that prints an array of prices to the console

```
double[] prices = {14.95, 12.95, 11.95, 9.95};
for (int i = 0; i < prices.length; i++)
{
   System.out.println(prices[i]);
}
```

The console output

```
14.95
12.95
11.95
9.95
```

Example 3: Code that computes the average of the array of prices

```
double sum = 0.0;
for (int i = 0; i < prices.length; i++)
{
   sum += prices[i];
}
double average = sum/prices.length;
```

Example 4: Another way to compute the average in a for loop

```
double sum = 0.0;
for (int i = 0; i < prices.length; sum += prices[i++]);
average = sum/prices.length;
```

Description

- You can use the length field of an array to determine how many elements are defined for the array.
- For loops are often used to process each element in an array.

Figure 10-3 How to use for loops with arrays

How to use enhanced for loops with arrays

In addition to the standard for loop, Java 5.0 provides an *enhanced for loop* that's designed especially for working with arrays and collections. The enhanced for loop is sometimes called a *foreach loop* because it's used to process each element in an array or collection. Figure 10-4 shows how this loop works.

As the syntax at the top of this figure shows, the enhanced for loop doesn't use separate expressions to initialize, test, and increment a counter variable like the for loop does. Instead, you declare a variable that will be used to refer to each element of the array. Then, within the loop, you can use this variable to access each array element.

To understand how this works, the first example in this figure shows how you can use an enhanced for loop to print the elements of an array of doubles. This example performs the same function as the second example in figure 10-3. In the enhanced for loop version, a variable named price is used to access each element in the prices array. Then, the statement within the for loop simply prints the price variable to the console. Notice that because the enhanced for loop keeps track of the current element automatically, no indexing is required.

The second example shows how to use an enhanced for loop to calculate the average value in the prices array. This example performs the same function as the third example in figure 10-3. Again, no indexing is required since the enhanced for loop automatically indexes the array.

The syntax of the enhanced for loop

```
for (type variableName : arrayName)
{
    statements
}
```

Example 1: Code that prints an array of prices to the console

```
double[] prices = {14.95, 12.95, 11.95, 9.95};
for (double price : prices)
{
   System.out.println(price);
}
```

The console output

```
14.95
12.95
11.95
9.95
```

Example 2: Code that computes the average of the array of prices

```
double sum = 0.0;
for (double price : prices)
{
   sum += price;
}
double average = sum/prices.length;
```

Description

- Java 5.0 provides a new form of the for loop called an *enhanced for loop*. The enhanced for loop simplifies the code required to loop through arrays. The enhanced for loop is sometimes called a *foreach loop* because it lets you process each element of an array.
- Within the parentheses of an enhanced for loop, you declare a variable with the same type as the array followed by a colon and the name of the array.
- With each iteration of the loop, the variable that's declared by the for loop is assigned the value of the next element in the array.

Note

- You can also use foreach loops to work with collections. See chapter 11 for details.

Figure 10-4 How to use enhanced for loops with arrays

More skills for working with arrays

Now that you've learned the basic skills for creating and working with arrays, you're ready to learn some additional skills for working with arrays. So in this topic, you'll learn how to use the Arrays class, the Comparable interface, and the System class to work with arrays. You'll also learn how to create a second variable to refer to an existing array.

The methods of the Arrays class

The Arrays class of the java.util package contains several static methods that you can use to compare, sort, and search arrays. In addition, you can use this class to assign a value to one or more elements of an array. Figure 10-5 describes these methods.

As you can see, you can use the fill method to assign a value to all or part of an array. You can use the equals method to compare two arrays to check whether they contain the same number of elements with the same values stored within each element. And you can use the sort method to sort all or part of an array. Note, however, that if you want to sort objects that are created from classes that you defined, such as the Product class, you must implement the Comparable interface as shown in figure 10-7.

The last method in this summary is the binarySearch method, which lets you search for an element with a specific value and return its index. Before you can use this method, though, you must use the sort method to sort the array. If you don't, you'll get an ArrayIndexOutOfBoundsException.

You can supply an array of primitive types or an array of objects as the array argument for any of the methods, and you can supply any primitive type or object as the value argument. However, you must make sure that the value type matches the array type. In addition, when you supply an index argument, you must make sure that the index falls within the bounds of the array. Otherwise, the method will throw an exception.

The Arrays class

```
java.util.Arrays
```

Static methods of the Arrays class

Method	Description
`fill(arrayName, value)`	Fills all elements of the specified array with the specified value.
`fill(arrayName, index1, index2, value)`	Fills elements of the specified array with the specified value from the index1 element to, but not including, the index2 element.
`equals(arrayName1, arrayName2)`	Returns a boolean true value if both arrays are of the same type and all of the elements within the array are equal to each other.
`sort(arrayName)`	Sorts the elements of an array into ascending order.
`sort(arrayName, index1, index2)`	Sorts the elements of an array into ascending order from the index1 element to, but not including, the index2 element.
`binarySearch(arrayName, value)`	Returns an int value for the index of the specified value in the specified array. Returns a negative number if the specified value is not found in the array. For this method to work properly, the array must first be sorted by the sort method.

Description

- All of these methods accept arrays of primitive data types and arrays of objects for the arrayName argument, and they all accept primitive types and objects for the value argument.
- All of the index arguments for these methods must be int types. If an index argument is less than zero or greater than one less than the length of the array, the method will throw an ArrayIndexOutOfBoundsException.
- If you use the sort method on an array of objects created from a user-defined class, such as the Product class, the class must implement the Comparable interface as shown in figure 10-7.

Figure 10-5 The methods of the Arrays class

Code examples that work with the Arrays class

Figure 10-6 presents several examples that illustrate how the methods of the Arrays class work. The first example shows how to use the fill method to assign a value to all of the elements in an array of int values. Here, the first statement creates an array of 5 int values. By default, this statement automatically initializes each element to 0. Then, the second statement uses the fill method of the Arrays class to set all five values to 1.

The second example shows how to use the fill method to fill just part of an array. Here, the second and third arguments for the method indicate that elements 1, 2, and 3 should be filled with a value of 100. This use of indexes is a little peculiar, since the index that specifies the end of the range to be filled is actually one greater than the end of the range. Thus, to fill elements 1 through 3, you specify 1 as the starting index and 4 as the ending index.

The third example shows how to use the equals method to compare two arrays. Here, the first two statements create two arrays of String objects. Both arrays have two elements with identical values. Then, an if statement uses the equality operator (==) to test whether the arrays are equal. The equality operator doesn't actually compare the values of the elements in these arrays, however. Instead, it tests whether the two array variables refer to the same array object. As a result, this comparison returns false. Next, an if statement uses the equals method of the Arrays class to compare the arrays. Because this method compares the values of each of the elements in the arrays, this comparison returns true.

The fourth example shows how to use the sort method to sort an array of int values. Here, the first statement creates an unsorted array of integers from 0 to 9, and the second statement uses the sort method to sort these values. After the sort, a for loop prints the contents of the array so you can see that the array has been sorted.

The fifth example shows how to use the binarySearch method. Here, the first statement creates an array of unsorted strings. Then, the second statement uses the sort method to sort this array. For strings, this will result in the array being sorted alphabetically from A to Z. As a result, the binarySearch method used in the third statement will return a value of 2, which means that the string is the third element of the array.

Example 1: Code that uses the fill method

```
int[] quantities = new int[5];
Arrays.fill(quantities, 1);          // all elements are set to 1
```

Example 2: Code that uses the fill method to fill 3 elements in an array

```
int[] quantities = new int[5];
Arrays.fill(quantities, 1, 4, 100);  // elements 1, 2, and 3 are set to 100
```

Example 3: Code that uses the equals method

```
String[] titles1 = {"War and Peace", "Gone With the Wind"};
String[] titles2 = {"War and Peace", "Gone With the Wind"};

if (titles1 == titles2)
    System.out.println("titles1 == titles2 is true");
else
    System.out.println("titles1 == titles2 is false");

if (Arrays.equals(titles1, titles2))
    System.out.println("Arrays.equals(titles1, titles2) is true");
else
    System.out.println("Arrays.equals(titles1, titles2) is false");
```

The console output

```
titles1 == titles2 is false
Arrays.equals(titles1, titles2) is true
```

Example 4: Code that uses the sort method

```
int[] numbers = {2,6,4,1,8,5,9,3,7,0};
Arrays.sort(numbers);
for (int num : numbers)
{
    System.out.print(num + " ");
}
```

The console output

```
0 1 2 3 4 5 6 7 8 9
```

Example 5: Code that uses the sort and binarySearch methods

```
String[] productCodes = {"mcbl", "jsps", "java"};
Arrays.sort(productCodes);
int index = Arrays.binarySearch(productCodes, "mcbl");   // sets index to 2
```

Figure 10-6 Code examples that work with the Arrays class

How to implement the Comparable interface

You can only use the sort method of the Arrays class to sort arrays of objects when the classes for those objects implement the Comparable interface. As a result, when you code your own classes, you need to implement the Comparable interface for any class that you need to sort. To do that, you must provide an implementation of the compareTo method of this interface. Figure 10-7 shows how you can do this for a simple Item class.

The code at the top of this figure shows how the Comparable interface is defined by the Java API. This interface provides a single method named compareTo that accepts an Object as an argument. This method should return a negative number if the current object is less than the passed object, 0 if the two objects are equal, and a positive number if the current object is greater than the passed object.

The Item class in this figure begins by declaring two private instance variables named number and description, a constructor that accepts values for these fields, and methods that return the values of these fields. Then, it provides a compareTo method that compares Item objects based on the values of the number fields. In other words, two items are considered equal if they have the same item number.

The compareTo method begins by casting the object passed to it to an Item object. Then, it uses if statements to compare the item numbers and determine whether to return -1, 0, or 1.

The code example after the Item class shows how you can sort an array of Item objects. Here, an array of three Item objects is created. Then, the sort method of the Arrays class is used to sort the array. Finally, an enhanced for loop is used to print the contents of the array. As you can see in the resulting output, the array is printed in item number sequence even though the array elements were created in a different sequence.

In this example, the objects are compared based on a numeric field. Because of that, you can use the greater than and less than operators to determine if one object is greater than or less than another. If you want to compare two objects based on a string field, however, you can't do that using these operators. Instead, you need to use the compareTo method of the String class. You'll learn more about how to use this method in chapter 12.

The Comparable interface defined in the Java API

```
public interface Comparable {
   int compareTo(Object obj);
}
```

An Item class that implements the Comparable interface

```
public class Item implements Comparable{
    private int number;
    private String description;

    public Item(int number, String description){
        this.number = number;
        this.description = description;
    }

    public int getNumber(){
        return number;
    }

    public String getDescription(){
        return description;
    }

    public int compareTo(Object o){
        Item i = (Item) o;
        if (this.getNumber() < i.getNumber())
            return -1;
        if (this.getNumber() > i.getNumber())
            return 1;
        return 0;
    }
}
```

Code that sorts an array of Item objects

```
Item[] items = new Item[3];
items[0] = new Item(102, "Duct Tape");
items[1] = new Item(103, "Bailing Wire");
items[2] = new Item(101, "Chewing Gum");
Arrays.sort(items);
for (Item i : items)
    System.out.println(i.getNumber() + ": " + i.getDescription());
```

The console output

```
101: Chewing Gum
102: Duct Tape
103: Bailing Wire
```

Description

- To implement the Comparable interface, you must define the compareTo method. Then, the sort method of the Arrays class uses the compareTo method to sort an array of objects created from that class.
- The compareTo method must return -1 if the current object is less than the passed object, 0 if the objects are equal, and 1 if the current object is greater than the passed object.

Figure 10-7 How to implement the Comparable interface

How to create a refererence to an array

The first example in figure 10-8 shows how to create a *reference* to an array by assigning an array variable to an existing array. Here, the grades variable and the percentages variable both refer to the same array. As a result, any change to the grades variable will be reflected by the percentages variable and vice versa. For instance, the third statement in this example sets percentages[1] to 70.2. Then, the last statement prints grades[1]. Because the percentages and grades variables actually refer to the same array, this statement prints the value 70.2.

Once you create an array, you can't change its size. However, you can use an existing array variable to refer to a larger or smaller array. When you do this, the reference to the original array is dropped, a new array is created, and the array variable is set to refer to the new array. For instance, suppose you create an array that contains 5 elements. Then, later in the program, you realize that you want that array to have 20 elements. To do this, you just reuse the array variable as shown in the second example and create a new array of 20 elements. When you do, any values you stored in the original 5-element array will be lost.

How to copy an array

If you want to create a copy of an array, you can use the arraycopy method of the System class as shown in this figure. Then, each array variable will point to its own copy of the array, and any changes that are made to one array won't affect the other array.

To use the arraycopy method, you specify the five arguments shown in the figure. First, you specify the source array and the starting index. Next, you specify the target array and the starting index. Then, you specify the total number of elements to copy. When you use the arraycopy method, the target array must already exist, and it must be large enough to hold the number of elements that you're copying. In addition, both arrays must be of the same type.

The third example in this figure shows how to make a copy of an entire array. Here, both index values are set to 0 and the intLength argument is set to the length of the grades array. As a result, this example copies all of the elements of the grades array into the percentages array.

The fourth example shows how to copy parts of one array into other arrays. Here, the first statement creates an array of four double values, and the second statement sorts these values from lowest to highest. Next, the third statement creates an array that can hold two double values, and the fourth statement copies the two lowest values into it. Then, the fifth statement creates an array that can hold two double values, and the sixth statement copies the two highest values into it.

How to create a reference to an array

Example 1: Code that creates a reference to an array

```
double[] grades = {92.3, 88.0, 95.2, 90.5};
double[] percentages = grades;
percentages[1] = 70.2;                          // changes grades[1] too
System.out.println("grades[1]=" + grades[1]);  // prints 70.2
```

Example 2: Code that reuses an array variable

```
double[] grades = new grades[5];
grades = new grades[20]
```

How to copy elements of one array to another

The syntax of the arraycopy method of the System class

```
System.arraycopy(fromArray, intFromIndex, toArray, intToIndex, intLength);
```

Example 3: Code that copies the values of an array

```
double[] grades = {92.3, 88.0, 95.2, 90.5};
double[] percentages = new double[grades.length];
System.arraycopy(grades, 0, percentages, 0, grades.length);
percentages[1] = 70.2;                          // doesn't change grades[1]
System.out.println("grades[1]=" + grades[1]);  // prints 88.0
```

Example 4: Code that copies part of one array into another array

```
double[] grades = {92.3, 88.0, 95.2, 90.5};
Arrays.sort(grades);
double[] lowestGrades = new double[2];
System.arraycopy(grades, 0, lowestGrades, 0, 2);
double[] highestGrades = new double[2];
System.arraycopy(grades, 2, highestGrades, 0, 2);
```

Description

- To create a *reference* to an existing array, code an assignment statement like the one shown in the first example. Then, two variables will point to the same array in memory.
- To copy the values of one array into another, use the arraycopy method of the System class as shown in the third and fourth examples.
- When you copy an array, the target array must be the same type as the sending array and it must be large enough to receive all of the elements that are copied to it.

Figure 10-8 How to refer to and copy arrays

How to work with two-dimensional arrays

So far, this chapter has shown how to work with an array that uses one index to store a single set of elements. You can think of that as a *one-dimensional array*. Now, you'll learn how to work with *two-dimensional arrays* that use two indexes to store data. You can think of a two-dimensional array as a table made up of rows and columns where each element in the array is at the intersection of a row and column.

If you're familiar with array processing in other languages such as C++ or even Visual Basic, you may be surprised to discover that Java doesn't directly support two-dimensional arrays in the same way those languages do. Instead, Java implements a two-dimensional array as an *array of arrays* where each element of the first array is itself an array. Although the syntax is different, the effect is nearly the same.

How to work with rectangular arrays

Figure 10-9 shows how to create and use the simplest type of two-dimensional array, called a *rectangular array*. In a rectangular array, each row has the same number of columns. For example, a 5x10 array consists of an array of five elements, each of which is a 10-element array. If you think of this rectangular array as a table, the 5-element array represents the table's rows, and each 10-element array represents the columns for one of the rows.

The syntax and code at the top of this figure show how to create a rectangular array. As you can see, you specify two sets of empty brackets following the array type. Then, you specify the number of rows and columns when you instantiate the array. Thus, the code example shown here declares and instantiates a rectangular array with 3 rows, each with two columns.

To refer to an element in a rectangular array, you specify two index values in separate sets of brackets. The first value refers to the row index, and the second value refers to the column index. Thus, numbers[1][0] refers to row 2, column 1 of the numbers array.

You can also create a rectangular array and assign values to its elements using a single statement. To do that, you use the same shorthand notation you use for one-dimensional arrays. However, you code each element of the array as a separate array as shown in this figure. Here, the numbers array is assigned three elements, each of which is a two-element array with the values {1, 2}, {3, 4}, and {5, 6}.

The last example in this figure shows how to use nested for loops to process the elements of a rectangular array. Here, the outer for loop uses the variable i to index the rows of the array, and numbers.length is used to determine the number of rows in the array. Then, the inner for loop uses the variable j to index the columns, and numbers[i].length is used to determine the number of columns in each row.

How to create a rectangular array

The syntax for creating a rectangular array

```
type[][] arrayName = new type[rowCount][columnCount];
```

A statement that creates a 3x2 array

```
int[][] numbers = new int[3][2];
```

How to assign values to a rectangular array

The syntax for referring to an element of a rectangular array

```
arrayName[rowIndex][columnIndex]
```

The indexes for a 3x2 array

```
[0][0]     [0][1]
[1][0]     [1][1]
[2][0]     [2][1]
```

Code that assigns values to the array

```
numbers[0][0] = 1;
numbers[0][1] = 2;
numbers[1][0] = 3;
numbers[1][1] = 4;
numbers[2][0] = 5;
numbers[2][1] = 6;
```

Code that creates a 3x2 array and initializes it in one statement

```
int[][] numbers = { {1,2} {3,4} {5,6} };
```

How to use nested for loops to process a rectangular array

Code that processes a rectangular array with nested for loops

```
int[][] numbers = { {1,2}, {3,4}, {5,6} };
for (int i = 0; i < numbers.length; i++)
{
    for (int j = 0; j < numbers[i].length; j++)
        System.out.print(numbers[i][j] + "  ");
    System.out.print("\n");
}
```

The console output

```
1  2
3  4
5  6
```

Description

- *Two-dimensional arrays* use two indexes and allow data to be stored in a table that consists of rows and columns. This can also be thought of as an *array of arrays* where each row is a separate array of columns.
- A *rectangular array* is a two-dimensional array whose rows all have the same number of columns.
- Although it's rarely necessary, you can extend this two-dimensional syntax to work with arrays that have more than two dimensions.

Figure 10-9 How to work with rectangular arrays

Although it's not shown in figure 10-9, you should realize that you can also use nested foreach loops to work with rectangular arrays. To do that, you declare an array variable in the outer for loop that you can use to refer to the rows in the array. Then, you declare a variable in the inner for loop that you can use to refer to the columns in each row. For example, figure 10-10 uses nested foreach loops to work with another type of two-dimensional array called a jagged array.

How to work with jagged arrays

A *jagged array* is a two-dimensional array in which the rows contain unequal numbers of columns. This is possible because each row of a two-dimensional array is actually a separate one-dimensional array, and Java doesn't require that each of these arrays be the same size. Figure 10-10 shows how to work with jagged arrays.

When you instantiate a jagged array, you specify the number of rows but not the number of columns. Then, you instantiate the array for each row separately, specifying as many columns as are necessary for that row. To illustrate, the first statement in the first example in this figure creates a jagged array named numbers that has 3 rows. Then, the next three statements create arrays of 10, 15, and 20 elements for the three rows of the numbers array.

The second example in this figure shows how you can initialize a jagged array using the shorthand notation. Here, a jagged array of strings is created with three rows. The first row contains three elements, the second row contains four elements, and the third row contains two elements.

In the third example, a jagged array of type int is created with four rows. Then, a for loop cycles through the rows and creates a different number of elements for each column array. The first time through the loop, i will be equal to 0 so the length of the array will be set to 1. The second time through the for loop, i will be equal to 1 so the length of the array will be set to 2. And so on.

For each column array, another for loop is used to initialize the element values. This loop uses a variable named j to index the columns. A variable named number is used to assign a value to each column. This variable is incremented within this for loop. As a result, the first row will have one element with the value 0. The second row will have two elements with the values 1 and 2. The third row will have three elements with the values 3, 4, and 5. And so on.

The fourth example in this figure uses nested for loops to print the contents of the array created in the third example. Here, each row is printed on a separate line so you can clearly see the number of elements it contains.

The fifth example shows how you can use nested foreach loops to produce the same output. In this example, the outer for loop accesses each element in the pyramid array as an array of int values named row. Then the inner for loop accesses each element in the row array as an int value named col.

The syntax for creating a jagged array

```
type[][] arrayName = new type[rowCount][];
```

Example 1: Code that creates a jagged array of integers

```
int[][] numbers = new int[3][];
numbers[0] = new int[10];
numbers[1] = new int[15];
numbers[2] = new int[20];
```

Example 2: Code that creates and initializes a jagged array of strings

```
String[][] titles = {{"War and Peace", "Wuthering Heights", "1984"},
                     {"Casablanca", "Wizard of Oz", "Star Wars", "Birdy"},
                     {"Blue Suede Shoes", "Yellow Submarine"}};
```

Example 3: Code that creates and initializes a jagged array of integers

```
int number = 0;
int[][] pyramid = new int[4][];
for (int i = 0; i < pyramid.length; i++)
{
    pyramid[i] = new int[i+1];
    for (int j = 0; j < pyramid[i].length; j++)
        pyramid[i][j] = number++;
}
```

Example 4: Code that prints the contents of the jagged array of integers

```
for (int i = 0; i < pyramid.length; i++)
{
   for (int j = 0; j < pyramid[i].length; j++)
      System.out.print(pyramid[i][j] + " ");
   System.out.print("\n");
}
```

The console output

```
0
1 2
3 4 5
6 7 8 9
```

Example 5: Code that uses foreach loops to print a jagged array

```
for (int[] row : pyramid)
{
    for (int col : row)
        System.out.print(col + " ");
    System.out.print("\n");
}
```

Description

- A *jagged array* is a two-dimensional array whose rows have different numbers of columns. When you create a jagged array, you specify the number of rows in the array, but you leave the size of each column array unspecified and set it later.

Figure 10-10 How to work with jagged arrays

Perspective

Now that you've finished this chapter, you should know how to work with one-dimensional and two-dimensional arrays. Although you'll use arrays in many applications, they may not always provide the functionality you need. In that case, you can use a more advanced data structure called a collection. You'll learn how to work with collections in the next chapter.

Summary

- An *array* is a special type of object that can store more than one primitive data type or object. The *length* (or *size*) of an array is the number of *elements* that are stored in the array. The *index* is the number that is used to identify any element in the array.
- For loops are often used to process arrays. Java 5.0 also introduced a new type of for loop, called an *enhanced for loop* or a *foreach loop*, that lets you process each element of an array without using indexes.
- You can use the Arrays class to fill, compare, sort, and search arrays. You can use an assignment statement to create a second *reference* to the same array. And you can use the arraycopy method of the System class to make a copy of an array.
- To provide for sorting a user-defined class, that class must implement the Comparable interface.
- A *one-dimensional array* provides for a single list or column of elements so just one index value is required to identify each element. In contrast, a *two-dimensional array*, or an *array of arrays*, can be used to organize data in a table that has rows and columns. As a result, two index values are required to identify each element.
- A two-dimensional array can be *rectangular,* in which case each row has the same number of columns, or *jagged,* in which case each row has a different number of columns.

Exercise 10-1 Use a one-dimensional array

In this exercise, you'll create an Array Test application so you can practice using one-dimensional arrays.

1. Open the ArrayTestApp class in the c:\java1.5\ch10 directory.
2. Create a one-dimensional array of 99 double values. Then, use a for loop to add a random number from 0 to 100 to each element in the array. For each value, use the random method of the Math class to get a double value between 0.0 and 1.0, and multiply it by 100.

3. Use an enhanced for loop to sum the values in the array. Then, calculate the average value and print that value on the console followed by a blank line. Compile and test this class.
4. Use the sort method of the Arrays class to sort the values in the array, and print the median value (the 50th value) on the console followed by a blank line. Then, test this enhancement.
5. Print the 9th value of the array on the console and every 9th value after that. Then, test this enhancement.

Exercise 10-2 Use a rectangular array

This exercise will guide you through the process of adding a rectangular array to the Future Value application. This array will store the values for up to ten of the calculations that are performed, and print a summary of those calculations when the program ends that looks something like this:

```
Future Value Calculations

Inv/Mo. Rate    Years   Future Value
$100.00 8.0%    10      $18,416.57
$125.00 8.0%    10      $23,020.71
$150.00 8.0%    10      $27,624.85

Press any key to continue . . .
```

1. Open the FutureValueApp application stored in the c:\java1.5\ch10 directory.
2. Declare variables at the beginning of the main method for a row counter and a rectangular array of strings that provides for 10 rows and 4 columns.
3. After the code that calculates, formats, and displays the results for each calculation, add code that stores the formatted values as strings in the next row of the array (you need to use the toString method of the Integer class to store the years value).
4. Add code to display the elements in the array at the console when the user indicates that the program should end. The output should be formatted as shown above. Then, compile and test the program by making up to 10 future value calculations. When you've got this working right, close the program.

Exercise 10-3 Sort an array of user-defined objects

In this exercise, you'll modify a Customer class so it implements the Comparable interface. Then, you'll sort an array of objects created from this class.

1. Open the Customer and SortedCustomersApp classes stored in the c:\java1.5\ch10 directory.

2. Add code to the Customer class to implement the Comparable interface. The compareTo method you create should compare the email field of the current customer with the email field of another customer. To do that, you can't use the > and < operators because the email field is a string. Instead, you'll need to use the compareToIgnoreCase method of the String class. This method compares the string it's executed on with the string that's passed to it as an argument. If the first string is less than the second string, this method returns a negative integer. If the first string is greater than the second string, it returns a positive integer. And if the two strings are equal, it returns 0.
3. Add code to the SortedCustomersApp class that creates an array of Customer objects that can hold 3 elements, and create and assign Customer objects to those elements. Be sure that the email values you assign to the objects aren't in alphabetical order. Sort the array.
4. Code a foreach loop that prints the email, firstName, and lastName fields of each Customer object on a separate line.
5. Compile and test the program. When you're sure it works correctly, close the program.

Exercise 10-4 Work with a deck of cards

In this exercise, you'll write an application that uses a variety of arrays and for loops to work with a deck of cards.

1. Open the CardDeckApp class in the c:\java1.5\ch10 directory.
2. Create an array whose elements hold the first initial of the four different suits in a card deck. Declare an array that can hold a representation of the cards in a deck of cards without jokers.
3. Write a method to load the card array, one suit at a time. (Use the numbers 11, 12, and 13 to represent Jacks, Queens, and Kings respectively, and use the number 1 to represent Aces.) Write another method to print the cards in the array, separating each card by a space and printing each suit on a separate line. Call these two methods from the main method. Compile the application and test it to be sure the array is loaded properly.
4. Write a method that shuffles the deck of cards. To do that, this method should get a number between 1 and 51 by multiplying the result of the random function by 50, converting it to an integer, and adding 1. Then, it should switch each card in the deck with the card that is the given number of cards after it (if there is one). This should be repeated 100 times to shuffle the deck thoroughly. Call this method from the main method, followed by the method that prints the cards array. Test the application to be sure that the cards are shuffled.
5. Declare a rectangular array that represents fours hands of cards with five cards each. Write a method that loads this array by dealing cards from the cards array. Be sure to deal one card at a time to each hand. Write a method that prints the hands, separating the cards in each hand by a space and printing each hand on a separate line. Test the application to be sure that the cards are dealt properly.

11

How to work with collections and generics

In this chapter, you'll learn how to work with collections. As you'll see, collections are similar to arrays but provide more advanced features. Along with collections, you'll learn how to use generics, a new feature of Java 5.0 that lets you specify the type of objects that can be stored in a collection. Because this chapter assumes that you already know how to work with arrays, you should read chapter 10 before reading this chapter.

An introduction to Java collections

Like an array, a *collection* is an object that can hold one or more other objects. However, unlike arrays, collections aren't a part of the Java language itself. Instead, collections are classes that are provided with the Java API. In the topics that follow, you'll learn how collections compare to arrays, you'll learn about the interfaces and classes in the Java collection hierarchy, and you'll learn about a new Java 5.0 feature called generics that make collections easier to work with.

A comparison of arrays and collections

Figure 11-1 presents a brief comparison of arrays and collections. As you can see, both arrays and collections can be used to store multiple occurrences of objects such as strings. You can also use arrays or collections to store objects created from user-defined classes such as Customer or Product. In addition, some collection classes—most notably the ArrayList class—actually use an array to store data. As a result, a collection based on the ArrayList class behaves much like an array.

Although arrays and collections have some similarities, they also have many differences. One important difference is that arrays are fixed in size. That means that if you initially create an array with 100 elements and then discover that you need to add 101 elements, you must create a new array large enough to hold 101 elements, copy the 100 elements from the first array to the new array, and then discard the original array. In contrast, collections are designed so that they can grow in size. When you create a collection, you don't specify the maximum size of the collection. Instead, you simply add as many elements to the collection as you want. Then, the collection will expand automatically to hold the elements you add.

Another difference between arrays and collections is that arrays can store primitive types, but collections can only store objects. Because of that, you have to use wrapper classes to store primitive types such as integers and doubles in a collection. You'll see examples of that later in this chapter.

Finally, you use indexes to work with the elements in an array, but you don't usually need to use indexes to work with the elements in a collection. This is illustrated in the two examples in this figure. Here, the first example stores three values in an array and then displays those values. The second example does the same thing using a collection created from the ArrayList class. Instead of using indexes to add the three values, the collection example uses the add method of the ArrayList class. In addition, this example uses an enhanced for loop to print the elements of the collection. Although you can use the enhanced for loop with arrays as well, you're much more likely to see arrays processed using the for loop since the enhanced for loop just became available with Java 5.0.

By the way, you shouldn't worry if you don't understand all of the code in the second example. You'll learn the details of working with the ArrayList class and some of the other collection classes later in this chapter. This example is simply meant to illustrate some of the differences between working with arrays and collections.

How arrays and collections are similar

- Both can store multiple occurrences of objects.
- Some collection types (such as ArrayList) use arrays internally to store data.

How arrays and collections differ

- An array is a Java language feature. Collections are classes in the Java API.
- Collection classes have methods that perform operations that arrays don't provide.
- Arrays are fixed in size. Collections are variable in size.
- Arrays can store primitive types. Collections can't.
- Indexes are almost always required to process arrays. Collections are usually processed without using indexes.

Example 1: Code that uses an array

```
String[] codes = new String[3];
codes[0] = "mcb2";
codes[1] = "java";
codes[2] = "jsps";
for (int i = 0; i < codes.length; i++)
    System.out.println(codes[i]);
```

Example 2: Code that uses a collection

```
ArrayList<String> codes = new ArrayList<String>();
codes.add("mcb2");
codes.add("java");
codes.add("jsps");
for (String s : codes)
    System.out.println(s);
```

Description

- A *collection* is an object that can hold other objects. Collections are similar to arrays, but are more flexible to use and are more efficient than arrays for many applications.

Figure 11-1 A comparison of arrays and collections

An overview of the Java collection framework

Figure 11-2 shows a simplified map of the Java *collection framework*. As you can see, the collection framework consists of a hierarchy of interfaces and classes. Here, the shaded boxes represent interfaces that define the basic collection types. The unshaded boxes represent classes that implement the collection interfaces.

The collection framework provides two main types of collections represented by two distinct class hierarchies. The first hierarchy begins with an interface named Collection. A *collection* is simply an object that can hold one or more objects. The Set and List interfaces inherit the Collection interface and define two distinct types of collections. A *set* is a collection of unique objects. In most cases, sets are also unordered. That means that sets don't retain information about the order of elements added to the set.

In contrast to a set, a *list* is an ordered collection of objects. A list always maintains some sort of order for the objects it contains. Depending on the type of list, the order might simply be the order in which the items were added to the list, or it might be a sorted order based on a key value. In addition, lists allow duplicate elements.

The second main type of collection is called a *map*, and it's defined by the Map interface. A map is similar to a collection, but its elements consist of *key-value pairs* in which each value element is associated with a unique key element. Each key must be associated with one and only one value. For example, a map might be used to store Customer objects mapped to customer numbers. In that case, the customer numbers are the keys and the Customer objects are the values. Note that even though the Map interface doesn't inherit the Collection interface, the term *collection* is often used to refer to both collections and maps.

Commonly used collection classes

Although Java provides more than 30 classes that implement the List, Set, or Map interfaces, you don't need to know how to use them all. The second table in this figure lists the five collection classes you'll probably use most often. Once you learn how to use these five classes, you shouldn't have much trouble learning how to use other collection classes if the need arises.

The ArrayList class implements an *array list*, which works much like a standard array. In fact, the ArrayList class uses an array internally to store the entries you add to the array list. The ArrayList class provides efficient access to the individual elements in the list. However, inserting an element into the middle of an array list can be inefficient because all of the elements after the insertion point must be moved to accommodate the inserted element.

The LinkedList class is an implementation of the List interface that uses a special structure called a *linked list* to store the list's elements. Each element in a linked list contains pointers to the elements immediately before and immediately after it. As a result, an element can be inserted into the middle of a linked list efficiently by simply adjusting the pointers in the elements before and after the inserted element. However, the elements in a linked list can't be retrieved as efficiently as the elements in an array list.

The collection framework

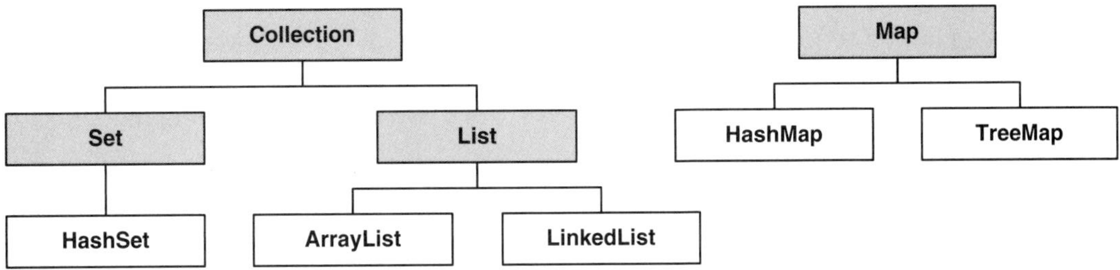

Collection interfaces

Interface	Description
Collection	Defines the basic methods available for all collections.
Set	Defines a type of collection in which no duplicate elements are allowed.
List	Defines a type of collection that maintains the order in which elements were added to the list.
Map	Defines a map, which is similar to a collection but holds one or more key-value pairs instead of simple elements. Each key-value pair consists of a key that uniquely identifies an entry and a value that provides data associated with a particular key.

Common collection classes

Class	Description
ArrayList	Works much like an array, but can be easily expanded to accommodate new elements. Very efficient for accessing individual elements in random sequence, but inserting elements into the middle of the list can be inefficient.
LinkedList	Similar to an array list, but with more features. Less efficient than an array list for accessing elements randomly, but more efficient when inserting items into the middle of the list.
HashSet	A collection that stores a set of unique values based on a *hash code*. Duplicates are not allowed. Objects you add to a hash set must implement a method called hashCode to generate a hash code for the object, which is used to ensure uniqueness.
HashMap	Similar to a hash set, but is based on the Map interface rather than the Set interface. As a result, a hash map stores key-value pairs whose keys must be unique.
TreeMap	Stores key-value pairs in a special arrangement called a *tree*. Entries in a tree map are automatically maintained in key sequence.

Description

- The Java *collection framework* is interface based, which means that each class in the collection implements one of the interfaces defined by the collection framework.
- The collection framework consists of two class hierarchies: Collection and Map. Collections store individual objects as elements. Maps store pairs of key objects and value objects in a way that lets you retrieve a value object based on its key.
- Although there are many classes in the Java collection framework, the most commonly used classes are the ArrayList, LinkedList, HashSet, HashMap, and TreeMap classes.

Figure 11-2 The Java collection framework and classes

Because ArrayList and LinkedList are the two most commonly used classes in the collection framework, much of this chapter focuses on those two classes. However, you'll also learn the basic skills for working with the HashMap and TreeMap classes. If you want to learn more about these classes, though, or you want to learn about the HashSet class, you shouldn't have any trouble doing that using the Java API documentation.

An introduction to generics

In previous versions of Java, the elements of a collection were defined as type Object. As a result, you could store any type of object as an element in a collection. At first, this flexibility might seem like an advantage. But with it comes two disadvantages. First, there's no way to guarantee that only objects of a certain type are added to a collection. For example, you can't limit an ArrayList so that it can hold only Product objects. Second, you must use casting whenever you retrieve an object from a collection. That's because an element can be any type of object. For example, to retrieve a Product object from a collection, you must cast the object to a Product.

Java 5.0 introduces a new feature called *generics* that addresses these two problems. The generics feature lets you specify the element type for a collection. Then, Java can ensure that only objects of the specified type are added to the collection. And any objects you retrieve from the collection are automatically cast to the correct type.

Figure 11-3 shows how the generics feature works. To specify a type when you declare a collection, you code the type in angle brackets immediately following the name of the collection class (such as ArrayList or LinkedList). You must usually do this twice: once when you use the collection class to declare the collection, and again when you use the constructor of the collection class to create an instance of the collection.

The first example in this figure shows a statement that declares and instantiates an instance of an array list collection named codes that will hold String objects. Here, <String> is specified following the ArrayList class name to indicate that the elements of the array list must be String objects. The second and third examples are similar, but they create collections that can hold integers and Product objects.

Notice in the second example that a *wrapper class* is specified as the type instead of the primitive type. That's necessary because a collection can only hold objects, not primitive types. But if you declare a collection with a wrapper type, you can store values of the related primitive type in that collection.

You can also create your own classes that use generics. To do that, you specify one or more type variables in angle brackets following the class name as shown in example 4. Here, the type variable is specified as E. Then, you can use this variable within the class anywhere you would normally specify a type. You'll see an example of a class that uses this technique later in this chapter.

Keep in mind that the generics feature is new for Java 5.0. As a result, most existing Java code doesn't use generics. You'll find information about using collection classes without using generics later in this chapter.

The syntax for specifying the type of elements in a collection

```
CollectionClass<Type> collectionName = new CollectionClass<Type>();
```

Example 1: A statement that creates an array list of type String

```
ArrayList<String> codes = new ArrayList<String>();
```

Example 2: A statement that creates an array list of integers

```
ArrayList<Integer> numbers = new ArrayList<Integer>();
```

Example 3: Code that creates a linked list of type Product

```
LinkedList<Product> products;
products = new LinkedList<Product>();
```

The syntax for declaring a class that uses generic types

```
public class ClassName<TypeVariable [,TypeVariable]...>{}
```

Example 4: A class statement for a class that implements a queue

```
public class GenericQueue<E>{}
```

Description

- *Generics* refers to a new feature of Java 5.0 that lets you create typed collections. A *typed collection* is a collection that can hold only objects of a certain type.
- To declare a variable that refers to a typed collection, you list the type in angle brackets (<>) following the name of the collection class.
- When you use a constructor for a typed collection, you specify the type variable in angle brackets following the constructor name.
- The type variable can't be a primitive type such as int or double. However, it can be a wrapper class such as Integer or Double. It can also be a user-defined class.
- If you do not specify a type for a collection, the collection can hold any type of object. However, the Java compiler will issue warning messages whenever you access the collection to warn you that type checking can't be performed for the collection.
- To create a *generic class* that lets you specify type information, specify one or more *type variables* in angle brackets following the class name on the class statement. Then, you can use the type variable within the class anywhere you would normally specify a type.

Figure 11-3 An introduction to generics

How to use the ArrayList class

The ArrayList class is one of the most commonly used Java collection classes. The following topics present an overview of this class along with several examples of how you can use it.

The ArrayList class

Figure 11-4 presents an overview of the ArrayList class, which is used to create a type of collection called an *array list*. An array list uses an array internally to store elements, so an array list is similar to an array in many ways. However, unlike an array, you can change the capacity of an array list after you've created it. In fact, an array list automatically adjusts its size as you add elements to it. So you don't have to write any special code to make sure that you don't exceed the capacity of an array list.

If adding an object to an array list causes the list to exceed the current capacity of the internal array, the ArrayList class automatically increases the capacity of the internal array. The documentation for the ArrayList class says that the method used to determine the new capacity of the array is unspecified. However, an examination of the source code for the ArrayList class reveals that the size of the internal array is increased by 50% plus 1. So, for example, if the current capacity of an array list is 1000, the array list will be expanded to a capacity of 1501.

Unfortunately, increasing the capacity of an array list is not an efficient operation, especially if the array list is large. First, the ArrayList class must create a new array of the expanded size. Then, the elements of the old array must be copied to the new array. Finally, the old array must be removed from memory.

The ArrayList class includes a constructor that lets you specify the initial capacity of the array list. If you don't provide this value, the array list is given a default capacity of 10 elements. Because expanding an array list is inefficient, you should always specify an appropriate initial capacity whenever you create an array list.

All three constructors in this figure show that the ArrayList class can be used to create a typed collection. This is indicated by the E that's enclosed in angle brackets following the class name. A capital letter E is the standard way of representing the type of elements that are stored in a collection.

The ArrayList class also has several methods that let you work with an array list. The ones you'll use most often are the add method, which lets you add an object to the list, and the get method, which lets you retrieve an object using an index number. You'll find code examples of these and several other methods of the ArrayList class in the next figure.

The ArrayList class

java.util.ArrayList

Constructors of the ArrayList class

Constructor	Description
ArrayList<E>()	Creates an empty array list with an initial capacity of ten objects of the specified type.
ArrayList<E>(intCapacity)	Creates an empty array list with the specified capacity.
ArrayList<E>(Collection)	Creates an array list containing the elements of the specified collection.

Common methods of the ArrayList class

Method	Description
add(object)	Adds the specified object to the end of the list.
add(index, object)	Adds the specified object at the specified index position.
clear()	Removes all elements from the list.
contains(object)	Returns true if the specified object is in the list.
get(index)	Returns the object at the specified index position.
indexOf(object)	Returns the index position of the specified object.
isEmpty()	Returns true if the list is empty.
remove(index)	Removes the object at the specified index position.
remove(object)	Removes the specified object.
set(index, object)	Sets the element at the specified index to the specified object.
size()	Returns the number of elements in the list.
toArray()	Returns an array containing the elements of the list.

Description

- An *array list* is a collection that's similar to an array, but can change its capacity as elements are added or removed. The ArrayList class uses an array to store the elements it contains.
- You can specify the type of elements to be stored in the array list by naming a type in angle brackets.
- You can specify the size of an array list when you create it, or you can let the array list default to an initial capacity of 10 elements.
- The capacity of an array list automatically increases whenever necessary.

Figure 11-4 The ArrayList class

Code examples that work with array lists

Figure 11-5 shows four code examples that use the ArrayList class. The first example creates an ArrayList of type String and adds three string values to it. Notice that the third call to the add method specifies an index value of 0. As a result, the string "warp" will be added as the first element in the array list, and the strings that were added before it ("mbdk" and "citr") will be moved down in the list.

Next, this example uses a standard for loop to print the elements in the array list. Inside the loop, the get method is called to retrieve each element by its index. Then, the println method is called to display the element. The resulting output shows the three strings in the order they're stored in the list.

The second example shows an alternate way to display the values in a collection. To do that, you simply specify the name of the collection in the println method. This implicitly calls the collection's toString method, which returns a string that lists the value of each element. Because the values are all listed on the same line and enclosed in brackets, this technique is useful only for collections with just a few elements.

The third example shows how to replace or delete elements in an array list. First, the set method is called to change the value of the element at index 1 to "wuth." Then, the remove method is used to delete the element whose value is "warp." Finally, the remove method is used to delete the element whose index is 1.

In the output for this example, you can see that the only remaining element in the collection is "wuth." You might be wondering why that element remains, since the element at index 1 was deleted by the third statement in this example. The reason is that the second statement deleted the element whose value is "warp." This element was at index 0, so when it was deleted, the elements after element 0 were moved up 1 position. As a result, element 1 ("wuth") was moved to element 0 and element 2 ("citr") was moved to element 1. Then, the third statement deleted "citr", not "wuth."

The fourth example shows code that works with an array list of type Integer. If you're new to Java, there's probably nothing remarkable about this example. However, if you've worked with collections in older versions of Java, you'll notice that no special coding is required to add int values to an array of Integers. That's because Java 5.0 automatically converts int values to Integer values and vice versa using a technique called *autoboxing*. In previous versions of Java, you had to call the constructor of the Integer class to create a new Integer object with the desired value. You'll see an example of this later in this chapter when we present techniques for working with legacy collections.

Example 1: Code that uses an array list of type String

```
// create an array list of type String
ArrayList<String> codes = new ArrayList<String>();

// add three strings
codes.add("mbdk");
codes.add("citr");
codes.add(0, "warp");

// print the array list
for (int i =0; i < codes.size(); i++)
{
    String code = codes.get(i);
    System.out.println(code);
}
```

Resulting output

```
warp
mbdk
citr
```

Example 2: Another way to display the contents of a collection

```
System.out.println(codes);
```

Resulting output

```
[warp, mbdk, citr]
```

Example 3: Code that replaces and deletes objects

```
codes.set(1,"wuth");
codes.remove("warp");
codes.remove(1);

System.out.print(codes);
```

Resulting output

```
[wuth]
```

Example 4: Code that uses an array list of type Integer

```
ArrayList<Integer> numbers = new ArrayList<Integer>();
numbers.add(1);
numbers.add(2);
numbers.add(3);

System.out.println(numbers);
```

Resulting output

```
[1, 2, 3]
```

Description

- When you use generics to create a collection that holds a wrapper type, the compiler automatically converts the primitive type to its wrapper type and vice versa using a technique called *autoboxing*.

Figure 11-5 Code examples that work with array lists

An Invoice application that uses an array list

The topics that follow present an Invoice application that lets the user enter one or more line items. This is similar to the Line Item application you've seen in earlier chapters, but the Invoice application stores the line items in an array list within an Invoice object.

An overview of the Invoice application

As figure 11-6 shows, the Invoice application lets the user enter a product code and quantity for one or more line items. As each line item is entered, the application adds it to the invoice and asks if the user wants to enter another line item. When the user is finished entering linc items, the application displays a list of the line items for the invoice. Then, it displays the total for all the invoices and ends.

The Invoice application uses six classes. The first four classes listed in this figure were presented in chapter 6. If you want to refresh your memory on how those classes work, you can refer back to that chapter to see the code for these classes. In this chapter, I'll present the code for the two new classes used by this application: the Invoice class, which represents the invoice entered by the user, and the InvoiceApp class, which contains the main method for the application.

As this figure shows, the Invoice class has one constructor (which accepts no parameters) and four methods. The addItem method adds a LineItem object to the invoice. The line item is stored within the Invoice object in an array list that can be accessed via the getLineItems method. The getInvoiceTotal method returns a double that's the sum of the totals for all the line items in the invoice. And the getFormattedTotal method returns this same value with a currency format.

Note that this application lets the user enter just one invoice, and it doesn't save the invoice when the application ends. A more realistic application would process more than one invoice, and the invoices would be saved to a file or database. In addition, the Invoice object would include additional information such as information about the customer, an invoice number, invoice date, and so on. The point of this application, though, is just to illustrate the use of an ArrayList.

Console output for the Invoice application

```
Welcome to the invoice application.

Enter product code: java
Enter quantity:     1
Another line item? (y/n): y

Enter product code: jsps
Enter quantity:     2
Another line item? (y/n): n

Code    Description                      Price    Qty    Total
----    -----------                      -----    ---    -----
java    Murach's Beginning Java 2        $49.50   1      $49.50
jsps    Murach's Java Servlets and JSP   $49.50   2      $99.00

                                         Invoice total:  $148.50
```

Classes used by the Invoice application

Name	Description	Figure
Product	Represents a Product object.	6-4
ProductDB	Provides a getProduct method that retrieves the Product object for a specified product code.	6-13
Validator	Provides methods that accept and validate user input.	6-20
LineItem	Represents an invoice line item, which includes a Product object, a quantity, and a total.	6-21
Invoice	Represents a single invoice. The line items are represented by an array list.	11-7
InvoiceApp	Contains the main method for the Invoice application.	11-8

The constructor and methods for the Invoice class

Constructor	Description
`Invoice()`	Creates an empty invoice.

Method	Description
`void addItem(LineItem lineItem)`	Adds the specified line item to the invoice.
`ArrayList getLineItems()`	Returns an ArrayList object that contains the line items for the invoice.
`double getInvoiceTotal()`	Returns a double that contains the sum of the totals for the line items in the invoice.
`String getFormattedTotal()`	Returns a String that contains the invoice total formatted as currency.

Description

- The user enters a product code and quantity for each line item to be added to the invoice. When the user indicates that all of the line items have been entered, the application displays each line item on a separate line along with the total for the invoice.

Figure 11-6 An overview of the Invoice application

The code for the Invoice class

Figure 11-7 presents the code for the Invoice class. This class defines one instance variable, which is an array list of LineItem objects named lineItems. This array list is used to store the line items for the invoice. The default constructor for the Invoice class instantiates the lineItems array list but doesn't add any line items to it.

The addItem method accepts a LineItem object as a parameter. This method consists of a single line that calls the add method of the lineItems array list to add the line item to the array list.

The getLineItems method provides access to the lineItems array list. Notice that the return type for this method (ArrayList<LineItem>) specifies the generic type of the array list that's returned to the caller. If you omitted the type here, the class would compile correctly. However, an error would occur when you tried to use the method.

The getInvoiceTotal method uses an enhanced for loop to process each LineItem element in the lineItems array list. Within this loop, the getTotal method is called for the current line item, and the result is added to the invoiceTotal variable. Then, the invoiceTotal variable is used as the method's return value.

Finally, the getFormattedTotal method uses the NumberFormat class to format the invoice total as a currency string. Notice that this method calls the getInvoiceTotal method to get the invoice total. That way, the getFormattedTotal method doesn't duplicate the code used to calculate the invoice total.

The code for the Invoice class

```
import java.text.NumberFormat;
import java.util.ArrayList;

public class Invoice
{
    // the instance variable
    private ArrayList<LineItem> lineItems;

    // the constructor
    public Invoice()
    {
        lineItems = new ArrayList<LineItem>();
    }

    // a method that adds a line item
    public void addItem(LineItem lineItem)
    {
        this.lineItems.add(lineItem);
    }

    // the get accessor for the line item collection
    public ArrayList<LineItem> getLineItems()
    {
        return lineItems;
    }

    // a method that gets the invoice total
    public double getInvoiceTotal()
    {
        double invoiceTotal = 0;
        for (LineItem lineItem : this.lineItems)
        {
            invoiceTotal += lineItem.getTotal();
        }
        return invoiceTotal;
    }

    // a method that returns the invoice total in currency format
    public String getFormattedTotal()
    {
        NumberFormat currency = NumberFormat.getCurrencyInstance();
        return currency.format(this.getInvoiceTotal());
    }
}
```

Figure 11-7 The code for the Invoice class

The code for the InvoiceApp class

Figure 11-8 shows the code for the InvoiceApp class, the main class for the Invoice application. First, it displays a welcome message. Then, it calls a method named getLineItems to get the line items for the invoice. Finally, it calls a method named displayInvoice to display the invoice's line items and total. Because both of these methods need access to the invoice data entered by the user, an Invoice object named invoice is declared at the class level. That way, the getLineItems method can add line items to the invoice and the displayInvoice method can retrieve the line items and calculate the invoice total.

The getLineItems method uses a while loop to let the user enter one or more line items. Within the while loop, the Scanner class and the Validator class are used to get a valid product code and quantity from the user. Then, the getProduct method of the ProductDB class is called to get a Product object for the code entered by the user. Next, the getLineItems method calls the addItem method of the invoice object to add the line item to the invoice. Because the addItem method accepts a LineItem object, a new instance of the LineItem class is created using the Product object and the quantity entered by the user.

After the line item has been added to the invoice, the user is asked whether he or she wants to enter another line item. The reply is saved in the choice variable, which is used to control the while loop.

The displayInvoice method is called when the user has finished entering line items. This method uses an enhanced for loop to process the line items. This for loop calls the getLineItems method of the invoice object to get an array list of LineItem objects. Then, it calls the getProduct method of the line item object to get the Product object for each line item so its code, name, and price can be displayed. After all the line items are displayed, the displayInvoice method calls the getFormattedTotal method of the invoice object to get the total of all the invoices in currency format. Then, this value is displayed at the console.

The code for the InvoiceApp class

```
import java.util.Scanner;

public class InvoiceApp
{
    public static Invoice invoice = new Invoice();

    public static void main(String args[])
    {
        System.out.println("Welcome to the invoice application.\n");
        getLineItems();
        displayInvoice();
    }

    public static void getLineItems()
    {
        Scanner sc = new Scanner(System.in);
        String choice = "y";
        while (choice.equalsIgnoreCase("y"))
        {
            // get the input from the user
            String productCode = Validator.getString(sc,
                "Enter product code: ");
            int quantity = Validator.getInt(sc,
                "Enter quantity:      ", 0, 1000);

            Product product = ProductDB.getProduct(productCode);
            invoice.addItem(new LineItem(product, quantity));

            // see if the user wants to continue
            choice = Validator.getString(sc, "Another line item? (y/n): ");
            System.out.println();
        }
     }

    public static void displayInvoice()
    {
        System.out.println("Code\tDescription\t\t\tPrice\tQty\tTotal");
        System.out.println("----\t-----------\t\t\t-----\t---\t-----");
        for (LineItem lineItem : invoice.getLineItems())
        {
            Product product = lineItem.getProduct();
            String s = product.getCode()
                + "\t" + product.getDescription()
                + "\t" + product.getFormattedPrice()
                + "\t" + lineItem.getQuantity()
                + "\t" + lineItem.getFormattedTotal();
            System.out.println(s);
        }
        System.out.println("\n\t\t\t\t\tInvoice total:\t"
            + invoice.getFormattedTotal() + "\n");
    }
}
```

Figure 11-8 The code for the InvoiceApp class

How to use the LinkedList class

The LinkedList class is similar to the ArrayList class, but it provides more features and uses a different technique to store its data. The topics that follow describe the LinkedList class and show some code examples that illustrate how you can use this class.

The LinkedList class

Figure 11-9 presents an overview of the LinkedList class, which creates a special type of list called a *linked list*. Unlike an array list, a linked list doesn't use an array to store its elements. Instead, the elements you add to a linked list are stored as separate objects. Each list element is stored along with a pointer to the object that precedes it and the object that follows it. As a result, the LinkedList class can use these pointers to navigate through the entire list.

Because the entries for a linked list aren't stored in an array, inserting an element into the middle of a linked list is more efficient than inserting an element into the middle of an array list. To insert an element into the middle of an array list, all of the elements that follow the insertion point must be moved down in the list. The more elements in the array list and the closer to the beginning of the array the insertion point is, the longer it takes to insert the element. In contrast, an element can be inserted into the middle of a linked list by simply adjusting the previous and next pointers for the elements that precede and follow the insertion point.

There is a trade-off to this efficiency, however. Although a linked list can be updated more quickly than an array list, it can't be accessed as quickly. Because all of the elements in an array list are stored in adjacent memory locations, access to those elements is fast. In contrast, access to the elements in a linked list is relatively slow because the pointers for the elements must be used.

For example, suppose you use the get method to access the 500th element in a linked list with more than 1,000 elements. To do that, the get method begins by accessing the first element in the list to get the pointer to the second element. It then accesses the second element to get a pointer to the third element. This process continues until the 500th element has been retrieved. In other words, to access a particular element in a linked list, all of the elements that precede it must be accessed.

(Actually, the get method first checks to see if the element being retrieved is closer to the first or last element in the list. If the element is closer to the last element, the search for the element begins at the last element and proceeds backwards until the desired element is located.)

When you develop a Java application that calls for a list, you should carefully consider whether to implement the collection using the ArrayList class or the LinkedList class. This is especially important if the list will contain a large number of elements. The larger the list, the more important the performance trade-offs of using an array list or a linked list become. In many cases, though, you'll use a linked list simply because you need the additional features that the LinkedList class provides.

The LinkedList class

`java.util.LinkedList`

A constructor for the LinkedList class

Constructor	Description
`LinkedList<E>()`	Creates an empty linked list using the specified type.

Common methods of the LinkedList class

Method	Description
`add(object)`	Adds the specified object to the list.
`add(index, object)`	Adds the specified object at the specified index position.
`addFirst(object)`	Adds the specified object to the beginning of the list.
`addLast(object)`	Adds the specified object to the end of the list.
`clear()`	Removes all elements from the list.
`contains(object)`	Returns true if the specified object is in the list.
`get(index)`	Returns the object at the specified index position.
`getFirst()`	Returns the first element in the list.
`getLast()`	Returns the last element in the list.
`indexOf(object)`	Returns the index position of the specified object.
`peek()`	Returns but doesn't remove the first element in the list.
`offer(object)`	Attempts to add the specified object to the end of the list. Returns true if the object was added. Returns false if the object is rejected.
`poll()`	Returns and removes the first element from the list. Returns null if the list is empty.
`remove()`	Returns and removes the first element from the list. Throws NoSuchElementException if the list is empty.
`remove(index)`	Removes and returns the object at the specified index position.
`remove(object)`	Removes the specified object.
`removeFirst()`	Removes and returns the first element of the list.
`removeLast()`	Removes and returns the last element of the list.
`set(index, object)`	Replaces the element at the specified index position with the specified object.
`size()`	Returns the number of elements in the list.
`toArray()`	Returns an array containing the elements of the list.

Description

- A *linked list* is a collection that's similar to an array list. However, the LinkedList class doesn't use an array to store its elements. Instead, each element in the list contains pointers that are used to refer to adjacent elements.
- You can specify the type of elements the linked list can contain by listing the type in angle brackets.
- The LinkedList class contains methods that let you perform more advanced operations than the ArrayList class.

Figure 11-9 The LinkedList class

Code examples that work with linked lists

Figure 11-10 shows four code examples that demonstrate the basic techniques for working with linked lists. The first example creates a linked list of type String and uses the add method to add three strings to the list. Then, it uses the println method to display the contents of the linked list by implicitly calling the list's toString method. As you can see, the strings are displayed in the order in which they were added to the list.

The second example shows code that uses the addFirst and addLast methods to add entries to the beginning and end of the list. As you can see in the console output for this example, the string added by the addFirst method appears first, followed by the three strings that were added in the first example, followed by the string that was added by the addLast method.

The third example shows code that uses an enhanced for loop to process all of the elements in the linked list. Note that you could also process the list using a standard for loop with an index variable and the get method. However, processing a linked list with an enhanced for loop is more efficient than processing it with a standard for loop. That's because the enhanced for loop is able to efficiently use the pointers stored with each list entry to access the next element in the list. For example, to move from the 100th element to the 101st element, the enhanced for loop simply uses the pointer to the next element. In contrast, the get method must start at the beginning of the list each time an element is accessed.

The fourth example shows code that uses the removeFirst and removeLast methods to retrieve and remove the first and last elements from the list. Notice that after these methods have been called, the list consists of just the three elements that were added in the first example.

Example 1: Code that creates a linked list of type String

```
// create a linked list of type String
LinkedList<String> codes = new LinkedList<String>();

// add three strings
codes.add("mbdk");
codes.add("citr");
codes.add(0, "warp");

System.out.println(codes);
```

Resulting output

```
[warp, mbdk, citr]
```

Example 2: Code that adds elements to the beginning and end of the list

```
codes.addFirst("wuth");
codes.addLast("wooz");

System.out.println(codes);
```

Resulting output

```
[wuth, warp, mbdk, citr, wooz]
```

Example 3: Code that uses an enhanced for loop to process the list

```
for (String s : codes)
    System.out.println(s);
```

Resulting output

```
wuth
warp
mbdk
citr
wooz
```

Example 4: Code that retrieves the first and last elements of the list

```
String firstString = codes.removeFirst();
String lastString = codes.removeLast();
System.out.println(firstString);
System.out.println(lastString);
System.out.println(codes);
```

Resulting output

```
wuth
wooz
[warp, mbdk, citr]
```

Figure 11-10 Code examples that work with linked lists

A class that uses a linked list to implement a generic queue

As figure 11-11 shows, a *queue* is a type of collection that lets you access elements on a first-in, first-out basis. Queues are used in many different types of data processing applications. For example, orders that are entered online at a web site are often queued so that they're processed in the order in which they were received.

A queue supports two basic operations: *push*, which adds an entry to the end of the queue, and *pull,* which retrieves the entry that's at the front of the queue. Note that whenever you pull an entry, the entry is removed from the queue. As a result, all of the other entries in the queue move up one position in the queue.

The LinkedList class provides the basic operations you need to implement a queue. The addLast method provides the push operation, and the removeFirst method provides the pull operation. Although the LinkedList class provides many other operations, most aren't used for queues.

The code in the first example in this figure shows a class that implements a simple queue based on the LinkedList class. Here, the class creates a linked list as a private class variable. Then, it exposes three methods: push, which calls the addLast method of the LinkedList class; pull, which calls the removeFirst method; and size, which calls the size method. When you use this class, all other features of the LinkedList class are effectively hidden.

Notice that the declaration for this class includes a type variable named E. This allows for any type of object to be stored in the queue. As you can see, this type variable is used when the linked list is created, it's used as the parameter type for the push method, and it's used as the return type for the pull method. So, for example, if the user specifies String for the queue type, the GenericQueue class creates a linked list of type String. In addition, the push method accepts a String parameter and the pull method returns a String value.

The second example shows how this works. The code in this example starts by creating a queue that will store strings. Then, it calls the push method three times to add three entries to the queue. Next, it uses the println method to display the number of entries in the queue. To do that, it calls the size method. Finally, it uses a while loop to pull and print each entry. This loop executes as long as the size method of the queue indicates that there is at least one more entry in the queue.

Basic methods of a class that implements a generic queue

Method	Description
push(element)	Adds the specified element to the end of the queue.
pull()	Retrieves and removes an element from the front of the queue.
size()	Returns the number of elements in the queue.

Example 1: Code for a GenericQueue class that implements a queue

```
import java.util.LinkedList;

public class GenericQueue<E>
{
    private LinkedList<E> list = new LinkedList<E>();

    public void push(E item)
    {
        list.addLast(item);
    }

    public E pull()
    {
        return list.removeFirst();
    }

    public int size()
    {
        return list.size();
    }
}
```

Example 2: Code that uses the GenericQueue class

```
GenericQueue<String> q1 = new GenericQueue<String>();
q1.push("Item One");
q1.push("Item Two");
q1.push("Item Three");
System.out.println("The queue contains " + q1.size() + " items");
while (q1.size > 0)
    System.out.println(q1.pull());
System.out.println("The queue now contains " + q1.size() + " items");
```

Resulting output

```
The queue contains 3 items
Item One
Item Two
Item Three
The queue now contains 0 items
```

Description

- A *queue* is a first-in, first-out collection. To implement a queue, you can use a linked list as shown above.
- A class that implements a queue is typically declared with a type variable that's used to specify the type of objects the queue will hold.

Figure 11-11 A class that uses a linked list to implement a generic queue

An enhanced version of the Invoice application

The following topics present an enhanced version of the Invoice application that was presented earlier in this chapter. This version illustrates one way to use a linked list in an application.

An overview of the enhanced Invoice application

Figure 11-12 shows the operation of the enhanced Invoice application. This version is similar to the version that was presented in figures 11-6 through 11-8. However, in addition to letting the user enter several line items for each invoice, it lets the user enter more than one invoice. These invoices are saved in a queue created using the GenericQueue class that was shown in figure 11-11. When the user finishes entering invoices, the application displays one line for each invoice that lists the invoice number and the invoice total. Then, it displays a total for all of the invoices.

Because the Invoice class doesn't provide for an invoice number, this application simply assigns sequential numbers to the invoices, starting with 1 for the first invoice entered. In addition, it doesn't save the invoice numbers with the invoices. Although I could have created another version of the Invoice class for this application that included an invoice number, that would have unnecessarily complicated the code without illustrating any additional features of the LinkedList class.

This application uses several classes in addition to the InvoiceApp class that's presented in the next figure. You saw the GenericQueue class in the last figure, and you saw the Invoice class in figure 11-7. The other classes—LineItem, Product, ProductDB, and Validator—are identical to the versions that were shown in chapter 6.

Console output for the enhanced Invoice application

```
Welcome to the invoice application.


Enter line items for invoice 1
Enter product code: java
Enter quantity:     1
Another line item? (y/n): n

Another invoice? (y/n): y


Enter line items for invoice 2
Enter product code: jsps
Enter quantity:     2
Another line item? (y/n): n

Another invoice? (y/n): n

You entered the following invoices:

Number  Total
------  -----
1       $49.50
2       $99.00
Total for all invoices: $148.50
```

Description

- This version of the Invoice application lets the user enter more than one invoice. The invoices are stored in a queue created from the GenericQueue class that was presented in figure 11-11.
- When the user has finished entering invoices, the application displays the invoice number and total for each invoice. Then, the application displays the total for all the invoices that were entered.
- The Invoice application assigns an invoice number to each invoice, starting with 1 for the first invoice entered. However, the invoice number isn't stored as a part of the Invoice object.

Figure 11-12 An overview of the enhanced Invoice application

The code for the InvoiceApp class

Figure 11-13 shows the code for the InvoiceApp class of the enhanced Invoice application. This code begins by declaring a static variable named invoices that will be used to store the invoices entered by the user. This variable is created from the GenericQueue class, and the type for the queue is specified as Invoice. As a result, the queue can be used for storing Invoice objects.

This class also declares an Invoice variable named invoice. This variable will be used to refer to the invoice that's currently being entered by the user. Notice that this statement doesn't instantiate an Invoice object. Instead, a new Invoice object will be instantiated each time the user indicates that there's another invoice to be entered.

After it displays a welcome message, the main method calls the getInvoices method. This method uses a while loop to get invoices from the user until the user indicates there are no more invoices to be entered. This loop begins by instantiating a new Invoice object and displaying a message that indicates the invoice number to be entered. Then, it calls the getLineItems method to get all of the line items for the invoice. The getLineItems method is almost identical to the getLineItems method you saw in figure 11-8, so I won't explain its operation here.

After the user has entered all of the line items for an invoice, the getInvoices method adds the invoice to the invoices collection by calling the push method. Then, it asks if the user wants to enter another invoice and increments the invoice number variable.

Code for the InvoiceApp class

Page 1

```
import java.util.Scanner;
import java.text.NumberFormat;

public class InvoiceApp
{
    private static GenericQueue<Invoice> invoices
        = new GenericQueue<Invoice>();

    private static Invoice invoice;

    private static Scanner sc;

    public static void main(String args[])
    {
        System.out.println("Welcome to the invoice application.\n");
        getInvoices();
        displayInvoices();
    }

    public static void getInvoices()
    {
        sc = new Scanner(System.in);
        int invoiceNumber = 1;
        String anotherInvoice = "y";
        while (anotherInvoice.equalsIgnoreCase("y"))
        {
            invoice = new Invoice();
            System.out.println("\nEnter line items for invoice "
                + invoiceNumber);
            getLineItems();
            invoices.push(invoice);

            // see if the user wants to continue
            anotherInvoice = Validator.getString(sc,
                "Another invoice? (y/n): ");
            System.out.println();
            invoiceNumber++;
        }
    }
```

Figure 11-13 The code for the InvoiceApp class (part 1 of 2)

When the user indicates there are no more invoices to enter, control returns to the main method. Then, this method calls the displayInvoices method to display the details for each invoice. This method uses a while loop that executes as long as the size method of the invoices collection indicates that there is at least one more invoice in the queue. Variables named invoiceNumber and batchTotal are used to keep track of the invoice numbers and totals for the invoices that were entered. Within the loop, the pull method is called to retrieve each Invoice object from the queue. Next, the println method is called to display the invoice number and the total for the invoice, the invoice number is incremented, and the invoice total is added to the batchTotal variable. After all of the invoices have been displayed, the batchTotal value is formatted and displayed.

Code for the InvoiceApp class

Page 2

```
    public static void getLineItems()
    {
        String anotherItem = "y";
        while (anotherItem.equalsIgnoreCase("y"))
        {
            // get the input from the user
            String productCode = Validator.getString(sc,
                "Enter product code: ");
            int quantity = Validator.getInt(sc,
                "Enter quantity:     ", 0, 1000);

            Product product = ProductDB.getProduct(productCode);
            invoice.addItem(new LineItem(product, quantity));

            // see if the user wants to continue
            anotherItem = Validator.getString(sc,
                "Another line item? (y/n): ");
            System.out.println();
        }
    }

    public static void displayInvoices()
    {
        System.out.println("You entered the following invoices:\n");
        System.out.println("Number\tTotal");
        System.out.println("------\t-----");
        double batchTotal = 0;
        int invoiceNumber = 1;
        while (invoices.size() > 0)
        {
            Invoice invoice = invoices.pull();
            System.out.println(invoiceNumber + "\t"
                + invoice.getFormattedTotal());
            invoiceNumber++;
            batchTotal += invoice.getInvoiceTotal();
        }
        NumberFormat currency = NumberFormat.getCurrencyInstance();
        System.out.println("Total for all invoices: "
            + currency.format(batchTotal));
    }
}
```

Figure 11-13 The code for the InvoiceApp class (part 2 of 2)

How to work with maps

The next two topics show you how to work with two classes that implement the Map interface: HashMap and TreeMap. These classes let you create collections in which objects can be accessed by using a key value. The main difference between a *hash map* and a *tree map* is that the entries in a hash map are not stored in any particular sequence, while the entries in a tree map are automatically sorted by key value.

The HashMap and TreeMap classes

Figure 11-14 presents the HashMap and TreeMap classes. Both of these classes implement the Map interface, which defines the basic behavior of a map. A *map* is a collection whose elements are pairs of keys and values. For example, you might use a map to store a collection of Product objects that can be accessed by a product code. In that case, the keys would be product codes and the values would be Product objects.

Unlike the other collections you've seen in this chapter, you specify two types when you declare and instantiate a map. The first, identified as K in the figure, represents the type of the map's keys. The second, identified as V, is the type of the map's objects. Typically, the key is a simple type such as String or Integer and the value is a user-defined type such as Product or Customer.

Like other collections, you use the get method to retrieve an object from a map. The get method accepts a single parameter that represents the key value for the object you want to retrieve. Then, the get method returns the value object that corresponds to the specified key. If the key isn't in the map, the get method returns null.

Although it's unlikely, it's possible for a key value to be in the map, but for the value associated with the key to be null. In that case, the get method will return null. Because of that, a null can mean that either the key isn't in the map, or the key is in the map but the value object associated with the key is null. To distinguish between these possibilities, you can use the containsKey method. This method returns true if the key is in the map and false if it isn't.

Unlike other types of collections, maps don't have an add method. Instead, the Map interface uses a method called put to add an element to a map. The put method accepts two arguments that represent the key and value. If the key is already in the map, the put method replaces the existing value.

Each element of a map implements an interface called Map.Entry. As this figure shows, this interface provides two methods that you can use to get the key and value for an entry: getKey and getValue. You'll see examples of how this interface is used in the next figure.

In case you're interested, a hash map and a tree map use different data structures to store their elements. A hash map uses a data structure called a *hash table*, and a tree map uses a structure called a *red-black tree*. The details of how these structures work are beyond the scope of this book. But if you're interested, you can go to any Web search page (such as www.google.com) and search for these structures by name.

The HashMap and TreeMap classes

```
java.util.HashMap
java.util.TreeMap
```

Common constructors of the HashMap and TreeMap classes

Constructor	Description
`HashMap<K,V>()`	Creates an empty HashMap using the specified types for the keys and values.
`TreeMap<K,V>()`	Creates an empty TreeMap using the specified types for the keys and values.

Common methods of the HashMap and TreeMap classes

Method	Description
`clear()`	Removes all entries from the map.
`containsKey(key)`	Returns true if the specified key is in the map.
`containsValue(value)`	Returns true if the specified value is in the map.
`entrySet()`	Returns a set of all the entries in the map as Map.Entry objects.
`get(key)`	Returns the value for the entry with the specified key. Returns null if the key isn't found.
`put(key, value)`	Adds an entry with the specified key and value, or replaces the value if an entry with the key already exists.
`remove(key)`	Removes the entry with the specified key.
`size()`	Returns the number of entries in the map.

Common methods of the Map.Entry interface

Method	Description
`getKey()`	Returns the key for the map entry.
`getValue()`	Returns the value for the map entry.

Description

- A *map* is a collection that contains values that are associated with keys. The two most commonly used classes that implement maps are HashMap and TreeMap.
- The main difference between a hash map and a tree map is that a tree map automatically maintains entries in order based on the key values. In contrast, a hash map doesn't maintain its entries in sorted order. If an application doesn't require that the entries be kept in order, a hash map is often more efficient than a tree map.
- Each entry of a map implements the Map.Entry interface in the java.util.Map package. You can use two of the methods provided by this interface to get the key and value for an entry.

Note

- You can use a custom class for the key objects of a hash map. To do that, the class must override the hashCode and equals methods inherited from Object. For more information, see the Java documentation.

Figure 11-14 The HashMap and TreeMap classes

Code examples that work with hash maps and tree maps

Figure 11-15 shows two code examples that work with maps. The only difference between these two examples is that the first one uses the HashMap class and the second one uses the TreeMap class. Other than the line that creates the map, the code for these two examples is identical. However, the resulting output is different.

Both examples start by declaring and creating a map named books. This map will be used to store book titles that are associated with codes. Because both the book titles and the book codes are strings, this statement specifies String for both the key and value type. Then, the next three statements use the put method to add three entries to the map.

Next, an enhanced for loop is used to display the entries in the map. Notice that the element type in this loop is Map.Entry. As a result, the statement within the loop can use the getKey and getValue methods of the Map.Entry interface to get the key and value objects for an entry. After this loop is executed, the get method is used to get the title of the book whose code is “mbdk” and that title is displayed at the console.

Notice in the resulting output for the first example that the books in the hash map aren’t stored in key sequence. In addition, they aren’t stored in the order in which they were added to the map. Instead, their positions in the collection are determined by a hashing function that converts the key values to index values. In contrast, the output for the second example shows that the books in the tree map are stored in key sequence.

Example 1: Code that uses a hash map

```
// create an empty hash map
HashMap<String, String> books = new HashMap<String, String>();

// add three entries
books.put("wooz", "Wizard of Oz");
books.put("mbdk", "Moby Dick");
books.put("wuth", "Wuthering Heights");

// print the entries
for (Map.Entry book : books.entrySet())
    System.out.println(book.getKey() + ": " + book.getValue());

// print the entry whose key is "mbdk"
System.out.println("\nCode mbdk is " + books.get("mbdk"));
```

Resulting output

```
wuth: Wuthering Heights
mbdk: Moby Dick
wooz: Wizard of Oz

Code mbdk is Moby Dick
```

Example 2: Code that uses a tree map

```
// create an empty tree map
TreeMap<String,String> books = new TreeMap<String, String>();

// add three entries
books.put("wooz", "Wizard of Oz");
books.put("mbdk", "Moby Dick");
books.put("wuth", "Wuthering Heights");

// print the entries
for (Map.Entry book : books.entrySet())
    System.out.println(book.getKey() + ": " + book.getValue());

// print the entry whose key is "mbdk"
System.out.println("\nCode mbdk is " + books.get("mbdk"));
```

Resulting output

```
mbdk: Moby Dick
wooz: Wizard of Oz
wuth: Wuthering Heights

Code mbdk is Moby Dick
```

Figure 11-15 Code examples that work with hash maps and tree maps

How to work with legacy collections

Java's collection classes have gone through several major overhauls over the years. Originally, Java included just a few collection classes, and they weren't very powerful. In the topics that follow, you'll be introduced to these classes. That way, you'll be familiar with them if you ever encounter code that uses them. In addition, you'll learn how to work with the classes in the collection framework without using generics. You'll see code like this in any application that was written before Java 5.0.

An introduction to legacy collection classes

Figure 11-16 presents a brief introduction to Java legacy collection classes. These classes are called *legacy classes* because although they are no longer the preferred classes, they are widely used in existing Java applications. Note that these classes have not been deprecated, so they are still fully supported by the Java API. However, you should use the newer collection framework classes for new application development.

The Vector class works much like the ArrayList class. In fact, the ArrayList class is in many ways simply an improved version of the Vector class. The HashTable class is an older class that has been replaced by the HashMap class. And the Stack class has been replaced by the LinkedList class.

The code example in this figure shows how to create a simple *vector*, add some string values to it, and display its contents using a for loop. If you compare this example with the first example in figure 11-5 that works with an array list, you'll find that they're similar. One difference is that the first statement in this figure declares the codes variable as a vector rather than as an array list. Another difference is that the object that's returned by the get method must be cast from the Object type to the String type.

Legacy collection classes

Class	Description
Vector	Provides features similar to the more powerful ArrayList class.
HashTable	Provides features similar to the more powerful HashMap class.
Stack	A type of Vector that implements a *stack*, which is a last-in, first-out list. The LinkedList class is now the preferred class for implementing a stack.

Code that uses a vector

```
// create a vector
Vector codes = new Vector();

// add three strings
codes.add("mbdk");
codes.add("citr");
codes.add(0, "warp");

// print the vector
for (int i =0; i < codes.size(); i++)
{
    String code = (String)codes.get(i);
    System.out.println(code);
}
```

Resulting output

```
warp
mbdk
citr
```

Description

- The collection hierarchy was introduced with Java 1.2. For compatibility reasons, Java still supports older collection classes such as Vector, HashTable, and Stack. However, you should avoid using these classes for new software development.
- The classes listed in this figure aren't deprecated. They are still fully supported as part of the Java API.
- The Vector class was the most commonly used legacy collection class. Because the newer ArrayList class is an improved version of the Vector class, the code used to work with a *vector* is similar to the code used to work with an array list.

Figure 11-16 An introduction to legacy collection classes

How to use an untyped collection

Figure 11-17 shows how to work with a collection whose type isn't specified. This type of collection, called an *untyped collection*, holds elements of type Object. This is the only type of collection that was available before Java 5.0.

The code at the top of this figure shows how you work with an untyped array list. After creating the array list, this code creates three Product objects and adds them to the list. Then, it uses a for loop to display the products. Within the for loop, the get method is used to retrieve each product. Because the array list is untyped, the get method returns an object of type Object. Then, this object must be cast to a Product object.

Although you can use code like this in applications you develop with Java 5.0, you're encouraged to use generics instead to create typed collections. In fact, if you use an untyped collection with Java 5.0, the compiler generates warning messages like the ones shown in this figure each time you add an element to the collection. Because these are only warning messages, the code will still compile and execute. If you ever see messages like this, however, you should consider modifying your code to use a typed collection.

Code that stores strings in an untyped array list

```
// create an untyped array list
ArrayList products = new ArrayList();

// add three productss
products.add(new Product("dctp", "Duct Tape", 4.95));
products.add(new Product("blwr", "Bailing Wire", 14.95));
products.add(new Product("cgum", "Chewing Gum", 0.95));

// print the array list
for (int i = 0; i < products.size(); i++)
{
    Product p = (Product)products.get(i);
    System.out.println(p.getCode() + "\t" + p.getDescription() + "\t"
        + p.getFormattedPrice());
}
```

Compiler warnings generated by the above code

```
H:\Java 1.5\examples\ch10\Untyped Arraylist\UntypedArrayList.java:13:
warning: [unchecked] unchecked call to add(E) as a member of the raw type
java.util.ArrayList
          products.add(new Product("dctp", "Duct Tape", 4.95));
                           ^
H:\Java 1.5\examples\ch10\Untyped Arraylist\UntypedArrayList.java:14:
warning: [unchecked] unchecked call to add(E) as a member of the raw type
java.util.ArrayList
          products.add(new Product("blwr", "Bailing Wire", 14.95));
                           ^
H:\Java 1.5\examples\ch10\Untyped Arraylist\UntypedArrayList.java:15:
warning: [unchecked] unchecked call to add(E) as a member of the raw type
java.util.ArrayList
          products.add(new Product("cgum", "Chewing Gum", 0.95));
                           ^
3 warnings

Tool completed successfully
```

Resulting output

```
dctp    Duct Tape       $4.95
blwr    Bailing Wire    $14.95
cgum    Chewing Gum     $0.95
```

Description

- Code written before Java 5.0 uses *untyped collections*, which don't use generics to specify the element type.
- Untyped collections hold elements of type Object. No special coding is required to add objects to an untyped collection. However, you must usually specify a cast to retrieve objects from an untyped collection.
- The Java 5.0 compiler generates a warning message whenever you add an element to an untyped collection.

Figure 11-17 How to use an untyped collection

How to use wrapper classes with untyped collections

Figure 11-18 shows another complication of working with untyped collections. In short, until Java 5.0, you couldn't add primitive data types directly to a collection. That's because the methods that add elements to a collection take an Object type as a parameter and, in Java, primitive types aren't derived from the Object class.

The solution to this problem is to use wrapper classes to create objects that contain the primitive values you want to add to the collection. Once you do that, the wrapper object can be stored in the collection.

The first example in this figure shows how this works. The code in this example creates instances of the Integer class to add three integer values to an untyped array list. If it had specified the integer values directly as arguments to the add method, the compiler would have generated an error.

To retrieve a primitive value from a collection, you can cast the retrieved value to the wrapper type as shown in the second example. Here, the result of the get method is cast to an Integer and then assigned to an int variable and displayed. Again, if you tried to assign the result of the get method to an int variable without casting, the compiler would have generated an error.

Wrapper classes for primitive types

Primitive type	Wrapper class
byte	Byte
short	Short
int	Integer
long	Long
float	Float
double	Double
char	Char
boolean	Boolean

Example 1: Code that adds integers to an untyped array list

```
ArrayList numbers = new ArrayList();

numbers.add(new Integer(1));
numbers.add(new Integer(2));
numbers.add(new Integer(3));
```

Example 2: Code that retrieves integers from the array list

```
for (int i = 0; i < numbers.size(); i++)
{
    int number = (Integer)numbers.get(i);
    System.out.println(number);
}
```

Resulting output

```
1
2
3
```

Description

- Because untyped collections hold elements of type Object, they can't hold primitive types. As a result, you must use wrapper classes to store primitive types in a collection.
- To add a primitive type to an untyped collection, create an instance of the appropriate wrapper class and pass the value you want it to hold to the constructor of that class.
- To retrieve an element that holds a primitive type, cast the element to the wrapper type. Because wrapper types can automatically be converted to their corresponding primitive types, you can assign the wrapper type to a primitive type variable without any explicit casting.

Figure 11-18 How to use wrapper classes with untyped collections

Perspective

Now that you've finished this chapter, you should know how to work with array lists and linked lists, the two most commonly used Java collections. You should also know how to use hash maps and tree maps to work with collections that store key-value pairs. Finally, you should know how to work with legacy collections in case you ever come across older programs that use them.

Summary

- A *collection* is an object that's designed to store other objects.
- The two most commonly used collection classes are ArrayList and LinkedList. An *array list* uses an array internally to store its data. A *linked list* uses a data structure with next and previous pointers.
- The *generics* feature, which became available with Java 5.0, lets you specify the type of elements a collection can store. This feature also lets you create *generic classes* that work with variable data types.
- A *map* is a collection that contains key-value pairs.
- The two most commonly used map classes are HashMap and TreeMap. The main difference between these two types of maps is that a *tree map* maintains its entries in key sequence and a *hash map* does not.
- Code that was written before Java 5.0 used *untyped collections*, which hold elements of type Object. To retrieve an element from an untyped collection, you typically have to use casting. To store primitive types in an untyped collection, you have to use *wrapper classes*.

Exercise 11-1 Use an array list

This exercise will guide you through the process of adding a rectangular array to the Future Value application. This array will store the values for each calculation that is performed, and print a summary of those calculations when the program ends that looks something like this:

```
Future Value Calculations

Inv/Mo. Rate    Years   Future Value
$100.00 8.0%    10      $18,416.57
$125.00 8.0%    10      $23,020.71
$150.00 8.0%    10      $27,624.85

Press any key to continue . . .
```

1. Open the FutureValueApp class stored in the c:\java1.5\ch11\FutureValueArrayList directory.
2. Declare a variable at the beginning of the main method for an array list that stores strings.
3. After the code that calculates, formats, and displays the results for each calculation, add code that formats a string with the results of the calculation, then stores the string in the array list.
4. Add code to display the elements in the array list at the console when the user indicates that the program should end. Then, test the program by making at least 3 future value calculations.

Exercise 11-2 Use a linked list

In this exercise, you'll modify the Future Value application you worked on in exercise 11-1 so it uses a linked list rather than an array list. In addition, you'll modify the code that displays the calculations so that the calculations are displayed in reverse order from the order in which they were entered.

1. Open the FutureValueApp class stored in the c:\java1.5\ch11\FutureValueArrayList directory and save it to the c:\java1.5\ch11\FutureValueLinkedList directory.
2. Change the variable declaration at the beginning of the main method from an array list to a linked list. Then, compile and test the application to see that it still works.
3. Modify the code that displays the calculations so it retrieves the elements of the linked list in reverse order. To do that, you'll need to use methods of the LinkedList class.
4. Compile and test the application again to be sure it works.

Exercise 11-3 Create a stack

In this exercise, you'll create a class called GenericStack that uses a linked list to implement a stack, which is a collection that lets you access entries on a first-in, last-out basis. Then, you'll create another class that uses the GenericStack class. The GenericStack class should implement these methods:

Method	Description
`push(element)`	Adds an element to the top of the stack.
`pop()`	Returns and removes the element at the top of the stack.
`peek()`	Returns but does not remove the element at the top of the stack.
`size()`	Returns the number of entries in the stack.

Create the GenericStack class

1. Start a new class named GenericStack that specifies a type variable that provides for generics. Then, save it in the c:\java1.5\ch11\GenericStack directory.
2. Declare a linked list that will hold the elements in the stack. Then, use the linked list to implement the methods shown above.
3. Compile the class.

Create a class that uses the GenericStack class

4. Open the GenericStackApp class in the c:\java1.5\ch11\GenericStack directory.
5. Declare a generic stack at the beginning of the main method that will store String objects.
6. Add code to the main method that uses the push method to add at least three items to the stack. After each item is added, display its value at the console (you'll need to use a string literal to do this). Then, use the peek method to return the first item and display that item, and use the size method to return the number of items in the stack and display that value. Next, use the pop method to return each item, displaying it as it's returned. Finally, use the size method to return the number of items again and display that value.
7. Compile and run the class. If it works correctly, your output should look something like this:

```
Push: Apples
Push: Oranges
Push: Bananas
The stack contains 3 items

Peek: Bananas
The stack contains 3 items

Pop: Bananas
Pop: Oranges
Pop: Apples
The stack contains 0 items
```

12

How to work with dates and strings

In section 1 of this book, you learned some basic skills for working with strings. In this chapter, you'll learn more about working with strings, and you'll learn how to work with dates. Because you'll use dates and strings in many of the applications that you develop, you should know how to use all of the skills presented in this chapter.

How to work with dates and times

Although Java doesn't have a primitive data type for working with dates and times, it does have several classes that you can use to work with dates and times. In this topic, you'll learn how to create objects that store dates and times, how to manipulate the values stored in those objects, and how to format those objects.

How to use the GregorianCalendar class to set dates and times

When you create dates and times, you usually use the GregorianCalendar class as shown in figure 12-1. Although you might think that a class named after a calendar would work mainly with dates, this class actually represents a point in time down to the millisecond.

This figure starts by showing four constructors of the GregorianCalendar class. The first constructor creates an object that contains the current date and time. The next three constructors create objects that contain values for a date and time that you specify. For instance, the second constructor creates a date and time using integer values for year, month, and day. In this case, Java sets the hour, minute, and second to 00. However, you can use the third or fourth constructors to set these values.

The statement in the first example shows how to get the current date and time. When you call this constructor, it sets the GregorianCalendar object equal to the current date and time. Java gets this date from your computer's internal clock. As a result, the date and time should be set correctly for your time zone.

The two statements in the second example show how to create a date using literals as arguments in the constructor of the GregorianCalendar class. Here, the first statement creates a GregorianCalendar object named startDate and sets the date to January 30, 2004. The second statement creates a GregorianCalendar object named startTime and sets it to 3:30 PM on July 20, 2007. Notice in both of these examples that the month is specified as an integer between 0 and 11, which might not be what you'd expect.

Like the first statement in the second example, the statement in the third example creates a GregorianCalendar object by supplying just a date. In this case, though, the year, month, and day are supplied as variables instead of literals.

When setting times, any values that you don't set will default to 0. The exception is if you use the first constructor shown in this figure, in which case the time is set to the current time. In addition, to set the hour, you must enter an integer between 0 and 23 where 0 is equal to midnight and 23 is equal to 11 PM. As a result, the first statement of example 2 and example 3 set the time to midnight (12:00:00 AM). The second statement of example 2 sets the hours to 15, which represents 3:00 PM, and the minutes to 30.

The GregorianCalendar class

```
java.util.GregorianCalendar;
```

Common constructors of the GregorianCalendar class

Method	Description
`GregorianCalendar()`	Creates a GregorianCalendar object set to the current date and time.
`GregorianCalendar(year, month, day)`	Creates a GregorianCalendar object set to the specified date.
`GregorianCalendar(year, month, day, hour, minute)`	Creates a GregorianCalendar object set to the specified date and time.
`GregorianCalendar(year, month, day, hour, minute, second)`	Creates a GregorianCalendar object set to the specified date and time.

Example 1: A statement that gets the current date

```
GregorianCalendar now = new GregorianCalendar();
```

Example 2: Statements that create dates with literals

```
GregorianCalendar startDate = new GregorianCalendar(2004, 0, 30);
GregorianCalendar startTime = new GregorianCalendar(2007, 8, 20, 15, 30);
```

Example 3: A statement that creates a date with variables

```
GregorianCalendar birthDate =
        new GregorianCalendar(birthYear, birthMonth, birthDay);
```

Description

- Year must be a four-digit integer.
- Month must be an integer from 0 to 11 with 0 being January and 11 being December.
- Day must be an integer from 1 to 31.
- Hour must be an integer from 0 to 23, with 0 being 12 AM (midnight) and 23 being 11 PM.
- Minute and second must be integers from 0 to 59.

Figure 12-1 How to use the GregorianCalendar class to set dates and times

How to use the Calendar and GregorianCalendar fields and methods

The GregorianCalendar class is a subclass of the Calendar class. As a result, it inherits all the public and protected fields and methods of the Calendar class. Then, the GregorianCalendar class overrides some of the methods of the Calendar class.

Once you create an object from the GregorianCalendar class, you can use the fields and methods shown in figure 12-2 to work with the object. The examples in this figure show how to use several of these fields and methods. Although these examples show how to work with the date portion of a GregorianCalendar object, you can use the same skills to work with the time portion. You can also find other fields and methods for working with dates and times in the API documentation for the Calendar and GregorianCalendar classes.

The first example shows how to use the set, add, and roll methods to change the value that's stored in a GregorianCalendar object. As you can see, you can use the same arguments for the set method that you used for the constructors of the GregorianCalendar class. In addition, you can use fields from the Calendar class, such as JANUARY and FEBRUARY, to set the month. Notice that when you use the add method to add 14 months to the date, the year is also increased. In contrast, when you use the roll method to roll the current month forward by 14 months, the year isn't affected. As a result, it only changes the month from August to October.

When you manipulate dates and times, you need to make sure to supply values that make sense. For example, since there are only 30 days in November, it doesn't make sense to use 31 as the day argument. If you do that, Java sets the date to December 1.

The second example shows how to use the get method to return various integer values that are stored in the GregorianCalendar object. Here, the year is 2005, the month is 1 (February), the day is 4, the day of the week is 6 (Friday), and the day of the year is 35 (the 31 days of January plus the 4 days of February).

The other two methods listed in this figure, setTime and getTime, work with Date objects. The setTime method sets a GregorianCalendar object to the date specified by a Date object, and the getTime method returns a Date object for a GregorianCalendar object. You'll learn more about Date objects in the next topic.

The Calendar class

```
java.util.Calendar;
```

Common fields of the Calendar class

```
DATE          DAY_OF_MONTH     DAY_OF_WEEK        DAY_OF_YEAR
HOUR          HOUR_OF_DAY      MINUTE             MONTH
SECOND        YEAR             MONDAY...SUNDAY    JANUARY...DECEMBER
```

Common methods of the Calendar and GregorianCalendar classes

Method	Description
`set(intYear, intMonth, ...)`	Sets the values for year, month, day, hour, minute, and second just as they are set in the constructor for the GregorianCalendar class.
`set(intField, intValue)`	Sets the specified field to the supplied value.
`setTime(Date)`	Sets the date and time values based on the supplied Date object.
`add(intField, intValue)`	Adds the supplied value to the specified field.
`roll(intField, intValue)`	Adds the supplied value to the specified field, but doesn't affect other fields.
`roll(intField, booleanValue)`	Increments the value of the specified field by 1 for true values and decrements the value of the field by 1 for false values.
`get(intField)`	Returns the int value of the specified field.
`getTime()`	Returns a Date object.

Example 1: Code that changes a GregorianCalendar object

```
GregorianCalendar endDate = new
   GregorianCalendar(2005, 0, 1);                    // January 1, 2005
endDate.set(2005, 2, 30);                            // March 30, 2005
endDate.set(2005, Calendar.MARCH, 30);               // March 30, 2005
endDate.set(Calendar.MONTH, Calendar.JANUARY);       // January 30, 2005
endDate.add(Calendar.MONTH, 5);                      // June 30, 2005
endDate.add(Calendar.MONTH, 14);                     // August 30, 2006
endDate.roll(Calendar.MONTH, 14);                    // October 30, 2006
endDate.roll(Calendar.MONTH, true);                  // November 30, 2006
endDate.roll(Calendar.DAY_OF_MONTH, false);          // November 29, 2006
```

Example 2: Code that accesses fields in a GregorianCalendar object

```
GregorianCalendar birthday = new
   GregorianCalendar(2005, Calendar.FEBRUARY, 4);   // Fri, Feb 4, 2005
int year = birthday.get(Calendar.YEAR);              // year is 2005
int month = birthday.get(Calendar.MONTH);            // month is 1
int day = birthday.get(Calendar.DAY_OF_MONTH);       // day is 4
int dayOfWeek = birthday.get(Calendar.DAY_OF_WEEK); // dayOfWeek is 6
int dayOfYear = birthday.get(Calendar.DAY_OF_YEAR); // dayOfYear is 35
```

Note

- For more information about these and other fields and methods, look up the Calendar and GregorianCalendar classes in the documentation for the Java API.

Figure 12-2 How to use the Calendar and GregorianCalendar fields and methods

How to use the Date class

Figure 12-3 shows how to use the Date class. Unlike the GregorianCalendar class, the Date class doesn't have fields that represent the year, month, day, and so on. Instead, the Date class represents a point in time by the number of milliseconds since January 1, 1970 00:00:00 Greenwich Mean Time (GMT). You need to use Date objects when you want to format a date as shown in the next figure. You may also find Date objects useful when you want to perform arithmetic operations on dates like subtracting one date from another.

To create a Date object, you can invoke the getTime method of a GregorianCalendar object as shown in the first example in this figure. Since the getTime method returns a Date object, you don't need to call either of the Date constructors. However, you can also use either of the constructors in this figure to create a Date object. The first constructor creates a Date object for the current date and time while the second constructor creates a Date object based on the number of milliseconds that are passed to it. The second example shows how to use the first constructor to create a Date object for the current date and time.

The third example shows how to use the toString and getTime methods of the Date class. The toString method returns a readable string that displays the day of the week, month, date, time, time zone, and year. The getTime method returns a long integer that represents the number of milliseconds since January 1, 1970 00:00:00 GMT.

The fourth example shows how Date objects can be useful when you want to calculate the elapsed time between two dates. First, two GregorianCalendar dates are converted to Date objects using the getTime method of the GregorianCalendar class. Next, the Date objects are converted to milliseconds using the getTime method of the Date class. Then, the starting date in milliseconds is subtracted from the ending date in milliseconds to get the elapsed milliseconds, and that result is divided by the number of milliseconds in a day to get the elapsed days. This type of routine is useful in many business programs.

The Date class

```
java.util.Date;
```

Common constructors

Constructor	Description
`Date()`	Creates a Date object for the current date and time based on your computer's internal clock.
`Date(longMilliseconds)`	Creates a Date object based on the number of milliseconds that is passed to it.

Common methods

Method	Description
`getTime()`	Returns a long value that represents the number of milliseconds for the date.
`toString()`	Returns a String object that contains the date and time formatted like this: Wed Aug 04 08:31:25 PDT 2004.

Example 1: A statement that converts a GregorianCalendar object to a Date object

```
Date endDate = gregEndDate.getTime();
```

Example 2: A statement that gets a Date object for the current date/time

```
Date now = new Date();
```

Example 3: Statements that convert Date objects to string and long variables

```
String nowAsString = now.toString();     // converts to a string
long nowInMS = now.getTime();            // converts to milliseconds
```

Example 4: Code that calculates the number of days between two dates

```
Date startDate = gregStartDate.getTime();
Date endDate = gregEndDate.getTime();
long startDateMS = startDate.getTime();
long endDateMS = endDate.getTime();
long elapsedMS = endDateMS - startDateMS;
long elapsedDays = elapsedMS / (24 * 60 * 60 * 1000);
```

Description

- A Date object stores a date and time as the number of milliseconds since January 1, 1970 00:00:00 GMT (Greenwich Mean Time).
- You need to convert GregorianCalendar objects to Date objects when you want to use the DateFormat class to format them as shown in the next figure.
- Date objects are also useful when you want to calculate the number of milliseconds (or days) between two dates.

Figure 12-3 How to use the Date class

How to use the DateFormat class to format dates and times

Figure 12-4 shows how to use the DateFormat class to convert a Date object to a string that you can use to display dates and times. In addition, it shows how to control the format of these strings. Since this class works similarly to the NumberFormat class, you shouldn't have much trouble using it.

Before you can format a date, you need to use one of the static methods of the DateFormat class to create a DateFormat object that has a particular format. When you do that, you can choose to return the date only, the time only, or the date and time. If you don't specify a format, the DateFormat object will use the default format. However, you can use one of the four DateFormat fields to override the default date format. Once you've created a DateFormat object that has the format you want, you can use its format method to apply the specified format to a Date object.

The first example shows how to format a Date object with the default format. Here, the getDateTimeInstance method is used to return both date and time. Since no arguments are supplied for this method, it will return a string that contains the current date and time with the default format, which should look something like this:

```
Jan 30, 2005 12:10:10 PM
```

The second example shows how to format a GregorianCalendar object with the default date format. Here, you can see that you start by using the getTime method to convert the GregorianCalendar object to a Date object. Then, you use the getDateInstance method to return a format with the date only. Since no arguments are supplied for this method, it will return a string that contains this date:

```
Dec 31, 2005
```

The third example shows how you can use the fields of the DateFormat class to override the default date format. Here, you can see how to use the SHORT field of the Calendar class, but the same skills apply to the other three fields. If you use the getDateTimeInstance method, you need to supply the first argument for the date and the second argument for the time. Since both of the arguments are specified as short in this example, they will return a date with a format something like this:

```
12/31/05 7:30 AM
```

When you use the LONG and FULL fields, the time portion of the date will end with an abbreviation for the current time zone. In this figure, the examples use the Pacific Standard Time (PST) time zone.

The DateFormat class

```
java.text.DateFormat;
```

Common static methods

Method	Description
`getDateInstance()`	Returns a DateFormat object with date, but not time.
`getTimeInstance()`	Returns a DateFormat object with time, but not date.
`getDateTimeInstance()`	Returns a DateFormat object with date and time.
`getDateInstance(intField)`	Same as above, but you can use the fields shown below to override the default date format.
`getTimeInstance(intField)`	Same as above, but you can use the fields shown below to override the default time format.
`getDateTimeInstance(intField, intField)`	Same as above, but you can use the fields shown below to override the default date and time formats.

Common fields

Style	Date example	Time example
`SHORT`	12/31/05	12:00 AM
`MEDIUM`	Dec 31, 2005	7:30:00 PM
`LONG`	December 31, 2005	7:30:00 AM PST
`FULL`	Saturday, December 31, 2005	7:30:00 AM PST

Common method

Method	Description
`format(Date)`	Returns a String object of the Date object with the format that's specified by the DateFormat object.

Example 1: Code that formats a Date object

```
Date now = new Date();
DateFormat defaultDate = DateFormat.getDateTimeInstance();
String nowString = defaultDate.format(now);
```

Example 2: Code that formats a GregorianCalendar object

```
GregorianCalendar gregEndDate = new GregorianCalendar(2005,11,31,7,30);
Date endDate = gregEndDate.getTime();
DateFormat defaultDate = DateFormat.getDateInstance();
String endDateString = defaultDate.format(endDate);
```

Example 3: Code that overrides the default date and time formats

```
DateFormat shortDate = DateFormat.getDateInstance(DateFormat.SHORT);
DateFormat shortTime = DateFormat.getTimeInstance(DateFormat.SHORT);
DateFormat shortDateTime =
    DateFormat.getDateTimeInstance(DateFormat.SHORT, DateFormat.SHORT);
```

Description

- You can use the DateFormat class to format Date objects in various ways.

Figure 12-4 How to use the DateFormat class to format dates and times

A DateUtils class that provides methods for handling dates

Although the date handling features of the Java API are powerful, they must frequently be used in combination to provide some of the most common operations needed by business applications. As a result, it's common for an application that uses dates to include a class like the one in figure 12-5. This class presents just a few of the date handling operations you may need to perform, but it should give you a good idea of what you can do with the date handling features.

The first method in the DateUtils class, getCurrentDate, returns a Date object that contains just the current date. To do that, it creates a GregorianCalendar object with the current date and time. Then, it uses the set method to set the hour, minute, and second to zero. Finally, it uses the getTime method to convert the GregorianCalendar object to a Date object. You might want to use a method like this to get a date that you can use to calculate the age of an invoice. In that case, you'll want to be sure that neither the invoice date or the current date contains a time so that the age is calculated properly.

The createDate method provides a simple way to create a Date object for a specific date with the hour, minute, and second set to zero. This method starts by creating a GregorianCalendar object for the specified date. Then, it uses the getTime method to convert the GregorianCalendar object to a Date object.

The stripTime method strips the hour, minute, and second from a Date object. It works by setting a GregorianCalendar object to the date and time specified by the Date object so the hour, minute, and second can be accessed. Then, it sets these values to zero and converts the result back to a Date object.

The daysDiff method calculates the difference between two Date objects in days. To do that, it starts by calling the stripTime method to remove the time-of-day component from both Date objects. That's important when you're working with Date objects that include times, because you don't want the time of day to be considered in the calculation.

Next, the daysDiff method uses the getTime method to convert the Date objects to long values. Then, it subtracts these two values to get the difference, which is expressed in milliseconds. To convert that value to days, it divides it by the number of milliseconds in a day, which is represented by the constant named MILLS_IN_DAY that's defined at the top of the class.

The code example at the bottom of this figure shows how you might use the DateUtils class in a simple application. This example determines the number of days between the current date and Christmas. The first two lines get the current date and then extract the current year using the get method. Next, a Date object named currentDate is set to the current date and another Date object named Christmas is set to December 25 of the current year. Then, an int variable named daysToChristmas is calculated by calling the daysDiff method. The rest of the code formats and displays the result.

The code for the DateUtils class

```
import java.util.*;
public class DateUtils
{
    static final int MILLS_IN_DAY = 24 * 60 * 60 * 1000;

    public static Date getCurrentDate()
    {
        GregorianCalendar currentDate = new GregorianCalendar();
        currentDate.set(Calendar.HOUR, 0);
        currentDate.set(Calendar.MINUTE, 0);
        currentDate.set(Calendar.SECOND, 0);
        return currentDate.getTime();
    }

    public static Date createDate(int year, int month, int day)
    {
        GregorianCalendar date = new GregorianCalendar(year, month, day);
        return date.getTime();
    }

    public static Date stripTime(Date date)
    {
        GregorianCalendar currentDate = new GregorianCalendar();
        currentDate.setTime(date);
        currentDate.set(Calendar.HOUR, 0);
        currentDate.set(Calendar.MINUTE, 0);
        currentDate.set(Calendar.SECOND, 0);
        return currentDate.getTime();
    }

    public static int daysDiff(Date date1, Date date2)
    {
        date1 = stripTime(date1);
        date2 = stripTime(date2);
        long longDate1 = date1.getTime();
        long longDate2 = date2.getTime();
        long longDiff = longDate2 - longDate1;
        return (int) (longDiff / MILLS_IN_DAY);
    }
}
```

Code that uses some of the DateUtils methods

```
GregorianCalendar currentGC = new GregorianCalendar();
int currentYear = currentGC.get(Calendar.YEAR);
Date currentDate = DateUtils.getCurrentDate();
Date christmas = DateUtils.createDate(currentYear, Calendar.DECEMBER, 25);
int daysToChristmas = DateUtils.daysDiff(currentDate, christmas);
DateFormat dateFormat = DateFormat.getDateInstance(DateFormat.LONG);
String formattedDate = dateFormat.format(currentDate);
System.out.println("Today is " + formattedDate);
System.out.println("There are " + daysToChristmas + " days until Christmas.");
```

Resulting output

```
Today is September 27, 2004
There are 89 days until Christmas.
```

Figure 12-5 A DateUtils class that provides methods for handling dates

An Invoice class that includes an invoice date

To show how you can use some of the date skills you just learned, figure 12-6 shows how to add a date to the Invoice class that was presented in chapter 11. As you can see, the constructor for this class sets the invoice date, which is declared as a Date object, to the current date. To do that, it uses the getCurrentDate method of the DateUtils class so that the invoice date doesn't include a time.

Two methods have also been added to this class to provide access to the invoice date. The getInvoiceDate method simply returns the invoice date as a Date object. The getFormattedDate method applies a short date format to the invoice date and returns it as a string.

To make the date classes available to this class, the two import statements at the beginning of the class have been changed. Now, instead of just importing the NumberFormat class of the java.text package and the ArrayList class of the java.util package, they import all of the classes in these packages. That way, the DateFormat class is available from the java.text package, and the GregorianCalendar, Calendar, and Date classes are available from the java.util package.

Code that adds a date to the Invoice class

```
import java.text.*;
import java.util.*;

public class Invoice
{
    private ArrayList<LineItem> lineItems;
    private Date invoiceDate;

    public Invoice()
    {
        lineItems = new ArrayList<LineItem>();
        invoiceDate = DateUtils.getCurrentDate();
    }

    public ArrayList<LineItem> getLineItems(){
        return lineItems;
    }

    public void addItem(LineItem lineItem)
    {
        this.lineItems.add(lineItem);
    }

    public double getInvoiceTotal()
    {
        double invoiceTotal = 0;
        for (LineItem lineItem : this.lineItems)
        {
            invoiceTotal += lineItem.getTotal();
        }
        return invoiceTotal;
    }

    public String getFormattedTotal()
    {
        NumberFormat currency = NumberFormat.getCurrencyInstance();
        return currency.format(this.getInvoiceTotal());
    }

    public Date getInvoiceDate()
    {
        return invoiceDate;
    }

    public String getFormattedDate()
    {
        DateFormat shortDate = DateFormat.getDateInstance(DateFormat.SHORT);
        return shortDate.format(invoiceDate);
    }
}
```

Figure 12-6 An Invoice class that includes an invoice date

How to work with the String class

In section 1, you learned how to create a String object and how to use two methods of the String class that compare two strings. Now, you'll learn some new ways to create String objects, and you'll learn how to use more of the methods of the String class.

Constructors of the String class

Figure 12-7 shows four constructors of the String class. The first constructor provides another way to create an empty string; the second constructor provides another way to create a string from a string; and the third and fourth constructors allow you to create a string from an array of char or byte types. Although none of these constructors are commonly used, the third and fourth constructors show that you can think of a string as an array of Unicode characters.

You may remember from chapter 3 that char is a primitive type that can hold a Unicode character with two bytes used for each character. That provides for over 65,000 unique characters. Now, you'll learn that a String variable can store an array of these Unicode characters.

Code examples that create strings

The first two examples in this figure show how to create a string. In example 1, the first statement uses the shorthand notation you learned how to use in chapter 2. Then, the second statement shows how to do the same task using a constructor of the String class. In example 2, the first statement initializes the new string from a string literal, and the second statement initializes it from a variable.

The third example creates a string from an array of characters. Here, the second statement converts the entire array of characters to a string named cityString1. Then, the third statement converts the first three characters in the array to a string named cityString2. Although there's little reason to create a string in this way, we included this example to demonstrate that an array of characters can be converted to a string. Note that literal char values must be enclosed in single quotes, not double quotes the way string literals are.

The fourth example creates a string from an array of bytes. Here, the first statement creates an array of bytes that represents the same characters as the characters that are used in the third example. That's because every character in the ASCII character set corresponds to a byte value. For example, the byte value of 68 represents the character *D*. Then, the second and third statements in this example work just like they did in the previous example.

The String class

```
java.lang.String
```

Common constructors of the String class

Constructor	Description
`String()`	Creates an empty string ("").
`String(arrayName)`	Creates a string from an array of char or byte types.
`String(arrayName, intOffset, intLength)`	Creates a string from a subset of an array of char or byte types.

Example 1: Two ways to create an empty string

```
String name = "";
String name = new String();
```

Example 2: Two ways to create a string from another string

```
String title = "Murach's Beginning Java 2";
String title = bookTitle;
```

Example 3: Two ways to create a string from an array of characters

```
char cityArray[] = {'D','a','l','l','a','s'};
String cityString1 = new String(cityArray);
String cityString2 = new String(cityArray, 0, 3);
```

Example 4: Two ways to create a string from an array of bytes

```
byte cityArray[] = {68, 97, 108, 108, 97, 115};
String cityString1 = new String(cityArray);
String cityString2 = new String(cityArray, 0, 3);
```

Notes

- For the fourth constructor shown above, the characters referred to by the intOffset and intLength arguments must fall within the array. Otherwise, the constructor will throw an IndexOutOfBoundsException.
- A char data type contains a single Unicode character, which is stored in two bytes. When you use the third and fourth constructors above, you can construct a String object from an array of char types. To code a literal char value, you use single quotes instead of double quotes as shown in the third example.
- Because a byte data type can hold the Unicode value for every character in the ASCII character set, you can also construct a String object from an array of bytes as shown in the fourth example.
- Since String objects are immutable, they can't grow or shrink. Later in this chapter, you'll learn how to work with StringBuilder objects that can grow and shrink.

Figure 12-7 How to create strings

Methods of the String class

In chapters 2 and 4, you learned how to use the equals and equalsIgnoreCase methods of the String class to compare strings. Now, figure 12-8 reviews these methods and introduces you to 16 more methods that you can use to work with strings. In the next figure, you'll see some examples that use some of these methods. You can also get more information about any of these methods by looking up the String class in the documentation for the Java API.

As you can see, we divided the methods presented in this figure into two categories. The first table lists methods that are used to manipulate the value of the string in one way or another. The first five of these methods return int values. The length method returns the total number of characters in the string. The indexOf and lastIndexOf methods return a value that represents an index within the string. This index value works as if the string was an array of characters. In other words, the index value for the first character in a string is 0, the index value for the second character is 1, and so on.

The next four methods return String objects. Here, the trim method returns the string, but it removes any spaces from the beginning and end of the string. The substring methods allow you to return part of a string by specifying index values. The replace method replaces all occurrences of a specified character with another character.

The split method returns an array of String objects. This method splits the string up into individual strings based on the delimiter string you specify. Actually, the delimiter string can be any *regular expression*, which is a complicated expression that can contain wildcards and other special characters. If you want to learn more about regular expressions, you can search the web for "java regular expression." In most cases, however, the delimiter string will be a single character or an escape sequence such as "\t" for tabs or "\n" for returns.

Finally, the last method in this table, charAt, returns the char value at the specified index.

The second table in this figure lists methods that are useful for comparing string values. The first five of these methods return boolean values. You've already seen the equals and equalsIgnoreCase methods, which compare strings and return a true value if the strings are equal. The startsWith and endsWith methods check whether a string starts or ends with a certain combination of characters and return a true value if it does. These methods work similarly to the equals method.

The last two methods are used to compare two strings to see which one is greater according to the sort order of the strings. These methods return an int value that's negative if the string is less than the specified string, zero if the strings are equal, and positive if the string is greater than the specified string. These methods are useful because you can't use normal comparison operators (such as < and >) with String objects.

Methods for manipulating strings

Method	Description
`length()`	Returns an int value for the number of characters in this string.
`indexOf(String)`	Returns an int value for the index of the first occurrence of the specified string in this string. If the string isn't found, this method returns -1.
`indexOf(String, startIndex)`	Returns an int value for the index of the first occurrence of the specified string starting at the specified index. If the string isn't found, this method returns -1.
`lastIndexOf(String)`	Returns an int value for the index of the last occurrence of the specified string in this string.
`lastIndexOf(String, startIndex)`	Returns an int value for the index of the last occurrence of the specified string in this string starting at the specified index.
`trim()`	Returns a String object with any spaces removed from the beginning and end of this string.
`substring(startIndex)`	Returns a String object that starts at the specified index and goes to the end of the string.
`substring(startIndex, endIndex)`	Returns a String object that starts at the specified start index and goes to, but doesn't include, the end index.
`replace(oldChar, newChar)`	Returns a String object that results from replacing all instances of the specified old char value with the specified new char value.
`split(delimiter)`	Returns an array of String objects that were separated in the original string by the specified delimiter.
`charAt(index)`	Returns the char value at the specified index.

Methods for comparing strings

Method	Description
`equals(String)`	Returns a boolean true value if the specified string is equal to the current string. This comparison is case-sensitive.
`equalsIgnoreCase(String)`	Returns a boolean true value if the specified string is equal to the current string. This comparison is *not* case-sensitive.
`startsWith(String)`	Returns a boolean true value if this string starts with the specified string.
`startsWith(String, startIndex)`	Returns a boolean true value if this string starts with the specified string starting at the start index.
`endsWith(String)`	Returns a boolean true value if the string ends with the specified string.
`compareTo(String)`	Returns an int that's less than zero if the string is less than the specified string, greater than zero if the string is greater than the specified string, and zero if the strings are equal.
`compareToIgnoreCase(String)`	The same as compareTo, but the case of the strings is ignored.

Note

- If you supply an index argument to the substring or charAt method that's negative or greater than the length of the string minus one, the method will throw a StringIndexOutOfBoundsException.

Figure 12-8 Methods of the String class

Code examples that work with strings

Figure 12-9 shows some examples of how you can use the methods of the String class. In particular, this figure provides some examples that use the String class to parse strings.

The first example shows how to parse the first name from a string that contains a full name. Here, the first statement sets the string to a string literal that includes a first and last name, and the second statement uses the trim method to remove any spaces from the beginning or end of the string. Then, the third statement uses the indexOf method to get the index of the first space in the string, which is the space between the first and last names. Finally, the last statement uses the substring method to set the first name variable equal to the string that begins at the first character of the string and ends at the first space character in the string.

The second example shows how to parse a string that contains an address into the components of the address. In this case, tab characters separate each component of the address. Here, the second statement uses the trim method to remove any spaces that may have been included at the beginning or end of the string. Next, the split method is used to separate the string into its individual components. Then, simple assignment statements are used to assign the components to individual strings. Note that this code doesn't account for an improperly formatted address string. In an actual application, you'd want to at least check the length of the addressParts array to make sure the string was successfully parsed into four components.

The third example shows how to add dashes to a phone number. To do that, this example creates a second string. Then, it uses the substring method to parse the first string and add the dashes at the appropriate locations in the string. In figure 12-11, you'll learn an easier way to accomplish this task.

The fourth example shows how to remove the dashes from a phone number. To do that, this example creates a second string. Then, it uses a for loop to cycle through each character in the first string. The only statement within this loop uses the charAt method to add all characters in the first string that are not equal to a dash to the second string. As a result, the second string won't contain any dashes. You'll learn another way to accomplish this task in figure 12-11.

The fifth example shows how to compare two strings to determine which one comes first based on the string's sort order. Here, two strings are created. Then, the compareToIgnoreCase method of the first string is used to compare the strings. If the result is less than zero, a message is printed indicating that the first string comes first in sequence. If the result is zero, the message indicates that the strings are equal. And if the result is greater than zero, the message indicates that the second string comes first.

Example 1: Code that parses a first name from a name string

```
String fullName = " Pamela Caldwell ";
fullName = fullName.trim();
int indexOfSpace = fullName.indexOf(" ");
String firstName = fullName.substring(0, indexOfSpace);
```

Example 2: Code that parses a string containing a tab-delimited address

```
String address = "805 Main Street\tDallas\tTX\t12345";
address = address.trim();
String[] addressParts = address.split("\t");
String street = addressParts[0];
String city = addressParts[1];
String state = addressParts[2];
String zip = addressParts[3];
```

Example 3: Code that adds dashes to a phone number

```
String phoneNumber1 = "9775551212";
String phoneNumber2 = phoneNumber1.substring(0, 3);
phoneNumber2 += "-";
phoneNumber2 += phoneNumber1.substring(3, 6);
phoneNumber2 += "-";
phoneNumber2 += phoneNumber1.substring(6);
```

Example 4: Code that removes dashes from a phone number

```
String phoneNumber3 = "977-555-1212";
String phoneNumber4 = "";
for(int i = 0; i < phoneNumber3.length(); i++)
{
   if (phoneNumber1.charAt(i) != '-')
      phoneNumber4 += phoneNumber3.charAt(i);
}
```

Example 5: Code that compares strings

```
String lastName1 = "Smith";
String lastName2 = "Lee";
int sortResult = lastName1.compareToIgnoreCase(lastName2);
if (sortResult < 0)
    System.out.println(lastName1 + " comes first.");
else if (sortResult == 0)
    System.out.println("The names are the same.");
else
    System.out.println(lastName2 + " comes first.");
```

Figure 12-9 Code examples that work with strings

How to work with the StringBuilder class

When you use the String class to work with strings, the string has a fixed length, and you can't edit the characters that make up the string. In other words, the String class creates strings that are *immutable*. Then, when you assign a new value to a string variable, the original String object is deleted and it's replaced with a new String object that contains the new value.

If you want more flexibility when working with strings, you can use the StringBuilder class. When you use this class, you create strings that are *mutable*. In other words, you can add, delete, or replace the characters in a StringBuilder object. This makes it easier to write some types of routines, and it can improve the efficiency of your code in some situations.

Note that the StringBuilder class is new for Java 5.0. It's designed to be a more efficient replacement for the StringBuffer class. Because the API for the StringBuffer class is identical to the API for the StringBuilder class, you can easily switch between StringBuffer and StringBuilder.

Constructors and methods of the StringBuilder class

Figure 12-10 shows three constructors and thirteen methods of the StringBuilder class. In the next figure, you'll see some examples that use these constructors and methods. As always, you can find more information on these constructors and methods by looking up the StringBuilder class in the documentation for the Java API.

To create a StringBuilder object, you can use one of the three constructors shown in this figure. The first constructor creates an empty StringBuilder object with a capacity of 16 characters. If you add characters to this StringBuilder object so the number of characters exceeds 16, Java will automatically increase the capacity.

Whenever possible, you should set the capacity to an appropriate value by using the second or third constructor shown in the figure. Otherwise, Java will have to allocate memory each time the capacity is exceeded, and that can cause your programs to run less efficiently. On the other hand, if you set a large capacity and use a small percentage of it, you waste memory.

Once you create a StringBuilder object, you can use the methods in this figure to work with the object. You can use the first three methods to check the capacity of the object or to check or set the length of the string. You can use the next six methods to add, edit, or delete strings or characters. And you can use the last four methods to return a String object or a character.

The StringBuilder class

`java.lang.StringBuilder`

Constructors of the StringBuilder class

Constructor	Description
`StringBuilder()`	Creates an empty StringBuilder object with an initial capacity of 16 characters.
`StringBuilder(intLength)`	Creates an empty StringBuilder object with an initial capacity of the specified number of characters.
`StringBuilder(String)`	Creates a StringBuilder object that contains the specified string plus an additional capacity of 16 characters.

Methods of the StringBuilder class

Methods	Description
`capacity()`	Returns an int value for the capacity of this StringBuilder object.
`length()`	Returns an int value for the number of characters in this StringBuilder object.
`setLength(intNumOfChars)`	Sets the length of this StringBuilder object to the specified number of characters.
`append(value)`	Adds the specified value to the end of the string.
`insert(index, value)`	Inserts the specified value at the specified index pushing the rest of the string back.
`replace(startIndex, endIndex, String)`	Replaces the characters from the start index to, but not including, the end index with the specified string.
`delete(startIndex, endIndex)`	Removes the substring from the start index to, but not including, the end index.
`deleteCharAt(index)`	Removes the character at the specified index.
`setCharAt(index, character)`	Replaces the character at the specified index with the specified character.
`charAt(index)`	Returns a char value for the character at the specified index.
`substring(index)`	Returns a String object that contains the characters starting at the specified index to the end of the string.
`substring(startIndex, endIndex)`	Returns a String object that contains the characters from the start index to, but not including, the end index.
`toString()`	Returns a String object that contains the string that's stored in the StringBuilder object.

Description

- StringBuilder objects are *mutable*, which means you can modify the characters in the string. The capacity of a StringBuilder object is automatically increased if necessary.
- The append and insert methods accept primitive types, objects, and arrays of characters.
- The StringBuilder class is new for Java 5.0. It's designed to replace the older StringBuffer class, which has identical constructors and methods but isn't as efficient.

Figure 12-10 Constructors and methods of the StringBuilder class

Code examples that work with the StringBuilder class

Figure 12-11 presents some examples that show how you can use the constructors and methods of the StringBuilder class. In particular, this figure shows how to add characters to the end of a string, insert characters into the middle of a string, and delete characters from a string.

The first example shows how to use the append method of the StringBuilder class. Here, the first statement creates an empty StringBuilder object with the default capacity of 16 characters. Then, the next three statements use the append method to add 10 characters to the end of the string. As a result, the length of the string is 10 and the capacity of the StringBuilder object is 16. (Note that the same effect can be achieved by using simple string concatenation. However, when you use concatenation, Java must create a new String object each time because the length of a String object can't be increased. In contrast, when you use the append method of the StringBuilder class, a new StringBuilder object isn't created because the length of a StringBuilder object can be increased.)

The second example adds dashes to the string that was created in the first example. Here, the first statement uses the insert method to insert a dash after the first three characters. This pushes the remaining numbers back one index. Then, the second statement uses the insert method to insert a dash after the seventh character in the string, which was the sixth character in the original string. This pushes the remaining four numbers in the string back one index.

The third example shows how to remove dashes from a phone number. Here, a loop cycles through each character, using the charAt method to check if the current character is a dash. If so, the deleteCharAt method is used to delete it. Since this causes all characters to the right of the dash to move forward one index, it's necessary to decrement the counter so the loop doesn't skip any characters.

The fourth example shows how to use the substring method of the StringBuilder class to separate the area code, prefix, and suffix components of a phone number. Here, the first statement uses a constructor to create a StringBuilder object from a String literal. Then, the next three statements use the substring method to create three String objects from the StringBuilder object. For example, the second statement specifies a substring that goes from the first character up to, but not including, the fourth character. (Note that the substring method works the same for the String class as it does for the StringBuilder class, so the same thing could be done with a simple string.)

The fifth example shows how a StringBuilder object automatically increases its capacity as the length of the string increases. Here, the first statement creates an empty StringBuilder object with a capacity of 8 characters, and the second statement uses the capacity method to check the capacity. Next, the third statement appends a string of 17 characters to the empty string. Since this causes the capacity of the StringBuilder object to be exceeded, Java automatically increases the capacity. The formula Java uses to increase the capacity is to double it and add 2 characters. As a result, the capacity of the name string is increased from 8 to 18 characters. Then, the last two statements check the length and capacity of the modified StringBuilder object.

Example 1: Code that creates a phone number

```
StringBuilder phoneNumber = new StringBuilder();
phoneNumber.append("977");
phoneNumber.append("555");
phoneNumber.append("1212");
```

Example 2: Code that adds dashes to a phone number

```
phoneNumber.insert(3, '-');
phoneNumber.insert(7, '-');
```

Example 3: Code that removes dashes from a phone number

```
for(int i = 0; i < phoneNumber.length(); i++)
{
   if (phoneNumber.charAt(i) == '-')
      phoneNumber.deleteCharAt(i--);
}
```

Example 4: Code that parses a phone number

```
StringBuilder phoneNumber = new StringBuilder("977-555-1212");
String areaCode = phoneNumber.substring(0,3);
String prefix = phoneNumber.substring(4,7);
String suffix = phoneNumber.substring(8);
```

Example 5: Code that shows how capacity automatically increases

```
StringBuilder name = new StringBuilder(8);
int capacity1 = name.capacity();    // capacity1 is 8
name.append("Raymond R. Thomas");
int length = name.length();         // length is 17
int capacity2 = name.capacity();    // capacity2 is 18 (2 * capacity1 + 2)
```

Figure 12-11 Code examples that work with the StringBuilder class

Perspective

Now that you've finished this chapter, you should be able to use the classes provided by the Java API to work with dates, and you should be able to use the String and StringBuilder classes to work with strings. These are skills that you will use often as you develop Java applications.

Summary

- You can use the GregorianCalendar, Calendar, Date, and DateFormat classes to create, manipulate, and format dates and times.
- You can use methods of the String class to locate a string within another string, return parts of a string, and compare all or part of a string. However, String objects are *immutable*, so you can't add, delete, or modify individual characters in a string.
- StringBuilder objects are *mutable*, so you can use the StringBuilder methods to add, delete, or modify characters in a StringBuilder object. Whenever necessary, Java automatically increases the capacity of a StringBuilder object.

Exercise 12-1 Add a due date to the Invoice application

For this exercise, you'll modify the Invoice class that's shown in figure 12-6 so that it contains methods that return a due date, calculated as 30 days after the invoice date. Then, you'll modify the Invoice application that was shown in chapter 11 to display the invoice date and due date for a batch of invoices.

1. Open the Invoice and InvoiceApp classes in the c:\java 1.5\ch12\Invoice directory.
2. Add two methods named getDueDate and getFormattedDueDate to the Invoice class. The getDueDate method should calculate and return a Date object that's 30 days after the invoice date. The getFormattedDueDate method should return the due date in the short date format. Compile the class.
3. Modify the displayInvoices method in the InvoiceApp class so that the invoice display includes columns for the invoice date and the due date in addition to the invoice number and total. Then, compile this class and run it to make sure it works.

Exercise 12-2 Calculate the user's age

In this exercise, you'll write a program that accepts a person's birth date from the console and displays the person's age in years. To make that easier to do, we'll give you a class that contains the code for accepting the birth date. The console output for the program should look something like this:

```
Welcome to the age calculator.
Enter the month you were born (1 to 12): 5
Enter the day of the month you were born: 16
Enter the year you were born (four digits): 1959
Your birth date is May 16, 1959
Today's date is Sep 27, 2004
Your age is: 45
```

1. Open the AgeCalculatorApp class in the c:\java 1.5\ch12\AgeCalculator directory.
2. Add code to this class that gets the current date and then uses the current year to validate the birth year the user enters. The user should not be allowed to enter a year after the current year or more than 110 years before the current year.
3. Add code to create, format, and print the user's birth date and to format and print the current date.
4. Add code to calculate and print the user's age.
5. Compile the class. Then, run it for a variety of dates to be sure it works.

Exercise 12-3 Parse a name

In this exercise, you'll write an application that parses full names into first and last name or first, middle, and last name, depending on whether the user enters a string consisting of two or three words. The output for the program should look something like this:

```
Welcome to the name parser.

Enter a name: Joel Murach

First name:  Joel
Last name:   Murach
```

1. Open the NameParserApp class in the c:\java 1.5\ch12\NameParser directory.
2. Add code to the main method that lets the user enter a full name as a string. Then, add code that separates the name into two or three strings depending on whether the user entered a name with two words or three. Finally, display each word of the name on a separate line. If the user enters fewer than two words or more than three words, display an error message. Also, make sure the application works even if the user enters one or more spaces before or after the name.
3. Compile the program and run it to make sure it works.

Exercise 12-4 Validate a social security number

In this exercise, you'll add a method named getSSN to the Validator class that was presented in chapter 6. Then, you'll use this method in a program to validate a social security number entered by the user.

1. Open the SSNValidatorApp and Validator classes in the c:\java1.5\ch12\SSNValidator directory.
2. Add a method named getSSN to the Validator class that accepts and validates a social security number. This method should accept a Scanner object and a string that will be displayed to the user as a prompt. After it accepts the social security number, this method should validate the entry by checking that the number consists of three numeric digits, followed by a hyphen and two numeric digits, followed by a hyphen and four numeric digits. If the user's entry doesn't conform to this format, the method should display an error message and ask the user to enter the number again. Compile the class.
3. Modify the SSNValidatorApp class so that it uses the getSSN method. Then, compile and run this class to make sure the validation works correctly.

13

How to handle exceptions

In chapter 5, you were introduced to the concept of exceptions and how to use the try statement to catch them. However, there's much more to exceptions than what was covered in that chapter. In this chapter, you'll learn the additional details you need to know to develop professional applications that handle all kinds of exceptions.

An introduction to exceptions

All applications encounter runtime errors. For example, a user may enter data that's not appropriate for the program, or a file that your program needs may get moved or deleted. These types of errors may cause a poorly-coded program to crash and cause the user to lose data. In contrast, when an error occurs in a well-coded program, the program will notify the user, save as much data as possible, clean up resources, and exit the program as smoothly as possible.

To help you handle errors, Java uses a mechanism known as *exception handling*. Before you learn how to handle errors, though, you need to learn about the exception hierarchy and the exception handling mechanism.

The exception hierarchy

In Java, an *exception* is an object that's created from the Exception class or one of its subclasses. An exception represents an error that has occurred, and it contains information about the error. All exception classes are derived from the Throwable class as shown by the diagram in figure 13-1.

As this diagram shows, two classes directly inherit the Throwable class: Error and Exception. The classes that inherit the Error class represent internal errors that you usually can't do anything about, such as problems with the Java runtime environment. As a result, you can ignore these errors most of the time. In contrast, you need to handle most of the exceptions that are derived from the Exception class.

The classes in the Exception subset are divided into two categories: (1) exceptions derived from the RuntimeException class and (2) all other exceptions. The exceptions derived from the RuntimeException class are called *unchecked exceptions* because the compiler doesn't force you to explicitly handle them. On the other hand, the compiler requires that you explicitly handle all other exceptions derived from the Exception class, either by catching them in the catch clause of a try statement or by throwing them up to the calling method in the throws clause of the method declaration. As a result, these exceptions are known as *checked exceptions*.

Unchecked exceptions often occur because of coding errors. For example, if a program attempts to access an array with an invalid index, Java will throw an ArrayIndexOutOfBoundsException, which is a type of IndexOutOfBoundsException. If you're careful when you write your code, you can usually prevent these types of exceptions from being thrown.

Checked exceptions, on the other hand, usually occur due to circumstances that are beyond the programmer's control, such as a missing file or a bad network connection. Although you can't avoid these exceptions, you can write code that handles them when they occur.

The Throwable hierarchy

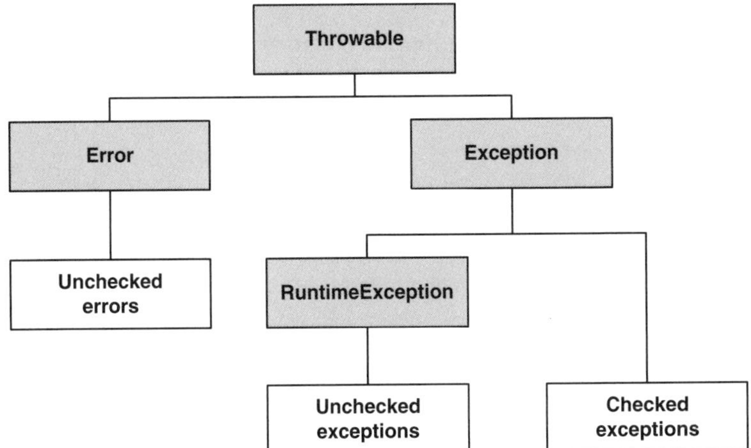

Common checked exceptions

```
ClassNotFoundException
IOException
    EOFException
    FileNotFoundException
NoSuchMethodException
```

Common unchecked exceptions

```
ArithmeticException
IllegalArgumentException
    NumberFormatException
IndexOutOfBoundsException
    ArrayIndexOutOfBoundsException
    StringIndexOutOfBoundsException
NullPointerException
```

Description

- An *exception* is an object of the Exception class or any of its subclasses. It represents a condition that prevents a method from successfully completing its function.
- The Exception class is derived from a class named Throwable. Two types of exceptions are derived from the Exception class: checked exceptions and unchecked exceptions.
- *Checked exceptions* are exceptions that are checked by the compiler. As a result, you must supply code that handles any checked exceptions or you won't be able to compile your program.
- *Unchecked exceptions* are not checked by the compiler. You can write code that handles unchecked exceptions. However, if you don't, any unchecked exceptions will cause your program to terminate. Note that unchecked exceptions don't directly inherit the Exception class. Instead, they inherit a class called RuntimeException, which in turn inherits the Exception class.
- Like the Exception class, the Error class is also derived from the Throwable class. However, the Error class identifies internal errors that are rare and can't usually be recovered from. As a result, you can usually ignore the Error class.

Figure 13-1 The exception hierarchy

How exceptions are propagated

Figure 13-2 shows how the exception handling mechanism works in Java. To start, when a method encounters a problem that can't be solved within that method, it *throws* an exception. This means that control of the program is transferred, or thrown, to another method.

Most of the time, exceptions are thrown by methods from classes in the Java API. Then, any method that calls a method that throws a checked exception must either throw the exception again or catch it and handle it. The code that catches and handles the exception is known as the *exception handler*.

Once a method throws an exception, the runtime system begins looking for the appropriate exception handler. To do this, it searches through the execution *stack trace,* also called the *call stack*. The stack trace is the list of methods that are called when you call one method, with the most recently called method listed first. In this diagram, for example, the stack trace when the code in MethodD executes is: MethodD, MethodC, MethodB, and MethodA.

This figure shows how MethodA calls MethodB, which calls MethodC, which calls MethodD. Here, MethodD may throw an exception. If it does, MethodD throws the exception up to MethodC, which throws it to MethodB, which throws it to MethodA, which catches it in a catch clause.

If you throw a checked exception all the way out of the program by coding a throws clause on each method in the call stack, including the main method, the program will terminate when the exception occurs. Then, Java will display information about the exception to the console.

Note that unchecked exceptions work the same way, except that you don't have to explicitly list unchecked exceptions in the throws clause of a method declaration. For example, suppose the try statement in MethodA also includes a catch clause that catches a runtime exception such as ArithmethicException. Then, if the code in MethodD throws ArithmeticException, the exception propagates up through MethodC and MethodB and is handled by the exception handler in MethodA, even though none of the method declarations include a throws clause that lists ArithmeticException.

How Java propagates exceptions

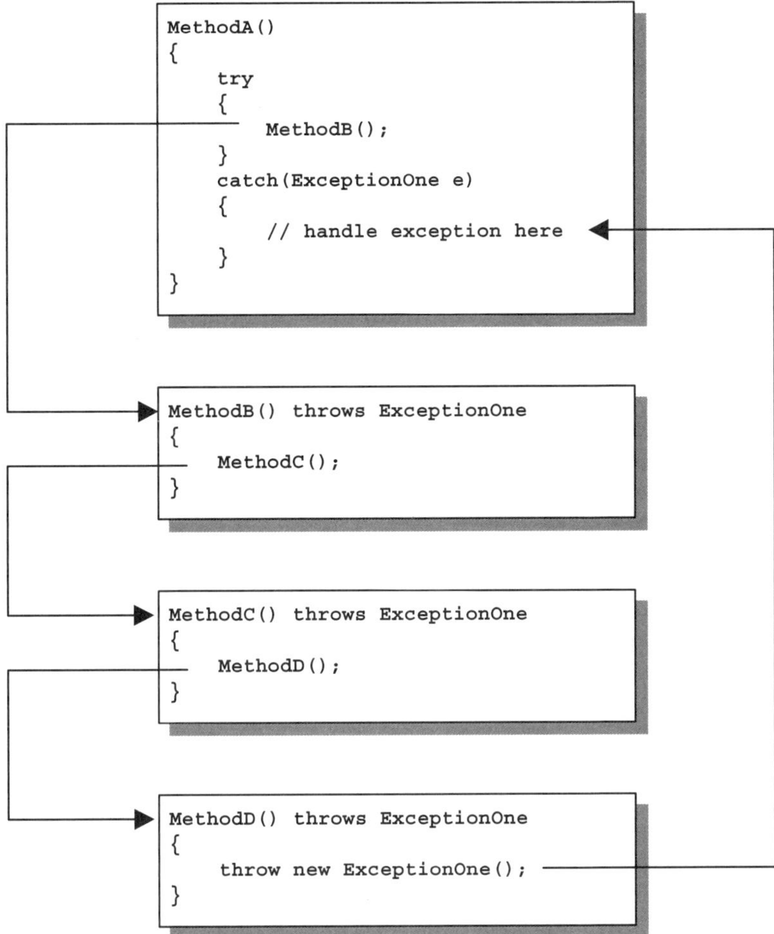
MethodA()
{
try
{
MethodB();
}
catch(ExceptionOne e)
{
// handle exception here
}
}
MethodB() throws ExceptionOne
{
MethodC();
}
MethodC() throws ExceptionOne
{
MethodD();
}
MethodD() throws ExceptionOne
{
throw new ExceptionOne();
}

Two ways to handle checked exceptions

- Throw the exception up to the calling method
- Catch the exception and handle it

Description

- When a method encounters a condition it can't handle, that method should throw an exception. This allows users of the method to handle the exception in a way that's appropriate for their programs. Many methods in the Java API throw exceptions.
- When a method calls another method that throws a checked exception, the method must either throw the exception up to its caller or catch the exception and handle it directly. Code that catches an exception is known as an *exception handler*.
- When an exception occurs, the runtime system looks for the appropriate exception handler. To do that, it looks through the *stack trace*, or *call stack*, which lists the methods that have been called until it finds a method that catches the exception.

Figure 13-2 How exceptions are propagated

How to work with exceptions

In the topics that follow, you'll learn some additional techniques for using the try statement. You'll also learn how to throw an exception, and you'll learn how to use some of the constructors and methods of the Throwable class.

How to use the try statement

Figure 13-3 shows how to code a try statement to catch exceptions. First, it shows the syntax for the try statement. Then, it shows a code example that uses a try statement in a loop to catch exceptions. The loop is set up so that it will continue to execute until no exception is thrown.

As you can see in the syntax, you should code the catch clauses of a try statement in the order in which you want exceptions to be caught. In general, that means you should list more specific exceptions before you list general exceptions. For example, if you want to catch both FileNotFoundException and IOException, you should list FileNotFoundException first because it's derived from IOException. For exceptions that are at the same level in the exception hierarchy (such as FileNotFoundException and EOFException), the order doesn't matter.

This syntax also shows that the try statement has a finally clause. The finally clause is executed whether or not an exception has been thrown. In practice, it isn't used much. But you need to understand how it works, so it's described in the next figure.

The code example in this figure shows how to code try/catch blocks. After the user enters a file name, the constructor of the RandomAccessFile class is called to create an object for the file with that name. Two exceptions can occur when this constructor is called. If the file doesn't exist, a FileNotFoundException will be thrown. If some other type of IO error occurs, an IOException will be thrown. In either case, an error message is displayed and the user is asked to enter another file name. The loop continues until the RandomAccessFile constructor completes successfully. Then, the boolean variable named validFileName is set to true so the loop can finish.

When you code too many try statements, you can easily clutter the logic of your methods with exception handling code. If possible, then, you should design your methods so they throw exceptions to another method that contains an appropriate exception handler. That way, you can code one exception handler that handles the exceptions from many methods. Another good coding practice is to code just one try statement within a method. Then, you can code catch blocks for each type of exception that can occur in the method.

One danger you should be aware of when working with try statements is that it's often tempting to create empty catch clauses for checked exceptions just to get your code to compile. That's okay, as long as you remember to add appropriate exception handling code later. Unfortunately, it's all too easy to forget to do that, so the exception never gets handled. Instead, the empty catch clause catches the exception, then ignores it. This is sometimes called *swallowing an exception*, and it's rarely an acceptable coding practice.

The syntax of the try statement

```
try
{
    // statements that can cause an exception to be thrown
}
catch (MostSpecificExceptionType e)
{
    // statements that handle the exception
}
catch (LeastSpecificExceptionType e)
{
    // statements that handle the exception
}
finally
{
    // statements that are executed whether or not an exception is thrown
}
```

Code that uses a try statement in a loop to validate user input

```
Scanner sc = new Scanner(System.in);

// get the file name from the user
RandomAccessFile file;
String fileName;
boolean validFileName = false;
while (!validFileName)
{
    System.out.print("File name: ");
    fileName = sc.next();
    try
    {
        file = new RandomAccessFile(fileName, "r");
        validFileName = true;
    }
    catch (FileNotFoundException e)
    {
        System.out.println("File not found.");
    }
    catch (IOException e)
    {
        System.out.println("An I/O error occurred.");
    }
    sc.nextLine();
}
System.out.println("File name accepted.");
```

Description

- You use the catch clause of the try statement to catch specific exception types.
- You should code the catch clauses in sequence from the most specific class in the Throwable hierarchy to the least specific class.
- A finally clause is executed whether or not an exception is thrown. See figure 13-4 for details.

Figure 13-3 How to use the try statement

How to use the finally clause

As you learned in the previous figure, the finally clause is executed whether or not an exception occurs. This clause is sometimes used to clean up resources that were used by a method. For example, you might close files or release database connections in a finally clause. Figure 13-4 shows three examples of how this clause can be used.

The first example shows the basic structure of a try statement with a finally clause. Here, code that might throw a FileNotFoundException is included within the try block of a try statement. Then, code that handles the FileNotFoundException is placed in the catch block. Code that should always be executed regardless of what happens in the try and catch blocks is placed in the finally block.

In this example, the try block returns an object that refers to a file if it executes successfully. However, the catch block returns a null value to indicate that the method did not execute successfully. Most of the time, return statements like these cause control to be returned to the calling method immediately. However, a finally block is always executed before control is returned to the calling method, even after a return statement is executed or an exception is thrown. For more detailed examples of this, you can refer to any of the chapters in section 5.

If the try and catch blocks don't include return statements, you can usually omit the finally clause and place the code after the try statement as shown in the second example. Here, the code that follows the try statement will be executed whether or not a FileNotFoundException is thrown, so placing this code in a finally clause isn't necessary.

The third example, however, shows that a finally clause is necessary if the code in the try block might throw an exception that isn't handled by the try statement. Here, the code in the try block might throw FileNotFoundException or IOException, but only FileNotFoundException is handled by the try statement. In this case, the code in the finally clause is executed if no exception is raised or if a FileNotFoundException is thrown. In addition, the code in the finally clause is executed if an IOException is thrown, before Java looks for an exception handler for this exception in the calling method. If you had simply placed the finally code after the try statement as in the second example, it wouldn't execute at all if an IOException was thrown.

Although you usually code a finally clause in a try statement that also has one or more catch clauses, it sometimes makes sense to code a try statement with no catch clauses but with a finally clause. If, for example, you want to throw an exception to another method, but you also want to clean up system resources, you can omit the catch clause and code a finally clause.

If you include a finally clause in a try statement, you should be aware that the exception handlers provided by the catch clauses are not in effect when the code in the finally block executes. Because of that, you'll need to enclose any statements in the finally block that might cause checked exceptions to be thrown within another try statement. For example, if you want to close a file in a finally

Example 1: Code that uses a finally clause

```
try
{
    // code that throws FileNotFoundException
    return productFile;
}
catch (FileNotFoundException e)
{
    // code that handles FileNotFoundException
    return null;
}
finally
{
    // code that's executed whether or not FileNotFoundException is thrown
}
```

Example 2: Code that doesn't use a finally clause

```
try
{
    // code that throws FileNotFoundException
}
catch (FileNotFoundException e)
{
    // code that handles FileNotFoundException
}
// code that's executed whether or not FileNotFoundException is thrown
```

Example 3: Code that uses a finally clause for an unhandled exception

```
try
{
    // code that throws FileNotFoundException or IOException
}
catch (FileNotFoundException e)
{
    // code that handles FileNotFoundException
}
finally
{
    // code that's executed whether or not FileNotFoundException or
    // IOException is thrown
}
// code that's executed whether or not FileNotFoundException is thrown
// but not if IOException is thrown
```

Description

- The code in the *finally block* is executed whether or not an exception is thrown.
- If the try statement is coded in a method that returns a value to its calling method, the code in the finally block is executed even if the code in the try block or a catch block issues a return statement.
- Unlike the code in a finally block, code that follows a try statement isn't executed if an exception is thrown but not handled by one of the catch clauses.

Figure 13-4 How to use the finally clause

clause, you must enclose the statement that closes the file within another try statement. This try statement would probably catch the IOException and print some information to the console, since there's not much you can do if an IOException occurs when you're trying to close a file because some other exception has already occurred.

How to use the throws clause

When you call a method from the Java API that throws a checked exception, you must either throw the exception or catch it. If you decide that you can't handle the exception properly in the method that you're coding, you code a throws clause on the method declaration as shown in figure 13-5. This throws the exception up to the calling method, which can handle it with an exception handler or throw it up to its calling method. If a method throws more than one exception, you use commas to separate the exceptions in the throws clause.

The first example in this figure shows how to code a method named getFileLength that throws an IOException. Here, the first statement in this method calls the constructor of the RandomAccessFile class, which may throw an IOException. (Actually, the constructor can also throw FileNotFoundException, but because FileNotFoundException is derived from IOException, it can be treated as an IOException.) Then, the next statement calls the length method of the RandomAccessFile object, which may also throw an IOException. As a result, the declaration for the getFileLength method uses a throws clause to identify this exception.

The second example shows how to code a method that calls the getFileLength method shown in the first example. Since this method starts by calling the getFileLength method, it must throw or handle IOException. In this example, the getRecordCount method uses a try statement to catch the exception.

The third example shows a method named getRecordCount that calls getFileLength without catching IOException. Here, the method declaration for the getRecordCount method includes a throws clause that throws the IOException up to the calling method.

This figure also shows an example of the type of error message that's generated by the compiler if you fail to catch or throw a checked exception. This error message would be generated if you omitted the throws clause in the method declaration shown in the third example.

The syntax for the declaration of a method that throws exceptions

```
modifiers returnType methodName([parameterList]) throws exceptionList {}
```

Example 1: A method that throws IOException

```
public static long getFileLength() throws IOException
{
    RandomAccessFile in = new RandomAccessFile("books.dat", "r");
    long length = in.length();
    return length;
}
```

Example 2: A method that calls getFileLength and catches IOException

```
public static int getRecordCount()
{
    try
    {
        long length = getFileLength();          // can throw IOException
        int recordCount = (int) (length / RECORD_SIZE);
        return recordCount;
    }
    catch (IOException e)
    {
        System.out.println("An IO error occurred.");
        return 0;
    }
}
```

Example 3: Code that calls getFileLength without catching IOException

```
public static int getRecordCount() throws IOException
{
    long length = getFileLength();          // can throw IOException
    int recordCount = (int) (length / RECORD_SIZE);
    return recordCount;
}
```

Compiler error generated if you don't catch or throw a checked exception

```
\java 1.5\examples\ch13\TestIOExceptionApp.java:26: unreported exception
java.io.IOException; must be caught or declared to be thrown
```

Description

- Any method that calls a method that throws a checked exception must either catch the exception or throw the exception up to the calling method. Otherwise, the program won't compile.
- To throw a checked exception up to the calling method, you code a throws clause in the method declaration. The throws clause must name each checked exception that's thrown up to the calling method.
- Although you can specify unchecked exceptions in the throws clause, the compiler doesn't force you to handle unchecked exceptions.

Figure 13-5 How to use the throws clause

How to use the throw statement

When you're coding a method, you may sometimes need to throw an exception as shown in figure 13-6. However, you should only throw an exception if the current method doesn't have the means to handle the exception, if you need to throw the exception for testing purposes, or if an exception handler needs to process an exception before it passes the exception up to the calling method.

To throw an exception, you code a throw statement that throws an object of an exception class. To do that, you usually use the new keyword to create an object from the exception class. When you create an object from the exception class, you can use the default constructor, which doesn't accept any arguments, or you can use a constructor that accepts a string that describes the exception in more detail.

The first example in this figure shows a method named calculateFutureValue that accepts three parameters and throws an IllegalArgumentException if any of these parameters are less than or equal to zero. It's a good coding practice for any public method to throw an IllegalArgumentException if the method is passed any parameters that have unacceptable values.

The second example shows how you might throw an exception to test an exception handler. This technique is useful for exceptions that are difficult to force otherwise. For example, you can easily test a handler for FileNotFoundException by providing a file name that doesn't exist. But testing a handler for IOException can be difficult. Sometimes, the easiest way is to explicitly throw the exception at the point you would expect it to occur. However, when you do this, the throw statement must be the last statement of the try clause, or it must be coded within an if statement. Otherwise, the code won't compile, and the compiler will display a message that indicates that the code contains unreachable statements.

The third example shows code that rethrows an exception after processing it. Here, the exception handler prints an error message that indicates an exception has occurred, then it rethrows the exception so that the calling method can handle it. Rethrowing an exception is easy. Since the catch clause receives the exception as an argument, you simply throw the variable specified in the catch clause. In this example, the catch clause assigns the IOException object to a variable named e. Then, the throw statement throws e.

The syntax of the throw statement

```
throw Throwable;
```

Example 1: A method that throws an unchecked exception

```
public double calculateFutureValue(double monthlyPayment,
        double monthlyInterestRate, int months)
{
    if (monthlyPayment <= 0)
        throw new IllegalArgumentException(
            "Monthly payment must be > 0");
    if (monthlyInterestRate <= 0)
        throw new IllegalArgumentException(
            "Interest rate must be > 0");
    if (months <= 0)
        throw new IllegalArgumentException(
            "Months must be > 0");
    // code to calculate and return future value goes here
}
```

Example 2: Code that throws an IOException for testing purposes

```
try
{
   throw new IOException();     // must be the last statement in the try block
}
catch (IOException e)
{
   // code to handle IOException goes here
}
```

Example 3: Code that rethrows an exception

```
try
{
    // code that throws IOException goes here
}
catch (IOException e)
{
   System.out.println("IOException thrown in getFileLength method.");
   throw e;
}
```

When to throw an exception

- When a method encounters a problem that prevents it from completing its task, such as when the method is passed unacceptable argument values.
- When you want to generate an exception to test an exception handler.
- When you want to catch an exception, perform some processing, then throw the exception again so it can be handled by the calling method.

Description

- You use the throw statement to throw an exception.
- You can name any object of type Throwable in a throw statement. To throw a new exception, use the new keyword to call the constructor of the exception class you want to throw. To throw an existing exception, you must first catch the exception with the catch clause of a try statement.

Figure 13-6 How to use the throw statement

How to use the constructors and methods of the Throwable class

Figure 13-7 shows how you can use the constructors and methods of the Throwable class to provide more descriptive error information when an exception occurs. As you can see, the second constructor for the Throwable class accepts an optional argument that lets you specify an error message that's stored in the exception object. And the methods of the Throwable class let you retrieve information from the exception object.

The first example in this figure shows code that creates an exception with the error message "An IO error has occurred." Then, in the exception handler, the getMessage method is used to retrieve and print this error message. In many cases, that's all you'll need to determine the cause of an error. However, not all errors return messages. Because of that, you may want to use the toString method instead of the getMessage method, which returns both the message and the name of the exception class. You can see the difference in the output from these two methods in this example.

Notice in this example that both of the statements in the catch block use the println method of the System.err object, which is the standard error output stream. Although this works the same as using the System.out object, the standard output stream, it's common to use the System.err object when displaying information about errors and exceptions. Then, it's possible to direct the standard output stream to one source (such as the console) and to direct the standard error output stream to another source (such as a log file).

The second example shows how you can use the printStackTrace method to access the stack trace, which prints each method that was called up to the point where the exception was thrown. Note that the printStackTrace method actually prints the stack trace to the standard error output stream. Although this output stream normally goes to the console, it can be redirected for logging purposes. The stack trace begins with the name of the exception class and the message. Then, it lists each method. In this example, only two methods are listed: getProductData is the method from which the exception was thrown, and main is the method that called getProductData.

Common constructors of the Throwable class

Constructor	Description
`Throwable()`	Creates a new exception with a null message.
`Throwable(message)`	Creates a new exception with the specified message.

Common methods of the Throwable class

Method	Description
`getMessage()`	Returns the message associated with the exception, if one is available.
`printStackTrace()`	Prints the stack trace to the standard error output stream along with the value of the toString method of the exception object.
`toString()`	Returns a string that includes the name of the class that the exception was created from, along with the message associated with the exception, if one is available.

Example 1: Code that throws an exception with a message

```
try
{
    throw new IOException("An IO error has occurred.");
}
catch (IOException e)
{
   System.err.println(e.getMessage());
   System.err.println(e.toString());
}
```

Resulting output

```
An IO error has occurred.
java.io.IOException: An IO error has occurred.
```

Example 2: Code that uses the printStackTrace method

```
try
{
    throw new IOException("An IO error has occurred.");
}
catch (IOException e)
{
    e.printStackTrace(); }
}
```

Resulting output

```
java.io.IOException: An IO error has occurred.
        at ProductTestApp.getProductData(ProductTestApp.java:14)
        at ProductTestApp.main(ProductTestApp.java:7)
```

Description

- The Throwable class (from which all exceptions are derived) has methods that let you retrieve a message that describes the exception, retrieve the name of the exception, or print a stack trace to the standard error output stream.
- When you create a new exception, you can pass a descriptive message to the constructor. If you omit the message, a null string is used.

Figure 13-7 How to use the constructors and methods of the Throwable class

How to work with custom exception classes

Although the Java API contains a wide range of exceptions, you may encounter a situation where none of those exceptions describes your exception accurately. If so, you can code a class that defines a custom exception as described in the following topics. Then, you can throw your exception just as you would throw any other exception.

How to create your own exception class

Figure 13-8 shows how to create your own custom exception class. Most of the time, you'll want to inherit the Exception class or one of its subclasses to create a checked exception. To illustrate, the first example in this figure shows an exception class named ProductDAOException that extends Exception. As a result, ProductDAOException is a checked exception. However, you can also code a class that defines an unchecked exception by inheriting the RuntimeException class or one of its subclasses.

By convention, all exception classes should have a default constructor that doesn't accept any arguments and another constructor that accepts a string argument. That way, your exception class will behave like the rest of the exception classes in the Java API. In the first example, you can see these two constructors. The second constructor calls the constructor of the Exception class, passing it the message that was passed via the parameter.

The second example shows code that throws the custom ProductDAOException. This example defines a method named getProduct, which calls a method named readProduct to retrieve a product object for a specified product code. The readProduct method throws an IOException, which is caught by the catch clause. The catch clause then throws a ProductDAOException.

The third example shows code that catches a custom exception. Here, the getProduct method is called in a try statement and the ProductDAOException is caught by the catch clause. In the event handler for the ProductDAOException, an error message is displayed at the console.

At first glance, it might seem that the custom exception defined by these examples isn't necessary. After all, couldn't the getProduct method simply throw IOException if an IO error occurs? Although it could, that would result in a poor design because it would expose too many details of the getProduct method's operation. An IOException can occur only when file I/O operations are used. As a result, throwing IOException would reveal that the getProduct method uses file I/O to access the product data.

What if the application is changed so that the product data is kept in a database instead of a file? In that case, the getProduct method wouldn't throw an IOException, it would throw some type of database exception. Then, any

Example 1: Code for the ProductDAOException class

```
public class ProductDAOException extends Exception
{
    public ProductDAOException()
    {
    }

    public ProductDAOException(String message)
    {
        super(message);
    }
}
```

Example 2: A method that throws the ProductDAOException

```
public static Product getProduct(String productCode)
    throws ProductDAOException
{
    try
    {
        Product p = readProduct(productCode);     // may throw IOException
        return p;
    }
    catch (IOException e)
    {
        throw new ProductDAOException(
            "An IO error occurred while retrieving the product.");
    }
}
```

Example 3: Code that catches the ProductDAOException

```
try
{
    Product p = getProduct("1234");
}
catch (ProductDAOException e)
{
    System.out.println(e.getmessage());
}
```

When to define your own exceptions

- When a method requires an exception that isn't provided by any of Java's exception types
- When using a built-in Java exception would inappropriately expose details of a method's operation

Description

- To define a checked exception, inherit the Exception class or any of its subclasses.
- To define an unchecked exception, inherit the RuntimeException class or any of its subclasses.
- By convention, each exception class should contain a default constructor that doesn't accept any arguments and another constructor that accepts a string argument.

Figure 13-8 How to create your own exception class

methods that call the getProduct method would have to be changed to handle the new exceptions. Creating a custom ProductDAOException for the getProduct method hides the details of how the getProduct method works from methods that call it. So even if the application is changed over to a database, the getProduct method can still throw ProductDAOException if an error occurs while retrieving a product object.

How to use exception chaining

You'll often throw custom exceptions in response to other exceptions that occur. For example, in the previous figure, ProductDAOException was thrown in response to IOException. Unfortunately, information about the underlying error that led to the ProductDAOException is lost. And that information might prove invaluable to determining what caused the ProductDAOException to occur.

Figure 13-9 shows how you can throw a custom exception without losing the details of the original exception that was thrown. This feature is called *exception chaining* because it lets you chain exceptions together. Whenever you create a custom exception type, it's a good practice to use exception chaining to avoid losing valuable debugging information.

To use exception chaining, you use an exception constructor that lets you specify an exception object as the cause for the new exception you're creating. Then, you can use the getCause method to retrieve the original exception object.

The first example in this figure shows a version of the ProductDAOException class that lets you specify a cause via the constructor. As you can see, the second constructor accepts a Throwable object as a parameter. Then, it passes this parameter on to the Exception constructor.

The second example shows code that throws a ProductDAOException in response to an IOException. Here, the IOException object is passed to the ProductDAOException constructor as an argument. That way, all of the information contained in the original IOException will be saved as part of the ProductDAOException object.

The third example shows code that catches a ProductDAOException and displays information about the cause of the exception. Here, an error message is displayed to indicate that a ProductDAOException has occurred. Then, the getCause method is used to retrieve the original exception, and the toString method is used to display information about the original exception.

Constructors and methods of the Throwable class for exception chaining

Constructor	Description
`Throwable(cause)`	Creates a new exception with the specified exception object as its cause.
`Throwable(message, cause)`	Creates a new exception with the specified message and cause.
Method	**Description**
`getCause()`	Returns the exception object that represents this exception's cause.
`initCause(cause)`	Sets the exception's cause to the specified exception. Note that this method can be called only once. If you initialize the cause via the constructor, you can't call this method at all.

Example 1: A custom exception class that uses exception chaining

```
public class ProductDAOException extends Exception
{
    public ProductDAOException()
    {
    }

    public ProductDAOException(Throwable cause)
    {
        super(cause);
    }
}
```

Example 2: Code that throws ProductDAOException with chaining

```
catch (IOException e)
{
    throw new ProductDAOException(e);
}
```

Example 3: Code that catches ProductDAOException and displays the cause

```
catch (ProductDAOException e)
{
    System.out.println("A ProductDAOException has occurred.");
    System.out.println(e.getCause().toString());
}
```

Resulting output

```
A ProductDAOException has occurred.
java.io.IOException: IOException
```

Description

- *Exception chaining* lets you maintain exception information for exceptions that are caught when new exceptions are thrown. Exception chaining uses the cause field, which represents the original exception that caused the current exception to be thrown.
- You can set the cause of an exception via the exception's constructor or by using the initCause method. You can retrieve an exception's cause by using the getCause method.

Figure 13-9 How to use exception chaining

How to work with assertions

An *assertion* is a new type of statement that was introduced with version 1.4 of Java. It lets you test that a condition is true at a particular point in your application. And that can help you to be more confident that the application is working correctly.

Assertions work differently than most Java statements because they can be enabled or disabled. By default, assertions are disabled so that an application will run efficiently. However, when you're testing and debugging an application, you'll want to enable assertions so that they're tested as the program executes.

How to code assert statements

Figure 13-10 shows how to code an assert statement. To start, you code the assert keyword followed by an expression that evaluates to true or false. Then, if you want to include a message that's displayed if the condition is false, you code a colon followed by a string expression.

The example in this figure shows an assert statement that specifies that the future value of a series of monthly investments should be greater than the sum of all of the investments. This is a reasonable assertion because the future value should include the investments plus the interest earned on those investments. Because the future value calculation isn't coded correctly in this figure, however, this condition will evaluate to false. As a result, if assertions are enabled, the assert statement will throw an AssertionError at runtime. Then, information like that shown in this figure is printed to the standard error stream.

How to enable and disable assertions

Figure 13-10 also shows how to enable and disable assertions. The technique you use depends on whether you're running a program from the command prompt or from TextPad. From the command prompt, you just code the –ea switch (think "enable assertions") after the java command. Then, the assertions are enabled for that execution of the program. If you're using TextPad, you enable assertions by adding the –ea switch to the parameters that are used when a program is run. Then, assertions are enabled for any program you run until you remove this switch. Note that you should add this switch to the beginning of the parameters or it may not work correctly.

Since assertions can be enabled or disabled, it's critical that they only test a Boolean condition and don't perform any tasks. For example, you wouldn't want an assert statement to update a counter variable. If it did, the application would work differently depending on whether assertions were enabled or disabled.

The syntax of the assert statement

```
assert booleanExpression [: message ];
```

Code that makes a reasonable assertion about a calculation

```
for (int i = 1; i <= months; i++)
{
    futureValue =
        (futureValue + monthlyInvestment) * monthlyInterestRate;
}
// future value should be at least monthlyInterest * months
assert (futureValue > monthlyInvestment * months) : "FV out of range";
```

The output that's displayed when an assertion exception is thrown

```
Exception in thread "main" java.lang.AssertionError: FV out of range
        at FutureValueApp.calculateFutureValue(FutureValueApp.java:152)
        at FutureValueApp.main(FutureValueApp.java:42)
```

TextPad's Preferences dialog box with the –ea switch set

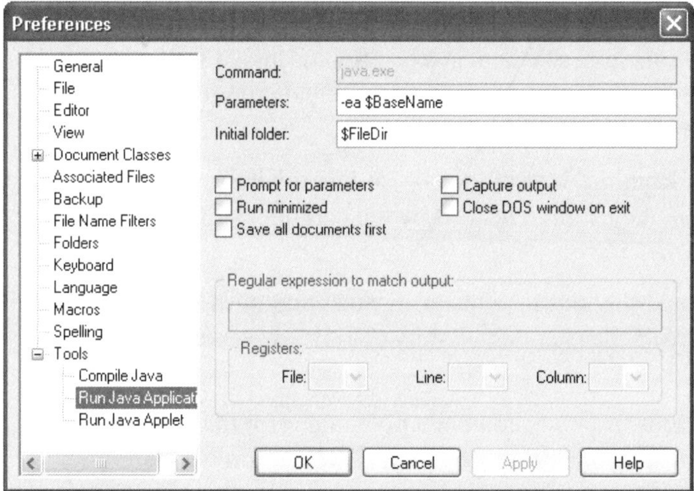

Description

- The assert statement was introduced with Java 1.4. You can use this statement to code an *assertion*, which is a condition that should be true at a particular point in your application.
- Assertions are disabled by default. To enable assertions when you run an application from the command prompt, enter the –ea switch after the java command. To enable assertions from TextPad, choose Configure→Preferences, expand the Tools group, select the Run Java Application option, and add –ea at the beginning of the Parameters text box.
- If assertions are enabled, the JRE evaluates assert statements and throws an AssertionError if the condition specified by the assert statement is false. If the assert statement specifies a message, the message is included in the AssertionError.
- An assert statement shouldn't include any code that performs a task. If it does, the program will run differently depending on whether assertions are enabled or disabled.

Figure 13-10 How to work with assertions

Perspective

In this chapter, you've learned the most important techniques for handling exceptions in Java. Unfortunately, exception handling is one of the more troublesome aspects of any serious application development. The essential problem of exception handling is that exceptions are usually thrown at the lowest levels of an application, but should be handled at the highest levels. For example, a getProduct method that retrieves Product objects probably has no idea what should be done if an IO error occurs. So this low-level method throws an exception that's handled by a higher-level method, which can write the exception to an error log, display an error message, or even terminate the application. In short, exception handling usually affects every level of an application's design.

Summary

- In Java, an *exception* is an object that's created from a class that's derived from the Exception class or one of its subclasses. When an exception occurs, a well-coded program notifies its users of the exception and minimizes any disruptions or data loss that may result from the exception.
- Exceptions derived from the RuntimeException class and its subclasses are *unchecked exceptions* because they aren't checked by the compiler. All other exceptions are *checked exceptions*.
- Any method that calls a method that *throws* a checked exception must either throw the exception by coding a throws clause or *catch* it by coding *try/catch/finally blocks* as an *exception handler*.
- When coding your own methods, if you encounter a potential error that can't be handled within that method, you can code a *throw statement* that throws the exception to another method. If you can't find an appropriate exception class in the Java API, you can code your own exception class.
- You can create custom exception classes to represent exceptions your methods might throw. This is often useful to hide the details of how a method is implemented.
- When you use custom exceptions, you can use *exception chaining* to save information about the cause of an exception.
- An *assertion* lets you test that a condition is true at a specific point in an application.

Exercise 13-1 Research Java exceptions

Examine the Java API documentation and make a list of three unchecked exception classes and three checked exception classes that aren't listed in figure 13-1. For each exception, give a brief description of a programming situation in which you might want to catch the exception.

Exercise 13-2 Throw and catch exceptions

In this exercise, you'll experiment with various types of exceptions and ways to handle them.

1. Open the ExceptionTesterApp class in the c:\java1.5\ch13 directory. This class provides a framework you can use to experiment with exceptions thrown and caught at different levels of the call stack. It consists of a main method that calls a method named Method1, which in turn calls a method named Method2, which in turn calls a method named Method3. Each method displays a message before and after it calls the next method, and indentation is used to indicate the level in the call stack. Compile and run this class to get a feel for how it works.
2. Add code to Method3 that throws an unchecked exception by attempting to divide an integer by zero. Compile and run the program and note where the exception is thrown.
3. Delete the code you just added to Method3. Then, add a statement to this method like the one in the first example in figure 13-5 that creates an object from the RandomAccessFile class. This class throws a checked exception named FileNotFoundException. Compile the class and note the error message that indicates that you haven't handled the exception.
4. Add the code necessary to handle the FileNotFoundException in Method1. To do that, you'll need to add throws clauses to the declarations of Method2 and Method3. You'll also need to add a try statement to Method1 that catches the exception. The catch block should display an error message. Run the program to make sure the exception handler works.
5. Remove the try statement from Method1 and add a throws clause to the declarations for Method1 and the main method. Then, run the program to see how a checked exception can propagate all the way out of a program.

Exercise 13-3 Use the finally clause

In this exercise, you'll experiment with the finally clause to see how it works.

1. Open the FinallyTesterApp class in the c:\java1.5\ch13 directory.
2. Modify the code in Method3 so that it contains a try statement that includes code that throws an IOException, a catch clause that handles the exception, and a finally clause. Add a statement to each clause of the try statement that prints information to the console so you can trace the execution of the program. Run the program to make sure that the catch clause catches the exception and that the finally clause is executed as expected.
3. Add an if statement to the try block that throws a NoSuchMethodException if a condition is true and the IOException if the condition is false. Use any condition you want, but be sure that it evaluates to true so the IOException won't be thrown. Instead of adding a catch clause to catch the new exception, add throws clauses to the Method1, Method2, and Method3 declarations so that the exception is thrown up to the main method.

4. Add a try statement to the main method, and call Method1 from within the try clause. Then, add a catch clause that catches the NoSuchMethodException and displays a message indicating that the exception has been caught. Run the application to verify that the code in the finally clause in Method3 is still executed, but the code that follows the try statement is not.

Exercise 13-4 Create a custom class

In this exercise, you'll experiment with custom classes and chained exceptions.

1. Create a custom checked exception class named TestException that contains two constructors: one that accepts no parameters and one that accepts a String message.
2. Open the CustomTesterApp class in the c:\java1.5\ch13 directory.
3. Add a statement to Method3 that throws a TestException without a message. (You'll also need to delete or comment out the last statement in Method3 or the compiler will flag it as unreachable.) Add the code necessary to catch this exception in Method2. The catch block should simply display a message at the console. Compile and run the program and observe its operation.
4. Modify your solution so that a custom message is passed to the TestException and is then displayed in the catch block. Compile and run the program to be sure that the custom message is displayed.
5. Add another constructor to the TestException class that accepts a Throwable object as a parameter.
6. Add a try statement to Method3 of the CustomTesterApp class. The try clause should throw an IOException, and the catch clause should throw a TestException, passing the IOException to its constructor.
7. Modify the catch block in Method2 that catches the TestException so that it displays the original cause of the exception. Compile and run the application to make sure it works.

Exercise 13-5 Use the assert statement

In this exercise, you'll add an assert statement to the Invoice application of chapter 4 so you can see how it works.

1. Open the InvoiceApp class in the c:\java1.5\ch13 directory. Notice that the statement that calculates the invoice total has been changed so that it adds the discount amount to the subtotal instead of subtracting it.
2. Add an assert statement that tests that the calculated invoice total is always less than or equal to the subtotal entered by the user. Include an appropriate message to be displayed if this assertion is false. Then, compile and run the application to see that this statement isn't executed by default.
3. Enable assertions, and then run the program again. This time, an assertion error should occur and the message you specified should be displayed.

14

How to work with threads

When you run a program in Java, the program runs in one or more threads. So far in this book, all of the programs have executed within a single thread. In this chapter, you'll learn how to develop programs that run in two or more threads that perform separate tasks. For example, you can use one thread to retrieve data from a database while another thread makes a complicated calculation. Then, the program can alternate between the two tasks so it runs more efficiently.

An introduction to threads

Before you learn how to develop applications that use two or more threads, you need to understand how threads work and when you would typically use them. You also need to be familiar with the classes and interfaces you use when you work with threads, and you need to understand the life cycle of a thread. That's what you'll learn in the topics that follow

How threads work

As figure 14-1 explains, a *thread* is a single flow of execution through a program. By default, Java applications use a single thread, called the *main thread*. This thread begins executing with the first statement of a program's main method and continues executing statements in sequence until the main method exits. The program may create additional objects and call additional methods, but the flow of control is always sequential, one statement at a time.

In some cases, single-threaded execution can be very inefficient. For example, imagine a program that performs two independent tasks. To accomplish the first task, the program must read data from a file, and this task spends most of its time waiting for file I/O operations to complete. As a result, the second task must wait too, even though it doesn't require any I/O operations.

The first diagram in this figure shows how this program might work when executed as a single thread. First, the program performs the first task. In this case, the CPU is idle while it waits for the I/O operations required by this task. When the first task is complete, the program runs the second task.

The second diagram shows how this program could benefit from being split into two threads, one to perform each task. As you can see, using two threads allows the two tasks to overlap, so the second task is executed while the first task waits on I/O operations. The result is that the two tasks finish sooner than they would if they were executed as a single thread.

Applications that perform several tasks that aren't dependent on one another benefit the most from *multithreading*. For example, the second task shown in this figure can only be overlapped with the first task if the second task doesn't depend on the results of the first task. If the second task depends on the results of the first task, some overlap may still be possible. But the two tasks must communicate with each other so they can coordinate their operations. As you'll learn later in this chapter, managing this sort of coordination can be challenging.

Typical uses for threads

In addition to showing the basics of how threads work, figure 14-1 lists three of the most common uses for threads. The first is to improve the performance of I/O operations. Any application that performs extensive I/O can benefit from multithreading. That's because I/O operations are thousands of times slower than CPU operations. So any program that reads data from a disk spends almost all of its time waiting for that information to be retrieved.

How using threads can improve performance

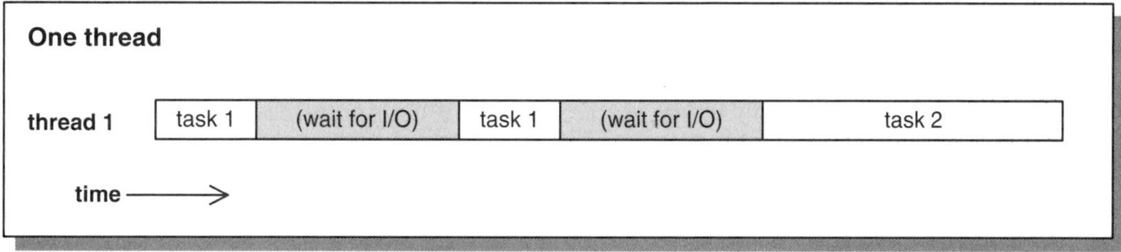

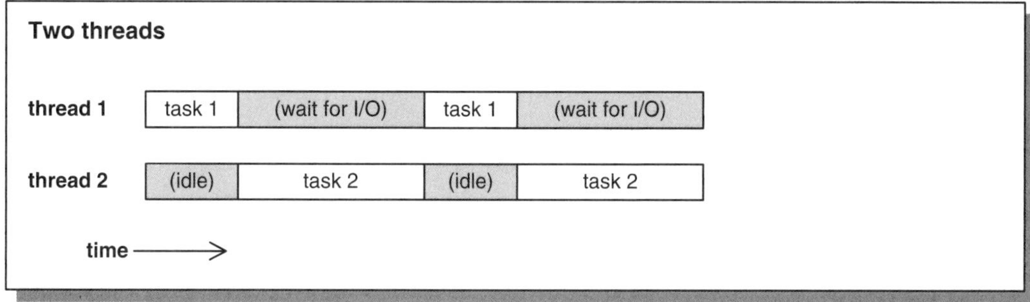

Typical uses for threads

- To improve the performance of applications with extensive I/O operations
- To improve the responsiveness of GUI applications
- To allow two or more users to run server-based applications simultaneously

Description

- A *thread* is a single sequential flow of control within a program. A thread often completes a specific task.
- By default, a Java application uses a single thread, called the *main thread*. However, some programs can benefit by using two or more threads to allow different parts of the program to execute simultaneously.
- On a computer that has just one *central processing unit*, or *CPU*, the threads don't actually execute simultaneously. Instead, a part of the Java virtual machine called the *thread scheduler* alternately lets portions of each thread execute. This gives the appearance that all of the tasks are running at the same time, and this can make an application work more efficiently.

Figure 14-1 How threads work

To give you some perspective on this, you should realize that the actual amount of time that the CPU spends waiting for I/O to complete is much greater than what's indicated in figure 14-1. In fact, since each of the blocks that show task 1 executing are about one half of an inch long, the blocks that show the CPU waiting for I/O would probably need to be about the length of a football field to show the wait time accurately. That's about how much slower disk operations are than CPU operations.

The second reason for using threads is to improve the responsiveness of programs that use graphical user interfaces. For example, when a user clicks a toolbar button, he or she expects the program to respond immediately, even if the program is busy doing something else. As you'll learn in section 4 of this book, all Java GUI programs are multithreaded to enable this type of responsiveness. So a basic understanding of how multithreading works will give you a head start when you start to learn GUI programming.

The final reason for using multithreading is to allow two or more users to run server-based applications, called *servlets*, simultaneously. You learned a little bit about servlets in chapter 1, and you can learn more about them in our book, *Murach's Java Servlets and JSP*. For now, you should just realize that each person who uses a servlet runs it in a separate thread, so the entire application must be multithreaded so that it can support multiple users.

Classes and interfaces for working with threads

Figure 14-2 presents two classes and an interface that you can use to create and work with threads and summarizes the key methods they provide. As you can see, the Thread class inherits the Object class, which means it has access to all of its public and protected methods. In addition, the Thread class implements the Runnable interface. Because the Runnable interface declares a single method named run, that means that the Thread class must implement this method.

To create a thread, you can use one of two techniques. First, you can define a class that inherits the Thread class. This class should overload the run method so it contains the code to be executed by the thread. Then, you can instantiate this class to create a thread.

The second way to create a thread is to define a class that implements the Runnable interface. This class must implement the run method to provide the code that's executed by the thread. Then, you pass an instance of this class to a constructor of the Thread class. This creates a thread that executes the Runnable object's code by calling its run method.

If these two techniques seem confusing right now, don't worry. They will become clearer when you see examples later in this chapter. For now, I just want you to be aware of the role of the Thread class and the Runnable interface. In short, the Thread class defines a thread, but the code that's executed by the thread can be provided by any class that implements the Runnable interface.

As you can see in this figure, the Object class also has some methods that can be used for threading. These methods are used to enable threads to easily communicate with each other. You'll learn about them later in this chapter.

Classes and interfaces used to create threads

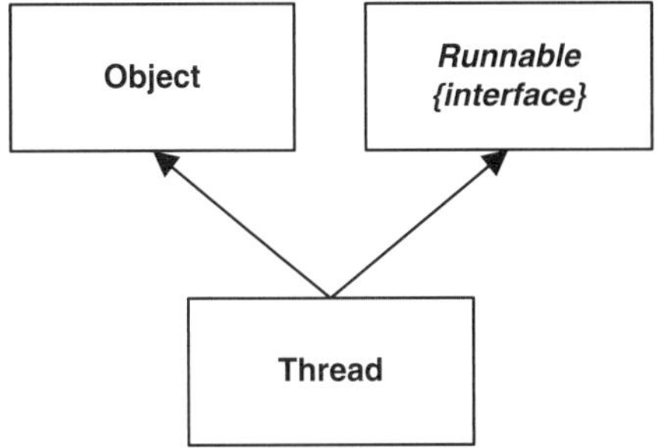

Summary of these classes and interfaces

Class/Interface	Description
Thread	A class that defines a thread. This class inherits the Object class and implements the Runnable interface.
Runnable	An interface that must be implemented by any class whose objects are going to be executed by a thread. The only method in this interface is the run method.
Object	The Object class has several methods that are used for threading. These methods are described in figure 14-11.

Key methods of the Thread class, Runnable interface, and Object class

Method	Class or interface	Description
start	Thread	Registers this thread with the thread scheduler so it's available for execution.
run	Runnable, Thread	An abstract method that's declared by the Runnable interface and implemented by the Thread class. The thread scheduler calls this method to run the thread.
sleep	Thread	Causes the current thread to wait (sleep) for a specified period of time so the CPU can run other threads.
wait	Object	Causes the current thread to wait until another thread calls the notify or notifyAll method for the current object.
notify	Object	Wakes up one arbitrary thread that's waiting on this object.
notifyAll	Object	Wakes up all the threads that are waiting on this object.

Two ways to create a thread

- Inherit the Thread class.
- Implement the Runnable interface, then pass a reference to the Runnable object to the constructor of the Thread class. This is useful if the thread needs to inherit a class other than the Thread class.

Description

- After you create a Thread object, you can call its start method so the thread scheduler can run the thread. Then, you can use the other methods shown above to manage the thread.

Figure 14-2 Classes and interfaces for working with threads

The life cycle of a thread

Figure 14-3 shows the life cycle of a thread and explains each of the five states a thread can be in. To create a thread, the programmer writes code that defines a class for the thread and instantiates a Thread object. When the Thread object is first instantiated, it is placed in the New state, which means that the thread has been created but is not yet ready to be run.

When the program is ready for the thread to be run, it calls the thread's start method. Although you might think that this causes the thread to begin execution, all it really does is change the state of the thread from New to Runnable. Once it's in the Runnable state, the thread joins a list of any other threads that are also in the Runnable state. Then, a component of the Java virtual machine called the *thread scheduler* selects one of the Runnable threads to be executed.

Note that Java doesn't have a separate state for the thread that's running. The state of the thread that's running, as well as all other threads that are eligible to be running, is Runnable. Note also that the thread scheduler may at any time decide that the thread that's currently running has been running long enough. Then, the thread scheduler will interrupt that thread and let one of the other Runnable threads run. This doesn't change the state of either thread.

A thread enters the Blocked state if a condition occurs that makes the thread temporarily not runnable. For example, a thread becomes Blocked when it is waiting for an I/O operation to complete. The thread will automatically be returned to the Runnable state when the I/O operation completes. A thread that's in Blocked state can't be selected for execution by the thread scheduler.

The Waiting state comes into play when threads need to coordinate their activities. You'll learn more about how this works later in this chapter. For now, just realize that a thread can voluntarily enter the Waiting state by calling the wait method. While in the Waiting state, the thread can't run. It will remain in Waiting state until another thread calls the notify or notifyAll method to let the thread know that it can resume.

Finally, when the run method of a thread finishes execution, the thread's state is changed to Terminated. Once a thread has entered the Terminated state, it remains there until the application ends.

The life cycle of a thread

① The Thread constructor is called to create a new instance of the Thread class
New
② The start method is called to designate the thread as runnable
④ The thread can become blocked for various reasons and will not run again until it is returned to the Runnable state
Blocked
③ The Java thread scheduler runs the thread as the processor becomes available
Runnable
Waiting
⑥ The thread ends when the run method terminates
Terminated
⑤ If the thread calls the wait method, it is put into the Waiting state and will remain there until another thread calls the notify or notifyAll method.

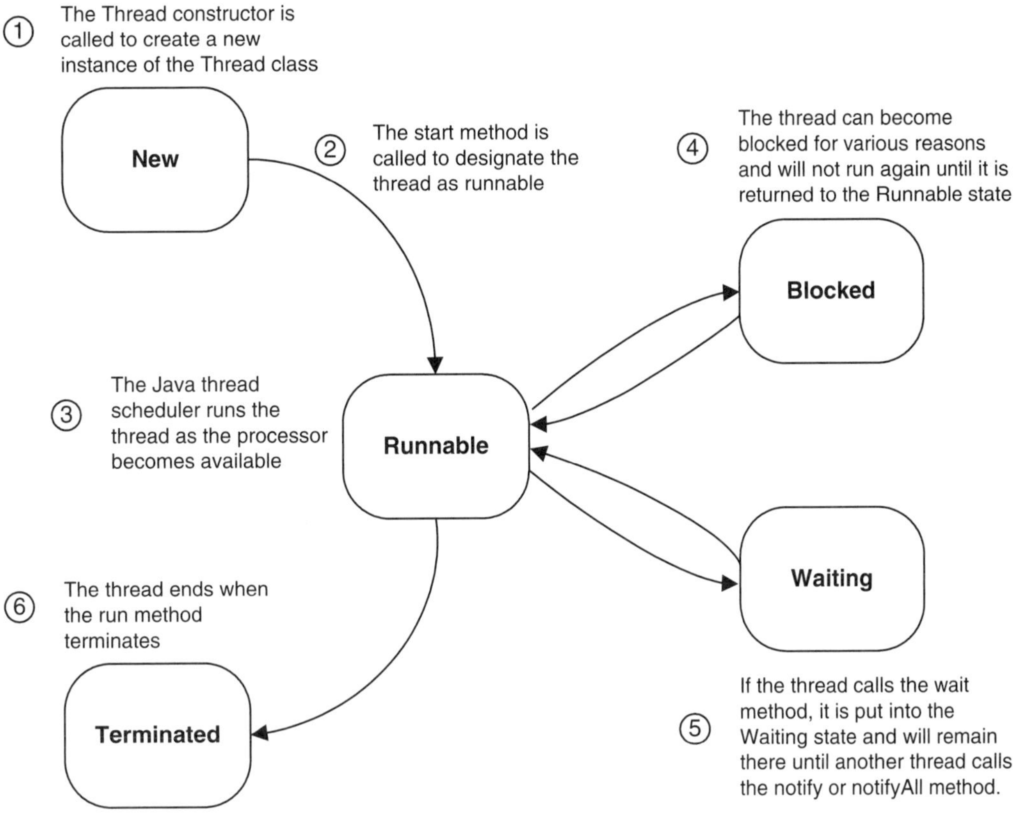

Thread states

State	Description
New	The thread has been created (its constructor has been called), but not yet started.
Runnable	The thread's start method has been called and the thread is available to be run by the thread scheduler. A thread in Runnable state may actually be running, or it may be waiting in the thread queue for an opportunity to run.
Blocked	The thread has been temporarily removed from the Runnable state so that it can't be executed. This can happen if the thread's sleep method is called, if the thread is waiting on I/O, or if the thread requests a lock on an object that's already locked. When the condition changes (for example, the I/O operation completes), the thread will be returned to the Runnable state.
Waiting	The thread has called its wait method so that other threads can access an object. The thread will remain in the Waiting state until another thread calls the notify or notifyAll method.
Terminated	The thread's run method has ended.

Description

- All threads have a life cycle that can include five states: New, Runnable, Blocked, Waiting, and Terminated.

Figure 14-3 The life cycle of a thread

How to create threads

In the topics that follow, you'll learn two ways to create a thread. But first, you'll learn more about the Thread class, which you must use regardless of how you create a thread.

Constructors and methods of the Thread class

The first table in figure 14-4 summarizes some of the constructors you can use to create Thread objects. The first constructor is used by default when you instantiate a class that inherits the Thread class. (Of course, you can also overload this constructor or define other constructors just as you can for any subclass.) The second constructor is used to create a thread from an object that implements the Runnable interface.

The third and fourth constructors let you specify the name of the thread that's created. By default, threads are named numerically. Since you don't typically refer to threads by name, the defaults are usually acceptable.

The second table in this figure presents some of the methods of the Thread class. You can use these methods to get information about a thread and to control when a thread runs and when it waits. Although most of these methods are self-explanatory, two require further explanation. First, you can use the setDaemon method to create a subordinate thread known as a *daemon thread* (pronounced *dee*-mon, not *day*-mon). When you create a daemon thread, that thread will end when the thread that started it ends. If you don't use this method to explicitly create a daemon thread, the thread is considered a *user thread*. User threads continue running even if the thread that created them ends.

Second, you use the setPriority method to set the priority of a thread. This method accepts an integer from 1 to 10 where 1 is the lowest priority and 10 is the highest priority. You'll learn more about how a thread's priority affects its execution later in this chapter.

The Thread class

```
java.lang.Thread;
```

Common constructors of the Thread class

Constructor	Description
`Thread()`	Creates a default Thread object.
`Thread(Runnable)`	Creates a Thread object from any object that implements the Runnable interface.
`Thread(String)`	Creates a Thread object with the specified name.
`Thread(Runnable, String)`	Creates a Thread object with the specified name from any object that implements the Runnable interface.

Common methods of the Thread class

Method	Description
`run()`	Implements the run method of the Runnable interface. This method should be overridden in all subclasses to provide the code that's executed by a thread.
`start()`	Places a thread in the Runnable state so it can be run by the thread scheduler.
`getName()`	Returns the name of a thread.
`currentThread()`	A static method that returns a reference to the currently executing thread.
`setDaemon(boolean)`	If the boolean value is true, marks a thread as a daemon thread. This means it's a subordinate thread that ends when the thread that created it ends.
`yield()`	A static method that causes the currently executing thread to pause so other threads can run.
`sleep(long)`	A static method that places the currently executing thread in the Blocked state for the specified number of milliseconds so that other threads can run.
`interrupt()`	Interrupts a thread.
`isInterrupted()`	Returns a true value if a thread has been interrupted.
`setPriority(int)`	Changes a thread's priority to an int value from 1 to 10.

Description

- By the default, the threads that you create explicitly are named numerically. If that's not what you want, you can specify the name on the constructor of the thread.
- By default, a thread is independent of the thread that created it. This is called a *user thread*. If that's not what you want, you can use the setDaemon method to create a *daemon thread*.
- The sleep method throws InterruptedException. Because this is a checked exception, you must throw or catch this exception when you use the sleep method.

Figure 14-4 Constructors and methods of the Thread class

How to create a thread by extending the Thread class

Figure 14-5 presents a procedure for creating a thread by extending the Thread class. To illustrate this procedure, this figure also presents a Count Down application that uses two threads to count down from 10 to 1. One of the threads counts the even numbers, and the other thread counts the odd numbers. Although this application isn't practical, it does illustrate the basic concepts for creating and working with threads.

This application consists of three classes. CountDownApp is the main class for the application. It contains the main method that's run when the application starts. CountDownEven is the class that counts down by even numbers, and CountDownOdd is the class that counts down by odd numbers. Before I explain how the CountDownApp class instantiates and starts the two threads, I'll describe how the CountDownEven and CountDownOdd classes work.

The CountDownEven class defines a thread that counts down by even numbers starting with 10. As you can see, it extends the Thread class. Then, it overloads the run method to provide the code that's executed when the thread is run. This method contains a for loop whose counter variable is initialized to 10 and decremented by 2 each time through the loop. Within this loop, the first statement calls the println method to display the name of the thread followed by the current value of the counter variable. To get the name of the current thread, the getName method is called. Then, the second statement calls the static yield method of the Thread class. This causes the current thread to pause so that the thread scheduler can run any other threads that are ready to be run.

The CountDownOdd class is almost identical to the CountDownEven class. In fact, the only difference is that its for statement initializes the counter variable to 9 rather than 10. That way, the CountDownOdd class counts down by odd numbers, starting with 9.

The CountDownApp class contains the main method for the application. The first two statements of the main method create instances of the CountDownEven and CountDownOdd classes, assigning them to Thread variables named count1 and count2. Then, the next two statements start the threads by calling their start methods. This places the threads in the Runnable state so the thread scheduler can run them.

Probably the most important thing to notice in this example is that this application never explicitly calls the run method of either thread. Instead, it calls the start method of each thread to make the threads Runnable. Then, the Java thread scheduler calls each thread's run method to actually execute the thread's code.

The output generated by the Count Down application is shown at the bottom of this figure. Each line begins by printing the name of the thread. Here, the name that's assigned to the CountDownEven thread is Thread-0, and the name that's assigned to the CountDownOdd thread is Thread-1. Then, each line prints the number that's generated by the for loop. Since both of these threads use the yield method, the scheduler switches between these two threads.

A procedure for creating a thread

1. Create a class that inherits the Thread class.
2. Overload the run method to perform the desired task.
3. Create the thread by instantiating an object from the class.
4. Call the start method of the thread object.

A Count Down application that starts two count-down threads

```
public class CountDownApp
{
    public static void main(String[] args)
    {
        Thread count1 = new CountDownEven();   // instantiate the countdown threads
        Thread count2 = new CountDownOdd();
        count1.start();                        // start the countdown threads
        count2.start();
    }
}

class CountDownEven extends Thread             // this class counts even numbers
{
    public void run()
    {
        for (int i = 10; i > 0; i-= 2)
        {
            System.out.println(this.getName() + " Count " + i);
            Thread.yield();                    // allow the other thread to run
        }
    }
}

class CountDownOdd extends Thread              // this class counts odd numbers
{
    public void run()
    {
        for (int i = 9; i > 0; i-= 2)
        {
            System.out.println(this.getName() + " Count " + i);
            Thread.yield();                    // allow the other thread to run
        }
    }
}
```

Resulting output

```
Thread-0 Count 10
Thread-1 Count 9
Thread-0 Count 8
Thread-1 Count 7
Thread-0 Count 6
Thread-1 Count 5
Thread-0 Count 4
Thread-1 Count 3
Thread-0 Count 2
Thread-1 Count 1
Press any key to continue . . .
```

Figure 14-5 How to create a thread by extending the Thread class

Incidentally, even though this application creates two threads, the main method still runs in its own thread. As a result, this program actually uses three threads: one for the main method, one for the CountDownEven class, and one for the CountDownOdd class.

How to create a thread by implementing the Runnable interface

Figure 14-6 shows a procedure for creating a thread by implementing the Runnable interface, and it presents a version of the Count Down application that uses this technique. Although this method of creating threads requires a little more code, it's also more flexible because it lets you define a thread that inherits a class other than the Thread class. As a result, it's used more often than the technique you saw in the previous figure.

You'll notice several differences in the code for this version of the application. First, because the CountDownEven and CountDownOdd classes don't inherit the Thread class, you can't instantiate Thread objects directly from them. Instead, you have to instantiate these classes to create Runnable objects. Then, you have to supply each object as an argument to the Thread constructor to create a thread. You can see the code that does this at the beginning of the main method.

Second, notice the differences in the code for the CountDownEven and CountDownOdd classes. To start, these classes implement the Runnable interface rather than extending the Thread class. Then, within the run method of each class, the first statement calls the static currentThread method of the Thread class to get a reference to the thread that's currently executing. That way, the getName method can be used to get the name of this thread. This isn't necessary in the version of this application that you saw in the last figure because the classes defined Thread objects. In this case, though, the classes define Runnable objects.

A procedure for creating a thread

1. Create a class that implements the Runnable interface.
2. Implement the run method to perform the desired task.
3. Create the thread by supplying an instance of the Runnable class to the Thread constructor.
4. Call the start method of the thread object.

A version of the Count Down application that uses the Runnable interface

```
public class CountDownRunnableApp
{
    public static void main(String[] args)
    {
        Thread count1 = new Thread(new CountDownEven());
        Thread count2 = new Thread(new CountDownOdd());
        count1.start();                     // start the countdown threads
        count2.start();
    }
}

class CountDownEven implements Runnable     // this class counts even numbers
{
    public void run()
    {
        Thread t = Thread.currentThread();
        for (int i = 10; i > 0; i-= 2)
        {
            System.out.println(t.getName() + " Count " + i);
            Thread.yield();                 // allow the other thread to run
        }
    }
}

class CountDownOdd implements Runnable      // this class counts odd numbers
{
    public void run()
    {
        Thread t = Thread.currentThread();
        for (int i = 9; i > 0; i-= 2)
        {
            System.out.println(t.getName() + " Count " + i);
            Thread.yield();                 // allow the other thread to run
        }
    }
}
```

Note

- The output from this code is identical to the output shown in figure 14-5.

Figure 14-6 How to create a thread by implementing the Runnable interface

How to manipulate threads

Once you've created a thread, Java provides several methods you can use to control how the thread executes. You use some of these methods in the run method of the thread class. You use others in the main method of the application that defines the threads, after you create the thread object but before you start the thread. The following topics show how to use these methods.

How to put a thread to sleep

The two versions of the Count Down application you've seen so far call the yield method to cause the threads to alternate execution. Figure 14-7 shows another way you can do that. Here, you can see another version of the Count Down application that uses the static sleep method instead of the yield method. The sleep method places a thread in Blocked state for a specified period of time. After the time expires, the thread is returned to Runnable state so the thread scheduler can resume its execution.

In this example, I purposely used different sleep intervals for the CountDownEven and CountDownOdd threads. The CountDownEven thread sleeps for one-half second (500 milliseconds) each time the for loop is executed, and the CountDownOdd thread sleeps for two full seconds (2000 milliseconds). As a result, the output counts down all ten numbers, but not in sequence.

Because the sleep method can throw InterruptedException, that exception must be either caught or thrown. As you'll learn in figure 14-9, this exception indicates that some other thread is attempting to interrupt the current thread while it is sleeping. How you deal with this exception depends on the application. In this case, the application simply ignores any attempts to interrupt the thread by catching the exception but not providing any code to process it. Normally, "swallowing" an exception like this is not a good programming practice. In this case, however, it's appropriate.

If you use the sleep method, you should also realize that it doesn't guarantee that the thread will wake up after the amount of time you specify. Instead, it simply guarantees that the thread will sleep for at least the amount of time you specify. When the time expires, the thread is returned to the Runnable state. But there's no guarantee that the thread scheduler will then immediately resume execution of the thread. So you shouldn't use the sleep method for applications that require precise timing.

A version of the Count Down application that uses sleep() rather than yield()

```
public class CountDownSleepApp
{
    public static void main(String[] args)
    {
        Thread count1 = new CountDownEven();    // instantiate the countdown threads
        Thread count2 = new CountDownOdd();
        count1.start();                         // start the countdown threads
        count2.start();
    }
}

class CountDownEven extends Thread              // this class counts even numbers
{
    public void run()
    {
        for (int i = 10; i > 0; i-= 2)
        {
            System.out.println(this.getName() + " Count " + i);
            try
            {
                Thread.sleep(500);              // sleep for 1/2 second
            }
            catch (InterruptedException e) {}  // ignore any interruptions
        }
    }
}

class CountDownOdd extends Thread               // this class counts odd numbers
{
    public void run()
    {
        for (int i = 9; i > 0; i-= 2)
        {
            System.out.println(this.getName() + " Count " + i);
            try
            {
                Thread.sleep(2000);             // sleep for 2 seconds
            }
            catch (InterruptedException e) {}  // ignore any interruptions
        }
    }
}
```

Resulting output

```
Thread-0 Count 10
Thread-1 Count 9
Thread-0 Count 8
Thread-0 Count 6
Thread-0 Count 4
Thread-1 Count 7
Thread-0 Count 2
Thread-1 Count 5
Thread-1 Count 3
Thread-1 Count 1
Press any key to continue . . .
```

Figure 14-7 How to put a thread to sleep

How to set a thread's priority

Figure 14-8 shows how to prioritize threads. When a thread is created, it's given a priority value between 1 and 10, where 10 is the highest priority and 1 is the lowest priority. Then, the thread scheduler takes these priorities into account when it determines which of several Runnable threads should be run next. In short, if two or more threads are ready to be run, the thread scheduler will always execute the one with the highest priority before it executes the ones with lower priorities.

In the example in this figure, the main method of the CountDownApp class sets the priority of the CountDownEven thread to the minimum priority and the CountDownOdd thread to the maximum priority. As you can see in the resulting output, this causes the thread scheduler to run the CountDownOdd thread to completion before executing the CountDownEven thread. Because of that, all of the odd numbers appear before any of the even numbers.

Note that this application uses the versions of the CountDownEven and CountDownOdd classes that use yield rather than sleep to alternate between threads. If these classes used sleep instead, the result would be different. That's because when the sleep method is executed for the CountDownOdd thread, that thread's state is changed to Blocked for the specified duration. Then, the thread scheduler would run the CountDownEven thread since the higher-priority CountDownOdd thread isn't Runnable.

Thread priorities let you create low-priority threads that will run when no other threads are running. For example, you could give a thread that loads data from a database a low priority so the data will load when all other threads have finished running. When you create a thread like this, though, it's still a good idea to include a yield method so the thread will yield to threads that have higher priorities if those threads become ready to run.

Note that if two or more Runnable threads have the same priority, the thread scheduler determines which one to run. Because the Java specifications don't indicate how the thread scheduler should do this, different Java implementations handle this situation differently. Most use a round-robin scheme that executes each thread in turn. But there's no guarantee of that, so you shouldn't count on it when you design a multithreaded application.

The setPriority method of the Thread class

Method	Description
`setPriority(int)`	Changes this thread's priority to an int value from 1 to 10.

Fields of the Thread class used to set thread priorities

Field	Description
`MAX_PRIORITY`	The maximum priority of any thread (an int value of 10).
`MIN_PRIORITY`	The minimum priority of any thread (an int value of 1).
`NORM_PRIORITY`	The default priority of any thread (an int value of 5).

A version of the Count Down application that sets thread priorities

```
public class CountDownPrioritiesApp
{
    public static void main(String[] args)
    {
        Thread count1 = new CountDownEven();       // instantiate the threads
        Thread count2 = new CountDownOdd();
        count1.setPriority(Thread.MIN_PRIORITY);   // set the thread priorities
        count2.setPriority(Thread.MAX_PRIORITY);
        count1.start();                            // start the threads
        count2.start();
    }
}
```

Resulting output

```
Thread-1 Count 9
Thread-1 Count 7
Thread-1 Count 5
Thread-1 Count 3
Thread-1 Count 1
Thread-0 Count 10
Thread-0 Count 8
Thread-0 Count 6
Thread-0 Count 4
Thread-0 Count 2
Press any key to continue . . .
```

Description

- If two or more runnable threads have different priorities, the thread scheduler executes the threads with the highest priority setting first.
- If two or more runnable threads have the same priority, the thread scheduler determines which thread to execute next. On most platforms, the threads are executed in a round-robin order.
- A thread can't yield to a thread with a lower priority.
- By default, every thread is given the priority of the thread that created it. If a thread is created from the main thread, it's given a priority of 5 by default.
- Since thread scheduling relies on the underlying system, the final result may vary depending on the platform.

Figure 14-8 How to set a thread's priority

How to interrupt a thread

In some cases, you may need to interrupt the thread that's currently executing. To do that, you use the interrupt method of the Thread class as shown in figure 14-9.

The application in this figure defines a thread named Counter that counts one-second intervals. This thread continues counting until the user types "stop" at the console and presses the Enter key. To accomplish this, the main method starts the Counter thread and then enters a while loop that uses the next method of the Scanner class to wait for the user to enter the word "stop." When that happens, the main method calls the Counter thread's interrupt method to interrupt the thread.

In the Counter thread's run method, several statements are required to properly detect that the thread has been interrupted. First, notice that the while loop repeats as long as the isInterrupted method of the thread returns a value of false. All threads maintain an internal flag that indicates whether the thread has been interrupted. If another thread calls the current thread's interrupt method, that flag is set to true. You can use the isInterrupted method to determine the setting of this flag.

Unfortunately, the isInterrupted method only works if the other thread (in this case, the main thread) calls the Counter thread's interrupt method while the Counter thread is executing. If the Counter thread is interrupted while it is in the Blocked state (for example, because it has called the sleep method), the thread's interrupted flag isn't set. Instead, InterruptedException is thrown. To allow the thread to be interrupted while it is sleeping, the sleep method shown in this figure is coded within a try/catch block. Then, when the catch clause catches the InterruptedException, it uses a break statement to terminate the while loop.

The output shown in this figure illustrates how this application works. Once the main method starts the Counter thread, this thread begins displaying numbers on the console at one-second intervals. Meanwhile, the main thread waits for the user to enter a string value at the console. When the user types "stop" and presses the Enter key, the main method calls the Counter thread's interrupt method. The Counter thread detects this, either by seeing that isInterrupted returns true or by catching the InterruptedException. In either case, the Counter thread terminates.

A Counter application that uses an interruptable thread

```
import java.util.Scanner;

public class CountInterruptApp
{
    public static void main(String[] args)
    {
        Thread counter = new Counter();          // instantiate the counter thread
        counter.start();                         // start the counter thread

        Scanner sc = new Scanner(System.in);
        String s = "";
        while (!s.equals("stop"))                // wait for the user to enter "stop"
            s = sc.next();
        counter.interrupt();                     // interrupt the counter thread
    }
}

class Counter extends Thread
{
    public void run()
    {
        int count = 0;
        while (!isInterrupted())
        {
            System.out.println(this.getName() + " Count " + count);
            count++;
            try
            {
                Thread.sleep(1000);
            }
            catch (InterruptedException e)
            {
                break;
            }
        }
        System.out.println("Counter interrupted.");
    }
}
```

Resulting output

```
Thread-0 Count 0
"stop" entered by user
Thread-0 Count 1
Thread-0 Count 2
stop
Counter interrupted.
Press any key to continue . . .
```

"stop" entered by user

Description

- One thread can interrupt another thread by calling the second thread's interrupt method.
- A thread should frequently check its isInterrupted method to see if it has been interrupted.
- If a thread is interrupted while it is sleeping, InterruptedException is thrown. In this case, the isInterrupted method won't indicate that the thread has been interrupted.

Figure 14-9 How to interrupt a thread

How to synchronize threads

So far, the threads you've seen execute independently of each other. These types of threads are known as *asynchronous threads*. In the next two topics, you'll learn how to work with threads that share resources and must be synchronized. These types of threads are known as *synchronous threads*.

How to create synchronized threads

Whenever you create an application that uses more than one thread, you need to think about any *concurrency* issues that the application might face. Concurrency issues result from conflicts that can occur when two or more threads attempt to access the same object at the same time. For example, suppose you create a multithreaded application that includes a method named calculateFutureValue that calculates future values using a for loop. If you then created a single instance of this object and let multiple threads call the calculateFutureValue method at the same time, the calculations would interfere with one another. Then, the results of most, if not all, of the threads would be inaccurate.

To solve this type of problem, you can synchronize the threads that have access to the object. To do that, you use the synchronized keyword as shown in figure 14-10. As you can see, you can code this keyword on a method declaration. Then, the Java virtual machine guarantees that when a thread calls the method, no other thread will be allowed to call it until the first thread is done with it.

The first example in this figure shows a synchronized version of the calculateFutureValue method. Because the synchronized keyword is used, this method can be used safely in a multithreaded application.

The second example shows that a method doesn't have to be long or complicated to require the synchronized keyword. Here, the method consists of a single statement that increments a variable and returns the incremented value. You might be tempted to think that this method wouldn't have to be synchronized. After all, if two threads call it at the same time, won't the first thread execute the method's single statement and exit before the second thread has a chance to execute the same statement? Not necessarily. The problem is that even a single statement like this can be compiled to several Java bytecode instructions. Because of that, the thread scheduler could switch to another thread between any of these instructions.

The synchronized keyword works by *locking* the object. Once the object is locked, no other thread can obtain a lock on the object until the synchronized method ends and the lock is released. Note that it is the object itself that's locked, not the synchronized method. As a result, when a thread calls a synchronized method, other threads are prevented from running any of the object's synchronized methods, not just the method called by the first thread. However, other threads aren't prevented from running unsynchronized methods. That's because an object's lock isn't checked when an unsynchronized method is called.

The syntax for creating a synchronized method

```
{public|private} synchronized returnType methodName([parameterList])
{
   statements
}
```

Example 1: A synchronized method that calculates future values

```
public synchronized double calculateFutureValue(double monthlyPayment,
double yearlyInterestRate, int years)
{
    int months = years * 12;
    double monthlyInterestRate = yearlyInterestRate/12/100;
    double futureValue = 0;
    for (int i = 1; i <= months; i++)
    {
        futureValue = (futureValue + monthlyPayment) *
                      (1 + monthlyInterestRate);
    }
    return futureValue;
}
```

Example 2: A synchronized method that increments an instance variable

```
public synchronized int getInvoiceNumber()
{
    return invoiceNumber++;
}
```

Description

- Whenever two or more threads can access an object, *concurrency* is an important issue. Concurrency problems can result because a thread running a method may be interrupted in the middle of the method so control can begiven to another thread that runs the same method. When that happens, the intermediate results from the first thread can affect the accuracy of the second thread.
- The synchronized keyword assures that only one thread at a time is allowed to execute any *synchronized method* of an object by *locking* the object. Any other thread that attempts to run any synchronized method for the object will be blocked until the first thread releases the lock by exiting the synchronized method.
- A thread can run an unsynchronized method of an object even if the object is locked. That's because the object isn't checked for a lock unless a synchronized method is executed.
- You should use synchronized methods whenever two or more threads might execute the same method. Even methods with just one line of code typically need to be synchronized.

Figure 14-10 How to create synchronized threads

How to use the wait and notifyAll methods to communicate among threads

When you use synchronized methods in a multithreaded application, you sometimes need a way for the threads to communicate with each other so they can coordinate their operations. For example, imagine an application in which two or more threads add orders to a queue, and two or more threads retrieve orders from the queue so they can be processed. For this application, the threads that add orders to the queue might need a way to notify the threads that retrieve the orders that an order is ready for processing.

As figure 14-11 shows, Java provides three methods you can use to accomplish this: wait, notify, and notifyAll. The wait method is used in a synchronized method to temporarily release the lock it holds on the current object. This places the thread object in the Waiting state until another method calls the notify or notifyAll method to return it to the Runnable state. (Although the notify and notifyAll methods perform similar functions, in practice, the notify method is rarely used. I'll explain why in a moment.)

To understand how this works, the first example in this figure shows code that might be used in a thread that retrieves orders from a queue. This code causes the thread to wait until an order is available in the queue before it retrieves the order. Here, a while loop tests the value returned by the queue's count method. If it is zero, meaning that no orders are available, the wait method is called. This places the thread in the Waiting state, allowing other threads to execute.

The second example shows code that might be used by a thread that adds orders to the queue. Here, the first statement adds an order to the queue. Then, the second statement calls the notifyAll method of the thread. This restores all the waiting threads to the Runnable state. That way, one of the threads can retrieve and process the order.

I mentioned previously that the notifyAll method is usually preferred over the notify method. The problem with the notify method is that it awakens only one waiting thread. This does not guarantee that the thread that was awakened will be able to process the order. That's why it's better to call notifyAll. This awakens all waiting threads. Each of these threads can then determine whether they can proceed.

This is also why the wait method is placed in a while loop in the first example. Since all waiting threads will be returned to the Runnable state when notifyAll is called, each thread must again test the condition it is waiting for (in this case, that at least one order is in the queue) before proceeding. If the condition has not been met, the thread should wait again.

If you're having trouble understanding the examples shown in this figure, don't worry. The rest of this chapter presents a complete version of the order queuing application that these examples are taken from. Once you see the complete application in operation, the wait and notifyAll methods should become clear.

Methods of the Object class for thread communication

Method	Description
`wait()`	Places the current thread in the Waiting state until another thread calls the notify or notifyAll method of the current object. This relinquishes the lock on the object so that other blocked threads can run. Throws InterruptedException.
`notify()`	Returns an arbitrary thread to the Runnable state.
`notifyAll()`	Returns all threads to the Runnable state so the scheduler can select one to run.

Example 1: Code that waits on a condition

```
while (orderQueue.count() == 0)       // if there are no orders ready, wait
{
    try
    {
        wait();
    }
    catch (InterruptedException e) {}
}
```

Example 2: Code that satisfies the condition and notifies other threads

```
orderQueue.add(order);               // add an order to the queue
notifyAll();                         // notify other threads
```

Description

- In some multithreaded applications, it's important for threads to inform one another when certain events have occurred or conditions have been met. The wait, notify, and notifyAll methods allow this type of communication.
- The wait method releases the lock on the current object so that other threads can execute synchronized methods. The effect of the wait method is to interrupt the current thread until another thread calls the notify or notifyAll method.
- The notifyAll method wakes up all of the threads that are waiting for the current object's lock. The Java thread scheduler then selects one of the threads for execution.
- The notify method is similar to the notifyAll method, but it wakes up only one arbitrarily selected thread. Since this thread may not be able to perform its function, the notifyAll method is typically used instead.
- The wait, notify, and notifyAll methods can only be used in synchronized methods. If you call one of these methods from an unsynchronized method, IllegalMonitorStateException will be thrown.

Figure 14-11 How to use the wait and notifyAll methods to communicate among threads

The Order Queue application

The following topics present a multithreaded application that demonstrates many of the threading concepts presented in this chapter. Before I present the code for this application, I'll present an overview of the application and its operation. Then, I'll summarize the various classes used by the application.

The operation of the Order Queue application

Figure 14-12 presents the operation of the Order Queue application. The diagram at the top of this figure shows how the application uses multiple OrderTaker threads to create orders and add them to the queue and multiple OrderHandler threads to remove orders from the queue and process them. The queue itself is managed by a class named OrderQueue that runs in its own thread (the main thread).

So you can focus on the threading aspects of this application, each order is represented by an Order object that consists of just an order number. Obviously, a more realistic Order object would include additional details, such as customer, product, and payment information.

The OrderTaker and OrderHandler classes are also simplified. In this application, the OrderTaker class simply creates a specified number of orders at one-second intervals, displaying a message on the console as each order is created. Similarly, the OrderHandler class retrieves an order from the queue, displays it on the console, and then waits two seconds before retrieving another order. In a more realistic application, the OrderTaker class would get input from a user about each order, and the OrderHandler class would print invoices, update customer information, and so on.

If you study the console output shown in this figure, you'll see that the Order Queue application begins by displaying information about the OrderTaker and OrderHandler threads. The number of OrderTaker and OrderHandler threads can easily be changed, as can the number of orders to be created by each OrderTaker thread. For this example, the application creates three OrderTaker threads, each of which creates three orders. As a result, a total of nine orders will be created. In addition, the application creates two OrderHandler threads.

After displaying this initial information, the application starts the OrderTaker and OrderHandler threads. Each OrderTaker thread displays a message when it creates an order, and each OrderHandler thread displays a message when it processes an order. As you can see, nine orders are created by the three OrderTaker threads, and nine orders are eventually processed by the two OrderHandler threads.

Incidentally, the design of the Order Queue application is based on a commonly-used design pattern called the *producer/consumer pattern*. This design pattern uses a queue to coordinate *producers*—objects that create items that need to be processed—with *consumers*—objects that process the items created by the producers.

The operation of the Order Queue application

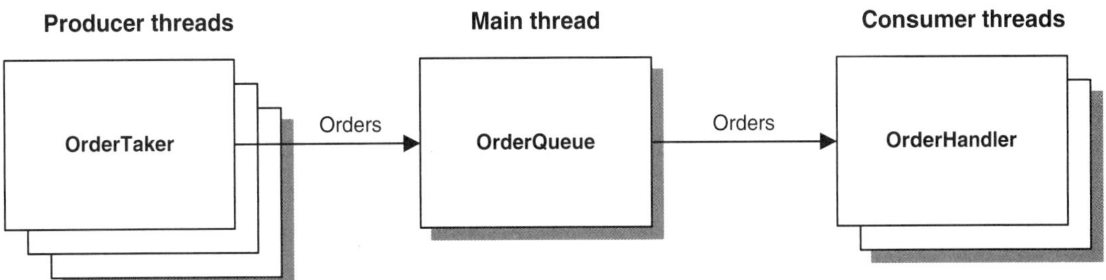

Console output from the Order Queue application

```
Starting the order queue.
Starting 3 order taker threads, each producing 3 orders.
Starting 2 order handler threads.

     OrderTaker threads              OrderHandler threads
============================    =============================
Order #1 created by Thread-1
Order #2 created by Thread-2
                                Order #1 processed by Thread-3
                                Order #2 processed by Thread-4

Order #3 created by Thread-0
Order #4 created by Thread-1
Order #5 created by Thread-2
Order #6 created by Thread-0
                                Order #3 processed by Thread-3
                                Order #4 processed by Thread-4

Order #7 created by Thread-1
Order #8 created by Thread-2
Order #9 created by Thread-0
                                Order #5 processed by Thread-3
                                Order #6 processed by Thread-4
                                Order #7 processed by Thread-3
                                Order #8 processed by Thread-4
                                Order #9 processed by Thread-3
```

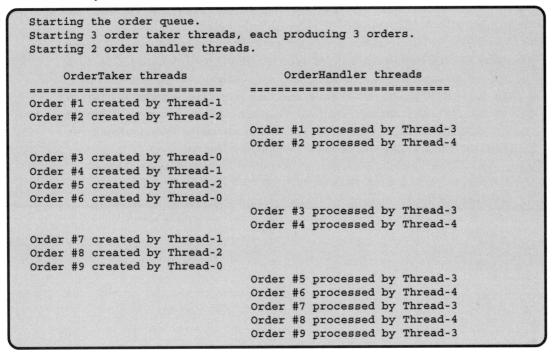

Description

- This application simulates a multithreaded ordering application in which multiple order takers, each running the application in a separate thread, generate orders that are added to a queue that runs in the application's main thread. The orders are then handled by multiple order-handling threads, which remove orders from the queue and display them on the console.
- Each OrderTaker thread creates orders at one-second intervals. Similarly, the OrderHandler threads retrieve orders at two-second intervals.
- This application creates three OrderTaker threads, each of which creates three orders before ending. It also creates two OrderHandler threads to process the orders.
- This application is an example of a common design pattern called *producer/consumer*, in which threads that produce objects place them in a queue so the objects can later be retrieved by threads that consume them.

Figure 14-12 The operation of the Order Queue application

The classes used by the Order Queue application

Figure 14-13 describes the four classes used by the Order Queue application. The first class is the Order class, which represents an individual order. To keep this application simple, the only information about an order that an Order object stores is the order number. The order number is passed to an order via its constructor. Then, this number can be retrieved by calling the toString method, which returns the order number in a formatted string (for example, "Order #1").

The OrderQueue class represents the queue used to store orders. This class uses a linked list internally to store the orders. It has two methods, both of which are synchronized. The pushOrder method adds an order to the queue, and the pullOrder method retrieves an order from the queue.

The OrderTaker class creates orders by adding them to the queue. It sleeps for one second between each order it creates. This class is designed to be run as a thread, so it extends the Thread class and implements the run method. Unlike the other thread classes you've seen, the OrderTaker class includes a constructor that accepts two parameters. The first parameter indicates how many orders the thread should create before ending. The second parameter holds a reference to the OrderQueue object that the orders should be added to.

The OrderHandler class retrieves orders from the order queue. It too is designed to run as a thread, so it extends the Thread class and defines its operations in the run method. It also includes a constructor that accepts a parameter that refers to the OrderQueue object that the orders should be retrieved from.

The Order class

Constructor	Description
`Order(int number)`	Creates an Order object with the specified number.
Method	**Description**
`toString()`	Returns a string in the form "Order #*n*," where *n* is the order number.

The OrderQueue class

Method	Description
`pushOrder(String order)`	Adds the specified order to the queue. For simplicity, the order is a String value.
`String pullOrder()`	Retrieves the first available order from the queue.

The OrderTaker class

Constructor	Description
`OrderTaker(int orderCount, OrderQueue queue)`	Creates a new order taker that adds the specified number of orders to the queue.
Method	**Description**
`run()`	Adds the number of orders specified by the constructor to the queue specified by the constructor, sleeping for one second between orders.

The OrderHandler class

Constructor	Description
`OrderHandler(OrderQueue queue)`	Creates a new order handler that reads orders from the specified queue.
Method	**Description**
`run()`	Retrieves orders from the queue specified by the constructor. A message is displayed on the console for each order retrieved, and the thread sleeps for two seconds between orders.

Description

- An Order object represents an order.
- An OrderQueue object uses a linked list to store orders created by the OrderTaker threads so they can be retrieved by the OrderHandler threads.
- An OrderTaker object runs in a separate thread, creates orders at one-second intervals, and adds them to a queue. The constructor lets you specify how many orders to create before the thread terminates.
- An OrderHandler object runs in a separate thread and removes orders from the queue at two-second intervals.

Figure 14-13 The classes used by the Order Queue application

The code for the OrderQueueApp class

The three parts of figure 14-14 show the code for the classes that make up the Order Queue application. To start, you can see the OrderQueueApp class, which contains the application's main method. This method begins by declaring three constants that store the number of OrderTaker threads to create, the number of orders to be created by each OrderTaker thread, and the number of OrderHandler threads to create. If you want, you can experiment with this application by varying these values and observing the effect your changes have on how the application runs.

Next, the main method creates an instance of the OrderQueue class and assigns it to a variable named queue. Then, it displays the starting information you saw in figure 14-12. Next, it uses two for loops to create and start the OrderTaker and OrderHandler threads. The first for loop creates the number of OrderTaker threads indicated by the TAKER_COUNT constant, and the second for loop creates the number of OrderHandler threads indicated by the HANDLER_COUNT constant. Notice that the queue variable is passed to each OrderTaker and OrderHandler constructor so these objects have access to the order queue. Notice also that the ORDER_COUNT constant is passed to the OrderTaker constructor so that those objects know how many orders to create.

The code for the Order class

To keep this application simple, the Order class just defines an instance variable named number, a constructor that accepts an order number as an argument, and a toString method that returns the order number in a displayable format. Otherwise, it would provide all the variables and methods related to an order.

The code for the OrderQueueApp class

```
public class OrderQueueApp
{
    public static void main(String[] args)
    {
        final int TAKER_COUNT = 3;      // number of OrderTaker threads
        final int ORDER_COUNT = 3;      // number of orders per OrderTaker thread
        final int HANDLER_COUNT = 2;    // number of OrderHandler threads

        OrderQueue queue = new OrderQueue();       // create the order queue

        System.out.println("Starting the order queue.");

        System.out.println("Starting " + TAKER_COUNT + " order taker threads, "
            + "each producing " + ORDER_COUNT + " orders.");
        for (int i = 0; i < TAKER_COUNT; i++)      // create OrderTaker threads
        {
            OrderTaker t = new OrderTaker(ORDER_COUNT, queue);
            t.start();
        }

        System.out.println("Starting " + HANDLER_COUNT
            + " order handler threads.\n");
        for (int i = 0; i < HANDLER_COUNT; i++)    // create OrderHandler threads
        {
            OrderHandler h = new OrderHandler(queue);
            h.start();
        }


        String s = "     OrderTaker threads      \t     OrderHandler threads    \n"
                + "===========================\t============================";
        System.out.println(s);

    }
}
```

The code for the Order class

```
public class Order
{
    private int number;

    public Order(int number)
    {
        this.number = number;
    }

    public String toString()
    {
        return "Order #" + number;
    }
}
```

Figure 14-14 The code for the Order Queue application (part 1 of 3)

The code for the OrderTaker class

The OrderTaker class begins by declaring a static variable named orderNumber. This variable will be used to supply the order numbers for the orders that are created by this class. As you can see, the private method named getOrderNumber returns this variable and then increments its value. This method is synchronized so that if two threads call it at the same time, each will receive a unique order number.

The constructor for the OrderTaker class accepts the order count and order queue as parameters and saves these values in instance variables. Then, the run method consists primarily of a while loop that creates the correct number of orders. The code within this loop creates a new order object using the result of the getOrderNumber method as the order number. Then, it calls the pushOrder method of the order queue to add the order to the queue. Finally, it calls the sleep method to place the thread in Blocked state for at least one second before creating another order.

The code for the OrderTaker class

```
public class OrderTaker extends Thread
{
    private static int orderNumber = 1;

    private int count = 0;
    private int maxOrders;
    private OrderQueue orderQueue;
    private String name;

    public OrderTaker(int orderCount, OrderQueue orderQueue)
    {
        this.maxOrders = orderCount;         // number of orders to create
        this.orderQueue = orderQueue;        // order queue
    }

    public void run()
    {
        int orderNumber;
        Order order;
        while (count < maxOrders)
        {
            order = new Order(getOrderNumber());
            orderQueue.pushOrder(order);     // add order to the queue
            System.out.println(order.toString() + " created by "
                + this.getName());
            count++;
            try
            {
                Thread.sleep(1000);          // delay one second
            }
            catch (InterruptedException e)
            {}                               // ignore interruptions
        }
    }

    private synchronized int getOrderNumber()
    {
        return orderNumber++;
    }

}
```

Figure 14-14 The code for the Order Queue application (part 2 of 3)

The code for the OrderHandler class

The OrderHandler class is simpler than the OrderTaker class. Its constructor accepts a reference to the order queue and saves it in an instance variable. Then, the run method consists of a never-ending while loop that calls the order queue's pullOrder method to get an order. The order is then displayed on the console, and the sleep method is called to place the thread in the Blocked state for at least two seconds before trying to retrieve another order.

The code for the OrderQueue class

To store the orders that are taken, the OrderQueue class uses a linked list to work with an order queue. If you haven't read chapter 11 yet, you may not understand the coding details for working with the linked list, but you can still focus on the code that works with threads.

As you can see, the pushOrder method is synchronized so only one thread can add an order to the queue at a time. It adds the order to the queue, and then calls the notifyAll method to wake up any threads that might be waiting to process orders.

The pullOrder method, which is also synchronized, uses a while loop to wait until the size method of the linked list indicates that there's at least one order available to be processed. Within the while loop, the wait method is called to place the OrderHandler thread in the Waiting state if an order isn't available. It remains in that state until one of the OrderTaker threads calls the pushOrder method, which in turn calls the notifyAll method to wake up any waiting threads.

Keep in mind that once an OrderHandler thread wakes up, the pullOrder method of the OrderQueue class is still in the while loop. So before an order is pulled from the queue, the size of the queue is checked to make sure that an order is still available. If so, the loop ends and the order is retrieved from the linked list and returned to the calling thread. If not, it means that another thread must have already processed the order, so the wait method is called again.

When you execute an application that uses threads, you should realize that the application doesn't end until all of its threads end. In this case, though, because the run method of the OrderHandler class contains a never-ending while loop, the OrderHandler threads never end. Because of that, you will have to end the application explicitly by closing the console window.

The code for the OrderHandler class

```
public class OrderHandler extends Thread
{
    private OrderQueue orderQueue;

    public OrderHandler(OrderQueue orderQueue)
    {
        this.orderQueue = orderQueue;
    }

    public void run()
    {
        Order order;
        while (true)
        {
            order = orderQueue.pullOrder();     // get next available order
            System.out.println("\t\t\t\t" + order.toString() + " processed by "
                + this.getName());
            try
            {
                Thread.sleep(2000);             // delay two seconds
            }
            catch (InterruptedException e) {}   // ignore interruptions
        }
    }
}
```

The code for the OrderQueue class

```
import java.util.LinkedList;

public class OrderQueue
{
    private LinkedList<Order> orderQueue = new LinkedList<Order>();

    public synchronized void pushOrder(Order order)
    {
        orderQueue.addLast(order);
        notifyAll();                            // notify any waiting threads
                                                // that an order has been added
    }

    public synchronized Order pullOrder()
    {
        while (orderQueue.size() == 0)          // if there are no orders in
                                                // the queue, wait
        {
            try
            {
                wait();
            }
            catch (InterruptedException e)
            {}
        }
        return orderQueue.removeFirst();
    }
}
```

Figure 14-14 The code for the Order Queue application (part 3 of 3)

Perspective

In this chapter, you learned the essential skills for working with threads. Frankly, threading is one of the most challenging topics in this book. So don't be too worried if you don't understand every detail of how it works. The best way to learn how to work with threads is to develop multithreaded applications. You'll get a chance to do that in the exercises that follow. Then, in the next section of this book, you'll learn how to use threading as you develop GUI applications.

You should be aware that several new threading features were introduced with Java 1.4 and Java 5.0. We didn't cover those features in this chapter, though, because they're used for more advanced aspects of multithreaded programming. For example, Java 1.4 introduced a new variable modifier called *volatile* that lets you share access to variables in unsynchronized methods. And Java 5.0 introduced a set of classes (java.util.concurrent, java.util.concurrent.atomic, and java.util.concurrent.locks) that provide more advanced threading features. You can refer to the Java documentation if you want to find out more about these features.

Summary

- A *thread* is a single sequential flow of control within a program that often completes a specific task.
- A *multithreaded application* consists of two or mores threads whose execution can overlap.
- Since a processor can only execute one thread at a time, the *thread scheduler* determines which thread to execute.
- *Multithreading* is typically used to improve the performance of applications with I/O operations, to improve the responsiveness of GUI operations, and to allow two or more users to run server-based applications simultaneously.
- You can create a thread by extending the Thread class and then instantiating the new class. Or, you can implement the Runnable interface and then pass a reference to the Runnable object to the constructor of the Thread class.
- You can use the methods of the Thread class to start a thread, to control when a thread runs, and to control when other threads are allowed to run.
- *Synchronized methods* can be used to ensure that two threads don't run the same method of an object simultaneously. When a thread calls a synchronized method, the object that contains that method is *locked* so that other threads can't access it.

Exercise 14-1 Create a Number Finder application

In this exercise, you'll create an application that generates a random number between 0 and 999, and then uses four threads to search for the number. When one of the threads finds the number, it should print a message on the console. The output from this application should look like this:

```
The number is 784
Target number 784 found by Thread-3
```

1. Open the NumberFinderThreadApp class in the c:\java1.5\ch14 directory. Review its code to see that it generates a random number between 0 and 999 and then displays it at the console.
2. Add a class named Finder that extends the Thread class to the NumberFinderThreadApp file. Then, add a constructor to this class that accepts three parameters: the number to search for, the number where the search should begin, and the number where the search should end.
3. Add a run method to the Finder class that searches for the number. This method should use a for loop to check each value in the specified range to determine if it matches the target value. If a match is made, the thread should display a message like the one shown above and terminate. Every ten times through the loop, the thread should yield to other threads.
4. Add code to the main method to create and start the four threads. The threads should check the following ranges: thread0, 0-249; thread1, 250-499; thread2, 500-749; and thread3, 750-999.
5. Compile the program. Then, run it two or more times to be sure it works correctly.

Exercise 14-2 Use the Runnable interface and the sleep method

In this exercise, you'll modify your solution to exercise 14-1 so that the Finder class implements the Runnable interface instead of extending the Thread class and so that it calls sleep rather than yield every ten times through the loop.

1. Open the NumberFinderThreadApp class you worked on in exercise 14-1. Then, change the class name to NumberFinderRunnableApp and save the class with this file name.
2. Modify the Finder class so it uses the Runnable interface. Then, compile the program and run it to make sure it works correctly.
3. Modify the Finder class so it uses the sleep method to cause the thread to sleep for 1 millisecond every ten times through the loop. Then, compile and test the program again.

Exercise 14-3 Add a Monitor thread to the Number Finder application

Because this exercise requires the use of a collection, you need to read chapters 10 and 11 before you do it. In this exercise, you'll modify your solution to exercise 14-2 so that the thread that finds the number notifies a Monitor thread, which then interrupts all of the Finder threads. When a Finder thread is interrupted, it should display a line indicating that it has been interrupted and then end. The resulting output should look like this:

```
The number is 20
Target number 20 found by Thread-1
Thread-2 interrupted
Thread-3 interrupted
Thread-4 interrupted
```

1. Open the NumberFinderRunnableApp class you worked on in exercise 14-2. Then, change the class name to NumberFinderMonitorApp and save the class with that file name.
2. Add a class named Monitor to the NumberFinderRunnableApp file. This class should define a thread by extending the Thread class. This class should include a method named addThread that adds a thread to a private collection of Thread objects. (You choose the type of collection.) It should also include a synchronized method named foundNumber that interrupts each thread in the threads collection. This method should also set a boolean instance variable to true to indicate that the number has been found. Then, the run method of this class can simply test this variable within a never-ending loop.
3. Modify the application's main method so that it creates and starts the Monitor thread, passes a reference to the Monitor thread to the Finder threads, and adds the four Finder threads to the Monitor thread.
4. Modify the Finder class so that its constructor accepts a reference to the Monitor thread. Then, modify the run method so that it calls the Monitor thread's foundNumber method if it finds the target number. Also modify this method so that a message is displayed when the thread is interrupted. Keep in mind that the thread may still be searching for the number when it's interrupted or it may have finished its search.
5. Compile the application and run it to be sure that it works correctly.

Section 4

GUI programming with Java

In this section, you'll learn how to develop graphical user interfaces (GUIs) for your applications. The first three chapters of this section show you how to create GUI applications using the popular Swing package. First, chapter 15 provides a basic introduction to creating a Swing interface. Then, chapter 16 shows how to use the most popular types of user interface controls, such as list boxes and radio buttons, and it shows you how to use a sophisticated layout manager to arrange those controls. Finally, chapter 17 shows you how to create professional GUI applications that include advanced event handling features and data validation.

Chapter 18 shows you how to develop a special type of program known as an *applet*. This type of program can be run within a web browser. To create the user interface for this type of program, you use the same skills as you do for creating a regular GUI. For this reason, you should read at least chapter 15 before you read chapter 18.

15

How to get started with Swing

So far in this book, all of the applications have been *console applications*. That means they interact with the user through a console window, one line at a time. Of course, console-style I/O was abandoned long ago in favor of *graphical user interfaces* (*GUIs*), such as the interface used by Microsoft Windows, by the Macintosh operating system, and by X Window on a Linux system.

In this chapter, you'll learn how to use a popular Java package called *Swing* to create applications that have a graphical user interface. Here, you'll learn how to create a simple GUI that includes labels, text boxes, and buttons. Then, you'll learn how to enhance a GUI in the two chapters that follow. When you're done, you'll be able to develop sophisticated GUIs of your own.

An introduction to the Swing classes

In this chapter, you'll learn how to create graphical user interfaces using classes from the javax.swing package. These classes are known as *Swing classes*, or the *Swing set*. The topics that follow present some general concepts that apply to all Swing classes.

The user interface for the Future Value Calculator application

Figure 15-1 presents the graphical user interface for the Future Value Calculator application that's presented in this chapter. This shows some of the terminology that Java uses for working with GUIs. For example, Java calls a "decorated" window a *frame*. That is, a frame is a window that contains a *title bar* that contains the Java icon, a title, a Minimize button, a Maximize button, and a Close button.

Within the frame is a *panel*. The panel in this figure contains ten controls: four *labels*, four *text fields*, and two *buttons*. Here, the fourth text field has been modified so it can display output but can't accept input from the user. In this chapter, you'll learn how to write the code that adds these *components* to the frame.

A user can use this application to calculate the future value of a monthly investment. To start, the user enters the numbers into the first three text fields. Then, the user can select the Calculate button by clicking on it or by pressing the Tab key to move the *focus* to the Calculate button and then pressing the spacebar. When this happens, the application displays the future value in the fourth text field.

By default, Swing components look and act the same on any platform. This is known as the *Metal look and feel*. However, these components look and act slightly different than the components that are native to a particular platform. For example, the user interface shown in this figure looks slightly different than a native Windows user interface. Although Swing provides classes that let programmers set the look and feel of a user interface to a particular platform, the Metal look and feel is appropriate for most programs. As a result, that's the look and feel that this book uses for all of its applications.

By the way, you should know that even though Swing applications work with graphical user interfaces, they still display a console window when you run them from a text editor such as TextPad. That's because a text editor runs an application by generating a batch file that's executed from the console window. Depending on how your system is configured, then, you may need to close this window to terminate the Swing application.

The user interface for the Future Value Calculator application

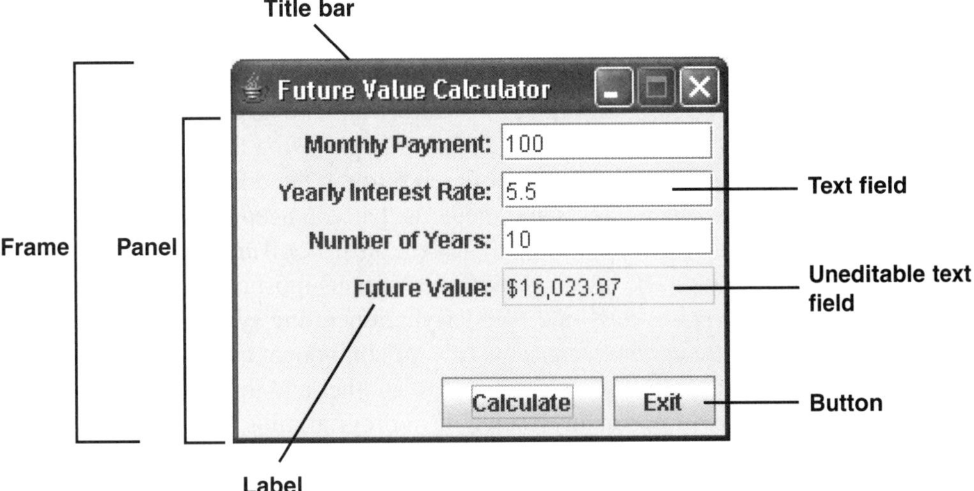

Description

- The window that contains the GUI is called a *frame*.
- The frame contains a *panel* that contains the controls that are displayed by the application.
- The panel in this figure contains ten controls: four *labels*, four *text fields*, and two *buttons*.
- The last text field in this figure is not editable. As a result, this text field can display output, but the user can't enter data into it.
- To calculate a future value, the user enters or changes the monthly payment amount, the yearly interest rate, and the number of years. Then, the user selects the Calculate button.
- To exit the program, the user selects the Exit button.
- To select a button, the user can click on the button or use the Tab key to move the focus to the button and then press the spacebar.
- This version of the Future Value Calculator application doesn't do any data validation, so it will throw an exception if the user enters invalid data.

Figure 15-1 The user interface for the Future Value Calculator application

The inheritance hierarchy for Swing components

Figure 15-2 presents a simplified inheritance hierarchy for user interface programming. Although the Java API contains an overwhelming number of classes and methods for GUI programming, this chapter and the next two chapters will teach you all of the concepts you need to begin using these classes. Once you understand these concepts, you can search through the documentation for the Java API to find the other classes and methods that you need.

When Java was first released, it contained only the *Abstract Window Toolkit* (*AWT*) for GUI programming. The java.awt package contains most of the classes for the AWT. Since these classes rely on the underlying operating system, they are often called *heavyweight components*. This type of component can make your code perform inconsistently from one system to another and thus difficult to debug. Instead of "write once, run anywhere," Java programming becomes "write once, debug everywhere."

That's why version 1.2 of Java introduced the Swing package for GUI programming. The Swing classes consist of *lightweight components*, which are written entirely in Java and don't rely on the underlying operating system as much. However, since Swing classes are derived from classes in the AWT, you need to understand how the AWT works. In fact, you need to use classes and methods from the AWT just to create a simple GUI like the one shown in this chapter.

The hierarchy shown in this figure includes a mixture of Swing and AWT classes. Many of the Swing classes shown in this figure also have corresponding AWT classes that aren't shown. You can tell which of the classes in this figure are Swing classes because they all begin with the letter J. Thus, JComponent, JFrame, and JPanel are all Swing classes as are the classes for the individual controls. In contrast, the Component, Container, Window, and Frame classes are AWT classes.

Although Swing frames are derived from the AWT Frame and Window classes, the other Swing components shown in this figure are derived from the JComponent class. In other words, Swing panels, labels, text fields, and buttons all inherit JComponent.

Note that all GUI components are derived from the Container class, which in turn is derived from the Component class. A *component* is an object with a graphical representation that can be drawn on the screen and that the user can interact with. A *container* is a component that can hold other components. For instance, a frame can hold a panel, a panel can hold buttons, buttons can hold text, and so on. Since all containers are components, a container can hold other containers. For example, you can create a panel that holds several buttons and then add the panel to another panel and add that panel to a frame. As you'll learn, a user interface usually consists of several panels that hold the buttons, labels, text boxes, and other controls the user interacts with directly.

The Component hierarchy

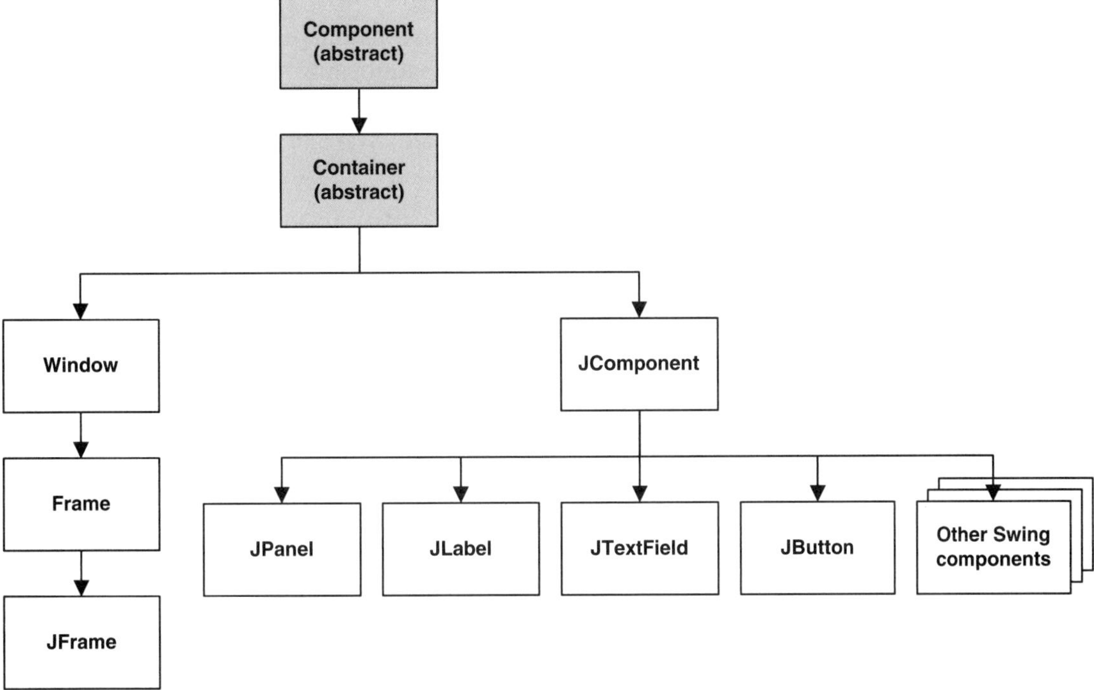

A summary of the classes

Class	Description
Component	An abstract base class that defines any object that can be displayed. For instance, frames, panels, buttons, labels, and text fields are derived from this class.
Container	An abstract class that defines any component that can contain other components.
Window	The AWT class that defines a window without a title bar or border.
Frame	The AWT class that defines a window with a title bar and border.
JFrame	The Swing class that defines a window with a title bar and border.
JComponent	A base class for Swing components such as JPanel, JButton, JLabel, and JTextField.
JPanel	The Swing class that defines a panel, which is used to hold other components.
JLabel	The Swing class that defines a label.
JTextField	The Swing class that defines a text field.
JButton	The Swing class that defines a button.

Description

- The *Abstract Window Toolkit* (*AWT*) is an older technology for creating GUIs that look and act a little different on different platforms. *Swing* is a newer technology that creates GUIs that are consistent from platform to platform.
- The AWT classes are stored in the java.awt package, while the Swing classes are stored in the javax.swing package. All Swing classes begin with the letter J.

Figure 15-2 The inheritance hierarchy for Swing components

Methods of the Component class

Figure 15-3 introduces you to some of the most commonly used methods of the Component class. Since all GUI components are ultimately derived from this class, you can use any of these methods with any component.

The first table in this figure presents some methods you can use to set the properties of a component. Here, the first three methods can be used to size and position a component. When you work with these methods, you use *pixels* as the unit of measurement. Pixels are the tiny dots that your monitor uses to display text and images. Although the number of pixels per screen varies depending on the resolution setting of the monitor, a typical setting is 800 pixels wide by 600 pixels tall. However, some people set their resolution as low as 640 by 480. As a result, if you want your components to fit on the screens of all computer users, you need to size and position your components for the lowest possible resolution.

Note that although you can use the setLocation method to set the exact position of a component, most Swing applications don't use this method. Instead, they rely on *layout managers* to automatically determine each component's position based on the size of the frame and the proximity of other components. You'll learn about layout managers later in this chapter.

The second table in this figure presents some methods you can use to return the properties of a component. With these methods, you can get the size, position, and name of a specific component.

The third table in this figure presents three other methods you can use to work with components. You can use the first two methods to determine if a component is enabled or visible. Then, you can use the requestFocusInWindow method to move the focus to the component.

Set methods

Method	Description
`setSize(intWidth, intHeight)`	Resizes this component using two int values.
`setLocation(intX, intY)`	Moves this component to the x and y coordinates specified by two int values.
`setBounds(intX, intY, intWidth, intHeight)`	Moves and resizes this component.
`setEnabled(boolean)`	If the boolean value is true, the component is enabled. If the boolean value is false, the component is disabled. A disabled component doesn't respond to user input or generate events.
`setVisible(boolean)`	Shows this component if the boolean value is true. Otherwise, hides it.
`setFocusable(boolean)`	Determines whether or not this component can receive the focus.
`setName(String)`	Sets the name of this component to the specified string.

Get methods

Method	Description
`getHeight()`	Returns the height of this component as an int.
`getWidth()`	Returns the width of this component as an int.
`getX()`	Returns the x coordinate of this component as an int.
`getY()`	Returns the y coordinate of this component as an int.
`getName()`	Returns the name of this component as a String.

Other methods

Method	Description
`isEnabled()`	Returns a true value if the component is enabled.
`isVisible()`	Returns a true value if the component is visible.
`requestFocusInWindow()`	Moves the focus to the component.

Description

- Since all GUI components are ultimately derived from the Component class, you can use its methods on any component.
- When you set the location and size of a component, the unit of measurement is *pixels*, which is the number of dots that your monitor uses to display a screen. The number of pixels per screen varies depending on the resolution setting.
- The preferred way to set the location of a component is to use a layout manager, as described in figures 15-10 and 15-11.

Figure 15-3 Methods of the Component class

How to work with frames

A *frame* is a window that has decorations such as a border, a title, a control menu, and buttons that let you minimize, maximize, and close the window. It also includes a *content pane* you can use to display other components. In the following topics, you'll learn how to create and display simple frames.

How to display a frame

Figure 15-4 shows a frame that doesn't contain any content. Then, it summarizes some methods that you can use to work with a frame. Finally, it shows some code for creating and displaying a frame.

In addition to the methods of the Component class that you saw in the previous figure, you can use methods of the Frame class to work with frames. This figure shows two methods of this class. As you work with frames, you can use these methods to control the behavior and appearance of each frame.

The first code example in this figure shows that the typical way to create a frame is to create a class that extends the JFrame class. In this example, the name of the frame class is FutureValueFrame. Within the constructor of this frame, the setTitle method is used to set the title of the frame, the setBounds method is used to set the size and position of the frame, and the setResizable method is used to keep the user from changing the size of the frame. Note that this example assumes that the class is included in the same file as the application's main class (shown in the second example). Because of that, it doesn't include a public modifier.

By default, all frames are 0 pixels by 0 pixels and are positioned in the top left corner of the screen. In this example, the top left corner of the frame begins 267 pixels to the right of the left edge of the screen and 200 pixels down from the top of the screen. The size of the frame is 267 pixels wide by 200 pixels tall. For a screen running at the 800 x 600 resolution, this setting will center the frame on the screen.

The second example shows an application class that contains a main method that creates an instance of the FutureValueFrame class and displays it. Here, the first statement of the main method creates an object from the FutureValueFrame class. Then, the second statement invokes the setVisible method to make the frame visible. Notice that this class starts with an import statement that imports the javax.swing package. However, it does not import the java.awt package. That's because the AWT classes that contain the methods you need for this application are inherited by the Swing classes.

A frame that doesn't contain any components

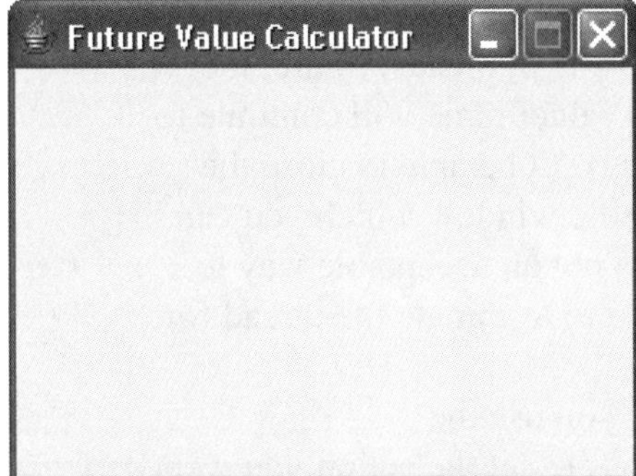

Common methods of the Frame class

Method	Description
`setTitle(String)`	Sets the title to the specified string.
`setResizable(boolean)`	If the boolean value is true, the user can resize the frame.

Example 1: A class that defines a frame

```
class FutureValueFrame extends JFrame
{
    public FutureValueFrame()
    {
        setTitle("Future Value Calculator");
        setBounds(267, 200, 267, 200);
        setResizable(false);
    }
}
```

Example 2: A class that displays the frame

```
import javax.swing.*;

public class FutureValueApp
{
    public static void main(String[] args)
    {
        JFrame frame = new FutureValueFrame();
        frame.setVisible(true);
    }
}
```

Description

- The contents of a frame are typically defined by a class that extends the JFrame class. To display the frame, the application's main method creates an instance of this frame class, and then calls its setVisible method to make the frame visible.
- In this example, the frame class is in the same file as the main application class. As a result, it doesn't include a public modifier.

Figure 15-4 How to display a frame

How to set the default close operation

When you create an instance of a frame like the one in the last figure, the frame runs in its own *thread*. As a result, the FutureValueFrame will continue to run even after the main method has ended, and you won't be able to close the frame properly. Instead, you'll be returned to a console window which you can close to manually terminate this thread. Since this is not an acceptable way to end a program, figure 15-5 provides the code needed to terminate the thread for a frame.

To close a frame or any other window properly, you use the setDefaultCloseOperation method of the JFrame class to set the action you want Swing to take when the user attempts to close the frame by clicking the frame's Close button or by choosing Close from the frame's control menu. Unfortunately, the default setting for this property is HIDE_ON_CLOSE, which means that the frame is hidden but not terminated. To create a frame that's terminated when the user closes it, use the setDefaultCloseOperation method to set the close action to EXIT_ON_CLOSE. That way, when the user closes the frame, Swing will exit the application.

The control menu for a frame

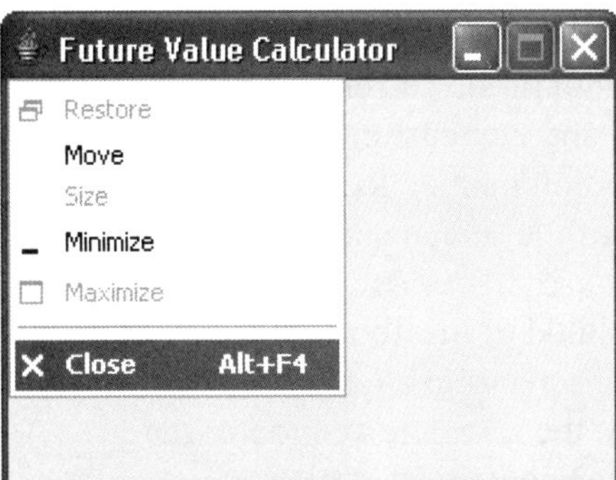

The setDefaultCloseOperation method of the JFrame class

Method	Description
`setDefaultCloseOperation(action)`	Sets the default close action for the frame.

Constants to set the default close operation

Constant	Description
`JFrame.EXIT_ON_CLOSE`	Exits the application when the user closes the window.
`WindowConstants.DO_NOTHING_ON_CLOSE`	Provides no default action, so the program must explicitly handle the closing event as described in chapter 17.
`WindowConstants.HIDE_ON_CLOSE`	Hides the frame when the user closes the window. This is the default action.
`WindowConstants.DISPOSE_ON_CLOSE`	Hides and disposes of the frame when the user closes the window.

A class that defines a closeable frame

```
class FutureValueFrame extends JFrame
{
    public FutureValueFrame()
    {
        setTitle("Future Value Calculator");
        setBounds(267, 200, 267, 200);
        setDefaultCloseOperation(JFrame.EXIT_ON_CLOSE);
    }
}
```

Description

- To close a frame, the user can click on the Close button in the upper right corner of the frame, press Alt+F4, or pull down the control menu and select the Close command.
- When you create an instance of a frame in an application, the frame runs in its own *thread*. As a result, the frame thread will continue to run even after the main method terminates. The application doesn't exit until the frame thread terminates.
- You can use the setDefaultCloseOperation method to cause the application to exit when the user closes the frame. Alternatively, you can add event-handling code to respond to the windowClosing event. You'll learn how to do that in chapter 17.

Figure 15-5 How to set the default close operation

How to center a frame using the Toolkit class

Figure 15-6 shows how to get the height and width of the current user's screen in pixels. To do that, you can use the Toolkit and Dimension classes of the java.awt package. Then, you can use the setLocation method to set the position of a frame relative to the height and width of the screen and the size of the frame.

To start, you use the static getDefaultToolkit method of the Toolkit class to get a Toolkit object that provides access to low-level screen functions. Then, you use the toolkit's getScreenSize method to return the screen resolution of the current system. This resolution is returned as a Dimension object, which provides fields for height and width.

The first example in this figure defines a method named centerWindow that centers a window. It accepts a Window object as a parameter. Then, it creates a Toolkit object and gets the current screen size. Finally, it uses the screen size and window size to set the correct location for the screen. The second example shows a constructor for a frame class that calls the centerWindow method. Since the FutureValueFrame class extends the JFrame class, which inherits the Window class, you can use the this keyword to pass an instance of the FutureValueFrame class to the CenterWindow method.

Two methods of the Toolkit class

Method	Description
`getDefaultToolkit()`	A static method that returns the Toolkit object for the current system.
`getScreenSize()`	Returns the screen resolution as a Dimension object.

Two fields of the Dimension class

Field	Description
`height`	Stores the height of this Dimension object as an int.
`width`	Stores the width of this Dimension object as an int.

Example 1: A method that centers a frame on the screen

```
private void centerWindow(Window w)
{
    Toolkit tk = Toolkit.getDefaultToolkit();
    Dimension d = tk.getScreenSize();
    setLocation((d.width-w.getWidth())/2, (d.height-w.getHeight())/2);
}
```

Example 2: The constructor for a class that defines a centered frame

```
FutureValueFrame()
{
    setTitle("Future Value Calculator");
    setSize(267, 200);
    centerWindow(this);
    setDefaultCloseOperation(JFrame.EXIT_ON_CLOSE);
}
```

Description

- The number of pixels per screen varies depending on the resolution setting of the user's monitor.
- To determine the number of pixels for the current screen, you can use a Toolkit object, or *toolkit*, to return a Dimension object that contains the number of pixels for the current screen.
- The Toolkit and Dimension classes are in the java.awt package, so you should provide an import statement for all the classes in this package when you use the technique shown above.

Figure 15-6 How to center a frame using the Toolkit class

How to work with panels, buttons, and events

Now that you know how to display and close a frame, you're ready to learn how to place other components on it. In the topics that follow, you'll learn how to add two types of components: panels and buttons. Then, you'll learn how to handle the event that's generated when a user selects a button.

How to add a panel to a frame

Figure 15-7 shows how to add a panel to a frame. To do that, you add the panel to the frame's *content pane*. Although other panes exist, you should place all components on the content pane.

The technique you use to add a pancl to a frame depends on whether you're using Java 5 or an earlier version of Java. With Java 5, you can use the add method of the JFrame class as illustrated in the first example in this figure. Note that although you can add other components such as buttons directly to a frame, you typically add components to a panel and then add the panel to the frame. This helps you organize the components so your code is easier to read and understand.

Prior to Java 1.5, the JFrame class didn't support the add method. As a result, you had to use the code shown in the second example to add a panel to a frame. Here, the first statement gets a reference to the content pane by calling the frame's getContentPane method. Then, the second statement uses the add method of the content pane to add the panel to the frame.

In case you're interested, the other panes in a frame provide various functions necessary to display and work with the components in the content pane. As its name suggests, the root pane is the pane that holds all other panes for the frame. The layered pane provides the ability to layer components so they visually overlap. This pane is used for features such as pop-up menus, floating toolbars, and drag-and-drop components. Finally, the glass pane (which isn't shown here) is a transparent pane that can be used to display elements on top of all other content in a frame. Since few Swing applications need to access any of these panes directly, you won't learn how to work with them in this book.

The JFrame structure

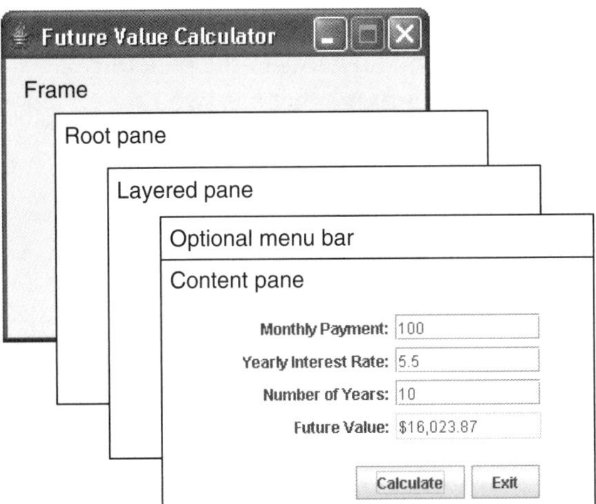

Method needed to add components to the content pane with Java 5

Class	Method	Description
JFrame	`add(Component)`	Adds a component to the frame's content pane.

A JFrame constructor that adds a panel to the content pane with Java 5

```
class FutureValueFrame()
{
    setTitle("Future Value Calculator");
    setSize(267, 200);
    centerWindow(this);
    setDefaultCloseOperation(JFrame.EXIT_ON_CLOSE);
    JPanel panel = new JPanel();
    this.add(panel);
}
```

Methods needed to add components to the content pane prior to Java 5

Class	Method	Description
JFrame	`getContentPane()`	Returns a Container object that represents the content pane.
Container	`add(Component)`	Adds a component (such as a JPanel) to this Container.

Code for adding a panel to the content pane prior to Java 5

```
Container contentPane = this.getContentPane();
contentPane.add(panel);
```

Description

- A JFrame object contains several *panes*. To add components to a frame, you add them to the *content pane* of the frame.
- A panel is a component that's used as a container for other components. The normal way to build a Swing user interface is to create a panel, add components such as labels, text boxes, and buttons to the panel, then add the panel to the content pane.

Figure 15-7 How to add a panel to a frame

How to add buttons to a panel

Figure 15-8 shows how to add buttons to a panel and how to add the panel to the frame's content pane. To start, this figure shows a frame that has two buttons. Then, it summarizes two constructors of the JButton class and three commonly used methods for working with buttons. Finally, it shows the code used to create the frame.

The two constructors of the JButton class shown in this figure let you create an empty button or a button that contains text. Usually, you'll use the second constructor to display text on the button so the user knows what its purpose is.

To work with the text displayed on a button, you can use the setText and getText methods that are summarized in this figure. You can also use the setEnabled method of the Component class to enable or disable a button. When you disable a button, the button is grayed out and it can't be selected.

The first code example in this figure defines a class for a panel that has two buttons. Here, the panel is named FutureValuePanel and it extends the JPanel class. It's common to use separate classes like this to define the panels used by an application.

The FutureValuePanel class begins by declaring two JButton objects, named calculateButton and exitButton. Then, the constructor for this class creates the button objects and adds the buttons to the panel.

The second example shows how to create an instance of the FutureValuePanel class and add it to the frame. Here, the first highlighted line creates an instance of the FutureValuePanel class by calling the FutureValuePanel constructor and assigns it to a variable of type JPanel. Then, the second highlighted line adds this panel to the frame.

Note that you could also define the panel variable as a FutureValuePanel type rather than a JPanel type. Because the FutureValuePanel class extends JPanel, the variable used to reference it can be either type. I usually declare panel variables as type JPanel, though, so I can assign any object derived from JPanel to the variable. But in this example, it doesn't matter.

If you run this application, you'll see a frame like the one shown at the top of this figure. Here, you can see that the size of the buttons are determined by the text that they display. You can also see that the frame displays the buttons in the top center of the frame. Later in this chapter, though, you'll learn how to control the layout that's used by frames and panels so you can display these buttons in the lower right corner of the frame.

A frame with two buttons

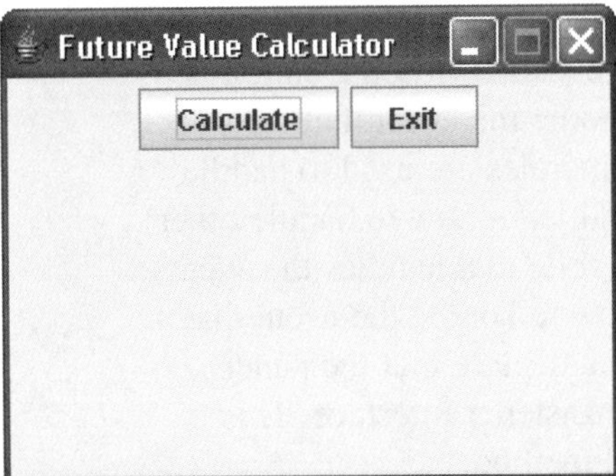

Common constructors of the JButton class

Constructor	Description
`JButton()`	Creates a button with no text.
`JButton(String)`	Creates a button with the text specified by the string.

Common methods of the JButton class

Method	Description
`setText(String)`	Sets the text of the button to the specified string.
`getText()`	Returns a String object for the text of this button.

Example 1: A JPanel class with two buttons

```
class FutureValuePanel extends JPanel
{
    private JButton calculateButton;
    private JButton exitButton;

    public FutureValuePanel()
    {
        calculateButton = new JButton("Calculate");
        this.add(calculateButton);
        exitButton = new JButton("Exit");
        this.add(exitButton);
    }
}
```

Example 2: A frame constructor that adds the panel to the frame

```
class FutureValueFrame()
{
    setTitle("Future Value Calculator");
    setSize(267, 200);
    centerWindow(this);
    setDefaultCloseOperation(JFrame.EXIT_ON_CLOSE);
    JPanel panel = new FutureValuePanel();
    this.add(panel);
}
```

Figure 15-8 How to add buttons to a panel

How to handle button events

Figure 15-9 shows how to write the code that's executed when a button is selected. Although this figure only shows how to handle the event that's generated when a user selects a button, the same principles are used to handle other types of events. In the next two chapters, you'll learn how to handle other types of events and more flexible ways to write the code that handles the events.

The procedure at the top of this figure shows how to handle the event that's generated when a user selects a button. In step 1, you declare that the panel class that contains the button implements the ActionListener interface. This interface contains one method: the actionPerformed method.

In step 2, you call the addActionListener method of the button to add an *event listener* that will listen for action events. The addActionListener method can take any object that implements the ActionListener interface. Since the button will be created in the panel class, and the panel class implements ActionListener, you can simply use the this keyword as the parameter. This indicates that the panel that contains this button will act as the listener for any action events that occur for the button.

In step 3, you implement the ActionListener interface by coding the actionPerformed method. This method, which must be public, handles the ActionEvent object that's passed to it when a button is selected. The first statement in the actionPerformed method uses the getSource method of the ActionEvent object to return the source of the event as an object of the Object class. Then, the second statement uses an if statement to check if the source of the event is equal to the Exit button. If so, it executes the exit method of the System class, which terminates the thread for the current frame. (The value that's passed to this method is a status code, where zero indicates a normal termination.)

The example in this figure shows how the three steps work when you code a class. This class defines a panel that contains two buttons, and it handles the events that are generated when a user selects either of these buttons. To start, the declaration for the class states that the panel implements the ActionListener interface. Then, both buttons are declared as instance variables within this class. That way, they're available to the constructor and the actionPerformed method. In the constructor, the code creates the buttons, adds the listener to both buttons, and adds the buttons to the panel.

In the actionPerformed method, the code gets the source object from the ActionEvent object. Then, it uses if/else statements to check the source object and execute the appropriate code for each button. If the source is the Exit button, the application exits. If the source is the Calculate button, the application changes the text of the Calculate button to "Clicked!" so the user will know that the button has been clicked. (Later in this chapter, you'll see a more realistic button event handler that calculates the future value when the user selects the Calculate button.)

How to handle an action event

1. Specify that the class that contains the button implements the ActionListener interface:

```
class FutureValuePanel extends JPanel implements ActionListener
```

2. Add an ActionListener object to the button by calling the addActionListener method:

```
exitButton.addActionListener(this);
```

3. Implement the ActionListener interface by coding the actionPerformed method:

```
public void actionPerformed(ActionEvent e)
{
   Object source = e.getSource();
   if (source == exitButton)
      System.exit(0);
}
```

A panel class that handles two action events

```
class FutureValuePanel extends JPanel implements ActionListener
{
    private JButton calculateButton;
    private JButton exitButton;

    public FutureValuePanel()
    {
        calculateButton = new JButton("Calculate");
        calculateButton.addActionListener(this);  // add an action listener
        this.add(calculateButton);

        exitButton = new JButton("Exit");
        exitButton.addActionListener(this);        // add an action listener
        this.add(exitButton);
    }

    public void actionPerformed(ActionEvent e)
    {
        Object source = e.getSource();
        if (source == exitButton)
            System.exit(0);
        else if (source == calculateButton)
            calculateButton.setText("Clicked!");
    }
}
```

Description

- When the user clicks a button, an *action event* is created and associated with the button. To handle this event, you use a class that implements the ActionListener interface, which is stored in the java.awt.event package.
- The ActionListener interface defines a single method named actionPerformed. The actionPerformed method can examine the ActionEvent object passed to it as a parameter to determine which button was clicked.
- System.exit(0) is commonly used in the actionPerformed method to terminate the application when the user clicks the Exit button.

Figure 15-9 How to handle button events

An introduction to layout managers

Although the Component class has methods that let you get and set the position of buttons and other components within a container, most Swing applications don't use these methods to control component layout. Instead, they rely on *layout managers* to determine the position of each component in a frame or panel. Swing comes with several different layout managers that use different techniques for controlling layout. The topics that follow show you how to use two of the most commonly used layout managers. By combining these layout managers, you can design an effective user interface. Then, in the next chapter, you'll learn more about using layout managers.

How to use the Flow layout manager

Figure 15-10 shows how to use the most common layout manager, called the *Flow layout manager*, to control the positioning of components within a panel. The Flow layout manager is used by default when you add buttons or other components to a panel. It adds components to the top of the container moving from left to right. When a container runs out of horizontal space, the Flow layout manager creates a new row and begins adding components to the new row. By default, this manager centers components horizontally.

To change the Flow layout manager to use left or right alignment, you start by creating a FlowLayout object using the second FlowLayout constructor listed in this figure. As you can see, this constructor accepts a field that specifies the alignment to be used. Then, you pass the layout manager object that's created to the panel's setLayout method.

The first frame in this figure shows what happens when five buttons are added to a panel using the Flow layout manager with center alignment. Here, you can see how the width of the frame and the widths of the buttons determine where the buttons are displayed. If you changed the width of the frame, however, the location of the buttons would change accordingly.

The code used to create this panel is shown in the first code example. Notice that, to make it clear how the controls should be aligned, I created a Flow layout manager and specified CENTER for the alignment. Since this is the default, however, this isn't necessary. Also notice that I didn't create variables for each button in this example. Instead, I passed the result of the JButton constructors directly to the panel's add method to add the button to the panel. In most cases, though, you'll want to assign the buttons you create to private instance variables so you can refer to them from anywhere in the class.

The second frame shows what happens when two buttons are added to a panel using the Flow layout manager with right alignment. The second code example shows how to create this panel. To do that, the first statement of the constructor uses the setLayout method to set the layout of the panel to a FlowLayout object with right alignment.

Two panels that use the Flow layout manager

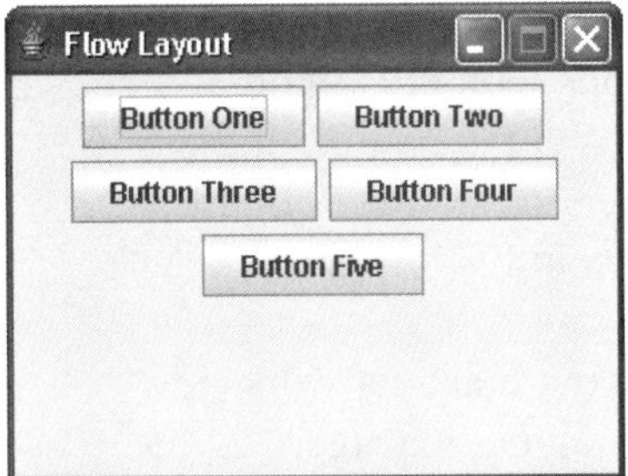

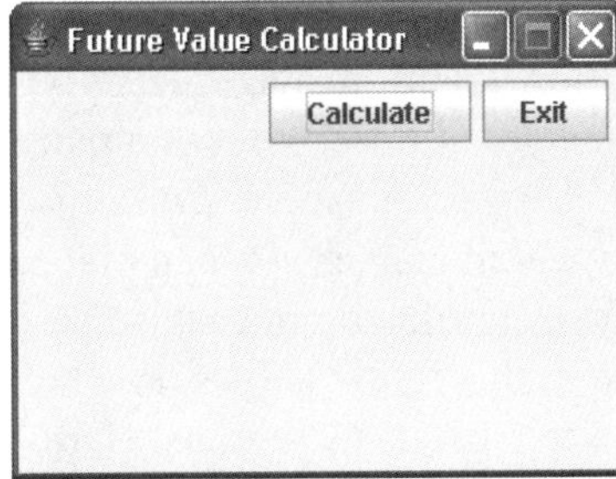

The setLayout method of the Container class

Method	Description
`setLayout(LayoutManager)`	Sets the layout manager for this container.

Two constructors of the FlowLayout class

Constructor	Description
`FlowLayout()`	Creates a Flow layout with centered alignment.
`FlowLayout(alignmentField)`	Creates a Flow layout with the specified alignment.

Alignment fields of the FlowLayout class

```
CENTER     LEFT     RIGHT
```

Example 1: Code that creates the centered button panel

```
class ButtonPanel extends JPanel
{
    public ButtonPanel()
    {
        this.setLayout(new FlowLayout(FlowLayout.CENTER));
        this.add(new JButton("Button One"));
        this.add(new JButton("Button Two"));
        this.add(new JButton("Button Three"));
        this.add(new JButton("Button Four"));
        this.add(new JButton("Button Five"));
    }
}
```

Example 2: Code that creates the right-aligned button panel

```
class FutureValuePanel extends JPanel
{
    private JButton calculateButton, exitButton;
    public FutureValuePanel()
    {
        this.setLayout(new FlowLayout(FlowLayout.RIGHT));
        calculateButton = new JButton("Calculate");
        this.add(calculateButton);
        exitButton = new JButton("Exit");
        this.add(exitButton);
    }
}
```

Figure 15-10 How to use the Flow layout manager

How to use the Border layout manager

Although the Flow layout manager lets you align buttons with the left or right edge of a container, it doesn't let you place the buttons at the bottom of the container. To do that, you can use the *Border layout manager* as shown in figure 15-11. With this layout manager, you can place components in five different regions of a container: north, south, east, west, or center.

The first frame in this figure shows how the Border layout manager works if you add one button to each of its regions. Here, the Border layout manager stretches the buttons so they are as wide as each region of the container. The first code example shows how to create this panel. The constructor for this panel begins by creating the five buttons, each with an appropriate label. Then, it creates a Border layout manager by calling the BorderLayout constructor, and it uses the setLayout method to apply the Border layout manager to the panel. Finally, it adds the buttons to the appropriate regions of the panel. Notice that the add method specifies the component as well as the region where the component should be added. If you don't specify a region, the component will be added to the center region.

The second frame in this figure shows what happens when you add two buttons to a panel with Flow layout and right alignment and then add that panel to the south region of a Border layout. In this case, the Border layout manager of the content pane will stretch the panel so it fits the entire south region, but the buttons will not be stretched. This shows how you can combine two or more layout managers to position components.

The second code example shows the code that creates the panel for the second frame. Here, the constructor for the panel begins by setting its layout manager to a new BorderLayout object. Then, it creates a new panel named buttonPanel with right alignment, and it applies the Flow layout manager to that panel. Next, it creates two buttons and adds them to the buttonPanel. Finally, it adds the buttonPanel to the south region of the main panel.

Two frames with panels that use the Border layout manager

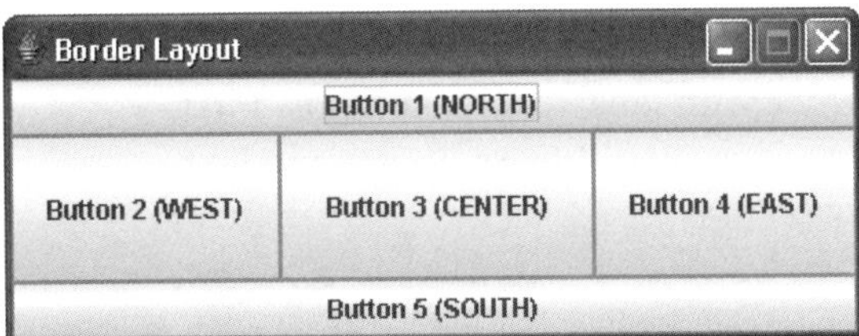

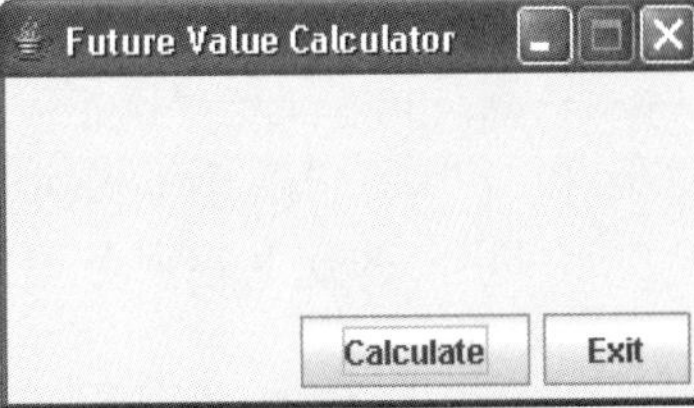

Common constructor and method of the BorderLayout class

Constructor	Description
`BorderLayout()`	Creates a Border layout manager.
Method	**Description**
`add(Component, regionField)`	Adds the component to the specified panel region.

Region fields of the BorderLayout class

```
NORTH    WEST    CENTER    EAST    SOUTH
```

Example 1: Code that creates the frame on the left

```
class BorderLayoutPanel extends JPanel
{
    public BorderLayoutPanel()
    {
        JButton button1 = new JButton("Button 1 (NORTH)");
        JButton button2 = new JButton("Button 2 (WEST)");
        JButton button3 = new JButton("Button 3 (CENTER)");
        JButton button4 = new JButton("Button 4 (EAST)");
        JButton button5 = new JButton("Button 5 (SOUTH)");

        this.setLayout(new BorderLayout());
        this.add(button1, BorderLayout.NORTH);
        this.add(button2, BorderLayout.WEST);
        this.add(button3, BorderLayout.CENTER);
        this.add(button4, BorderLayout.EAST);
        this.add(button5, BorderLayout.SOUTH);
    }
}
```

Example 2: Code that creates the frame on the right

```
class BorderLayoutPanel extends JPanel
{
    public BorderLayoutPanel()
    {
        this.setLayout(new BorderLayout());
        JPanel buttonPanel = new JPanel();
        buttonPanel.setLayout(new FlowLayout(FlowLayout.RIGHT));
        JButton calculateButton = new JButton("Calculate");
        JButton exitButton = new JButton("Exit");
        buttonPanel.add(calculateButton);
        buttonPanel.add(exitButton);
        this.add(buttonPanel, BorderLayout.SOUTH);
    }
}
```

Figure 15-11 How to use the Border layout manager

How to work with labels and text fields

The next two topics show you how to work with labels and text fields. First, you'll learn how to use labels to display text. Then, you'll learn how to use text fields to get input from a user and to display output.

How to work with labels

Figure 15-12 shows how to use the JLabel class to add *labels* to a panel. Labels are typically used to display text that identifies other components. Because of that, they don't receive the focus when the user presses the Tab key or clicks on them.

The JLabel constructors in this figure show two ways to create a label. Most of the time, you'll use the constructor that accepts a string argument to create a label that contains text. However, you can also create a blank label and then use the setText method later to set the text for the label.

The first code example in this figure creates a simple panel with a single label. The first statement in the panel class declares a variable to hold the label. Then, the class constructor calls the JLabel constructor to create the label and assign it to this variable, and it adds the label to the panel. When this panel is displayed in a frame, it will use the default layout manager for a panel, which is the Flow layout with centered alignment. That means the label will be centered at the top of the frame as shown in the first frame at the top of this figure.

The second code example shows how to add four labels to a panel with right alignment. Here, a Flow layout manager with right alignment is created and assigned to the panel. Then, the four labels are created and added to the panel. The result is shown in the second frame in this figure.

In the first code example, a variable is created to hold the label. That way, the label can be referred to later in the program. If you don't need to refer to a label, however, you can pass the label object that's created when you call the JLabel constructor directly to the add method of the panel as shown in the second example. I prefer to create variables to hold labels regardless of whether they will be referred to later, though. That way, it's clear what controls each panel contains.

If you look up the JLabel class in the documentation for the Java API, you'll see that this class contains many constructors and methods not shown in this figure. These constructors and methods let you associate a label with a component and provide keystroke shortcuts for the associated component. Now that you understand the basic skills for working with labels, you should be able to learn how to use these additional constructors and methods on your own.

Two panels that display labels

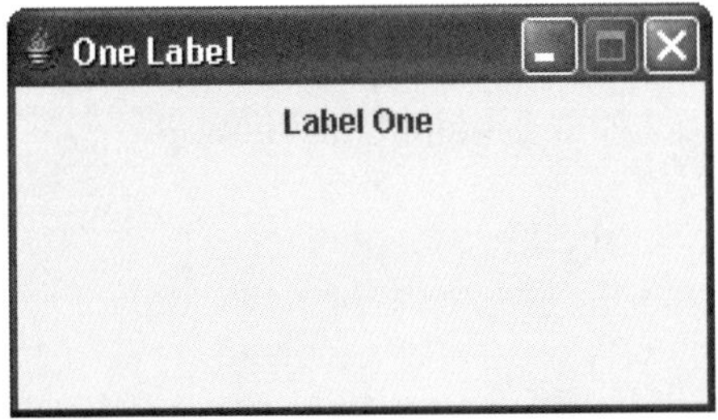

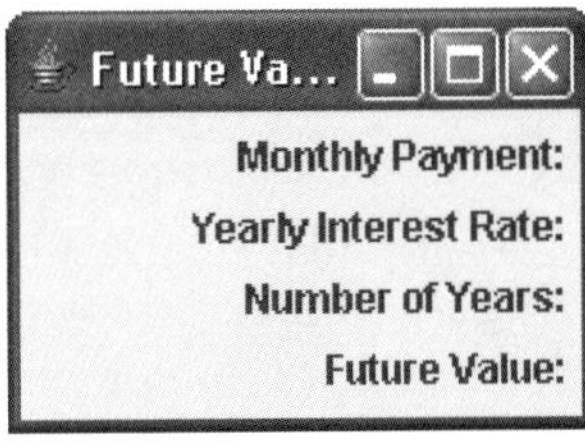

Common constructors and methods of the JLabel class

Constructor	Description
`JLabel()`	Creates a blank label.
`JLabel(String)`	Creates a label with the text specified by the string.
Method	**Description**
`getText()`	Returns the text in this text field as a String.
`setText(String)`	Sets the text in this field to the specified string.

Example 1: A class that creates the panel on the left

```
class LabelPanel extends JPanel
{
    private JLabel labelOne;

    public LabelPanel()
    {
        labelOne = new JLabel("Label One");
        this.add(labelOne);
    }
}
```

Example 2: A class that creates the panel on the right

```
class FutureValuePanel extends JPanel
{
    public FutureValuePanel()
    {
        this.setLayout(new FlowLayout(FlowLayout.RIGHT));
        this.add(new JLabel("Monthly Payment:"));
        this.add(new JLabel("Yearly Interest Rate:"));
        this.add(new JLabel("Number of Years:"));
        this.add(new JLabel("Future Value:"));
    }
}
```

Description

- The JLabel class defines a *label* component that can be used to display text on the panel.
- If you need to refer to a label in code, you can assign it to a variable and then add that variable to the panel as shown in the first example above. Otherwise, you can create the label and add it to the panel in a single statement as shown in the second example.

Figure 15-12 How to work with labels

How to work with text fields

Figure 15-13 shows how to use the JTextField class to add *text fields* to a panel. This figure also shows how you can use text fields to get input, and how you can use a uneditable text field to display output.

To start, this figure summarizes two constructors of the JTextField class. The first constructor accepts an argument that specifies the length of the field, and the second constructor accepts arguments that specify a default string and the length of the field. When you specify the length of a field, you specify the maximum number of characters that you want the field to be able to display. However, due to variations in fonts and operating systems, this measurement isn't completely consistent. As a result, it's usually a good coding practice to specify a slightly larger value for the length of the text field. Otherwise, the text field may not be wide enough to display all of its text. (Note that this setting doesn't prevent the user from entering more than the specified number of characters. It just sets the width of the text field.)

This figure also presents some of the methods of the JTextField class. You'll see how some of these methods are used in the two examples in this figure.

The first example shows how to create two text fields and add them to a panel. Here, the first statement calls the JTextField constructor to create a text field and assign it to the textFieldOne variable. The initial contents of the text field is set to "Test" and the size of the text field is set to approximately 20 characters wide. Then, the next statement adds the text field to the panel. The next two statements create another text field, this one with no initial text and a column width of 10. When you display this panel, it appears as shown in the first frame in this figure. Then, the user can use the Tab key to move between the text fields. In addition, the user can enter and edit the text in these fields.

The second code example shows a method that modifies the second text field created by the first example. Here, the first statement uses the getText method of the first text field to return the text that's stored in that field, and it assigns that text to a String variable named data. The second statement uses the setText method to set the text of the second text field to the text that was retrieved from the first field. The third statement uses the setColumns method to change the width of the second text field to 20. And the fourth statement uses the setEditable method to modify the second text field so that the user won't be able to enter any text into this field. When a text field can't be edited, its border is grayed out as shown in the second frame in this figure.

Two versions of a panel that displays two text fields

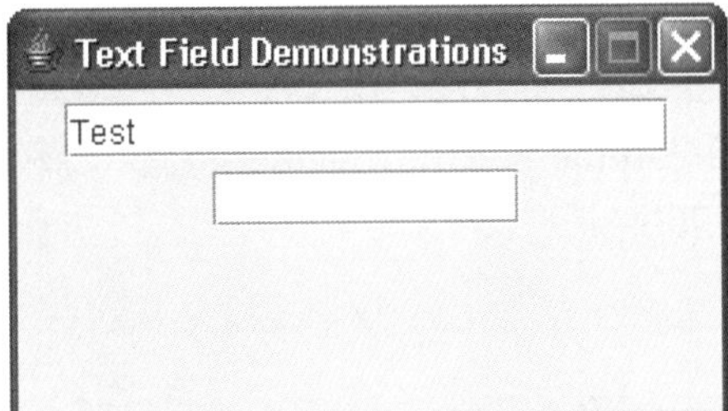

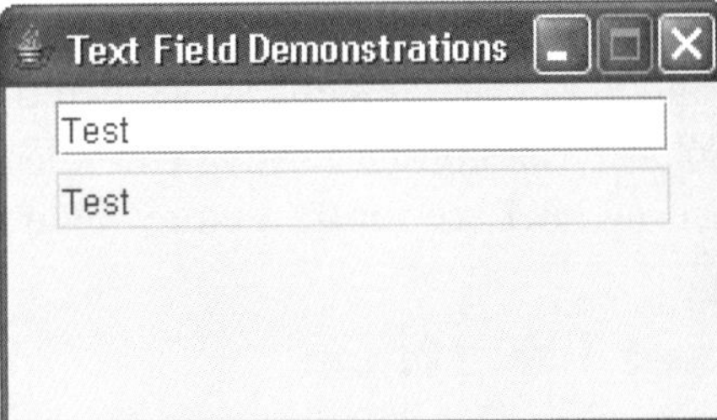

Common constructors and methods of the JTextField class

Constructor	Description
`JTextField(intColumns)`	Creates a text field with the specified number of columns.
`JTextField(String, intColumns)`	Creates a text field that starts with the text specified by the string and contains the specified number of columns.

Method	Description
`getText()`	Returns the text in this text field as a String object.
`setText(String)`	Sets the text in this field to the specified string.
`setColumns(intSize)`	Sets the number of columns to the specified value.
`setEditable(boolean)`	Determines whether or not the field can be edited.
`setFocusable(boolean)`	Determines whether or not the field can receive the focus.

Example 1: A class that creates the panel on the left

```
class TextFieldPanel extends JPanel
{
    private JTextField textFieldOne, textFieldTwo;

    public TextFieldPanel()
    {
        textFieldOne = new JTextField("Test", 20);
        this.add(textFieldOne);
        textFieldTwo = new JTextField(10);
        this.add(textFieldTwo);
    }
}
```

Example 2: Code that modifies the second text field as shown above

```
public void modifyFields()
{
    String data = textFieldOne.getText();
    textFieldTwo.setText(data);
    textFieldTwo.setColumns(20);
    textFieldTwo.setEditable(false);
}
```

Description

- The JTextField class defines a *text field* into which the user may input data. A text field can also be defined so that it can only display data.

Figure 15-13 How to work with text fields

The Future Value Calculator application

In this chapter, you've learned all the skills you need to design a simple graphical user interface. Now, you'll learn how to put all these skills together to create an interface for the Future Value Calculator application.

The user interface

Figure 15-14 begins by showing the user interface for the Future Value Calculator application. This user interface uses three panels. The outermost panel is the FutureValuePanel, and it uses a Border layout. Then, the displayPanel is added to the center region of the FutureValuePanel, and the buttonPanel is added to the south region of the FutureValuePanel. Both the displayPanel and the buttonPanel use a Flow layout with right alignment.

The code

All of the code for the Future Value Calculator application is stored in a single file named FutureValueApp. This class starts by importing the classes needed by the application, including the AWT and Swing classes. Then, the main method creates and displays a FutureValueFrame.

The FutureValueFrame class defines the frame of the application. Its constructor sets the title and size for the frame and calls the centerWindow method to center the frame on the screen. Then, it calls the setResizable method so the user can't change the size of the frame, and it sets the default close action so that the application is ended if the user closes the frame. Finally, it creates an instance of the FutureValuePanel and adds it to the frame.

The declaration for the FutureValuePanel class, shown on page 2 of this listing, extends the JPanel class and implements the ActionListener interface. Then, the declarations for the instance variables identify the controls that will be added to this panel: four labels, four text fields, and two buttons.

The constructor for this class begins by creating the display panel that will hold the labels and text boxes. Then, it creates a FlowLayout object with right alignment and assigns it to this panel. After that, it creates the labels and text boxes and adds them to the panel.

Next, on page 3, the constructor creates the button panel that will hold the two buttons. Like the display panel, this panel is assigned Flow layout with right alignment. Then, the buttons are created and added to the panel. Finally, the constructor sets the layout manager for the FutureValuePanel class to a BorderLayout object, and the display panel and button panel are added to it.

The last method in this application is the actionPerformed method, which is called when the user selects one of the buttons. This method begins by determining the source of the action event. If it is the Exit button, the application is terminated.

The panels of the user interface

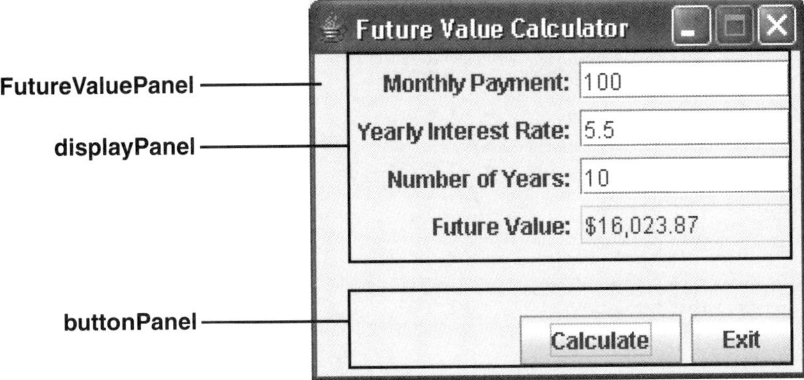

The code for the classes

Page 1

```
import java.awt.*;
import java.awt.event.*;
import javax.swing.*;
import java.text.*;

public class FutureValueApp
{
    public static void main(String[] args)
    {
        JFrame frame = new FutureValueFrame();
        frame.setVisible(true);
    }
}

class FutureValueFrame extends JFrame
{
    public FutureValueFrame()
    {
        setTitle("Future Value Calculator");
        setSize(267, 200);
        centerWindow(this);
        setResizable(false);
        setDefaultCloseOperation(JFrame.EXIT_ON_CLOSE);
        JPanel panel = new FutureValuePanel();
        this.add(panel);
    }

    private void centerWindow(Window w)
    {
        Toolkit tk = Toolkit.getDefaultToolkit();
        Dimension d = tk.getScreenSize();
        setLocation((d.width-w.getWidth())/2, (d.height-w.getHeight())/2);
    }
}
```

Figure 15-14 The Future Value Calculator application (part 1 of 3)

The code for the classes

Page 2

```
class FutureValuePanel extends JPanel implements ActionListener
{
    private JTextField  paymentTextField,
                        rateTextField,
                        yearsTextField,
                        futureValueTextField;
    private JLabel      paymentLabel,
                        rateLabel,
                        yearsLabel,
                        futureValueLabel;
    private JButton     calculateButton,
                        exitButton;

    public FutureValuePanel()
    {
        // display panel
        JPanel displayPanel = new JPanel();
        displayPanel.setLayout(new FlowLayout(FlowLayout.RIGHT));

        // payment label
        paymentLabel = new JLabel("Monthly Payment:");
        displayPanel.add(paymentLabel);

        // payment text field
        paymentTextField = new JTextField(10);
        displayPanel.add(paymentTextField);

        // rate label
        rateLabel = new JLabel("Yearly Interest Rate:");
        displayPanel.add(rateLabel);

        // rate text field
        rateTextField = new JTextField(10);
        displayPanel.add(rateTextField);

        // years label
        yearsLabel = new JLabel("Number of Years:");
        displayPanel.add(yearsLabel);

        // years text field
        yearsTextField = new JTextField(10);
        displayPanel.add(yearsTextField);

        // future value label
        futureValueLabel = new JLabel("Future Value:");
        displayPanel.add(futureValueLabel);

        // future value text field
        futureValueTextField = new JTextField(10);
        futureValueTextField.setEditable(false);
        futureValueTextField.setFocusable(false);
        displayPanel.add(futureValueTextField);
```

Figure 15-14 The Future Value Calculator application (part 2 of 3)

The code for the classes

Page 3

```
        // button panel
        JPanel buttonPanel = new JPanel();
        buttonPanel.setLayout(new FlowLayout(FlowLayout.RIGHT));

        // calculate button
        calculateButton = new JButton("Calculate");
        calculateButton.addActionListener(this);
        buttonPanel.add(calculateButton);

        // exit button
        exitButton = new JButton("Exit");
        exitButton.addActionListener(this);
        buttonPanel.add(exitButton);

        // add panels to main panel
        this.setLayout(new BorderLayout());
        this.add(displayPanel, BorderLayout.CENTER);
        this.add(buttonPanel, BorderLayout.SOUTH);
    }

    public void actionPerformed(ActionEvent e)
    {
        Object source = e.getSource();
        if (source == exitButton)
            System.exit(0);
        else if (source == calculateButton)
        {
            double payment =
                Double.parseDouble(paymentTextField.getText());
            double rate = Double.parseDouble(rateTextField.getText());
            int years = Integer.parseInt(yearsTextField.getText());
            double futureValue =
                FinancialCalculations.calculateFutureValue(
                payment, rate, years);
            NumberFormat currency = NumberFormat.getCurrencyInstance();
            futureValueTextField.setText(currency.format(futureValue));
        }
    }
}
```

Figure 15-14 The Future Value Calculator application (part 3 of 3)

If the actionPerformed method is executed as a result of the user selecting the Calculate button, the getText method is used to retrieve the values the user entered into the first three text fields. Then, these text values are converted to numeric values and passed to the calculateFutureValue method of the FinancialCalculations class you saw in figure 6-15 of chapter 6. Finally, a currency format is applied to the result of this calculation, and this value is assigned to the fourth text field.

To keep this application simple, it doesn't do any data validation. So if the user enters an invalid number into any of the text fields, the program will end with an unhandled exception. In chapter 17, though, you'll learn how to add proper data validation to this program.

Perspective

Now that you've finished this chapter, you should be able to create a graphical user interface that can accept user input, display output, and respond appropriately when the user selects a button. In particular, you learned how to work with components like frames, panels, labels, text boxes, and buttons. Although that's a good start, there's much more to developing GUIs than that.

In the next two chapters, then, you'll expand on this base of knowledge. There, you'll learn how to work with other types of components. You'll learn how to use a more sophisticated layout manager. You'll learn more about handling events. And you'll learn some techniques for validating data. When you're done with these chapters, you'll be able to develop GUIs at a professional level.

As you learn how to develop GUIs with code, you may remember from chapter 1 that integrated development environments (IDEs) like Eclipse and BlueJ provide drag-and-drop tools that make it much easier to create a GUI. The trouble is that you still need to understand the code that's generated by the IDE because you often have to modify or enhance it. That's why you need to master the coding skills before you start using an IDE.

Summary

- You can use *Swing* components to create graphical user interfaces that are platform independent and more bug-free than GUIs developed with the older GUI technology known as the *Abstract Window Toolkit* (*AWT*).
- All Swing classes inherit the Component and Container classes, are stored in the javax.swing package, and begin with the letter J. Since all Swing components inherit the Component class, you can call any methods of the Component class from any Swing component.
- You can use Swing components to create a *frame* that contains a title bar and a border. Then, you can add *panels*, *labels*, *text fields*, and *buttons* to the *content pane* of that frame.

- You can use the Toolkit class to get the height and width of a user's screen in *pixels*. Then, you can use this information to center the frames you create on the screen.
- When coding a graphical user interface, you write code that handles *events* that are initiated by the user. To do that, you must write code that defines a *listener* that listens for each event and responds when an event occurs.
- You can use *layout managers*, such as the *Flow layout manager* and the *Border layout manager*, to control how components are displayed within a frame or panel. When using these layout managers, it's common to nest one panel within another panel.

Exercise 15-1 Create a Swing version of the Invoice application

In this exercise, you'll create a Swing version of the Invoice application that was presented in figure 2-18 of chapter 2. The application should have a user interface that looks something like this:

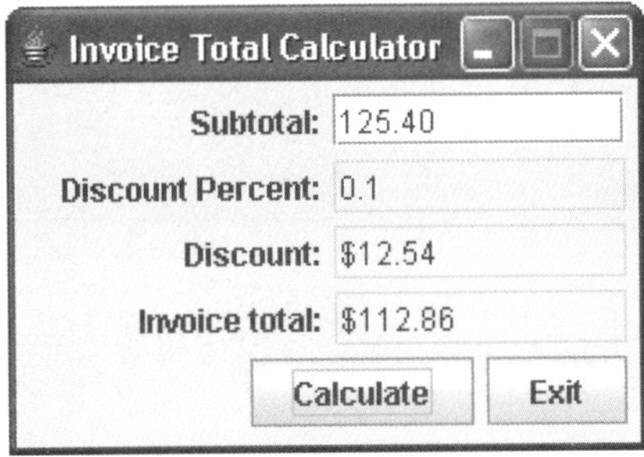

1. Open the InvoiceApp.java file in the c:\java1.5\ch15 directory. This file contains a public InvoiceApp class with an empty main method.
2. Add a class that defines the frame shown above. This frame should be centered on the screen, it should not be resizable, and closing it should end the application. This frame should be displayed when the application starts.
3. Add a class that defines a panel with the controls shown above, using a Flow layout manager to align the controls. Implement the ActionListener interface for this class so it will respond to the user selecting the Exit or Calculate button. If the user selects the Exit button, the application should end. If the user selects the Calculate button, the application should calculate and display the discount percent, discount amount, and invoice total. (The discount percent should be 20% if the subtotal is greater than or equal to $200, 10% if the subtotal is less than $200 but greater than or equal to $100, and 0% if the subtotal is less than $100.) Create an instance of this class and add it to the frame from the frame class.
4. Add the import statements needed by this application. Then, compile the application and run it to be sure it works correctly.

Exercise 15-2 Enhance the Invoice application

In this exercise, you'll enhance the Invoice application that you created for exercise 15-1.

1. Open the InvoiceApp.java file in the c:\java1.5\ch15 directory.
2. Modify the Invoice application so it uses three panels. The main panel should use Border layout and should serve only as a container for the other two panels. The labels and text fields should be added to a second panel that uses Flow layout, and the buttons should be added to a third panel that uses Flow layout. Add the second panel to the center region of the main panel and add the third panel to the south region of the main panel.
3. Modify the actionPerformed method so that if the value entered by the user can't be converted to a valid number, the application clears all the text fields and doesn't perform any calculations. To do that, you need to use a try/catch statement within this method.
4. Add a third button labeled Clear to the left of the other buttons. If the user selects this button, the application should clear the contents of all four text fields.
5. Compile the application and test it to be sure these changes work.

16

How to work with controls and layout managers

In the last chapter, you learned how to code a graphical user interface by using the most common controls and layout managers. Now, you'll learn how to code a graphical user interface using more sophisticated controls and layout managers. When you complete this chapter, you should be able to develop GUIs that provide a variety of functions.

Incidentally, two of the controls that are presented in this chapter require some knowledge of arrays and some of the examples use array lists. So if you haven't already read chapters 10 and 11, you should probably do that before you read this chapter.

How to work with components

In the last chapter, you learned how to work with four Swing components: panels, labels, text fields, and buttons. In the figures that follow, you'll learn how to use seven more components to enhance the user interfaces you create.

A summary of the Swing components presented in this chapter

Figure 16-1 summarizes the Swing components that are presented in this chapter and shows a Swing frame that uses most of these components. As you can see, this chapter presents five new Swing controls: text areas, check boxes, radio buttons, combo boxes, and lists.

In addition, this chapter presents two Swing components that are used in conjunction with other components. The border component lets you add a border to another component such as a panel. In the frame in this figure, for example, a border is used to group two radio buttons in a panel. The scroll pane component lets you add scroll bars to another component like the list component in this figure.

You should be aware that Swing offers many other components besides the ones listed here. Once you learn how to use these basic components, however, you should have no trouble using the API documentation to learn how to use the others.

A frame with several new types of components

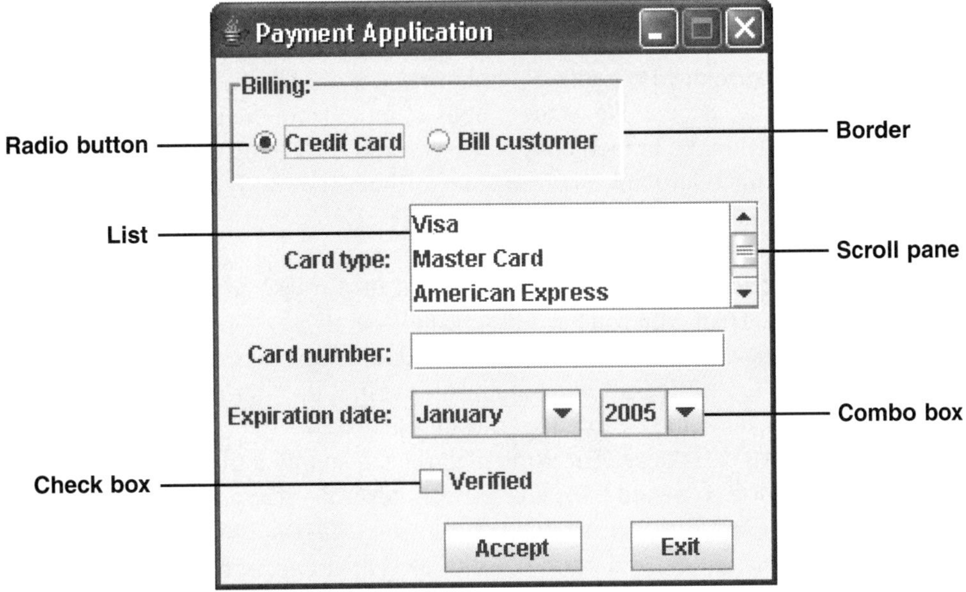

Swing controls presented in this chapter

Control	Class	Description
Text area	JTextArea	A text area lets the user enter more than one line of text.
Check box	JCheckBox	A check box lets the user select or deselect an option.
Radio button	JRadioButton	A radio button lets the user select an option from a group of options.
List	JList	A list lets the user select one or more items from a list of items.
Combo box	JComboBox	A combo box lets the user select a single item from a drop-down list of items. A combo box can also let the user enter text into the text portion of the combo box.

Components that enhance controls

Component	Class	Description
Border	JBorder	A border can be used to visually group components or to enhance the appearance of an individual component.
Scroll pane	JScrollPane	A scroll pane contains scroll bars that can be used to scroll through the contents of other controls. Scroll panes are typically used with text area and list controls.

Description

- Swing offers many different types of controls besides labels, text boxes, and buttons. The most commonly used are text areas, check boxes, radio buttons, lists, and combo boxes.
- The JBorder and JScrollPane classes create components that are used to enhance the appearance or operation of other components.

Figure 16-1 A summary of the Swing components presented in this chapter

How to work with text areas

In the last chapter, you learned how to use a text field to get one line of input from a user. Now, figure 16-2 shows you how to use the JTextArea class to create a *text area* that can accept one or more lines of input from the user. Text areas are similar to text fields. In fact, both classes extend the JTextComponent class, which provides many of the basic functions for both classes. For example, the getText and setText methods are defined by the JTextComponent class, so they're available to both text fields and text areas.

When you create a text area, you specify the number of rows and columns you want it to contain. Then, you can use the setLineWrap and setWrapStyleWord methods to determine how the text wraps from one line to the next. By default, the text doesn't wrap at all. As a result, the user must press the Enter key to start a new line of text. If you want the text to wrap automatically, you must call the setLineWrap method and supply a true value as the argument. In addition, wrapped lines are split wherever the line reaches the end of the text area, even if that's in the middle of a word. To make sure that the text is wrapped between words, you must also call the setWrapStyleWord method and supply a true value as the argument.

The first code example in this figure shows how to add a text area to a panel. Here, the first statement declares a text area variable. Then, the second statement creates a text area with 7 rows and 20 columns and assigns to it the variable. The next two statements set the wrapping for the text area. Finally, the last statement adds the text area to the panel where it's defined.

The second example shows how to retrieve the text that's displayed in a text area as a string. To do that, you use the getText method just as you do for text fields.

Before I go on, you should realize that if the text area contains more lines than can be displayed in the number of rows you specified when you created the text area, Swing will attempt to increase the size of the text area to display all of its text. If that's not possible, however, some of the text won't be displayed. You can avoid that problem by using a scroll pane in combination with the text area as shown in the next figure.

A frame with a text area

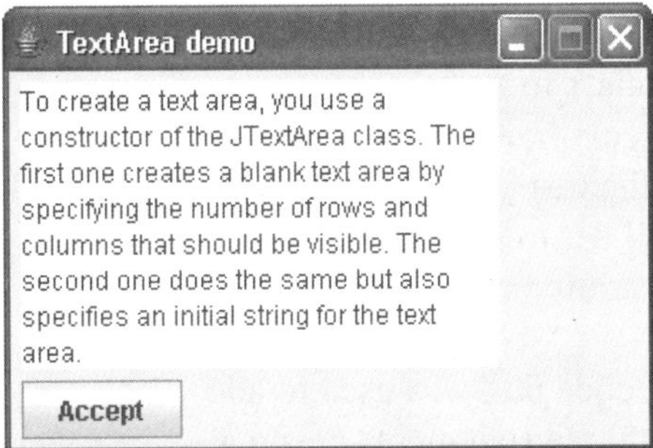

Common constructors of the JTextArea class

Constructor	Description
`JTextArea(intRows, intCols)`	Creates an empty text area with the specified number of rows and columns.
`JTextArea(String, intRows, intCols)`	Creates a text area with the specified number of rows and columns starting with the specified text.

Some methods that work with text areas

Method	Description
`setLineWrap(boolean)`	If the boolean value is true, the lines will wrap if they don't fit.
`setWrapStyleWord(boolean)`	If the boolean value is true and line wrapping is turned on, wrapped lines will be separated between words.
`append(String)`	Appends the specified string to the text in the text area.
`getText()`	Returns the text in the text area as a String.
`setText(String)`	Sets the text in the text area to the specified string.

Example 1: Code that creates the text area

```
private JTextArea commentTextArea;
commentTextArea = new JTextArea(7, 20);
commentTextArea.setLineWrap(true);
commentTextArea.setWrapStyleWord(true);
add(commentTextArea);
```

Example 2: Code that gets the text stored in the text area

```
String comments = commentTextArea.getText();
```

Description

- In contrast to a text field, a *text area* can be used to enter and display more than one line of text.
- You can use the setLineWrap and setWrapStyleWord methods to provide for wrapping the lines in the text area when necessary and breaking these lines between words.
- When you create a text area, you specify the number of rows and columns for the area. If the text area is going to receive more text than can be viewed at one time, you should add the text area to a scroll pane as described in figure 16-3.

Figure 16-2 How to work with text areas

How to work with scroll panes

Figure 16-3 shows how to use the JScrollPane class to add a component such as a text area to a *scroll pane*. Here, you can see a frame that includes a text area that has a vertical scroll bar. That way, if the text is too long to be displayed in the text area, the user can use the scroll bar to see all of the text. Later in this chapter, you'll see how you can use a scroll pane to scroll through the items in a list control.

The first code example in this figure shows the code that was used to add the text area in this figure to a scroll pane. The first three statements create a text area just like the one in the previous figure. Then, the fourth statement creates a scroll pane object, passing the text area to the scroll pane's constructor. Finally, the last line adds the scroll pane to the panel where it's defined.

If you use the first constructor to create a scroll pane, vertical and horizontal scroll bars will be displayed as needed. If that's not what you want, you can use the second scroll pane constructor to control when vertical and horizontal scroll bars are displayed as shown in the second example. In this case, the scroll pane will always display a vertical scroll bar and never display a horizontal scroll bar.

A frame that displays a text area in a scroll pane

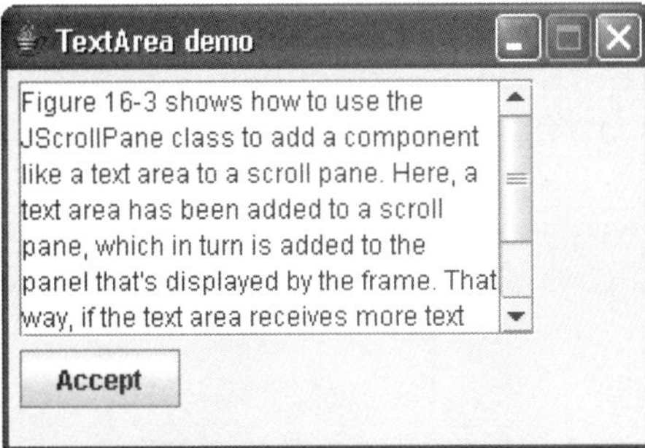

Common constructors of the JScrollPane class

Constructor	Description
`JScrollPane(Component)`	Creates a scroll pane that displays the specified component, along with vertical and horizontal scrollbars as needed.
`JScrollPane(Component, vertical, horizontal)`	Creates a scroll pane that displays the specified component and uses the specified vertical and horizontal policies.

Fields of the ScrollPaneConstants interface that set scrollbar policies

Field	Description
`VERTICAL_SCROLLBAR_ALWAYS`	Always display a vertical scrollbar.
`VERTICAL_SCROLLBAR_AS_NEEDED`	Display a vertical scrollbar only when needed.
`VERTICAL_SCROLLBAR_NEVER`	Never display a vertical scrollbar.
`HORIZONTAL_SCROLLBAR_ALWAYS`	Always display a horizontal scrollbar.
`HORIZONTAL_SCROLLBAR_AS_NEEDED`	Display a horizontal scrollbar only when needed.
`HORIZONTAL_SCROLLBAR_NEVER`	Never display a horizontal scrollbar.

Example 1: Code that uses a scroll pane with the text area

```
private JTextArea commentTextArea = new JTextArea(7, 20);
commentTextArea.setLineWrap(true);
commentTextArea.setWrapStyleWord(true);
JScrollPane commentScroll = new JScrollPane(commentTextArea);
add(commentScroll);
```

Example 2: Code that creates a scroll pane and sets the scroll bar policies

```
JScrollPane commentScroll = new JScrollPane(commentTextArea,
    ScrollPaneConstants.VERTICAL_SCROLLBAR_ALWAYS,
    ScrollPaneConstants.HORIZONTAL_SCROLLBAR_NEVER);
```

Description

- A *scroll pane* can be used when the contents of another component won't fit in the space allotted to the component. The scroll pane displays horizontal and vertical scroll bars so the user can scroll to see the entire contents of the component displayed by the scroll pane.
- You can add any component to a scroll pane, but they're typically used for text areas and lists.
- You can set the vertical and horizontal scroll bar policies to control how the scroll pane displays vertical and horizontal scroll bars.

Figure 16-3 How to work with scroll panes

How to work with check boxes

Figure 16-4 shows how to use a *check box*. Here, if the box is checked, the Address text area is enabled so the user can enter a mailing address. Otherwise, the Address text area is disabled.

To create a check box, you can use one of the two constructors of the JCheckBox class shown in this figure. Since check boxes are unchecked by default, you need to use the second constructor to create a box that is checked. Otherwise, you can use the setSelected method to check or uncheck a box after it has been created.

The first code example shows how to use the JCheckBox class to add a check box to a panel. Here, the first statement declares the check box and the second statement creates the check box. Because a check box is a type of button (both the JCheckBox and JButton classes are derived from the AbstractButton class), it generates action events when the user clicks it. To handle these events, the third statement adds an action listener to the check box. Then, the fourth statement adds the check box to a panel.

The action listener is necessary only if you want the application to immediately respond when the user clicks the check box. In many cases, this isn't necessary. Instead, you just need to check the status of the check box when the user clicks some other button on the form. In that case, you can use a statement like the one shown in the second example. Here, a boolean variable named addToList is declared and set to the result of the isSelected method. Thus, if the check box is checked, the addToList variable will be set to true. Otherwise, it will be set to false.

The third code example shows how you can code an actionPerformed method for an action listener for a check box. Here, the ActionEvent object's getSource method is used to determine whether the source of the action event is the mailingCheckBox component. If it is, an if statement tests to see if the check box is checked. If so, the addressTextArea component is enabled so the user can enter an address. Otherwise, the text area is disabled.

A frame with a check box

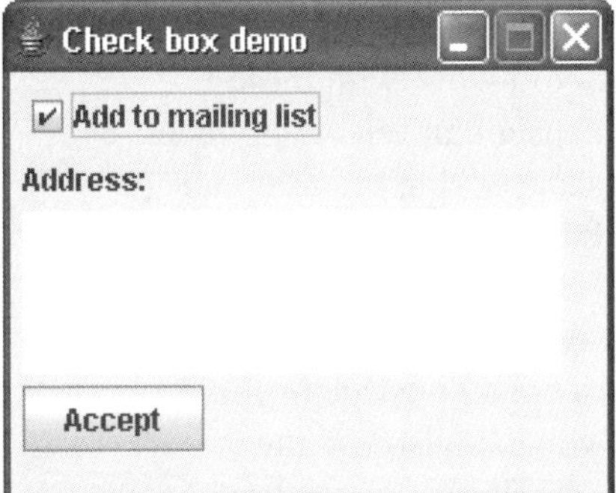

Common constructors of the JCheckBox class

Constructor	Description
JCheckBox(String)	Creates an unselected check box with a label that contains the specified string.
JCheckBox(String, boolean)	Creates a check box with a label that contains the specified string. If the boolean value is true, the check box is selected.

Some methods that work with check boxes

Method	Description
isSelected()	Returns a true value if the check box is selected.
setSelected(boolean)	Checks or unchecks the check box depending on the boolean value.
addActionListener(ActionListener)	Adds an action listener to the check box.

Example 1: Code that creates the check box

```
private JCheckBox mailingCheckBox;
mailingCheckBox = new JCheckBox("Add to mailing list", true);
mailingCheckBox.addActionListener(this);
add(mailingCheckBox);
```

Example 2: Code that checks the status of the check box

```
boolean addToList = mailingCheckBox.isSelected();
```

Example 3: An actionPerformed method for the check box

```
public void actionPerformed(ActionEvent e)
{
    Object source = e.getSource();
    if (source == mailingCheckBox)
    {
        if (mailingCheckBox.isSelected())
            addressTextArea.setEnabled(true);
        else
            addressTextArea.setEnabled(false);
    }
}
```

Figure 16-4 How to work with check boxes

How to work with radio buttons

Figure 16-5 shows how to use *radio buttons*. When you work with these buttons, you must put them in a *button group*. Then, the user can select only one button from the group. In the frame in this figure, you can see that the user can select one of three shipping methods: USPS (the Post Office), UPS, or Federal Express.

Like a check box, a radio button is not selected by default. When you create a group of radio buttons, then, you'll typically use the second constructor for one of the radio buttons to select it initially. However, you can also use the setSelected method to select a radio button, just as you can with a check box.

The first example shows how to add the three radio buttons shown in this figure to a panel and a button group. Here, the first statement declares the three radio buttons. Then, the next three statements create radio buttons with the appropriate labels. Next, the radio buttons are added to the panel.

The last four statements in this example create a button group using the ButtonGroup class and then add the buttons to that group. A button group creates a logical grouping of radio buttons. At any given moment, only one of the radio buttons in a button group can be selected. If the user clicks one of the radio buttons in a button group, the clicked radio button is selected and the radio button that was previously selected is deselected.

The second code example shows how to determine which of the three radio buttons is selected and assigns an appropriate string value to the shipVia variable. It does this by using an if/else statement that tests the isSelected method of each radio button in the group.

Like the JCheckBox and JButton classes, the JRadioButton class inherits the AbstractButton class. As a result, you can use an action listener with a radio button just as you can with a check box or regular button. You use the addActionListener method to add an action listener object to the radio button. Then, in the class that implements the ActionListener interface, you code the actionPerformed method to handle the event.

A frame with three radio buttons

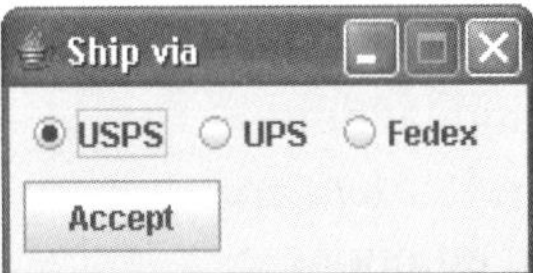

Common constructors and methods of the JRadioButton class

Constructor	Description
`JRadioButton(String)`	Creates an unselected radio button with the specified text.
`JRadioButton(String, boolean)`	Creates a radio button with the specified text. If the boolean value is true, the radio button is selected.
Method	**Description**
`isSelected()`	Returns a true value if the radio button is selected.
`addActionListener(ActionListener)`	Adds an action listener to the radio button.

Common constructors and methods of the ButtonGroup class

Constructor	Description
`ButtonGroup()`	Creates a button group used to hold a group of buttons.
Method	**Description**
`add(AbstractButton)`	Adds the specified button to the group.

Example 1: Code that creates the three radio buttons and adds them to a panel

```
private JRadioButton uspsRadioButton, upsRadioButton, fedexRadioButton;
uspsRadioButton = new JRadioButton("USPS", true);
upsRadioButton = new JRadioButton("UPS");
fedexRadioButton = new JRadioButton("Fedex");
add(uspsRadioButton);
add(upsRadioButton);
add(fedexRadioButton);
ButtonGroup shipViaGroup = new ButtonGroup();
shipViaGroup.add(uspsRadioButton);
shipViaGroup.add(upsRadioButton);
shipViaGroup.add(fedexRadioButton);
```

Example 2: Code that determines which radio button is selected

```
if (uspsRadioButton.isSelected())
    shipVia = "USPS";
else if (upsRadioButton.isSelected())
    shipVia = "UPS";
else if (fedexRadioButton.isSelected())
    shipVia = "Federal Express";
```

Description

- *Radio buttons* let the user choose one from among several options.
- You must add each radio button in a set of options to a ButtonGroup object. Selecting a radio button automatically deselects all other radio buttons in the same button group.

Figure 16-5 How to work with radio buttons

How to work with borders

Figure 16-6 shows how to add a *border* to a component. Although adding borders is an esthetic consideration that doesn't affect functionality, borders are important for two reasons. First, they let you visually group related components. This is especially important for radio buttons. Second, they let you add a title to a group of related components. The frame shown in this figure shows how the three radio buttons from the previous figure appear when displayed with a border.

You might expect that to create a border for a component, you would simply call a method to set the border style. Unfortunately, it isn't that simple. First, you must create a Border object with the style settings that you want to use. You do that by calling one of the static methods of the BorderFactory class listed in this figure. This table shows six methods that create four different types of borders: plain line borders, etched borders, beveled borders, and titled borders. Then, you call the component's setBorder method, passing the Border object as a parameter.

To complicate matters, the methods that create etched and beveled borders don't let you specify a title. So if you want to create an etched or beveled border with a title, you must first create the etched or beveled border. Then, you pass this Border object as a parameter to the createTitledBorder method. The result is a Border object that has both a title and an etched or beveled border.

The code example in this figure shows how to add a border to a panel that contains three radio buttons. The unshaded lines of this example are the same as the code in the last figure. The shaded lines show the code that creates a panel with a border and adds radio buttons to it. The first shaded line creates a panel object named shipViaPanel. Then, the next line uses the createEtchedBorder method of the BorderFactory class to create an etched Border object. The third line uses the createTitledBorder method to add a title to this Border object. Then, the setBorder method of the shipViaPanel object applies this border to the panel. The remaining lines add the radio buttons to the shipViaPanel and add the shipViaPanel to the main panel for the frame.

Although it's not shown here, you must import the javax.swing.border package to work with borders. That's because the Border interface that all of the borders implement is stored in this package.

Radio buttons with an etched and titled border

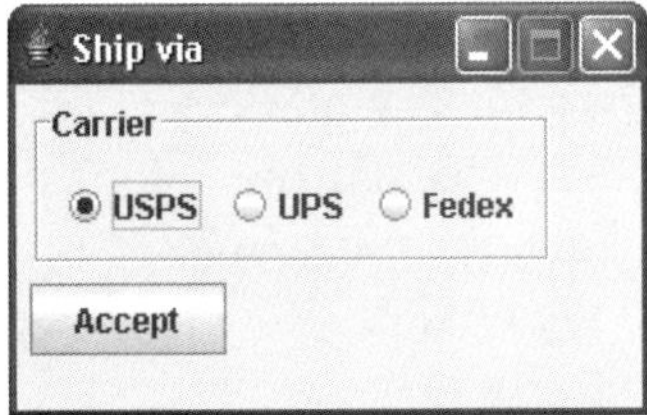

Static methods of the BorderFactory class

Method	Description
`createLineBorder()`	Creates a line border.
`createEtchedBorder()`	Creates an etched border.
`createLoweredBevelBorder()`	Creates a lowered bevel border.
`createRaisedBevelBorder()`	Creates a raised bevel border.
`createTitledBorder(String)`	Creates a line border with the specified title.
`createTitledBorder(Border, String)`	Adds the specified title to the specified border.

Method of the JComponent class used to set borders

Method	Description
`setBorder(Border)`	Sets the border style for a component.

Code that creates bordered radio buttons

```
uspsRadioButton = new JRadioButton("USPS", true);
upsRadioButton = new JRadioButton("UPS");
fedexRadioButton = new JRadioButton("Fedex");
ButtonGroup shipViaGroup = new ButtonGroup();
shipViaGroup.add(uspsRadioButton);
shipViaGroup.add(upsRadioButton);
shipViaGroup.add(fedexRadioButton);

JPanel shipViaPanel = new JPanel();
Border shipViaBorder = BorderFactory.createEtchedBorder();
shipViaBorder = BorderFactory.createTitledBorder(shipViaBorder, "Carrier");
shipViaPanel.setBorder(shipViaBorder);
shipViaPanel.add(uspsRadioButton);
shipViaPanel.add(upsRadioButton);
shipViaPanel.add(fedexRadioButton);
add(shipViaPanel);
```

Description

- *Borders* are used to visually group controls such as radio buttons or to enhance the appearance of controls.
- To place controls in a border, you must create a panel, create a border and apply it the panel, and add the controls to the panel.
- Because a border only groups controls visually, you must still use a ButtonGroup object to group radio buttons logically.
- To set borders as shown above, you must import the javax.swing.border package.

Figure 16-6 How to work with borders

How to work with combo boxes

Figure 16-7 shows how to work with the JComboBox class, which creates a *combo box* component. A combo box is a control that lets the user choose from one of several options in a drop-down list. Depending on how the combo box is configured, the user may also be able to type data directly into the box. In effect, a combo box is a combination of a text field and a drop-down list.

The frames at the top of this figure show a combo box in use. In the first frame, the combo box resembles a text field with a drop-down arrow to its right. When the user clicks this arrow, a scrollable list of selections is displayed as shown in the second frame. When the user makes a selection, the drop-down list retracts and the selected item is displayed in the text portion of the combo box.

The first code example in this figure shows how to use the JComboBox class to create a combo box. The first statement of this example declares an array of Product objects. Then, the second statement calls a private method that returns an ArrayList that contains Product objects. To keep this example simple, this method isn't shown here. However, you can find several versions of this method in the chapters in section 5. After the array list is loaded, the JComboBox constructor is called to create a combo box object, which is assigned to a previously declared variable named productComboBox. Then, an enhanced for loop is used to add the description of each product to the combo box by calling its addItem method. Finally, the combo box is added to the panel. Notice that this code doesn't set the item that's initially selected in the list. That's because, by default, the first item in the list is selected. If that's not what you want, you can use the setSelectedIndex method to select an item.

The second code example shows how to determine which product the user selected. Here, the getSelectedIndex method is called to retrieve the index of the item selected by the user. Then, this index is used to get the selected product from the products array list.

By default, combo boxes aren't editable, so the user can't change the value that's in the combo box. Although that's usually what you want, you can use the setEditable method to make the combo box editable. Then, the user can type the text of an item into the combo box instead of selecting an item from the list. If you do this, keep in mind that the user might enter invalid data. As a result, you'll have to add some data validation code to prevent invalid entries.

Although the example shown in this figure adds String objects to the combo box, the addItem method lets you add any type of object. As a result, this example could have added the Product objects directly to the combo box. Then, the combo box would call each product's toString method to get the text to display for the object. Since the Product class overrides the toString method to return the product description, the result would be the same as calling the getDescription method of the product. However, because the Product objects are stored in the combo box, you can simply use the getSelectedItem method to get the selected item rather than using the getSelectedIndex method to get the index of the selected item and then using that index in a get method to get the selected product from the array list.

A frame with a combo box

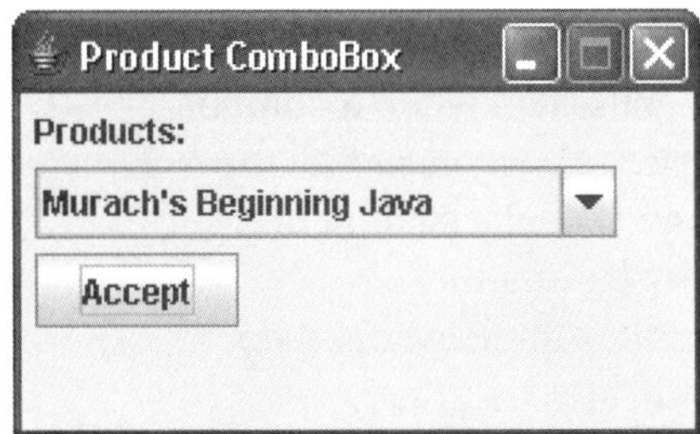

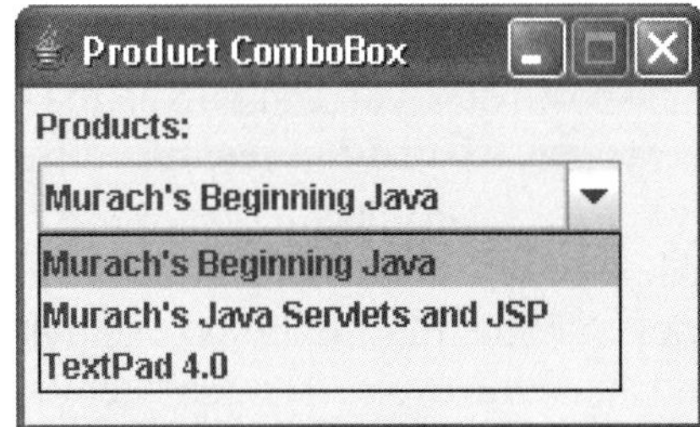

Common constructors of the JComboBox class

Constructor	Description
`JComboBox()`	Creates an empty combo box.
`JComboBox(Object[])`	Creates a combo box with the objects stored in the specified array.

Some methods that work with combo boxes

Method	Description
`getSelectedItem()`	Returns an Object type for the selected item.
`getSelectedIndex()`	Returns an int value for the index of the selected item.
`setSelectedIndex(intIndex)`	Selects the item at the specified index.
`setEditable(boolean)`	If the boolean value is true, the combo box can be edited.
`getItemCount()`	Returns the number of items stored in the combo box.
`addItem(Object)`	Adds an item to the combo box.
`removeItemAt(int)`	Removes the item at the specified index from the combo box.
`removeItem(Object)`	Removes the specified item from the combo box.
`addActionListener(ActionListener)`	Adds an action listener to the combo box.
`addItemListener(ItemListener)`	Adds an item listener to the combo box (see figure 16-8).

Example 1: Code that creates the combo box

```
private ArrayList<Product> products;
products = getProducts();          // returns an ArrayList of products
productComboBox = new JComboBox();
for (Product p : products)
    productComboBox.addItem(p.getDescription());
add(productComboBox);
```

Example 2: Code that determines which item was selected

```
int i = productComboBox.getSelectedIndex();
Product p = products.get(i);
```

Description

- A *combo box* lets the user choose one of several items from a drop-down list.
- To populate the list in a combo box, you can pass an array to the constructor. Alternatively, you can use the addItem method to add individual items to the list.

Figure 16-7 How to work with combo boxes

How to use event listeners with a combo box

Figure 16-8 shows how you can handle the events generated when a combo box selection changes. As you can see, two different types of events are raised by a combo box: *item events* and *action events*. When a user selects an item from a combo box or when the application changes it by calling the setSelectedIndex method, the combo box actually generates three events: two item events and an action event. The first item event indicates that the previously selected item has been deselected. The second item event indicates that a new item has been selected. And the action event indicates that the selection has changed.

Because two item events are generated each time the selection changes, it's usually best to handle the action event instead. If you use the item event, however, you'll need to implement the ItemListener interface shown in this figure. This interface declares a method named itemStateChanged that you must code in any class that implements the interface. As you can see, this method accepts a single argument of the ItemEvent type. You can use the getSource method of the ItemEvent class to get the source of the event just as you can with an action listener. In addition, you can use the getItem method to get the selected item, and you can use the getStateChanged method to determine whether an item was selected or deselected.

The code examples in this figure show you how to use the action event with a combo box. The first example shows how you add an action listener to the combo box by calling the addActionListener method. Then, the second example shows how you can code the actionPerformed method to handle the event. Here, the if statement determines whether the combo box is the source of the event. (Remember that action events are also generated by other components such as buttons, check boxes, and radio buttons.) If so, the selected product is retrieved and the price text box is set to display the price of the selected product.

Notice in the first code example that before the action listener is added to the combo box, the setSelectedIndex method is called to select the first item in the list. Although this isn't required since this item is selected by default, it brings up an important point. That is, the setSelectedIndex method must be called before the action listener is added to the combo box. That's because the setSelectedIndex method generates an action event that can't properly be dealt with in the constructor code. Specifically, the action event handler refers to the price text box, which isn't created until after the combo box is created. If I had called the addActionListener method before the setSelectedIndex method, the action event listener would be called from the constructor code before the price text box was created, and the statement that refers to the price text box would fail with a null pointer exception.

A frame that uses an action event listener to update the display based on the user's selection

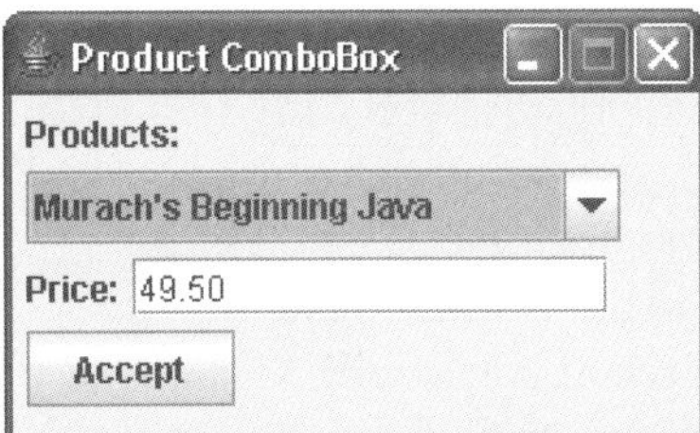

The actionPerformed method of the ActionListener interface

Method	Description
`void actionPerformed(ActionEvent e)`	Invoked when an item is selected.

The itemStateChanged method of the ItemListener interface

Method	Description
`void itemStateChanged(ItemEvent e)`	Invoked when an item is selected or deselected.

Common methods of the ItemEvent class

Method	Description
`getSource()`	Returns the source of the event.
`getItem()`	Returns the selected item.
`getStateChanged()`	Returns an int value that indicates whether an item was selected or deselected. The field names for these values are SELECTED and DESELECTED.

Example 1: Code that creates the combo box

```
products = getProducts();
productComboBox = new JComboBox();
for (Product p : products)
    productComboBox.addItem(p.getDescription());
productComboBox.setSelectedIndex(0);
productComboBox.addActionListener(this);
add(productComboBox);
```

Example 2: Code that implements the ActionListener interface for the combo box

```
public void actionPerformed(ActionEvent e)
{
    Object source = e.getSource();
    if (source == productComboBox)
    {
        int i = productComboBox.getSelectedIndex();
        Product p = products.get(i);
        priceTextField.setText(p.getFormattedPrice());
    }
}
```

Figure 16-8 How to use event listeners with a combo box

How to work with lists

Figure 16-9 shows how to work with the JList class to create a *list*. The frame at the top of this figure shows a list that displays products. As you can see, there are more products than can fit in the list at once, so a scroll bar is used to allow the user to scroll through the entries. As with a text area, the JList class doesn't provide scroll bars. As a result, you must add the list to a scroll pane to create a scrollable list. Since nearly all lists will require a scroll bar, you'll almost always use the JList component in combination with a scroll pane.

The first code example shows how to create the list shown at the top of the figure. First, a method called getProductDescriptions is called to retrieve a simple array of descriptions. Although the code for this method isn't shown, you shouldn't have any trouble imagining how it would work. It simply calls the getProducts method that's used elsewhere in this book, creates an array that contains each of the product's descriptions, and returns this array to the caller. Next, the JList constructor is called and the array of product descriptions is passed as a parameter to the constructor. This creates a list that displays the values in the array.

Next, a series of set methods are called to configure the properties of the list. The setFixedCellWidth and setVisibleRowCount methods set the width of the list and number of rows that are visible at one time. The setSelectedIndex method sets the initial selection to the first item in the list. (Unlike a combo box, the first item isn't selected by default.) And the setSelectionMode method sets the *selection mode* of the list so that only one selection is allowed. (In figure 16-10, you'll learn how to work with lists that allow multiple selections.)

The second code example shows how to access the value of the item selected by the user. Here, the getSelectedValue method retrieves the selected value. Because this value is returned as an Object, it must be cast to a String to assign it to a String variable. Note that you can also use the getSelectedIndex method to return the index of the selected item and then use that index to retrieve the product description from the array.

You may have noticed that, unlike the JComboBox class, the JList class doesn't include an addItem method. That's because, by default, the list of items displayed by a list is immutable. In other words, you can't add or change items once the list has been created. Instead, you pass an array that contains the list items to the JList constructor. Later in this chapter, however, you'll learn how to create a list from an object that implements the ListModel interface. Then, you can add and delete objects from the list.

A frame that includes a list

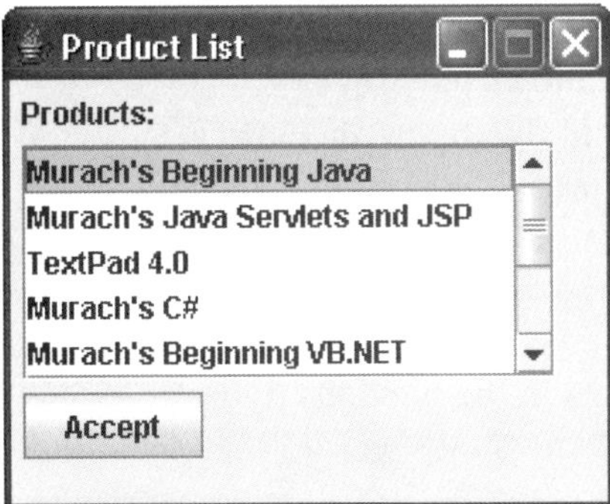

Common constructors of the JList class

Constructor	Description
`JList(Object[])`	Creates a list that contains the objects stored in the specified array of objects.
`JList(ListModel)`	Creates a list using the specified list model as described in figure 16-11.

Some methods of the JList class

Method	Description
`getSelectedValue()`	Returns the selected item as an Object type.
`getSelectedIndex()`	Returns an int value for the index of the selected item.
`isSelectedIndex(intIndex)`	Returns a true value if the item at the specified index is selected.
`setFixedCellWidth(intPixels)`	Sets the cell width to the specified number of pixels. Otherwise, the width of the list is slightly wider than the widest item in the array that populates the list.
`setVisibleRowCount(intRows)`	Sets the visible row count to the specified int value. This only works when the list is displayed within a scroll pane.
`setSelectionMode(mode)`	Sets the selection mode. To allow single selections, specify ListSelectionModel.SINGLE_SELECTION. For other options, see figure 16-10.
`setSelectedIndex(intIndex)`	Selects the item at the specified index.

Example 1: Code that creates the list

```
descriptions = getProductDescriptions(); // returns an array of
                                         // descriptions
productList = new JList(descriptions);
productList.setFixedCellWidth(200);
productList.setVisibleRowCount(5);
productList.setSelectedIndex(0);
productList.setSelectionMode(ListSelectionModel.SINGLE_SELECTION);
add(new JScrollPane(productList));
```

Example 2: Code that gets the selected item

```
String s = (String)productList.getSelectedValue();
```

Figure 16-9 How to work with lists

How to work with multiple selections in a list

Figure 16-10 shows how you can create a list that allows the user to select more than one item from the list. The frame at the top of this figure includes a list that allows multiple selections. In addition, the frame includes a text area that displays the products that were selected when the user clicked the Accept button.

The first code example shows how to create the list shown in this figure. This code is almost identical to the code that was shown in the previous figure. In fact, the only difference is that the setSelectionMode method specifies that the list will allow multiple selections. As this figure shows, the ListSelectionModel interface defines three fields you can pass to this method. You use the SINGLE_SELECTION field to limit the list to one selection. If you specify SINGLE_INTERVAL_SELECTION, the user can select a range of items by clicking the first item in the range and then holding down the Shift key and clicking the last item in the range. If you specify MULTIPLE_INTERVAL_SELECTION (as this example does), the user can select any combination of items in the list by holding down the Ctrl key while selecting items. The user can also use the Shift key to create a range of selections, then hold down the Ctrl key and click to start another range and hold the shift key and click to mark the end of that range. In this way, the user can create a selection that consists of multiple ranges of selections, which is why this type of selection mode is called *multiple interval selection.*

The second code example in this figure shows an action event handler that processes the entries selected in a list that allows multiple selections. Here, the getSelectedValues method returns an array that includes all of the selected objects. Then, a for loop is used to create a string that lists each selection on a separate line. Finally, the resulting string is assigned to the text area.

Notice in the for loop that each object in the array retrieved by the getSelectedValues method must be cast to a String object. That's because the getSelectedValues method returns an array of type Object. You might be tempted to think you could declare the selections array as an array of strings and let Java automatically convert the array of objects to an array of strings. Unfortunately, Java's automatic type conversion feature isn't that sophisticated, so you have to cast each element in the array to a String object.

A list that allows multiple selections

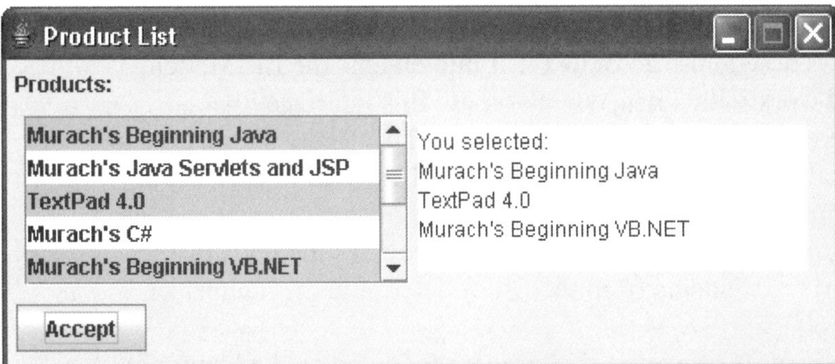

Fields of the ListSelectionModel interface used to set the selection mode

Field	Description
`SINGLE_SELECTION`	Allows just one selection.
`SINGLE_INTERVAL_SELECTION`	Allows a single range of selections.
`MULTIPLE_INTERVAL_SELECTION`	Allows multiple ranges of selections. This is the default.

Methods of the JList class used to process multiple selections

Method	Description
`getSelectedValues()`	Returns an array of Object types for the selected items.
`getSelectedIndices()`	Returns an array of ints corresponding to the indices of the selected items.

Example 1: Code that creates the list

```
descriptions = getProductDescriptions(); // returns an array of
                                         // descriptions
productList = new JList(descriptions);
productList.setFixedCellWidth(200);
productList.setVisibleRowCount(5);
productList.setSelectedIndex(0);
productList.setSelectionMode(
    ListSelectionModel.MULTIPLE_INTERVAL_SELECTION);
add(new JScrollPane(productList));
```

Example 2: Code that displays the selections

```
public void actionPerformed(ActionEvent e)
{
    Object source = e.getSource();
    if (source == acceptButton)
    {
        Object[] selections = productList.getSelectedValues();
        String s = "";
        for (Object o : selections)
            s += (String)o + "\n";
        productTextArea.setText("You selected:\n" + s);
    }
}
```

Figure 16-10 How to work with multiple selections in a list

How to work with list models

Figure 16-11 shows how to use an object that implements the ListModel interface to create and work with a list. When you use this interface, the contents of the list are managed by a *list model* object. This figure shows how to use the DefaultListModel class, which implements the ListModel interface, to create a list whose items can be changed after the list is created. As you can see in the table in this figure, the DefaultListModel class provides methods that let you add, delete, or retrieve elements from the list or determine the number of elements in the list.

The frame at the top of this figure includes a text field and an Add button. To add an item to the list, the user types the text to be added to the list into the text field and clicks the Add button. The text is then added to the list.

The first code example shows how to create this list. First, it calls the getProductDescriptions method to get an array of product descriptions. Instead of passing this array to the JList constructor, however, it creates a DefaultListModel object named productListModel and then uses a for loop to add each element of the descriptions array to the list model. (Although it isn't shown in this figure, the productListModel variable is declared as an instance variable of type DefaultListModel.) Then, the next statement passes the list model object to the JList constructor. The rest of this code is the same as the corresponding code in the previous figure.

The second code example shows the actionPerformed method of an action listener that adds a new item to the list when the user clicks the Add button. After determining that the event source is the Add button, this code gets the text the user entered into the Description text field and then calls the addElement method of the list model object to add the string to the list.

A frame that lets you add elements to a list

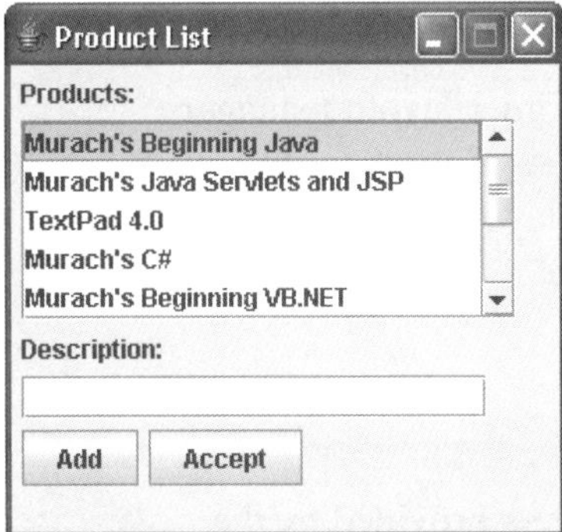

Some methods of the DefaultListModel class

Method	Description
`addElement(Object)`	Adds the specified object to the list.
`contains(Object)`	Returns a true value if the list contains the specified object.
`get(int)`	Returns an Object type for the element at the specified position.
`removeElementAt(int)`	Removes the element at the specified position.
`size()`	Returns the number of elements in the list.
`clear()`	Removes all entries from the list.

Example 1: Code that creates the list

```
String[] descriptions = getProductDescriptions();
productListModel = new DefaultListModel();
for (String s : descriptions)
    productListModel.addElement(s);
productList = new JList(productListModel);
productList.setFixedCellWidth(220);
productList.setSelectedIndex(0);
productList.setVisibleRowCount(5);
add(new JScrollPane(productList));
```

Example 2: Code that adds an element to the list

```
public void actionPerformed(ActionEvent e)
{
    Object source = e.getSource();
    if (source == addButton)
    {
        String s = descriptionTextField.getText();
        productListModel.addElement(s);
    }
}
```

Description

- To modify the contents of a list, you must first create a *list model* to access the data displayed by the list. Then, you pass the list model to the list via the JList constructor.
- The list model can be any object that implements the ListModel interface. The most commonly used model is the DefaultListModel class.

Figure 16-11 How to work with list models

How to work with layout managers

In chapter 15, you were introduced to the Flow and Border layout managers. Now, you'll be introduced to the rest of the layout managers of the Java API, and you'll learn how to use one of the most sophisticated layout managers, the Grid Bag layout manager.

A summary of the layout managers

Figure 16-12 presents a summary of the layout managers provided by the Java API. After the Flow and Border layout managers that you learned about in the last chapter, you can see the Card layout manager, the Box layout manager, the Grid layout manager, and the Grid Bag layout manager.

The first frame shown in this figure illustrates the Box layout, which arranges components in a single row either vertically or horizontally. To set the direction of the layout, you use the constructor of the BoxLayout class. The first code example in this figure shows the code used to create the box layout panel that's displayed by the first frame. Here, the setLayout method specifies a new BoxLayout object that uses Y_AXIS orientation, which means that the components added to the panel will be stacked vertically.

The second frame in this figure uses the Grid layout manager, which uses a rectangular grid to lay out components. With this layout, each rectangle in the grid is of equal size. To set the grid up, you specify the number of rows and columns in the constructor of the GridLayout class, and then pass the GridLayout object to the setLayout method of a panel or other container. Then, you add the components to the container.

If you use the Grid layout manager, you should realize that Swing sometimes adjusts the number of columns you specify based on the contents of the panel. For example, if you create a Grid layout with 4 rows and 3 columns and then add 8 components to the panel, the Grid layout manager will use just two columns instead of three.

Although the Box and Grid layouts aren't used much, they're easy to use if you ever need them. To learn more about these layout managers, you can look them up in the documentation of the Java API. (They're stored in the java.awt package.)

The Card layout manager lets you create a panel in which components are organized into tabs. Because this layout manager has been replaced by the JTabbedPane control, however, you shouldn't use it. To find out more about the JTabbedPane control, you can refer to the Java API documentation.

In contrast to the other layout managers, the Grid Bag layout manager is flexible and sophisticated. Because of that, it's used commonly. You'll learn how to work with this layout manager in the next two figures.

Examples of the Box and Grid layouts

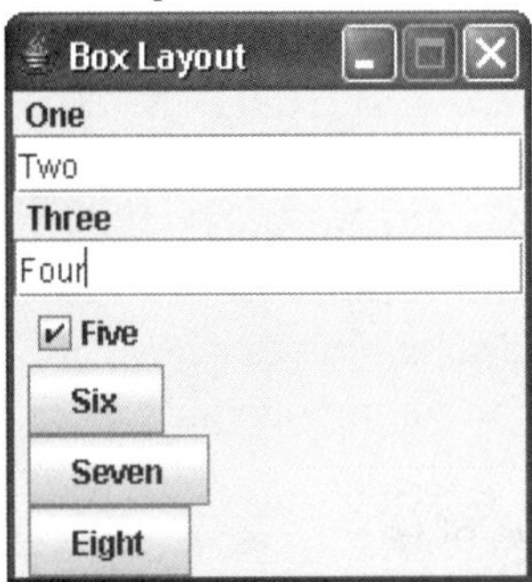

Summary of the layout managers

Layout manager	Description
FlowLayout	Lays out components from left to right as shown in chapter 15.
BorderLayout	Lays out components in five regions as shown in chapter 15.
CardLayout	Lays out components on a card where only one card is visible at a time. Rather than using this class, you can use the JTabbedPane class.
BoxLayout	Lays out components in a horizontal or vertical row of cells as shown above.
GridLayout	Lays out components in a rectangular grid of cells where each cell is the same size as shown above.
GridBagLayout	Lays out components horizontally and vertically in a rectangular grid as shown in the next two figures.

Example 1: Code that creates the Box layout panel

```
class BoxLayoutPanel extends JPanel
{
    public BoxLayoutPanel()
    {
        setLayout(new BoxLayout(this, BoxLayout.Y_AXIS));
        add(new JLabel("One"));
        add(new JTextField("Two"));
        add(new JLabel("Three"));
        add(new JTextField("Four"));
        add(new JCheckBox("Five"));
        add(new JButton("Six"));
        add(new JButton("Seven"));
        add(new JButton("Eight"));
    }
}
```

Example 2: Code that creates a Grid layout manager

```
setLayout(new GridLayout(4, 2));
```

Note

- The Box layout and Grid layout managers automatically resize each component to fill the available space. This often results in unattractive panel layouts, as shown above. You can avoid this problem by creating additional panels to hold the component or components you want in each cell and then adding these panels to the panel that uses Box or Grid layout.

Figure 16-12 A summary of the layout managers

How to work with the Grid Bag layout manager

Figure 16-13 shows how to work with the *Grid Bag layout manager*. Here, you can see a user interface with this layout along with the grid that's used to align the components in this user interface. When you use this layout manager, components can differ in size and be aligned both horizontally and vertically. Like the Grid layout, the Grid Bag layout uses a rectangular grid to lay out the components. But unlike the Grid layout, the Grid Bag layout allows components to be displayed in more than one cell.

To use the Grid Bag layout, you specify the location and size of each component within the grid. To do that, you can use the six-step procedure shown in this figure.

In step 1, you sketch the GUI and divide it into rows and columns. From this, you can see how many rows and columns each component will occupy. For instance, the sketch in this figure shows that the panel that contains the radio buttons will start at x = 0 and y = 0 and use 3 columns and 1 row. Similarly, the text field will start at x = 1 and y = 2 and use 1 row and 2 columns.

In step 2, you set the container's layout manager by calling the constructor of the GridBagLayout class. However, this class doesn't hold the size and positioning information. So in step 3, you create an object of the GridBagConstraints class to hold this constraint information.

In step 4, you set the constraints for each component. You'll learn more about how to do that in the next figure. Then, in step 5, you use the add method of the Container class with the component and its constraints as arguments. Finally, as step 6 shows, you repeat steps 4 and 5 for each component of the layout.

This figure also shows the pack method of the Window class, which is inherited by the JFrame class. This method lets you avoid the tedious task of manually setting the size of a frame. It's especially useful with the Grid Bag layout manager. Rather than use the setSize method for a frame that's formatted with the Grid Bag layout manager, you should use the pack method. (With other layout managers, the pack method often doesn't work as you'd expect.)

A user interface that uses the Grid Bag layout

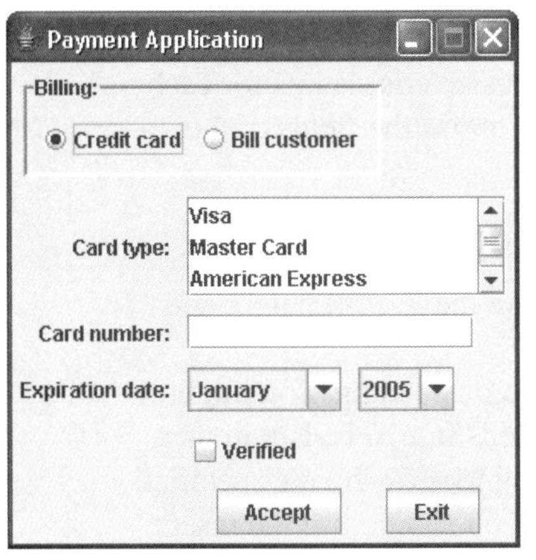

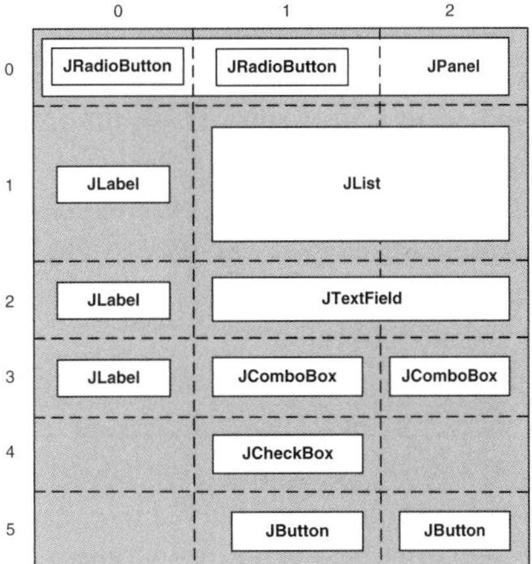

How to work with the Grid Bag layout

1. Diagram or sketch the user interface and divide it into rows and columns as shown above.
2. Set the layout to an object of the GridBagLayout class:

```
setLayout(new GridBagLayout());
```

3. Create a GridBagConstraints object to hold positioning data:

```
GridBagConstraints c = new GridBagConstraints();
```

4. Set the constraints in the GridBagConstraints object as shown in the next figure:

```
c.gridx = 0;
c.gridy = 0;
c.gridwidth = 3;
c.gridheight = 1;
c.insets = new Insets(5, 5, 5, 5);      // sets space around the cell
```

5. Use the add method of the Container class that specifies the component and its constraints:

```
add(Component, GridBagConstraints)
```

6. Repeat steps 4 and 5 until all components have been added.

The pack method of the Window class

Method	Description
`pack()`	Resizes the window to accommodate the components it contains.

Description

- The Grid Bag layout manager lets you organize a user interface using cells in a grid.
- When you use the Grid Bag layout manager, it's helpful to use the pack method of the Window class to set the frame size. That way, the size of the frame will automatically be set to accommodate the components that are added to it.

Figure 16-13 How to work with the Grid Bag layout manager

How to set the constraints for a Grid Bag layout

Figure 16-14 shows how to set the positioning and size constraints for each component in a Grid Bag layout. To do that, you need to use the fields of the GridBagConstraints class.

The first four fields in this figure let you set the size and position of each component. You use the gridx and gridy fields to set the starting position for the cell. You use the gridheight and gridwidth fields to state the overall height and width of the component in cells.

The names of the ipadx and ipady fields are a little misleading. You might suspect that they create padding that's used between cells in pixels. But in fact, they cause the size of each component added to the cell to grow by the specified amount. To create visual space between components, you should use the insets field instead. This field takes an Insets object that specifies the amount of empty space to leave at the top, bottom, left, and right of the cell.

The weightx and weighty fields specify how to distribute the extra space when the overall layout doesn't take up the whole container area. By default, the weightx and weighty values are set to 0 so the cells are spaced as close together as possible. If you want some extra space to appear between the cells, you can set these values to 100 for all components. Note, however, that the weightx and weighty fields don't work well in conjunction with the insets field. So if you use the insets field, I recommend you leave the weight fields set to 0.

The anchor field aligns components within a cell. If, for example, you want to align a component on the left edge of a cell, you can set the anchor constraint to WEST. To right-align a component in a cell, set the anchor field to EAST. The default setting is CENTER.

You use the fill constraint to determine what to do with any extra space in the cell. If, for example, you want a component to grow vertically so it fills the entire cell, you can set the fill constraint to the VERTICAL field. You'll usually leave this field set to the default value (NONE).

You can specify RELATIVE for the gridx, gridy, gridheight, and gridwidth fields to use relative positioning for component layout. For example, you can specify RELATIVE for the gridx constraint to place a component to the right of the previous field.

You can also specify REMAINDER for the gridwidth or gridheight field to specify when a component is the last in a row or column. That way, the layout manager knows to move on to the next row or column.

At this point, you should realize that using the Grid Bay layout manager can be tedious, but it's not that difficult. After you set the layout for the container to GridBagLayout and create the GridBagConstraints object, you just set the constraints for each component and add it to the container. This is an efficient way to design and code a layout for most applications.

Fields of the GridBagConstraints class

Field	Description
`gridx`	An int value that specifies the leftmost cell that the component occupies.
`gridy`	An int value that specifies the topmost cell that the component occupies.
`gridheight`	An int value that specifies the number of vertical cells that a component occupies.
`gridwidth`	An int value that specifies the number of horizontal cells that a component occupies.
`ipadx`	An int value that specifies the amount of internal horizontal padding to be added to each control.
`ipady`	An int value that specifies the amount of internal vertical padding to be added to each control.
`insets`	An Insets object that specifies the amount of empty space to leave on each side of the cell.
`weightx`	A double value that specifies how extra horizontal space is distributed if the resulting layout is horizontally smaller than the area allotted.
`weighty`	A double value that specifies how extra vertical space is distributed if the resulting layout is vertically smaller that the area allotted.
`anchor`	An int value that specifies the alignment of a component within a cell. You can use the fields below to set this constraint.
`fill`	An int value that specifies what to do with extra space in a cell. You can use the fields below to set this constraint.

Fields of the GridBagConstraints class that set the anchor field

```
CENTER      NORTHEAST      WEST      SOUTHEAST
NORTH       EAST           SOUTH
```

Fields of the GridBagConstraints class that set the fill field

```
NONE        HORIZONTAL     VERTICAL  BOTH
```

Other fields of the GridBagConstraints class

Field	Description
`RELATIVE`	For the gridx and gridy fields, this field specifies that the component will be placed next to the last added component. For the gridwidth and gridheight fields, this field specifies that the component will be the next-to-last component in a row or column.
`REMAINDER`	For the gridwidth and gridheight fields, this field specifies that a component is the last component in a row or column.

A constructor for the Insets class

Constructor	Description
`Insets(intTop, intBottom, (intLeft, intRight)`	Creates an Insets object with the specified spacing for the top, bottom, left, and right of each cell.

Description

- In most cases, you should set the insets field to create some visual space between cells. Otherwise, the components in the layout will appear jammed together.

Figure 16-14 How to set the constraints for a Grid Bag layout

An application that uses the Grid Bag layout manager

Figure 16-15 presents the code for the application that creates and uses the Payment frame that was shown in figure 16-13. Note that this frame uses all of the controls that were presented in this chapter except for a text area. As a result, you can study this code to see how the various types of Swing components are used together. Because most of this code is straightforward, I'll just point out some of the highlights.

First, the constructor of the PaymentFrame class uses the pack method rather than the setSize method to set the size of the frame. It calls the pack method after it adds the payment panel to the frame. Then, it calls the centerWindow method to center the window on the screen. Note that for the centerWindow method to work properly, it must be called after the pack method. That's because the pack method changes the size of the window to accommodate the components it contains.

The code that lays out the controls is found in the PaymentPanel class, which begins at the bottom of the first page of this listing. The code for this class starts by declaring the class variables that will be used to refer to the controls used by this application: two radio buttons, a list, a text field, two combo boxes, a check box, two buttons, and three labels.

The code for the Payment application

Page 1

```
import java.awt.*;
import java.awt.event.*;
import javax.swing.*;
import javax.swing.border.*;

public class PaymentApp
{
    public static void main(String[] args)
    {
        JFrame frame = new PaymentFrame();
        frame.setVisible(true);
    }
}

class PaymentFrame extends JFrame
{
    public PaymentFrame()
    {
        setTitle("Payment Application");
        setResizable(false);
        setDefaultCloseOperation(JFrame.EXIT_ON_CLOSE);
        JPanel panel = new PaymentPanel();
        this.add(panel);
        this.pack();
        centerWindow(this);
    }

    private void centerWindow(Window w)
    {
        Toolkit tk = Toolkit.getDefaultToolkit();
        Dimension d = tk.getScreenSize();
        setLocation((d.width-w.getWidth())/2, (d.height-w.getHeight())/2);
    }
}

class PaymentPanel extends JPanel implements ActionListener
{
    private JRadioButton creditCardRadioButton,
                         billCustomerRadioButton;
    private JList        cardTypeList;
    private JTextField   cardNumberTextField;
    private JComboBox    monthComboBox,
                         yearComboBox;
    private JCheckBox    verifiedCheckBox;
    private JButton      acceptButton,
                         exitButton;
    private JLabel       cardTypeLabel,
                         cardNumberLabel,
                         expirationDateLabel;
```

Figure 16-15 An application that uses the Grid Bag layout manager (part 1 of 4)

The constructor for the PaymentPanel class begins by setting the panel's layout manager to a GridBagLayout object. Next, it creates a beveled border that will be used to group the radio buttons. It then creates the various components used by the application and adds them to the panel.

As you review the code for the PaymentPanel constructor, you'll notice that the add methods that add the components to the PaymentPanel call a private method named getConstraints. You'll find this method at the bottom of page 3. The getConstraints method returns a GridBagConstraints object created using the values for the x, y, width, height, and anchor values passed to it as parameters. In addition, three other grid constraints fields (insets, ipadx, and ipady) are given default values. This method saves a lot of repetitive coding.

In the actionPerformed method shown on page 4, if the event source is the Accept button, a message that contains the information the user selected is formatted and displayed in a dialog box. (You'll learn how to use the JOptionPane class in the next chapter, so don't worry if you don't completely understand this code now.) Then, the controls are initialized so the user can make another selection.

If the event source is one of the radio buttons, the enableCreditCardControls method shown at the end of this listing is called to either enable or disable the credit card controls. For example, if the user clicks the Credit Card radio button, the controls are enabled so the user can enter credit card information. But if the user clicks the Bill Customer radio button, the credit card controls are disabled.

The code for the Payment application

Page 2

```
public PaymentPanel()
{
    setLayout(new GridBagLayout());

    Border loweredBorder
        = BorderFactory.createBevelBorder(BevelBorder.LOWERED);

    // radio button panel
    JPanel radioPanel = new JPanel();
    ButtonGroup billingGroup = new ButtonGroup();
    radioPanel.setLayout(new FlowLayout(FlowLayout.LEFT));
    radioPanel.setBorder(
        BorderFactory.createTitledBorder(loweredBorder, "Billing:"));

    // credit card radio button
    creditCardRadioButton = new JRadioButton("Credit card", true);
    creditCardRadioButton.addActionListener(this);
    billingGroup.add(creditCardRadioButton);
    radioPanel.add(creditCardRadioButton);

    // bill customer radio button
    billCustomerRadioButton = new JRadioButton("Bill customer");
    billCustomerRadioButton.addActionListener(this);
    billingGroup.add(billCustomerRadioButton);
    radioPanel.add(billCustomerRadioButton);

    add(radioPanel, getConstraints(0,0,3,1, GridBagConstraints.WEST));

    // card type label
    cardTypeLabel = new JLabel("Card type:");
    add(cardTypeLabel, getConstraints(0,1,1,1, GridBagConstraints.EAST));

    // card type list
    String[] cardNames
         = {"Visa", "Master Card", "American Express", "Other"};
    cardTypeList = new JList(cardNames);
    cardTypeList.setFixedCellWidth(170);
    cardTypeList.setSelectionMode(ListSelectionModel.SINGLE_SELECTION);
    cardTypeList.setVisibleRowCount(3);
    JScrollPane cardTypeScrollPane = new JScrollPane(cardTypeList);
    add(cardTypeScrollPane,
         getConstraints(1,1,2,1, GridBagConstraints.WEST));

    // card number label
    cardNumberLabel = new JLabel("Card number:");
    add(cardNumberLabel,
         getConstraints(0,2,1,1, GridBagConstraints.EAST));

    // card number text field
    cardNumberTextField = new JTextField(15);
    add(cardNumberTextField,
         getConstraints(1,2,2,1, GridBagConstraints.WEST));
```

Figure 16-15 An application that uses the Grid Bag layout manager (part 2 of 4)

The code for the Payment application

Page 3

```
        // expiration date label
        expirationDateLabel= new JLabel("Expiration date:");
        add(expirationDateLabel,
            getConstraints(0,3,1,1, GridBagConstraints.EAST));

        // month combo box
        String[] months = { "January", "February", "March", "April",
                            "May", "June", "July", "August", "September",
                            "October", "November", "December" };
        monthComboBox = new JComboBox(months);
        add(monthComboBox, getConstraints(1,3,1,1, GridBagConstraints.WEST));

        // year combo box
        String[] years = { "2005", "2006", "2007", "2008", "2009", "2010" };
        yearComboBox = new JComboBox(years);
        add(yearComboBox, getConstraints(2,3,1,1, GridBagConstraints.WEST));

        // verified check box
        verifiedCheckBox = new JCheckBox("Verified");
        add(verifiedCheckBox,
            getConstraints(1,4,1,1, GridBagConstraints.WEST));

        // calculate button
        acceptButton = new JButton("Accept");
        acceptButton.addActionListener(this);
        add(acceptButton, getConstraints(1,5,1,1, GridBagConstraints.EAST));

        // exit button
        exitButton = new JButton("Exit");
        exitButton.addActionListener(this);
        add(exitButton, getConstraints(2,5,1,1, GridBagConstraints.CENTER));
    }

    // a method for setting grid bag constraints
    private GridBagConstraints getConstraints(int gridx, int gridy,
    int gridwidth, int gridheight, int anchor)
    {
        GridBagConstraints c = new GridBagConstraints();
        c.insets = new Insets(5, 5, 5, 5);
        c.ipadx = 0;
        c.ipady = 0;
        c.gridx = gridx;
        c.gridy = gridy;
        c.gridwidth = gridwidth;
        c.gridheight = gridheight;
        c.anchor = anchor;
        return c;
    }
```

Figure 16-15 An application that uses the Grid Bag layout manager (part 3 of 4)

The code for the Payment application

Page 4

```
    public void actionPerformed(ActionEvent e)
    {
        Object source = e.getSource();
        if (source == exitButton)
            System.exit(0);
        else if (source == acceptButton)
        {
            String msg = "";
            if (creditCardRadioButton.isSelected())
            {
                msg = "Bill " + (String)cardTypeList.getSelectedValue() +
                    "\nNumber + " + cardNumberTextField.getText() +
                    "\nExpiration date: " +
                    (String)monthComboBox.getSelectedItem() +
                    ", " + (String)yearComboBox.getSelectedItem();
                if (verifiedCheckBox.isSelected())
                    msg+= "\nCard has been verified.";
                else
                    msg+= "\nCard has not been verified.";
            }
            else
                msg = "Customer will be billed.";
            JOptionPane.showMessageDialog(this, msg);
            cardTypeList.setSelectedIndex(0);
            cardNumberTextField.setText("");
            monthComboBox.setSelectedIndex(0);
            yearComboBox.setSelectedIndex(0);
            verifiedCheckBox.setSelected(false);
        }
        else if (source == creditCardRadioButton
                || source == billCustomerRadioButton)
        {
            if (creditCardRadioButton.isSelected())
                enableCreditCardControls(true);
            else if (billCustomerRadioButton.isSelected())
                enableCreditCardControls(false);
        }
    }

    private void enableCreditCardControls(boolean enable)
    {
        cardTypeLabel.setEnabled(enable);
        cardTypeList.setEnabled(enable);
        cardNumberLabel.setEnabled(enable);
        cardNumberTextField.setEnabled(enable);
        expirationDateLabel.setEnabled(enable);
        monthComboBox.setEnabled(enable);
        yearComboBox.setEnabled(enable);
        verifiedCheckBox.setEnabled(enable);

    }
}
```

Figure 16-15 An application that uses the Grid Bag layout manager (part 4 of 4)

Perspective

In this chapter, you learned how to work with some new components and the events generated by these components. In addition, you learned how to use the most sophisticated layout manager available from the Java API. You should now be able to create significant user interfaces on your own. However, you still need to know some additional techniques for working with events. And you need to know how to provide for data validation so that users can't enter invalid data. You'll learn these skills in the next chapter.

Summary

- You can create a *text area* that can store one or more lines of text, and you can use many of the same techniques to work with text fields and text areas.
- You can create two or more *radio buttons* that you can add to a *button group*. Then, the user can select one of the buttons in the group. You can also create a *check box* that lets a user check or uncheck the box.
- A *combo box* lets a user select an item from a drop-down list of items, and a *list* lets a user select one or more items from a list of items.
- You can add a component like a text area or list to a *scroll pane*, and you can add a *border* to any component.
- The *Grid Bag layout manager* is the most sophisticated and flexible layout manager. When you use the Grid Bag layout manager, you use the fields of the GridBagConstraints class to position components in a grid.

Exercise 16-1 Modify the Future Value application

For this exercise, you'll modify the Future Value application presented in chapter 15 so that it uses a combo box, a list, and the Grid Bag layout manager. When you're done, the user interface should look something like this:

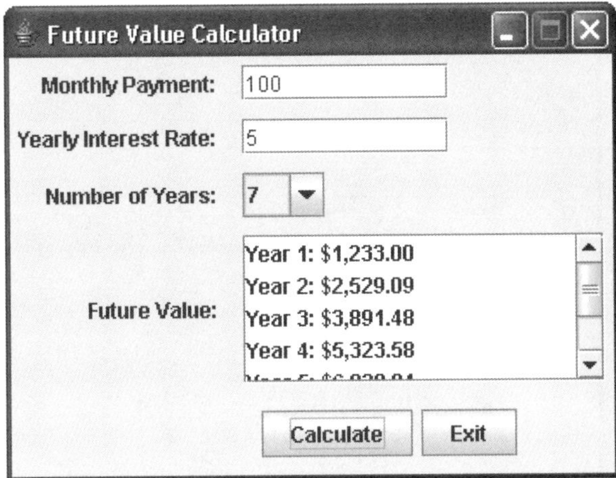

1. Open the FutureValueApp class in the c:\java1.5\ch16\FutureValue directory.
2. Modify the panel so that it uses the Grid Bag layout manager rather than the Flow layout manager. If you want to, you can use the getConstraints method that's shown in part 3 of figure 16-15 to help set the grid bag constraints.
3. Replace the Number of Years text field with a combo box that contains the values 1 through 20.
4. Replace the Future Value text field with a list that displays five rows and uses a vertical scroll bar.
5. Modify the action event listener for the Calculate button so that instead of calculating a single future value, it calculates the future value for each year up to the year selected via the combo box and adds a string showing the calculation for each year to the list.
6. Compile the program, then test it to be sure it works correctly.

Exercise 16-2 Create a Pizza Calculator application

For this exercise, you'll develop an application that calculates the price of a pizza based on its size and toppings. The user interface for this application should look something like this:

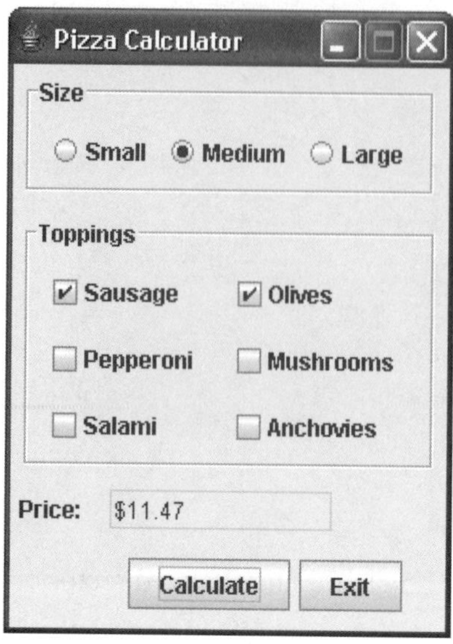

1. Decide what layout manager or combination of layout managers you want to use to implement the user interface, and then sketch the user interface and its rows and columns.
2. Open the PizzaOrderApp.java file in the c:\java1.5\ch16\PizzaOrder directory. This file contains a public PizzaOrderApp class with an empty main method.
3. Add the code necessary to implement this application. When the user selects a size and toppings for the pizza and clicks the Calculate button, the application should calculate the price of the pizza and display that price in the text field. To calculate the price of the pizza, add the price of the selected toppings to the base price of the pizza:

Item	Price
Small pizza	$6.99
Medium pizza	$8.99
Large pizza	$10.99
Sausage	$1.49
Pepperoni	$1.49
Salami	$1.49
Olives	$0.99
Mushrooms	$0.99
Anchovies	$0.99

4. Compile the program and test it to be sure it works correctly.

17

How to handle events and validate data

In this chapter, you'll learn several important Swing programming techniques related to event handling. First, you'll learn alternative ways to code the event listeners that handle high-level events such as button clicks and combo box selections. Then, you'll learn how to handle low-level events such as focus events and keyboard events. Finally, you'll learn how to incorporate data validation into your event handling code.

How to handle events

In chapter 15, you learned how to handle the event that occurs when the user clicks a button. Then, in chapter 16, you learned how to handle events that occur on other controls, like check boxes and combo boxes. Now, this chapter starts by presenting some conceptual information about events. Then, it presents several techniques you can use to implement event handling code.

The Java event model

Figure 17-1 shows how event handling works. Here, the first diagram shows how an event that's generated by a JButton component is handled. When the user selects the JButton component (either by clicking the button with the mouse or by moving the focus to the button and pressing the space bar), the JButton component generates an ActionEvent object. The ActionEvent object contains important information about the event, such as a reference to the component that generated the event (in this case, a JButton object). Next, the ActionEvent object is sent to an ActionListener object. The ActionListener object contains the code that responds to the event. For example, if the button happens to be the Exit button, the ActionListener responds to the ActionEvent object by terminating the application.

The second diagram is more general and introduces some key event-processing terminology. It shows that objects that generate events are called *event sources*, and the object that's created when an event occurs is called an *event object.* The event objects are sent to objects called *event listeners*. An event listener contains the code necessary to respond to a particular type of event.

Every class that represents an event source object has one or more methods that allow you to *register* event listeners for the events that can be generated by the object. For example, the JButton class has an addActionListener method that lets you register an ActionListener object with the JButton object. In effect, this method lets you inform the JButton object that your application is interested in processing action events that occur for this button.

What happens when a button is pressed

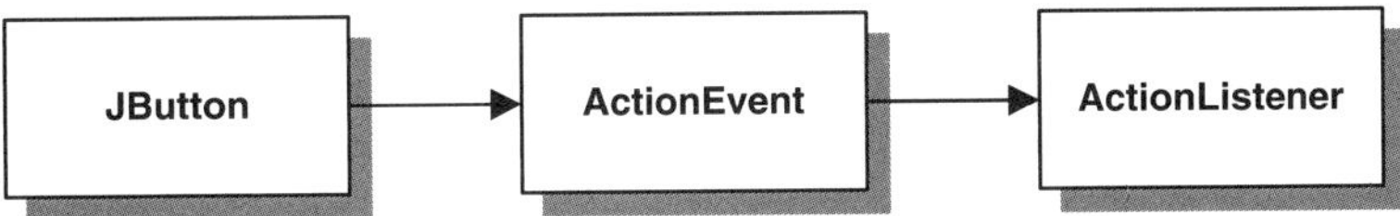

What happens when any event occurs

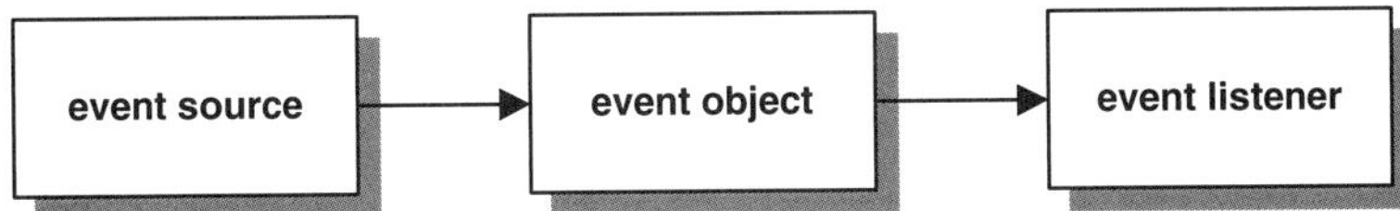

Description

- GUI applications depend on *events* that represent user interactions such as clicking a button or selecting an item from a list.
- All events are represented by an *event object* that derives from the EventObject class. The event object contains information about the event that occurred.
- An *event listener* is an object tht responds to an event. The class that defines an event listener must implement an event listener interface.
- A component that generates an event is called an *event source*.
- To respond to an event, an application must *register* an event listener object with the event source that generates the event. The class for the event source provides a method for registering event listeners. Then, when the event occurs, the event source creates an event object and passes it to the event listener so the event listener can respond to the event.

Figure 17-1 The Java event model

Two types of Java events

The tables in figure 17-2 summarize some common actions along with their events and listeners. These tables divide the events into two categories: *semantic events* and *low-level events*. In general, semantic events represent high-level user interactions with controls, while low-level events represent less specific events such as mouse movements or clicks or keyboard presses. In many cases, a semantic event can be generated in response to several different types of low-level events. For example, an ActionEvent is generated for a button if the user clicks the button with the mouse or if the user moves the focus to the button and presses the space bar. As a result, the semantic event (ActionEvent) can be triggered by either of two low-level events (KeyEvent or MouseEvent).

Whenever possible, you should write code to deal with semantic events rather than low-level events. For example, although you could add both a KeyEvent and a MouseEvent listener to a JButton object to respond to both key presses and mouse events, it's much easier to just use an ActionListener.

As you can see in these tables, some components generate more than one event. For example, when a user selects an item from a combo box, the combo box generates both an ActionEvent object and an ItemEvent object. You can provide listeners for either of these events. Sometimes, you'll choose the type of event that is more specific to the component, like an item event for a combo box because the user selects an item. Sometimes, you'll choose the type of event that works for most or all of the components on a panel, like the action event that can be used for buttons, combo boxes, radio buttons, check boxes, and scroll bars. Or, you can add both listeners and handle both events.

Since the Java event model depends on the Abstract Window Toolkit (AWT), most of the classes and interfaces in this figure are stored in the java.awt package and the java.awt.event package. However, some event classes and interfaces were added with the introduction of Swing and are stored in the javax.swing.event package. For instance, the javax.swing.event package contains the classes and interfaces that are used to respond to the selection of a list item and the change of a text component. To respond to these events, then, you must import the javax.swing.event package.

Semantic events

Action	Event object	Listener interface
Button clicked	ActionEvent	ActionListener
Combo box item selected	ActionEvent ItemEvent	ActionListener ItemListener
List item selected	ListSelectionEvent	ListSelectionListener
Text component changed	DocumentEvent	DocumentListener
Radio button selected	ActionEvent ItemEvent	ActionListener ItemListener
Check box selected	ActionEvent ItemEvent	ActionListener ItemListener
Scroll bar repositioned	AdjustmentEvent	AdjustmentListener

Low-level events

Action	Event object	Listener interface
Window changed	WindowEvent	WindowListener
Focus changed	FocusEvent	FocusListener
Key pressed	KeyEvent	KeyListener
Mouse moved or clicked	MouseEvent	MouseListener

Description

- Two types of events exist in Java: *semantic events* and *low-level events*. A semantic event is related to a specific component such as clicking a button or selecting an item from a list. Low-level events are less specific like clicking a mouse button, pressing a key on the keyboard, or closing a window.
- Most events and listeners are stored in the java.awt.event package, but some of the newer events and listeners are stored in the javax.swing.event package.
- Some user actions create more than one event. For example, both an ActionEvent and an ItemEvent are created when a user selects an item in a combo box. You can use listeners to respond to either of these events.

Figure 17-2 The two types of Java events

How to structure event handling code

Figure 17-3 shows a general procedure for handling events in a Swing application. In step 1 of this procedure, you create a class that implements the appropriate event listener interface. For example, to handle action events, you must declare a class that implements the ActionListener interface. This class must provide an implementation of the method or methods declared by the event listener interface. In the case of the ActionListener interface, a single method named actionPerformed is declared. As a result, your event listener class must provide an implementation for the actionPerformed method.

In step 2, you *register* an instance of the class you created in step 1 to the event source. To do this, you create an instance of the event listener class and then pass it to the appropriate method of the event source. For example, components that generate action events have a method called addActionListener. You use this method to register ActionListener objects that listen for action events.

This figure also lists four ways you can implement an event listener interface. The first is to have the panel class itself implement the event listener interface. Alternatively, you can create a separate class to define the event listener. This class can be a completely separate class, or it can be an *inner class* that's nested within the panel class or a special type of inner class called an *anonymous inner class*. You'll learn about these alternatives later in this chapter.

Finally, this figure indicates that if you have several components that generate the same event, you must decide whether to handle these events with a common event listener or provide a separate event listener for each component. For example, if your panel has two buttons, you can provide a single listener that handles the action event for both buttons, or you can provide a separate action event listener for each button. If you choose to use a common event listener, the event listener code is more complicated because it must determine which component generated the event. If you use separate event listeners, your code is more complicated because it has to include a separate class to listen for each component's events.

Note that this figure doesn't describe all of the possible alternatives for coding event listeners. As you gain experience with event listening, you'll see that there are still other ways to structure your event handling code besides these, including combinations of the techniques shown in this figure. However, the alternatives listed here and described in the next few figures will give you a good introduction to the flexibility of Java's event handling model.

Two steps to handle any event

1. Create a class that implements the appropriate listener interface. In this class, you must code an implementation of the appropriate listener interface method to respond to the event.
2. Register an instance of the listener class to the event source by calling the appropriate add*event*Listener method

Four options for implementing the listener interface

- Implement it in the panel itself
- Implement it in a separate class
- Implement it in an inner class within the panel
- Implement it in an anonymous inner class

Two options for handling multiple event sources

- Create one listener that handles all events for the panel
- Create a separate listener for each event

Description

- Although the basic procedure for handling events is straightforward, it is also very flexible. As a result, many variations are available.
- An event listener can be any object that implements the appropriate listener interface. As a result, you can place the code that responds to the events in a variety of locations.
- If two or more components generate the same event, you can provide a single listener to handle all the event sources, or you can provide a separate listener for each event source.

Figure 17-3 How to structure event handling code

How to implement an event listener in a panel class

Figure 17-4 shows how you can implement an event listener directly in a panel class. Here, the FutureValuePanel class both extends the JPanel class and implements the ActionListener interface. As a result, this class both defines the panel and serves as the listener for action events generated by the panel's components.

The FutureValuePanel class begins by declaring class variables for two buttons. These variables need to be declared at the class level so they can be accessed from both the class constructor, where the components are instantiated and added to the panel, and the actionPerformed method, where they are used to determine which button the user clicked to trigger the action event. In general, it's best to declare class variables for all of the components in the panel so you can access them from any method in the panel class.

In the constructor, the addActionListener methods register the FutureValuePanel object itself as a listener for action events generated by both of the buttons in the panel. They do this by specifying the this keyword as the ActionListener parameter. That's possible because the class implements the ActionListener interface.

The actionPerformed method is called whenever the user clicks either the Calculate button or the Exit button. This method calls the ActionEvent object's getSource method to get the object that generated the event. Then, it uses an if/else statement to respond accordingly, depending on which button was clicked. If the Exit button was clicked, the actionPerformed method terminates the application. Otherwise, it changes the text displayed by the Calculate button to "Clicked!" so the user knows that the button has been clicked. (Of course, in an actual application, this code would do something more useful. I coded this example this way to keep the code short so you can focus on how it's structured.)

The advantage of this technique is that it is simple. The disadvantage, however, is that it mixes the code that controls the panel's appearance with the code that controls its operation. That's not a problem for small panels with just a few controls, but for large applications with complicated user interfaces, mixing these code elements isn't a good idea. As a result, you should opt for one of the techniques presented in the following figures for more complicated applications.

Code for a panel that implements the ActionListener interface

```
class FutureValuePanel extends JPanel implements ActionListener
{
    private JButton calculateButton;
    private JButton exitButton;

    public FutureValuePanel()
    {
        calculateButton = new JButton("Calculate");
        calculateButton.addActionListener(this);
        this.add(calculateButton);

        exitButton = new JButton("Exit");
        exitButton.addActionListener(this);
        this.add(exitButton);
    }

    public void actionPerformed(ActionEvent e)
    {
        Object source = e.getSource();
        if (source == exitButton)
            System.exit(0);
        else if (source == calculateButton)
            calculateButton.setText("Clicked!");
    }
}
```

Description

- The easiest way to implement a listener interface is in the class that defines the panel or frame that contains the components that generate the events.
- When the panel or frame class itself implements the listener, you can specify the this keyword as the parameter to the method that registers the listener.
- This is the technique that was used by the Future Value application presented in chapter 15 and the Payment application presented in chapter 16.

Figure 17-4 How to implement an event listener in a panel class

How to implement an event listener as a separate class

Figure 17-5 shows how you can separate the code that creates a panel from the code that handles the events that are generated by the panel's components. In this case, two separate classes are defined. The FutureValuePanel class extends the JPanel class and defines the panel and its components. Then, the FutureValueActionListener class implements the ActionListener interface and handles the action events for the FutureValuePanel class.

The advantage of this technique is that it separates the code that controls the appearance of the user interface from the code that controls its behavior. Then, because the listener is defined by a separate class, you have to explicitly instantiate this class before you can register it as an event listener for any of the panel's components. That's what the first statement in the constructor of the FutureValuePanel class in this figure does. Notice that because the FutureValueActionListener class implements the ActionListener interface, an instance of this class can be assigned to a variable with the ActionListener type. After the ActionListener object is created, it is passed to the addActionListener method of the buttons.

A major disadvantage of using separate classes in this way is that the ActionListener object doesn't have direct access to the components on the panel. And, the code that processes the events for a panel invariably needs to access some of these components. The actionPerformed method in this figure, for example, needs to access the button components to determine which button the user clicked. As a result, you must provide some way for the event listener class to access the components in the panel class.

The easiest way to do that is to declare the components as public in the panel class and then pass a reference to the panel object to the listener class via its constructor. You can see how this works in the figure. Here, the calculateButton and exitButton variables are declared as public in the FutureValuePanel class. Then, when the FutureValuePanel class creates an instance of the FutureValueActionListener class, it uses the this keyword to pass a reference to itself to the constructor of the action listener class so that the action listener can refer to the panel. As you can see, the constructor of the FutureValueActionListener class stores this reference in a private variable named panel. Then, the actionPerformed method can access the panel buttons through this variable.

Code for a panel that uses a separate listener class

```
class FuturevaluePanel extends JPanel
{
    public JButton calculateButton;
    public JButton exitButton;

    public FutureValuePanel()
    {
        ActionListener listener =
            new FutureValueActionListener(this);
        calculateButton = new JButton("Calculate");
        calculateButton.addActionListener(listener);
        this.add(calculateButton);

        exitButton = new JButton("Exit");
        exitButton.addActionListener(listener);
        this.add(exitButton);
    }
}
```

Panel class

```
class FutureValueActionListener implements ActionListener
{
    private FutureValuePanel panel;

    public FutureValueActionListener(FutureValuePanel p)
    {
        this.panel = p;
    }

    public void actionPerformed(ActionEvent e)
    {
        Object source = e.getSource();
        if (source == panel.exitButton)
            System.exit(0);
        else if (source == panel.calculateButton)
            panel.calculateButton.setText("Clicked!");
    }
}
```

Listener class

Description

- If you implement a listener as a separate class, you'll need to provide a way for the listener class to access the source components and any other panel components that are required to respond to the event. One way to do that is to pass the panel to the constructor of the listener class and declare the components that need to be referred to as public.

Figure 17-5 How to implement an event listener as a separate class

How to implement an event listener as an inner class

One way to eliminate the complexity of accessing panel components from the listener class is to create the listener class as an *inner class* as described in figure 17-6. If you've read chapter 9, you should already understand how inner classes work. But now, you'll see that they're particularly useful for implementing event listeners.

As you can see in this figure, an inner class is a class that's nested within another class. In this example, the listener class (FutureValueActionListener) is an inner class of the panel class (FutureValuePanel). The FutureValuePanel class extends the JPanel class and contains the code that controls the appearance of the panel. The FutureValueActionListener class implements the ActionListener interface and contains the code that handles any action events raised for the panel.

The class declaration for the inner class is coded within the containing class (FutureValuePanel). As a result, the inner class has access to all the members of the containing class. For example, it can access the calculateButton and exitButton variables that are declared in the FutureValuePanel class. As a result, it's not necessary to declare the button variables as public or to pass the panel object to the constructor of the action listener class.

Code that implements the listener as an inner class

```
class FutureValuePanel extends JPanel
{
    private JButton calculateButton;
    private JButton exitButton;

    public FutureValuePanel()
    {
        ActionListener listener =
            new FutureValueActionListener();
        calculateButton = new JButton("Calculate");
        calculateButton.addActionListener(listener);
        this.add(calculateButton);

        exitButton = new JButton("Exit");
        exitButton.addActionListener(listener);
        this.add(exitButton);
    }

    class FutureValueActionListener
        implements ActionListener
    {
        public void actionPerformed(ActionEvent e)
        {
            Object source = e.getSource();
            if (source == exitButton)
                System.exit(0);
            else if (source == calculateButton)
                calculateButton.setText("Clicked!");
        }
    }
}
```

Panel class

Inner listener class

Description

- An *inner class* is a class that is contained within another class.
- An inner class has access to all of the members of its *containing class*. Because of that, inner classes are often used to implement event listeners.

Figure 17-6 How to implement an event listener as an inner class

How to implement separate event listeners for each event

All of the event listeners you've seen so far in this book have included code that determines which component generated the event. As figure 17-7 shows, however, you can often eliminate this code by creating a separate event listener for each component in a panel. For example, the code in this figure defines two event listeners as inner classes of the FutureValuePanel class. The first one, CalculateListener, handles the action event for the Calculate button. The second one, ExitListener, handles the action event for the Exit button.

These event listeners don't have to call the getSource method to determine which component generated the action event. Instead, the CalculateListener class can assume that the source is the Calculate button and the ExitListener class can assume that the Exit button is the source. As an added benefit, the FutureValuePanel constructor doesn't have to create a variable to hold a reference to the event listener. Instead, each listener's constructor is called directly from the statement that calls the addActionListener method to register the listener.

Because these advantages are minor and are offset by the need to create additional classes and instantiate additional objects, most programmers prefer to create event listener classes that listen for events from multiple components. Even so, you should at least consider the technique presented in this figure, especially for applications with complicated user interfaces.

Code that implements separate listeners for each event

```
class FutureValuePanel extends JPanel
{
    private JButton calculateButton;
    private JButton exitButton;

    public FutureValuePanel()
    {
        calculateButton = new JButton("Calculate");
        calculateButton.addActionListener(new CalculateListener());
        this.add(calculateButton);

        exitButton = new JButton("Exit");
        exitButton.addActionListener(new ExitListener());
        this.add(exitButton);
    }

    class CalculateListener implements ActionListener
    {
        public void actionPerformed(ActionEvent e)
        {
            calculateButton.setText("Clicked!");
        }
    }

    class ExitListener implements ActionListener
    {
        public void actionPerformed(ActionEvent e)
        {
            System.exit(0);
        }
    }
}
```


Description

- You can eliminate the code in the event listener class that determines the event source by creating a separate listener class for each component that raises the event. Then, you simply register an instance of each event listener class with the appropriate event source.

Figure 17-7 How to implement separate event listeners for each event

How to implement event listeners as anonymous inner classes

Some programmers prefer to use a Java feature called an *anonymous inner class* (usually just called an *anonymous class*) to implement event handlers. An anonymous class is a special type of inner class that isn't given a name and, as a result, doesn't require a separate class declaration. Instead, you declare the class body in the same statement that instantiates the class as shown in figure 17-8.

The syntax for creating an anonymous class for an event listener is shown at the top of this figure. As you can see, you code the new keyword, followed by the name of the listener interface the anonymous class will implement, followed by an empty set of parentheses. This is followed immediately by the body of the anonymous class enclosed in a set of braces. Note that the body of an anonymous class can't include a constructor. That's because the constructor must have the same name as the class, and an anonymous class doesn't have a name.

The code example in this figure uses anonymous classes to create the event listeners for the two buttons in the Future Value application. For the Calculate button, the addActionListener method creates an instance of an anonymous class that extends the ActionListener interface. The body for this anonymous class declares an actionPerformed method that uses the setText method of the button to change the text displayed by the Calculate button to "Clicked!".

Similarly, the addActionListener method for the Exit button creates an instance of an anonymous class that implements the ActionListener interface. This time, the actionPerformed method calls System.exit(0) to terminate the application.

Most programmers who use anonymous classes for event listeners do so because it results in concise code and because it places the code that handles the events generated by a component close to the code that creates the component. However, other programmers prefer not to use them because they think that the code that creates a component should be separated from the code that handles the events for the component.

If you choose to use anonymous classes for event listeners, you can often simplify your code by creating separate methods that actually do the work required by each event listener and then calling those methods from the anonymous classes. For example, suppose the actionPerformed method for the anonymous class used by the Calculate button required several hundred lines of code. Rather than include this code directly in the anonymous class, you could create a calculateFutureValue method for the FutureValuePanel class. Then, the actionPerformed method of the anonymous class could simply call the calculateFutureValue method.

The syntax for creating an anonymous class for an event listener

```
new ListenerInterface() { class-body }
```

Code that implements event listeners as anonymous classes

```
class FutureValuePanel extends JPanel
{
    private JButton calculateButton;
    private JButton exitButton;

    public FutureValuePanel()
    {
        calculateButton = new JButton("Calculate");
        calculateButton.addActionListener(
            new ActionListener()
            {
                public void actionPerformed(ActionEvent e)
                {
                    calculateButton.setText("Clicked!");
                }
            } );
        this.add(calculateButton);

        exitButton = new JButton("Exit");
        exitButton.addActionListener(
            new ActionListener()
            {
                public void actionPerformed(ActionEvent e)
                {
                    System.exit(0);
                }
            } );
        this.add(exitButton);
    }
}
```

Calculate button listener (anonymous inner class)

Exit button listener (anonymous inner class)

Panel class

Description

- An *anonymous inner class* is a class that is both declared and instantiated in one statement. Anonymous inner classes are often used as event listeners.
- To create an anonymous inner class for an event listener, specify the interface name for the event listener after the new keyword followed by parentheses. Then, follow this immediately with the class body enclosed in braces.
- Because anonymous inner classes force you to mix the code that creates a panel with the code that responds to the panel's events, I recommend that you avoid using them for any but the simplest event listeners.

Figure 17-8 How to implement event listeners as anonymous inner classes

How to code low-level events

So far, you've learned how to handle the semantic events that are generated by controls. Now, you'll learn how to work with low-level events, such as a mouse being moved or the user pressing a key on the keyboard.

A summary of low-level events

The first table in figure 17-9 presents a summary of low-level events. To handle these events, you need to implement the appropriate listener interfaces. Then, you need to add the listener to a component. Notice that, unlike the listeners for semantic events that often require only a single method, the listeners for low-level events require two or more methods.

The first five events in this figure can occur on any component. In other words, the Component class contains methods that let you add these event listeners to any component, as shown in the second table in this figure. The last event can be used only with the Window class because only this class has an addWindowListener method.

In the next two figures, you'll learn how to work with the FocusListener and KeyListener interfaces. Then, if you want to learn more about the rest of the low-level events, you can look up the interfaces for these events in the documentation for the Java API. All of these interfaces are stored in the java.awt.event package.

Common low-level events and listeners

Event	Interface	Methods
Moving the focus	FocusListener	`void focusLost(FocusEvent e)` `void focusLost(FocusEvent e)`

Pressing or releasing a key	KeyListener	`void keyPressed(KeyEvent e)`
		`void keyReleased(KeyEvent e)`
		`void keyTyped(KeyEvent e)`

Moving or dragging the mouse	MouseMotionListener	`void mouseDragged(MouseEvent e)` `void mouseMoved(MouseEvent e)`

Clicking the mouse	MouseListener	`void mouseClicked(MouseEvent e)`
		`void mouseEntered(MouseEvent e)`
		`void mouseExited(MouseEvent e)`
		`void mousePressed(MouseEvent e)`
		`void mouseReleased(MouseEvent e)`

Moving or sizing a component	ComponentListener	`void componentHidden(ComponentEvent e)`
		`void componentMoved(ComponentEvent e)`
		`void componentResized(ComponentEvent e)`
		`void componentShown(ComponentEvent e)`

Working with the window	WindowListener	`void windowActivated(WindowEvent e)`
		`void windowClosed(WindowEvent e)`
		`void windowClosing(WindowEvent e)`
		`void windowDeactivated(WindowEvent e)`
		`void windowDeiconified(WindowEvent e)`
		`void windowIconified(WindowEvent e)`
		`void windowOpened(WindowEvent e)`

Methods that add low-level listeners

Event source	Method
Component	`addFocusListener(FocusListener)`
Component	`addKeyListener(KeyListener)`
Component	`addMouseMotionListener(MouseMotionListener)`
Component	`addMouseListener(MouseListener)`
Component	`addComponentListener(ComponentListener)`
Window	`addWindowListener(WindowListener)`

Description

- Low-level listeners let you handle events such as mouse movements or key presses.
- The source for all of these events except the WindowListener event is the Component class. As a result, you can register listeners for these events with any object that derives from Component. That includes frames, panels, and controls such as buttons, labels, and text fields.
- The source for the WindowListener event is the Window class.

Figure 17-9 A summary of low-level events

How to work with focus events

Figure 17-10 shows how to work with *focus events*. To start, this figure describes the two methods declared by the FocusListener interface. You must provide implementations for these methods when you implement FocusListener. Next, this figure describes three methods you can use to get information about the FocusEvent object that's created when a focus event occurs. Then, it describes the selectAll method of the JTextComponent class, which is used by the first code example presented in this figure.

This example shows a class named AutoSelect that implements the FocusListener interface. The focusGained method in this class determines whether the component that generated this event is an instance of the JTextField class. If so, this method casts the component to a JTextField type and then calls the component's selectAll method to select all of the text in the text field. In effect, this class causes the text field to automatically select all of its contents whenever it receives the focus. For some data entry applications, this can result in faster data entry.

Note that this class also implements the focusLost method, but it leaves this method's body empty. As a result, the AutoSelect class doesn't do anything when a component loses focus. However, because the focusLost method is declared by the FocusListener interface, it must be implemented by any class that implements FocusListener.

The second code example shows how to use the AutoSelect class as a focus listener for a text field. Here, the addFocusListener method of the text field is called and passed a new instance of the AutoSelect class.

Methods of the FocusListener interface

Method	Description
`void focusGained(FocusEvent e)`	Invoked when a component that implements a focus listener gains the focus.
`void focusLost(FocusEvent e)`	Invoked when a component that implements a focus listener loses the focus.

Common methods of the FocusEvent class

Method	Description
`getComponent()`	Returns the component where the event occurred.
`isTemporary()`	Returns true if the focus is a temporary change.
`getOppositeComponent()`	A method introduced with JDK 1.4 that returns the other component involved in the focus change.

A method of the JTextComponent class

Method	Description
`selectAll()`	Selects all of the text in the text component.

Example 1: A class that implements the FocusListener interface

```
public class AutoSelect implements FocusListener
{
    public void focusGained(FocusEvent e)
    {
        if (e.getComponent() instanceof JTextField)
        {
            JTextField t = (JTextField) e.getComponent();
            t.selectAll();
        }
    }

    public void focusLost(FocusEvent e) {}
}
```

Example 2: A text field that uses the focus listener

```
paymentTextField = new JTextField(10);
paymentTextField.addFocusListener(new AutoSelect());
displayPanel.add(paymentTextField);
```

Description

- A *focus event* occurs when the focus moves to or from a component.
- To implement a focus listener, you must implement both of the methods of the FocusListener interface.
- The AutoSelect class in this figure automatically selects all the text in a text field whenever the user moves the focus to the text field.

Figure 17-10 How to work with focus events

How to work with keyboard events

Figure 17-11 shows how to work with *keyboard events* that result from keys being pressed. To start, it describes the three methods that must be coded to implement the KeyListener interface. Then, it describes some of the methods of the KeyEvent class. Next, it describes a method of the InputEvent class, which is inherited by the KeyEvent class.

The first code example in this figure shows a class named NumFilter that prevents the user from entering non-numeric characters into a text field. The keyTyped method of this class starts by calling the getKeyChar method of the KeyEvent object to get a char that represents the key that was pressed. Then, it uses an if statement to check if the user pressed a key other than a numeral, a decimal point, or a plus or minus sign. If so, the consume method of the KeyEvent object is called to stop the event processing. Although the code in this example helps reduce data entry errors by preventing the user from entering non-numeric characters, you should realize that the value could still be invalid. For example, the user could still enter an invalid number such as "3.2+48-2."

The second code example shows how to register an instance of the NumFilter class with a text field so the field will accept only numeric characters. Again, keep in mind that additional data validation must be done to make sure the user enters a valid numeric value.

Notice that the NumFilter class declares all three methods of the KeyListener interface, even though the keyTyped method is the only method that contains any statements. In the next figure, you'll learn how you can use adapter classes so you don't have to code these empty methods.

Methods of the KeyListener interface

Method	Description
`void keyPressed(KeyEvent e)`	Invoked when a key is pressed.
`void keyReleased(KeyEvent e)`	Invoked when a key is released.
`void keyTyped(KeyEvent e)`	Invoked when a key is pressed and released.

Common methods of the KeyEvent class

Method	Description
`getKeyCode()`	Returns an int code that represents the key pressed.
`getKeyChar()`	Returns a char that represents the key pressed.
`isControlDown()`	Returns a boolean that indicates if the Ctrl key is down.
`isAltDown()`	Returns a boolean that indicates if the Alt key is down.
`isShiftDown()`	Returns a boolean that indicates if the Shift key is down.

A method of the InputEvent class

Method	Description
`consume()`	Stops further processing of the event.

Example 1: A class that implements the KeyListener interface

```
public class NumFilter implements KeyListener
{
    public void keyTyped(KeyEvent e)
    {
        char c = e.getKeyChar();
        if (   c != '0' && c != '1' && c != '2'
            && c != '3' && c != '4' && c != '5'
            && c != '6' && c != '7' && c != '8'
            && c != '9' && c != '.' && c != '+' && c != '-')
            e.consume();
    }

    public void keyPressed(KeyEvent e) {}

    public void keyReleased(KeyEvent e) {}
}
```

Example 2: A text field that uses the key listener

```
paymentTextField = new JTextField(10);
paymentTextField.addKeyListener(new NumFilter());
displayPanel.add(paymentTextField);
```

Description

- A *keyboard event* occurs when a user presses, releases, or presses and releases a key.
- This example uses the keyTyped method to limit the user's input to numeric data.
- The KeyEvent class inherits the InputEvent class.

Figure 17-11 How to work with keyboard events

How to work with adapter classes

Since it can be tedious to code all the methods in a low-level listener interface just to use one of them, the Java API provides an *adapter class* for each of its listener interfaces. An adapter class is a class that implements all the methods of a listener interface but doesn't code any statements within these methods. Then, your listener class can inherit the adapter class and override any methods you want to code.

Figure 17-12 shows how to work with adapter classes. To start, it summarizes five adapter classes that correspond to five of the listener interfaces. Then, it shows versions of the AutoSelect and NumFilter classes that you saw in the last two figures that extend the adapter classes rather than implement the listener interfaces. As you can see, these versions of the AutoSelect and NumFilter classes don't contain empty methods. The implementation for these empty methods is provided by the FocusAdapter and KeyAdapter classes.

Common adapter classes

Class	Interface
WindowAdapter	WindowListener
FocusAdapter	FocusListener
KeyAdapter	KeyListener
MouseAdapter	MouseListener
MouseMotionAdapter	MouseMotionListener

Example 1: The AutoSelect class using FocusAdapter

```
public class AutoSelect extends FocusAdapter
{
    public void focusGained(FocusEvent e)
    {
        if (e.getComponent() instanceof JTextField)
        {
            JTextField t = (JTextField) e.getComponent();
            t.selectAll();
        }
    }
}
```

Example 2: The NumFilter class using KeyAdapter

```
public class NumFilter extends KeyAdapter
{
    public void keyTyped(KeyEvent e)
    {
        char c = e.getKeyChar();
        if (   c != '0' && c != '1' && c != '2'
            && c != '3' && c != '4' && c != '5'
            && c != '6' && c != '7' && c != '8'
            && c != '9' && c != '.' && c != '+' && c != '-')
            e.consume();
    }
}
```

Description

- An *adapter class* is a class that implements all the methods of a listener interface as empty methods. Then, an event listener class that inherits an adapter class must override only the methods that the program needs.
- Using an adapter class makes it unnecessary to code empty methods for the methods your application doesn't need to implement.

Figure 17-12 How to work with adapter classes

How to validate Swing input data

In chapter 5, you learned how to validate input data for console applications. Then, in chapter 6, you saw an example of a Validator class that uses static methods to help validate data for console applications. In the topics that follow, you'll see that you can use similar techniques to validate the input data for Swing applications.

How to display error messages

When you validate data in a Swing application, you need to be able to display an error message to inform the user that an invalid entry has been detected. The easiest way to do that is to display the error message in a separate dialog box as shown at the top of figure 17-13. To display a dialog box like this, you use the showMessageDialog method of the JOptionPane class as described in this figure.

The four parameters accepted by this method are the parent component that determines the location of the dialog box, the message to be displayed, the title of the dialog box, and a message type parameter that determines which of the icons listed in the figure should be displayed. The parent component parameter can be the control that's being validated or the panel or frame that contains the control. It can also be null, in which case the dialog box will be centered on the screen.

The code example in this figure shows how to display a simple error message. Here, I used the this keyword as the parent component. For that to work, this code must appear in a class that extends the Component class or a class derived from it, such as JFrame or JPanel. The error message itself is provided via a String variable, and the title is coded as a literal string. Finally, the message type is JOptionPane.ERROR_MESSAGE, which displays an error icon.

An error message displayed in a JOptionPane dialog box

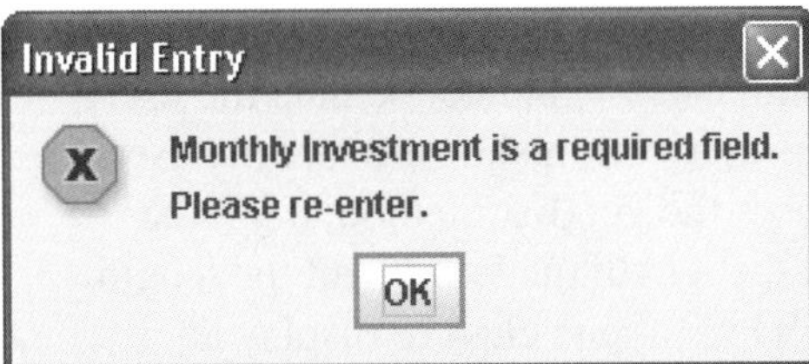

The showMessageDialog method of the JOptionPane class

Syntax

```
showMessageDialog(parentComponent, messageString, titleString,
  messageTypeInt);
```

Arguments

Argument	Description
parentComponent	An object representing the component that's the parent of the dialog box. If you specify null, the dialog box will appear in the center of the screen.
messageString	A string representing the message to be displayed in the dialog box.
titleString	A string representing the title of the dialog box.
messageTypeInt	An int that indicates the type of icon that will be used for the dialog box. You can use the fields of the JOptionPane class for this argument.

Fields used for the message type parameter

Icon displayed	Field
(none)	PLAIN_MESSAGE
i	INFORMATION_MESSAGE
!	WARNING_MESSAGE
X	ERROR_MESSAGE
?	QUESTION_MESSAGE

Code that displays the dialog box shown above

```
String message = "Monthly Investment is a required field.\n"
    + "Please re-enter.";
JOptionPane.showMessageDialog(this,         // assumes "this" is a component
    message, "Invalid Entry",
    JOptionPane.ERROR_MESSAGE);
```

Description

- The showMessageDialog method is a static method of the JOptionPane class that is commonly used to display dialog boxes with error messages for data validation.
- You can also use the JOptionPane class to accept input from the user. For more information, see the API documentation for this class.

Figure 17-13 How to display error messages

How to validate the data entered into a text field

Figure 17-14 shows two techniques you can use to validate the data the user enters into a text field. The first code example checks to make sure that the user has entered data into the field. To do that, it uses the getText method to get the text the user entered as a string. Then, it uses the length method to get the length of the string. If the length is zero, it uses the JOptionPane class to display an error message in a dialog box. Then, it calls the text field's requestFocusInWindow method to move the focus to the text field after the user closes the dialog box. Finally, it sets a boolean variable named validData to false. This variable can be tested elsewhere in the program to determine if the user has entered correct data into all input fields.

The second example shows how to check that the user entered a numeric value. Here, the parseDouble method of the Double class is used to parse the text entered by the user to a double value. This conversion is placed within a try statement. Then, if a NumberFormatException occurs, the catch block catches the exception, displays an error message, moves the focus to the text field, and sets the validData variable to false.

Example 1: Code that checks if an entry has been made

```
if (investmentTextField.getText().length() == 0)
{
    JOptionPane.showMessageDialog(this, "Monthly Investment is "
        + "a required field.\nPlease re-enter.",
        "Invalid Entry", JOptionPane.ERROR_MESSAGE);
    investmentTextField.requestFocusInWindow();
    validData = false;
}
```

Example 2: Code that checks if an entry is a valid number

```
try
{
    double d = Double.parseDouble(investmentTextField.getText());
}
catch (NumberFormatException e)
{
    JOptionPane.showMessageDialog(this, "Monthly Investment "
        + "must be a valid number.\nPlease re-enter.",
        "Invalid Entry", JOptionPane.ERROR_MESSAGE);
    investmentTextField.requestFocusInWindow();
    validData = false;
}
```

Description

- Like console applications, Swing applications should validate all data entered by the user before processing the data.
- When an entry is invalid, the program needs to display an error message and give the user another chance to enter valid data.
- To test whether a value has been entered into a text field, you can use the getText method of the text field to get a string that contains the text the user entered. Then, you can check whether the length of that string is zero by using its length method.
- To test whether a text field contains valid numeric data, you can code the statement that converts the data in a try block and use a catch block to catch a NumberFormatException.

Figure 17-14 How to validate the data entered into a text field

The SwingValidator class

Figure 17-15 shows a class named SwingValidator that I created to validate the data entered into a text component. Like the Validator class that was presented in chapter 6, this class uses static methods to perform common validation functions. Each of the three public methods in this class returns a boolean value to indicate whether or not the component passed the validation test. The private method is called to display an error message in a dialog box when an error is detected by one of the public methods.

Each of the public methods accepts two parameters. The first parameter is the control to be validated, and the second parameter is a string that contains the name of the field being validated. Notice that the first parameter is of type JTextComponent. Since both the JTextField and JText Area classes are derived from the JTextComponent class, that means these methods can be used with both text fields and text areas.

The isPresent method determines whether or not the user has entered data into a text component. The code in this method is similar to the code you saw in the first example in the previous figure. The isInteger method determines whether the value entered is a valid integer, and the isDouble method determines whether the value is a valid double value. The code in these methods is similar to the code you saw in the second example in the previous figure. Of course, you can easily extend this class to perform other types of tests, such as checking for valid dates or checking that a number or date is within a valid range.

The code for the SwingValidator class

```
import javax.swing.*;
import javax.swing.text.JTextComponent;

public class SwingValidator
{
    public static boolean isPresent(JTextComponent c, String title)
    {
        if (c.getText().length() == 0)
        {
            showMessage(c, title + " is a required field.\n"
                + "Please re-enter.");
            c.requestFocusInWindow();
            return false;
        }
        return true;
    }

    public static boolean isInteger(JTextComponent c, String title)
    {
        try
        {
            int i = Integer.parseInt(c.getText());
            return true;
        }
        catch (NumberFormatException e)
        {
            showMessage(c, title + " must be an integer.\n"
                + "Please re-enter.");
            c.requestFocusInWindow();
            return false;
        }
    }

    public static boolean isDouble(JTextComponent c, String title)
    {
        try
        {
            double d = Double.parseDouble(c.getText());
            return true;
        }
        catch (NumberFormatException e)
        {
            showMessage(c, title + " must be a valid number number.\n"
                + "Please re-enter.");
            c.requestFocusInWindow();
            return false;
        }
    }

    private static void showMessage(JTextComponent c, String message)
    {
            JOptionPane.showMessageDialog(c, message, "Invalid Entry",
                JOptionPane.ERROR_MESSAGE);
    }
}
```

Figure 17-15 The SwingValidator class

How to validate multiple entries

Figure 17-16 shows how you can create a single method to handle the validation testing for all of the controls on a frame. The first two examples show two different ways to code this method, named isValidData. Notice that both of these examples call the static methods of the SwingValidator class you saw in figure 17-15 to perform the validation tests for each control.

The code in the first example uses a series of nested if statements to test each condition that must be met for the input data to be considered valid. For example, the first two if statements test that the user entered a value for the monthly investment and that the value is a double. Similarly, the last two if statements test that the user entered a value for the number of years and that the value was an int. If any of these validation tests fails, a false value is returned to the calling method. If all of the validation tests succeed, the last statement in the method returns a true value to the calling method.

The second example performs the same validation tests as the first example, but it uses a compound conditional expression in a single return statement. Here, the validation tests are combined using the && (and) operator. That way, this compound expression will return a true value only if each of the separate calls to the SwingValidator methods returns a true value. If any of the SwingValidator calls returns a false value, the expression returns a false value.

Note that it's important to use the short-circuit and operator (&&) rather than the normal and operator (&). That way, if one of the SwingValidator calls returns a false value, the rest of the conditions aren't tested. As a result, an error message is displayed only for the first validation test that fails.

The third example in this figure shows how to call the isValidData method from an action event listener. As you can see, this method is called before the data is processed. That way, you can be sure that the data processing code will work correctly.

Example 1: Code that validates multiple entries with a series of if statements

```
public boolean isValidData()
{
    // validate investmentTextField
    if (!SwingValidator.isPresent(investmentTextField, "Monthly Investment"))
        return false;
    if (!SwingValidator.isDouble(investmentTextField, "Monthly Investment"))
        return false;

    // validate rateTextField
    if (!SwingValidator.isPresent(rateTextField, "Interest Rate"))
        return false;
    if (!SwingValidator.isDouble(rateTextField, "Interest Rate"))
        return false;

    // validate yearsTextField
    if (!SwingValidator.isPresent(yearsTextField, "Number of Years"))
        return false;
    if (!SwingValidator.isInteger(yearsTextField, "Number of Years"))
        return false;

    return true;
}
```

Example 2: Code that validates multiple entries with a compound condition

```
public boolean isValidData()
{
    return SwingValidator.isPresent(investmentTextField, "Monthly Investment")
        && SwingValidator.isDouble(investmentTextField, "Monthly Investment")
        && SwingValidator.isPresent(rateTextField, "Interest Rate")
        && SwingValidator.isDouble(rateTextField, "Interest Rate")
        && SwingValidator.isPresent(yearsTextField, "Number of Years")
        && SwingValidator.isInteger(yearsTextField, "Number of Years");
}
```

Example 3: Code that calls the isValidData method

```
public void actionPerformed(ActionEvent e)
{
    Object source = e.getSource();
    if (source == calculateButton)
    {
        if (isValidData())
        {
            // code that processes the data
        }
    }
}
```

Description

- When more than one field needs to be validated, it is best to put all the validation logic in a separate method that returns a boolean value to indicate whether or not the data is valid.
- The first and second examples above show two alternatives for validating multiple entries. Both use the static methods of the SwingValidator class.

Figure 17-16 How to validate multiple entries

The Product Maintenance application

The next two topics present the specifications and code for a Swing version of the Product Maintenance application that was first presented in chapter 8. This version uses many of the techniques presented in this chapter.

The specifications

Figure 17-17 presents the specifications for the Swing version of the Product Maintenance application. As you can see, the main frame for this application lets the user add, edit, or delete products.

To add a product, the user clicks the Add button. This causes the product code, description, and price text fields to be cleared and enabled so the user can enter data for the new product. In addition, the Add, Edit, and Delete buttons are disabled and the Accept and Cancel buttons are enabled. The user can then enter data for the new product and click the Accept button to add the product to the products data store and the combo box. Or, the user can click the Cancel button to cancel the entry. Either way, the frame reverts to its original state: the text fields are disabled, the Add, Edit, and Delete buttons are enabled, and the Accept and Cancel buttons are disabled.

To edit an existing product, the user first selects the product from the combo box. The product's data then appears in the text fields, which are still disabled so they can't be changed. Then, the user clicks the Edit button. This enables the description and price text fields (the application doesn't allow the user to change the product code), disables the Add, Edit, and Delete buttons, and enables the Accept and Cancel buttons. The user can then edit the description or price and click the Accept button to save the changes to the products data store. Or, the user can click the Cancel button to cancel the changes.

To delete a product, the user selects the product from the combo box and clicks the Delete button. This deletes the product from the products data store and removes it from the combo box.

The Product Maintenance application uses the same class design as the version that was presented in chapter 8. It includes a class named DAOFactory that gets an object that implements the ProductDAO interface. This data access object has methods that retrieve all of the products, retrieve a single product based on its product code, add a product, update a product, and delete a product. You may want to review chapter 8 (specifically, figure 8-9) for more information about how this class design works.

The Product Maintenance frame

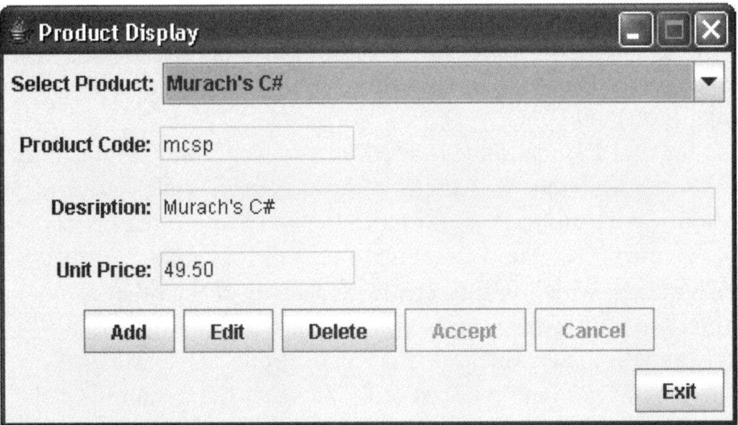

Typical dialog boxes displayed when invalid data is entered

Description

- The Product Maintenance application lets the user add, edit, or delete products. It is similar to the Product Maintenance application that was presented in chapter 8, but it uses a Swing interface rather than a console interface.
- To add a new product, the user clicks the Add button. Then, the Product Code, Description, and Unit Price text fields as well as the Accept and Cancel buttons are enabled. The user enters data for the new product and clicks the Accept button to accept the new product or the Cancel button to cancel the entry.
- To edit a product, the user chooses the product from the combo box, then clicks the Edit button. The data for the selected product is shown in the text fields, and the text fields are enabled. The user enters any necessary changes and then clicks the Accept button to accept the changes or the Cancel button to cancel the changes.
- To delete a product, the user chooses the product from the combo box and then clicks the Delete button.
- The Swing controls for this application are displayed in three panels within the main panel. The selector panel contains the combo box and the logic necessary to select a product. The product panel contains the labels and text fields for the product data. And the button panel contains the buttons and their event listeners.
- The class diagram for this application is almost identical to the class diagram that was shown in figure 8-9 of chapter 8. The only difference is that this application uses the SwingValidator class rather than the Validator class to do its data validation.

Figure 17-17 The specifications for the Product Maintenance application

The code

Figure 17-18 presents the code for the Product Maintenance application. Although it is eight pages long, its operation isn't that complex. Because of that, I'll just describe the highlights here.

To begin, the frame for this application (ProductMaintenanceFrame) is made up of four panels, named ProductMaintenancePanel, ProductSelectorPanel, ProductDisplayPanel, and ProductButtonPanel. The frame and each of the panels are declared as separate classes. The frame constructor creates an instance of the ProductMaintenancePanel class, which in turn creates instances of the other three panel classes. In addition, separate listener classes are used to handle the action events for the buttons. Note that the ProductSelectorPanel, ProductDisplayPanel, and ProductButtonPanel classes are inner classes of the ProductMaintenancePanel class as are the listener classes.

The ProductMaintenancePanel class, shown on pages 1 and 2 of this listing, begins by declaring instance variables for the data access object, an array list that will hold all the products, and a Product object that will be used to hold a new or modified product. It also declares variables for the three panel objects it will create. Then, the constructor of this class uses the data access object to populate the array list, and it creates instances of the panel classes.

The ProductSelectorPanel class, shown on pages 2 and 3, is responsible for displaying a combo box that lists all the products and responding appropriately when the user selects a product. To respond to this event, this class implements the ActionListener interface. The constructor of this class creates the combo box and calls the fillComboBox method to add the products to it. Then, it calls the addItemListener method to set the ProductSelectorPanel object as the listener for action events generated by the combo box.

Notice that the fillComboBox method sets a boolean variable named filling to true. Then, the actionPerformed method, which handles action events for the combo box, tests this variable. If it's true, the event is ignored. That way, action events aren't processed while the combo box is being filled.

The fillComboBox method is also called each time the product list changes. To accomplish that, this method is declared as public so it can be called from the appropriate classes. Similarly, the selectProduct method, which selects an item in the combo box, and the getCurrentProduct method, which gets a product from the combo box, are declared as public so they can be called from other classes.

The ProductDisplayPanel class, shown on pages 3 through 5, manages the text fields that are used to display and edit product data. The constructor for this class creates the labels and text fields that are displayed on the panel. Since the text fields are declared as public, they can be accessed from other classes in the application. In addition, the text fields are initially set so they are not editable and can't receive the focus. These properties change when the user adds or edits a product.

This class has six public methods. The showProduct method simply displays the code, description, and price for a specified product in the text fields. The clearFields method sets all three text fields to empty strings. And the getProduct method creates a new Product object using the data entered into the text fields.

The code for the Product Maintenance application **Page 1**

```
import java.awt.*;
import java.awt.event.*;
import javax.swing.*;
import java.util.ArrayList;

public class ProductMaintenanceApp
{
    public static void main(String[] args)
    {
        JFrame frame = new ProductMaintenanceFrame();
        frame.setVisible(true);
    }
}

class ProductMaintenanceFrame extends JFrame
{
    public ProductMaintenanceFrame()
    {
        setTitle("Product Display");
        setResizable(false);
        setDefaultCloseOperation(JFrame.EXIT_ON_CLOSE);
        this.add(new ProductMaintenancePanel());
        this.pack();
        centerWindow(this);
    }

    private void centerWindow(Window w)
    {
        Toolkit tk = Toolkit.getDefaultToolkit();
        Dimension d = tk.getScreenSize();
        setLocation((d.width-w.getWidth())/2, (d.height-w.getHeight())/2);
    }
}

class ProductMaintenancePanel extends JPanel
{
    ProductDAO productDAO;
    ArrayList<Product> products;
    Product newProduct = null;

    ProductSelectorPanel selectorPanel;
    ProductDisplayPanel productPanel;
    ProductButtonPanel buttonPanel;

    public ProductMaintenancePanel()
    {
        // fill the products ArrayList
        productDAO = DAOFactory.getProductDAO();
        products = productDAO.getProducts();
```

Figure 17-18 The code for the Product Maintenance application (part 1 of 8)

The code for the Product Maintenance application **Page 2**

```
        // add the panels
        setLayout(new GridBagLayout());
        selectorPanel = new ProductSelectorPanel();
        add(selectorPanel, getConstraints(0,0,1,1, GridBagConstraints.EAST));
        productPanel = new ProductDisplayPanel();
        add(productPanel, getConstraints(0,1,1,1, GridBagConstraints.EAST));
        buttonPanel = new ProductButtonPanel();
        add(buttonPanel, getConstraints(0,2,1,1, GridBagConstraints.EAST));
        // set the initial product to be displayed
        productPanel.showProduct(products.get(0));
        selectorPanel.selectProduct(products.get(0));
    }

    // a method for setting grid bag constraints
    private GridBagConstraints getConstraints(int gridx, int gridy,
    int gridwidth, int gridheight, int anchor)
    {
        GridBagConstraints c = new GridBagConstraints();
        c.insets = new Insets(5, 5, 5, 5);
        c.ipadx = 0;
        c.ipady = 0;
        c.gridx = gridx;
        c.gridy = gridy;
        c.gridwidth = gridwidth;
        c.gridheight = gridheight;
        c.anchor = anchor;
        return c;
    }

    class ProductSelectorPanel extends JPanel implements ActionListener
    {
        public JComboBox    productComboBox;
        private JLabel      productLabel;

        boolean filling = false;            // used to indicate the combo
                                            // box is being filled
        public ProductSelectorPanel()
        {
            // set panel layout
            setLayout(new FlowLayout(FlowLayout.LEFT));

            // product label
            productLabel = new JLabel("Select Product:");
            add(productLabel);

            // product combo box
            productComboBox = new JComboBox();
            fillComboBox(products);
            productComboBox.addActionListener(this);
            add(productComboBox);
        }
```

Figure 17-18 The code for the Product Maintenance application (part 2 of 8)

The code for the Product Maintenance application Page 3

```
    public void actionPerformed(ActionEvent e)
    {
        if (!filling)
        {
            Product p = (Product)productComboBox.getSelectedItem();
            productPanel.showProduct(p);
        }
    }

    public void fillComboBox(ArrayList<Product> a)
    {
        filling = true;
        productComboBox.removeAllItems();
        for (Product p : a)
            productComboBox.addItem(p);
        filling = false;
    }

    public void selectProduct(Product p)
    {
        productComboBox.setSelectedItem(p);
    }

    public Product getCurrentProduct()
    {
        return (Product) productComboBox.getSelectedItem();
    }
}

class ProductDisplayPanel extends JPanel
{
    public JTextField   codeTextField,
                        descriptionTextField,
                        priceTextField;
    private JLabel      codeLabel,
                        descriptionLabel,
                        priceLabel;

    public ProductDisplayPanel()
    {
        // set panel layout
        setLayout(new GridBagLayout());

        // code label
        codeLabel = new JLabel("Product Code:");
        add(codeLabel, getConstraints(0,0,1,1, GridBagConstraints.EAST));

        // code text field
        codeTextField = new JTextField(10);
        codeTextField.setEditable(false);
        codeTextField.setFocusable(false);
        codeTextField.addFocusListener(new AutoSelect());
        add(codeTextField, getConstraints(
            1,0,1,1, GridBagConstraints.WEST));
```

Figure 17-18 The code for the Product Maintenance application (part 3 of 8)

In addition, the setAddMode, setEditMode, and setDisplayMode methods call the setEditable and setFocusable methods of the text fields, passing a value that depends on whether the user is adding, editing, or displaying a product.

The ProductButtonPanel class, shown on pages 5 and 6, displays the application's buttons. This panel contains two panels: one for the maintenance buttons (Add, Edit, Delete, Accept, and Cancel) and one for the Exit button. It also contains a public method named setAddEditMode that's used to enable or disable the maintenance buttons depending on the operation that's being performed.

Notice in the code that creates the buttons that a different listener object is used to respond to the action event for each button. You can see the classes that are used to create these objects on pages 6 through 8. Each one implements the ActionListener interface and includes an actionPerformed method.

The AddListener class responds to the user clicking the Add button. Its actionPerformed method starts by creating a new Product object and clearing the data entry fields. Then, it calls the button panel's setAddEditMode method and the product panel's setAddMode method so the user can enter data for a new product. Note that this method doesn't actually add a new product. That's done after the user enters the data for the product and clicks the Accept button.

The EditListener class responds to the user clicking the Edit button. Its actionPerformed method simply calls the setAddEditMode and setEditMode methods so the user can edit the product. Again, the product isn't actually updated until the user clicks the Accept button.

In contrast, the actionPerformed method in the DeleteListener class actually deletes the selected product. To do that, it starts by getting the current product. Then, it deletes the product from the data store, and it removes the product from the products array list. Next, it reloads the combo box so it doesn't contain the deleted product, and it updates the combo box and the product panel to display the first product in the combo box.

If the user clicks the Accept button, the actionPerformed method of the AcceptListener class begins by calling the isValid method shown on page 8 to validate the input data. Notice that this method checks the newProduct variable for a null value to determine whether or not a new product is being added. If so, the product code field is validated. Otherwise, it isn't.

Assuming the data is valid, the actionPerformed method either adds a new product or updates an existing product depending on whether newProduct is null. To add a new product, it starts by getting the values for the product. Then, it adds the object to the data store, it refreshes the combo box so it includes the new product, and it selects that product. To update an existing product, it gets the current product and then creates a new product from the new values. Then, it assigns the new values to the existing product, updates the product in the data store, and updates the display. Finally, this method resets the controls on the form so the user can perform another operation.

If the user clicks the Cancel button, the actionPerformed method of the CancelListener class is executed. This method sets the newProduct variable to null, restores the panel to display mode, and calls the product panel's showProduct method to redisplay the data for the current product. This effectively discards any changes made by the user.

The code for the Product Maintenance application **Page 4**

```
        // description label
        descriptionLabel = new JLabel("Desription:");
        add(descriptionLabel, getConstraints(
            0,1,1,1, GridBagConstraints.EAST));

        // description text field
        descriptionTextField = new JTextField(30);
        descriptionTextField.setEditable(false);
        descriptionTextField.setFocusable(false);
        descriptionTextField.addFocusListener(new AutoSelect());
        add(descriptionTextField, getConstraints(1,1,1,1,
            GridBagConstraints.WEST));

        // price label
        priceLabel = new JLabel("Unit Price:");
        add(priceLabel, getConstraints(0,2,1,1, GridBagConstraints.EAST));

        // price text field
        priceTextField = new JTextField(10);
        priceTextField.setEditable(false);
        priceTextField.setFocusable(false);
        priceTextField.addFocusListener(new AutoSelect());
        priceTextField.addKeyListener(new NumFilter());
        add(priceTextField, getConstraints(
            1,2,1,1, GridBagConstraints.WEST));
    }

    public void showProduct(Product p)
    {
        codeTextField.setText(p.getCode());
        descriptionTextField.setText(p.getDescription());
        priceTextField.setText(p.getFormattedPrice());
    }

    public void clearFields()
    {
        codeTextField.setText("");
        descriptionTextField.setText("");
        priceTextField.setText("");
    }

    // return a Product object with the data in the text fields
    public Product getProduct()
    {
        Product p = new Product();
        p.setCode(codeTextField.getText());
        p.setDescription(descriptionTextField.getText());
        p.setPrice(Double.parseDouble(priceTextField.getText()));
        return p;
    }
```

Figure 17-18 The code for the Product Maintenance application (part 4 of 8)

The code for the Product Maintenance application

Page 5

```
        public void setAddMode()
        {
            codeTextField.setEditable(true);
            codeTextField.setFocusable(true);
            codeTextField.requestFocusInWindow();
            descriptionTextField.setEditable(true);
            descriptionTextField.setFocusable(true);
            priceTextField.setEditable(true);
            priceTextField.setFocusable(true);
        }

        public void setEditMode()
        {
            descriptionTextField.setEditable(true);
            descriptionTextField.setFocusable(true);
            descriptionTextField.requestFocusInWindow();
            priceTextField.setEditable(true);
            priceTextField.setFocusable(true);
        }

        public void setDisplayMode()
        {
            codeTextField.setEditable(false);
            codeTextField.setFocusable(false);
            descriptionTextField.setEditable(false);
            descriptionTextField.setFocusable(false);
            priceTextField.setEditable(false);
            priceTextField.setFocusable(false);
        }
    }

    class ProductButtonPanel extends JPanel
    {
        public JButton addButton,
                       editButton,
                       deleteButton,
                       acceptButton,
                       cancelButton,
                       exitButton;

        public ProductButtonPanel()
        {
            // create maintenance button panel
            JPanel maintPanel = new JPanel();
            maintPanel.setLayout(new FlowLayout(FlowLayout.CENTER));

            // add button
            addButton = new JButton("Add");
            addButton.addActionListener(new AddListener());
            maintPanel.add(addButton);

            // edit button
            editButton = new JButton("Edit");
            editButton.addActionListener(new EditListener());
            maintPanel.add(editButton);
```

Figure 17-18 The code for the Product Maintenance application (part 5 of 8)

The code for the Product Maintenance application

Page 6

```
        // delete button
        deleteButton = new JButton("Delete");
        deleteButton.addActionListener(new DeleteListener());
        maintPanel.add(deleteButton);

        // accept button
        acceptButton = new JButton("Accept");
        acceptButton.setEnabled(false);
        acceptButton.addActionListener(new AcceptListener());
        maintPanel.add(acceptButton);

        // cancel button
        cancelButton = new JButton("Cancel");
        cancelButton.setEnabled(false);
        cancelButton.addActionListener(new CancelListener());
        maintPanel.add(cancelButton);

        // create exit button panel
        JPanel exitPanel = new JPanel();
        exitPanel.setLayout(new FlowLayout(FlowLayout.RIGHT));

        // exit button
        exitButton = new JButton("Exit");
        exitButton.addActionListener(new ExitListener());
        exitPanel.add(exitButton);

        // add panels to the ProductButtonPanel
        setLayout(new BorderLayout());
        add(maintPanel, BorderLayout.CENTER);
        add(exitPanel, BorderLayout.SOUTH);
    }

    public void setAddEditMode(boolean e)
    {
        addButton.setEnabled(!e);
        editButton.setEnabled(!e);
        deleteButton.setEnabled(!e);
        acceptButton.setEnabled(e);
        cancelButton.setEnabled(e);
    }
}

class AddListener implements ActionListener
{
    public void actionPerformed(ActionEvent e)
    {
        newProduct = new Product();
        productPanel.clearFields();
        buttonPanel.setAddEditMode(true);
        productPanel.setAddMode();
    }
}
```

Figure 17-18 The code for the Product Maintenance application (part 6 of 8)

The code for the Product Maintenance application

Page 7

```
class EditListener implements ActionListener
{
    public void actionPerformed(ActionEvent e)
    {
        buttonPanel.setAddEditMode(true);
        productPanel.setEditMode();
    }
}

class DeleteListener implements ActionListener
{
    public void actionPerformed(ActionEvent e)
    {
        Product p = productPanel.getProduct();
        productDAO.deleteProduct(p);
        products.remove(p);
        selectorPanel.fillComboBox(products);
        selectorPanel.selectProduct(products.get(0));
        productPanel.showProduct(products.get(0));
        selectorPanel.productComboBox.requestFocusInWindow();
    }
}

class AcceptListener implements ActionListener
{
    public void actionPerformed(ActionEvent e)
    {
        if (isValidData())
        {
            if (newProduct != null)
            {
                newProduct = productPanel.getProduct();
                productDAO.addProduct(newProduct);
                products.add(newProduct);
                selectorPanel.fillComboBox(products);
                selectorPanel.selectProduct(newProduct);
                newProduct = null;
            }
            else
            {
                Product p = selectorPanel.getCurrentProduct();
                Product newProduct = productPanel.getProduct();
                p.setDescription(newProduct.getDescription());
                p.setPrice(newProduct.getPrice());
                productDAO.updateProduct(p);
                selectorPanel.fillComboBox(products);
                selectorPanel.selectProduct(p);
                productPanel.showProduct(
                    selectorPanel.getCurrentProduct());
            }
            productPanel.setDisplayMode();
            buttonPanel.setAddEditMode(false);
            selectorPanel.productComboBox.requestFocusInWindow();
        }
    }
```

Figure 17-18 The code for the Product Maintenance application (part 7 of 8)

The code for the Product Maintenance application — Page 8

```
        public boolean isValidData()
        {
            if (newProduct != null)
                return SwingValidator.isPresent(
                       productPanel.codeTextField, "Product Code")
                    && SwingValidator.isPresent(
                       productPanel.descriptionTextField, "Description")
                    && SwingValidator.isPresent(
                       productPanel.priceTextField, "Unit Price")
                    && SwingValidator.isDouble(
                       productPanel.priceTextField, "Unit Price");
            else
                return SwingValidator.isPresent(
                       productPanel.descriptionTextField, "Description")
                    && SwingValidator.isPresent(
                       productPanel.priceTextField, "Unit Price")
                    && SwingValidator.isDouble(
                       productPanel.priceTextField, "Unit Price");
        }
    }

    class CancelListener implements ActionListener
    {
        public void actionPerformed(ActionEvent e)
        {
            if (newProduct != null)
            {
                newProduct = null;
            }
            productPanel.setDisplayMode();
            productPanel.showProduct(selectorPanel.getCurrentProduct());
            buttonPanel.setAddEditMode(false);
            selectorPanel.productComboBox.requestFocusInWindow();
        }
    }

    class ExitListener implements ActionListener
    {
        public void actionPerformed(ActionEvent e)
        {
            System.exit(0);
        }
    }
}
```

Figure 17-18 The code for the Product Maintenance application (part 8 of 8)

Perspective

In this chapter, you've learned how to handle events generated by Swing controls and how to validate the data entered by the user. Now, if you understand the Product Maintenance application that's presented at the end of this chapter, you've come a long way. Once you master the data access skills that are presented in the next chapter, you'll have a solid set of skills for developing Java applications at a professional level.

If you're overwhelmed by all of the options for handling events, take heart. As you work with Swing applications, you'll find that each technique is useful in certain situations. Eventually, you'll come to appreciate Swing's flexibility.

One programming technique I didn't cover in this chapter is the new Swing data validation framework, which was introduced with Java 1.4. The data validation framework is based on focus events. As a result, it automatically invokes data validation code whenever the focus leaves a component such as a text field. Although the data validation framework is flexible, it's also tricky to program. If you want to learn more about it, consult the InputVerifier class in the Java API documentation.

Summary

- An *event* is an object that's generated by user actions or by system events. An event *listener* is an object that implements a listener interface.
- A *semantic event* is an event that's related to a specific component like clicking on a button. In contrast, a *low-level event* is a less specific event like clicking the mouse.
- To handle an event, you must implement the appropriate listener interface. Then, you must add an object created from the listener class to the appropriate component by using the add*event*Listener method, and you must code the methods of the listener interface.
- The class that creates the component that generates events can also serve as the listener for those events. In that case, you specify *this* in the add*event*Listener method.
- You can also use separate classes to listen for events. The benefit of this is that it separates the code that controls the appearance of the user interface from the code that manages the application's behavior.
- *Inner classes* are often used as event listeners because they can easily access the fields and methods of the class that contains them.
- *Anonymous inner classes* are sometimes used as event listeners because they let you easily create classes that are instantiated only once.
- To make it easier to code the listener interfaces for low-level events, the Java API includes *adapter classes* that contain empty methods for all of the methods in the listener interface.

Exercise 17-1 Implement an event listener as a separate class

1. Open the FutureValueApp file in the c:\java1.5\ch17\FutureValue directory, and save it in the c:\java1.5\ch17\FutureValueSeparateClass directory.
2. Review the code for this application to see that the ActionEvent listener for the Calculate and Exit buttons are implemented by the FutureValuePanel class.
3. Run the application to refresh your memory on how it works.
4. Modify the application so that the ActionEvent listener for the Calculate and Exit buttons is implemented in a separate class rather than by the FutureValuePanel class.
5. Compile the application, and test it to be sure it still works correctly.

Exercise 17-2 Implement an event listener as an inner class

1. Open the FutureValueApp file in the c:\java1.5\ch17\FutureValue directory, and save it in the c:\java1.5\ch17\FutureValueInnerClass directory.
2. Modify the file so that the ActionEvent listener for the Calculate and Exit buttons is implemented as an inner class within the FutureValuePanel class.
3. Compile the application, and test it to be sure it works correctly.

Exercise 17-3 Implement separate event listeners

1. Open the FutureValueApp file in the c:\java1.5\ch17\FutureValue directory, and save it in the c:\java1.5\ch17\FutureValueSeparateListeners directory.
2. Modify the file so that the ActionEvent listeners for the Calculate and Exit buttons are implemented as separate inner classes within the FutureValuePanel class.
3. Compile the application, and test it to be sure it works correctly.

Exercise 17-4 Implement the event listeners as anonymous inner classes

1. Open the FutureValueApp file in the c:\java1.5\ch17\FutureValue directory, and save it in the c:\java1.5\ch17\FutureValueAnonymousClasses directory.
2. Modify the file so that the ActionEvent listeners for the Calculate and Exit buttons are implemented as anonymous inner classes in the statements that call the addActionListener method for each button.
3. Compile the application, and test it to be sure it works correctly.

Exercise 17-5 Add low-level events to the Future Value application

1. Open the FutureValueApp file in the c:\java1.5\ch17\FutureValue directory.
2. Add low-level event listeners to this application so (1) the user is prevented from entering non-numeric characters into the text fields, and (2) the characters in each text field are selected automatically when the text field receives the focus.
3. Compile the application, and test it to be sure it works correctly.

Exercise 17-6 Add data validation to the Future Value application

1. Open the FutureValueApp file in the c:\java1.5\ch17\FutureValue directory.
2. Add data validation to the Future Value application so the user is prevented from omitting data or entering non-numeric data in the text fields. Use the SwingValidator class in the c:\java1.5\ch17\FutureValue directory to handle the validation. The user must enter data into all three of the text fields. In addition, the monthly investment and interest rate text fields must be valid double values, and the number of years text field must be an integer.
3. Compile the application, and test it by entering invalid data.

18

How to develop applets

In this chapter, you'll learn how to develop an applet, a special type of application that can be downloaded from an Internet or intranet server and run on a client computer within a web browser. Applets are unique to Java, and they helped fuel the remarkable growth of Java in its early days. In recent years, though, other technologies such as servlets, JSP, and DHTML scripting have taken over many of the tasks that used to be performed with applets. Nevertheless, applets are still commonly used for some types of applications such as online games.

An introduction to applets

This topic begins by showing a simple applet. Then, it discusses some security issues that apply to applets. Finally, it gives an overview of the classes and methods that you use to work with applets.

The Future Value Calculator applet

Figure 18-1 shows the Future Value Calculator application that was presented in chapter 15 after it has been converted to an *applet*. The main difference between this applet and the application is that an applet can be stored on a web server. For example, the applet shown in this figure is stored on the web server for the murach.com website. Then, this applet can be downloaded and run within a web browser that's running on a client machine. Another difference is that the applet doesn't include an Exit button. That's because it runs within a browser, not a frame. As a result, you have to exit from the applet by closing the browser or by navigating to another page.

A brief history of applets

Applets were introduced with version 1.0 of the JDK, which was released in 1996. In the early days of applets, both the Netscape and Internet Explorer browsers included versions of the JRE so that applets could be run within the browser. However, the version of the JRE that was included with Microsoft's Internet Explorer differed slightly from the version of the JRE that was provided by Sun and included with the Netscape browser. Worse, after version 1.1 of the JDK, Microsoft stopped upgrading its version of the JRE that was included with the Internet Explorer. As a result, when later versions of the JDK became available, the Internet Explorer couldn't run applets that used any of the newer Java features, including Swing.

To get around this problem, Sun developed the *Java Plug-in*. This piece of software is similar to other browser plug-ins such as Apple QuickTime that extend the browser's capabilities. It allows the browser to run Sun's current version of the JRE instead of the outdated and nonstandard version that's included by default with the Internet Explorer. Before the user can run an applet for the first time, the JRE, which includes the Java Plug-in, must be downloaded and installed. Sun maintains a website (www.java.com) that makes it easy for users to download and install the JRE and the Java Plug-in.

Another way to get around this problem is to develop applets that only use features in versions 1.0 and 1.1 of the JDK. This means that you must use AWT components instead of Swing components, and you can't use any of the features that were added to Java after version 1.1. However, Microsoft has recently agreed to stop enhancing its version of the JRE that's included with Internet Explorer and to phase out use of the JRE by 2007. This means that the Java Plug-in will be the only way to run Java applets in the future. As a result, neither Microsoft nor Sun recommend developing applets that rely on the JRE that's built into Internet Explorer.

The Future Value Calculator applet

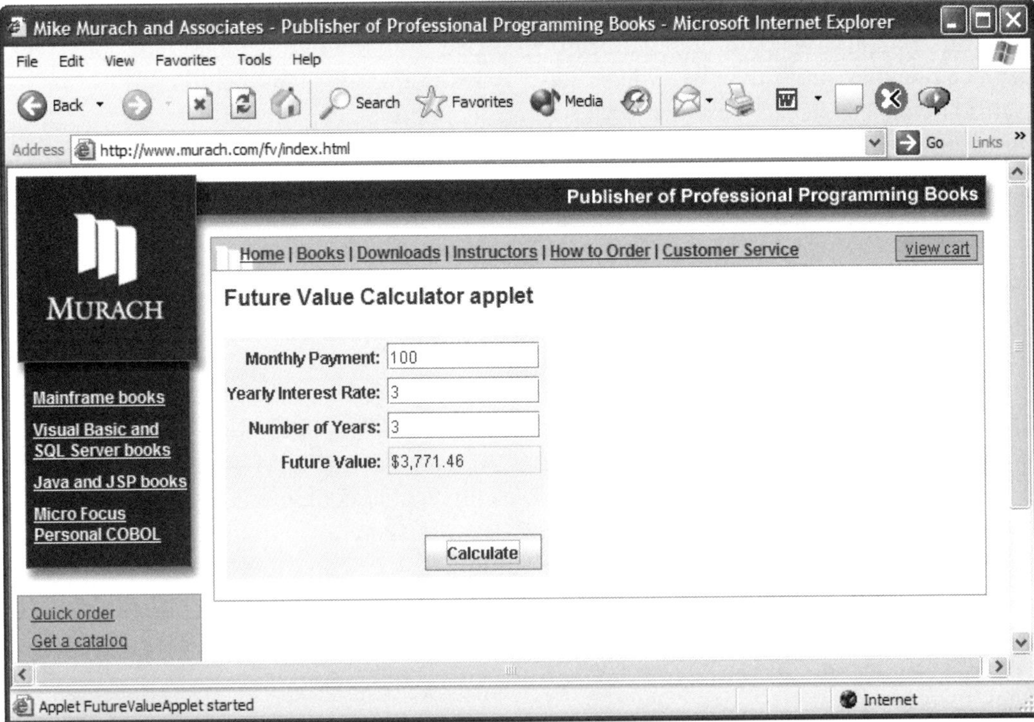

Description

- An *applet* is a special type of application that can be downloaded from an Internet or intranet server and run on the client's computer within a web browser.
- The *Java Plug-in* is included as part of the JRE. It is a browser plug-in that allows a web browser to use a version of the JRE that's newer than the one that's included with the browser.
- For a client machine to run applets, a current version of the JRE and Java Plug-in must be installed on the client.
- When you install the current version of the JDK, the current version of the JRE and Java Plug-in are automatically installed on your machine. For example, installing JDK 5.0 also installs version 5.0 of the JRE and Java Plug-in.
- If a user attempts to run an applet without first installing the current version of the Java Plug-in, a prompt will be displayed indicating that the Java Plug-in must be downloaded.
- The JRE and Java Plug-in can be downloaded from www.java.com. If necessary, you can provide a link to this site from your web page.

Applet security issues

Since applets were designed to be downloaded from the Internet and to be run on client systems, they have more security restrictions than applications. This prevents applets from intentionally or accidentally damaging the client system.

Figure 18-2 lists some of these security restrictions. This shows that an applet can't access any files or databases on the client system, and it can't access much information about the client system. In fact, an applet can only access the information it needs to run, such as the Java version and type of operating system that's used by the client.

Although applets have tight security restrictions by default, you can loosen these security restrictions. To do that, you can create a *signed applet* that shows that the applet comes from a trusted source. Then, an applet could, for example, read files from the client system's hard drive.

Although applets can't read and write files on a client computer, they can read and write files on Internet, intranet, and network servers. To do that, an applet can send and receive data from other programs located on the host server. This way, another program can read and write files and transfer the data back and forth to the applet. However, this requires some networking techniques that aren't presented in this book. That's why this chapter focuses on applets that don't work with files or databases.

What an applet can't do

- Read, write, or delete files or databases on the client system.
- Access information about the files or databases on the client system.
- Run programs on the client system.
- Access system properties for the client system except the Java version, the name and version of the operating system, and the characters used to separate directories, paths, and lines.
- Make network connections to other servers available to the client system.

What an applet can do

- Display user interface components and graphics.
- Send keystrokes and mouse clicks back to the applet's server.
- Make network connections to the applet's server.
- Call public methods from other applets on the same web page.

Description

- To prevent applets from damaging a client system or from making it possible to damage a client system, security restrictions limit what an applet can do.
- To overcome these security restrictions, you can create a *signed applet*. This indicates that the applet comes from a trusted source. Then, you can add rights to the signed applet.

Figure 18-2 Applet security issues

The inheritance hierarchy for applets

Figure 18-3 begins by presenting the inheritance hierarchy for the JApplet class that's stored in the javax.swing package. In the next figure, you'll learn how to extend this class to define an applet that uses Swing components.

The JApplet class inherits the older Applet class that's stored in the java.applet package. This class contains the methods that control the execution of an applet.

The JApplet class also inherits the Component, Container, and Panel classes. As a result, you can call methods of these classes to work with the applet, to place other components on the applet, and to handle the events that are generated for the applet. Since you've already learned how to use these classes, you should already have most of the skills that you need for developing applets.

Four methods of an applet

Figure 18-3 also introduces the four methods of the Applet class that are used to control the execution of any applet. Since the browser automatically calls these methods, you don't need to call them explicitly. However, when you write the code for an applet, you need to override one or more of these methods to provide the functionality of your applet. In the next figure, for example, you'll see how to override the init method to initialize an applet.

The inheritance hierarchy for a Swing applet

```
java.awt.Component
    java.awt.Container
        java.awt.Panel
            java.applet.Applet
                javax.swing.JApplet
```

Four methods of the Applet class

Method	Description
`public void init()`	Called when the browser first loads the applet.
`public void start()`	Called after the init method and every time the user moves to the web page for the applet.
`public void stop()`	Called before the destroy method and every time the user moves to another web page.
`public void destroy()`	Called when the user exits the browser.

Description

- To create a Swing applet, you define a class that extends the JApplet class. This class is stored in the javax.swing package, and it inherits the Applet class in the java.applet package.
- Once you define a class that extends the JApplet class, you can override any of the four methods of the Applet class that's stored in the java.applet package. These methods are called automatically by the browser as indicated above, and they control the execution of the applet.
- The JApplet class also inherits the Component, Container, and Panel classes. As a result, you can call methods of these classes when you code an applet.

Figure 18-3 The inheritance hierarchy and methods of an applet

How to develop and test applets

In this topic, you'll learn how to develop and test an applet. More specifically, you'll learn how to write the code for an applet, how to code the web page for the applet, how to test the applet using a tool that comes with the JDK, how to convert the web page so it will run in a browser, and how to test the applet from a browser.

How to code an applet

Instead of showing you how to code an applet from scratch, figure 18-4 shows you how to convert the Future Value Calculator application that was presented in chapter 15 (figure 15-14) to an applet. That way, you can focus on the code that's specific to an applet and not get distracted by the code for the Swing components.

To start, this figure shows a class named FutureValueApplet that extends the JApplet class. This class begins by overriding the init method of the Applet class. This is the method that's called when the web browser loads the applet. It consists of just two statements. The first statement creates a JPanel object from the FutureValuePanel class. Then, the second statement adds the JPanel object to the content pane. If you've read chapter 15, you shouldn't have any trouble understanding these statements. In fact, these same two statements are included in the constructor of the FutureValueFrame class that's presented in figure 15-14, and they work the same within a frame as they do within an applet.

This figure also presents an outline of the code for the FutureValuePanel class. This outline indicates the changes that need to be made to the FutureValuePanel class that was presented in chapter 15 to make it work with an applet. As you can see, all references to the Exit button need to be removed. In other words, this class shouldn't contain an instance variable that refers to the Exit button, the constructor shouldn't create an Exit button, and the actionPerformed method shouldn't handle the event that's generated when the user clicks the Exit button.

The code for the Future Value Calculator applet

```
import java.awt.*;
import javax.swing.*;

public class FutureValueApplet extends JApplet
{
    public void init()
    {
        JPanel panel = new FutureValuePanel();
        this.add(panel);
    }
}
```

How to modify the code for the FutureValuePanel class so it can be used with an applet

```
public class FutureValuePanel extends JPanel implements ActionListener
{
    // the declarations should not include an Exit button

    public FutureValuePanel()
    {
        // the constructor should not create an Exit button
    }

    public void actionPerformed(ActionEvent e)
    {
        // the ActionListener should not respond to the Exit button
    }
}
```

Description

- The two statements in the init method of the FutureValueApplet class are also in the constructor of the FutureValueFrame class that was presented in chapter 15 (figure 15-14). These statements add an instance of the FutureValuePanel class to the content pane.
- Any panels that are added to an applet's content pane should not contain any code that attempts to exit from the pane. For example, to convert the FutureValuePanel class of chapter 15 so it can be used for an applet, you need to remove all code that displays and responds to the Exit button.

Figure 18-4 How to code an applet

How to code the HTML page for an applet

Figure 18-5 shows the code for an HTML page that includes an applet. To code an HTML page, you can use the HTML *tags* described in this figure. To code a tag, you start with a tag name (like <html>) and end with the tag name preceded by a slash (like </html>). As you code, you'll often need to nest one tag within another tag. For instance, the HTML tag marks the start and end of an HTML page, so all of the other tags are nested within it. Similarly, the HEAD tag is coded around all code that makes up the header for the page, such as the TITLE tag that defines the text that's displayed in the browser's title bar.

The BODY tag is coded around all of the code that makes up the body of the HTML page. In this figure, for example, the H1 tag displays "Future Value Calculator applet" as a level-1 heading. Then, the APPLET tag tells the browser to display the specified applet with the specified width and height.

When you code the APPLET tag, you can use the *attributes* shown in this figure to provide information about the applet. In particular, you use the CODE attribute to specify the class file for the applet, and you use the WIDTH and HEIGHT attributes to specify the size of the applet in pixels. Within the APPLET tag, the P tag defines a paragraph that will be displayed if the browser can't display the applet. Just before this tag, an HTML comment is used to describe the P tag.

Once you code the APPLET tag, you can use the HTML Converter application described in figure 18-7 to generate the OBJECT and EMBED tags from the APPLET tag. These tags are used by the Internet Explorer and Netscape browsers and contain many complex attributes that aren't described in this figure.

To enter and edit an HTML page, you can use any text editor, but you must save the HTML page in a file with *html* or *htm* as the extension. For example, you might want to save the HTML page for the Future Value Calculator applet with a file name of "future_value.html." Although TextPad has some features for working with HTML, you may want to get a text editor that's designed specifically for working with HTML if you work with it more extensively.

Unlike Java, HTML is not case-sensitive. As a result, you can use whatever capitalization you like when coding HTML tags and attributes. In practice, however, lowercase letters are often used for HTML tags as shown in this chapter.

An HTML page that includes the Future Value Calculator applet

```
<html>
  <head>
    <title>Future Value Calculator applet</title>
  </head>

  <body>
    <h1>Future Value Calculator applet</h1>
    <applet code = "FutureValueApplet.class" width = 240 height = 175>
      <!-- If the browser can't display the applet, display this HTML -->
      <p>This applet requires version 1.5 or later of Java.</p>
    </applet>
  </body>
</html>
```

Some HTML tags

Tag	Description
`<html></html>`	Marks the beginning and end of an HTML document.
`<head></head>`	Marks the beginning and end of the head of the HTML document.
`<title></title>`	Defines the title that's displayed in the title bar of the browser.
`<body></body>`	Marks the beginning and end of the body of the HTML document.
`<h1></h1>`	Displays the enclosed text as a level-1 header.
`<p></p>`	Displays the enclosed text as a paragraph.
`<applet></applet>`	Defines an applet within the HTML page. After you code this tag, you can use the HTML Converter as described in figure 18-7 to convert this tag to OBJECT and EMBED tags.
`<object></object>`	Defines an object within the HTML page. Internet Explorer uses this tag to define applets.
`<embed></embed>`	Embeds an application within the HTML page. Netscape uses this tag to define applets.

Some attributes for working with the APPLET tag

Attribute	Description
`code`	Specifies the class name of the code to be executed.
`width`	Specifies the width of the applet in pixels.
`height`	Specifies the height of the applet in pixels.

An HTML comment

```
<!-- This is an HTML comment -->
```

Description

- The *Hypertext Markup Language* (HTML) is the language that's used to create web pages. Each HTML *tag* begins with the tag name and ends with the tag name prefixed by a forward slash. Within a tag, you can set the *attributes* for the tag.
- Although HTML isn't case-sensitive, the name of the Java applet class is.

Figure 18-5 How to code the HTML page for an applet

How to test an applet with the Applet Viewer

Figure 18-6 shows how to view an applet with the Applet Viewer, a tool that's included in the JDK. You can use the Applet Viewer to test applets without using a web browser. Then, once you're confident that the applet is working correctly, you can use the HTML Converter application described in the next figure so you can test the applet in a browser.

To run the Applet Viewer from TextPad, you open the source code for the applet and select the Run Java Applet command from the Tools menu or press Ctrl+3. If you use this technique, you should realize that you don't need to create the HTML page first. That's because TextPad will automatically create a temporary HTML page for you if one doesn't already exist. If an HTML page does exist, however, TextPad will provide a dialog box that lets you select that HTML page.

To run the Applet Viewer from the command prompt, you must code an HTML page for the applet. Then, you start the command prompt, navigate to the directory that holds the HTML file, and enter the appletviewer command followed by the name of the HTML file.

When you use the Applet Viewer, you should realize that it only displays the applet, not any other text that's included in the HTML file. Nevertheless, this is a quick way to test an applet before you run the HTML Converter and do the final testing using a web browser.

An applet in the Applet Viewer

How to run the Applet Viewer from TextPad

- Open the source code file for the applet. Then, select the Run Java Applet command from the Tools menu or press Ctrl+3.
- If you have not created an HTML page for the applet or the page is stored in a different directory than the applet, TextPad will automatically create a temporary HTML page for you. Otherwise, the Applet Viewer will use the existing HTML page.

How to run the Applet Viewer from the command prompt

- Start the command prompt, and navigate to the directory that contains the HTML page you want to test. Then, enter the appletviewer command followed by the name of the HTML page like this:

```
C:\java1.5\ch18\FutureValue>appletviewer future_value.html
```

Description

- The Applet Viewer that's included in the JDK lets you test an applet before you run it in a browser.
- When you run the Applet Viewer, you will see the applet but you won't see any other elements that are defined by the HTML page.

Note

- If you have already created the HTML page for the applet and used the HTML Converter to convert the page as described in figure 18-7, the Applet Viewer may display the applet twice: once for the OBJECT tag and once for the EMBED tag.

Figure 18-6 How to test an applet with the Applet Viewer

How to convert the HTML page for an applet

To convert the APPLET tag in an HTML page to the OBJECT and EMBED tags that are used by the Internet Explorer and Netscape browsers, you can use the Java Plug-in HTML Converter application. To start this application from Windows, you can use the Windows Explorer to navigate to the JDK's bin directory. Then, you can double-click on the HtmlConverter.exe file. This displays the HTML Converter dialog box shown in figure 18-7.

From the HTML Converter dialog box, you can specify the file or files that you want to convert. Then, the folder for the backup files will be set automatically, which is usually what you want. To convert the HTML files, you just click on the Convert button. When you do, the converter moves the original HTML files to the backup directory before it converts them. In this figure, for example, the future_value.html file in the C:\java1.5\ch18\FutureValue folder will be stored in the C:\java1.5\ch18\FutureValue_BAK folder before it's converted.

By default, the HTML converter creates an HTML page that's designed to work with the Internet Explorer (IE) and Netscape (Navigator) browsers on the Windows and Solaris operating systems. That's adequate for most applets. If you need to create a page that can be used by other browsers and operating systems, however, you can select a different Template File option.

To create an HTML page that will help users upgrade their JREs to version 5.0 (1.5) or higher, the HTML Converter uses the second Java Versioning option by default. Then, if the user doesn't have version 5.0 or higher, the newest version will be downloaded automatically if possible. If that's not what you want, you can select the first Java Versioning option. Then, the applet will use only JRE version 5.0. If that version isn't installed, it will be downloaded automatically if possible, even if a newer version is available. Sometimes the converted web page won't be able to automatically download the JRE. In that case, the converted web page will redirect the user to a page on the java.sun.com web site where the user can manually download the appropriate version of the JRE.

The HTML Converter dialog box

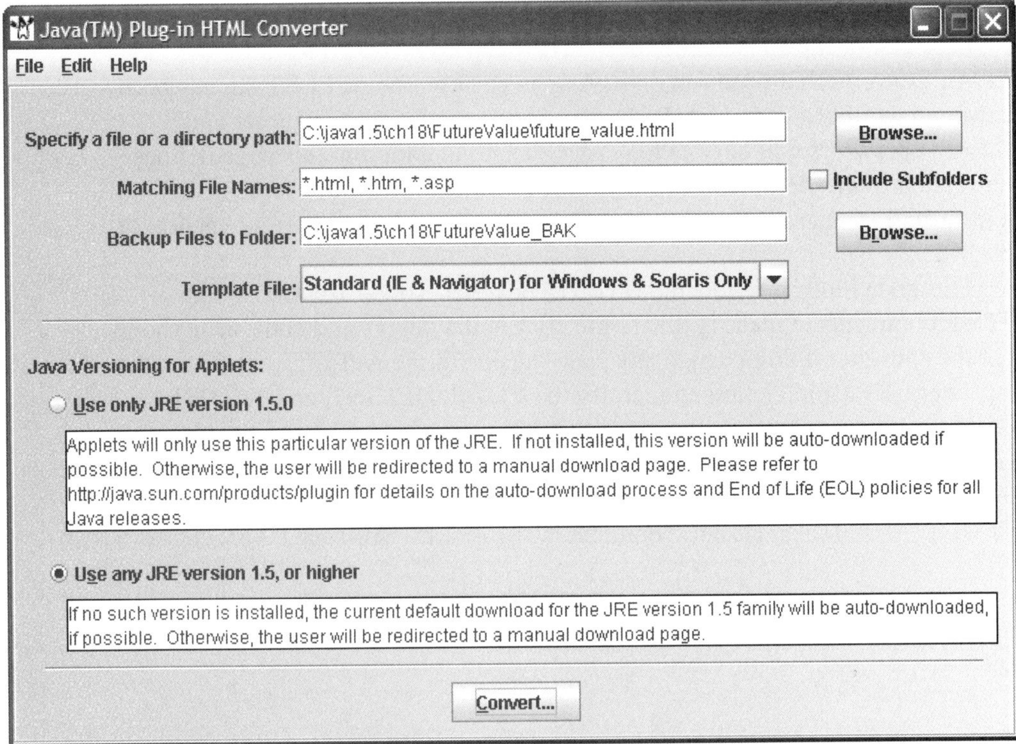

How to use the HTML Converter with Windows

1. Open the Windows Explorer and navigate to your JDK's bin folder (typically C:\Program Files\Java\jdk1.5.0\bin).
2. Double-click the HtmlConverter.exe file to display the Java Plug-in HTML Converter dialog box.
3. Use the HTML Converter dialog box to specify the HTML files that you want to convert, along with the backup directory for the original HTML files if necessary.
4. Click the Convert button to convert the files.

Description

- You can use the Matching File Names text field to limit or expand the types of files that the HTML Converter attempts to convert.
- You can use the Include Subfolders check box to include all subfolders in the conversion.
- You can use the Template File combo box to create HTML files that work with different browsers and operating systems.
- You can use the Java Versioning radio button to create HTML files that help the user automatically or manually download the appropriate version of the JRE.

Figure 18-7 How to convert the HTML page for an applet

The code for the converted HTML page

Figure 18-8 shows the code for the HTML file in figure 18-5 after the HTML Converter has been run on it. As you can see, the APPLET tag has been converted to OBJECT and EMBED tags so that the Internet Explorer and Netscape browsers will be able to read the page. In addition, this page defines the version of the JRE that's used by the applet, and it includes some code that helps install or upgrade the JRE on systems that don't have a current version of the JRE.

This code illustrates how the HTML Converter works. To start, it adds HTML comments to identify where the conversion begins and ends. This shows that the converter didn't change any code outside of the APPLET tag. Then, the converter uses capital letters to identify the CODE, HEIGHT, and WIDTH attributes that were specified by the APPLET tag, and it uses lowercase letters for the other tags that it generated. This makes it easy to see which tags were generated. Finally, the converter stores the APPLET tag that was in the original HTML page within an HTML comment in the new HTML page.

The HTML file in figure 18-5 after the conversion process

```
<html>
    <head>
        <title>Future Value Calculator applet</title>
    </head>

    <body>
        <h1>Future Value Calculator applet</h1>
        <!--"CONVERTED_APPLET"-->
<!-- HTML CONVERTER -->
<object
    classid = "clsid:8AD9C840-044E-11D1-B3E9-00805F499D93"
    codebase = "http://java.sun.com/update/1.5.0/jinstall-1_5-windows-
i586.cab#Version=1,5,0,0"
    WIDTH = 240 HEIGHT = 175 >
    <PARAM NAME = CODE VALUE = "FutureValueApplet.class" >
    <param name = "type" value = "application/x-java-applet;version=1.5">
    <param name = "scriptable" value = "false">

    <comment>
    <embed
            type = "application/x-java-applet;version=1.5" \
            CODE = "FutureValueApplet.class" \
            WIDTH = 240 \
            HEIGHT = 175
        scriptable = false
        pluginspage = "http://java.sun.com/products/plugin/index.html#download">
        <noembed>
            <p>This applet requires version 1.5 or later of Java.</p>
            </noembed>
    </embed>
    </comment>
</object>

<!--
<APPLET CODE = "FutureValueApplet.class" WIDTH = 240 HEIGHT = 175>
<p>This applet requires version 1.5 or later of Java.</p>
</APPLET>
-->
<!--"END_CONVERTED_APPLET"-->

    </body>
</html>
```

Description

- The HTML Converter inserts HTML comments to show where the conversion begins and ends.
- The HTML Converter converts the APPLET tag to the OBJECT and EMBED tags that are used by the Internet Explorer and Netscape browsers, respectively.
- The HTML Converter stores the original APPLET tag within an HTML comment.
- The HTML Converter uses capital letters for attributes that were coded in the original APPLET tag and lowercase letters for other tags that were generated.

Figure 18-8 The code for the converted HTML page

How to test an applet from a web browser

Since the Java Plug-in is automatically installed on your system when you install the JDK on your computer, you can view an applet in your browser as shown in figure 18-9. Then, you can test the applet to make sure it runs properly within the browser. As you do that, you can use the Java Console to view debugging information.

If you're using version 5.0 of the JRE and you run an applet within a browser, the Java icon is displayed at the right side of the taskbar. Then, you can display the Java Console by right-clicking on this icon and selecting the Open Console command. If that doesn't work, you may be able to display the Java Console by selecting an item from one of the menus of your web browser. If not, your browser may have disabled the Java Console. To enable it, you can check the "Enable Java Console" option located in your browser's advanced options.

Once you display the Java Console, you can use it to view any debugging information that the applet has printed to the console using println statements as well as any exceptions that have been thrown by the applet at run time. The Java Console shown in this figure illustrates how this works. It begins by displaying some general information about the current system and a list of commands that you can use to work with the Java Console. Then, it displays three lines that were printed to the console by println statements in the panel.

How to deploy an applet

If you have access to a web server, you can deploy an applet by using an FTP application to upload the HTML page and class files for the applet to the server. That's all there is to it. Then, the applet is available to any client computer that has a web browser and security clearance to view that HTML page.

If the client computer doesn't have the current version of the JRE and Java Plug-in installed, a dialog box will be displayed prompting the user to install the Java Plug-in. If the user agrees to install it, the browser will download and launch the installer. Then, the user can respond to the dialog boxes that are displayed to install the Java Plug-in. After a successful installation, the user will see a Java icon at the right side of the taskbar, which indicates that the JRE and Java Plug-in are running.

A Swing applet with the Java Console displayed

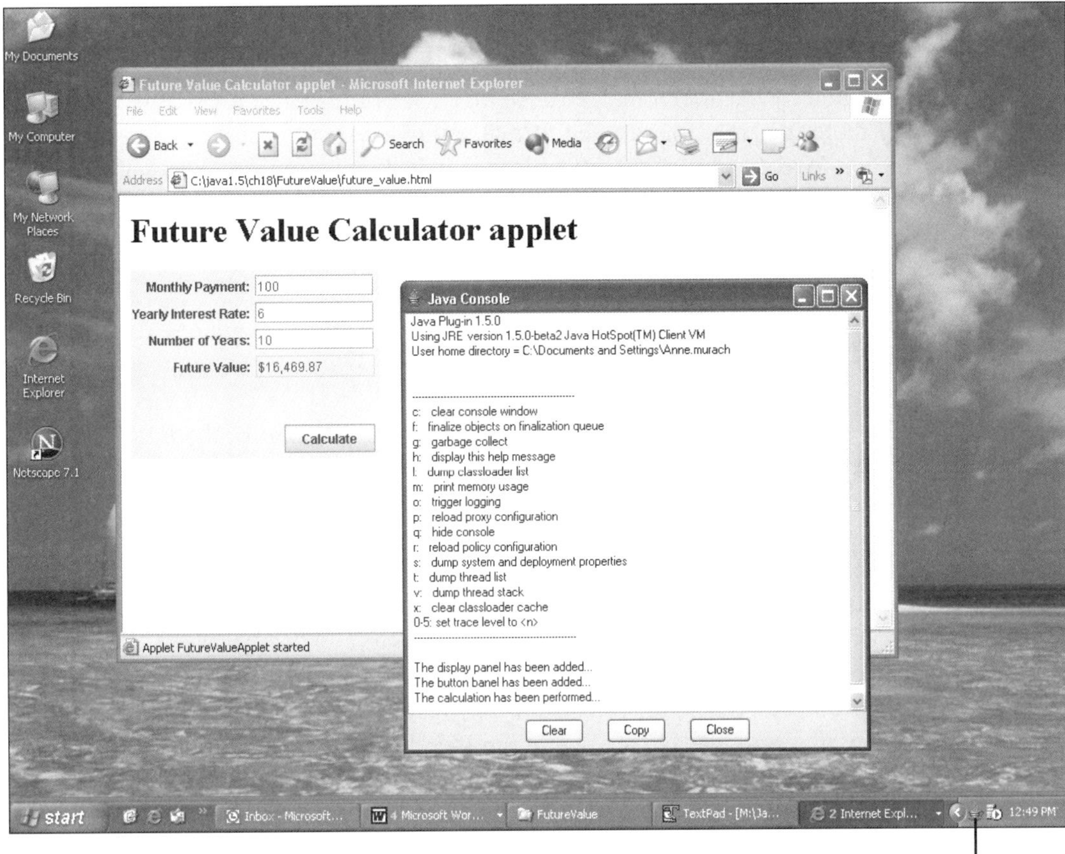

How to test a Swing applet

1. Start your web browser, display the applet's HTML page by entering its address, and test the applet to make sure it's working correctly.
2. If necessary, display the Java Console to view the output from println statements or information about any exceptions that have been thrown.

How to display the Java Console

- If you're using version 5.0 or later of the JDK, right-click the Java icon in the task bar and select the Show Console command.

How to work with the Java Console

- You can press any of the letters shown in the Java Console to execute the related command. Although most of these letters execute advanced functions that go beyond the scope of this book, you can press *c* to clear all messages from the Java Console window, and you can press *q* to close (quit) the Java Console window.

Figure 18-9 How to test an applet from a web browser

How to use JAR files with applets

When you deploy an applet, it's common to store the applet file and all other files required by the applet in a *Java Archive* (*JAR*) file. Since a JAR file stores one or more files in a compressed format, using a JAR file can dramatically improve the download time of the applet. In addition, the browser can retrieve all the files it needs for the applet from the server with a single request. As a result, you'll want to use JAR files whenever you deploy an applet, especially if the applet needs to access other files.

How to create and work with JAR files

Figure 18-10 shows how to use the JAR tool that comes as part of the JDK. In particular, it shows how to use the JAR command to create and update a JAR file, to list the contents of a JAR file, and to extract files from a JAR file.

To use the JAR command, you start a command prompt and navigate to the directory that contains the files you want to add to the JAR file. Then, you type the JAR command followed by one or more of the six options that are summarized in this figure. For example, to create a JAR file with verbose output, you specify c to create the file, f to specify the name of the file, and v to specify verbose output. After that, you specify the name of the JAR file followed by any files you want to include in the JAR file. When you do that, you can use the wildcard character (*) to specify all files of a particular type. For example, you can use *.class to add all of the class files in a directory to the JAR file. Or, you can separate each file name with a space.

The examples in this figure show how to work with the JAR command. Here, the first example shows how to create a JAR file named FutureValue.jar that contains all of the class files in the current directory. The second example shows how to add the SwingValidator.class file to the JAR file. The third example shows how to extract these files from the JAR file. And the fourth example shows how to list the contents of the JAR file.

Since you usually want to get feedback about each JAR command, you typically use the verbose output option, especially when working with the create, update, and extract options. The first three examples in this figure illustrate the output from this option. In the first example, the output shows the three files that were added to the JAR file and how much they were compressed. In the second example, the output shows the one class that was added to the JAR file and how much it was compressed. And in the third example, the output shows the four files that were extracted.

The syntax for using the JAR tool at the command line

```
jar [options] JARFileName File1 File2 File3 ...
```

Common options of the JAR tool

Option	Description
c	Creates a new JAR file and adds the specified files to it.
f	Specifies the second argument as the JAR file name.
u	Updates an existing JAR file by adding or replacing files.
x	Extracts the files from the specified JAR file.
t	Lists the contents of the specified JAR file.
v	Creates verbose output that includes compression information about the files that are stored in a JAR file.

An example that creates a JAR file

```
C:\java1.5\ch18\FutureValue>jar cfv FutureValue.jar *.class
added manifest
adding: FinancialCalculations.class(in = 437) (out= 336)(deflated 23%)
adding: FutureValueApplet.class(in = 452) (out= 298)(deflated 34%)
adding: FutureValuePanel.class(in = 2966) (out= 1583)(deflated 46%)
```

An example that updates a JAR file

```
C:\java1.5\ch18\FutureValue>jar ufv FutureValue.jar SwingValidator.class
adding: SwingValidator.class(in = 2022) (out= 1010)(deflated 50%)
```

An example that extracts files from a JAR file

```
C:\java1.5\ch18\FutureValue>jar xfv FutureValue.jar
  created: META-INF/
 inflated: META-INF/MANIFEST.MF
 inflated: FinancialCalculations.class
 inflated: FutureValueApplet.class
 inflated: FutureValuePanel.class
 inflated: SwingValidator.class
```

An example that lists the contents of a JAR file

```
C:\java1.5\ch18\FutureValue>jar tf FutureValue.jar
META-INF/
META-INF/MANIFEST.MF
FinancialCalculations.class
FutureValueApplet.class
FutureValuePanel.class
SwingValidator.class
```

Description

- To use the JAR tool, start the command prompt and navigate to the directory where the files you want to archive are stored. Then, issue the JAR command.
- To operate on all the files with a given extension, you can use the wildcard character (*).

Figure 18-10 How to create and work with JAR files

How to include a JAR file that contains an applet in an HTML page

Once you create a JAR file that contains all of the files needed by an applet, you can specify the JAR file in the HTML page that contains the applet as shown in figure 18-11. To do that, you use the ARCHIVE attribute of the APPLET tag to specify the name of the JAR file. Notice that you still need to use the CODE attribute to specify the class file that defines the applet so the browser knows what code to execute to start the applet. Then, every time it needs another file, it looks for that file in the JAR file. If it can't find it there, it requests the file from the server. However, requesting additional files from the server can significantly decrease the performance of your applet. As a result, you should try to include all the files that the applet needs within the JAR file.

The ARCHIVE attribute of the APPLET tag

Attribute	Description
archive	Specifies the archive file (such as a JAR file) to be downloaded.

How to include a JAR file in an HTML page

```
<html>
  <head>
    <title>Future Value Calculator applet</title>
  </head>

  <body>
    <h1>Future Value Calculator applet</h1>
    <applet
      archive = "FutureValueApplet.jar"
      code = "FutureValueApplet.class"
      width = 240
      height = 175>
        <!-- If the browser can't display this applet, display this -->
        <p>This applet requires version 1.5 or later of Java.</p>
    </applet>
  </body>
</html>
```

Description

- To improve the download time for your applets, you can place all the files needed by the applet in one JAR file. Then, you can use the ARCHIVE attribute of the APPLET tag to specify the name of the JAR file.

Figure 18-11 How to include a JAR file that contains an applet in an HTML page

Perspective

In this chapter, you learned how to develop applets. You also learned about some of the limitations of applets that have led web programmers to use other methods for developing web applications. As a result, before you begin developing a project that relies heavily on applets, you should review this technology to make sure that it's appropriate for your project.

In particular, if you want to develop web applications that store data in a file or database on the server, you should consider using servlets and Java Server Pages (JSP). Then, all processing is done on the server and the server returns standard HTML to the browser. The second book in this series, *Murach's Java Servlets and JSP*, shows how to use servlets and JSP to create web applications.

Summary

- An *applet* is a special type of application that's stored on a web server and runs within a web browser on a client machine.
- To view an applet, the client computer must have the appropriate version of the *Java Runtime Environment* (*JRE*) and the *Java Plug-in* installed. The Java Plug-in is part of the JRE.
- Since applets are downloaded from remote servers and run on client machines, they have stricter security restrictions than applications. To get around these restrictions, it's possible to create a *signed applet*.
- You can use the JApplet class to create an applet that can use Swing components and all of the current features of Java.
- You can use the Applet Viewer to test an applet outside of its HTML page.
- You can use the *Hypertext Markup Language* (*HTML*) to create a web page. Within the HTML file, you use *tags* to define the elements of the page. And within some tags, you define *attributes* that provide additional information.
- To add an applet to a web page, you include an APPLET tag with CODE, HEIGHT, and WIDTH attributes.
- Before you deploy an applet, you should run the Java Plug-in HTML Converter to convert the HTML page so it works with the appropriate browsers and operating systems.
- To test an applet and its HTML page, you view the HTML page in a web browser. Then, you can use the Java Console to view the debugging information.
- You can use a *Java Archive file* (*JAR file*) to store the files required by an applet in a compressed format. Then, you can modify the HTML page for the applet so it uses this JAR file.

Exercise 18-1 Develop a Payment applet

In this exercise, you'll modify the Payment application you saw in chapter 16 so that it can be run as an applet.

1. Open the PaymentApp class in the c:\java1.5\ch18\Payment directory and review its code.
2. Open a new file, and cut and paste the code for the PaymentPanel class from the PaymentApp file to the new file. Give this class public access, add any required import statements, save the file as PaymentPanel, and compile it.
3. Delete the import statements that aren't needed from the PaymentApp file, then compile the file and run the application to see that it still works.
4. Create a class named PaymentApplet that displays the payment panel. When you're done, compile the applet class to make sure that it compiles cleanly.
5. Open the payment.html file and review the starting code. This file contains all the tags needed for the Payment applet except the APPLET tag. Add an APPLET tag that displays the PaymentApplet at 300 by 300 pixels, and then save the file.
6. Use the Applet Viewer to view and test the applet. When you're done, click the Exit button to see that an exception is thrown indicating that the applet doesn't have the proper security clearance to access the current thread.
7. Modify the PaymentPanel class so it doesn't include an Exit button, and compile this class. Then, run the PaymentApp class and test it. This application won't display an Exit button anymore, but you can still close it by clicking the Close button in the upper right corner.
8. Use the Applet Viewer to run and test the PaymentApplet class. This time, you'll have to exit from the applet by closing the browser window. Now, you have an application (PaymentApp) and an applet (PaymentApplet) that both use the same panel class.
9. Run the HTML Converter to convert the payment.html page. Then, open the payment.html page that's in the Payment directory and review the new code. Also, open the payment.html page that's in the Payment_BAK directory to see that it contains the original code.
10. Use your web browser to test the HTML page and the applet. Since the JRE and Java Plug-in were automatically installed when you installed the JDK, the applet should work properly.
11. Modify the actionPerformed method of the PaymentPanel class so that when you click the Accept button, a message is printed to the console indicating that the payment was accepted. Then, compile the class and run the applet from the browser again. This time, display the Java Console and view the statement that's printed to the console when you click the Accept button.

Exercise 18-2 Store the Payment applet in a JAR file

In this exercise, you'll create a JAR file that contains the class files for the Payment applet that you created for exercise 18-1.

1. Use the JAR tool to create a JAR file named payment.jar that contains only the class files needed by the Payment applet.
2. Replace the payment.html file that's in the Payment directory with the payment.html file that's in the Payment_BAK directory. Modify the payment.html page so it uses the JAR file you created in step 1.
3. Use the HTML Converter to convert the HTML page. Then, use your web browser to display the HTML page to see that it still works with the JAR file.
4. If you have access to a web server, use an FTP program to upload the payment.html and payment.jar files to the web server. Then, run the Payment applet from the web server. If you have access to systems that don't have the current version of Java installed, test this applet on these systems to see what happens.

Section 5

Data access programming with Java

In the last section, you learned how to create user interfaces that get input from the user. But unless you save that data to a file or database, the data is lost when the program ends. That's why Java provides classes that let you work with files and databases. You'll learn about those classes in this section.

In chapter 19, you'll learn how to work with the data in text files and binary files. In chapter 20, you'll learn how to work with data using XML. And in chapter 21, you'll learn how to work with the data in a database.

Since the chapters in this section have been designed as independent modules, you can read them in any order you like. For example, if you want to learn how to use XML right away, you can jump to chapter 20. Or, if you want to begin working with databases, you can jump to chapter 21.

19

How to work with text and binary files

In this chapter, you'll learn how to work with two types of files: text files and binary files. Although binary files are used more often in business applications, text files are appropriate for some applications. For random access, though, you have to use binary files.

When you work with files, you frequently use arrays and collections (chapters 10 and 11). You need to be able to handle the exceptions thrown by I/O operations (chapter 13). And you may need to parse strings for some applications (chapter 12). As a result, you may want to review those chapters when you come upon the code in this chapter that uses those features.

Introduction to files and directories

Java provides a File class that you can use to perform some basic operations on files and directories. You'll learn how to use this class in the next two topics.

Constructors and methods of the File class

Figure 19-1 introduces you to the File class that's stored in the java.io package. To start, this figure shows one constructor of the File class. Then, it summarizes over a dozen methods of the File class that you can use for working with files and directories.

You can use the first group of methods in this figure to test a file or directory. For example, you can use the first three methods to check whether a file exists and whether you can read from or write to the file. And you can use the next two methods to test whether the path name refers to a file or a directory.

You can use the second group of methods to get information about a file or directory. To return the name of the file or directory, for example, you can use the getName method. To return the path name of the file or directory, you can use the getPath or getAbsolutePath methods. To return the length of the file in bytes or the time that the file was last modified, you can use the length and lastModified methods. And to return arrays that describe the available drives, directories, and files, you can use the listRoots, listFiles, and list methods.

You can use the last group of methods to work with files and directories. For instance, you can use the setReadOnly method to create a file or directory that only allows read operations, and you can use the delete method to delete a file or directory. Before you can delete a directory, though, the directory must be empty. Since all four of the methods in this group return a boolean value that indicates whether the operation was successful, you can write code that checks the return values whenever you need to know if the method ran successfully.

The File class

`java.io.File`

One constructor of the File class

Constructor	Description
`File(StringPath)`	Creates a File object that refers to the specified path name.

Methods that check a File object

Method	Description
`exists()`	Returns a true value if the path name exists.
`canRead()`	Returns a true value if the path name exists and a program can read from it.
`canWrite()`	Returns a true value if the path name exists and a program can write to it.
`isDirectory()`	Returns a true value if the path name exists and refers to a directory.
`isFile()`	Returns a true value if the path name exists and refers to a file.

Methods that get information about a File object

Method	Description
`getName()`	Returns the name of the file or directory as a String object.
`getPath()`	Returns the path name as represented in the constructor as a String object.
`getAbsolutePath()`	Returns the absolute path name as a String object.
`length()`	Returns the length of the file in bytes as a long type.
`lastModified()`	Returns a long value representing the time that the file was last modified as the number of milliseconds since January 1, 1970.
`listRoots()`	A static method that returns an array of File objects representing the drives available to the current system.
`listFiles()`	If the object refers to a directory, this method returns an array of File objects for the files and subdirectories of this directory.
`list()`	If the object refers to a directory, this method returns an array of String objects for the files and subdirectories of this directory.

Methods that work with File objects

Method	Description
`setReadOnly()`	Makes the object read-only. If successful, this method returns a true value.
`createNewFile()`	Creates a new file for the file represented by the File object if one doesn't already exist. Returns a true value if the file is created. This method throws IOException.
`mkdirs()`	Creates a new directory for the directory represented by this File object including any necessary but non-existent parent directories. Returns a true value if the directory is created.
`delete()`	Deletes the file or directory represented by the File object. If successful, this method returns a true value. A directory can only be deleted if it's empty.

Figure 19-1 Constructors and methods of the File class

Code examples that work with directories and files

The first example in figure 19-2 shows how to create a new directory. To do this, the first statement initializes a string that refers to a directory. In this case, the directory is the java 1.5\files directory on the C drive. Then, the second statement creates a File object for this directory. Finally, an if statements checks whether this directory already exists. If not, the last statement calls the mkdirs method to create the directory and any necessary subdirectories. For example, the mkdirs method will create both the java 1.5 directory and the files subdirectory if neither directory exists.

The second example shows how to create a new file. To do this, the first two statements create a File object that refers to a file named products.txt in the c:\java 1.5\files directory. Then, if the file doesn't already exist, the last statement calls the createNewFile method to create the file. In this example, an *absolute path name* is supplied to the constructor of the File class. In other words, this example specifies the entire path and file name for the file. However, if you want to create a File object that refers to a file that's in the same directory as the application, you can use a *relative path name*. To do that, you just specify the name of the file.

The third example shows how to get information about the file that was created by the first two examples. The output below this example shows the result of the three statements. First, the getName method returns the name of the file. Then, the getAbsolutePath method returns the full path for the file. Finally, the canWrite method returns a true value to show that the file is not read-only.

The fourth example shows how to list the names of the files and subdirectories in a directory. To start, an if statement checks whether the directory exists and whether it is a directory. If both are true, the first statement in the if block prints the name of the directory to the console. Then, the second statement prints a string to the console, and a for loop prints the file name of each file in the directory. To do this, the for loop uses the list method to return an array of String objects where each String object represents a file name. In this example, the directory only contains two files. However, it could also contain additional subdirectories.

While the first four examples show you everything you need to work with files on the local computer, the fifth example shows you how to use the *Universal Naming Convention* (*UNC*) to work with files on a remote computer. To use the UNC, you code two front slashes (//), followed by the host name and the share name. In this case, the dirName variable refers to a file located on a computer named server on the C share drive in the editorial directory.

If you're used to working with Windows, you may be surprised to find that you use a front slash instead of a backslash to separate the parts of a path. That's because Java uses the backslash to identify escape characters. This makes it cumbersome to use backslashes when specifying paths. However, using a front slash works equally well for both Windows and other operating systems such as Linux. The output for these examples shows that Windows systems automatically convert the front slash to a backslash when necessary.

Example 1: Code that creates a directory if it doesn't already exist

```
String dirName = "c:/java 1.5/files/";
File dir = new File(dirName);
if (!dir.exists())
    dir.mkdirs();
```

Example 2: Code that creates a file if it doesn't already exist

```
String fileName = "products.txt";
File productsFile = new File(dirName + fileName);
if (!productsFile.exists())
    productsFile.createNewFile();
```

Example 3: Code that displays information about a file

```
System.out.println("File name:       " + productsFile.getName());
System.out.println("Absolute path:   " + productsFile.getAbsolutePath());
System.out.println("Is writable:     " + productsFile.canWrite());
```

Resulting output

```
File name:       products.txt
Absolute path:   c:\java 1.5\files\products.txt
Is writable:     true
```

Example 4: Code that displays information about a directory

```
if (dir.exists() && dir.isDirectory())
{
    System.out.println("Directory: " + dir.getAbsolutePath());
    System.out.println("Files: ");
    for (String filename : dir.list())
        System.out.println("     " + filename);
}
```

Resulting output

```
Directory: c:\java 1.5\files
Files:
     customers.txt
     products.txt
```

Example 4: Code that specifies a directory and file on a remote server

```
String dirName = "//server/c/editorial/customers.txt";
```

Description

- When coding directory names, you can use a front slash to separate directories. This works equally well for Windows and other operating system.
- To identify the name and location of a file, you can use an *absolute path name* to specify the entire path for a file, or you can use a *relative path name* to specify the path of the file relative to another directory.
- To create a File object that represents a file on a remote computer, you can use the *Universal Naming Convention* (*UNC*). To do that, code two slashes (//) followed by the host name and the share name.

Figure 19-2 Code examples that work with directories and files

Introduction to file input and output

This topic begins by introducing you to the types of files and streams that you can use for file input and output. Then, it presents an example that introduces the code that's needed to perform input and output operations on a file. Finally, it shows how to handle the exceptions that occur most frequently when you perform input and output operations.

How files and streams work

Figure 19-2 presents the two types of files and the two types of streams that you use when you do *I/O operations* (or *file I/O*). In a *text file*, all of the data is stored as characters with one character per byte on disk. Often, the fields and records in this type of file are separated by delimiters like tabs and new line characters. In the text file in this figure, the fields are separated by tabs and the records by new line characters.

In contrast, the data in a *binary file* is stored in a different format that can read and write the primitive data types. In the example in this figure, you can see that some of the bytes in this format can't be read by a text editor. Here, two non-character bytes are written before the code and description fields of each product record, and the price field is written in a non-character format that isn't readable by a text editor. Also, since the records in a binary file don't end with new line characters, one record isn't displayed on each line when a binary file is opened by a text editor.

To handle I/O operations, Java uses *streams*. You can think of a stream as the flow of data from one location to another. For instance, an *output stream* can flow from the internal memory of an application to a disk file, and an *input stream* can flow from a disk file to internal memory. When you work with a text file, you use a *character stream*. When you work with a binary file, you use a *binary stream*.

Although this chapter shows you how to use streams with disk files, Java also uses streams with other types of devices. For instance, you can use an output stream to send data to the console or to a network connection. In fact, the System.out and System.err objects are the standard output streams that are used for printing data to the console. Similarly, you can use an input stream to read data from a source like a keyboard or a network connection. In fact, the System.in object that's used by the Scanner class is a standard input stream that is used for reading data from the keyboard.

When you save a text or binary file, you can use any extension for the file name. In this book, we have used *txt* as the extension for all text files and *dat* for all binary files. For instance, the text file in this figure is named products.txt, and the binary file is named products.dat.

A text file that's opened by a text editor

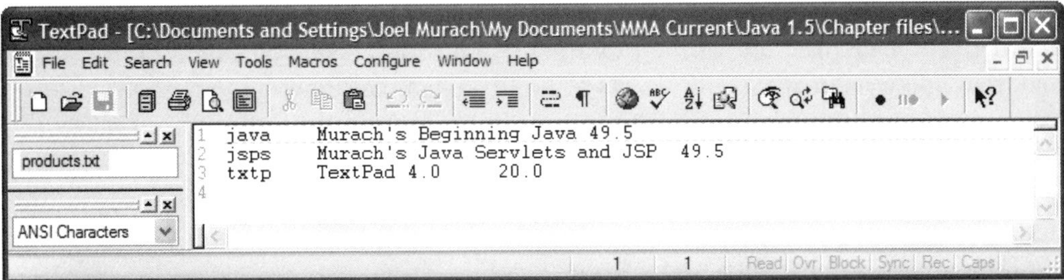

A binary file that's opened by a text editor

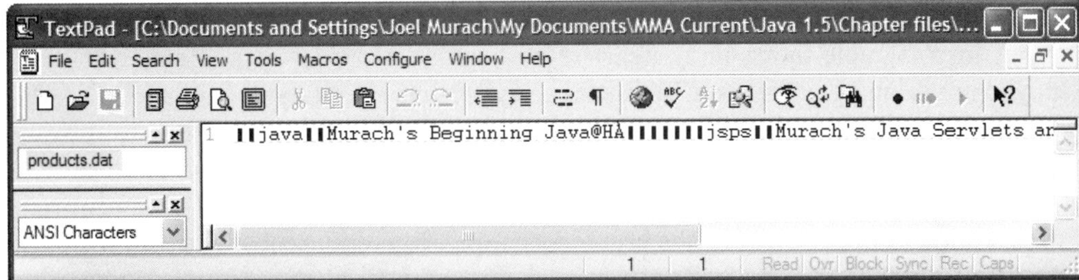

Two types of files

File	Description
Text	A file that contains characters. The fields and records in this type of file are often delimited by special characters like tab and new line characters.
Binary	A file that may contain characters as well as other non-character data types that can't be read by a text editor.

Two types of streams

Stream	Description
Character	Used to transfer text data to or from an I/O device.
Binary	Used to transfer binary data to or from an I/O device.

Description

- An *input file* is a file that is read by a program; an *output file* is a file that is written by a program. Input and output operations are often referred to as *I/O operations* or *file I/O*.
- A *stream* is the flow of data from one location to another. To write data to a file from internal storage, you use an *output stream*. To read from a file into internal storage, you use an *input stream*.
- To read and write *text files*, you use *character streams*. To read and write *binary files*, you use *binary streams*.
- Streams are not only used with disk devices, but also with input devices like keyboards and network connections and output devices like PC monitors and network connections.

Figure 19-3 How files and streams work

A file I/O example

To give you an overview of file I/O, figure 19-4 shows code you can use to read from and write to a text file. To start, the first example shows an import statement for the java.io package. This statement is necessary because most of the classes for working with file I/O are stored in the java.io package. As a result, any class that works with file I/O typically imports all of the classes in this package.

The second example shows how to create a File object that refers to a file named products.txt. In this example, no directory is specified for the file. Because of that, this File object refers to a file that's stored in the same directory as the class that contains this statement.

The third example shows three steps for writing data to a file. In the first step, you create an output stream. To create a stream that has all the functionality that you need for an application, you can *layer* two or more streams into a single stream. To layer streams in Java, you use an object of one class as the argument for the constructor of another class. In this example, a BufferedWriter object is used as the argument of the PrintWriter constructor, and a FileWriter object is used as the argument of the BufferedWriter constructor.

The BufferedWriter object adds a block of internal memory known as a *buffer* to the stream. This causes the data in the stream to be stored in a buffer before it is written to the output device. Then, when the buffer is full, or when the stream is closed, all of the data in the buffer is *flushed* to the disk file in a single I/O operation. Similarly, when you use a buffer for input, a full buffer of data is read in a single I/O operation.

The benefit of buffering is that it reduces the number of I/O operations that are done by a disk device. If, for example, a buffer can hold 4000 bytes of data, only one write or read operation is required to flush or fill the buffer. In contrast, if the data is written or read one field at a time, 4000 bytes might require hundreds of I/O operations. For each I/O operation, the disk has to rotate to the starting disk location. Since this rotation is extremely slow relative to internal operations, buffering dramatically improves the performance of I/O operations. That's why you should use buffers for all but the most trivial disk operations.

In the second step of the third example, the println method of the output stream is used to write the data to a file. And in the third step, the close method of the output stream closes the stream and flushes any data that's in the buffer to the file.

The fourth example reads the data that was written by the third example. In the first step, it creates a buffered input stream for the products file. Then, it reads the first line of that file, and it prints that line to the console. Finally, it closes the input stream, which flushes the buffer and frees all system resources associated with the input stream.

Because this figure is only intended to give you an idea of how file I/O works, you shouldn't worry if you don't understand it completely. As you progress through this chapter, you'll learn about all of the classes and methods shown here in more detail.

Example 1: Import all classes in the java.io package

```
import java.io.*;
```

Example 2: Create a File object

```
File productsFile = new File("products.txt");
```

Example 3: Write data to a file

Step 1: Open a buffered output stream

```
PrintWriter out = new PrintWriter(
                  new BufferedWriter(
                  new FileWriter(productsFile)));
```

Step 2: Write data to the stream

```
out.println("java\tMurach's Beginning Java 2\t49.50");
```

Step 3: Close the stream and flush all data to the file

```
out.close();
```

Example 4: Read data from a file

Step 1: Open a buffered input stream

```
BufferedReader in = new BufferedReader(
                    new FileReader(productsFile));
```

Step 2: Read data from the stream and print it to the console

```
String line = in.readLine();
System.out.println(line);
```

Step 3: Close the stream

```
out.close();
```

Resulting output

```
java    Murach's Beginning Java 2        49.50
```

Description

- The java.io package contains dozens of classes that can be used to create different types of streams that have different functionality. The java.nio package contains even more classes for working with I/O.
- To get the functionality you need for a stream, you often need to combine, or *layer*, two or more streams. You'll learn more about how this works as you progress through this chapter.
- To make disk processing more efficient, you can use a *buffered stream* that adds a block of internal memory called a *buffer* to the stream.
- When working with buffers, you often need to *flush* the buffer. This sends all data in the buffer to the I/O device. One way to do that is to close the I/O stream.

Figure 19-4 A file I/O example

How to work with I/O exceptions

If you've read chapter 13, you know the basic skills for handling exceptions. In fact, you have already been introduced to some of the exceptions that are thrown by I/O operations. Now, figure 19-5 summarizes three types of checked exceptions that must be handled when you're working with file I/O. It also shows a typical way to prevent or handle these types of exceptions. You'll see other examples like this throughout this chapter.

All exceptions that are thrown by classes that perform file I/O operations inherit the IOException class. In particular, an EOFException may be thrown when a program attempts to read beyond the end of a file, and a FileNotFoundException is thrown when a program attempts to open a file that doesn't exist.

To prevent an exception such as a FileNotFoundException, you can use code like that shown in the first example in this figure. This code attempts to read data from a file. Before it does that, though, it uses the exists method of the file to be sure that the file exists. If it does, it creates an input stream and reads the first record in the file. Then, it uses a while loop to read the remaining records in the file as long as the string that's returned isn't null, which indicates that the end of the file has been reached. If it has, the loop ends.

To handle any other I/O exceptions that might occur as the file is processed, the statements that create the input stream and read the file are coded within a try statement. Then, a catch clause catches the IOException and prints it to the console.

The second example shows how a close method can be used to close any input or output stream that implements the Closeable interface. As of version 5.0 of the J2SE, most input and output streams implement this interface. As a result, this method can be used to close most input and output streams.

To start, this method checks whether the stream is null. This prevents the NullPointerException that would be thrown if you tried to call the close method from a stream that wasn't initialized. If the stream is not null, the close method is called. If the close method throws an IOException exception, the catch clause prints the exception to the console.

A subset of the IOException hierarchy

```
IOException
    EOFException
    FileNotFoundException
```

Common I/O exceptions

Exception	Description
`IOException`	Thrown when an error occurs in I/O processing.
`EOFException`	Thrown when a program attempts to read beyond the end of a file.
`FileNotFoundException`	Thrown when a program attempts to open a file that doesn't exist.

Example 1: Code that handles I/O exceptions

```
BufferedReader in = null;
try
{
    if (productsFile.exists())  // prevent the FileNotFoundException
    {
        in = new BufferedReader(
             new FileReader(productsFile));

        String line = in.readLine();

        while(line != null)
        {
            System.out.println(line);
            line = in.readLine();
        }
    }
    else
        System.out.println(productsFile.getPath() + " doesn't exist");
}
catch(IOException ioe)  // catch any other IOExceptions
{
    System.out.println(ioe);
}
finally  // close the stream even if an exception was thrown
{
    this.close(in);  // call the close method
}
```

Example 2: A method that closes a stream

```
private void close(Closeable stream)
{
    try
    {
        if (stream != null) // prevent a NullPointerException
            stream.close();
    }
    catch(IOException ioe)
    {
        System.out.println("Unable to close stream: " + ioe);
    }
}
```

Figure 19-5 How to work with I/O exceptions

How to work with text files

When working with text files, you need to layer two or more classes to create a character input or output stream. You'll learn how to do that in the topics that follow. In addition, you'll learn how to use the methods of these classes to work with text files. Then, you'll see a complete class that you can use to read and write Product objects to a text file.

How to connect a character output stream to a file

Before you can write to a text file, you need to create a character output stream, and you need to connect that stream to a file. To do that, you must layer two or more of the classes in the Writer hierarchy as shown in figure 19-6. As you can see, you use the methods of the PrintWriter class to write data to the output stream, you use the BufferedWriter class to create a buffer for the output stream, and you use the FileWriter class to connect the stream to a file.

Although it's typically a good coding practice to use a buffer, the first example in this figure shows how to connect to a file without using a buffer. Here, the first statement creates a FileWriter object by passing a file name to the constructor of the FileWriter class. Then, the second statement creates a PrintWriter object by passing the FileWriter object to the constructor of the PrintWriter class.

The second example shows a more concise way to write the first example. Here, you don't assign the PrintWriter object to a named variable. Instead, you nest the call to the constructor of the PrintWriter class within the constructor of the FileWriter class. You can align these nested constructor calls any way you like. In this example, the whole statement is coded on one line, but it's often easier to read if each constructor call is coded on a separate line as shown in the next three examples.

The third example shows how to include a buffer in the output stream. To do that, you use a BufferedWriter object in addition to a FileWriter and PrintWriter object. Also notice in this example that a File object named productsFile is passed to the FileWriter constructor rather than a file name. This is the most common way to create a FileWriter object, and it's the technique you'll see throughout this chapter.

The fourth example shows how to append data to an existing file. To do that, you set the second argument of the FileWriter constructor to true. If you don't code a value for this argument, the existing data in the file is overwritten.

By default, the data in an output stream is flushed from the buffer to the disk when the buffer is full. However, if you set the second argument of the PrintWriter constructor to true, the *autoflush feature* is turned on. Then, the buffer is flushed each time the println method is executed.

A subset of the Writer hierarchy

```
Writer <<abstract>>
    BufferedWriter
    PrintWriter
    OutputStreamWriter
        FileWriter
```

Classes used to connect a character output stream to a file

PrintWriter	contains the methods for writing data to a text stream
→BufferedWriter	creates a buffer for the stream
→FileWriter	connects the stream to a file

Constructors of these classes

Constructor	Throws
`PrintWriter(Writer[, booleanFlush])`	None
`BufferedWriter(Writer)`	None
`FileWriter(File[, booleanAppend])`	IOException
`FileWriter(StringFileName[, booleanAppend])`	IOException

Example 1: How to connect without a buffer (not recommended)

```
FileWriter fileWriter = new FileWriter("products.txt");
PrintWriter out = new PrintWriter(fileWriter);
```

Example 2: A more concise way to code example 1

```
PrintWriter out = new PrintWriter(new FileWriter("products.txt"));
```

Example 3: How to connect to a file with a buffer

```
PrintWriter out = new PrintWriter(
                  new BufferedWriter(
                  new FileWriter(productsFile)));
```

Example 4: How to connect for an append operation

```
PrintWriter out = new PrintWriter(
                  new BufferedWriter(
                  new FileWriter(productsFile, true)));
```

Example 5: How to connect with the autoflush feature turned on

```
PrintWriter out = new PrintWriter(
                  new BufferedWriter(
                  new FileWriter(productsFile)), true);
```

Description

- The Writer class is an abstract class that's inherited by all of the classes in the Writer hierarchy. To learn more about the Writer hierarchy, see the Java API documentation.
- By default, the output file is overwritten. If that's not what you want, you can specify true for the second argument of the FileWriter constructor to append data to the file.
- If you specify true for the second argument of the PrintWriter constructor, the *autoflush feature* flushes the buffer each time the println method is called.

Figure 19-6 How to connect a character output stream to a file

The constructors in figure 19-6 should help you understand how to layer output streams. Here, you can see that the PrintWriter constructor accepts any class derived from the Writer class. As a result, you can supply a BufferedWriter object or a FileWriter object as an argument of the PrintWriter constructor. Similarly, since the BufferedWriter constructor also accepts any Writer object, you can supply a FileWriter object as an argument of the BufferedWriter constructor.

How to write to a text file

Figure 19-7 shows how to write to a text file. To do that, you use the print and println methods to send data to the file. These methods work like the print and println methods of the System.out object, but they print data to the output stream instead of printing data to the console.

Once you're done printing data to the output stream, you can use the close method to close the output stream. This flushes the buffer and frees any system resources that are being used by the output stream. Or, if you want to keep the output stream open, you can use the flush method to flush all the data in the stream to the file. Either way, you need to throw or catch the IOException that can be thrown by these methods.

The first example in this figure shows how to append a string and an object to a text file named log.txt. To start, the FileWriter constructor creates a FileWriter object that can append data to the file. If no file named log.txt exists in the current directory, this statement will create the file. Then, the print method prints a string, and the println method prints a Date object that represents the current date and time. Using a Date object as an argument of the println method automatically calls the toString method for that object.

The second example in this figure shows how to write the data that's stored in a Product object to a *delimited text file*. In this type of file, one type of *delimiter* is used to separate the *fields* (or *columns*) that are written to the file, and another type of delimiter is used to separate the *records* (or *rows*). In this example, the tab character (\t) is used as the delimiter for the fields, and the new line character is used as the delimiter for the records. That way, the code, description, and price for one product are stored in the same record separated by tabs. Then, the new line character ends the data for that product, and the data for the next product can be stored in the next record.

Common methods of the PrintWriter class

Method	Throws	Description
`print(argument)`	None	Writes the character representation of the argument type to the file.
`println(argument)`	None	Writes the character representation of the argument type to the file followed by the new line character. If the autoflush feature is turned on, this also flushes the buffer.
`flush()`	IOException	Flushes any data that's in the buffer to the file.
`close()`	IOException	Flushes any data that's in the buffer to the file and closes the stream.

Example 1: Code that appends a string and an object to a text file

```
// open an output stream for appending to the text file
PrintWriter out =    new PrintWriter(
                     new BufferedWriter(
                     new FileWriter("log.txt", true)));

// write a string and an object to the file
out.print("This application was run on ");
Date today = new Date();
out.println(today);

// flush data to the file and close the output stream
out.close();
```

Example 2: Code that writes a Product object to a delimited text file

```
// open an output stream for overwriting a text file
PrintWriter out =    new PrintWriter(
                     new BufferedWriter(
                     new FileWriter(productsFile)));

// write the Product object to the file
out.print(product.getCode() + "\t");
out.print(product.getDescription() + "\t");
out.println(product.getPrice());

// flush data to the file and close the output stream
out.close();
```

Description

- To write a character representation of a data type to an output stream, you use the print and println methods of the PrintWriter class. If you supply an object as an argument, these methods will call the toString method of the object.
- To create a *delimited text file*, you delimit the *records* in the file with one *delimiter*, such as a new line character, and you delimit the *fields* of each record with another delimiter, such as a tab character.
- To prevent data from being lost, you should always close the stream when you're done using it. Then, the program will flush all data to the file before it closes the stream.

Figure 19-7 How to write to a text file

How to connect a character input stream to a file

Before you can read characters from a text file, you must connect the character input stream to a file. Figure 19-8 shows how to do that with a buffer and a File object. As you can see in the example in this figure, you supply the FileReader class as the argument of the constructor of the BufferedReader class. This creates a stream that uses a buffer and has methods that you can use to read data.

If you look at the constructors for the BufferedReader and FileReader classes, you can see why this code works. Since the constructor for the BufferedReader object accepts any object in the Reader hierarchy, it can accept a FileReader object that connects the stream to a file. However, the BufferedReader object can also accept an InputStreamReader object, which can be used to connect the character input stream to the keyboard or to a network connection rather than to a file.

A subset of the Reader hierarchy

```
Reader <<abstract>>
    BufferedReader
    InputStreamReader
        FileReader
```

Classes used to connect to a file with a buffer

BufferedReader	contains methods for reading data from the stream
→FileReader	connects the stream to a file

Constructors of these classes

Constructor	Throws
`BufferedReader(Reader)`	None
`FileReader(File)`	FileNotFoundException
`FileReader(StringFileName)`	FileNotFoundException

How to connect a character input stream to a file

```
BufferedReader in = new BufferedReader(
                    new FileReader(productsFile));
```

Description

- The Reader class is an abstract class that's inherited by all of the classes in the Reader hierarchy. To learn more about the Reader hierarchy, check the documentation for the Java API. All classes in the java.io package that end with Reader are members of the Reader hierarchy.
- Although you can read files with the FileReader class alone, the BufferedReader class improves efficiency and provides better methods for reading character input streams.

Figure 19-8 How to connect a character input stream to a file

How to read from a text file

The two examples in figure 19-9 show how to read the two text files that are written by the examples in figure 19-7. In the first example, the first statement uses the readLine method to read the first record in the log file. Then, a while loop prints the current record to the console and reads the next record. When the readLine method attempts to read past the end of the file, it returns a null, which causes the while loop to end. Then, the close method is called to flush the buffer and close the input stream.

The second example shows how to read a record from the products file. To do that, it uses the readLine method. Then, because this file is a delimited text file, it parses the string into its individual columns. To do that, it uses the split method of the String class to split the string into an array. In this example, the tab character is supplied as the argument of the split method since this is the character that's used to divide the fields in the record. (If you're not familiar with how the split method works, please see chapter 12.)

This example continues by creating a Product object from the data in the columns array. Since the product code and description are strings, the columns that contain these values can be passed directly to the constructor of the Product object. However, the price column must be converted from a String object to a double value. In this example, the parseDouble method of the Double class is used to do that.

The last statement in this example calls the close method. That flushes the buffer and frees any system resources.

Although you can also use the read method to read a text file, that's not common. That's because it reads a single character, and it returns an int value that represents the ASCII code for the character. Then, to get the character, you must cast the return type to a char value.

If you know the structure of the data in the input stream that you're working with, you may occasionally need to skip a specific number of characters. To do that, you can use the skip method. When you call this method, it tries to move forward in the file the specified number of characters without reading new characters into the stream. However, if this method encounters the end of the file or can't continue for some other reason, it returns the actual number of characters that were skipped.

Common methods of the BufferedReader class

Method	Throws	Description
`readLine()`	IOException	Reads a line of text and returns it as a string.
`read()`	IOException	Reads a single character and returns it as an int that represents the ASCII code for the character. When this method attempts to read past the end of the file, it returns an int value of -1.
`skip(longValue)`	IOException	Attempts to skip the specified number of characters, and returns an int value for the actual number of characters skipped.
`close()`	IOException	Closes the input stream and flushes the buffer.

Example 1: Code that reads the records in a text file

```
// read the records of the file
String line = in.readLine();
while(line != null)
{
    System.out.println(line);
    line = in.readLine();
}

// close the input stream
in.close();
```

Sample output

```
This application was run on Tue Oct 19 09:21:42 PDT 2004
This application was run on Wed Oct 20 10:14:12 PDT 2004
```

Example 2: Code that reads a Product object from a delimited text file

```
// read the next line of the file
String line = in.readLine();

// parse the line into its columns
String[] columns = line.split("\t");
String code = columns[0];
String description = columns[1];
String price = columns[2];

// create a Product object from the data in the columns
Product p = new Product(code, description, Double.parseDouble(price));

// print the Product object
System.out.println(p);

// close the input stream
in.close();
```

Sample output

```
Code:        java
Description: Murach's Beginning Java
Price:       $49.50
```

Figure 19-9 How to read from a text file

An interface for working with file I/O

In chapter 8, you saw a ProductDAO interface that defines I/O methods and constants for a data access object. Now, figure 19-10 presents a similar interface that you can use to access data. As you can see, this interface extends the ProductReader, ProductWriter, and ProductConstants interfaces. Since these interfaces are similar to the interfaces that were presented in chapter 8, you shouldn't have trouble understanding how they work. In fact, the only difference is that the ProductReader interface shown here uses an array list to store Product objects instead of using a string to store the product data. In the next figure, you'll see an example of a class that implements this interface for a text file.

To start, the ProductReader interface defines two methods that you can use to get product data from a file or database. Here, the getProduct method returns a single Product object for the product with the specified product code, and the getProducts method returns an ArrayList object that contains Product objects for all the products in a file or database.

The ProductWriter interface defines three methods that you can use to write product data to a file or database. Each of these methods accepts a Product object and returns a boolean value that indicates whether or not the operation was successful.

Finally, the ProductConstants interface defines two constants. Here, the CODE_SIZE constant specifies the maximum number of characters in a product's code, and the DESCRIPTION_SIZE constant specifies the maximum number of characters in a product's description.

As you learned in chapter 8, you must implement all five methods defined by the ProductReader and ProductWriter interfaces when you code a class that implements the ProductDAO interface. In addition, you have the option of using the constants stored in the ProductConstants interface. In this chapter, you'll see two examples of file I/O classes that implement the ProductDAO interface. The first example, shown in the next figure, doesn't use any constants from the ProductConstants interface. However, the second example, shown in the last figure, does use these constants.

The ProductDAO interface

```
public interface ProductDAO
    extends ProductReader, ProductWriter, ProductConstants {}
```

The ProductReader interface

```
import java.util.ArrayList;

public interface ProductReader
{
    Product getProduct(String code);
    ArrayList<Product> getProducts();
}
```

The ProductWriter interface

```
public interface ProductWriter
{
    boolean addProduct(Product p);
    boolean updateProduct(Product p);
    boolean deleteProduct(Product p);
}
```

The ProductConstants interface

```
public interface ProductConstants
{
    int CODE_SIZE = 4;
    int DESCRIPTION_SIZE = 40;
}
```

Figure 19-10 An interface for working with file I/O

A class that works with a text file

Figure 19-11 shows a complete class named ProductTextFile that can be used to read and write products to a text file. This class implements the ProductDAO interface shown in figure 19-10. As a result, it includes all five public methods defined by the ProductReader and ProductWriter interfaces. In addition, it includes some private methods that are used by these methods.

To start, this class defines an instance variable and a constant. Here, the File object named productsFile will be used to connect to the products file. Then, the FIELD_SEP constant defines the tab character as the character that's used to separate the columns in the products file.

The constructor for the ProductTextFile class initializes the instance variable. To do that, it creates a File object for a file named products.txt that's stored in the same directory as the ProductTextFile class. As a result, if the ProductTextFile class is stored in the c:\java1.5\ch19 directory, the products.txt file will be stored in that directory too.

The first method in this class, checkFile, provides code that checks whether the products file exists. If not, this method creates the products file that's defined by the File object named productsFile. Since this method creates the file if it doesn't exist, it can be used to prevent a FileNotFoundException from being thrown. As you'll see, this method is called by both the saveProducts and getProducts methods.

The saveProducts method accepts an ArrayList object that contains Product objects, and it writes all of these Product objects to the file. If this operation is successful, it returns a true value. If an IOException is thrown, this method returns a false value to indicate that the save operation wasn't successful. Either way, this method attempts to close the output stream by passing it to the close method that's defined later in the class.

The saveProducts method starts by calling the checkFile method to make sure that the products.txt file exists and to create it if it doesn't. Then, it creates a buffered output stream that connects to the products file. Finally, this method uses a loop to write each product in the array list to the file. To do that, it uses the FIELD_SEP constant to separate each field in a product record, and it uses the println method to insert a new line character at the end of each product record.

The code for the ProductTextFile class

Page 1

```
import java.io.*;
import java.util.*;

public class ProductTextFile implements ProductDAO
{
    private File productsFile = null;
    private final String FIELD_SEP = "\t";

    public ProductTextFile()
    {
        productsFile = new File("products.txt");
    }

    private void checkFile() throws IOException
    {
        // if the file doesn't exist, create it
        if (!productsFile.exists())
            productsFile.createNewFile();
    }

    private boolean saveProducts(ArrayList<Product> products)
    {
        PrintWriter out = null;
        try
        {
            this.checkFile();

            // open output stream for overwriting
            out = new PrintWriter(
                  new BufferedWriter(
                  new FileWriter(productsFile)));

            // write all products in the array list
            // to the file
            for (Product p : products)
            {
                out.print(p.getCode() + FIELD_SEP);
                out.print(p.getDescription() + FIELD_SEP);
                out.println(p.getPrice());
            }
        }
        catch(IOException ioe)
        {
            ioe.printStackTrace();
            return false;
        }
        finally
        {
            this.close(out);
        }
        return true;
    }
```

Figure 19-11 A class that works with a text file (part 1 of 3)

The close method can be used to close any input or output stream that implements the Closeable interface. Since this method is described in figure 19-5, you should understand how it works. Within this class, this method is used to close the output stream that's used by the saveProducts method, and it's used to close the input stream that's used by the getProducts method.

The getProducts method returns an ArrayList object that stores all of the Product objects in the products file. This method starts by calling the checkFile method to be sure the file exists. If it doesn't, it creates the file. Then, it creates a buffered input stream. Next, it declares and initializes an ArrayList object named products that can store Product objects.

To create the Product objects, this method starts by reading the first record from the products file into a string variable. Then, it uses a while loop to process the records in the file until the end of the file is reached. As you learned earlier in this chapter, you can test for an end-of-file condition by checking the string that's returned by the readLine method for a null.

Within the while loop, the first statement uses the FIELD_SEP constant to split the line into its three columns (code, description, and price). Then, this loop creates a Product object from the values in these columns and adds the Product object to the array list. Finally, this loop reads the next line in the file.

If an IOException is thrown somewhere in the getProducts method, this method returns a null. That way, any method that calls the getProducts method can test whether it executed successfully by checking the array list it returns for a null. Whether or not an exception is thrown, the finally clause attempts to close the input stream. To do that, the input stream is passed to the close method you saw earlier in this class.

In this class, the catch clauses in the saveProducts, getProducts, and close methods print the stack trace to the console. This is useful when you're testing and debugging a program, but it might not be appropriate when you put a program into production. As a result, before putting a class like this into a production environment, you might want to change the way that exceptions are handled. Instead of printing the stack trace, for example, you might want to write an error message to a log file. Or, you might want to throw a custom exception that indicates that a generic access error has occurred. For more information on how to create a custom exception, see chapter 13.

The code for the ProductTextFile class **Page 2**

```
    private void close(Closeable stream)
    {
        try
        {
            if (stream != null)
                stream.close();
        }
        catch(IOException ioe)
        {
            ioe.printStackTrace();
        }
    }

    public ArrayList<Product> getProducts()
    {
        BufferedReader in = null;
        try
        {
            this.checkFile();

            in = new BufferedReader(
                 new FileReader(productsFile));

            ArrayList<Product> products = new ArrayList<Product>();

            // read all products stored in the file
            // into the array list
            String line = in.readLine();
            while(line != null)
            {
                String[] columns = line.split(FIELD_SEP);
                String code = columns[0];
                String description = columns[1];
                String price = columns[2];

                Product p = new Product(
                    code, description, Double.parseDouble(price));
                products.add(p);

                line = in.readLine();
            }
            return products;
        }
        catch(IOException ioe)
        {
            ioe.printStackTrace();
            return null;
        }
        finally
        {
            this.close(in);
        }
    }
```

Figure 19-11 A class that works with a text file (part 2 of 3)

The getProduct method returns a Product object for a product that matches the specified product code. To search for the product, this method starts by calling the getProducts method to return a products array list. Then, the getProduct method loops through each product in the products array list until it finds one with the specified product code. Finally, it returns that product. If no product is found with the specified code, this method returns a null.

The addProduct method starts by calling the getProducts method to return a products array list. Then, it calls the add method of the ArrayList class to add the product to the array list. Finally, it calls the saveProducts method to save the modified products array list to the products file so that the array list and the file contain the same data. Notice that the addProduct method returns the boolean value that's returned by the saveProducts method. That way, if the saveProducts method returns a true value, the addProduct method will also return true.

The deleteProduct method is similar. It starts by calling the getProducts method to return a products array list. Then, it calls the remove method of the ArrayList class to remove the product from the array list. Finally, it calls the saveProducts method to save the array list to the products file, and it returns the boolean value that's returned by that method.

The updateProduct method works a little differently. This method updates the data for an existing product with the data in a new Product object. Like the addProduct and deleteProduct methods, this method begins by calling the getProducts method to get the products array list. But then, it uses the getProduct method to get the old Product object with the same product code as the new Product object. Next, it gets the index for the old product, and it removes that product from the array list. Then, it inserts the new product into the array list where the old product used to be. Finally, it calls the saveProducts method to save the array list to the products file, and it returns a value that indicates whether the save operation was successful.

If you review the code for this class, you'll notice that the entire products file is read each time the getProducts and getProduct methods are called. Worse, the entire products file is read and written each time the addProduct, deleteProduct, and updateProduct methods are called. Obviously, this isn't an efficient way to read and write data to and from a file. As a result, it wouldn't make sense to use this class for a file that contained thousands of records. However, for smaller files, code like this will work fine. That's because buffered streams allow you to work with files relatively efficiently, and because the operating system may cache the data anyway.

One technique for enhancing the performance of this class is to store the products array list as an instance variable. Then, you don't have to read the products array list each time one of the methods in this class is called. This increases efficiency by reading the file only when necessary. However, this technique also raises several tricky debugging issues. For example, it's probably a good idea to code the getProducts method so it returns a deep clone of the products array list. Otherwise, the calling method may obtain a reference to the products array list that's stored in the ProductTextFile class. Then, that calling method can modify the Product objects within that array list, which can lead to unpredictable results.

The code for the ProductTextFile class

Page 3

```
    public Product getProduct(String code)
    {
        ArrayList<Product> products = this.getProducts();
        for (Product p : products)
        {
            if (p.getCode().equals(code))
                return p;
        }
        return null;
    }

    public boolean addProduct(Product p)
    {
        ArrayList<Product> products = this.getProducts();
        products.add(p);
        return this.saveProducts(products);
    }

    public boolean deleteProduct(Product p)
    {
        ArrayList<Product> products = this.getProducts();
        products.remove(p);
        return this.saveProducts(products);
    }

    public boolean updateProduct(Product newProduct)
    {
        ArrayList<Product> products = this.getProducts();

        // get the old product and remove it
        Product oldProduct = this.getProduct(newProduct.getCode());
        int i = products.indexOf(oldProduct);
        products.remove(i);

        // add the updated product
        products.add(i, newProduct);

        return this.saveProducts(products);
    }
}
```

Figure 19-11 A class that works with a text file (part 3 of 3)

How to work with binary files

To connect a binary stream to a binary file, you use a technique that's similar to the technique you use to connect a character stream to a text file. However, the methods you use to read and write binary data are different from the methods you use to read and write character data. In the topics that follow, you'll learn how to work with the data that's stored in a binary file.

How to connect a binary output stream to a file

To create a binary output stream that's connected to a file, you can layer three streams in the OutputStream hierarchy as shown in figure 19-12. Here, the first example shows how to create a File object named productsFile that refers to a binary file. This works just like it does for a text file. However, the file extension for a binary file is typically different than the extension for a text file. In this case, the extension is *dat*.

The second and third examples both create a buffered stream and connect to the binary file specified in the first example. In the second example, the code creates an output stream that will delete all data in the existing file before it writes the new data to the file. However, the third example shows how you can append data to the end of a file. To do that, you set the second argument of the FileOutputStream constructor to true.

The constructors shown in this figure should help you understand how to layer binary output streams. Here, you can see that the DataOutputStream constructor accepts any class in the OutputStream hierarchy. As a result, you can supply a BufferedOutputStream object as an argument of the DataOutputStream constructor. Similarly, since the BufferedOutputStream constructor also accepts any OutputStream object, you can supply a FileOutputStream object as an argument of the BufferedOutputStream constructor. Then, to create a FileOutputStream object, you can supply a File object or file name that refers to a binary file.

A subset of the OutputStream hierarchy

```
OutputStream <<abstract>>
    FileOutputStream
    FilterOutputStream
        BufferedOutputStream
        DataOutputStream <<implements DataOutput interface>>
```

Classes used to connect a binary output stream to a file

DataOutputStream	writes data to the stream
→BufferedOutputStream	creates a buffer for the stream
→FileOutputStream	connects the stream to a file

Constructors of these classes

Constructor	Throws
`DataOutputStream(OutputStream)`	None
`BufferedOutputStream(OutputStream)`	None
`FileOutputStream(File[, booleanAppend])`	FileNotFoundException
`FileOutputStream(StringFileName[, booleanAppend])`	FileNotFoundException

Example 1: A File object that refers to a binary file

```
File productsFile = new File("products.dat");
```

Example 2: How to connect to a file with a buffer

```
DataOutputStream out = new DataOutputStream(
                       new BufferedOutputStream(
                       new FileOutputStream(productsFile)));
```

Example 3: How to connect for an append operation

```
DataOutputStream out = new DataOutputStream(
                       new BufferedOutputStream(
                       new FileOutputStream(productsFile, true)));
```

Description

- The OutputStream class is an abstract class that's inherited by all of the classes in the OutputStream hierarchy. To learn more about the OutputStream hierarchy, check the documentation for the Java API.
- All classes in the java.io and java.util.zip packages that end with OutputStream are members of the OutputStream hierarchy.
- The FilterOutputStream class is a superclass of all classes that filter binary output streams.
- By default, the output file is overwritten. If that's not what you want, you can specify true for the second argument of the FileWriter constructor to append data to the file.
- Although a buffer isn't required, it makes output operations more efficient.

Figure 19-12 How to connect a binary output stream to a file

How to write to a binary file

If you look back at figure 19-12, you can see that the DataOutputStream class implements the DataOutput interface. As a result, you can call any of the methods of the DataOutput interface from an output stream that includes a DataOutputStream object. Some of the most commonly used methods of this interface are summarized in figure 19-13.

You can use the first four methods in this figure to write primitive data types to a binary output stream. For example, you can use the writeInt method to write an int value to a binary output stream. To read these data types, you sometimes need to know how many bytes each data type uses. That's why we've included the number of bytes used by each data type in this figure.

You can use the writeChars and writeUTF methods to write strings to a binary output stream. When you use the writeChars method, it writes two bytes per character. When you use the writeUTF method, it starts by writing a two-byte number that indicates the length of the string. Then, it writes the *UTF* (*Universal Text Format*) representation of the string. Although this usually writes each ASCII character as one byte, it may write some Unicode characters as two or three bytes. In general, you can use the writeUTF method whenever it's okay to write strings with lengths that vary. But when you need to write strings that have equal lengths, you need to use the writeChars method. Later in this chapter, you'll learn why.

This figure also summarizes the size, flush, and close methods of the DataOutputStream class. You can use these methods if you need to check the number of bytes that have been written to the stream, or if you need to flush data from the buffer. As always, you should use the close method to close the stream when you're done working with it.

The example in this figure shows how to write the data that's stored in a Product object to a binary file. To start, the writeUTF method is used to write the product's code and description, which are String objects. Then, the writeDouble method is used to write the product's price to the file. Finally, the last statement closes the output stream, which flushes all data to the file and releases the resources that were used by the stream object.

Note that all of the methods shown here can throw an IOException. As a result, you must either throw or catch this exception. Otherwise, you won't be able to compile your code.

Common methods of the DataOutput interface

Method	Throws	Description
`writeBoolean(boolean)`	IOException	Writes a 1-byte boolean value to the output stream.
`writeInt(int)`	IOException	Writes a 4-byte int value to the output stream.
`writeDouble(double)`	IOException	Writes an 8-byte double value to the output stream.
`writeChar(int)`	IOException	Writes a 2-byte char value to the output stream.
`writeChars(String)`	IOException	Writes a string using 2 bytes per character to the output stream.
`writeUTF(String)`	IOException	Writes a 2-byte value for the number of bytes in the string followed by the UTF representation of the string, which typically uses 1 byte per character.

Methods of the DataOutputStream class

Method	Throws	Description
`size()`	None	Returns an int for the number of bytes written to this stream.
`flush()`	IOException	Flushes any data that's in the buffer to the file.
`close()`	IOException	Flushes any data that's in the buffer to the file and closes the stream.

Code that writes data to a binary file

```
// write a Product object to the file
out.writeUTF(product.getCode());
out.writeUTF(product.getDescription());
out.writeDouble(product.getPrice());

// flush data to the file and close the output stream
out.close();
```

Description

- Since the DataOutputStream class implements the DataOutput interface, you can call any of the methods shown above from a DataOutputStream object.
- The writeUTF method uses the *Universal Text Format (UTF)*. First, this method writes a two-byte number for the number of bytes in the string. Then, it writes the characters using the Universal Text Format. For most strings, UTF uses one byte per character.

Figure 19-13 How to write to a binary file

How to connect a binary input stream to a file

To create a binary input stream, you can layer three streams from the InputStream hierarchy as shown in figure 19-14. The example in this figure shows how you do that. As in all of the examples in this chapter, the productsFile variable in this example refers to a File object.

The constructors of the classes shown here explain how you can layer these streams. For example, the DataInputStream constructor accepts an InputStream object. As a result, you can use an object created from any class in the InputStream hierarchy as an argument. Similarly, since the BufferedInputStream constructor also accepts any object of the InputStream hierarchy, it can accept a FileInputStream object. Finally, the FileInputStream constructor accepts a File object or file name.

A subset of the InputStream hierarchy

```
InputStream {abstract}
    FileInputStream
    FilterInputStream
        BufferedInputStream
        DataInputStream {implements DataInput interface}
```

Classes used to connect a binary input stream to a file

DataInputStream	reads data from the stream
→BufferedInputStream	creates a buffer for the stream
→FileInputStream	connects the stream to the file

Constructors of these classes

Constructor	Throws
`DataInputStream(InputStream)`	None
`BufferedInputStream(InputStream)`	None
`FileInputStream(File)`	FileNotFoundException
`FileInputStream(StringFileName)`	FileNotFoundException

How to connect a binary input stream to a file

```
DataInputStream in = new DataInputStream(
                     new BufferedInputStream(
                     new FileInputStream(productsFile)));
```

Description

- The InputStream class is an abstract class that's inherited by all of the classes in the InputStream hierarchy. To learn more about the InputStream hierarchy, check the documentation for the Java API.
- All classes in the java.io and java.util.zip packages that end with InputStream are members of the InputStream hierarchy.
- The FilterInputStream class is a superclass of all classes that filter binary input streams.
- Although a buffer isn't required, it makes input operations more efficient.

Figure 19-14 How to connect a binary input stream to a file

How to read from a binary file

If you look back at figure 19-14, you can see that the DataInputStream class implements the DataInput interface. As a result, you can call any of the methods of the DataInput interface from an input stream that includes a DataInputStream object. Some of the most commonly used methods of this interface are summarized in figure 19-15.

You can use the first four methods in this figure to read primitive data types from a binary input stream. For example, you can use the readInt method to read an int value from a binary input stream. To read these data types, you sometimes need to know how many bytes each data type uses. That's why the number of bytes used by each data type is included in this figure.

You can use the readUTF method to read binary data that's stored in the Universal Text Format that was described earlier in this chapter. Usually, that means that you'll use the readUTF method to read data that was written with the writeUTF method.

You can use the skipBytes method to skip a specified number of bytes in an input stream. If for some reason it can't skip that number of bytes, though, the method skips as many bytes as it can and returns an int value for the actual number that it skipped. This can happen, for example, if the method reaches the end of the file before it skips the specified number of bytes.

Although the read methods in this figure correspond to the write methods shown earlier in this chapter, there is no corresponding read method for the writeChars method. As a result, to read strings written by the writeChars method, you need to create a loop that reads in each character using the readChar method. The next figure shows an example of how to do this.

When working with a binary input stream, you can also use some methods from the DataInputStream class. In particular, you can use the available method to return the number of bytes in the file that haven't been read, and you can use the close method to close the input stream and release any resources used by it.

The example in this figure shows show how to read the data for a Product object from a binary file. To start, the first two statements use the readUTF method to read the product's code and description. This will only work if these fields were written using the writeUTF method as shown in figure 19-13. Then, the third statement uses the readDouble method to read the product's price. Again, this will only work if the product's price was written using the writeDouble method.

Once the three fields have been read, the fourth statement uses the fields to create a Product object. Notice that, unlike the example that works with a text file, this example doesn't convert the price from a string to a double value. That's because the price was written to the file and read from the file as a double value. Finally, the last statement uses the close method to close the file. As always, this statement is necessary to flush the buffer and free any system resources that are being used by the stream.

Note that all of the methods shown in this figure can throw an IOException that's checked by the compiler. As a result, you must either throw or catch this exception. Otherwise, you won't be able to compile your code.

Common methods of the DataInput interface

Method	Throws	Description
`readBoolean()`	EOFException	Reads 1 byte and returns a boolean value.
`readInt()`	EOFException	Reads 4 bytes and returns an int value.
`readDouble()`	EOFException	Reads 8 bytes and returns a double value.
`readChar()`	EOFException	Reads 2 bytes and returns a char value.
`readUTF()`	EOFException	Reads and returns the string encoded with UTF.
`skipBytes(int)`	EOFException	Attempts to skip the specified number of bytes, and returns an int value for the actual number of bytes skipped.

Common methods of the DataInputStream class

Method	Throws	Description
`available()`	IOException	Returns the number of bytes remaining in the file.
`close()`	IOException	Closes the stream.

Code that reads a Product object from a binary file

```
// read product data from a file
String code = in.readUTF();
String description = in.readUTF();
double price = in.readDouble();

// create the Product object from its data
Product p = new Product(code, description, price);

// close the input stream
in.close();
```

Description

- Since the DataInputStream class implements the DataInput interface, you can call any of the methods shown above from an object of this class.
- The readUTF method reads characters that were written with the Universal Text Format.

Figure 19-15 How to read from a binary file

Two ways to work with binary strings

Figure 19-16 illustrates two ways you can read and write binary strings. First, you can use the readChar and WriteChars methods to read and write strings using two bytes per character. Second, you can use the readUTF and writeUTF methods to read and write strings with one byte per character using the Universal Text Format.

The first example shows how the writeUTF method differs from the writeChars method. This example starts by creating a string that contains 23 characters (22 regular characters plus one new line character). Then, the first group of statements starts by calling the writeUTF method to write the string to the stream. Then, it calls the size method to return the number of bytes that were written, and it prints the number of bytes that were written to the console. As you can see, the writeUTF method wrote 25 bytes: two bytes that indicate the length of the string and one byte for each of the 23 characters in the string.

The next group of statements starts by calling the writeChars method to write the same string. Then, it calculates the number of bytes that were written to the stream. To do that, it subtracts the number of bytes written by the writeUTF method from the total number of bytes written to the stream. Finally, it prints the number of bytes that were written to the console. In this case, 46 bytes, or two bytes per character, were written to the stream. If you open this test file in a text editor as shown here, you can see the difference between how these two strings are stored.

The second example reads the strings that were written by the writeUTF and writeChars methods. To start, the first statement in this example calls the available method to get the total number of bytes in the file. Then, the first group of statements calls the readUTF method to read the string that was written by the writeUTF method. After the string has been read, the next statement calculates the total number of bytes that were read. To do that, it subtracts the number of bytes that are left in the file from the total number of bytes in the file. Then, the last statement in this group prints a message to the console that indicates the number of bytes that were read. In this case, 25 bytes were read, which is the same number of bytes that were written by the writeUTF method.

The second group of statements uses the readChar method within a loop to read the string that was written by the writeChars method. To read the appropriate number of characters, the loop is executed the number of times indicated by the length method of the original string variable. In other words, before you can use the readChar method, you need to know how many characters are in the string. Within the loop, the first statement appends the char value that's read from the binary file to the String variable named string2. Then, the second statement keeps a running count of the number of characters that have been read (2 bytes per character) so it can be printed to the console when the loop ends.

For many applications, you can use the writeUTF and readUTF methods to write and read string data. However, if you need to make sure that each string has the same length, you have to use the writeChars and readChar methods. You'll see an example of how to do that later in this chapter.

Example 1: Two ways to write a binary string

```
// create a test string
String testString = "This is a test string.\n";

// use the writeUTF method
out.writeUTF(testString);
int writeSize1 = out.size();
System.out.println("writeUTF writes " + writeSize1 + " bytes.");

// use the writeChars method
out.writeChars(testString);
int writeSize2 = out.size() - writeSize1;
System.out.println("writeChars writes " + writeSize2 + " bytes\n");

out.close();
```

Resulting output

```
writeUTF writes 25 bytes.
writeChars writes 46 bytes.
```

The file opened in a text editor

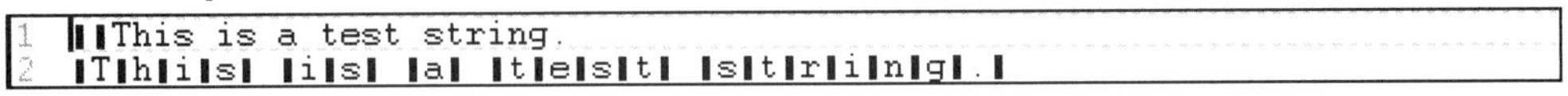

```
1 ▮▮This is a test string.
2 ▮T▮h▮i▮s▮ ▮i▮s▮ ▮a▮ ▮t▮e▮s▮t▮ ▮s▮t▮r▮i▮n▮g▮.▮
```

Example 2: Two ways to read a binary string

```
// get total bytes
int totalBytes = in.available();

// use the readUTF method
String string1 = in.readUTF();
int readSize1 = totalBytes - in.available();
System.out.println("readUTF reads " + readSize1 + " bytes.");

// use the readChar method
int readSize2 = 0;
String string2 = "";
for (int i = 0; i < testString.length(); i++)
{
    string2 += in.readChar();
    readSize2 += 2;
}
System.out.println("readChar reads " + readSize2 + " bytes.\n");
```

Resulting output

```
readUTF reads 25 bytes.
readChar reads 46 bytes.
```

Figure 19-16 Two ways to work with binary strings

How to work with random-access files

So far in this chapter, you've learned how to use streams to read and write files sequentially. That means that you read or write one record after another, from the first record in a file to the last. As a result, you have to read the first 49 records in a file before you can read the 50th record in the file. Files that you access sequentially are known as *sequential-access files* (or just *sequential files*).

Now, you'll learn how to access a binary file randomly using a RandomAccessFile object. A binary file that you access randomly is known as a *random-access file*. This type of file lets you move a *pointer* (or *cursor*) to any location in the file. Then, you can read or write from that point, which means you can read the 50th record in a file without reading the first 49 records in the file. This type of access is far more efficient than sequential access for many types of business applications.

How to connect to a random-access file

Figure 19-17 shows how to create a RandomAccessFile object. To do that, you can use either of the constructors shown in this figure. The first one accepts a File object, and the second one accepts a string that specifies the file name.

Both constructors accept a second argument that specifies the mode for the random-access file. Here, you can specify "r" to open the file in read-only mode, "rw" to open the file in read-write mode, and "rws" or "rwd" to open the file in one of the synchronized read-write modes. The difference between the two synchronized modes is that the rws mode updates the data stored in the file as well as the *metadata* for the file, while the rwd mode updates just the data. The metadata includes information about the file such as its size and the date it was last modified. Since updating the metadata requires an additional file I/O operation, the rws mode isn't as efficient as the rwd mode.

You should use one of the synchronized modes when your program needs to allow two or more users to update the same random-access file at the same time. That way, one user won't be able to update the file while another user is updating the same part of the file. In practice, though, you'll probably want to use a database for any program that needs to allow two or more users to update the same data. That's because databases provide features that make it easier to handle this type of problem.

Notice that when you work with a random-access file, you can't use a buffer. That's because you normally read or write just one record at a time. As a result, buffering isn't as critical as it is for working with sequential-access files where you often need to read and write the entire file.

Constructors of the RandomAccessFile class

Constructor	Throws
`RandomAccessFile(File, stringMode)`	FileNotFoundException
`RandomAccessFile(StringFileName, stringMode)`	FileNotFoundException

Access mode values

Value	Description
r	Open for reading only.
rw	Open for reading and writing. If the file doesn't already exist, an attempt will be made to create it.
rws	Open for reading and writing and also require that every update to the data stored in the file or the metadata for the file be written synchronously to the underlying storage device.
rwd	Open for reading and writing and also require that every update to the data stored in the file be written synchronously to the underlying storage device.

Example 1: A File object that refers to a binary file

```
File file = new File("products.dat");
```

Example 2: How to create a read-write RandomAccessFile object

```
RandomAccessFile productsFile = new RandomAccessFile(file, "rw");
```

Example 3: How to create a read-only RandomAccessFile object

```
RandomAccessFile productsFile = new RandomAccessFile(file, "r");
```

Example 4: How to create a synchronized read-write object

```
RandomAccessFile productsFile = new RandomAccessFile(file, "rws");
```

Description

- You can use the classes in the OutputStream and InputStream hierarchies to read and write files sequentially. A file you access sequentially is called a *sequential-access file*. When you work with a sequential-access file, you read from the beginning of the file to the end of the file, and you can add data only at the end of the file.
- You can use the RandomAccessFile class to read and write files randomly. A file you access randomly is called a *random-access file*. When you work with a random-access file, you can move a *pointer* to any point in the file. Then, you can read and write data starting at that point. This lets you modify part of a file without affecting the rest of the file.
- If you use one of the synchronized read-write modes, only one user at a time can update the file. Since the rwd mode doesn't update the metadata with each operation, it reduces the number of IO operations and runs slightly faster than the rws mode.
- The *metadata* for a file includes information about the file such as its size, the date it was last modified, and so on.

Figure 19-17 How to connect to a random-access file

How to read to and write from a random-access file

Figure 19-18 shows how to read and write random-access files. To start, it shows that this class implements both the DataOutput and DataInput interfaces you saw in figures 19-13 and 19-15. As a result, you can call the methods of those interfaces to write and read random-access files.

In addition, you can use the four methods summarized in this figure that are specific to random-access files. Of these four methods, the seek method makes random access possible. This method lets you move the pointer to any location in the file without reading the records before that point. To use this method, you supply a long value that specifies the number of bytes from the beginning of the file that you want to move the pointer to. This lets you move the pointer forward or backward through the file. If you try to move the pointer beyond the end of the file, the pointer will be moved just beyond the last byte in the file so you can write a record at the end of the file.

The other three methods let you work with the length of a file and close a file. For instance, you can use the length method to return a long value that indicates the length of a file in bytes. You can also use the setLength method to change the length of a random-access file. If you use this method to make a random-access file shorter, it will truncate the file, thus deleting any data stored after the new length. When you're done working with a RandomAccessFile object, you can use the close method to close it and free the resources that are used by this object.

When you write data to a random-access file, each field of a record should have the same length as the same field in other records so that each record will have the same length. That way, you can easily calculate the number of bytes that marks the beginning of the field or record that you want to access. Then, you can use the seek method to move the pointer to that field or record.

To illustrate, the first example in this figure shows how to use a RandomAccessFile object to write three records that contain two fields. Here, the first statement opens a random-access file in read-write mode. Then, a loop writes each record to the file using methods provided by the DataOutput interface. Within this loop, the first statement uses the writeChars method to write a string using two bytes per character. Since each string has four characters, this statement always writes eight bytes. Then, the second statement writes a double value, which always uses eight bytes.

The second example shows how to read the third record in the random-access file that was written by the first example. Here, the first statement initializes a constant that specifies the record length. Then, the second statement opens the file in read-only mode. The next two statements specify the record to read (the third record) and use the seek method to move the pointer to the beginning of that record. After that, the next group of statements reads the data of the third record. To do that, the writeChar method is called four times from within a loop to read all four characters of the first field, and the readDouble method is called to read the double value of the second field.

Two interfaces implemented by the RandomAccessFile class

```
DataOutput    (see figure 19-13)
DataInput     (see figure 19-15)
```

Methods of the RandomAccessFile class used for input and output

Method	Throws	Description
`seek(long)`	IOException	Sets the pointer to the specified number of bytes from the beginning of the file. If the pointer is set beyond the end of the file, the pointer will be moved to the end of the file.
`length()`	IOException	Returns a long for the number of bytes in the file.
`setLength(long)`	IOException	Sets the length of the file to the specified number of bytes.
`close()`	IOException	Closes the file.

Example 1: Code that writes data to a file

```
RandomAccessFile productsFile = new RandomAccessFile(file, "rw");

// write 3 records that contain codes and prices to the file
String[] codes = {"java", "jsps", "txtp"};
double[] prices = {49.5, 49.5, 20.0};
for (int i = 0; i < codes.length; i++)
{
    productsFile.writeChars(codes[i]);
    productsFile.writeDouble(prices[i]);
}

productsFile.close();
```

Example 2: Code that reads data from a file

```
final int RECORD_LENGTH = 16;  // 4 chars @ 2 bytes per char +
                               // 1 double @ 8 bytes

RandomAccessFile productsFile = new RandomAccessFile(file, "r");

// move the pointer to the third record
int recordNumber = 3;
productsFile.seek((recordNumber - 1) * RECORD_LENGTH);

// read the third record
String code = "";
for (int i = 0; i < 4; i++)
    code += productsFile.readChar();
double price = productsFile.readDouble();

productsFile.close();
```

Description

- When writing to a random-access file, it's a common coding practice to write each record with the same number of bytes. This makes it possible to move the file pointer to the start of each record in the file.

Figure 19-18 How to read to and write from a random access file

How to read and write fixed-length strings

When you write strings to a random-access file, you need to write each string with a fixed number of characters. In other words, you need to write *fixed-length strings*. If, for example, you want to create a field that stores last names, you might decide to use 20 characters for that field. Then, when you write a last name that has fewer than 20 characters, you can pad the field so it contains 20 characters. One way to do that is to add Unicode zeros to the end of the field. Then, when you read the field, you read characters until the first Unicode zero is encountered.

To illustrate, figure 19-19 shows how to code a class named IOStringUtils. This class contains two static methods that you can use for writing and reading fixed-length strings. Then, the next figure shows how you can call these methods from another class.

Within the IOStringUtils class, the writeFixedString method contains code that writes a fixed-length string. This method accepts three arguments and throws an IOException. The first argument is a DataOutput object, which is usually a RandomAccessFile object. The second argument is a String object that contains the string to be written. The third argument is an int value that specifies the length of the fixed-length string. Within the method, a loop writes each character of the string to the file. If the string is shorter than the specified length, the method writes Unicode zeros until it reaches the specified length.

Conversely, the readFixedString method reads the fixed-length strings that were written by the writeFixedString method, discarding any Unicode zeros. This method accepts two arguments and throws an IOException. The first argument is a DataInput object, which can be either a RandomAccessFile object or a DataInputStream object. The second argument is an int value that specifies the length of the fixed-length string. Within the method, the code reads characters and builds a string. If it reads a Unicode zero, it stops adding characters to the string. Otherwise, it reads until it reaches the specified length. Then, it returns the string.

A class that writes and reads fixed-length strings

```
import java.io.*;

public class IOStringUtils
{
    public static void writeFixedString(DataOutput out, int length,
    String s) throws IOException
    {
        for (int i = 0; i < length; i++)
        {
            if (i < s.length())
                out.writeChar(s.charAt(i)); // write char
            else
                out.writeChar(0);           // write unicode zero
        }
    }

    public static String getFixedString(DataInput in, int length)
    throws IOException
    {
        StringBuilder sb = new StringBuilder();
        for (int i = 0; i < length; i++)
        {
            char c = in.readChar();
            // if char is not Unicode zero add to string
            if (c != 0)
                sb.append(c);
        }
        return sb.toString();
    }
}
```

Description

- When you write strings to a random-access file, you need to write *fixed-length strings*. That way, the length of the strings won't vary from one record to another, and all of the record lengths in the file will be the same.
- You can create a class like the IOStringUtils class shown above that contains static methods to write and read fixed-length strings.
- The writeFixedString method writes the characters of an input string to an output file followed by Unicode zeros for any unused positions in the fixed-length output string.
- The getFixedString method reads a string written by the writeFixedString method, but stops appending characters to the StringBuilder object when the first Unicode zero is read.

Figure 19-19 How to read and write fixed-length strings

A class that works with a random-access file

Figure 19-20 presents the complete code for the ProductRandomFile class. Like the ProductTextFile class, this class implements the ProductDAO interface shown in figure 19-10.

To start, this class declares two instance variables. The first instance variable defines a RandomAccessFile object named productsFile, and the second instance variable defines an ArrayList object named productCodes.

Next, this class defines three constants that are available to the entire class. The PRICE_SIZE constant indicates that the size of the price field is 8 bytes since it is a double value. Then, the RECORD_SIZE constant calculates the size of each record in the file. To do that, it uses the CODE_SIZE and DESCRIPTION_SIZE constants that are stored in the ProductConstants interface shown in figure 19-10. After that, the DELETION_CODE constant defines a string that's used to indicate that a product has been marked for deletion. In this case, the string contains four spaces. In other words, if a product has a code of four spaces, it has been marked for deletion.

The constructor for the ProductRandomFile class initializes the two instance variables of the class. The first statement initializes the productsFile variable by opening a random-access file named products.ran in read-write mode. Then, the second statement initializes the productCodes variable by calling the getCodes method that's coded later in this class. Since the constructor of the RandomAccessFile class can throw a FileNotFoundException, these statements are coded within a try statement. Then, the catch clause that catches this exception prints the stack trace to the console.

After the constructor, the finalize method overrides the finalize method of the Object class. This method is called when Java determines that there are no more references to this object. When that happens, the code in this method closes the random-access file. To do that, it uses an if statement to prevent a NullPointerException from occurring, and it uses a catch clause to catch the IOException that may be thrown by the close method. Notice that this method is declared as public even though you don't call it directly from your applications.

The next four methods in this class are private methods that are used to read records from the products file. The first method, getRecordCount, returns the number of records in the file. To do that, it calculates the number of records in the file by dividing the total number of bytes in the file by the number of bytes in each record. Since the length method returns a long value, the result of this calculation must be cast to an int value.

The code for the ProductRandomFile class **Page 1**

```
import java.io.*;
import java.util.*;

public class ProductRandomFile implements ProductDAO
{
    private RandomAccessFile productsFile = null;
    private ArrayList<String> productCodes = null;

    private final int PRICE_SIZE = 8;  // doubles are 8 bytes
    private final int RECORD_SIZE =
        CODE_SIZE * 2 +          // from the ProductConstants interface
        DESCRIPTION_SIZE * 2 +   // from the ProductConstants interface
        PRICE_SIZE;
    private final String DELETION_CODE = "    ";

    public ProductRandomFile()
    {
        try
        {
            productsFile = new RandomAccessFile("products.ran", "rw");
            productCodes = this.getCodes();
        }
        catch(FileNotFoundException fnfe)
        {
            fnfe.printStackTrace();
        }
    }

    public void finalize()
    {
        try
        {
            if (productsFile != null)
                productsFile.close();
        }
        catch(IOException ioe)
        {
            ioe.printStackTrace();
        }
    }

    //**************************************************
    // Private methods for reading products
    //**************************************************

    private int getRecordCount() throws IOException
    {
        int recordCount = (int) productsFile.length() / RECORD_SIZE;
        return recordCount;
    }
```

Figure 19-20 A class that works with a random-access file (part 1 of 4)

The getRecordNumber method accepts a string that contains a product code and returns the record number for that product code. To do that, it compares each string in the productCodes array list with the specified product code. If it finds a match, it returns the current position in the array. Otherwise, it returns an int value of -1 to indicate that the record wasn't found.

The getRecord method accepts an int value that specifies the record number for a record and returns a Product object for that record. To start, this method checks if the record number is greater than or equal to zero and less than the total number of records. If so, the record number is valid and the method continues by creating a Product object from the data that's stored in the record and returning it to the calling method. Otherwise, the method returns a null to indicate that no product exists for that record number.

To create the Product object, the getRecord method uses the seek method to position the pointer at the beginning of the specified record. Then, the readFixedString method of the IOStringUtils class is used to read the product's code and description, and the readDouble method is used to read the product's price. Finally, these values are passed to the constructor of the Product class to create a Product object.

The getCodes method creates an array list that contains every product code that's stored in the file. To start, this method declares an array list of strings. Then, it uses a loop to read each product code from the file into the array. To do that, this method uses the getRecordCount method to return the number of records in the file, it uses the seek method to skip to the beginning of each record, and it uses the static readFixedString method of the IOStringUtils class to read the string for the product code. When the loop completes, the array list is returned to the calling method. If an exception is encountered as the product codes are read, however, the stack trace is printed to the console and a null is returned to indicate that the getCodes method did not complete successfully.

The code for the ProductRandomFile class

Page 2

```
private int getRecordNumber(String productCode)
{
    for (int i = 0; i < productCodes.size(); i++)
    {
        String code = productCodes.get(i);
        if (productCode.equals(code))
            return i;
    }
    return -1;  // no record matches the product code
}

private Product getRecord(int recordNumber) throws IOException
{
    if (recordNumber >= 0 && recordNumber < this.getRecordCount())
    {
        productsFile.seek(recordNumber * RECORD_SIZE);

        String code = IOStringUtils.getFixedString(
            productsFile, CODE_SIZE);
        String description = IOStringUtils.getFixedString(
            productsFile, DESCRIPTION_SIZE);
        double price = productsFile.readDouble();

        Product product = new Product(code, description, price);
        return product;
    }
    else
        return null;
}

private ArrayList<String> getCodes()
{
    try
    {
        ArrayList<String> codes = new ArrayList<String>();
        for (int i = 0; i < this.getRecordCount(); i++)
        {
            productsFile.seek(i * RECORD_SIZE);
            codes.add(IOStringUtils.getFixedString(
                productsFile, CODE_SIZE));
        }
        return codes;
    }
    catch(IOException ioe)
    {
        ioe.printStackTrace();
        return null;
    }
}
```

Figure 19-20 A class that works with a random-access file (part 2 of 4)

The next two methods in this class are public methods that return Product objects. Both of these methods catch any IOException that might be thrown. This prevents any of the implementation details of this class (such as the type of exceptions) from being exposed to other classes, and it makes it easier for programmers to use these methods since they don't have to handle these exceptions.

If either of these methods encounter an IOException, its catch clause executes two statements. The first statement prints the stack trace to the console, which can help the programmer who is coding this class determine the cause of the error during the testing and debugging phase. Then, the second statement returns a null. This indicates to the programmer who is using this class that the operation wasn't completed successfully.

The getProducts method returns an array list that contains all the Product objects in the file that haven't been marked for deletion. To do that, this method begins by creating an ArrayList object named products that can store Product objects. Then, it uses a loop to create a Product object for each record. Within the loop, an if statement checks if the product code for the record is equal to the DELETION_CODE constant. If not, the product has not been marked for deletion. Then, the getProduct method is called to get the Product object for the record, and the Product object is added to the array list.

The getProduct method accepts a product code. If the random-access file contains a record with this product code, this method returns a Product object that contains the data that's stored in that record. To do that, it calls the getRecordNumber method to get the record number of the record with the specified product code. Then, it calls the getRecord method to get the record with that number and create a Product object from the data in that record.

Note that if a record with the specified product code isn't found, the getRecordNumber method returns –1. Then, the getRecord method returns a null because –1 is an invalid record number. In that case, the Product object that's returned to the calling method is null.

The code for the ProductRandomFile class **Page 3**

```
//*****************************************************
// Public methods for reading products
//*****************************************************

public ArrayList<Product> getProducts()
{
    ArrayList<Product> products = new ArrayList<Product>();
    try
    {
        for (int i = 0; i < productCodes.size(); i++)
        {
            // if record has been marked for deletion,
            // don't add to products array list
            if (!productCodes.get(i).equals(DELETION_CODE))
            {
                Product product = this.getRecord(i);
                products.add(product);
            }
        }
    }
    catch(IOException ioe)
    {
        ioe.printStackTrace();
        return null;
    }
    return products;
}

public Product getProduct(String productCode)
{
    try
    {
        int recordNumber = this.getRecordNumber(productCode);
        Product product = this.getRecord(recordNumber);
        return product;
    }
    catch(IOException ioe)
    {
        ioe.printStackTrace();
        return null;
    }
}
```

Figure 19-20 A class that works with a random-access file (part 3 of 4)

The next method in this class is a private method named writeProduct that's used to write the data for a product to the file. This method accepts a Product object and a record number. It uses the record number to move the pointer to the position in the file where the record is to be written. Then, it writes the data in the Product object to the file. To write the product code and description fields, it uses the writeFixedString method of the IOStringUtils. To write the price field, it uses the writeDouble method. If an exception is thrown by any of these statements, this method prints the stack trace and returns a false value.

The next three methods are public methods that can be used to add, update, and delete the products stored in the products file. All three of these methods accept a Product object as an argument.

The addProduct method writes the data in the Product object that's passed to it to the end of the random-access file. To do that, it adds the product code to the productCodes array list. Then, it calls the getRecordNumber method to get the record number of the new product. Finally, it calls the writeProduct method to write the new product at the position indicated by the record number, which should be at the end of the file. If the writeProduct method executes successfully, it returns a true value. That value is then returned to the method that called the addProduct method.

The updateProduct method writes the data that's stored in the Product object that's passed to it over the record that has the same product code. To do that, it starts by calling the getRecordNumber method to get the record number for the product. If this record number isn't equal to –1, which indicates that the product was found, this method calls the writeProduct method to write the data for the specified Product object over the data for the current record. However, if the product code isn't found, this method returns a false value and doesn't update the record.

The deleteProduct method marks the specified Product object for deletion. To do that, the first statement gets the record number for the Product by calling the getRecordNumber method. If this method returns a value other than –1, indicating that the product was found, the set method of the productCodes array list is used to set the product code of the specified product to the value that's stored in the DELETION_CODE constant. Then, a new Product object is created with a product code equal to the DELETION_CODE constant, a description of an empty string, and a price of zero. Finally, the deleteProduct method calls the writeProduct method to write the new Product object to the file. If this write operation is successful, this method returns a true value. If this operation isn't successful, or if the product wasn't found, this method returns a false value.

Since the deleteProduct method doesn't actually delete the record from the file, you may want to include another method in this class that deletes all the records that have been marked for deletion. Then, you can run that method periodically to remove unnecessary data from the file. To do that, this method could use the getProducts method to read all the products that haven't been marked for deletion. Then, it could write all of these products to the file, overwriting any existing records. Finally, it could use the setLength method of the RandomAccessFile class to set the length of the file based on the number of records that remain, which would truncate any leftover data at the end of the file.

The code for the ProductRandomFile class Page 4

```
    //**************************************************
    //* Private methods for writing products
    //**************************************************

    private boolean writeProduct(Product product, int recordNumber)
    {
        try
        {
            productsFile.seek(recordNumber * RECORD_SIZE);
            IOStringUtils.writeFixedString(
                productsFile, CODE_SIZE, product.getCode());
            IOStringUtils.writeFixedString(
                productsFile, DESCRIPTION_SIZE, product.getDescription());
            productsFile.writeDouble(product.getPrice());
            return true;
        }
        catch(IOException ioe)
        {
            ioe.printStackTrace();
            return false;
        }
    }

    //**************************************************
    //* Public methods for writing products
    //**************************************************

    public boolean addProduct(Product product)
    {
        productCodes.add(product.getCode());
        int recordNumber = this.getRecordNumber(product.getCode());
        return this.writeProduct(product, recordNumber);
    }

    public boolean updateProduct(Product product)
    {
        int recordNumber = this.getRecordNumber(product.getCode());
        if (recordNumber != -1)
            return this.writeProduct(product, recordNumber);
        else
            return false;
    }

    public boolean deleteProduct(Product product)
    {
        int recordNumber = this.getRecordNumber(product.getCode());
        if (recordNumber != -1)
        {
            productCodes.set(recordNumber, DELETION_CODE);
            Product p = new Product(DELETION_CODE, "", 0);
            return this.writeProduct(product, recordNumber);
        }
        else
            return false;
    }
}
```

Figure 19-20 A class that works with a random-access file (part 4 of 4)

Perspective

In this chapter, you learned how to read and write text files sequentially, and you learned how to read and write binary files sequentially and randomly. If you've already read the chapters in section 4, this means that now at last you can see how all of the classes and methods in a business application work together. That includes presentation classes like JFrame and JPanel classes, business classes like Product and Invoice classes, and data storage classes like the ProductTextFile and ProductRandomFile classes.

Now that you've seen how to work with text files and binary files, you might want to take a moment to consider the advantages and disadvantages of each. For example, since you don't need to convert int and double values to strings and back, binary files make it easier to work with numbers. However, text files are often easier to share with other programs. For example, the data in a text file can be viewed in a text editor or a web browser.

As you work with files, remember that they are only one option for storing data. Another option is to store data in a database. Because databases provide sophisticated features for organizing and managing data, they're used for most serious applications. You'll learn how to work with databases in chapter 21. But first, the next chapter will show you how to work with data using XML.

Summary

- A *text file* stores data as characters. A *binary file* stores data in a binary format.
- In a *delimited text file*, *delimiters* are used to separate the *fields* and *records* of the file.
- You use *character streams* to read and write text files and *binary streams* to read and write binary files. To get the functionality you need, you can *layer* two or more streams.
- A *buffer* is a block of memory that is used to store the data in a stream before it is written to or after it is read from an I/O device. When an output buffer is full, its data is *flushed* to the I/O device.
- When you work with I/O operations, you'll need to catch or throw three types of checked exceptions: IOException, FileNotFoundException, and EOFException.
- To identify a file when you create a File object, you can use an *absolute path name* or a *relative path name*. To identify a file on a remote computer, you can use the *Universal Naming Convention (UNC)*.
- The File class provides many methods that you can use to check whether a file or directory exists, to get information about a File object, and to create or delete directories and files.

- You can use the classes in the Writer and Reader hierarchies to work with a text file. You can use the classes in the OutputStream and InputStream hierarchies to work with a binary file. You can also use the methods of the DataOutput and DataInput interfaces to work with binary files.
- You can use the RandomAccessFile class to access a binary file randomly rather than sequentially. When you use a *random-access file*, you can position a *pointer* to any location in the file.
- When you work with random-access files, you store string values as *fixed-length strings*. That way, the files have the same number of bytes for each field within each record.

Exercise 19-1 Work with a text file

In this exercise, you'll create an application that maintains the name of the class that's used to create the ProductDAO object for the Product Maintenance application of chapter 8 in a text file. Then, you'll modify the Product Maintenance application so it uses the object specified in the text file.

Create the DAO Maintenance application

1. Open the DAOFile and DAOMaintApp classes in the c:\java1.5\ch19\ProductMaintenance directory.
2. Add code to the DAOFile class so that it can read and write a string that contains the name of a ProductDAO class to a text file named dao.txt. To do that, you'll need to add code to the constructor to initialize the File object, and you'll need to add code to the getDAOName and setDAOName methods so they read and write to the file.
3. Display the DAOMaintApp class, and add the code needed to create a DAOFile object and to get and set the name of the ProductDAO object in the file that the DAOFile object refers to. Test this application by changing the name of the ProductDAO class to ProductTextFile. The output should look like this:

```
Welcome to the DAO Maintenance application

The current ProductDAO class is: ProductRandomFile

Do you want to change this? (y/n): y

Enter the name of a valid ProductDAO class: ProductTextFile

The current ProductDAO class is: ProductTextFile

Do you want to change this? (y/n): n
```

4. To be sure that the dao.txt file was changed correctly, open it in a text editor.

Modify the Product Maintenance application

5. Open the DAOFactory class and modify it so it uses the DAOFile class to read the string in the dao.txt file and return the appropriate DAOFactory object. It should provide for ProductTextFile and ProductRandomFile objects.
6. Open the ProductMaintApp class and test it to make sure it works correctly. If the name of the class in the dao.txt file is anything other than ProductTextFile or ProductRandomFile, this class will throw an exception.
7. Modify the ProductMaintApp class so it prevents the exception that's thrown if an invalid ProductDAO class is specified.

Exercise 19-2 Work with a binary file

In this exercise, you'll enhance the Product Maintenance application so it can use a binary file.

1. Open the ProductTextFile class in the c:\java1.5\ ProductMaintenance directory. Change the class name to ProductBinaryFile, and save the class with this name.
2. Modify this class so it uses a binary file named products.dat. Be sure to store the product code and description as UTF characters.
3. Modify the DAOFactory class so it provides for the ProductBinaryFile class.
4. Run the DAOMaintApp application to change the ProductDAO class to ProductBinaryFile. Then, run the ProductMaintApp application to see if it works with the binary file. Make sure to leave at least three product records in the binary file.
5. Use a text editor to open the products.dat file. Note that it's easier to read the data that's stored in the text file.

Exercise 19-3 Improve the exception handling

In this exercise, you'll improve the way that exceptions are handled by the ProductMaintApp and ProductTextFile classes.

1. Open the ProductMaintApp class and modify it so it displays an error message and exits the application if the getProducts method returns a null.
2. Open the ProductTextFile class and comment out the line in the catch clause of the getProducts method that prints the stack trace to the console. Then, add a statement like this that throws an IOException to the beginning of the getProducts method:

```
if (true)
    throw new IOException(
        "This is a test of the getProducts method.");
```

3. Test these changes to make sure they're working correctly. To do that, run the DAOMaintApp application to set the name of the ProductDAO class to ProductTextFile. Then, run the ProductMaintApp application and enter the list command. If this works, comment out the statement you added that throws the IOException.
4. Modify the ProductMaintApp class so it responds appropriately if the addProduct or deleteProduct method returns a false value. Test this exception by commenting out the line in the catch clause of the saveProducts method that displays the stack trace and adding a statement near the beginning of this method that throws an IOException. Test these changes.
5. Modify the ProductTextFile class so it writes exceptions to a text file named errorLog.txt instead of printing them to the console. To do that, add a method named printToLogFile that accepts an IOException as an argument. This method should append two records to the log file: one that indicates the date and time the exception occurred and one that contains information about the exception.
6. Modify the getProducts and saveProducts methods so they call the printToLogFile method when an error occurs. Test these changes. When you're sure this works correctly, comment out the statement you added that throws the IOException and compile the class again.

Exercise 19-4 Enhance the random-access processing

In this exercise, you'll modify the ProductRandomFile class so it works more efficiently.

1. Use the DAOMaintApp application to specify the ProductRandomFile class as the ProductDAO class.
2. Open the ProductRandomFile class in the c:\java1.5\ch19\ProductMaintenance directory and review its code. Note that the getProducts method does not use a buffered input stream.
3. Modify the getProducts method so it uses a buffered DataInputStream to read each product in the products.ran file sequentially, creates a Product object for each product that isn't marked for deletion, and adds the Product object to the products array list. Be sure to check that the file exists before you process it.
4. Test this change by running the ProductMaintApp application.

Exercise 19-5 Update the random-access file

In this exercise, you'll add a method to the RandomAccessFile class that can be used to permanently delete the records in the products.ran file that have been marked for deletion. Then, you'll write the code to call this method.

1. Open the ProductRandomFile and RandomMaintApp classes in the c:\java1.5\ch19\ProductMaintenance directory.
2. Add a method named commitDeletions to the ProductRandomFile class. This method should delete all the records from the products.ran file that are marked for deletion and return the number of records that were deleted. (If an IOException occurs, it should return –1.) To do that, you can write all the products in the products array list to the file, and you can use the setLength method to set the file to the appropriate length. To make this code work, you'll need to close the RandomAccessFile object so that the new file length is applied. Also, be sure to reopen the file for random access, and reinitialize the productCodes array so it contains only the current products.
3. Display the RandomMaintApp class and note that it's similar to the ProductMaintApp class but contains only commit, help, and exit commands. Add the code to this class to implement the commitDeletions method that's executed when the user enters the commit command. If the commit operation is successful, it should display the number of records that were deleted. Otherwise, it should display an appropriate error message. Test this class to be sure it works correctly. To do that, you'll need to use the ProductMaintApp application to delete one or more records before you run the RandomMaintApp application.

20

How to work with XML

XML provides a standard way of storing data. Although XML is often used to exchange data between applications, particularly web-based applications, it can also be used to store structured data in a file. In this chapter, you'll learn the basics of creating XML documents, and you'll learn how to store those documents in a file. Because the classes at the end of this chapter use an array list, you may want to review chapters 10 and 11 before you read this chapter.

Introduction to XML

The topics that follow introduce you to the basics of XML. Here, you'll learn what XML is, how it is used, and the rules you must follow to create a simple XML document.

An XML document

XML (*Extensible Markup Language*) provides a standard way to structure data by using *tags* that identify each data element. In some ways, XML is similar to HTML, the markup language that's used to format HTML documents on the World Wide Web. As a result, if you're familiar with HTML, you'll have no trouble learning how to create *XML documents*.

Figure 20-1 shows a simple XML document that contains data for three products. Each product has a code, description, and price. In the next two figures, you'll learn how the tags in this XML document work. But even without knowing those details, you can pick out the code, description, and price for each of the three products represented by this XML document.

You can also use XML files as an alternative to the text and binary files described in chapter 19. Later in this chapter, for example, you'll see a ProductXMLFile class that uses an XML file. You can use this class with the Product Maintenance application you first saw in chapter 8.

Data for three products

Code	Description	Price
java	Murach's Beginning Java 2	49.50
jsps	Murach's Java Servlets and JSP	49.50
zjcl	Murach's OS/390 and z/OS JCL	62.50

The products.xml document

```
<?xml version="1.0" encoding="utf-8" ?>
<!--Product data--><Products>
  <Product Code="java">
    <Description>Murach's Beginning Java 2</Description>
    <Price>49.50</Price>
  </Product>
  <Product Code="jsps">
    <Description>Murach's Java Servlets and JSP</Description>
    <Price>49.50</Price>
  </Product>
  <Product Code="zjcl">
    <Description>Murach's OS/390 and z/OS JCL</Description>
    <Price>62.50</Price>
  </Product>
</Products>
```

Description

- *XML*, which stands for *Extensible Markup Language*, is a method of structuring data using special *tags*.
- The *XML document* in this figure contains data for three products. Each product has an *attribute* named Code and *elements* named Description and Price. You'll learn more about attributes and elements in the next two figures.
- XML can be used to exchange data between different systems, especially via the Internet.
- XML documents that are stored in a file can be used as an alternative to binary files, text files, or even database systems for storing data.
- When XML is stored in a file, the file name usually has an extension of xml.

Figure 20-1 An XML document

XML tags, declarations, and comments

Figure 20-2 shows how XML uses tags to structure the data in an XML document. Here, each XML tag begins with the < character and ends with the > character. As a result, the first line in the XML document in this figure contains a complete XML tag. Similarly, the next three lines also contain complete tags. In contrast, the fifth line contains two tags, <Description> and </Description>, with a text value in between.

The first tag in any XML document is an *XML declaration*. This declaration identifies the document as an XML document and indicates which XML version the document conforms to. In this example, the document conforms to XML version 1.0. In addition, the declaration usually identifies the character set that's being used for the document. In this example, the character set is UTF-8, the most common one used for XML documents in English-speaking countries.

An XML document can also contain comments. These are tags that begin with <!-- and end with -->. Between the tags, you can type anything you want. For instance, the second line in this figure is a comment that indicates what type of data is contained in the XML document. It's often a good idea to include similar comments in your own XML documents.

XML elements

Elements are the building blocks of XML. Each element in an XML document represents a single data item and is identified by two tags: a *start tag* and an *end tag*. The start tag marks the beginning of the element and provides the element's name. The end tag marks the end of the element and repeats the name, prefixed by a slash. For example, <Description> is the start tag for an element named Description, and </Description> is the corresponding end tag.

It's important to realize that XML does not provide a pre-defined set of element names the way HTML does. Instead, you create your own element names to describe the contents of each element. Also, since XML names are case-sensitive, <Product> and <product> are not the same.

A complete element consists of the element's start tag, its end tag, and the *content* between the tags. For example, <Price>49.50</Price> indicates that the content of the Price element is 49.50. And <Description>Murach's Beginning Java 2</Description> indicates that the content of the Description element is *Murach's Beginning Java 2*.

Besides content, elements can contain other elements, known as *child elements*. This lets you add structure to a *parent element*. For example, a parent product element can have child elements that provide details about each product, such as the product's description and price. In this figure, for example, you can see that the start tag, end tag, and values for the Description and Price elements are contained between the start and end tags for the Product element. As a result, Description and Price are children of the Product element, and the Product element is the parent of both the Description and Price elements.

An XML document

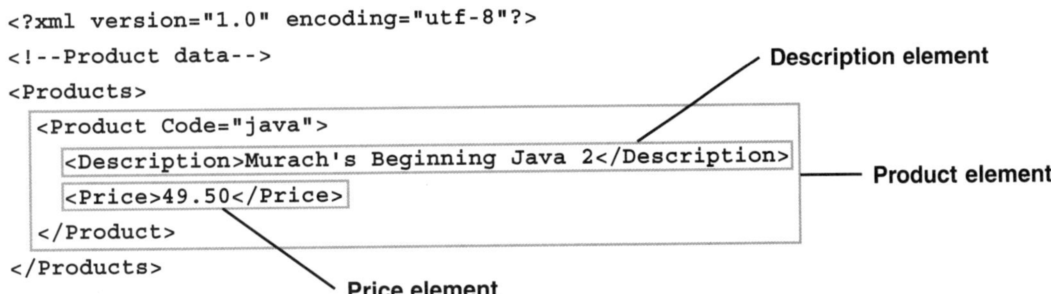

<?xml version="1.0" encoding="utf-8"?>
<!--Product data-->
<Products>
<Product Code="java">
<Description>Murach's Beginning Java 2</Description>
<Price>49.50</Price>
</Product>
</Products>
Description element
Product element
Price element

XML tags, declarations, and comments

- Each XML tag begins with < and ends with >.
- The first line in an XML document is an *XML declaration* that indicates which version of the XML standard is being used for the document. In addition, the declaration usually identifies the standard character set that's being used. For documents in English-speaking countries, UTF-8 is the character set that's commonly used.
- You can use the <!-- and --> tags to include comments in an XML document.

Elements

- An *element* is a unit of XML data that begins with a *start tag* and ends with an *end tag*. The start tag provides the name of the element and contains any attributes assigned to the element (see figure 20-3 for details on attributes). The end tag repeats the name, prefixed with a slash (/). You can use any name you want for an XML element.
- The text between an element's start and end tags is called the element's *content*. For example, <Description>Murach's Beginning Java 2</Description> indicates that the content of the Description element is the string *Murach's Beginning Java 2*.
- Elements can contain other elements. An element that's contained within another element is known as a *child element*. The element that contains a child element is known as the child's *parent element*.
- Child elements can repeat within a parent element. For instance, in the example above, the Products element can contain more than one Product element. Similarly, each Product element could contain repeating child elements.
- The highest-level parent element in an XML document is known as the *root element*. An XML document can have only one root element.

Figure 20-2 XML tags, declarations, comments, and elements

As the XML document in figure 20-1 shows, an element can occur more than once within an XML document. In this case, the document has three Product elements, each representing a product. Since each of these Product elements contains Description and Price elements, these elements also appear three times in the document.

Although this example doesn't show it, a given child element can also occur more than once within a parent. For example, suppose you want to provide for products that have more than one category. You could do this by using a Category child element to indicate the category of a product. Then, for a product that belongs to multiple categories, you simply include multiple Category child elements within the Product element for that product.

The highest-level parent element in an XML document is known as the *root element*, and an XML document can have only one root element. In the examples in figures 20-1 and 20-2, the root element is Products. For XML documents that contain repeating data, it is common to use a plural name for the root element to indicate that it contains multiple child elements.

XML attributes

As shown in figure 20-3, *attributes* are a concise way to provide data for XML elements. In the products XML document, for example, each Product element has a Code attribute that provides an identifying code for the product. Thus, <Product Code="java"> contains an attribute named Code whose value is *java*.

Here again, XML doesn't provide a set of pre-defined attributes. Instead, you create attributes as you need them, using names that describe the content of the attributes. If an element has more than one attribute, you can list the attributes in any order you wish. However, you must separate the attributes from each other with one or more spaces. In addition, each attribute can appear only once within an element.

When you plan the layout of an XML document, you will often need to decide whether to use elements or attributes to represent each data item. In many cases, either one will work. In the products document, for example, I could have used a child element named Code rather than an attribute to represent each product's code. Likewise, I could have used an attribute named Description rather than a child element for the product's description.

Because attributes are more concise than child elements, it's often tempting to use attributes rather than child elements. Keep in mind, though, that an element with more than a few attributes soon becomes unwieldy. As a result, most designers limit their use of attributes to certain types of data, such as identifiers like product codes or customer numbers.

An XML document

```
<?xml version="1.0" encoding="utf-8" ?>
<!--Product data-->
<Products>
  <Product Code="java">
    <Description>Murach's Beginning Java 2</Description>
    <Price>49.50</Price>
  </Product>
</Products>
```

Code attribute

Description

- You can include one or more *attributes* in the start tag for an element. An attribute typically consists of an attribute name, an equal sign, and a string value in quotes.
- If an element has more than one attribute, the order in which the attributes appear doesn't matter, but the attributes must be separated by one or more spaces.

When to use attributes instead of child elements

- When you design an XML document, you can use either child elements or attributes to represent the data for an element. The choice of whether to implement a data item as an attribute or as a separate child element is often a matter of preference.
- Two advantages of attributes are that they can appear in any order and they are more concise because they do not require end tags.
- Two advantages of child elements are that they are easier for people to read and they are more convenient for long string values.

An introduction to DTDs

By now, you can begin to see that XML provides a flexible way to store structured data. However, the XML standard provides for other tools that you can use to work with an XML document. One of the most useful is a *schema*, which you can use to define a list of conditions that an XML document must follow. For example, figure 20-4 shows how to use a *Document Type Definition (DTD)* to define the conditions for the products.xml document that was shown in figure 20-1.

Although a DTD is optional, you can use a DTD to make sure that various XML documents use the same format. For example, if various suppliers were sending you information about their products, you could supply them with a DTD to make sure that they all used a compatible format. This provides a way to create a standard set of tags for a certain application.

In a DTD, each XML element is declared in an ELEMENT declaration. If an element has children, that element must declare the children by listing the names in order, separated by commas. For example, the Product element DTD in this figure contains Description and Price elements in that order.

To specify that a child element may occur zero or one time, you can code a question mark after the element name. To specify that a child element may occur zero or more times, you can code an asterisk after the element name. And to specify that an element must occur one or more times, you can code a plus sign after the element name. If you don't code any of these characters after an element name, the element must occur one and only one time.

If an element contains text, you code the #PCDATA (parsed character data) keyword for that element. In this figure, for example, you can see that this keyword is coded for both the Description and Price elements.

To specify the attributes for an element, you use the ATTLIST declaration. This declaration specifies the element to which the attribute belongs, the name of the attribute, and the attribute type. If an attribute contains character data, you code the CDATA keyword. (Notice that you don't prefix this keyword with the # character.) In addition, an attribute declaration can include the #REQUIRED keyword to show that the attribute is required. In this figure, the Code attribute of the Product element is required, and it can store character data.

This figure also shows an XML document that uses a DOCTYPE declaration to refer to a DTD that's stored in an external file. Here, the DOCTYPE declaration is coded after the XML declaration but before the start tag of the root element, and this declaration points to a DTD file named products.dtd. (Because a path isn't specified for this file, it must be stored in the same directory as the products.xml file.) That way, you can easily validate this XML document against the specified DTD.

Rules for the products.xml document

- The document must contain one and only one Products element.
- The document can contain multiple Product elements. Each of these Product elements must contain two elements named Description and Price.
- Each Product element must contain one attribute named Code that holds a string.
- The Description and Price elements can contain text data, but they can't contain child elements.

A DTD that implements these rules

```
<?xml version="1.0" encoding="UTF-8"?>
<!-- DTD for the products.xml file. -->
<!ELEMENT Products (Product*)>
<!ELEMENT Product (Description, Price)>
<!ATTLIST Product
          Code CDATA #REQUIRED
>
<!ELEMENT Description (#PCDATA)>
<!ELEMENT Price (#PCDATA ) >
```

How to specify a DTD file in an XML document

```
<?xml version="1.0" encoding="UTF-8"?>
<!DOCTYPE Products SYSTEM "products.dtd">
<Products>
    <Product Code="java">
        <Description>Murach's Beginning Java</Description>
        <Price>49.5</Price>
    </Product>
    <Product Code="jsps">
        <Description>Murach's Java Servlets and JSP</Description>
        <Price>49.5</Price>
    </Product>
</Products>
```

Description

- XML allows you to set conditions that must be enforced on an XML document. To define these conditions, you use a *schema language* to create a *schema*. *Document Type Definition (DTD)* is a schema language that's part of standard XML.
- You use the ELEMENT declaration in a DTD to define the names of the elements and the types of data they will contain. You use the ATTLIST declaration to define the names of the attributes and the types of data they will contain.
- By default, each child element must occur one time. To specify that a child element can occur zero or one time, code a question mark after the name of a child element on the parent element declaration. To specify that the child element can occur zero or more times, code an asterisk. And to specify that a child element can occur one or more times, code a plus sign.
- In an XML document, you can use a DOCTYPE declaration to refer to a DTD that's stored in a DTD file.

Figure 20-4 An introduction to DTDs

How to view and edit an XML file

When working with XML files, you often need to view or edit the data they contain. To view the data that's stored in an existing XML file, you can use a web browser. To enter or edit the data that's stored in an XML file, you can use a text editor.

How to view an XML file

The browser shown in figure 20-5 displays the XML document that's stored in a file named products.xml. This shows that a browser is able to read the XML tags and display an XML document in a structured format that's easy to read. When you view an XML document in a browser, you can click on the minus sign (-) to the left of an element to collapse the element. Then, you can click on the plus sign (+) to expand the element.

To view an XML file that's available on a local drive in a browser, you can use the Windows Explorer to navigate to that file. Then, you can right-click on it, and select the Open command from the resulting menu. Alternatively, you can enter the path and file name directly into the browser. If the XML file is stored on an intranet or the Internet, you can open the file by entering its web address in the browser.

How to edit an XML file

To edit an XML file, you can open it with a text editor. Then, you can enter new tags and data, or you can edit the existing tags and data. Although you can use a text editor such as TextPad to work with an XML file, you'll want to use a text editor that's specifically designed for working with XML if you work with XML files often. One such editor is Altova XMLSpy, and it's shown in figure 20-5.

An XML editor like XMLSpy makes it easier to edit XML documents. For example, tags, content, attributes, values, and comments are color-coded so you can easily tell them apart. When you type a start tag, the XML editor automatically adds the end tag and positions the cursor between the start and end tags. In addition, child elements are indented automatically.

A good XML editor such as XMLSpy also contains features that make it easy to create and work with DTD files like the one shown in figure 20-4. For example, XMLSpy includes an Assign DTD command that let's you assign a DTD to an XML file, and it provides a Validate command that will check an XML file to make sure it adheres to the rules specified by the DTD.

If you're interested in using XMLSpy, you can learn more about it from Altova's website (www.altova.com). The Home Edition of XMLSpy is designed for entry-level developers and students, and it is available as a free download.

An XML document in a browser

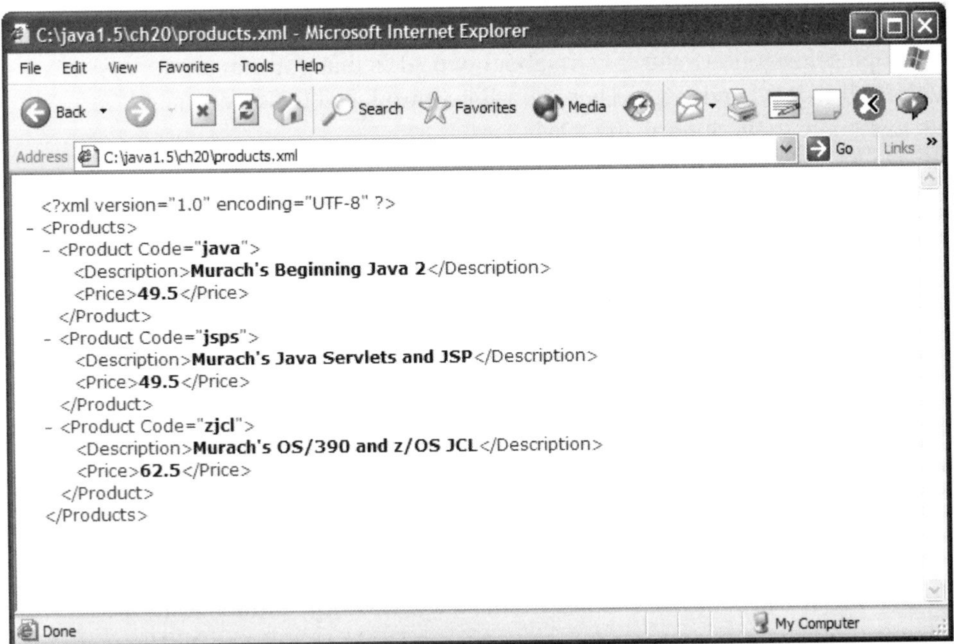

An XML document in an XML editor

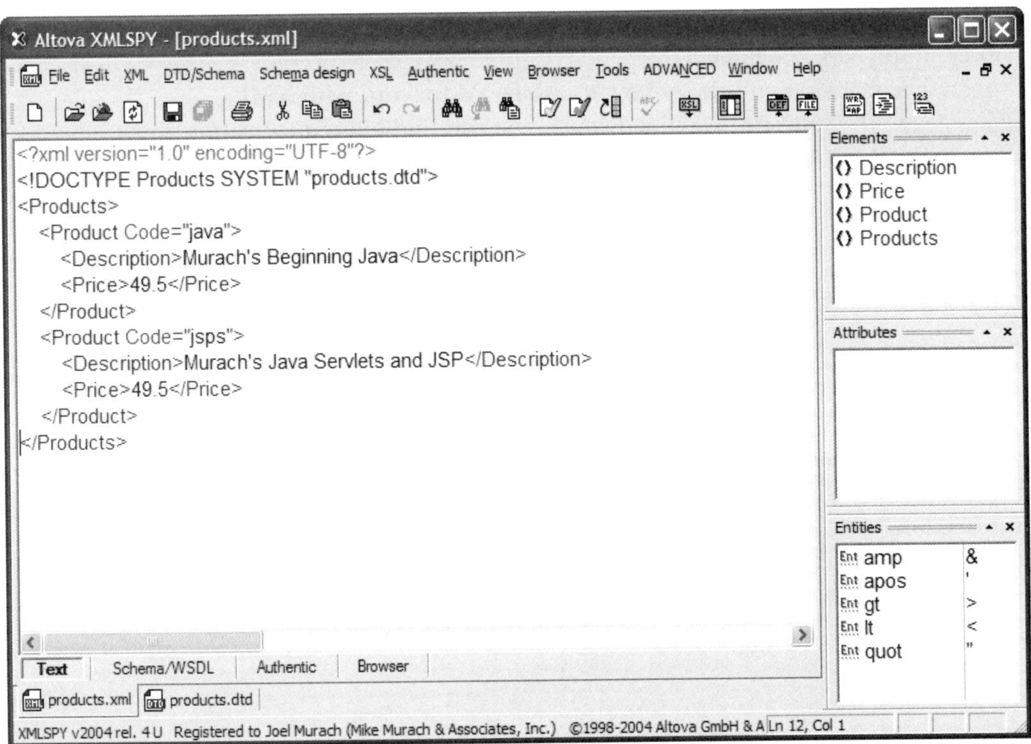

Figure 20-5 How to view and edit an XML file

Introduction to XML APIs

In the topics that follow, you'll learn about two APIs that you can use to work with XML: DOM and SAX. Then, you'll be introduced to some general concepts that apply to working with DOM.

An introduction to XML APIs

Figure 20-6 presents the pros and cons of the two major APIs for working with XML documents. J2SE has included support for both of these XML APIs since version 1.4.

SAX is the *Simple API for XML*. Originally, this XML API was a Java-only API, but versions are now available for other languages too. Although SAX is fast and memory efficient, it is read-only. However, it allows an application to read only the tags, text, and comments that are needed. As a result, it's commonly used to read large XML documents.

DOM stands for *Document Object Model*. This XML standard was developed by the World Wide Web Consortium (www.w3c.org). Although DOM isn't as fast or memory efficient as SAX, you can use DOM to write an XML document to a file. Unlike SAX, DOM begins by reading the entire XML document into memory, storing the document as a collection of objects. Then, you can use object-oriented programming techniques to work with the data stored in the XML document.

In this chapter, you'll learn how to use DOM to work with XML documents. If you're interested, however, you can find more information about working with SAX and other XML APIs on the Java web site.

SAX is

- Memory efficient
- Read-only
- Typically used for working with documents larger than 10 megabytes

DOM is

- Memory intensive
- Read-write
- Typically used for working with documents smaller than 10 megabytes

Description

- The *Simple API for XML* (*SAX*) and the *Document Object Model* (*DOM*) are the two standard XML APIs.
- J2SE has provided support for both of these XML APIs since version 1.4.
- When you use SAX, you can read only the parts of the XML document that you need.
- When you use DOM, the entire XML document structure is read into memory.
- You can find more information about these and other XML APIs on the World Wide Web.

Figure 20-6 An introduction to XML APIs

The DOM tree

Figure 20-7 presents a *DOM tree* for the XML document that contains the data for a single product. This tree is a collection of objects that represent the XML document after it's been read into memory.

The DOM tree is a collection of related *nodes*. Each node can have a *parent node*, zero or more *child nodes*, and zero or more *sibling nodes*. For example, Node B has one sibling node (Node C), one child node (Node D) and one parent node (Node A). Node H has one parent node (Node F), no child nodes, and no sibling nodes.

Each node has a *node type*. For example, Node A is a Document type, Node B is an Element type, Node C is a Comment type, Node E is an Attr type, and Node H is a Text type. In the next figure, you'll learn that these types correspond to Java objects. However, these types are defined by DOM, regardless of what language you use to access the DOM tree.

Every DOM tree contains one document node that defines the DOM tree. This node must contain one and only one child element node, but it can contain other types of nodes such as a comment node. Any element node in a DOM tree can contain multiple child elements. For example, Node D contains three child elements. However, unlike element nodes, comment nodes and text nodes can't contain children.

In a DOM tree, any element node that contains text contains a text node that stores the textual data. A common error in DOM processing is to navigate to an element node and expect it to contain the data that is stored in that element. For example, Node F in this figure is the node for the Description element. However, this node doesn't hold the value for the description. Instead, it contains a child text node (Node H) that holds the value for the description.

The structure of the DOM tree for the Product XML document

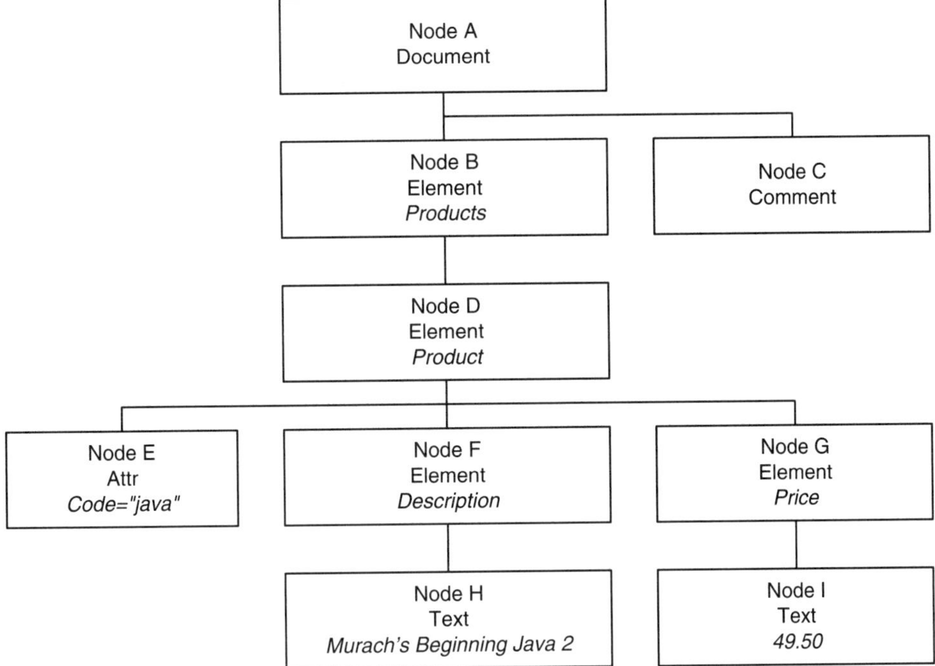

Description

- You can use the DOM API to load an XML document into a *DOM tree*. Then, you can use the DOM API to work with the data in the XML document.
- A DOM tree is a collection of *nodes*. Each node may have a *parent node*, one or more *child nodes*, and one or more *sibling nodes*.
- Each node has a *node type* that indicates whether the node represents the document, an element, an attribute, a text value, or a comment.

Figure 20-7 The DOM tree

How to use DOM to work with XML

Now that you've learned some basic concepts about SAX and DOM, the topics that follow will show you how to use DOM to work with an XML document. Interestingly, the Java API uses SAX to read a DOM tree from a file.

Interfaces for working with the DOM tree

Figure 20-8 shows the Node interface hierarchy that's used to work with a DOM tree. Here, the Node interface represents a node on a DOM tree. Then, the Document, Element, Text, Comment, and Attr interfaces that extend the Node interface define the types of nodes available from a DOM tree. This shows that Document, Element, Text, Comment, and Attr objects can also be cast to Node objects.

In the rest of this chapter, you'll learn how to use these interfaces to work with a DOM tree. However, if you want to learn more about the methods that are available from these interfaces, you can always look them up in the documentation for the JDK. They're all stored in the org.w3c.dom package. This package contains Java interfaces that conform to the DOM specification developed by the World Wide Web Consortium (W3C).

The DOM package

```
org.w3c.dom
```

The interfaces in the DOM package

```
Node
    Document
    Element
    CharacterData
        Text
        Comment
    Attr
```

Description

- The Node interface represents a single node in the DOM tree.
- The Document, Element, Text, Comment, and Attr interfaces represent the different types of nodes available in a DOM tree.
- You can use the methods of these interfaces to work with the nodes of a DOM tree.
- Since the Document, Element, CharacterData, Attr, Text, and Comment interfaces inherit the Node interface, you can use any of the methods of the Node interface to work with nodes.
- These interfaces are located in the org.w3c.dom package. As a result, you must import this package to work with a DOM tree.

Figure 20-8 Interfaces for working with the DOM tree

How to create an empty DOM tree

Figure 20-9 shows how to create a Document object that represents an empty DOM tree. Before you can create the Document object, you need to use the DocumentBuilderFactory class to create a DocumentBuilder object. Then, you can call the newDocument method of that object to create an empty Document object.

For this code to work, you must import the javax.xml.parsers and org.w3c.dom packages. In addition, you need to handle the ParserConfigurationException that's thrown by the newDocumentBuilder method of the DocumentBuilderFactory class.

Classes for creating an empty DOM tree

```
javax.xml.parsers.DocumentBuilderFactory
javax.xml.parsers.DocumentBuilder
javax.xml.parsers.ParserConfigurationException
```

Common methods of the DocumentBuilderFactory class

Method	Description
`newInstance()`	A static method that returns a DocumentBuilderFactory object.
`newDocumentBuilder()`	Returns a DocumentBuilder object and throws a ParserConfigurationException.

A common method of the DocumentBuilder class

Method	Description
`newDocument()`	Returns a Document object.

Code that creates an empty DOM tree

```
DocumentBuilderFactory dbf = DocumentBuilderFactory.newInstance();
DocumentBuilder db = dbf.newDocumentBuilder();
Document doc = db.newDocument();
```

Description

- You can use a DocumentBuilderFactory object to create a DocumentBuilder object. Then, you can use the DocumentBuilder object to create a Document object that contains an empty DOM tree.

Figure 20-9 How to create an empty DOM tree

How to build a DOM tree

Once you have a Document object that represents a DOM tree, you can create nodes and add them to the tree as shown in figure 20-10. To do this, you can use the methods of the Document, Node, Element, and Text interfaces.

The first example shows how to create the root element (Products), and append it to the document node. Then, the second example shows how to create a comment and append it to a node. In this case, the comment is appended to the document node. As a result, it's displayed before the root element in the XML document. However, you can display a comment before any node by appending the comment to that node.

The third example shows how to create a Product element and append it to the Products element. The fourth example shows how to create an attribute, set its value, and add it to the Product element. To do that, you call the setAttribute method from the Product element and specify the name and value of the attribute. The fifth example shows how to create an element that contains text. To do that, this example creates the Description element and appends it to the Product element. Then, it creates a text node, sets the value of that node, and then appends it to the Description element.

When you create a comment, text, or element node, you must append the node to another node or it won't be placed in the DOM tree. To do that, you can use the appendChild method that's defined in the Node interface. However, if you call the appendChild method from a node that can't have children, such as a text node or a comment node, the appendChild method will throw a DOMException. As a result, you must throw or handle this exception when you work with this method. You must also throw or handle this exception when you use the setAttribute and setNodeValue methods.

Common methods of the Document interface

Method	Description
`createElement(StringName)`	Returns an Element object with the specified name.
`createComment(StringText)`	Returns a Comment object that contains the specified text.
`createTextNode(StringText)`	Returns a Text object that contains the specified text.

Common method of the Node interface

Method	Description
`appendChild(childNode)`	Sets the specified node as a child of the current element.

Common method of the Element interface

Method	Description
`setAttribute(name, value)`	Sets an attribute with the specified name and value.

Common method of the Text interface

Method	Description
`setNodeValue(StringText)`	Sets the text for the node.

Example 1: Code that creates and appends the root element

```
Element productsElement = doc.createElement("Products");
doc.appendChild(productsElement);
```

Example 2: Code that creates and appends a comment

```
Comment comment = doc.createComment("Product Information");
doc.appendChild(comment);
```

Example 3: Code that creates and appends an element

```
Element productElement = doc.createElement("Product");
productsElement.appendChild(productElement);
```

Example 4: Code that sets an attribute

```
productElement.setAttribute("Code", "java");
```

Example 5: Code that creates and appends an element that contains text

```
Element descriptionElement = doc.createElement("Description");
productElement.appendChild(descriptionElement);
Text descriptionText = doc.createTextNode("Description");
descriptionText.setNodeValue("Murach's Beginning Java 2");
descriptionElement.appendChild(descriptionText);
```

Description

- The createElement, setAttribute, setNodeValue, and appendChild methods throw a DOMException.

Figure 20-10 How to build a DOM tree

How to write a DOM tree to a file

Now that you know how to create a Document object that contains a DOM tree, you're ready to *transform* that document into an input source that can be written to an output stream. More specifically, figure 20-11 shows how to write a DOM tree to a file. (In case you haven't read chapter 19, a stream is the flow of data from one location to another. To write data to a file from internal storage, you use an output stream.)

To write a DOM tree to a file, you must follow three steps. First, you must define the DOM tree as the input source. To do that, you create a DOMSource object by passing the Document object to the constructor of this class. Second, you must define the file to be used as the output destination. To do that, you can create a StreamResult object by passing a string to the constructor for this class that specifies the path and file name for the file. Third, you must create a Transformer object and then use the transform method of that object to write the input source to the output stream.

To obtain a Transformer object, you use the newInstance method of the TransformerFactory class to get a TransformerFactory object. Then, you call the newTransformer method of that object to get a Transformer object. Before you call the transform method, though, you may want to set some properties that affect the output of the XML document. To specify that the document can use indentation, for example, you can use the setOutputProperty method as shown in this figure. This also adds a new line character at the end of each element, which can make an XML file easier to read when opened in a text editor.

Classes for writing a DOM tree to a file

```
javax.xml.transform.dom.DOMSource
javax.xml.transform.stream.StreamResult
javax.xml.transform.TransformerFactory
javax.xml.transform.Transformer
javax.xml.transform.OutputKeys
```

Common constructors of the DOMSource and StreamResult classes

Constructor	Description
`DOMSource(Document)`	Creates an input source for the specified DOM document.
`StreamResult(StringFileName)`	Creates an output stream for the file with the specified name.

Common methods of the TransformerFactory class

Method	Description
`newInstance()`	A static method that returns a TransformerFactory object.
`newTransformer()`	Returns a Transformer object and throws a TransformerConfigurationException.

Common methods of the Transformer class

Method	Description
`setOutputProperty(name, value)`	Sets the name and value of an output property. The OutputKeys class contains constants for many possible property names.
`transform(xmlSource, target)`	Transforms the XML document into a stream and sends it to the target. Throws a TransformerException.

Code that writes a DOM tree to a file

```
// prepare the input source (the DOM document)
DOMSource inputDoc = new DOMSource(doc);

// prepare the output file
StreamResult outputFile = new StreamResult("products.xml");

// write the DOM document to the file
TransformerFactory tFactory = TransformerFactory.newInstance();
Transformer t = tFactory.newTransformer();
t.setOutputProperty(OutputKeys.INDENT, "yes");
t.transform(inputDoc, outputFile);
```

Description

- You can use a TransformerFactory object to create a Transformer object. Then, you can use the Transformer object to write an XML document to a file.
- By default, an XML document is written as one continuous string, which can make it difficult to read. To indent elements and to add a new line character at the end of each element, use the setOutputProperty method to set the indent property to "yes."

Figure 20-11 How to write a DOM tree to a file

How to read a DOM tree from a file

Figure 20-12 shows how to read a Document object that represents a DOM tree from an XML document that's stored in a file. To do that, you use the DocumentBuilderFactory class to create a DocumentBuilder object just as you do when you create an empty DOM tree. Instead of creating a new Document object from the DocumentBuilder object, however, you create an InputSource object that you can use to read an existing XML document from an XML file into a Document object. To create an InputSource object, you can pass a string that refers to the XML file to the constructor of the InputSource class.

Before you create the DocumentBuilder object, you can use the methods of the DocumentBuilderFactory class to set conditions for the DOM tree that's returned. For example, you can use the setIgnoringComments method to tell the parser that's created by the DocumentBuilderFactory to ignore comments. By default, the parser that's created includes comments. As a result, if you don't want to include comments, you can provide a true value for the setIgnoringComments method. In most cases, you'll use this method only if you don't intend to update the XML document. Otherwise, the comments won't be included when you update the XML file.

If you look at the packages that are used in this example, you can see that the InputSource class is stored in the org.xml.sax package. In addition, the parse method of the DocumentBuilder class throws a SAXException. This shows that this code uses the SAX API to read a DOM tree from a file. Because this is handled for you automatically, however, all you need to do is import the org.xml.sax package and throw or catch the SAXException. You also need to import the java.io package and throw or catch the IOException when you use the parse method.

Classes for reading a DOM tree from a file

```
javax.xml.parsers.DocumentBuilderFactory
javax.xml.parsers.DocumentBuilder
org.xml.sax.InputSource
```

Common constructor of the InputSource class

Constructor	Description
InputSource(StringFileName)	Creates an input source for the file with the specified name.

Common method of the DocumentBuilderFactory class

Method	Description
setIgnoringComments(boolean)	Specifies whether the parser will ignore comments. By default, this value is set to false.

Common method of the DocumentBuilder class

Method	Description
parse(inputFile)	Specifies the source of the XML data and returns a Document object. Throws a SAXException and an IOException.

Code that reads a DOM tree from a file

```
// get the DocumentBuilderFactory object and set its properties
DocumentBuilderFactory dbf = DocumentBuilderFactory.newInstance();
dbf.setIgnoringComments(true);

// get the DocumentBuilder object
DocumentBuilder db = dbf.newDocumentBuilder();

// specify the XML file and read it
InputSource inputFile = new InputSource("products.xml");
Document doc = db.parse(inputFile);
```

Note

- The newInstance and newDocumentBuilder methods of the DocumentBuilderFactory are described in figure 20-9.

Figure 20-12 How to read a DOM tree from a file

How to read the nodes of a DOM tree

Figure 20-13 shows how to read the nodes of a Document object that represents a DOM tree. The example in this figure reads all of the Product elements from the products.xml file, gets the code, description, and price for each element, creates a Product object using these values, and then stores the Product object in an array list. After it creates the array list, this example uses the getDocumentElement method to return the root element of the Document object. Then, it uses the getElementsByTagName method of the Document object to obtain a NodeList object that contains a collection of element nodes that represent the products.

Once it gets the NodeList object, it uses two methods to loop through all of the element nodes contained within the NodeList object. First, it uses the getLength method to return the number of elements in the list. Second, it uses the item method to return a specified item in the list. Notice that since the item method returns a Node object, that object must be cast to an Element object for this code to work.

After it gets the Element object for a product, it uses the methods shown in this figure to get its attribute and child elements. To get the value for the Code attribute, it calls the getAttribute method of the Element interface. However, getting the values of the Description and Prices elements is more complicated. To start, you must use the getElementsByTagName method to get a NodeList object for the element. Then, you must use the item method to get the first Node object in the list, and you must cast it to an Element object. (You get the first Node object because each Product element can have only one Description and one Price node.) Next, you invoke the getFirstChild method to return the text node for the element. Finally, you use the getNodeValue method to return the value of the node.

The code in this figure assumes that you know the structure of the XML document and that it's acceptable to hard code the names of the XML elements and attributes. However, for many types of applications, you may not know the exact structure of the DOM tree, or you may not want to hard code the names of the elements. Fortunately, the Node interface provides many more methods that aren't shown in this figure that you can use to determine the structure of an XML document and retrieve values from this structure.

Common method of the Document interface

Method	Description
`getDocumentElement()`	Returns an Element object for the root of the DOM tree.

Common methods of the Element interface

Method	Description
`getElementsByTagName(name)`	Returns a NodeList object that contains a collection of Node objects for the specified tag name.
`getAttribute(name)`	Returns a string that contains the value of the specified attribute.
`getFirstChild()`	Returns a Node object for the first child node.

Common methods of the NodeList interface

Method	Description
`getLength()`	Returns the number of Node objects in the NodeList object.
`item(index)`	Returns the Node object at the specified index.

Common method of the Text interface

Method	Description
`getNodeValue()`	Returns the text from a text node.

Code that reads all Product elements into a products array list

```
ArrayList<Product> products = new ArrayList<Product>();
Element root = doc.getDocumentElement();
NodeList productsList = root.getElementsByTagName("Product");
for (int i = 0; i < productsList.getLength(); i++)
{
    Element productElement = (Element) productsList.item(i);

    String code = productElement.getAttribute("Code");

    NodeList descriptionList =
        productElement.getElementsByTagName("Description");
    Element descriptionElement = (Element) descriptionList.item(0);
    Text descriptionText = (Text) descriptionElement.getFirstChild();
    String description = descriptionText.getNodeValue();

    NodeList priceList = productElement.getElementsByTagName("Price");
    Element priceElement = (Element) priceList.item(0);
    Text priceText = (Text) priceElement.getFirstChild();
    String priceString = priceText.getNodeValue();
    double price = Double.parseDouble(priceString);

    Product p = new Product(code, description, price);
    products.add(p);
}
```

Figure 20-13 How to read the nodes of a DOM tree

How to modify the nodes of a DOM tree

You can use the methods shown in figure 20-14 to add, update, and delete the nodes of a DOM tree. In this figure, the code examples work with child elements of the root element. To return an Element object for the root element, you use the getDocumentElement method as shown in the first example.

To add a new node, you start by creating a Node object as described earlier in this chapter. To create an element node, for example, you use the createElement method of the Document interface as shown in the first example. Then, you can use the appendChild method to add that node to the end of the list of child nodes for a node.

To add a node to the beginning or middle of the list of child nodes, you use the insertBefore method. To do that, you need to retrieve an existing Node object as described in figure 20-13. Then, you can use the insertBefore method to insert the new Node object before the existing Node as shown in the second example. If you supply a null value for the second argument, this method will add the node to the end of the list of child nodes just as it would if you used the appendChild method.

To update an element, you can use the replaceChild method as shown in the third example. Before you can use this method, though, you'll need to create the new Node object, and you'll need to read the Node object to be replaced. If you only want to update the value of a text node, you might want to use the setNodeValue method to update the value that's stored in the element instead of creating an entirely new element and replacing the old element with the new one. Similarly, if you only want to update an element node's attribute value, you might want to use the setAttribute method.

To delete an element, you start by retrieving the Node object that you want to remove. Then, you call the removeChild method from the parent node and specify the child node that you want to delete as illustrated in the fourth example.

Methods of the Node interface for adding, updating, and deleting elements

Method	Description
appendChild(childNode)	Inserts the new node at the end of any existing child nodes.
insertBefore(newChild, refChild)	Inserts the new node before the reference node. If you code a null value for the reference node, this method inserts the new child at the end of any existing child nodes.
replaceChild(newChild, oldChild)	Replaces the specified child node with a new child node.
removeChild(childNode)	Removes the specified child node.

Example 1: Code that appends an element to the root element after all other child nodes

```
Element root = doc.getDocumentElement();
Element newProductElement = doc.createElement("Product");
root.appendChild(newProductElement);
```

Example 2: Code that inserts an element before another child node

```
root.insertBefore(newProductElement, firstProductElement);
```

Example 3: Code that updates an element

```
root.replaceChild(newProductElement, oldProductElement);
```

Example 4: Code that removes an element

```
root.removeChild(productElement);
```

Description

- The appendChild, insertBefore, removeChild, and replaceChild methods shown above throw a DOMException.
- If you want to modify one or more values stored in a node instead of replacing the entire node, you can use the setAttribute and setNodeValue methods described in figure 20-10.

Figure 20-14 How to modify the nodes of a DOM tree

Two classes that work with XML files

Now that you know the details for writing Java code that uses DOM to work with an XML document, you're ready to see how that code fits within an application. In the next topic, then, you'll see a utility class that contains some common methods for working with XML. Then, you'll see a class that uses this utility class to work with product data.

A utility class that works with XML files

As you use Java to work with XML, you'll find yourself repeating the same operations over and over. To make it easier to perform these operations, you can create a utility class like the one shown in figure 20-15. This class contains static methods for creating an empty DOM tree, reading a DOM tree from a file, and writing a DOM tree to file. In addition, it contains methods for getting and setting the values of an element's text node. If you have any trouble understanding how the code in these methods work, you can refer to the figures presented earlier in this chapter.

This class starts by importing all of the packages needed to use DOM to work with an XML file. To start, it imports the org.w3c.dom package so you can use the interfaces that define the nodes of a DOM tree. Then, it imports the javax.xml.parsers, org.xml.sax, and java.io packages so you can read a DOM tree from a file and provide for exceptions. Finally, it imports the javax.xml.transform, javax.xml.transform.dom, and javax.xml.transform.stream packages so you can write a DOM tree to a file.

To create an empty Document object, you can call the getNewDocument method. To read a Document object from an XML file, you can call the getDocumentFromFile method. And to write a Document object to a file, you can use the writeDocumentToFile method. To use either the getdocumentFromFile or writeDocumentToFile method, you must supply a string that specifies the XML file to use. You must also supply the XML document to be written to the file when you use the writeDocumentToFile method.

To get the value of an element's text node, you can use the getTextNodeValue method. To use this method, you must supply the parent element and the name of the element. Then, this method retrieves the child element from the nodes collection for that element, and it gets the value of the text node for that element.

To add an element that contains a child text node to a DOM tree, you can use the addTextNodeElement method. To use this method, you must supply the Document object, the parent element, the name of the element you wish to add, and the value of its text node.

When you use these methods, you must handle the exceptions that they throw. For example, the getDocumentFromFile method throws three exceptions. As a result, when you call this method, you must either throw or catch these exceptions.

The code for the XMLUtil class

```
import org.w3c.dom.*;                    // for working with a DOM tree
import javax.xml.parsers.*;              // for reading a DOM tree from a file
import org.xml.sax.*;
import java.io.*;
import javax.xml.transform.*;            // for writing a DOM tree to a file
import javax.xml.transform.dom.*;
import javax.xml.transform.stream.*;

public class XMLUtil
{
    public static Document getNewDocument()
    throws ParserConfigurationException
    {
        DocumentBuilderFactory dbf = DocumentBuilderFactory.newInstance();
        DocumentBuilder db = dbf.newDocumentBuilder();
        return db.newDocument();
    }

    public static Document getDocumentFromFile(String xmlFile)
    throws ParserConfigurationException, SAXException, IOException
    {
        DocumentBuilderFactory dbf = DocumentBuilderFactory.newInstance();
        DocumentBuilder db = dbf.newDocumentBuilder();
        InputSource in = new InputSource(xmlFile);
        return db.parse(in);
    }

    public static String getTextNodeValue(Element parent, String tagName)
    {
        NodeList list = parent.getElementsByTagName(tagName);
        Element element = (Element) list.item(0);
        Text text = (Text) element.getFirstChild();
        return text.getNodeValue();
    }

    public static void addTextNode(Document doc, Element parent,
    String elementName, String elementValue)
    {
        Element element = doc.createElement(elementName);
        parent.appendChild(element);
        Text text = doc.createTextNode(elementName);
        text.setNodeValue(elementValue);
        element.appendChild(text);
    }

    public static void writeDocumentToFile(String xmlFile, Document doc)
    throws TransformerException
    {
        DOMSource in = new DOMSource(doc);
        StreamResult out = new StreamResult(xmlFile);
        Transformer transformer =
            TransformerFactory.newInstance().newTransformer();
        transformer.setOutputProperty(OutputKeys.INDENT, "yes");
        transformer.transform(in, out);
    }
}
```

Figure 20-15 A utility class that works with XML files

A class that works with an XML file

Figure 20-16 presents the complete code for the ProductXMLFile class. If you've read chapter 19, you'll see that, like the ProductTextFile and ProductRandomFile classes presented in that chapter, this class implements the ProductDAO interface. If you haven't read chapter 19, you may want to review figure 19-10 to see how this interface is defined.

The ProductXMLFile class starts by declaring four instance variables. The first instance variable defines a String named productsFile that will store the name of the XML file. The second instance variable defines a Document object named doc that will store the XML document. The third instance variable defines an Element object named root that will store the root element of the XML document. And the fourth instance variable defines a NodeList object named productsList that will store the collection of product nodes.

The constructor for this class initializes the instance variables of the class. To start, the first statement initializes the productsFile variable by setting the name of the products file to products.xml. Then, the second statement calls the getDocument method to initialize the XML document. Next, the third statement initializes the root element of the XML document. Finally, the fourth statement initializes the productsList object so it contains one Element object for each Product element stored in the XML document.

The getDocument method reads the XML file and returns the Document object for the XML document that's stored in the file. To get the XML document from the file, it uses the getDocumentFromFile method of the XMLUtil class. If an exception is thrown anywhere in the getDocument method, this method returns a null. That way, any programmer that calls this method can assume that the method executed successfully if the Document object is not null.

To catch the exceptions that may be thrown, the getDocument method includes a catch block that catches all exceptions of the Exception type. That way, you can use a single catch block to catch the three types of exceptions that may be thrown by the getDocumentFromFile method of the XMLUtil class.

The getProducts method returns an ArrayList object that contains Product objects that are created from the Product elements stored in the XML document. This method starts by declaring and initializing an ArrayList object that can store Product objects. Then, it uses a loop to create a Product object from each Product element in the nodes list and to add each Product object to the array list.

Within the loop, the first statement returns an Element object for the Product element at the specified index. The next statement gets the value of the Code attribute for that element. The two statements after that use the getTextNodeValue method of the XMLUtil class to get the string values for the Description and Price elements. The next statement converts the price string to a double value. Once all the data has been retrieved from the XML element, the last two statements in the loop create the Product object and add it to the array list.

The code for the ProductXMLFile class

Page 1

```
import org.w3c.dom.*;
import java.util.*;

public class ProductXMLFile implements ProductDAO
{
    private String productsFile = null;
    private Document doc = null;
    private Element root = null;
    private NodeList productsList = null;

    public ProductXMLFile()
    {
        productsFile = "products.xml";
        doc = this.getDocument();
        root = doc.getDocumentElement();
        productsList = doc.getElementsByTagName("Product");
    }

    private Document getDocument()
    {
        try
        {
            // read the XML document from XML file
            doc = XMLUtil.getDocumentFromFile(productsFile);
            return doc;
        }
        // catch ParserConfigurationException, SAXException, IOException
        catch(Exception e)
        {
            return null;
        }
    }

    public ArrayList<Product> getProducts()
    {
        // declare the products array list
        ArrayList<Product> products = new ArrayList<Product>();

        // create Product objects from the Product elements
        for (int i = 0; i < productsList.getLength(); i++)
        {
            Element productElement = (Element) productsList.item(i);

            String code = productElement.getAttribute("Code");
            String description =
                XMLUtil.getTextNodeValue(productElement, "Description");
            String priceString =
                XMLUtil.getTextNodeValue(productElement, "Price");
            double price = Double.parseDouble(priceString);

            Product p = new Product(code, description, price);
            products.add(p);
        }
        return products;
    }
```

Figure 20-16 A class that works with an XML file (part 1 of 3)

The getProduct method returns a Product object for the product that matches the specified product code. To get the product, this method loops through the products in the XML document. If no Product element is found with a Code attribute that matches the specified code, this method returns a null. However, if the Code attribute of a Product element matches the specified code, this method creates a Product object from the Product element and returns it. To get the description and price for the product, it uses the getTextNodeValue method of the XMLUtil class.

The private getProductIndex method works similarly to the getProduct method. Instead of returning a Product object, however, it returns an index that identifies the Product element's position in the XML document. If no Product element is found with a Code attribute that matches the specified code, this method returns a value of -1 to indicate that the specified code doesn't exist in the XML document.

The private saveProducts method writes the XML document to the XML file. To do that, it calls the writeDocumentToFile method of the XMLUtil class, passing it the string that contains the name of the file and the Document object that contains the XML document. If the writeDocumentToFile method is successful, the saveProducts method returns a true value. If the writeDocumentToFile method throws an exception, however, the saveProducts method returns a false value to indicate that the save operation wasn't successful.

The code for the ProductXMLFile class **Page 2**

```
public Product getProduct(String code)
{
    // loop through Product nodes and return Product object if found
    for (int i = 0; i < productsList.getLength(); i++)
    {
        Element productElement = (Element) productsList.item(i);

        String productCode = productElement.getAttribute("Code");
        if (code.equals(productCode))
        {
            String description =
                XMLUtil.getTextNodeValue(productElement, "Description");
            String priceString =
                XMLUtil.getTextNodeValue(productElement, "Price");
            double price = Double.parseDouble(priceString);
            Product product = new Product(code, description, price);
            return product;
        }
    }
    return null;
}

private int getProductIndex(String code)
{
    // loop through Product nodes and return Product index if found
    for (int i = 0; i < productsList.getLength(); i++)
    {
        Element productElement = (Element) productsList.item(i);

        String productCode = productElement.getAttribute("Code");
        if (code.equals(productCode))
        {
            return i;
        }
    }
    return -1;
}

private boolean saveProducts()
{
    try
    {
        // write the XML document to the products file
        XMLUtil.writeDocumentToFile(productsFile, doc);
        return true;
    }
    // catch ParserConfigurationException, TransformerException
    catch(Exception e)
    {
        return false;
    }
}
```

Figure 20-16 A class that works with an XML file (part 2 of 3)

The private getElementFromProduct method returns an XML element that's created from the Product object that's passed to this method. To do that, the first statement creates an Element object for the Product element. Then, the second statement sets the Code attribute for that element equal to the product's code. Next, the third and fourth statements call the addTextNode method of the XMLUtil class to add the Description and Price elements to the Product element. To do that, the document, the Product element, the name of a child element, and the value of that element is passed to the addTextNode method. Finally, this method returns the Product element.

The addProduct method begins by adding the product to the XML document. To do that, it uses the getElementFromProduct method to create an Element object that contains the data of the Product object, and it uses the appendChild method to add the element to the XML document. Then, it calls the saveProducts method to save the modified XML document to the XML file. That way, the XML document and the XML file will contain the same data. Also, because the saveProducts method returns a boolean value that indicates whether it was successful, the addProduct method returns the same boolean value. In other words, if the saveProducts method returns a true value, the addProduct method will also return a true value.

The deleteProduct method begins by calling the getProductIndex method to get the index of the specified product from the XML document. If the getProductIndex method returns a value of -1, it means that the product wasn't found. Then, this method returns a false value to indicate that the operation wasn't successful. Otherwise, this method gets the product element at the specified index and then calls the removeChild method to remove that element from the XML document. Finally, like the addProduct method, this method saves the modified XML document to the XML file and returns a boolean value that indicates whether the save operation was successful.

The updateProduct method updates the data for an existing product with the data for a new product that has the same product code. To do that, it starts by calling the getProductIndex method to get the index for the product that has the same code as the new product. Then, if the index is not equal to -1, this method updates and saves the XML document. To do that, it gets the existing Product element at the specified index. Then, it uses the getElementFromProduct method to create a new Product element from the specified product. Next, it uses the replaceChild method to replace the existing element with the new element. Finally, it saves the modified XML document to the XML file by calling the saveProducts method, and it returns a value that indicates whether the save operation was successful.

If you review the code for this class, you'll see that it only reads the XML document from the XML file when the class is instantiated and the constructor is executed. As a result, the getProducts and getProduct methods run efficiently since they don't need to read the XML file. In contrast, the addProduct, deleteProduct, and updateProduct methods write the entire XML document to the XML file. Because of that, these methods may not run as efficiently, especially if the XML document contains thousands of Product elements.

The code for the ProductXMLFile class **Page 3**

```
    private Element getElementFromProduct(Product p)
    {
        Element pe = doc.createElement("Product");
        pe.setAttribute("Code", p.getCode());
        XMLUtil.addTextNode(doc, pe, "Description", p.getDescription());
        XMLUtil.addTextNode(doc, pe, "Price", Double.toString(p.getPrice()));
        return pe;
    }

    public boolean addProduct(Product p)
    {
        Element pe = this.getElementFromProduct(p);
        root.appendChild(pe);
        return this.saveProducts();
    }

    public boolean deleteProduct(Product p)
    {
        int i = this.getProductIndex(p.getCode());
        if (i != -1)
        {
            // update the XML document
            Element pe = (Element) productsList.item(i);
            root.removeChild(pe);
            return this.saveProducts();
        }
        else
            return false;
    }

    public boolean updateProduct(Product newProduct)
    {
        int i = this.getProductIndex(newProduct.getCode());
        if (i != -1)
        {
            // update the XML document
            Element oldElement = (Element) productsList.item(i);
            Element newElement = this.getElementFromProduct(newProduct);
            root.replaceChild(newElement, oldElement);
            return this.saveProducts();
        }
        else
            return false;
    }
}
```

Figure 20-16 A class that works with an XML file (part 3 of 3)

Perspective

In this chapter, you learned the basic concepts and terms for working with XML. In addition, you learned some specific skills for using Java and DOM to work with the data in XML files. With that as background, you should be able to learn how to use Java to work with other XML APIs such as SAX.

Summary

- *XML* provides a standard way to structure data by using *tags* that identify data items.
- An *element* begins with a *start tag* and ends with an *end tag*. An element can contain data in the form of *content* that appears between the tags. It can also contain *child elements*.
- An *attribute* consists of a name and value that appear within an element's start tag.
- A *DTD* (*Documentation Type Definition*) is a *schema* that defines the structure of an XML document. This schema can be enforced when a document is read or written.
- You can use a web browser to view XML data, and you can use any text editor to edit an XML file, but it's helpful to use a text editor that's designed for working with XML.
- *SAX* (the *Simple API for XML*) can be used to read an XML document.
- *DOM* (the *Document Object Model*) is an API that can be used to build a DOM tree, work with the nodes of a tree, read an XML document from a file, and write an XML document to a file.
- Java provides interfaces that let you work with the document, element, text, comment, and attribute nodes of a DOM tree.

Exercise 20-1 Work with an XML file

In this exercise, you'll write code that works with an XML document that's stored in a file. When you complete this exercise, the console output should look like this:

```
The XML document has been read from the products.xml file.

Products list:
java    Murach's Beginning Java                          $49.50
jsps    Murach's Java Servlets and JSP                   $49.50

XML Tester has been added to the XML document.

Products list:
java    Murach's Beginning Java                          $49.50
jsps    Murach's Java Servlets and JSP                   $49.50
test    XML Tester                                       $77.77

XML Tester has been deleted from the XML document.

Products list:
java    Murach's Beginning Java                          $49.50
jsps    Murach's Java Servlets and JSP                   $49.50

The XML document has been written to the products.xml file.
```

1. Use a web browser to view the products.xml file in the c:\java1.5\ch20 directory. Experiment with collapsing and expanding elements. Then, open this file in a text editor.
2. Open the XMLTesterApp class that's stored in the c:\java1.5\ch20\XMLTester directory. Run this application to see how it works. At this point, it prints messages to the console, but it doesn't work with the XML file.
3. Add code to the readProductsDoc method that reads an XML document from the products.xml file and stores it in a DOM tree. Be sure to catch any exceptions that may be thrown. Compile this class to make sure it doesn't contain any compile-time errors.
4. Add code to the printProductsDoc method that prints the XML document to the console. To do that, you can create a Product object from each Product element. Then, you can use the printProduct method to print each Product object. Compile this class and test it. At this point, the application should print three identical product lists, and those lists should match the data that's stored in the products.xml file.
5. Add code to the addProduct method that adds the specified product to the XML document. Then, compile and test the application. At this point, the application should add the "XML Tester" product to the second and third product lists. However, since this method only adds the product to the XML document, not the file, this product won't appear in the products.xml file.

6. Add code to the writeProductsDoc method that writes the XML document to the products.xml file. Then, compile and test the application again. When you do, it should write the "XML Tester" product to the products.xml file each time you run it.
7. Add code to the deleteProduct method that deletes all occurrences of the specified product from the XML document. To do that, you can delete all Product elements with the given product code. Compile and test the application. When you do, it should delete all of the "XML Tester" products.

Exercise 20-2 Modify the ProductXMLFile class

In this exercise, you'll modify the code for the ProductXMLFile class, and you'll use this class with the Product Maintenance application to maintain the data in the products.xml file.

1. Open the ProductXMLFile and ProductMaintApp classes that are stored in the c:\java1.5\ch20\ProductMaintenance directory. Review this code and run the application to make sure you understand how it works.
2. Add a private method named getProductFromElement to the ProductXMLFile class that accepts an Element object and returns a Product object. Then, write the code for this method.
3. Modify the getProducts and getProduct methods so they use the getProductFromElement method to convert the Product elements to Product objects.
4. Test the application to be sure that the changes work. To verify that the data is being saved correctly, you can view the XML file.

21

How to use JDBC to work with databases

In this chapter, you'll learn how to use JDBC to work with data that's stored in a database. As you will see, databases provide data management features that aren't offered with files. That's why databases are used for most serious business applications.

How a relational database is organized

In 1970, Dr. E. F. Codd developed a model for a new type of *database* called a *relational database*. This type of database eliminated some of the problems that were associated with earlier types of databases like hierarchical databases. By using the relational model, you can reduce data redundancy, which saves disk storage and leads to more efficient data retrieval. You can also view and manipulate data in a way that is both intuitive and efficient. Today, relational databases are the de facto standard for database applications.

How a table is organized

A relational database stores data in *tables*. Each table contains *rows* and *columns* as shown in figure 21-1. In practice, rows and columns are often referred to by the traditional terms, *records* and *fields*. That's why this book uses these terms interchangeably.

In a relational database, a table has one column that's defined as the *primary key*. The primary key uniquely identifies each row in a table. That way, the rows in one table can easily be related to the rows in another table. In this table, the ProductCode column is the primary key.

The software that manages a relational database is called the *database management system* (*DBMS*) or *relational database management system* (*RDBMS*). The DBMS provides features that let you design the database. After that, the DBMS manages all changes, additions, and deletions to the database. Three of the most popular database management systems are Oracle, Microsoft's SQL Server, and IBM's DB2. In recent years, MySQL has also become popular. This DBMS is fast, easy-to-use, and free for most purposes. However, it doesn't provide all of the features that Oracle, MS SQL Server, and DB2 provide.

In addition to these database management systems, Access databases are also popular for some types of applications. In particular, Access databases are useful for small departmental applications. One difference between Access and most other database management systems is that Access doesn't require a piece of software known as a database server to be running on the computer that stores the database. As a result, you don't need to install a database server to use Java to work with an Access database. Because of that, we use an Access database in the examples in this chapter and in the exercises at the end of the chapter.

The Products table

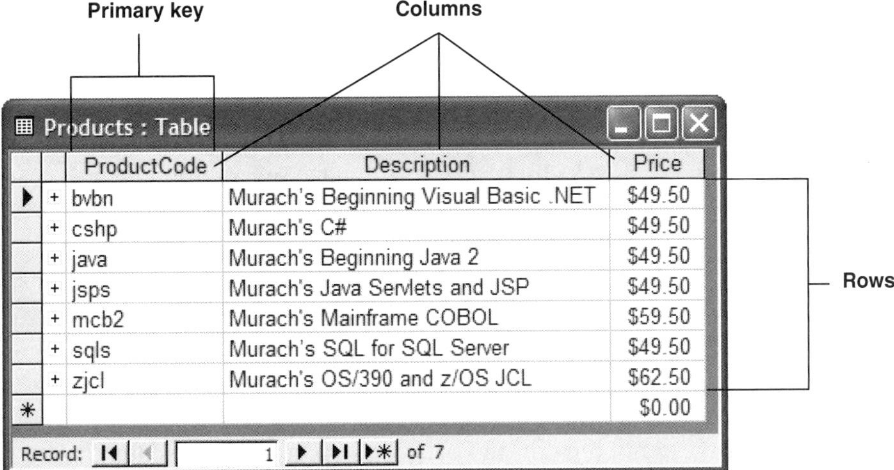

Description

- A *relational database* uses *tables* to store and manipulate data. Each table contains one or more *records*, or *rows*, that contain the data for a single entry. Each row contains one or more *fields*, or *columns*, with each column representing a single item of data.
- Most tables contain a *primary key* that uniquely identifies each row in the table.
- The software that manages a relational database is called a *database management system* (*DBMS*). Four popular database management systems today are Oracle, Microsoft's SQL Server, IBM's DB2, and MySQL.

Note

- In addition to the database management systems mentioned above, Access databases are popular for applications with a smaller number of users. Unlike other database management systems, you don't have to have a piece of software known as a database server running on your system to use an Access database.

Figure 21-1 How a table is organized

How the tables in a database are related

Figure 21-2 shows how a relational database uses the values in the primary key field to relate one table to another. Here, each ProductCode field in the LineItems table contains a value that identifies one row in the Products table. Since the ProductCode field in the LineItems table points to a primary key in another table, it's called a *foreign key*. Often, a table will have several foreign keys.

In this figure, each row in the Products table relates to one or more rows in the LineItems table. As a result, the Products table has a *one-to-many relationship* with the LineItems table. Although a one-to-many relationship is the most common type of relationship between tables, you can also have a *one-to-one relationship* or a *many-to-many relationship*. However, a one-to-one relationship between two tables is rare since the data can be stored in a single table. In contrast, a many-to-many relationship between two tables is typically implemented by using a third table that has a one-to-many relationship with both of the original tables.

Incidentally, the primary key in the LineItems table is the LineItemID field. It is automatically generated by the DBMS when a new record is added to the database. This type of primary key is often appropriate for tables like Invoice, Employee, and Customer tables.

The relationship between the Products and LineItems tables

Primary key

Products : Table

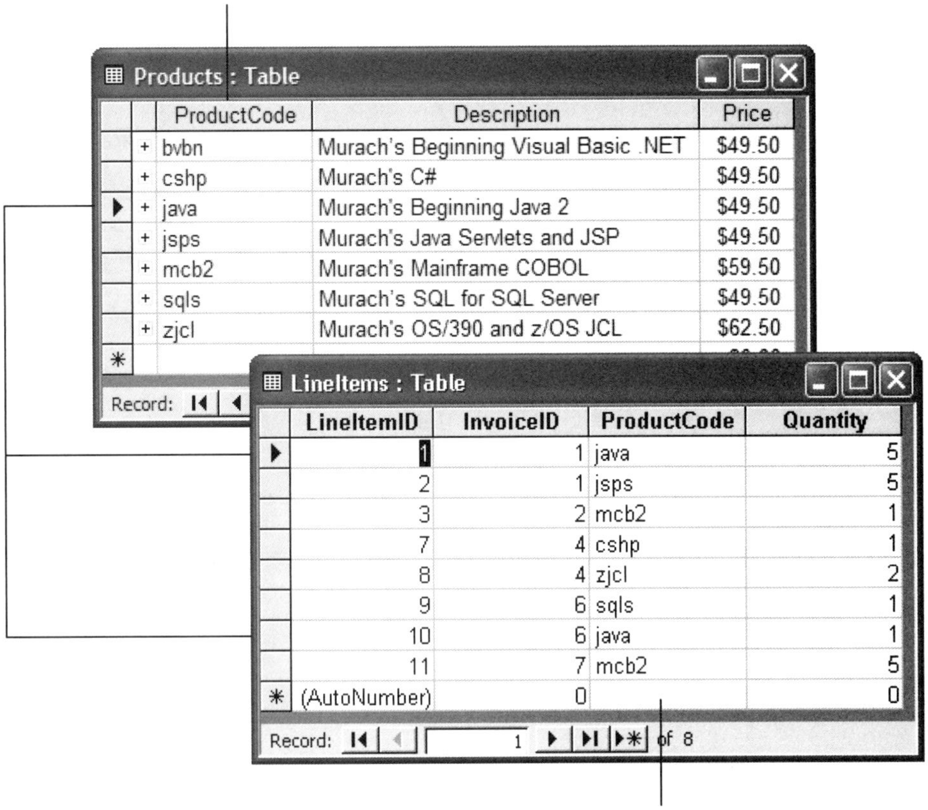

	ProductCode	Description	Price
+	bvbn	Murach's Beginning Visual Basic .NET	$49.50
+	cshp	Murach's C#	$49.50
+	java	Murach's Beginning Java 2	$49.50
+	jsps	Murach's Java Servlets and JSP	$49.50
+	mcb2	Murach's Mainframe COBOL	$59.50
+	sqls	Murach's SQL for SQL Server	$49.50
+	zjcl	Murach's OS/390 and z/OS JCL	$62.50
*			

Record:

LineItems : Table

LineItemID	InvoiceID	ProductCode	Quantity
1	1	java	5
2	1	jsps	5
3	2	mcb2	1
7	4	cshp	1
8	4	zjcl	2
9	6	sqls	1
10	6	java	1
11	7	mcb2	5
(AutoNumber)	0		0

Record: 1 of 8

Foreign key

Description

- The tables in a relational database are related to each other through their key fields. For example, the ProductCode field is used to relate the Products and LineItems tables. The ProductCode field in the LineItems table is called a *foreign key* because it identifies a related row in the Products table.
- Three types of relationships can exist between tables. The most common type is a *one-to-many relationship* as illustrated above. However, two tables can also have a *one-to-one relationship* or a *many-to-many relationship*.

How the fields in a database are defined

Figure 21-3 shows how a DBMS defines a field in a database. In particular, it shows how the DBMS defines a name and data type for each field. Although this figure shows a Microsoft Access database, all relational databases require a name and a data type for each field. In addition, any modern relational database will let you set other properties for each field in the database such as a default value for new rows, whether the field is required, and so on.

This figure shows the names and data types for the fields in the Products table. Here, the key icon to the left of the ProductCode field indicates that it is the primary key for the table. This field and the Description field are defined with the Text data type, which maps to the String type in Java. In contrast, the Price field is defined with the Currency data type, which maps to the double type in Java.

When a DBMS defines a field as a required field, an application must provide a value for the field when it tries to add a record to the database. For some applications, though, you can supply a *default value* for the field. That way, if the application tries to add a new record without specifying a value for the field, the DBMS will use the default value.

The design of the Products table in Access 2002

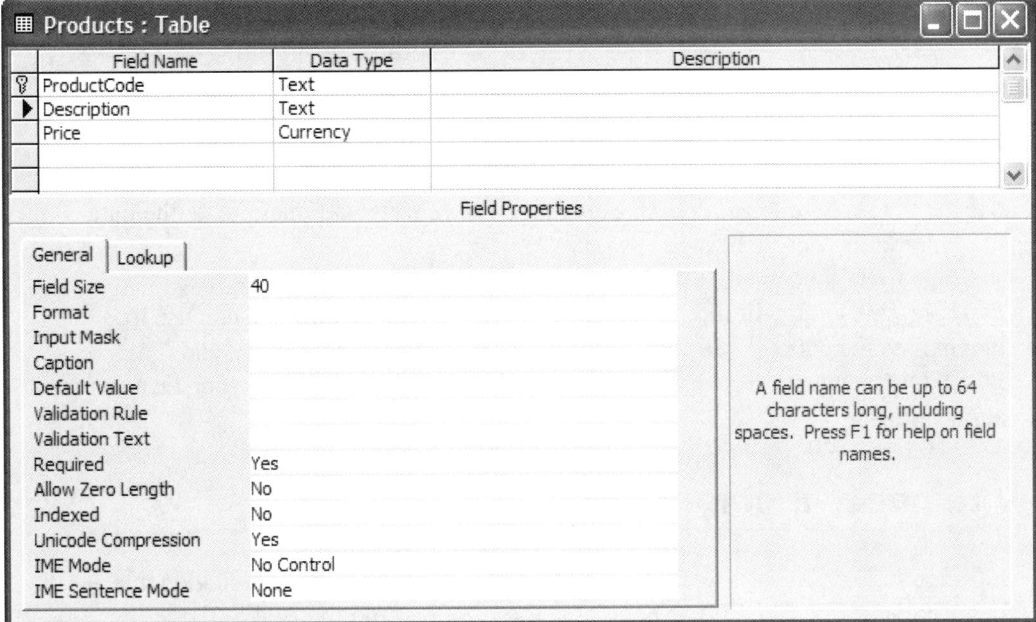

Description

- A database management system requires a name and data type for each field. Depending on the data type, you may be able to specify other attributes for the field such as the field size, whether the field is required by new rows or not, and so on.
- If you specify a *default value* for a field, that value is used for the field in a new record when no other value is supplied.

Figure 21-3 How the fields in a table are defined

How to use SQL to work with the data in a database

Structured Query Language (*SQL*) is a standard language that you can use to communicate with any modern DBMS. This language can be divided into two parts. The *Data Definition Language* (*DDL*) lets you define the tables in a database. The *Data Manipulation Language* (*DML*) lets you manipulate the data that's stored in those tables.

Since you'll normally use database software to define the tables in a database, this topic will focus on the four SQL statements that you can use to manipulate the data in a database: the SELECT, INSERT, UPDATE, and DELETE statements. These are the statements that you will use in your Java applications.

How to query a single table

Figure 21-4 shows how to use a SELECT statement to *query* a single table in a database. The SELECT statement is the most commonly used SQL statement. It returns a *result set* (or *result table*) that contains the rows and columns that are specified by the SELECT statement.

In the syntax summary for this statement, the capitalized words are SQL keywords and the lowercase words represent the items that you must supply. To separate the items in a statement, you can use one or more spaces, and you can use indentation whenever it helps improve the readability of a statement. Unlike Java, SQL is not case-sensitive. As a result, you can use whatever capitalization you like when referring to SQL keywords. In this chapter, we capitalize all SQL keywords to make it easy to tell the difference between these keywords and other parts of the SQL language such as column names. However, in practice, many programmers use lowercase for SQL keywords when writing SQL statements.

The first example in this figure shows how to retrieve three columns from the Products table. Here, the SELECT clause identifies the three columns and the FROM clause identifies the table. Then, the WHERE clause limits the number of rows that are retrieved by specifying that the statement should only retrieve rows where the value in the Price field is greater than 50. Last, the ORDER BY clause indicates that the retrieved rows should be sorted in ascending order (from A to Z) by the ProductCode field.

The result set is a logical table that's created temporarily within the database. Here, the *current row pointer*, or *cursor*, keeps track of the current row. If you make a change to the data in a result set, the change is also made to the table that the result set was created from.

As you might guess, queries can have a significant effect on the performance of a database application. The more columns and rows that a query returns, the more traffic the network has to bear. As a result, when you design queries, you should try to keep the number of columns and rows to a minimum.

SELECT syntax for selecting from one table

```
SELECT field-1 [, field-2] ...
FROM table-1
[WHERE selection-criteria]
[ORDER BY field-1 [ASC|DESC] [, field-2 [ASC|DESC] ...]]
```

A SELECT statement that gets selected columns and rows

```
SELECT ProductCode, Description, Price
FROM Products
WHERE Price > 50
ORDER BY ProductCode ASC
```

The result set defined by the SELECT statement

	ProductCode	Description	Price
▶	mcb2	Murach's Mainframe COBOL	$59.50
	zjcl	Murach's OS/390 and z/OS JCL	$62.50

A SELECT statement that returns all columns and rows

```
SELECT * FROM Products
```

Description

- The SELECT statement is used to perform a *query* that retrieves rows and columns from a database.
- The *result set* (or *result table*) is the set of records that are retrieved by a query.
- The *current row pointer*, or *cursor*, identifies the current row in a result set. You can use this pointer to identify the row you want to update or delete from a result set. Any change to the result set is reflected in the table that the result set is based on.
- To select all of the columns in a table, you can code an asterisk (*) instead of coding field names.
- For efficiency, you should code your queries so the result set has as few rows and as few columns as possible.

How to join data from two or more tables

Figure 21-5 shows how to use the SELECT statement to retrieve data from two tables. Since the data from the two tables is joined together into a single result set, this type of operation is known as a *join*. In this figure, for example, the SELECT statement joins data from the Products and LineItems tables into a single result set.

An *inner join* is the most common type of join. When you use an inner join, which is sometimes called an *equi-join*, the records from the two tables in the join are included in the result set only if their related fields match. These matching fields are specified in the SELECT statement. In this figure, for example, records from the Products and LineItems tables are included only if the value of the ProductCode field of the Products table is equal to the ProductCode field of the LineItems table. In other words, if there isn't any data in the LineItems table for a product, that Product won't be added to the result set.

Please note in this SELECT statement that the last field in the query, the Total field, is calculated by multiplying Price and Quantity. In other words, a field by the name of Total doesn't actually exist in the database. This type of field is called a *calculated field*, and it exists only in the results of the query.

Another type of join is an *outer join*. With this type of join, all of the records in one of the tables are included in the result set whether or not there are matching records in the other table. In a *left outer join*, all of the records in the first table (the one on the left) are included in the result set. In a *right outer join*, all of the records in the second table are included. To illustrate, assume that the SELECT statement in this figure had used a left outer join. In that case, all of the records in the Products table whose price is greater than 50 would have been included in the result set...even if no matching record was found in the LineItems table.

Although this figure only shows how to join data from two tables, you can extend this syntax to join data from additional tables. If, for example, you want to create a result set that includes data from three tables named Customers, Invoices, and LineItems, you could code the FROM clause of the SELECT statement like this:

```
FROM Customers
    INNER JOIN Invoices
        ON Customers.CustomerID = Invoices.CustomerID
    INNER JOIN LineItems
        ON Invoices.InvoiceID = LineItems.InvoiceID
```

Then, you could include any of the fields from the three tables in the field list of the SELECT statement.

This figure also shows an alternate SQL syntax that lets you join two tables by using the WHERE clause instead of the FROM clause. Using this syntax, the FROM clause lists all of the tables in the result set. Then, the WHERE clause identifies the join by using the AND keyword to connect all of the selection criteria that must be satisfied. This is an older syntax for joins that is still used by some database management systems.

SELECT syntax for joining two tables

```
SELECT field-1 [, field-2] ...
FROM table-1
   {INNER | LEFT OUTER | RIGHT OUTER} JOIN table-2
   ON table-1.field-1 {=|<|>|<=|>=|<>} table-2.field-2
[WHERE selection-criteria]
[ORDER BY field-1 [ASC|DESC] [, field-2 [ASC|DESC] ...]]
```

A SELECT statement that retrieves and sorts selected fields and records from the Products table

```
SELECT ProductCode, Description, Price, Quantity,
       Price * Quantity AS Total
FROM Products
   INNER JOIN LineItems
   ON Products.ProductCode = LineItems.ProductCode
WHERE Price > 50
ORDER BY ProductCode ASC
```

Another way to write the SELECT statement shown above

```
SELECT ProductCode, Description, Price, Quantity,
       Price * Quantity AS Total
FROM Products, LineItems
WHERE Products.ProductCode = LineItems.ProductCode AND Price > 50
ORDER BY ProductCode ASC
```

The result set defined by the SELECT statement

	ProductCode	Description	Price	Quantity	Total
▶	mcb2	Murach's Mainframe COBOL	$59.50	1	$59.50
	mcb2	Murach's Mainframe COBOL	$59.50	5	$297.50
	zjcl	Murach's OS/390 and z/OS JCL	$62.50	2	$125.00

Description

- A *join* lets you combine data from two or more tables into a single result set.
- An *inner join*, or *equi-join*, returns records from both tables, but only if their related fields match. An *outer join* returns records from one table in the join (the LEFT or RIGHT table) even if the records aren't matched by records in the other table.

How to add, update, and delete data in a table

Figure 21-6 shows how to use the INSERT, UPDATE, and DELETE statements to add, update, or delete one or more records in a database. The queries done by these SQL statements are sometimes referred to as *action queries* because they actually change the data in a database.

The first syntax and example for the INSERT statement show how to use this statement to add one record to a database. To do that, the statement supplies the names of the fields that are going to receive values in the new record, followed by the values for those fields.

In contrast, the second syntax and example for the INSERT statement show how to add multiple records to a table. To do that, you include a SELECT statement within the INSERT statement. Then, the SELECT statement selects the fields and records from one table, and the INSERT statement adds those records to another table. In this example, the SELECT statement selects all of the fields from the records in the Invoices table that have been paid in full (AmountDue = 0), and inserts them into the InvoiceArchive table. In this case, you don't have to specify the list of fields because both tables have the same fields.

Similarly, the syntax and examples for the UPDATE statement show how to update a single record and a group of records. In the first example, the UPDATE statement updates the Description and Price fields in the record where ProductCode is equal to "casp". In the second example, the Price field is updated to 49.95 in all of the records where Price is equal to 49.50.

Last, the syntax and examples for the DELETE statement show how to delete a single record or a group of records. Here, the first example deletes the record from the Products table where the ProductCode equals "casp". Since each record contains a unique value in the ProductCode field, this only deletes a single record. However, in the second example, many records in the Invoices table may have an AmountDue field that equals 0. As a result, this statement deletes all invoices whose balance has been paid in full. That way, the Invoices table will only contain unpaid invoices.

When you issue an INSERT, UPDATE, or DELETE statement from a Java application, you usually work with one record at a time. You'll see this illustrated by the ProductsDB class shown later in this chapter. Action queries that affect more than one record are typically used by database administrators and programmers using tools provided by the DBMS.

How to add records

INSERT syntax for adding a single record

```
INSERT INTO table-name [(field-list)]
   VALUES (value-list)
```

A statement that adds a single record

```
INSERT INTO Products (ProductCode, Description, Price)
   VALUES ('casp', 'ASP.NET Web Programming with C#', '54.50')
```

INSERT syntax for adding multiple records

```
INSERT INTO table-name [(field-list)]
   SELECT-statement
```

A statement that adds multiple records

```
INSERT INTO InvoiceArchive
   SELECT * FROM Invoices WHERE AmountDue = 0
```

How to update records

UPDATE syntax

```
UPDATE table-name
   SET expression-1 [, expression-2] ...
   WHERE selection-criteria
```

A statement that updates a single record

```
UPDATE Products
   SET Description = 'Murach''s ASP.NET Web Programming with C#',
       Price = '49.50'
   WHERE ProductCode = 'casp'
```

A statement that updates multiple records

```
UPDATE Products
   SET Price = '49.95'
   WHERE Price = '49.50'
```

How to delete records

DELETE syntax

```
DELETE FROM table-name
   WHERE selection-criteria
```

A statement that deletes a single record

```
DELETE FROM Products WHERE ProductCode = 'casp'
```

A statement that deletes multiple records

```
DELETE FROM Invoices WHERE AmountDue = 0
```

Figure 21-6 How to add, update, and delete data in a table

An introduction to Java database drivers

When you use *JDBC* (*Java Database Connectivity*) to work with a database, you need to use a database driver to communicate with the database. In the next two topics, you'll learn about four types of drivers that work with Java, and you'll learn how to configure one type of standard database driver.

The four driver types

Figure 21-7 shows four ways a Java application can access a database. To start, the Java application uses the JDBC driver manager to load a *database driver*. Then, the Java application can use one or more of the driver types to connect to the database and manipulate the data.

You can use a type-1, *JDBC-ODBC bridge driver* to connect to a database through *ODBC* (*Open Database Connectivity*), a standard way to access databases. Since ODBC drivers exist for most modern databases, a type-1 driver provides a way to connect Java with almost any type of database. And since a type-1 driver is included with the J2SE, it's available to all Java programmers. However, in order for a type-1 driver to work, an ODBC data source must be registered on the client machine as shown in the next figure.

You can use a type-2, *native protocol partly Java driver* to connect to a database without using ODBC. However, like ODBC, this driver requires that some binary code be installed on each client machine. As a result, you'll want to use a type-3 or type-4 driver if you plan to distribute the application on multiple client machines.

You can use a type-3, *net protocol all Java driver* to connect to a database by converting JDBC calls to an independent net protocol that's used by a specific vendor. Then, the vendor's middleware software, which runs on a server, will convert the net protocol into calls in the native protocol that's used by the DBMS. Since the middleware software can typically convert the net protocol into the native DBMS protocol for multiple databases, this solution is the most flexible.

You can also use a type-4, *native protocol all Java driver* to connect to a database. This type of driver, which runs on a server, converts JDBC calls directly to the native DBMS protocol. Since most DBMS protocols are proprietary, these types of drivers are typically available from the database vendors. For example, there are type-4 drivers available for Oracle, Microsoft SQL Server, IBM DB2, and MySQL.

Although this chapter shows how to connect to a database using both a type-1 and type-3 driver, you'll want to use a type-3 or type-4 driver for any serious application. You can download type-3 and type-4 drivers for most databases from the Java web site (servlet.java.sun.com/products/jdbc/drivers) or from the database vendor's web site. The documentation for these drivers typically shows how to install and configure the driver so it runs on a server.

Four ways to access a database

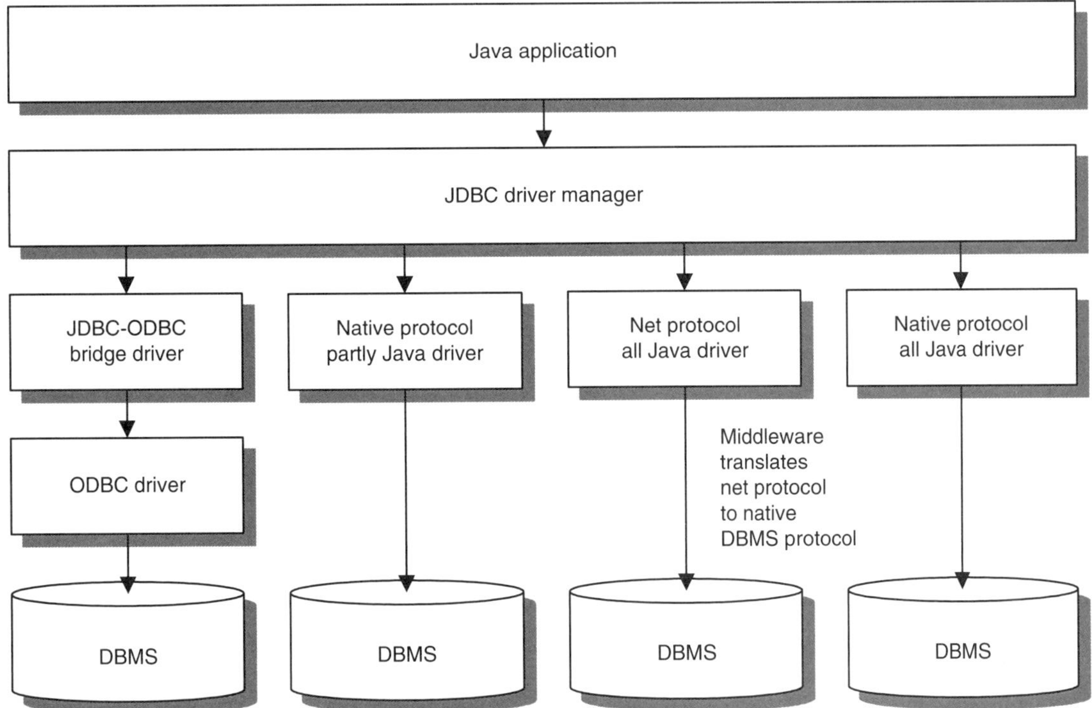

The four types of Java drivers

Type 1 A *JDBC-ODBC bridge driver* converts JDBC calls into ODBC calls that access the DBMS protocol. This data access method requires that the ODBC drivers be installed on the client machines.

Type 2 A *native protocol partly Java driver* converts JDBC calls into calls in the native DBMS protocol. Since this conversion takes place on the client, some binary code must be installed on the client machine.

Type 3 A *net protocol all Java driver* converts JDBC calls into a net protocol that's independent of any native DBMS protocol. Then, middleware software running on a server converts the net protocol to the native DBMS protocol. Since this conversion takes place on the server side, no installation is required on the client machine.

Type 4 A *native protocol all Java driver* converts JDBC calls into a native DBMS protocol. Since this conversion takes place on the server side, no installation is required on the client machine.

Notes

- To get information about the drivers that are currently available, check the Java web site at java.sun.com/products/jdbc and click on the List of Drivers Available link.
- Since type-1 and type-2 drivers require some client-side installation, they're not a good solution for Internet applications.

Figure 21-7 The four driver types

How to configure an ODBC driver

To use a JDBC-ODBC bridge driver, you need to configure the ODBC data source on each client machine. In contrast, to use a type-3 or type-4 driver, you don't need to do any configuration on the client machines. However, you still need to install the driver and configure the ODBC data source on the server machine.

Figure 21-8 shows how to register an ODBC data source for a machine running under Windows. During this procedure, you must specify the type of ODBC driver, the name you want to use for the data source, and the location and name of the database. In this example, the ODBC driver is the Microsoft Access Driver, and the name of the data source is MurachDB.

How to register an ODBC data source

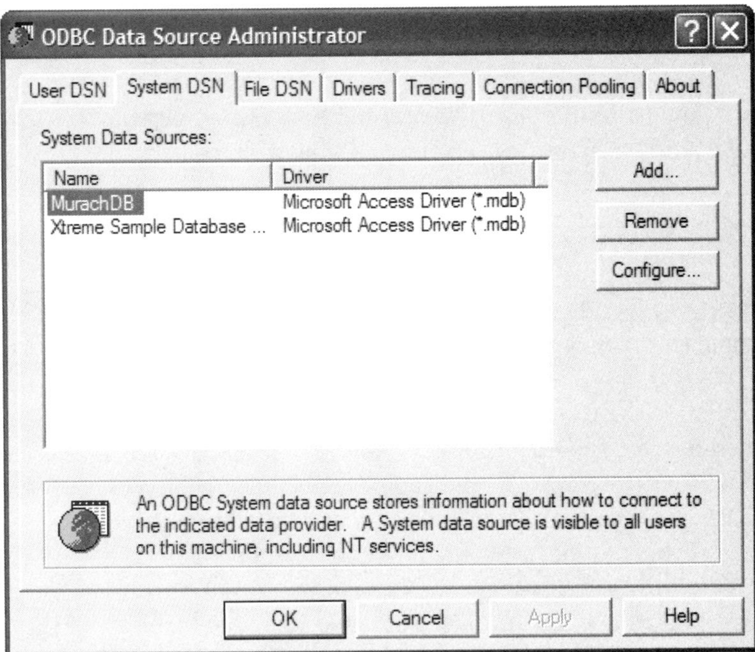

How to install the client driver for an ODBC data source

1. Start the ODBC Data Source Administrator. To do that under Windows 98/2000, go to the Control Panel and select the ODBC Data Sources (32 bit) icon. To do that under Windows NT/XP, go to the Control Panel and select the Performance and Maintenance icon, then the Administrative Tools icon, and then double-click the Data Sources (ODBC) icon.
2. From the ODBC Data Source Administrator, click on the System DSN tab, and then click on the Add button to add a data source.
3. From the Create New Data Source dialog box, select the type of database and click on the Finish button. Then, enter a name for the data source and locate and identify the data source. When you're done, the ODBC Data Source Administrator should look similar to the dialog box shown above.

Description

- The procedure above will vary depending on the operating system and on the type of database. However, the general idea is the same. You must select a type of ODBC driver, you must provide a name for the data source, and you must locate and identify the data source.

Figure 21-8 How to configure an ODBC driver

How to use Java to work with a database

Now that you know about the four types of drivers and how to configure an ODBC data source, you're ready to write Java code that works with a database.

How to connect to a database

Figure 21-9 shows the syntax and code needed to use JDBC to connect to a database. The first example shows how to use the JDBC-ODBC bridge driver that comes as a part of JDK 5.0 to connect to the MurachDB database. To start, you use the forName method of the Class class to load the driver. Then, you use the getConnection method of the DriverManager class in the java.sql package to return a Connection object. (This package contains all of the classes, interfaces, and exceptions you'll learn about in this chapter.) To do that, you must supply at least a URL for the database. In addition, you typically have to supply a user name and a password.

The URL (Uniform Resource Locator) for these drivers starts with "jdbc". Then, for JDBC-ODBC bridge drivers, the subprotocol is "odbc" and the database URL is the name that you used when you configured the ODBC data source. In this example, the default user name and password for a Microsoft Access database are used. However, if the security for the database was enabled, you would need to supply a valid user name and password for the database.

The second example shows how to use a type-3 driver named JDataConnect to connect to the MurachDB database. A trial version of this driver can be downloaded from JNetDirect's website (www.jnetdirect.com). Once you download this driver, you can read the documentation to learn how to install and load it. When you do, you'll find that the driver class ($Driver.class) is stored in a package (JData2_0.sql) within a JAR file. By default, this JAR file is installed into the directory shown in this figure. Since this JAR file isn't part of the Java API, you must set the class path to the JAR file so Java can find the class for this driver. Then, you can load the driver by specifying the package and class for the driver (JData2_0.sql.$Driver.class) in the forName method of the Class class.

All of the connection code in the second example is similar to the code in the first example except for the URL specification. Here, the subprotocol is the JDataConnect protocol, and the URL points to the computer that the database is running on. In this case, the database is running on a network server. To point to this server, this example uses a URL that specifies the server's name (DBSERVER) followed by the name of the ODBC data source (MurachDB). However, you can test this driver by placing it on your computer and using the localhost keyword rather than the server's name.

Since the JDataConnect driver uses a net protocol to communicate with an ODBC data source, you must configure the ODBC data source on the computer that the JDataConnect driver is installed on. In addition, you must make sure

URL syntax

```
jdbc:subprotocolName:databaseURL
```

How to connect to the MurachDB database with the JDBC-ODBC bridge driver

```
Connection connection = null;
try
{
    // load the JDBC-ODBC bridge driver
    Class.forName("sun.jdbc.odbc.JdbcOdbcDriver");

    // use the DriverManager to create a Connection object
    String dbUrl = "jdbc:odbc:MurachDB";
    String username = "Admin";
    String password = "";
    connection = DriverManager.getConnection(dbUrl, username, password);
}
catch(ClassNotFoundException e)
{
    System.err.println("Database driver not found.");
}
catch(SQLException e)
{
    System.err.println("Error connecting to the database: " + e);
}
```

How to connect to the MurachDB database with a type-3 driver named JDataConnect

```
// add the path for the JAR file to the classpath:
// C:\JNetDirect\JDataConnect\JARs\JData2_0.jar

// load the type-3 driver
Class.forName("JData2_0.sql.$Driver");   // class path must be set correctly

// use the DriverManager to create a Connection object
String dbUrl = "jdbc:JDataConnect://DBSERVER/MurachDB";
String username = "Admin";
String password = "";
connection = DriverManager.getConnection(dbUrl, username, password);
```

Description

- All of the interfaces, classes, and exceptions for using JDBC that are presented in this chapter are stored in the java.sql package.
- The forName method of the Class class throws a ClassNotFoundException.
- The getConnection method of the DriverManager class throws a SQLException.
- Since the Connection object will often be used by more than one method in a class, it's typically declared so it's available to the entire class.
- Sun doesn't recommend using the ODBC bridge driver that comes as part of the J2SE for serious applications. This driver doesn't support all the features of the JDBC 2.0 API.
- To learn more about downloading and installing the JDataConnect driver, check the JNetDirect website (www.jnetdirect.com).

Figure 21-9 How to connect to a database

that the JDataConnect driver is running on that computer. To do that, you can start the JDataAdmin program that's installed when you install the JDataConnect driver. Then, you can click the Service Control tab and the Start Service button.

Although figure 21-9 only shows the exception handling code for the first example, you need to provide exception handling code whenever you connect to a database. To start, you must handle the ClassNotFoundException that's thrown by the forName method of the Class class. Then, you must handle the SQLException that's thrown by the getConnection method of the DriverManager class. In general, it's good programming practice to catch both of these exceptions. That way, if an error occurs, you can tell whether it's because the code couldn't load the driver class (ClassNotFoundException) or because it couldn't connect to the database (SQLException).

In practice, connecting to the database is often the most time consuming and frustrating part of working with a database. So if some of your colleagues have already made a connection to the database you need to use, by all means get help from them. That can save you hours of frustration.

How to return a result set

Figure 21-10 shows how to use Statement objects to return ResultSet objects. The first example shows how to create a forward-only, read-only result set. Here, the createStatement method is called from a Connection object to return a Statement object. Then, the executeQuery method is called from the Statement object to execute an SQL SELECT statement that's coded as a string. This SELECT statement uses the wildcard character to select all fields and rows from the Products table.

The second example shows how to create a scrollable, updateable result set. To do this, the code supplies two arguments for the createStatement method of the Connection object.

The first argument uses a field from the ResultSet class to specify the type of result set. In this example, the argument specifies that the result set should be scrollable, and it should display changes that have been made by other users to the data that's in the result set. Although this is the most flexible type of result set, it also requires the most system resources. In contrast, a scrollable result set that isn't sensitive to changes requires fewer resources.

The second argument in this example specifies the concurrency of the result set. Here, the concurrency has been set to updateable. That means that you can update the values in the result set, and those values will be stored in the database.

When you return a result set, you need to make sure that your driver supports the features of the result set. For example, some older drivers may only support version 1.0 of the JDBC API. Since scrollable and updateable result sets were added in version 2.0 of the JDBC API, this means that those drivers don't support these types of result sets. In addition, not all drivers will support version 3.0 of the JDBC API. This version is included with version 5.0 of the JDK and includes newer features such as allowing multiple result sets to be open at the same time.

How to create a forward-only, read-only result set

```
Statement statement = connection.createStatement();
ResultSet rs = statement.executeQuery("SELECT * FROM Products");
```

How to create a scrollable, updateable result set

```
Statement statement = connection.createStatement(
    ResultSet.TYPE_SCROLL_SENSITIVE,
    ResultSet.CONCUR_UPDATABLE);

String query = "SELECT ProductCode, Description, Price "
             + "FROM Products ORDER BY ProductCode ASC";

ResultSet rs = statement.executeQuery(query);
```

Five ResultSet fields that set type and concurrency

Constant	Description
TYPE_FORWARD_ONLY	Creates a result set where the cursor can only move forward (default).
TYPE_SCROLL_INSENSITIVE	Creates a result set where the cursor can scroll through the result set but won't display changes made by others to the result set.
TYPE_SCROLL_SENSITIVE	Creates a result set where the cursor can scroll through the result set and will display changes made by others to the result set.
CONCUR_READ_ONLY	Creates a read-only result set (default).
CONCUR_UPDATABLE	Creates an updateable result set.

Description

- The createStatement method of a Connection object creates a Statement object. Then, the executeQuery method of the Statement object executes a SELECT statement that returns a ResultSet object.
- By default, the createStatement method creates a forward-only, read-only result set. However, you can set the type and concurrency of a Statement object by coding the fields above for the two arguments of the createStatement method.
- Both the createStatement and executeQuery methods throw an exception of the SQLException type. As a result, any code that returns a result set will need to catch or throw this exception.

Figure 21-10 How to return a result set

How to move the cursor through a result set

Figure 21-11 shows how to move the cursor through a result set. To start, this figure shows 14 methods of the ResultSet object. Since the ResultSet object is created from the ResultSet interface, it's up to the driver software to fully implement these methods. As a result, older drivers may not support some of the methods that were added in versions 2.0 and 3.0 of the JDBC API. That includes the methods for working with scrollable result sets.

If the result set is a forward-only result set, you'll only be able to use the next method to move through the result set as shown in the first example. In this example, the next method is coded as the condition for a while loop. As a result, the first time the next method is called, it attempts to move the pointer to the first record in the result set. If it is successful, it returns a true value. Within the loop, you can write code like the code shown in the next figure that works with the current record. Once the loop has moved through all of the records in the result set, the next method will return a false value and the loop will end.

If the result set is scrollable, you can use the next, previous, first, last, absolute, and relative methods to move the cursor through the result set as shown in the second example. Here, the first statement moves the cursor to the first row in the result set, and the second statement moves the cursor to the last row. Then, the first if statement moves the cursor to the previous row if the cursor isn't on the first row, and the second if statement moves the cursor to the next row if the cursor isn't on the last row. Finally, the fifth statement moves the cursor to the fourth record in the result set; the sixth statement moves the cursor back two rows; and the seventh statement moves the cursor forward three rows.

Like the next method, all of these methods return a boolean value that indicates whether the cursor has been moved to a valid row. For example, the previous method returns a true value until it reaches the first row of the result set or until it hits a row that's invalid for other reasons. Since all of these methods throw an exception of the SQLException type, you either need to throw or catch this exception when you're working with these methods.

Methods of a ResultSet object that work with a result set

Method	Description
`beforeFirst()`	Moves the cursor before the first row in this result set.
`afterLast()`	Moves the cursor after the last row in this result set.
`first()`	Moves the cursor to the first row in this result set.
`previous()`	Moves the cursor up to the previous row in this result set.
`next()`	Moves the cursor down to the next row in this result set.
`last()`	Moves the cursor to the last row in this result set.
`absolute(intRow)`	Moves the cursor to the row specified by the int value where 1 is the first row, 2 is the second row, and so on.
`relative(intRow)`	Moves the cursor the number of rows specified relative to the current row.
`isBeforeFirst()`	Returns a true value if the cursor is positioned before the first row.
`isAfterLast()`	Returns a true value if the cursor is positioned after the last row.
`isFirst()`	Returns a true value if the cursor is positioned on the first row.
`isLast()`	Returns a true value if the cursor is positioned on the last row.
`close()`	Releases the result set's JDBC and database resources.
`getRow()`	Returns an int value that identifies the current row of the result set.

How to work with a forward-only result set

```
while(rs.next())
{
    // code that works with each record
}
```

How to work with a scrollable result set

```
rs.first();
rs.last();
if (rs.isFirst() == false)
   rs.previous();
if (rs.isLast() == false)
   rs.next();
rs.absolute(4);
rs.relative(-2);
rs.relative(3);
```

Description

- When you create a result set, the cursor is positioned before the first record. As a result, the first time you call the next method, it will move to the first record in the result set.
- The first, previous, next, last, absolute, and relative methods all return a true value if the new row exists and a false value if the new row doesn't exist or the result set is empty.
- All of the methods in this figure throw an exception of the SQLException type.

Figure 21-11 How to move the cursor through a result set

How to return data from a result set

Figure 21-12 shows how to return data from the current record in a result set. In particular, it shows how to use the getString and getDouble methods of the ResultSet object to return strings and double values. However, the same principles can be used for any of the get methods of the ResultSet object.

The four methods in this figure show the two types of arguments accepted by the get methods. The first and third get methods accept an int value that specifies the number of the column in the result set, where 1 is the first column, 2 is the second column, and so on. The second and fourth get methods accept a string value that specifies the name of the column in the result set. Although the get methods that specify the column index require less typing, using the get methods that specify the column name can be more flexible. For example, they will work regardless of the sequence in which the columns are returned.

The first example shows how to use column indexes to return data from a result set named rs. Here, the first two statements use the getString method to return the code and description for the current product while the third statement uses the getDouble method to return the price of the product. Since these methods use column indexes, the first column in the result set must contain the product code, the second column must contain the description, and the third column must contain the price.

The second example shows how to use column names to return data from a result set. Since this code uses the column names, the order of the columns in the result set doesn't matter. However, the column names must exist in the result set. If not, an SQLException will be thrown indicating that a column wasn't found.

The third example shows how you can use the get methods to create a Product object from a row in a result set. Here, the constructor for the Product object uses three values that are returned by the get methods to create a new Product object. Since objects are often created from data that's stored in a database, code like this is used frequently.

If you look up the ResultSet interface in the documentation for the API, you'll see that get methods exist for all of the primitive types as well as for other types of data. For example, get methods exist for the Date, Time, and Timestamp classes that are a part of the java.sql package. In addition, they exist for *BLOB objects* (*Binary Large Objects*) and *CLOB objects* (*Character Large Objects*). These types of objects are used for storing large objects such as multimedia files in databases.

Methods of a ResultSet object that return data from a result set

Method	Description
`getString(intColumnIndex)`	Returns a String from the specified column number.
`getString(StringColumnName)`	Returns a String from the specified column name.
`getDouble(intColumnIndex)`	Returns a double value from the specified column number.
`getDouble(StringColumnName)`	Returns a double value from the specified column name.

Code that uses column indexes to return fields from the Products result set

```
String code = rs.getString(1);
String description = rs.getString(2);
double price = rs.getDouble(3);
```

Code that uses column names to return the same fields

```
String code = rs.getString("ProductCode");
String description = rs.getString("Description");
double price = rs.getDouble("Price");
```

Code that creates a Product object from the result set

```
Product p = new Product(rs.getString("ProductCode"),
                        rs.getString("Description"),
                        rs.getDouble("Price"));
```

Description

- The get methods of a ResultSet object can be used to return all eight primitive types. For example, the getInt method returns the int type and the getLong method returns the long type.
- The get methods of a ResultSet object can also be used to return some objects such as dates and times. For example, the getDate, getTime, and getTimestamp methods return objects of the Date, Time, and Timestamp classes of the java.sql package.
- Although they aren't widely used, the getBlob and getClob methods can be used to return *BLOB objects* (*Binary Large Objects*) and *CLOB objects* (*Character Large Objects*).

Figure 21-12 How to return data from a result set

How to modify data in a database

Figure 21-13 shows how to use Java to modify the data in a database. First, it shows how to use the executeUpdate method of a Statement object to execute SQL statements that add, update, and delete data. Then, this figure shows how to use methods that were introduced with the JDBC 2.0 API to add, update, and delete data. Since the executeUpdate method has been a part of Java since version 1.0 of the JDBC API, this method should work for all JDBC drivers. In contrast, the methods of the JDBC 2.0 and 3.0 APIs may not work with older JDBC drivers. For example, these methods don't work with the JDBC-ODBC bridge driver that's included with the JDK 5.0.

To use the executeUpdate method, you pass an SQL statement to the database. In these examples, the code adds, updates, and deletes a product in the Product table. To do that, the code combines data from a Product object with the appropriate SQL statement. For the UPDATE and DELETE statements, the SQL statement uses the product's code in the WHERE clause to select a single product.

When you work with the 2.0 methods of the JDBC, you don't have to use SQL statements. Instead, you just call methods of the ResultSet object to add, update, and delete records from the current result set. In these examples, you can assume that the ResultSet object named rs contains three columns and many rows.

To add a record, you call the moveToInsertRow method to move the cursor to a special buffer area that's used to construct a new row. Then, you call the appropriate update method for each column in the row. For example, you call the updateString method for a string, or the updateDouble method for a double value. Here, the first argument specifies the name of the column and the second argument specifies the value of the column. When you're done providing values for all of the columns in the row, you call the insertRow method to commit the changes to the database. Then, you can call the moveToCurrentRow method to move back to the row that you were on before you called the moveToInsertRow method.

To update or delete a row, you start by moving to that row using the methods that were described earlier in this chapter. Then, you can update the row by calling the appropriate update method for any of the columns that you wish to update and by calling the updateRow method after that. Or, you can delete a row by calling the deleteRow method.

Depending on the driver that you're using, the modifications that you make to a result set may cause some problems. For example, when you add a row, you may not be able to move to that row. Worse, when you delete a row, an invalid row may remain in the result set where the deleted row used to be. Then, if you try to move to that row, your application will throw an SQLException. The best way to solve these problems is to get a better driver or change the way your program retrieves data. However, you can also solve these problems by closing the result set and opening it again. Although that isn't efficient, it will refresh all the rows in the result set.

How to use the executeUpdate method to modify data

How to add a record

```
String insertStatement =
    "INSERT INTO Products (ProductCode, Description, Price) " +
    "VALUES ('" + p.getCode() + "', " +
            "'" + p.getDescription() + "', " +
            "'" + p.getPrice() + "')";
int count = statement.executeUpdate(insertStatement);
```

How to update a record

```
String updateStatement =
    "UPDATE Products SET " +
        "ProductCode = '" + p.getCode() + "', " +
        "Description = '" + p.getDescription() + "', " +
        "Price = '" + p.getPrice() + "' " +
    "WHERE ProductCode = '" + p.getCode() + "'";
int count = statement.executeUpdate(updateStatement);
```

How to delete a record

```
String deleteStatement =
    "DELETE FROM Products " +
    "WHERE ProductCode = '" + p.getCode() + "'";
int count = statement.executeUpdate(deleteStatement);
```

How to use methods from JDBC 2.0 and later to modify data

How to add a record

```
rs.moveToInsertRow();
rs.updateString("ProductCode", p.getCode());
rs.updateString("Description", p.getDescription());
rs.updateDouble("Price", p.getPrice());
rs.insertRow();
rs.moveToCurrentRow();
```

How to update a record

```
rs.updateString("ProductCode", p.getCode());
rs.updateString("Description", p.getDescription());
rs.updateDouble("Price", p.getPrice());
rs.updateRow();
```

How to delete a record

```
rs.deleteRow();
```

Description

- The executeUpdate method is an older method that works with most JDBC drivers. The newer methods may not work properly with older JDBC drivers.
- The executeUpdate method returns an int value that identifies the number of records that were affected by the update.
- When you delete a record, the result set may contain an invalid row where the deleted row used to be. To solve this problem, you can close the result set and reopen it.

Figure 21-13 How to modify data in a database

How to work with prepared statements

Figure 21-14 shows how to use a prepared SQL statement to return a result set or to modify data. When you use a *prepared statement*, you include placeholders in the statement for parameters whose values will vary. Then, before you execute the statement, you set the values of those parameters. Since the database can cache and reuse prepared statements, they execute faster than regular statements. In addition, it's easier to read and write the code for the SQL statement. As a result, you should use prepared statements whenever possible.

The first example in this figure shows how to use a prepared statement to create a result set that contains a single product. Here, the first statement uses a question mark (?) placeholder to identify the parameter for the SELECT statement, which is the code for the product. The second statement uses the prepareStatement method of the Connection object to return a PreparedStatement object. The third statement uses a set method (the setString method) of the PreparedStatement object to set a value for the first parameter in the SELECT statement. And the fourth statement uses the executeQuery method of the PreparedStatement object to return a ResultSet object.

The second example shows how to use a prepared statement to execute an UPDATE query that requires three parameters. Here, the first statement uses three question marks (?) to identify the three parameters of the UPDATE statement, and the second statement creates the PreparedStatement object. Then, the next three statements use the set methods to set the three parameters in the order that they appear in the UPDATE statement. The last statement uses the executeUpdate method of the PreparedStatement object to execute the UPDATE statement. The third and fourth examples show how to insert and delete records with prepared statements.

These examples show that the type of SQL statement that you're using determines whether you use the executeQuery method or the executeUpdate method. If you're using a SELECT statement to return a result set, you use the executeQuery method. But if you're using an INSERT, UPDATE, or DELETE statement, you use the executeUpdate method. This holds true whether you're using a Statement object or a PreparedStatement object.

The executeUpdate method returns an int value that indicates the number of rows that were successfully updated. In this example, the SQL statements only modify a single record, so this value isn't that useful. However, if the SQL statements modified multiple records, this count would be more useful.

By default, the prepareStatement method of the Connection object creates a forward-only, read-only result set. However, you can set the type and concurrency of a PreparedStatement object just as you can for Statement objects as shown in figure 21-10. That way, you can create a scrollable, updateable result set from a prepared statement.

How to use a prepared statement

To return a result set

```
String selectProduct =
    "SELECT ProductCode, Description, Price " +
    "FROM Products " +
    "WHERE ProductCode = ?";
PreparedStatement ps = connection.prepareStatement(selectProduct);
ps.setString(1, p.getCode());
ResultSet rs = ps.executeQuery();
```

To update a record

```
String updateProduct =
    "UPDATE Products " +
    "SET Description = ?, Price = ? " +
    "WHERE ProductCode = ?";
PreparedStatement ps = connection.prepareStatement(updateProduct);
ps.setString(1, p.getDescription());
ps.setDouble(2, p.getPrice());
ps.setString(3, p.getCode());
int count = ps.executeUpdate();
```

To insert a record

```
String insertProduct =
    "INSERT INTO Products (ProductCode, Description, Price) " +
    "VALUES (?, ?, ?)";
PreparedStatement ps = connection.prepareStatement(insertProduct);
ps.setString(1, p.getCode());
ps.setString(2, p.getDescription());
ps.setDouble(3, p.getPrice());
int count = ps.executeUpdate();
```

To delete a record

```
String deleteProduct =
    "DELETE FROM Products " +
    "WHERE ProductCode = ?";
PreparedStatement ps = connection.prepareStatement(deleteProduct);
ps.setString(1, p.getCode());
int count = ps.executeUpdate();
```

Description

- To specify a parameter, type a question mark (?) in the SQL statement.
- To supply values for the parameters in a prepared statement, use the set methods of the PreparedStatement interface. For a complete list of set methods, look up the PreparedStatement interface of the java.sql package in the documentation for the Java API.
- To execute a SELECT statement, use the executeQuery method. To execute an INSERT, UPDATE, or DELETE statement, use the executeUpdate method.

Figure 21-14 How to work with prepared statements

Two classes for working with databases

In the last two chapters, you learned how to code classes that implement the ProductDAO interface (see figure 19-10) so you can use that .interface to store data in files. Now, you'll learn how to code a ProductDB class that implements the ProductDAO interface so you can use that interface to store data in a database. But first, you'll be introduced to a utility class that you can use to solve a common problem that you may encounter when using a Statement object to store strings in a database.

A utility class for working with strings

In an SQL statement that specifies column values, you use the single quote (') to identify the beginning and end of the data for each column. As a result, if you try to insert a string that contains a single quote as shown in the first example of figure 21-15, the database will interpret that quote as the end of the string. Then, an exception will be thrown when the database isn't able to interpret the rest of the SQL statement. To fix this problem, you can prefix the single quote with another single quote as shown in the second example. In other words, you can code two single quotes to tell the database that you want to include a single quote in the string, not end the string.

The DBUtil class shown in this figure contains a method named fixDBString that you can use to fix the single quotes for any string that's passed to it. If the string that's passed to this method is null, the method returns a null and ends. This prevents a NullPointerException. Otherwise, this method loops through each character in the string. Then, each time it finds a single quote, it adds another single quote immediately before that single quote. When it's done, it returns the resulting string.

To use the fixDBString method, you can use code like that shown at the bottom of this figure. This code creates a statement that inserts a row into the Products table. Because the product description can contain single quotes, the fixDBString method is used to process this string.

If you use prepared statements as shown in figure 21-14, you should realize that this problem is handled for you automatically. As a result, you only need to use code like the code shown in this figure if you aren't using prepared statements. This is yet another reason to use prepared statements.

A SQL statement that causes an error

```
"INSERT INTO Products (ProductCode, Description, Price) " +
"VALUES ('java', 'Murach's Beginning Java 2', '49.50')";
```

A SQL statement that works

```
"INSERT INTO Products (ProductCode, Description, Price) " +
"VALUES ('java', 'Murach''s Beginning Java 2', '49.50')";
```

A utility class for working with strings

```
public class DBStringUtil
{
    // handle strings that contain one or more apostrophes (')
    private static String fixDBString(String s)
    {
        // if the string is null, return it
        if (s == null)
            return s;

        // add an apostrophe before each existing apostrophe
        StringBuilder sb = new StringBuilder(s);
        for (int i = 0; i < sb.length(); i++)
        {
            char ch = sb.charAt(i);
            if (ch == 39)  //39 is the ASCII code for an apostrophe
                sb.insert(i++, "'");
        }
        return sb.toString();
    }
}
```

Code that uses this class

```
Statement statement = connection.createStatement();
String insert =
    "INSERT INTO Products (ProductCode, Description, Price) " +
    "VALUES ('" + p.getCode() + "', " +
            "'" + DBUtils.fixDBString(p.getDescription()) + "', " +
            "'" + p.getPrice() + "')";
statement.executeUpdate(insert);
```

Description

- SQL uses single quotes to indicate the beginning and end of the value of a column. If you need to store a single quote in a column value, you have to code two consecutive single quotes.

Figure 21-15 A utility class for working with strings

A class that works with a database

Figure 21-16 presents the complete code for the ProductDB class. This class works with the data in the Products table of the MurachDB database. Like the ProductTextFile and ProductRandomFile classes presented in chapter 19 and the ProductXMLFile class presented in chapter 20, this class implements the ProductDAO interface shown in figure 19-10. If you have already read chapter 19 or 20, you shouldn't have any trouble understanding how the ProductDB class works.

To start, this class declares an instance variable that defines a Connection object that provides the connection to the database. Then, the constructor for this class initializes that instance variable by calling the connect method.

To initialize the Connection object, the connect method starts by calling the static forName method of the Class class to load the JDBC-ODBC bridge driver. Then, it sets the URL for the ODBC data source named MurachDB, and it sets the default user name (Admin) and password (empty string) for a Microsoft Access database. Finally, it uses the static getConnection method of the DriverManager class to load the database driver and connect to the database. If the connect method isn't able to connect to the database, it will print an appropriate error message to the console.

The getProducts method returns an ArrayList object that contains all of the Product objects that are stored in the Products table of the MurachDB database. This method starts by declaring and initializing an ArrayList object that can store Product objects. Then, it creates a string that contains a SQL statement that selects the ProductCode, Description, and Price fields from the Products table and sorts them in ascending order. To create a PreparedStatement object for the SQL statement, this method calls the prepareStatement method of the Connection object. Then, to return a ResultSet object that contains this data, this method calls the executeQuery method of the PreparedStatement object.

Once the ResultSet object has been returned, the getProducts method uses a loop to read each record in the result set. Within the loop, the first two statements use the getString method of the ResultSet object to return strings for the ProductCode and Description columns of the result set. Then, the third statement uses the getDouble method of the ResultSet object to return a double value for the Price column. Finally, this loop creates the Product object and adds it to the products array list.

After the loop finishes executing, the close methods of the ResultSet and PreparedStatement objects are called to immediately free the system resources that are used by these objects. When you code these statements, you must be sure to close the result set before you close the prepared statement. Otherwise, an SQLException will be thrown.

The code for the ProductDB class

Page 1

```
import java.util.*;
import java.sql.*;

public class ProductDB implements ProductDAO
{
    private Connection connection = null;

    public ProductDB()
    {
        this.connect();  // initializes connection
    }

    private void connect()
    {
        try
        {
            Class.forName("sun.jdbc.odbc.JdbcOdbcDriver");

            String url = "jdbc:odbc:MurachDB";
            String username = "Admin";
            String password = "";
            connection = DriverManager.getConnection(url, username, password);
        }
        catch(ClassNotFoundException e)
        {
            System.err.println("Database driver not found.");
        }
        catch(SQLException e)
        {
            System.err.println("Error connecting to the database: " + e);
        }
    }

    public ArrayList<Product> getProducts()
    {
        try
        {
            ArrayList<Product> products = new ArrayList<Product>();

            String query = "SELECT ProductCode, Description, Price "
                         + "FROM Products ORDER BY ProductCode ASC";
            PreparedStatement ps = connection.prepareStatement(query);
            ResultSet rs = ps.executeQuery();
            while(rs.next())
            {
                String code = rs.getString("ProductCode");
                String description = rs.getString("Description");
                double price = rs.getDouble("Price");

                Product p = new Product(code, description, price);
                products.add(p);
            }
            rs.close();
            ps.close();
            return products;
        }
```

Figure 21-16 A class that works with a database (part 1 of 3)

If an SQLException is thrown anywhere in the getProducts method, this method returns a null. Otherwise, the getProducts method returns the products array list. That way, any programmer that calls this method can assume that the method executed successfully if the products array list is not null.

The getProduct method returns a Product object for a product that matches the specified product code. To do that, it uses a prepared SQL statement to return a result set. Then, it calls the next method of the result set to attempt to move the cursor to the first row in the result set. If successful, this method continues by reading the description and price fields from the row and creating a Product object from these fields. Then, it closes the result set and prepared statement and returns the Product object. However, if no product record contains a product code that matches the specified code, this method returns a null to indicate that the product couldn't be found. In addition, if an SQLException is thrown anywhere in this method, this method returns a null to indicate that it was not successful.

The addProduct method begins by creating a prepared SQL statement that inserts the data that's stored in the Product object that's passed to it into the Products table. If this update is successful, this method returns a true value. However, if an SQLException is thrown anywhere in this method, this method returns a false value to indicate that it was not successful.

The code for the ProductDB class

Page 2

```
        catch(SQLException sqle)
        {
            return null;
        }
    }

    public Product getProduct(String code)
    {
        try
        {
            String selectProduct =
                "SELECT ProductCode, Description, Price " +
                "FROM Products " +
                "WHERE ProductCode = ?";
            PreparedStatement ps = connection.prepareStatement(selectProduct);
            ps.setString(1, code);
            ResultSet rs = ps.executeQuery();

            if (rs.next())
            {
                String description = rs.getString("Description");
                double price = rs.getDouble("Price");
                Product p = new Product(code, description, price);
                rs.close();
                ps.close();
                return p;
            }
            else
                return null;
        }
        catch(SQLException sqle)
        {
            return null;
        }
    }

    public boolean addProduct(Product p)
    {
        try
        {
            String insert =
                "INSERT INTO Products (ProductCode, Description, Price) " +
                "VALUES (?, ?, ?)";
            PreparedStatement ps = connection.prepareStatement(insert);
            ps.setString(1, p.getCode());
            ps.setString(2, p.getDescription());
            ps.setDouble(3, p.getPrice());
            ps.executeUpdate();
            ps.close();
            return true;
        }
        catch(SQLException sqle)
        {
            return false;
        }
    }
```

Figure 21-16 A class that works with a database (part 2 of 3)

The deleteProduct method uses a prepared SQL statement to delete the product record that has the same product code as the Product object that's passed to it. Like the addProduct method, the deleteProduct method returns a true value if the operation is successful, and it returns a false value if an SQLException is thrown anywhere in the method.

The updateProduct method uses a prepared SQL statement to update an existing product in the Products table with the data that's stored in the Product object that's passed to it. This method will only work if the Product object has a product code that exists in the Products table, and that's what you usually want. Like the addProduct and deleteProduct methods, this method returns a boolean value that indicates whether the operation was successful.

If you review the code for this class, you'll see that it only uses methods from the JDBC 1.0 API. That's because this is still the most common way to use JDBC to work with databases. In addition, when you use this technique, you can be sure that your code will work with most database drivers…even the JDBC-ODBC bridge driver that comes with JDK 5.0. The downside of this technique is that it requires the Java programmer to understand SQL. However, SQL is easy to learn, and most programmers who work with databases already know how to use it. In fact, some programmers prefer using SQL so they have direct control over the SQL statement that's sent to the database.

You may also notice that this class doesn't close the Connection object. That's okay for most applications because the Connection object is automatically closed when Java determines that there aren't any more references to it. In this case, it will be closed sometime after the user exits the application.

Another option would be to modify the class so the Connection object isn't an instance variable. Then, each method that needs a connection could open a connection, do its processing, and close the connection. For example, you could modify the connect method so it returns a Connection object. Then, the getProducts method could call the connect method to return a Connection object, use that connection to retrieve the product records, and close the connection when it's done with it. The advantage of this approach is that all the resources used by the Connection object will be freed immediately. This might be necessary if the application was used by a large number of users and the number of open database connections was an issue. The disadvantage is that your application will need to open a database connection each time it calls a method that needs a connection. Since opening a database connection is a relatively time-consuming process, this may have a negative impact on the performance of your application.

Finally, you may notice that the record set and prepared statement objects that are used by the methods in this class aren't closed if an SQLException is thrown. Since this exception should rarely be thrown, this code is probably acceptable. And, if an SQLException is thrown, Java will close these objects automatically when it determines that there are no more references to them. In this case, they'll be closed sometime after the method that declares them ends. If you wanted to close these objects explicitly when an SQLException was thrown, you could code the close methods in a finally clause. Then, the objects would be closed regardless of whether the method was successful.

The code for the ProductDB class

Page 3

```
    public boolean deleteProduct(Product p)
    {
        try
        {
            String delete =
                "DELETE FROM Products " +
                "WHERE ProductCode = ?";
            PreparedStatement ps = connection.prepareStatement(delete);
            ps.setString(1, p.getCode());
            ps.executeUpdate();
            ps.close();
            return true;
        }
        catch(SQLException sqle)
        {
            return false;
        }
    }

    public boolean updateProduct(Product p)
    {
        try
        {
            String update =
                "UPDATE Products SET " +
                    "Description = ?, " +
                    "Price = ? " +
                "WHERE ProductCode = ?";
            PreparedStatement ps = connection.prepareStatement(update);
            ps.setString(1, p.getDescription());
            ps.setDouble(2, p.getPrice());
            ps.setString(3, p.getCode());
            ps.executeUpdate();
            ps.close();
            return true;
        }
        catch(SQLException sqle)
        {
            return false;
        }
    }
}
```

Figure 21-16 A class that works with a database (part 3 of 3)

An introduction to working with metadata

When you work with a result set, you can get data about the definition of the result set. This type of information is known as *metadata*. For example, the metadata of a result set includes the number of columns, names of the columns, and the data type that's stored in each column. Although working with metadata is an advanced skill that you don't need for normal business applications, this topic gives you a taste of what you can do with it.

How to work with metadata

Figure 21-17 shows the basic skills for working with metadata. First, this figure shows how to return a ResultSetMetaData object from a ResultSet object. Then, it shows five methods that are commonly used to work with metadata.

When you use the last four methods in this figure, you use an integer value to specify the column, where 1 is the first column, 2 is the second column, and so on. The difference between the second and third methods is that the second method returns the *name* that the DBMS uses to identify the column while the third method returns the *label* that's used as a heading for GUIs and reports. If a label hasn't been defined for a column, the DBMS often uses the column name as a default. The difference between the fourth and fifth methods is that the fourth method returns an int type that represents an SQL data type while the fifth method returns the name of the SQL data type.

The first example shows a static method that returns the column names for a result set. This method accepts a ResultSet object as a parameter and returns an ArrayList object that contains all of the column names. To do that, the first statement initializes an ArrayList object that can store strings. Then, the second statement gets the ResultSetMetaData object from the result set that has been passed to the method, and the third statement uses the getColumnCount method to get the column count. After that, a for loop cycles through all of the columns in the result set and uses the getColumnName method to add each column name to the array list. The last statement in this method returns the array list.

The second example shows a static method that returns the data for each row in a result set. This method also accepts a ResultSet object as a parameter and returns an ArrayList object. However, the array list that's returned in this example is a two-dimensional array list. That way, the outer array list can store one inner array list for each row in the result set. To do that, this method uses a while loop to cycle through all of the records in the result set. Inside the outer loop, the inner loop cycles through each column in the result set using the getColumnType method to check the data type for the column. Depending on the data type, the appropriate get method is used to add the data to the inner array list. In this example, the code uses the fields of the Types class to check for the VARCHAR and INTEGER types. In addition, this code checks for the SQL data type with an int value of 2 (which corresponds to the CURRENCY type that's used by Microsoft Access).

How to use the getMetaData method to create a ResultSetMetaData object

```
ResultSetMetaData metaData = resultSet.getMetaData();
```

Methods of a ResultSetMetaData object for working with meta data

Method	Description
`getColumnCount()`	Returns the number of columns in this RecordSet object as an int type.
`getColumnName(intColumn)`	Returns the name of this column as a String object.
`getColumnLabel(intColumn)`	Returns the label of this column as a String object.
`getColumnType(intColumn)`	Returns an int type that represents the SQL data type that's used to store the data in this column.
`getColumnTypeName(intColumn)`	Returns a String object that identifies the SQL data type that's used to store the data in this column.

A method that returns the column names of a result set

```
public static ArrayList<String> getColumnNames(ResultSet results)
throws SQLException
{
    ArrayList<String> columnNames = new ArrayList<String>();
    ResultSetMetaData metaData = results.getMetaData();
    int columnCount = metaData.getColumnCount();
    for (int i = 1; i <= columnCount; i++)
        columnNames.add(metaData.getColumnName(i));
    return columnNames;
}
```

A method that returns the rows of a result set

```
public static ArrayList<ArrayList> getRows(ResultSet results)
throws SQLException
{
    ArrayList<ArrayList> rows = new ArrayList<ArrayList>();
    ResultSetMetaData metaData = results.getMetaData();
    while (results.next())
    {
        ArrayList<Object> row = new ArrayList<Object>();
        for (int i = 1; i <= metaData.getColumnCount(); i++)
        {
            if (metaData.getColumnType(i) == Types.VARCHAR)
                row.add(results.getString(i));
            else if (metaData.getColumnType(i) == Types.INTEGER)
                row.add(new Integer(results.getInt(i)));
            else if (metaData.getColumnType(i) == 2)
                row.add(new Double(results.getDouble(i)));
        }
        rows.add(row);
    }
    return rows;
}
```

Description

- You can use the fields of the Types class of the java.sql package to specify an int value for a SQL data type.

Figure 21-17 How to work with metadata

How SQL data types map to Java data types

Figure 21-18 shows how some of the most common SQL data types map to the Java data types. Some of these conversions are intuitive. For example, the SQL INTEGER type corresponds to the Java int type. However, some of these conversions aren't as intuitive. For example, the SQL REAL type maps to the Java float type.

When you write code that converts SQL types to Java types, you can use the constants in the Types class of the java.sql package to refer to the SQL types as shown in the previous figure. And if a constant doesn't exist for the data type, you can use an int value to refer to the data type. To get the int value for a data type in your result set, you can use the getColumnType method described in the previous figure. Or, to get the string that describes the data type, you can use the getColumnTypeName. For example, the Microsoft Access field that defines the Price column uses a non-standard Currency data type. In an SQL result set, the int value for this data type is 2 and the name for this data type is CURRENCY.

How SQL data types map to Java data types

SQL data type	Java data type
VARCHAR, LONGVARCHAR	String
BIT	boolean
TINYBIT	byte
SMALLINT	short
INTEGER	int
BIGINT	long
REAL	float
DOUBLE	double
VARBINARY, LONGVARBINARY	byte[]
NUMERIC	java.math.BigDecimal
DATE	java.sql.Date
TIME	java.sql.Time
TIMESTAMP	java.sql.Timestamp

Description

- To get the SQL data type that's used in the column of a result set, you can use the getColumnType and getColumnTypeName methods of the ResultSetMetaData class.

Figure 21-18 How SQL data types map to Java data types

Perspective

Now that you've finished this chapter, you should understand how to use JDBC to store data in a database and to retrieve data from a database. Although there's much more to learn about working with databases, those are the essential skills. To enhance your database skills, you can learn more about SQL, you can learn more about database management systems like Microsoft SQL Server or MySQL, and you can learn more about the other JDBC features.

Summary

- A *relational database* uses tables to store and manipulate data. Each table contains one or more *rows*, or *records*, while each row contains one or more *columns*, or *fields*.
- A *primary key* is used to identify each row in a table. A *foreign key* is a key in one table that is used to relate rows to another table.
- Each database is managed by a *database management system* (*DBMS*) that supports the use of the *Structured Query Language* (*SQL*). To manipulate the data in a database, you use the SQL SELECT, INSERT, UPDATE, and DELETE statements.
- The SELECT statement is used to return data from one or more tables in a *result set*. To return data from two or more tables, you *join* the data based on the data in related fields.
- An *inner join* returns a result set that includes data only if the related fields match. An *outer join* returns a result set that includes data from all of the rows in one table plus the data from the rows in the other table that match the related fields.
- Before you use JDBC to access data in a database, you have to connect the application to a database through a *database driver*.
- A Java program can use one of four driver types to access a database. *Type-1* and *type-2 drivers* run on the client's machine, while *type-3* and *type-4 drivers* can run on a server machine.
- When working with databases, you often need to handle ClassNotFoundException and SQLException.
- You can use JDBC to execute SQL statements that select, add, update, or delete one or more records in a database. You can also control the location of the *cursor* in the result set.
- You can use *prepared statements* to supply parameters at a later time in SQL statements.
- You can return a list of the column names and types in a result set by using *metadata*. To do this, you may need to convert SQL data types to Java data types.

Exercise 21-1 Work with JDBC

In this exercise, you'll install an ODBC driver for the MurachDB database, and you'll write JDBC code that works with the MurachDB database.

1. Install an ODBC data source named MurachDB for the MurachDB database that's in the c:\java1.5\database directory as described in figure 21-8. This database is in Microsoft Access 2000 format. If the ODBC driver for Microsoft Access on your system doesn't support the Access 2000 format, use the database named MurachDB97 instead, but still use MurachDB as the name for the data source.
2. Open the DBTesterApp class that's in the c:\java1.5\ch21\DBTester directory. Review the code and then run the application. It should print all of the records in the Products table to the console. Then, it should print several blank products to the console.
3. Write the code for the printFirstProduct method. Use column names to retrieve the column values. Then, compile the class and run the application. You can tell if this method is working correctly if it prints the first product in the list of products that's printed by the printProducts method.
4. Write the code for the printLastProduct method. Note that to move to the last product in the result set, you'll need to use a scrollable result set. Compile the class and then test the application.
5. Write the code for the printProductByCode method. Use a prepared statement to create the result set, and use indexes to retrieve the column values. Compile the class and test the application.
6. Write the code for the insertProduct method. This method should begin by checking if a product with the specified product code exists in the database. If so, this method should display an error message. Otherwise, it should add the product to the database and print the product that was added to the console.
7. Compile the class and test the insertProduct method. To do that, you will need to run the application twice. The first time, the product should be added to the database. The second time, the product should appear in the list of products, but then an error message should be displayed indicating that the product already exists.
8. Repeat steps 6 and 7 for the deleteProduct method. You can use this method to delete the product that was added by the insertProduct method. Compile the class and test the method.

Exercise 21-2 Modify the ProductDB class

In this exercise, you'll modify the ProductDB class of figure 21-16 so it works differently. However, the ProductMaintApp class that uses this class should still work the same.

1. Make sure an ODBC data source named MurachDB is installed for the MurachDB database that's in the c:\java1.5\database directory as shown in figure 21-8 and as described in step 1 of exercise 21-1.
2. Open the ProductMaintApp class that's in the c:\java1.5\ch21\ProductMaint directory. Run this application and test it. It should work the same as it did in previous chapters.
3. Open the ProductDB class and review its code. Note how the Connection object isn't explicitly closed by this class.
4. Delete the instance variable for the Connection object and delete the statement in the constructor that calls the connect method to initialize this instance variable.
5. Modify the declaration for the connect method so it returns a Connection object. Then, modify the code for this method so it creates a Connection object and returns it.
6. Modify the getProducts, addProduct, updateProduct, and deleteProduct methods so they call the connect method to return a Connection object, use this connection object, and close it when they're done with it.
7. Compile and test the application. It should work the way it did before. Since this application opens and closes the database connection more often, however, you may notice that it runs more slowly.

Appendix A

How to use the downloadable files for this book

The single topic in this appendix describes the files for this book that are available for download from our web site and tells you how you can use them.

How to use the downloadable files

Throughout this book, complete applications have been used to illustrate the material presented in each chapter. To help you understand these applications, you can download the source code and data for some of these applications from our web site. Then, you can view the source code and run them.

These files come in a single download that also includes the source code and data you'll need for the exercises at the end of each chapter. Figure A-1 describes how you download, install, and use these files.

When you download the single install file and execute it, it will install all of the files for this book in the murach\java5 directory on your C drive. Within this directory, you'll find a directory named exercises that contains a directory named java1.5 that contains all of the files and directories you'll need for the exercises presented in this book. Before you use these files and directories, though, you'll want to copy (not move) the java1.5 directory that contains them to the root directory of your C drive. That way, it will be easy to locate the files and directories you need as you're working on the exercises. In addition, if you make a mistake and want to restore a file to its original state, you can do that by copying it from the directory where it was originally installed.

You'll also find a directory named applications within the c:\murach\java5 directory. This directory contains the source code for the applications presented in this book. Within this directory, you'll find chapter directories, and within the chapter directories you'll find a directory that contains the source files for each application. You can view the source code for these applications as you read each chapter, and you can compile and run these applications to experiment with them.

What the downloadable files for this book contain

- The source code and data for selected applications presented in the book
- The starting source code and data for all of the exercises included in the book

How to download and install the files for this book

- Go to www.murach.com, and go to the page for *Murach's Beginning Java 2, JDK 5.*
- Click the link for "FREE download of the book applications." Then, download "All book files." This will download one file named jav5_allfiles.exe to the root directory of your C drive.
- Use the Windows Explorer to find the exe file on your C drive. Then, double-click this file and respond to the dialog boxes that follow. This installs the files in directories that start with c:\murach\java5.

How to prepare your system for doing the exercises

- Some of the exercises have you start from existing applications. The source code for these applications is in the c:\murach\java5\exercises\java1.5 directory. Before you do the exercises, you'll want to copy (not move) the java1.5 subdirectory and all of its subdirectories to the root directory of the C drive. From that point on, you can find the programs and files that you need in directories like c:\java1.5\ch01, c:\ java1.5\ch02, c:\java1.5\files, and c:\java1.5 \database.

How to use the source code for the applications presented in this book

- The source code for the applications presented in this book can be found in the subdirectories of the c:\murach\java5\applications directory. Then, you can view, compile, and run the source code for each application in each chapter of this book.

Notes for other versions of the JDK

- If you're using JDK 1.5 (5.0) or later, you should be able to compile and run all of these applications.
- If you're using JDK 1.4 or earlier, you can view the source code, but you won't be able to compile and run applications that use the features of Java introduced with JDK 1.5. To solve this problem, you can download and install version 1.5 of the JDK as described in chapter 1.

Figure A-1 How to use the downloadable files for this book

Index

B

C

D

E

F

G

H

I

J

K

L

M

N

O

P

Q

R

S

T

U

V

W

X

Y

What software you need for this book

- The Java Development Kit 5.0 (JDK 5.0) or higher for the Java 2 Platform, Standard Edition 5.0 (J2SE 5.0). You can download this software for free from http://java.sun.com. Then, you can install and configure this software as described in chapter 1.
- A text editor that's designed for working with Java, such as TextPad. You can download a trial version of this software for free from www.textpad.com. Then, you can install and configure this software as described in chapter 1.

The downloadable files for this book

- Complete source code for the applications presented in this book so you can view, compile, and run the code for the applications as you read each chapter.
- Starting source code for the exercises presented at the end of each chapter so you can get more practice in less time.
- Data for the applications and exercises.

How to download the files for this book

- Go to www.murach.com, and go to the page for ***Murach's Beginning Java 2, JDK 5.***
- Click the link for "FREE download of the book applications." Then, download "All book files." This will download one file named jav5_allfiles.exe to the root directory of your C drive.
- Use the Windows Explorer to find the exe file on your C drive. Then, double-click this file and respond to the dialog boxes that follow. This installs the files in directories that start with c:\murach\java5.
- From that point on, you can find the applications in folders like c:\murach\java5\applications, and you'll find the starting points for the exercises in the c:\murach\java5\exercises folder.

How to prepare your system for the exercises

- Before you do the exercises, you'll want to copy (not move) the java1.5 subdirectory and all of its subdirectories from c:\murach\java5\exercises to the root directory of the C drive. From that point on, you can find the starting points for the exercises you need in directories like c:\java1.5\ch01, c:\java1.5\ch02, c:\java1.5\files, and c:\java1.5\database.